WESTERN FEVER
THE LIFE AND TIMES OF GIDEON TRUESDELL

WESTERN FEVER
THE LIFE AND TIMES OF GIDEON TRUESDELL

RICHARD C. FRITZ

© 2023 by Richard C. Fritz
All Rights Reserved
No part of this book may be reproduced in any form or by any electronic or mechanical means including information storage and retrieval systems without permission in writing from the publisher, except by a reviewer who may quote brief passages in a review.

Sunstone books may be purchased for educational, business, or sales promotional use. For information please write: Special Markets Department, Sunstone Press, P.O. Box 2321, Santa Fe, New Mexico 87504-2321.
Printed on acid-free paper

Library of Congress Cataloging-in-Publication Data

Names: Fritz, Richard C., 1957- author.
Title: Western fever : the life and times of Gideon Truesdell / Richard C. Fritz.
Other titles: Life and times of Gideon Truesdell
Description: Santa Fe : Sunstone Press, [2023] | Summary: "A meticulously researched story of the life and times of Gideon Truesdell (1811-1882), who struggled to amass a fortune, only to lose everything, and had to start over in one of the roughest towns in the old Southwest, where his family became intimately acquainted with Billy the Kid"-- Provided by publisher.
Identifiers: LCCN 2023005312 | ISBN 9781632934611 (paperback) | ISBN 9781632935359 (hardback)
Subjects: LCSH: Truesdell, Gideon, 1811-1882. | Businessmen--Biography. | Silver City (N.M.)--Biography. | Kenosha County (Wis.)--Biography.
Classification: LCC F802.G7 F75 2023 | DDC 978.9692092--dc23/eng20230303
LC record available at https://lccn.loc.gov/2023005312

WWW.SUNSTONEPRESS.COM
SUNSTONE PRESS / POST OFFICE BOX 2321 / SANTA FE, NM 87504-2321 /USA
(505) 988-4418

Dedicated to the pioneer spirit that settled this country.

CONTENTS

Preface : 11
The Research and Writing of *Western Fever* : 11

1 / Holland Land Purchase : 19

  The Truesdells Settle in the Holland Land Purchase, Circa 1803
  Widow Truesdell Brings Her Family to the Holland Land Purchase, 1806
  Gideon Truesdell Catches a Bad Case of Western Fever, 1836
  Wisconsin Territory, circa 1836
  Troubled Times on the Wisconsin Frontier; the Arrival of Judge James Doty, Morgan Martin, Panic of 1837, and the Winnebago War
  Gideon and Julia Truesdell Arrive on the Wisconsin River
  Clearing the Land, Building a Cabin, and Planting Crops in the Wilderness During the Summer of 1837
  Draper, Fay & Company, Sawmill Owners
  Creating a Government in the Wilderness, 1839
  Rafting Lumber from Draper's Rapids to St. Louis, Circa 1839–1841
  Draper, Fay & Company and Gideon Truesdell File for Bankruptcy
  Gideon and Julia Truesdell Settle in Southport, Wisconsin, 1843
  Catherine and Charles Durkee
  Charles Durkee & Company, General Merchants
  The Origins of Durkee, Truesdell & Company
  Gideon Truesdell and Joseph Hackley's Trip to the California Gold Fields, 1849

2 / Durkee, Truesdell & Company : 109

>Gideon Truesdell & Company, 1850–1852
>Durkee, Truesdell & Company, 1852–1871
>Schooner Challenge
>Southport & Beloit Plank Road Company
>Durkee, Truesdell & Company: Wholesale Lumber Dealers and Manufacturers
>Kenosha Pier Company, 1857
>Kenosha and Beloit Railroad, 1853
>The City Bank of Kenosha
>U.S. Senator Charles Durkee
>Durkee, Truesdell & Company, Muskegon, Michigan, 1856
>Levi Truesdell, Joseph Hackley, and William Glue
>Durkee, Truesdell & Company, Chicago Lumber Dealers
>Saloons, Whorehouses and Loggers
>Collapse of Durkee, Truesdell & Company, 1857

3 / Surviving the Panic of 1857 and Organizing the Truesdell Lumber Company : 215

>Surviving the Panic of 1857
>Joseph Hackley, Superintendent of the Durkee, Truesdell & Company Mill
>Chicago Wholesale Lumber Market, Circa 1859
>Foreclosing on the Trowbridge & Wing Mill and Organizing J.H. Hackley & Company
>Life in a Lumber Town: Muskegon, Michigan
>G. Truesdell & Son, General Merchants
>Logging Camps and Log Drives
>Muskegon Booming Company
>G.J. and Louisa Truesdell
>The Typical Life of a Lumberjack in the Woods
>Chicago's Franklin Street Wholesale Dock
>Logging Operations Along the White, Muskegon and Grand Rivers
>Chicago, Grand Haven & Muskegon Ship Line
>Charles Hackley's $70,000 Train Ride

    Gideon Truesdell Semi-Retires from the Lumber Business a Millionaire, 1865

4 / Largest Dairy Farm in Wisconsin : 293

    G. Truesdell & Son Farms, Pleasant Prairie, Wisconsin
    Gideon Truesdell Wins 66th Assembly Seat in the Wisconsin Legislature, 1867
    Gideon Truesdell & Son Farms, Circa 1867
    Gideon Truesdell's Farm, Kenosha County, Best Improvements and Largest Farm in the State of Wisconsin
    Illinois & Wisconsin Dairyman's Association and Northwest Dairyman's Association
    A Good Time in the Town of Pleasant Prairie Among the Dairymen
    Northwest Dairyman's Convention, Kenosha, Wisconsin, 1870
    Cutting Feed for Livestock and Dairy Farming in Kenosha County
    The Development of the Cheese-Making Industry in Kenosha County: The Model Farm of Gideon Truesdell
    Gideon Truesdell Drills for Salt
    Truesdell's City Mills Flour, 1866
    The Halliday House (Formerly Durkee House) Fire, 1871
    Governor Charles Durkee and the Old Settlers Picnic, May 1st, 1869
    Truesdell, Wisconsin, 1871

5 / Chicago Fire Bankrupts Gideon Truesdell : 367

    The 1871 Chicago Fire Destroys over $750,000 of Gideon Truesdell's Wealth
    The Night America Burned
    Total Devastation and Mayhem in Chicago
    Gideon Truesdell Reorganizes Debt, 1872
    Panic of 1873: End of the Road for Gideon Truesdell
    Gideon Truesdell's Dairy Farm Destroyed by Fire, 1873
    Creditors Push Gideon Truesdell into Bankruptcy, 1874
    Gideon Truesdell declared Bankrupt

6 / Silver City, New Mexico : 399

Silver City, New Mexico Territory
Early Prospectors, Apache Depredations, and Primitive Equipment
The Two Ikes Mine, Chloride Flats Mining District
G.J. Truesdell Brings a Steam Mill to Silver City
Wisconsin Mining Company
The Two Ikes Mine and the Wisconsin Mill Begin Manufacturing Thirty Pound Bricks of Silver
Wisconsin Mining Company Plagued by Problems
Gideon and Julia Truesdell Arrive in Silver City, 1874
Gideon Truesdell Re-organizes the Wisconsin Mining Company
Mining Company fails: Gideon Truesdell Starts Over in Silver City at the age of Sixty-four
Truesdell Ranch, 1875
G. Truesdell & Son, Grocers and Dealers in Provisions
Clifton, Arizona, and the Longfellow Mine
Henry Antrim A.K.A. Billy the Kid and Truesdell's Star Hotel
Silver City, Mercantile hub of the Southwest
Law and Order in Southwest New Mexico
G.J. and Louisa Truesdell
Apache Depredations
Truesdell, Lyons & Campbell Cattle Company, Tombstone, Arizona, 1879
Gideon Truesdell, Dead at the Age of Seventy-one

Truesdell Genealogy Chart : 522

Bibliography : 524

PREFACE

The Research and Writing of *Western Fever*

During the 1970s James Michener's *Centennial* became a best seller that were turned into landmark mini-series that grabbed the attention of millions of people, including a real estate developer named Patrick Truesdell.

He wanted to hire somebody to research his ancestors who lived in Kenosha during the 1840s, so he placed a "help wanted" advertisement in the *Kenosha News* that caught my eye because even crummy jobs were hard to find that summer. I had just graduated from high school, and was working for an electrical contractor stockpiling cash for tuition and books, but once the job was over, I knew I would still need money.

I gave Mr. Truesdell a call at Truesdell's Auction & Galleries, and learned that he wanted somebody to dig through old courthouse records. I hadn't done this type of work before so I was thorough, which caused him to ask me to travel to New York, Michigan, and New Mexico between semesters to see what I could dig up.

I returned with hundreds of copies of documents back when courthouses only had one Xerox machine in the building, and an "out of order" sign meant taking pages and pages of notes. I also brought back some local history books that I was able to purchase, which gave me a feel for the various communities that Gideon Truesdell lived in.

It was a good start, and there were a few surprises like the Billy the Kid connection. He lived with the Truesdells for five months, and academic scholars agree they knew him well. There was a close relationship because Louisa Truesdell cared for his mother when she was dying of tuberculosis.

A few months into the research, Mr. Truesdell was thrilled with what I found, and this occurred at a time when nobody had heard of the

Richard C. Fritz

Internet. At the age of nineteen, I really didn't know what I was looking for but I began running across stray pieces of information.

I knew from old Kenosha County courthouse records that Gideon Truesdell was declared bankrupt in Chicago, and I spent months trying to determine if there was still a file somewhere with his name on it. I knew this was important because it would give us a financial snapshot of his holdings in 1873, and from there I could reconstruct a lot of information. My research at that stage was very amateurish, but I was running across a lot of interesting information.

He was declared bankrupt a long, long time ago so I wasn't sure anything existed, but since I was able to go back a hundred years in the Kenosha courthouse, I figured I should be able to do the same. The only drawback was that there were entire buildings in Chicago that housed records, whereas in Kenosha there were five or six filing cabinets in the basement of the old courthouse.

In 1977, while visiting the extremely busy Cook County Clerk of Court's office in Chicago, a secretary took pity on me and pointed me in the right direction. This was right after *Roots* was on television and it seemed like everybody was researching their families. All you had to do is say "I'm looking for information about my family," and employees would give you a hostile look.

I had learned to preface my request with "I'm working my way through college and I was hired to do some research," which usually worked. I mentioned that I wasn't even sure if the bankruptcy papers still existed until she snapped "young man, the federal government never throws anything out," as if any idiot would know this. She was right; I found a 233-page file "In the matter of Gideon Truesdell" was sitting out on Pulaski Road in a federal records archive.

Another discovery was the confidential R.G. Dun & Company credit reports at Harvard, which gave detailed information about Gideon Truesdell, Harvey Durkee, and Durkee, Truesdell & Company. These reports weren't 100% accurate but valuable in so many other ways.

While waiting for an archivist to photocopy the entire bankruptcy file from 1873, which I learned was rarely done, an archivist asked if I had checked Gideon's income tax records.

I had never heard about a person's tax records becoming a matter of public record, but during the 1860s the larger tax returns were often published in the newspapers, and it came from records that were warehoused in the federal archives.

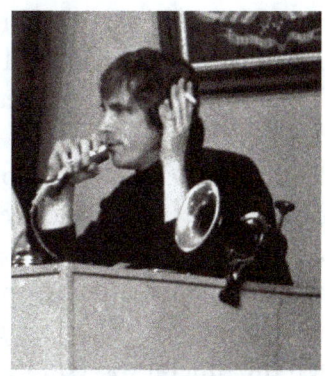

Pat Truesdell running an auction with a cigarette in one hand and a glass of scotch nearby.

One of Pat's 32 Victorian homes being moved across town before renovation work began.

After traveling around the country between semesters Mr. Truesdell asked me to swing by Sacramento where he lived, and when he heard that accounting was my major, he asked me to look at his books, which were a complicated mess with over $60,000 of past-due bills lying in a box. (That was $60,000 in 1976 dollars!) I was there for a few weeks, and I put together a list of accounts payable, although after I left, I'm sure he went back to the cigar box system of accounting. He always regarded paying bills, taxes, and record keeping as a pain-in-the-neck.

As interesting as my research was, by the end of my second year of college my part-time job ended when interest rates ruined Mr. Truesdell's real estate business. I hadn't been paid. I later discovered that appearances notwithstanding, he was strapped for cash right from the start of our relationship although I didn't figure this out until it was too late. He was an interesting guy, and one of the best stories I heard him tell was how he bought an old string of pearls.

This was back in the late 1960s when he would drive out to the old farming towns looking for farmhouses that belonged to older people, much the same as they do on *American Pickers*. At one particular farmhouse he noticed what he thought was a leftover Christmas wreath on the front door, that turned out to be a funeral wreath. Back in those days, this wasn't unusual in rural areas when the funeral was conducted from the home, but when Pat pulled into the driveway, he had no idea that this wreath signified a death in the family.

An older man opened the door and invited Pat into the house. "I've got a lot of my wife's stuff you can buy cheap" he grunted, and sold him a couple of boxes of decent jewelry. On his way downstairs Pat sensed there was something odd about the sale, because there wasn't any haggling, and just about everyone haggled over the price.

"Is there anything else you might be interested in selling," he asked? He thought for a couple of seconds before mentioning that his wife had a string of pearls if the price were right. Pat said that he would have to see them before he could make an offer so the old man walked over to a set of double doors, slid them open, and ushered him into an old-fashioned parlor where a casket stood in front of the windows.

"Funeral's tomorrow," he said as he opened the casket. After Pat got a grip on himself, he realized that the necklace was worth at least $4,000 but he thought that he could get it for a lot less. "They're beautiful but there isn't much of a market for them, and she probably wanted to be buried with them," he said feigning disinterest. The old man grunted that she would never know, and Pat said "I understand...they're worth nothing in the ground." The old man said that he was glad that she was dead, and Pat figured that she had been sick for a long time.

Pat said that he really couldn't go any higher than $600, which was true because that's all the cash he had left, and much to Pat's surprise the old man agreed. When the old man didn't make any attempt to remove the pearls, Pat leaned over the casket, unclasped the pearls, and heard the old man mumble "I want to get rid of everything that bitch owned."

During the 1980s a few descendants ran across my research, and they were interested in who Gideon and Julia Truesdell were. In 1984, Hattie

Truesdell Hector traveled to Silver City, and somebody gave her my last known address. She got in touch with me, and was stunned to discover that I had over a thousand pages of research about her great grandfather. "My Dad's family was dirt poor.... how could they possibly have had that kind of money?" She was very interested in my research, and I was looking for a descendent to pass the torch too. I sent her what had become the "Truesdell mess" and she was very pleased to have it.

I really hadn't thought about Gideon Truesdell until 1991, when Jerry Weddle gave me a call inquiring about the Truesdells. After considerable research in Silver City, he ran across my work, and asked if I knew where he could find pictures of the Truesdells for the book he was writing about Billy the Kid's early years in Silver City. I gave him a few names and addresses, and he was able to locate the pictures that appear in *Antrim was my Stepfather's Name: The Boyhood of Billy the Kid*.

It was a thoroughly researched and superbly written book, and it has earned a place in the relatively small collection of books that are recognized by the academic community as definitive works. When it comes to Billy the Kid, you can discard about 80% of the books and magazine articles because most of it is fiction bordering on fantasy.

During the 1990s a wealth of information found its way to the Internet, and after some preliminary searches I found a lot of new information. I would say the Internet and access to online newspaper collections easily tripled the volume of source materials that I now had at my fingertips. I discovered some fascinating historical overlays.

Gideon's partner in Durkee, Truesdell & Company was Charles Durkee, who was friends with a lot of important people in Washington where he served as a Congressman and Senator. He was on a first-name basis with Andrew Johnson, Chief Justice Salmon P. Chase, Secretary of State William Seward, and Secretary of the Treasury William Fessenden.

His brother, Harrison Durkee, was a charter member (1837) of the New York Stock Exchange, and was intimately connected with railroad tycoons Cornelius Vanderbilt and Erastus Corning. I also ran across the "lost Durkee millions," a spectacular lawsuit against the federal government for $64 million ($1.9 billion today), when he had become a supplier of coal, provisions, and railroad ties for which he was paid in Union Pacific and Central Pacific bonds.

Another surprise was Gideon's Chicago attorney, who happened to be a close friend of Abraham Lincoln's, and during the 1860 campaign he spent the night at Henry and Althea Blodgett's Waukegan residence. Gideon's other attorney, and he kept several of them busy because he would sue at the drop of a hat, was Orson Head, stage and screen legend Orson Welles' great grandfather. Gideon was also a partner in the Kenosha Pier Company, one of the largest on Lake Michigan, where John V. Ayer, was a partner, and he was Gerald Ford's great, grandfather.

I found these unexpected historical twists and turns fascinating, and after a fifteen-year gap in my research, I found my interest renewed, more out of curiosity than a historic sense of duty. At the age of forty I found Gideon's life and times far more interesting than I did at nineteen, and had been told that I had unearthed a lot of history. Nothing earth shattering, but a detailed look at life 175 years ago in specific towns.

I'm not a writer but I always thought I could hire others to turn what I had into a regional history, which is what Professor Buenker suggested many years earlier when I submitted a copy of my thesis. During the early 1990s I recruited the first of four writers, mostly graduate students, to reduce over a thousand pages of complicated research into a manuscript, which in hindsight was a mistake.

Each person had their own interpretation of the story with a distinct bias that crept into their writing. They described some people in a way I knew they weren't, sensationalized research data that should have been left alone, and included notes from interviews that should have been used as background information. It wasn't what I envisioned, because I knew the story they presented was inaccurate, and misleading in many areas.

When they failed to put together what I envisioned as "the story" I was ready to give up, and yet I wasn't quite ready to throw the "Truesdell mess" into the garbage. I asked the University of Wisconsin if they had any interest in the papers, and they did but only if they were indexed and organized.

I began this complicated task whenever time and motivation permitted, putting the papers in order similar to the chapters in this book, tracking down information that I gave away to family members decades earlier, and filling in a few gaps. But plugging these holes only raised more questions and increased my curiosity so I kept digging as time permitted.

Twelve years later this caused me to take another stab at telling the story, only this time I figured I'd write it myself and have somebody else clean it up. I pushed ahead with years where I did next to nothing, and years where I spent a fair amount of time pulling things together.

Writing something this complex was a challenge, but when I ran across Cicero's advice to the historian it pushed me in the right direction. "The first law for the historian is that he shall never dare utter an untruth. The second is that he shall suppress nothing that is true, moreover, there shall be no suspicion of partiality in his writing, or of malice."

I knew mistakes were inevitable, so I sent a couple of drafts to some academic people for review, because my greatest concern was accuracy, although for a long time I wasn't so sure that I would ever have the time to get this project completed. It needed so much work and I had so little time.

Soliciting help from the academic community improved the accuracy of the information, and in some instances, they sent me information that helped amplify what I had or caused me to discard a page or two when my research didn't fit. I considered the time period in which Truesdell lived to be a critical part of the back-story, and *Kenosha News* Editor and historian Don Jensen thought that what I had was a collection of discreet stories about the frontier.

Once in a while I ran across descendents or they ran across me, all of whom were helpful and courteous, and who tried to put me in touch with the family keeper of old diaries, letters, and yellowed newspaper clippings. The story really began back in 1900, when Gideon Truesdell's sister-in-law sat down and recited the family history to a grandson. She was married to Gideon's younger brother.

It was told by Rhoda Truesdell (1815–1905) who at the time was eighty-five, and what she recited was typed into five pages thirty-nine years later. During the 1900s her grandson began writing letters to family members, and thirty years later another branch of the family began looking for information. This led to letters between Gideon's great grandson, E. Frances Devos and distant cousins. Gideon's grandsons, Gideon and Chauncey Truesdell, tried to explain what they remembered, and people who had lost touch decades ago began talking to one another.

In 1952, Chauncey's son, who was Vice President of Zenith, sent his father a television. A talk show on NBC asked "old timers" to write about their experiences, and Chauncey sent two pages that included a few paragraphs about Billy the Kid. Robert Mullins of the Haley Memorial Library & History Center, conducted an interview that contradicted some long-accepted details of Billy the Kid's life as a teenager, and scholars accepted this interview as a critical piece of history.

Gideon was an interesting person but I'm not so sure he was that

Richard C. Fritz   17

fascinating, at least no more so than a lot of other pioneers. But he was typical of so many settlers who came to the frontier with little more than a fierce determination to succeed, and they worked unbelievably hard to overcome obstacles. It took plenty of guts and perseverance for the people in this story to have survived, much less prospered.

During the 1830s the opportunities in the Old Northwest Territory were unlimited, but doing business in the wilderness, bank failures, crooked politicians, land grant frauds, crop failures, and the limitations of life during that era were staggering. Those who got ahead had to be at the top of their game to overcome monumental challenges.

When it came to telling "the story" I thought the best way to make sense of the research was to tie it together with the times in which Gideon and Julia Truesdell lived. If you've ever wondered what it was like to live 175 years ago, I think you'll find the first-hand accounts in this story just as fascinating as I did.

—Richard Fritz

1

HOLLAND LAND PURCHASE

The Truesdells Settle in the Holland Land Purchase, circa 1803

Like most distinguished westerners-to-be, Gideon J. Truesdell began life as an easterner. On October 20, 1811, he was born in a cabin built in the wilderness by his parents in what was known as the Holland Land Purchase, 55 miles southeast of Buffalo, New York.[1] As his father had joined the great westward journey from east of the Hudson River, the edge of civilization in those days, Gideon would do the same at the age of twenty-five.[2]

Gideon's family had been in this country for over 175 years after having arrived in 1630 aboard the Winthrop Fleet from England to escape "the plague," and his mother was a Mayflower descendent.[3] This branch of the Truesdell family had most recently lived in Whitehall, New York, near the Hudson River, where they farmed with enough success to make buying fresh soil on the frontier possible.[4] The country was young, and Gideon J. Truesdell's father, Gideon R. (1789–1847), and his uncles had fought in the War of 1812.[5]

It was 22 years after George Washington became the first president of the new United States, which were expanding rapidly, mostly to the west. By the time Gideon J. was born, there were 17 states in the union with the Hudson River becoming the edge of civilization. The wilderness west of the Hudson River was mostly inhabited by Indians and wild animals.

In 1806, the Truesdells, along with many of their neighbors, left Whitehall looking for good soil.[6] Before land management, growing the same crop depleted the soil of essential nutrients. Instead of harvesting 120 bushels per acre, crop yields dropped to 18 to 20 bushels after twenty years of growing the same thing. The Truesdells found fresh soil in the Holland

Land Purchase, 200 miles west of the Hudson River where they could triple their annual yield of wheat, at least until they depleted the fertility of the soil, as they had back in Whitehall, and had to search for fresh soil.

The syndicate of Dutch bankers who had founded the Holland Land Company owned 3.2 million acres between Buffalo and the Genesee River in western New York. They hired thirty-one year old Joseph Ellicott to survey the land and divide it into six square mile townships. In March 1798, he proceeded by hiring draftsmen, cooks, axe-men, camp workers and 150 surveyors. Among Ellicott's surveyors, according to family tradition, were Gideon J. Truesdell's grandfather, Gideon, and his neighbor from down the road, Elizur Webster.[7]

Each surveying party was assigned to measure townships and ranges that tied into boundaries established by Ellicott. They also took detailed notes describing lakes, rivers, streams, valleys, standing timber, and mineral deposits.[8] The observations of the surveyors were important when determining the price of the land.

Diary accounts tell us that the survey was a miserable one as illness and death took a toll on surveyors and their livestock. There were serious supply shortages of food and supplies, yet there was enough alcohol floating around to fuel arguments that turned into drunken brawls.[9] By the end of the year most of the work had been completed except for isolated areas. The western survey ended abruptly on December 7, 1778, when a blizzard blanketed the area.[10]

Whatever his experience with the survey crew, it was the opening of the Holland Land Company office in the back of a roadside tavern at Clarence Hollow that caused Gideon's close friend and neighbor, thirty-six year old Elizur Webster, to buy a parcel of land that he intended to sell to his neighbors.[11] Webster was a descendant of John Webster, a colonial governor of Connecticut, and a successful farmer.

The relationship between the Truesdell and Webster families was close; they owned farms on the Whitehall-Hampton township border and worshipped at the same Baptist Church where Elizur's sister married Gideon Truesdell's son, John.

During the spring of 1803, Elizur traveled to the Holland Land Purchase with his sixteen year old brother, William, to purchase land. A cousin, Jabez Warren (1761–1810) was already there surveying roads for the land company. He advised Elizur to buy land along a tributary of the Genesee River at what was then called Allen's Creek (Oatka Creek today).[12]

Elizur rode south a few miles until he came to a creek where the Senecas camped and where a heavily-wooded valley straddled a creek with good water-power. This was critical, because in those days sawmills, gristmills, and tanneries were powered by a water-wheel that drove the equipment.

Since he didn't bring any surveyor's tools, Elizur made a measuring stick from bark. With a compass and stick, he surveyed a 3,600 acre claim that was off by no more than 30 feet when surveyed many years later with proper instruments.[13]

Throughout the summer of 1803, Elizur and William Webster spent most of their time chopping down trees, and bartered a few acres with another settler to build a cabin.[14] Before returning to Whitehall/Hampton for the winter, they had hundreds of logs cut and stacked down by the creek for a sawmill that Simeon Hovey (1776–1862) was building for Webster.[15] Hovey, a carpenter, had bartered his skills for a 10 acre parcel. Over the winter, he carved the gears for a waterwheel on his wife's kitchen table.[16]

Joseph Ellicott and William Johnson representing the Holland Land Company completing the survey in 1804 in Buffalo. Photo courtesy of the Buffalo and Erie County Historical Society.

The Holland Land Company had dozens of loggers clearing trees for a roadway that would run westerly all the way to Buffalo, and another that would run north and south between the settlements north to Rochester and south to Belmont, New York.

The land was thick with trees and undergrowth with trails "brushed out by wood choppers." Cutting a trail through the dense wilderness was slow and arduous work with mules pulling logs out of the roadway. For heavier work an ox was preferable because they could pull a 500 hundred pound log from a dead-stop but they moved at an agonizingly slow pace.

Early trails were called "avenues of convenience," and built to facilitate the movement of crops while allowing prospective settlers to inspect the land before buying. A pathway was cut through the wilderness by strong young men who were paid $40 ($16,000 today) per mile, with two-thirds payable in land and one-third in cash. To make it easier for travelers, the Holland Land Company offered free land at ten mile intervals to anyone who would build a tavern or inn.

Building a roadway meant clearing the underbrush, leveling riverbanks and streams for easier crossings, draining swamps, and building bridges across low lying areas with logs. Large trees were left standing, which meant roadways had irregular twists and turns, but despite their primitive construction they greatly improved travel time throughout the 3.2 million acres in the Holland Land Purchase.

During the spring of 1804, several families traveled through the wilderness from the Baptist settlement of Whitehall and Hampton, mostly Baptists, to the land they bought in the Holland Purchase.[17] Two years later Dorcas Truesdell sold the remainder of her husband's land, and by the time she and her children arrived in the settlement of South Warsaw, there were forty dwellings scattered on the land Elizur Webster sold to his friends and neighbors a few years earlier.[18]

From *History of the Town of Warsaw* (New York, page 53):

> Life was far more hazardous than anything we can imagine when settlements were small and distances between farms was great. When Artemas Shattuck was trapped by a falling tree in a freak accident, he was spun upside down with his foot stuck, and he was left suspended high in the air where he couldn't touch the ground, or pull himself into a sitting position on a branch.
>
> He yelled for help until he began suffering extreme pain from hanging upside down by a foot for hours. He continued yelling but was three-fourths of a mile away from the nearest cabin, and the weather was starting to turn cold. He knew that he would soon lose consciousness from hanging upside down, which meant that he

would be dead by morning unless he did something extreme. He ran through a list of options, and the only one that made sense was severing his foot.

He realized that even then there was a good chance that he might bleed to death, but if he did nothing he was as good as dead. He pulled out of his hip pocket an old Barlow knife, and cut off the leg of his boot and sock, and with a piece of line that he had in his pocket, he tied-off his ankle as tightly as possible to stop the flow of blood. After mentally preparing himself for the pain and gore he took a deep breath, carefully severed his ankle, and left his foot in the cleft of the tree.

Shattuck slide down the tree trunk, and crawled to his dinner basket where he bound-up the stump with a napkin. He cut a stick, and hobbled or crawled on his hands and knees through the snow towards his cabin. When he arrived within a few rods of his place he was discovered by his family. Exhausted and almost ready to pass out from the pain and loss of blood, he was brought indoors and resuscitated.

Widow Truesdell Brings Her Family to the Holland Land Purchase, Circa 1806

According a descendant who did extensive research, Gideon Truesdell (1756–1799), father of Gideon R. and grandfather of Gideon J., was one of the surveyors hired by Joseph Ellicott, which seems plausible because he had been appointed to several positions in Whitehall that dealt with surveying

Some descendants believe Gideon died around 1830 but the weight of evidence suggests he died at age forty-two or forty-three soon after the survey ended, possibly from pneumonia or an accident, and several years before his family moved to the Holland Purchase.[19] He was still living in 1799 because his wife Dorcas gave birth to a daughter the following spring.[20] But his death is corroborated by the 1800 federal census where Dorcas is listed as the head of the household, and the 1804 Whitehall tax assessment where she is listed as a "widow."[21]

Although deceased, 562 acres had been purchased in the name of "Gideon Truesdell," but which one? The father was dead, and the son, Gideon R. Truesdell (1789–1847), was fourteen years old and still a minor.

Since it would be years before the land could be entered at a courthouse, Webster probably listed the land in Gideon's name, knowing it had already been inherited by Gideon's widow, Dorcas, who would divide it between her children at a later date.

Before the family left Whitehall for the Holland Land Purchase, the connection with the Webster family became even closer when Gideon and Dorcas' son, twenty-four year old John Truesdell (1784–1838), married Elizur Webster's sister, Betsy (1789–1870) on January 16th, 1806.[22]

Before leaving the Whitehall farm, Dorcas and her children loaded several wagons with possessions needed in the heavily-wooded wilderness: cast iron skillets, pots, utensils, clay bowls, a spinning wheel, rifles, traps, carpentry tools, and farm implements with breeding stock tethered behind slow-moving wagons.

It wouldn't have been an easy trip for Mrs. Truesdell with children ranging in age from six to twenty-four. A fifteen year old daughter, Dorcas, was deaf, although she learned how to read, write, speak, and eventually married.[23]

When the Truesdells arrived in the Holland Land Purchase, their 562 acres were unevenly divided between Gideon and Dorcas' children.[24] Cabins were built as a son or daughter married with each family operating their own farm, mostly for their own personal use, while operating a sawmill, tannery, grist mill, match factory, and hotel. About a quarter of each brother's property was left as a woodland to supply firewood for the next 50 years.

In addition to farming, each son started a small business. According to family legend, the patriarch of the family, Gideon Truesdell (1756–1799), made saddles, leather harnesses, and shoes, measuring each foot with long straws from a broom. The shoes were so well made they could be worn on either foot for five to ten years.

A couple of decades came and went before settlements were scattered throughout the Holland Land Purchase, all with mail service in a day when such correspondence was their only link with the outside world. At best, during the 1820s mail moved slowly by mail carriers with a leather bag of letters slung over their shoulder as they traveled on post roads. These were government roads between post offices, and anyone caught operating a private mail service was severely punished. A letter for one of the Truesdells would have first passed through the Batavia land office.

Primitive trails were chopped through the woods between settlements, with barely enough room for a covered wagon, horses, and breeding stock tethered behind the last wagon. Picture courtesy of the Monmouth County Park System.

A letter would have been addressed to "John Truesdell, Batavia - #9 - First Range." Batavia was the closest land office and "9" was the section of land he owned.[25] At Batavia, mail was passed to the next person riding 30 miles south to the designated area, where it was delivered to a general store or tavern to be picked up.

In 1808, nineteen year old Gideon R. Truesdell (1789–1847) fell in love with the girl down the road, twenty year old Polly Bannister (1788–1856), who lived with her uncles at what was then called Bannister's Settlement.[26] They probably met at church, and as a teenager she came from Windsor County, Vermont along the Connecticut River to the Holland Land Purchase.[27] On October 20, 1811, Gideon J. Truesdell, the subject of this biography, was born along with the following brothers and sisters.[28]

Polly Diadema Truesdell (King), 1809–1902
Jeremiah Crandall Truesdell, 1810–1860
Gideon J. Truesdell, 1811–1882
Amos Truesdell, 1813–1885
Levi Truesdell, 1815–1887
Ezra Truesdell, 1817–1895
Clarissa Truesdell (Davis), 1819–1906

A few years after Gideon's birth, and in addition to his 166-acre farm, his father bought farmland about four miles south at Bannister's

Settlement.²⁹ At a time when most people farmed 20 to 40 acres Gideon R. had hundreds of acres in cultivation, which required a lot of manpower but generated a very good income. It was an era when farmers made up a large proportion of the population and often enjoyed a status as prosperous community leaders, but not without lots of hard work and perseverance.

Gideon and Polly had five sons who, like children on other farms, were accustomed to hard work because by the time they were teenagers they were working sixteen hour days during the planting and harvesting seasons. They learned to work from dawn to dusk, and thought nothing of it because they were working alongside of their parents. Boys as young as five or six spent summers chopping weeds in the wheat fields with a small, specially made hoe while the girls helped their mother with the endless procession of household chores. Children followed their parents' example of living frugally with decisions made with common sense, and we know from descendants that the family read passages from the Bible every night.³⁰ (Dorcas was descended from Elder John Crandall (1612–1675), a prominent Rhode Island Baptist clergyman who died defending the Narragansett Indians.)

Pioneer cabin pictures courtesy of Museum of Appalachia.

Six years after they arrived in the Holland Land Purchase, the United States was at war again with England. At a time when there wasn't an organized army, volunteer militias from each state were activated. When the call went out, thirty year old Jeremiah Truesdell, twenty-five year old Solomon, twenty-three year old Gideon R., and twenty-two year old Timothy Truesdell joined Nobles Regiment in the light infantry.³¹

Regiments from the Holland Purchase were called to fight during the "War on the Niagara Frontier." Although their length of service was only a little more than a month, the action pulled hundreds of men from their work in the fields during the fall harvest.[32] During another call to arms, Timothy Truesdell stayed behind to harvest crops while his brothers were away on the shores of Lake Erie.

The previous decade had been difficult for settlers due to high property taxes and land payments. When the fighting began, another tax was imposed to pay for the war, which everyone had to pay or risk losing their property. This forced housewives to spin cloth from flax so they had something to trade for goods at the general store so they could conserve enough cash to pay their taxes. Not surprisingly, some farmers smuggled food across the Niagara River to the British at inflated prices so they could pay high wartime taxes.

The fighting began on September 8, 1812, when a hundred New York soldiers crossed the Niagara River into Canada to seize the schooners Caledonia and Detroit, but due to a calm wind they couldn't sail back, and were only able to beach them against the Canadian shoreline. After stealing about $150,000 worth of furs, they set the Detroit on fire.

A few days later, when the Truesdells crossed the river to fight the British there were heavy casualties. General VanRensselaer sent for reinforcements but when 1,200 soldiers saw wagon after wagon piled with dead soldiers, they refused to cross the river. They would fight to protect New York farms and settlements but not to defend foreign soil.

The 800 soldiers who had crossed the river were badly outnumbered, and about 1,000 Americans were wounded, captured or killed. Sometimes the British recruited the Indians, mostly Algonquins, to strip dead militia soldiers of their clothes and scalp them. Some militia soldiers surrendered, but the Truesdell brothers managed to escape and found their way back to their farms.[33]

On November 3, 1812, when Noble's Regiment was disbanded, the Truesdells and in-law Daniel Bannister returned home. Two years later when they were once again called to duty, Solomon Truesdell spent a month in Churchill's Militia while his brother Timothy was assigned to Captain Bronson's New York Volunteers.[34]

After the fighting was over Gideon R. Truesdell (1789–1847) returned to his cabin in South Warsaw along Truesdell Road, where several years earlier, at the age of seventeen he had begun clearing land to plant wheat, a cash crop he could sell to grain elevators in Buffalo for a high price due to demand.

Corn, which didn't sell for nearly as much but had myriad uses, was mixed with tall grass and fed to the cattle. Husks were used to stuff mattresses, and cobs were turned into corks for jugs or tool handles. Four bushels of corn could feed a hog until he tipped the scales at over four hundred pounds, and a hand full of kernels fed a flock of chickens. In addition to harvesting hay from fields for winter feed, every farmer planted a few acres of barley to supplement their livestocks diet.

Battle of Lake Erie, September 10th, 1813, by William Henry Powell. Painting courtesy of the U.S. Senate Archives.

A lazy farmer squandered his grass when he didn't rotate grazing animals to other pastures so it could grow back. Grass (hay) cut early in the season weighed less but was far more nutritious whereas grass cut late in the season created a larger tonnage but was less nutritious.

One agricultural journal warned farmers not to cut more grass than they could rake and bundle by late afternoon, because once the sun set moisture from dew contaminated the grass with mold. Shocks of wheat had to be turned over in the fields so the sun could thoroughly dry them out before separating the wheat from the chaff.

In 1827, sixteen year old Gideon J. Truesdell (1811–1882), the subject of this biography, bought 80 acres near the tiny hamlet of Portageville,

New York, with a small down payment and his father's signature.[35] His ambitious nature is clearly evident even at this age because he got started earlier than most young men. He lived his entire life at a fast pace. A year later, his fifteen year old brother, Amos Truesdell (1813–1885), bought 80 acres and they cleared about half their land for farming.[36]

A young man could clear an acre in about a week with an axe and a mule. But a half dozen men could clear an acre in a day, and since there were over sixty-five Truesdell and Bannister cousins living in the area, Gideon and Amos probably were able to line-up a small army of kinfolk to help them clear their land for farming.

Most land was cleared during the winter, because except for tending to the livestock there wasn't much work to do. The ground was frozen, which made chopping down trees and grubbing the underbrush much easier, when young men slashed through the woods at a rapid pace from dawn to dusk.

Trees were pulled to the side of the field by mules, and left to dry for a year before they were burned the following spring. Piles of ashes were shoveled into barrels because they were a cash crop. "Asheries" paid top dollar, and 10 acres yielded about five 100-pound barrels of potash. Gideon and Amos probably loaded about a ton of ashes into wagons for their agonizingly slow trip to the nearest ashery 55 miles northwest in Buffalo. After selling twenty barrels, Gideon and Amos would have been able to pay their workers a good wage, and still had enough left over to purchase an expensive cast iron plow.

Winter storms and chilly temperatures kept Gideon and Amos indoors working on projects in front of the fireplace. Many husbands and wives made shingles because lumberyards paid top dollar for them. They would have brought two-foot bolts of wood indoors, and using a cleaving tool split them from the grain into shingles. By spring, they would have had a couple thousand of them stacked in the barn ready to sell to one of the yards in Buffalo or Rochester. Another winter occupation was woodworking. Based on family tradition Gideon, Amos, and Ezra were skilled cabinetmakers who filled orders for chests of drawers, tables and chairs, bed frames, or dressers during the winters.[37]

It was in nearby Mt. Morris, New York, that Gideon, 22, met Julia Ann Torrey (1813–1878).[38] In 1833, he married this kindhearted, hard working, and beautiful twenty year old farm girl.[39] Like Gideon, she came from a successful farming family, and was deeply religious with several ministers among her kinfolk, including her grandfather.

Two years later, Gideon's twenty-two year old brother, Amos, tied the knot with twenty year old Rhoda Mills, who came to America from London, England. They were married by Reverend William Arthur, father of the twenty-first president of the United States.[40] To accommodate the newlyweds, the brothers built another cabin a few hundred feet from the barn; Gideon and Julia's cabin on one side, Amos and Rhoda's were on the other.[41]

At age eighty-seven, Rhoda dictated several accounts of what she remembered about pioneer life to her grandchildren, recalling that she and Gideon's wife, Julia, were close friends.[42] This would have been only natural because their husbands were close, and turned to each other throughout their lives for support.[43] While Gideon and Amos worked in the fields, slaughtered pigs, milked cows, and shoveled manure their wives shared the cooking, washing, spinning of wool, quilting, canning fruits, and hundreds of other chores.[44]

Gideon Truesdell Catches a Bad Case of Western Fever, 1836

Since the age of sixteen, Gideon had been farming although a lot longer since he had been helping his father since a small child. But by the age of twenty-five things weren't moving fast enough to suit him. His father had done well as a farmer in "Magnificent Genesee County," but farming was a plodding and methodical lifestyle, and a yearly crapshoot where their yearly income hinged on the fall harvest. Too much or too little rain could leave a farmer with little to show for a year's work. A farmer was always rolling the dice with Mother Nature with as many years coming up twos as sevens.

His brother Jeremiah had also ruled out farming, at least for the time being, and was working as a stone mason in Buffalo. It seems likely that Gideon and Amos heard from him that the Buffalo & Black Rock was looking for loggers to build bridges for a small strap-line railroad to improve movement around a rapidly growing port city.[45]

Horse-drawn railroads were cutting edge transportation during the early 1800s for moving people and freight around large cities. Little more than stagecoaches or flatbed wagons modified with smaller iron wheels, a streetcar ran on steel straps nailed to wooden rails. The Buffalo & Black

Pictures courtesy of Buffalo and Erie County Historical Society.

Although Gideon and Amos had driven wagons loaded with wheat to the Buffalo grain elevators, it's doubtful that they experienced much of life beyond their farms and sleepy little Portageville. Based on a family narrative, Gideon and Amos landed winter jobs that paid well, and we know from Amos' widow that during the fall of 1834, twenty-three year old Gideon and twenty-one year old Amos, began working on a Buffalo & Black Rock railroad construction crew.[46]

After harvesting their crops, they probably hitched a ride to Buffalo and shared a room, becoming temporary residents of a big city with a population of 15,000. Rooms were scarce and it was common for three or four men to share a bed in a boarding house, sleeping in shifts with day workers using the bed at night and night workers sleeping during the day. If Gideon and Amos stayed with their brother Jeremiah and his wife, which seems plausible, they would have been far more comfortable and saved boarding fees.[47]

The following winter, the Truesdells were working for the Buffalo & Niagara Falls line, which had acquired the Buffalo & Black Rock when tracks were extended to Niagara Falls.[48] They moved up a notch, because instead of chopping down trees, they were part of a crew building bridges and trestles using mule power to move heavy beams. They used ropes, pulleys and muscle to notch a twenty-foot log weighing 600 to 800 pounds into place five or six stories above the ground.[49]

In January 1835, Gideon's wife Julia gave birth to a child, but, according to Portageville cemetery records, she died five months later.[50] Their infant daughter, Maude, was buried in the family plot with the Genesee River flowing below a beautiful bluff, the first of many infants that were stillborn or died within a few weeks or months after their birth.

The presumption that death follows a long and productive life belongs in another century. Accidents, epidemics, pneumonia, childbirth and archaic medical practices took their toll. Nearly every family could expect to lose at least one child, and childbirth was the great killer of young women.

In Buffalo, docks on the riverfront were crowded with freight-forwarding houses. Freight originating in New York City was brought up the Hudson River in schooners, and loaded aboard packet boats sailing west along the Erie Canal. Once they reached Buffalo at the eastern end of Lake Erie, the cargo was loaded aboard ships sailing to ports on the Great Lakes. During the winter over 100 schooners froze in the Buffalo harbor with crew members living aboard to save living expenses. After the spring thaw, the sleepy port came alive again.

Taverns along the riverfront were crowded with men talking about the western frontier, a world of land that could be bought for $1.25 an acre, sky high crop yields, commercial outposts of unheard-of opportunities, native stands of pine ripe for the harvesting, and tales of ordinary men striking it rich in the Old Northwest Territory.

Men returning from the frontier discussed where trading posts were located along rivers, which rivers would settle first due to superb geography, the best locations for mills, friendly or hostile Indians and how much protection they could expect from military forts. Newspapers of the day described young men with a burning desire to settle on the frontier as having caught a "case of western fever," and by 1836 Gideon had surely caught it.

Gideon's father and grandfather had pushed westward looking for opportunities. Now, it was time for him to take his turn in the generational push for a better life. The newspapers were full of stories of ordinary men striking it rich on the frontier, and for an ambitious young man like Gideon, these stories would have made it impossible for him to go back to farming. But where were the best opportunities for a young man without a lot of money?

For years, the area on the western side of Lake Michigan had been part of the Michigan Territory, but in 1836 it was about to be split off into a new territory when Michigan petitioned for statehood. It would be an incredible opportunity for young men tough enough to try their luck on the unsettled frontier among the Indians and wild animals. The government would sell cheap land to encourage settlement, and the right parcel of land along a river or developing settlement could make a young man affluent. The beneficiary of the occupation of Indian land was the lumber industry with farmers not far behind.

It had been a decade since Gideon cleared the trees off his land. Now, during the autumn of 1836 and after the crops were in the barn, he was anxious to take a look at the Wisconsin frontier. He dragged his twenty-three year old brother Amos along for a look at the land west of Lake Michigan between Milwaukee and Chicago. They traveled to Buffalo where they boarded a schooner sailing through the Great Lakes to Milwaukee. There were 2,893 people living on either side of the Milwaukee River, many of whom were speculators looking to buy land.[51] When they got off the boat, hucksters were waiting for them with maps selling for the inflated price of $1.35 ($69 today). They were drawn from old Jesuit maps leftover from the late 1700s, but weren't terribly accurate although they did give a rough idea of where rivers, streams, and Indian trails were located in relation to military trails.

Wisconsin Territory, Circa 1836

When a territory had 100,000 residents it could petition for statehood, and in 1836 that's exactly what the Michigan legislature did. The result was that the land east of Lake Michigan, plus the Upper Peninsula became the State of Michigan. The land west of Lake Michigan and south of Lake Superior became the Wisconsin Territory, which included Minnesota, Iowa and parts of the eastern Dakotas.

Gideon and Amos didn't leave behind a diary account of their trip through the Great Lakes, but Nelson and Thomas Olin did when they made a similar trip in 1836 from Buffalo to Green Bay.[52]

After spending the night at a tavern in Buffalo, the Olins had to walk three miles to catch the steamer, United States, headed for Cleveland and Detroit, where the Olins spent two days looking for another ship sailing to Green Bay. After a few days, the Jacob Barker pulled into Detroit ready to set sail north to St. Ignace Bay between the Upper and Lower Peninsula of Michigan. They took their chances, hoping to catch a ride aboard a ship sailing directly to Green Bay, a gateway to the Midwest through the Fox River and its tributaries and a portage to the Wisconsin River. Since the 1700s, fur traders and settlers followed a series of rivers southwesterly from

Green Bay to the Mississippi River, which eventually brought them to St. Louis.

When the Olins asked the captain if he could take them north to the Straits of Mackinac, he replied, "Yes, if you can put up with my fare… lie on the deck, a billet of wood for a pillow, and find your own grub. If you have no blankets, you can have an old sail for a covering."[53] They went ashore, bought some crackers and jumped on board just as the ship was pulling away from the dock.[54]

Of their nautical interlude, the Olins said, "When we entered the crooked river with strong headwinds, it seemed almost impossible to make any headway. The river was full of vessels that couldn't move an inch, and the captains were thunderstruck to see the Jacob Barker sailing so easily and gracefully past them. Finally, by tacking from one side of the river to the other, he worked his vessel up into Lake Huron where he had fair sailing, but we had headwinds the greater part of the way to within ten miles of Mackinac, where we encountered a thick, heavy fog and then calm. We did not stir an inch for twenty-four hours.[55]

"We were stuck in Mackinac for two weeks while waiting for a ship heading to Green Bay, but found a place on the Mackinac. She sailed along smooth until we passed the light ship and came into grand old Lake Michigan, where the waves seemed from one-half to one mile high, threatening any moment to send the old craft to the bottom….we ran to the mouth of Green Bay just as the sun was setting, a sailor continually sounding the bottom (this was done with a lead sinker attached to a rope with knots every six feet; a fathom was six feet) crying at the top of his voice 'SEVEN FATHOMS – SIX FATHOMS – FIVE FATHOMS – FOUR FATHOMS.' When he cried out four fathoms the captain's eyes bugged out, yelling that this wasn't the mouth of the bay because the water there was 24 feet deep.

"As the Captain had never been in the bay and the water was growing shallow fast, he became alarmed and ordered the helmsman 'put her about.' No, said the pilot, it is the mouth of the bay surely, keep her on her way. But the Captain's orders prevailed. She was put about, sails lowered, and she was allowed to drift all night. As soon as it was light the sails were hoisted and we were again on our way toward the mouth of the bay.

"When about a mile from the dock we saw a boat coming to meet us and when in hailing distance those on deck wanted to know if there was anyone on board who wished to work, who could handle a jack plane and a saw. We gave them encouragement to that effect and after we landed, they came up and wished to hire us.

"I was at work on the bank of the Fox River on June 8, when a large man about six feet two inches in height came along, and he being a little the worse for strong drink I concluded. He said to me 'young man, what are you doing here?' I am making holes in this timber and getting it ready to build a house. 'What are you getting for your work?' One dollar per day, I said. 'Oh, go to Milwaukee. There you can do better.' I said I would think about it. He said his name was Solomon Juneau. (A fur trader, land speculator and one of the founders of Milwaukee.) He had come to the Bay to prove up his preemption and would return in the course of a week or ten days.

"He wished that my brother and I would return with him. With a pack horse to carry his grub he had come through on the trail, and would probably return that way if no boat came along. In the course of the next week Juneau brought his business to a close and on June 17 the old steamer Michigan came into sight and soon hauled up to the dock. Juneau boarded the vessel to see if Captain Blake would take five or six passengers on board bound for Milwaukee. The captain at first refused for he knew nothing about the place, and did not know whether he could anchor there.

"His anchors were insufficient in case of a storm, but finally he concluded to take us on and run us in as near as he dared and set us ashore in the yawl. It was near midnight when we came in sight of a light. The command was given to 'keep her off-keep her off more-there may be large boulders far out from this point, keep her out.' Juneau was called out to say whether the light he saw were near Milwaukee.

"'Yes, that light is in Orendorf's shanty. You're all right Captain. Steer straight for that light and you are all right.' The boat was run in as near as the captain thought prudent, the anchors cast overboard, and the yawl ordered down. With passengers and trunks on board, the yawl started for the shore.

"As we neared the beach, the retreating waves carried us back into the lake in spite of all we were able to do and the yawl filled with water. A second effort was made, but we were again carried back to the retreating waves. Another rush was made for the shore and when near the beach the sailors sprang out of the boat, grabbed it and hauled it out on the beach

Richard C. Fritz   35

in spite of the waves. Such was the landing of passengers from the first steamboat that ever came into the bay at Milwaukee."[56]

Having followed a parallel journey through the Great Lakes, Gideon and Amos would have rented horses from a Milwaukee livery stable and rode south on the Green Bay Military Trail, which took them through untouched land that was perfect for farming, roughly twelve miles west of Lake Michigan. When they reached the Chicago River neither brother was impressed. Inflated land prices and swampy land caused them to keep looking. They returned to Milwaukee, taking the much busier lakeshore path that was within eyesight of Lake Michigan, passing through dozens of small settlements that had developed along rivers or streams emptying into the lake.[57] Sometimes a traveler got lucky, and were able to hitch a ride aboard a schooner sailing between Chicago and Milwaukee with their horses stabled on deck.

Due to the Treaty of Cedar Point (1836) along the Wisconsin River in the "pinery," stands of valuable timber, mainly white pine, were waiting near riverbanks to be harvested by the likes of Gideon Truesdell and other ambitious young men. But chopping down trees in the wilderness, building a water-powered sawmill, and rafting the lumber 426 miles to St. Louis would require an incredible amount of tenacity. Life on the frontier was tough, dangerous, and a young man's game.

Not that they had any say in the matter, the Menominee Indians had just sold a strip of land 48 miles long and three miles on each side of the Wisconsin River to the government amounting to four million acres. Settlers would need lumber, and there was enough timber on this strip for the next sixty years. Those who got there first could file claims on the best locations where there were rapids powerful enough to run a sawmill. By locking up a parcel along the river, a shrewd frontiersman could start a logging company to supply the mills that were sure to follow.

There was an acute shortage of lumber that would last for another five years across the developing Midwest, with lumber selling for 500% more on the frontier than back east. It was a risky proposition, starting a logging company in the middle of the wilderness among the Indians and wild animals, and rafting the lumber down a treacherous river. But if everything fell into place Gideon stood to make a small fortune, and by the end of his exploratory trip he was ready to risk everything he had for a shot at something much bigger than farming.

But he would have to roll the dice without his brother Amos, who wanted no part of such a complicated scheme, and returned to his farm. He bought his brother's 80 acres and continued to farm for the next 14 years before moving to land in Deerfield, Illinois.[58] As close as the brothers were, they never really understood each other, and many years later Amos told a grandson without a trace of recrimination that "Gid took too many chances."[59] And he did.

Troubled Times on the Wisconsin Frontier; the Arrival of Judge James Doty, Morgan Martin, Panic of 1837, and the Winnebago War

James Doty (1799–1865) arrived in the Wisconsin Territory after studying for the bar exam, and at age nineteen was appointed to a clerkship with the Michigan Territorial Court. He came from a prominent family with heavy-duty connections, and was a Mayflower descendent. He resigned his clerkship so he could serve as Governor Lewis Cass's aide on an inspection tour of the western side of the Territory through what would become Wisconsin, Minnesota, and Iowa. As the Governor's protégé, his career was fast-tracked until he had contacts at the highest levels of the Democratic Party. Despite being a youthful looking twenty-four year old, his friends pulled some strings in the Monroe Administration to get him appointed to a federal judgeship.

Judges, especially in sparsely populated territories, often ascended to the bench because of their politics, not brilliance, and the courts were badly run. Outcomes depended on judges' political affiliations more so than the law, although Doty followed the law and did a respectable job under difficult circumstances. As a new territory where the law wasn't always enforced, he was instructed to bring justice to the frontier. This was a tall order because for years the frontier had been run by autocratic army officers and Indian agents, many who made a fortune "double-dipping" by charging the Indians and U.S. government for the same thing.

His first high-profile prosecution was of a military officer who struck and jailed a fur trader. In the past nobody cared, but with a U.S. Attorney and a judge investigating the matter the officer had some explaining to do. In another case, when an Indian agent heard that a lumberman was logging Indian land, he had him arrested and thrown into jail without due process.

Judge Doty's cousin, Morgan Martin (1805–1887), joined him on the Wisconsin frontier, and was destined to become somebody of note in the emerging territory. When he arrived in Green Bay in 1827, he was just twenty-two years old, and there were about 100 residents, mainly of French or French-Menominee ancestry. The following year he traveled with Judge Doty, U.S. Marshall Thomas Rowland and Deputy Marshall William Meldrum from Green Bay to the Fox River and then down the Wisconsin River to Prairie du Chien where it emptied into the Mississippi. Six men were hired to paddle a large canoe that could hold twelve tons of passengers, provisions, cooking equipment, tents and cots. The passengers spent lazy days floating down the river talking, napping, and stopping for meals where their servants cooked along the shoreline. The men got out, stretched their legs, and walked along the riverfront.

Besides passing through pristine, untouched countryside they had important work to do, because two American adults and their child had been murdered. A very public scalping and a big celebration got the government's attention, and to avoid further issues tribal leaders turned over the culprits. The depredations began when white settlers arrogantly took over their lead mining ranges along the Wisconsin-Illinois border. Lead mining had long been the Winnebagos' largest source of income, and by 1828, there were over 10,000 easterners and Europeans mining a large tonnage of lead on their land. This unwanted encroachment robbed them of a significant share of their yearly income, and added another layer of tensions on the frontier.

By the time the government got involved the situation had escalated to several murders by a small band of angry Indians. Again, to avoid problems with the U.S. Army, tribal leaders wisely turned over the eight men responsible for the killings, signed a peace treaty, and sold the lead mining ranges to the United States in a scenario that was becoming quite normal. Trying to "civilize" the Indians had been a failure. Sending them to reservations where they could live among their people, raise crops, and butcher livestock became the government's remedy to an immensely complicated problem.

Since most of the Wisconsin Territory belonged to several tribes, Governor Henry Dodge was ordered by the Department of Interior to bring them to the bargaining table. The government wanted to pressure them to sell millions of acres but the Chief's objected to several clauses in the treaty. They were highly intelligent tribal leaders who could see through their empty promises, and the Chippewas insisted on retaining hunting and fishing rights so they could continue feeding their people.

Governor Dodge showed them the boundaries of the purchase on a map, said that the government would pay them $700,000 ($179 million today) with a down payment, and that the remaining balance would be paid in yearly installments over a 20-year period. Half-bloods would receive a "donation" of $100,000, and the Indians would first have to spend most of this money to satisfy unpaid debts to traders like the American Fur Company.

Chief Flat Mouth argued heatedly about the "unpaid debts" clause because many of the debtors were dead or had been killed while trapping furs for the white man. As far as he was concerned, once a man died, his debts died with him. He argued that for decades fur traders lived on Chippewa land, ate their animals, fished in their streams, and used their wood for fuel and building materials without asking permission or paying them a cent. He insisted that these unpaid debts didn't exist, and argued that the annuity should be forever since the land would be gone forever. Sixty years later their grandchildren would be left with nothing while the white man had everything, and yet it's doubtful that the Indians could continue to live as they had because their way of life was rapidly becoming a thing of the past.

Officials tried to appease them with the promise they could fish and hunt as long as the government allowed, but made it clear that the land would no longer belong to them. Cash payments were to be made in gold coins until the fur companies came up with an even better arrangement. They would issue promissory notes, which were worthless except at a trading post where traders determined the exchange rate. It was a way for the white man to get his hands on more of their money, because in 1837 trading posts collected over $360,000 ($85 million today) from the first Indian treaty payments from four tribes.[60]

Prior to the Treaty of Cedar Point, and at a time when most of the land was still owned by the Indians, the Secretary of War's office in Washington had to issue permits to businessmen that wanted to conduct logging operations on Indian land.[61] Before a single tree could be chopped down, they had to come to an agreement with tribal leaders, who sometimes accepted horses, guns, or whiskey for the privilege of removing trees from their land.

In 1827, well before the Treaty of Cedar Point, frontiersman Daniel Whitney was given permission from the Winnebagos to chop down trees on their land, for which he traded gun powder, lead shot, tobacco, seed corn, and other goods.[62] He hired 22 Stockbridge Indians from the Green

Bay area to chop down trees and work in this mill, which he turned over to his nephew, David Whitney (1804–1838).[63] Since the Stockbridge tribe were prohibited from hunting on Winnebago land, Whitney had to ship provisions 126 miles southwest from Green Bay to Fort Winnebago, at the portage between the Fox and Wisconsin rivers. Then, north through the woods to his field operations at the mouth of the Yellow River, where it emptied into the Wisconsin River.[64]

When soldiers at Fort Winnebago noticed pack mules loaded with provisions going north, they reported this to their superiors. Major David Twiggs ordered one of Whitney's men to send the Stockbridge workers away because he knew this could lead to trouble. The Stockbridge Indians were a transplanted New York tribe cutting trees on Winnebago land.[65]

Whitney ignored Twiggs, whom he had absolutely no respect for, and told his men to take trails that bypassed Fort Winnebago. When the Major learned they were still cutting trees and making shingles, he sent an officer, 12 soldiers, and a U.S. Indian agent to Whitney's camp where they found over 200,000 shingles.[66] They pushed the Indians off Winnebago land, burned most of the shingles, and took enough to shingle a new barracks at the fort.

Whitney sued the Major for $3,000 ($720,000 today) for the "molestation" of his business but dropped his lawsuit due to a lack of evidence.[67] Twiggs brought a criminal case against Whitney for trespassing on Indian lands but his case went nowhere.[68]

"All of us knew Twiggs bore a bad character,"[69] recalled attorney Morgan Martin. Later, while stationed in Texas just prior to the Civil War, Twiggs released federal installations to the Confederacy without permission and was immediately relieved of his command. His true character surfaced, and he was exposed as a liar and a traitor.

In 1831, prior to the treaties ceding small parcels of Indian land to the white man, Daniel Whitney received permission from the War Department to build another mill upstream from his shingle mill with his nephew David Whitney (1804–1838). He added a log cabin that served as a trading post, lodging and living quarters for David's wife and five young children. A cook was hired and a clerk to run the trading post while Whitney was away on business, paddling his canoe to different settlements as far away as St. Louis. She was the first white woman in the area, and a true frontier wife who endured her share of hardships and perils but managed to gain the respect of the Indians.[70]

The Indians referred to this place as Nekoosa, at the southern end of the 48-mile strip of forests ceded to the United States by the Menominee tribe. The French-Canadian explorers and fur traders called it Point Basse because it was at the point below the last rapids of the Wisconsin River, and were subsequently called Whitney's Rapids. The river ran twenty-one miles from elevated highlands to lowland marshes. In 1837, this became the destination of Gideon and Julia Truesdell.

Northwest Trading Company's trading post on the Snake River. There was a small living quarters, trading post, and warehouse for storing furs or merchandise. This trading post is very similar to Whitney's at Whitney's Rapids. Drawing courtesy of the Minnesota Historical Society.

Deep in the wilderness along the Wisconsin River the pristine forests were untouched by the white man, the animal population vastly outnumbered the settlers, and some of the Indians weren't pleased to see them while other tribes were friendly. The winters were unbelievably cold with days where it did nothing but snow, and the only trail going north into the woods was a washed-out dirt Indian trail.

Gideon and Julia were entering a world that can legitimately be called the great unknown. It was a vast expanse of wilderness, and they could travel for days without seeing another white person.

Gideon and Julia Truesdell Arrive on the Wisconsin River, 1837

When Wisconsin became a territory, the northern parts were largely inhabited by Indians and a few French-Canadian traders. Most of the population was in the southwest corner in the lead mining regions along the Mississippi. Commerce from Lake Michigan flowed to settlements where ships dropped anchor offshore, and signaled with lanterns to send a scow that could navigate shallow waters littered with rocks.

Getting any closer to the shoreline was out of the question due to rapidly changing depths that could wreck the bottom of a $3,500 ($530,000 today) schooner. A scow was launched from the shoreline that could ferry around eight tons of passengers and freight, but transferring freight and rowing the scow through choppy water to and from the shoreline was very exhausting and physical work.

Territorial roads ran southwesterly from the old French-Canadian enclave of Green Bay on the western shores of Lake Michigan to the Mississippi River at Prairie du Chien. Three large and diverse river networks ran throughout the territory, which allowed Indians and settlers to travel great distances. Many fur trappers preferred following this network of rivers to the Illinois River until it emptied into the Mississippi, and thence to St. Louis.

Despite millions of acres of trees there were only two sawmills in the entire territory located near Green Bay. Lumber for the territorial capitol building were rafted from Pennsylvania down the Allegheny to the Ohio River past Cincinnati, and finally to St. Louis, where it was loaded aboard a side wheeler and brought to Prairie du Chien at the confluence of the Mississippi and Wisconsin Rivers. Thousands of boards were dropped into the water with the currents washing them ashore, where they were loaded into wagons for the 42-mile trip to the temporary capitol in Belmont. In 1836, a legislative hall and boarding house for the delegates were completed just a few days before the first session.

Newspapers were full of stories about the new territory, with tales of ordinary men striking it rich on the frontier. Under the preemption law, a man could contract to buy land for $1.25 an acre, with the balance due in three to four years when the government survey was completed. Gideon was smart enough to realize that he needed to get to the Wisconsin River ahead of the flood of eastern lumbermen, and file claims on a couple thousand acres, including key parcels adjacent to rapids that could be damned for waterpower. This meant leaving his Portageville farm as soon as the snow thawed and the roads were navigable.

The fastest way to get to Wisconsin was through the Great Lakes, but since Gideon brought 15 to 20 loggers, 10 or more covered wagons, 20 horses or mules and implements, he took the overland route. Since he was about to start a logging company in a remote area where less than 20 white people lived in a 500-mile radius, he recruited workers from back home to chop down trees in the woods for a percentage of the profits. With lumber selling for 500% more than back east this would have been a golden opportunity, and worth rolling the dice. Gideon and his men traveled in a convoy of covered wagons loaded with tools, saws, axes and enough food to last them until reaching the Wisconsin River.

We know from a Truesdell descendent that "somebody named Gideon" traveled with them as far as Indiana, which matches other timelines.[71] Jeremiah Truesdell (1782–1837) was about to buy fresh soil because after 30 years of farming the soil was exhausted, a good reason for an easterner to head west.

The Truesdell convoy followed the Buffalo Road to Buffalo, New York, then another trail that paralleled Lake Erie's eastern shoreline. Six or seven days later they rolled into Erie, Pennsylvania, an old French military outpost.

Like other wagon trains, at dusk each afternoon the Truesdell party circled their wagons for protection and built a fire for cooking. They let their horses graze but corralled them inside the perimeter with somebody standing guard to protect them from theft, but more likely coyote or wolf attacks. If it was raining, they hung a tarp off the back of a wagon over the fire, with Julia cooking under the most trying conditions with her clothing soaked by the time the meal was served. If the trail was navigable, even during a storm the wagons kept rolling in the interests of making time.

Before stopping for the day, a couple of men hunted game for that night's supper, which Julia would have cooked in a stew with vegetables, flour, and bread. We know from the 1840 census that none of the loggers traveling with Gideon brought wives. According to the census taker, a "chore boy" was living with Gideon and Julia.[72] This didn't necessarily mean that the child was put to work doing chores, but more likely the only designation available for a non-family person living with them.

Mississippi River steamboats being loaded with freight and passengers. Picture courtesy of the *Steamboat Times*.

This turned out to be six year old Bradley S. Truesdell (1831–1846) that were listed in a family genealogy.[73] He probably didn't find his way to Gideon and Julia's doorstep just in time for their cross-country trip, but had been living with them for a year or two. In those days' churches found good homes for orphans, of which there were many, and that might have been how he found his way to their home. He was named after Julia Truesdell's deceased younger brother, Bradley S. Torrey (1831–1832).[74]

Traveling across washed-out trails was hard on wagons so when they stopped for the night a couple of men had "wheel duty," checking wheels, spokes or axles and making repairs before the next morning. If they could avoid breakdowns, they could make good travel time. Nobody went far without spare parts, a tar bucket, water barrels, or a pail of axle grease. Tar was used to water proof the gaps between boards so the wagon could float across numerous rivers or streams. Horses are strong swimmers due to their enormous lung capacity, which enables them to float naturally when they encounter deep water, and pull a fully loaded wagon across a river.

Another important job was filling 15 to 20 water barrels each day for livestock and people. Each of the wagons had a barrel on each side which held about 45 gallons each. When they ran low the convoy stopped by a fast-moving stream because deadly bacteria lurked in slow-moving water. A bucket brigade passed wooden pails back and forth until each barrel was topping off. When filled, the convoy had about 900 gallons of fresh water to get them through the next day or two.

Gideon's convoy reached the Chicago River in early May 1837, and the settlement was a scattering of haphazard cabins and shacks along the southside of the river.[75] They crossed the river using a rickety draw bridge that had to be hoisted open by twelve men. After crossing into the newly organized Wisconsin Territory, they traveled 180 miles northwest across Indian trails until reaching Fort Winnebago and the Wisconsin River. A trail that had been cobbled together by fur trader Daniel Whitney would bring them to Grand Rapids, where a trading post and sawmill were located, and had become a gathering place for people living on the river.

When Truesdell and his loggers arrived, they found large tracts of 200 year old pine trees towering 120-160 feet with trunks four to seven feet wide. All of the settlers along the river were there for the same reason, to chop down trees, build sawmills, and build rafts so they could transport lumber, lath, and shingles 422 miles downriver to St. Louis. The one thing they had in common was an intense desire to beat the odds, and they pushed ahead against incredible odds with perseverance and grim determination. A person couldn't have survived that first winter unless they were tough as nails.

Searching for a site with strong water power to run sawmill, Gideon traveled 10 miles north of Whitney's Rapids, to a point several miles above Grand Rapids.[76] Although Gideon's prospective claim was among marshy terrain and cranberry bogs, the rapids there had a five-foot drop that could be dammed for water power. The site faced two islands. The smaller became part of Gideon's "jackknife claim," which he filed by carving his initials and the date with a jackknife on trees around the perimeter. Even though the land hadn't been surveyed, as long as the soil was broken, a cabin built, and somebody living there it belonged to him.

When the land survey was completed four years later, Gideon bought the land for $1.25 per acre ($495 today). If the person was a United States citizen, he could buy land at a low price; otherwise, land was sold through auctions at prices few foreign land syndicates could afford. The federal government did a superb job of blocking wealthy speculators from buying the land in 20,000-acre parcels, and then renting it to tenant farmers like English feudal lords.

His claim was 130 miles north of the land office in Mineral Point, the frontier metropolis of the oldest settlement in the territory, a lead mining (bullets) district with a population over 5,000 and a busy land office that encouraged outlying areas to send one representative to file claims, but even then, people stood in line for hours waiting their turn to speak with overworked and exhausted clerks.

During the 1830s there were two primary lumber markets in the Midwest; Galena, Illinois and St. Louis, which meant that the lumber cut along the Wisconsin and St. Croix Rivers would end up there. Back when the Galena lead mines were essential to manufacturing bullets, the town became much larger than Chicago, and the largest outpost in Illinois. But their yards sold a much smaller volume than St. Louis yards, and paid about a third less due to the limited amount of lumber they could sell. St. Louis lumberyards, on the other hand, shipped a massive tonnage into the western territories and the lower Mississippi River.

Clearing the Land, Building a Cabin, and Planting Crops in the Wilderness during the Summer of 1837

"Men of enterprise" arrived on the Wisconsin River looking for sites adjacent to rapids with enough power to run a mill.[77] These far-sighted pioneers were risk-takers with capital or sufficient credit to buy land, harvest acres of trees, mill roughly 12,000 feet of lumber per acre, and sell the lumber for $58 ($8,700 today) per 5,000 feet to lumberyards in St. Louis, Missouri, due to scarcity.[78]

Frontiersman Paul Kingston's twenty-nine year old son-in-law, Harrison Fay (1808–1850) arrived on the Wisconsin River with fifty-two year old Joshua Draper (1785–1861) in June, 1837. They knew that lumber would be in great demand, and that a sawmill would be a good investment. By the time they arrived every parcel with access for water power had been claimed, so they struck a deal to buy twenty-six acres of Gideon's land by the rapids.[79] Since he had no plans to build his own sawmill, he was willing to come to an arrangement with Harrison Fay and Joshua Draper.

While Gideon was away filing claims on a couple thousand acres at the land office, his loggers were busy clearing a site for a boarding house, and a barn for their livestock, wagons, tools, and provisions. The land had clusters of trees that would have been used to build a large cabin and barn, with the branches turned into a lattice of roof joists or split rails for fences to protect their crops from wild animals. Pulling stumps required more time and manpower than they had, so crops were planted around tree stumps, a common frontier occurrence.

According to one pioneer account, settlers without a plow used oxen to plow their fields by lashing their horns together in a makeshift harness, so they could pull a plow made from a thick tree branch with the end carved into a blade. It was primitive but it worked.

A shallow well was dug, and firewood stockpiled for that first winter which was bound to be cold, freezing, and nasty. Instead of building his cabin on the riverbank Gideon decided to build on higher ground about a quarter mile from a river that experienced severe spring and autumn flooding. Whether he learned about this from others or felt that it was smarter to build on higher ground has never been determined, but it was a smart move.

Rocks were used to build a foundation so the first row of logs didn't begin to rot the day they were laid, and this foundation lasted for 75 years because a county surveyor stumbled across the remnants. He described the outline of a large cabin with a long room with a fireplace, and a smaller room at the opposite end with a fireplace where Gideon and Julia no doubt slept with six year old Bradley.

The long room would have been where Julia cooked their food in several pots suspended over a fire in an open stone fireplace; the rest of the room probably consisted of a table and benches where 15 to 20 people were seated for meals, playing cards, checkers or other indoor activities when a harsh Wisconsin winter trapped them indoors for days at a time.

The loggers slept in a loft where the heat from the fireplaces drifted upstairs, but with sub-zero temperatures, even indoors it would have been chilly when outdoor wind chills reached 30 below zero. Everyone stayed warm wearing buffalo robes.

Their wagons, horses, mules, and cows were protected from the harsh elements in a barn that was connected to the cabin by a passageway, a common frontier design that allowed them to check on their livestock without having to venture outside. The passageway had an outhouse and washstands, which made life a little easier in a forbidding climate. But it was still very cold, and one old timer recalled that the only difference between the indoor and outdoor temperature was the absence of a howling wind and sub-zero wind chills.

A typical northern Wisconsin winter with lots of snow and cold temperatures. Pictures courtesy of the author.

During the summer of 1837, Gideon picked an area north of his cabin with the fewest trees and planted about 16 acres of wheat, corn, vegetables and perhaps berries and fruits, which would have been harvested and canned 90 days later before the weather turned cold. This little farm was vital to their survival, and run by his brother-in-law, twenty year old Kirkland Torrey, who grew up on a New York farm.[80] One of his jobs was growing enough vegetables, fruits, and having enough bacon, ham, and other meats curing while hung from the rafters in the barn.

Unlike many who nearly starved during their first winter on the frontier, settlers along the Wisconsin River had plenty of food. We know from diary entries there were thousands of wild turkeys in the woods and, after chopping a hole in the ice, they could have had a 20-pound basket of fresh fish every day.

Julia Truesdell, with the help of her brother Kirkland, would have sweated over a hot fire for weeks as they preserved and canned fruits and vegetables for the winter in crockery jugs sealed with wax. Nearby cranberry bogs would have provided her with an abundance of fruit that were easy to pick. She and her brother prepared three meals a day for the crew with the accompanying washing of pots, pans, dishes and tableware. Then there was a mountain of dirty laundry, which required two tubs elevated over an open fire with clothing scrubbed clean on a washboard, using soap made with lye from ashes.

We know that the Indians were friendly, and often bartered with settlers. Strong Indian teenagers swapped chores like splitting firewood, catching fish or wild game, and cleaning the animals. Their pay was the pelts from these animals, which they traded each fall when trading companies gathered on the two islands across from the Draper & Fay sawmill.

Julia, or more likely her brother, would have been up before the crack of dawn to start a fire so he could begin cooking a simple breakfast for the men, with the standard fare consisting of eggs, corn bread, bacon or ham, and coffee. By the time the men were ready to start chopping down trees, Kirkland would have been busy preparing several kettles of stew for the men that several hours later he brought to where they were working, with a couple of loaves of bread and coffee. He would also have sent kettles of fruit cobbler, probably cranberry since they grew profusely along the river, for a morning and afternoon high energy snack since carbohydrates fueled the logger's energy.

Julia must have had an abundance of inner strength. She was remembered as a lady of great kindness and common sense, whereas Gideon was described as somewhat brusque, a man of few words, although his sister-in-law described him as "gruff but kindhearted."[81]

As cold as a Wisconsin winter was, summers were hot, sticky and uncomfortable due to a massive mosquito population.[82] Diary accounts tell us that almost everyone wore long sleeves, and many battled malaria at one time or another. There was probably a reason the creek that ran through Truesdell's land across the river was named "Mosquito Creek." In addition to lots of daily struggles, the woods were populated by thousands of timber wolves, panthers, lynx, and wildcats which made it difficult to tell who was predator and prey.

About a month after Gideon and Julia arrived on the river, Robert Wakely (1808–1893), his wife Mary and their two boys ran across David Whitney while in St. Louis.[83] They had lived in Genesee County, New York, about 25 miles north of Gideon and Julia's farm, but spent a year or two in Ohio before rafting down the Ohio River with their five and three year old boys.[84] Wakely was looking for opportunities on the frontier, and bought a raft of lumber near Pittsburgh for $6 per thousand feet, and floated it down the Monongahela and Ohio Rivers until reaching Cincinnati, where he sold it for at least twice what he paid.[85] That money became his grubstake on the Wisconsin River.

David Whitney encouraged the Wakelys to settle near his trading post at Whitney's Rapids (Point Basse). The Wakelys caught a ride on a steamship traveling upriver until they reached Prairie du Chien at the confluence of the Mississippi and Wisconsin Rivers. He had permission from Daniel Whitney to use one of the keelboats he kept docked there for the trip upriver to his trading post. Thy spent several days sailing 140 miles northeast against the 20 mph currents until reaching Whitney's trading post.

Typical frontier boarding house with a loft where the men slept, with each log squared with a broad axe and detail of side of the house. Pictures courtesy of Mallard's Crossing Historical Village.

There was lots of wildlife along the river. Pictures courtesy of the author.

While in St. Louis, he asked David Whitney what type of business would do best along the Wisconsin River. David and Maria had been letting travelers passing through the area sleep on their floor until they ran out of room. Whitney didn't hesitate to urge him to open "a tavern," which had a broad interpretation, and usually including a dormitory upstairs for indoor sleeping for the flood of settlers that were sure to follow. Wakely built a cabin that served meals, liquor, and offered a place to sleep.[86] About 300 feet at the end of a path was a stub-dock on the riverfront with a sign that advertised "Wakelys Tavern."

After a decade on the frontier Wakely was able to replace his log cabin with a hotel, warehouse, and sawmill. His frontier gamble paid off because he was now affluent. Meanwhile, he indulged in politics, served on committees and held public office. After ten years on the frontier, he was an important man and possibly his tavern's best customer. Famously, he rode a horse into a Portage County court room where he serenaded a startled judge to the amusement of everyone but the judge, who angrily ordered Wakely locked up in a hotel room until he sobered up for the ride home. A lot of drunks were killed in those days when they collided with a low-lying branch at a full gallop.

Draper, Fay & Company, Sawmill Owners

Paul Kingston (1783–1864) came to the United States from Ireland at the age of twenty with his younger brother, and opened a general store in Missouri where they made money rafting freight down the Mississippi River to New Orleans before moving to the Illinois River, where the Kingstons were listed as storekeepers.[87]

By 1830, they had already made a healthy profit buying and selling riverfront lots in the Chicago area as far away as the Du Page River.[88] With Chicago River land prices soaring due to talk of a canal, Kingston sold out at the top of the market and reinvested his profits where prices were low, 75 miles north in Racine, Wisconsin. He became acquainted with Richard Bushnell, a builder who loaned his profits at 25% interest, and a speculator who owned considerable land near Kingston in the southeastern corner of the Wisconsin Territory.

With a string of successful real estate investments, Kingston would have had no difficulty finding a banker with money to lend. He organized Draper, Fay & Company with his son-in-law, Harrison Fay, and Joshua Draper to build a sawmill.[89] Court documents show a leveraged deal but with lumber selling for $12.00 per thousand feet in St. Louis, they expected a large return on their investment.[90]

The logs for this sawmill would come from Gideon's loggers, and instead of rafting them to the Draper & Fay mill like other mills, which would have been impossible since the currents ran in the opposite direction, he built a plank road where horses and oxen pulled logs from "an unusually fine stand of pine" through the marshy terrain.

Water-wheel picture courtesy of Evolution of the Sawmill and an "up and down" sash saw at Old Stockbridge, Massachusetts.

We don't know much about Joshua Draper, other than he came to the Wisconsin River with over twenty years of sawmill experience, and that he arrived as early as April 1837 because he had mail waiting for him at the Milwaukee post office.[91] In those days people sent mail "general delivery" to a post office, and the recipient picked it up when he arrived in town.

He knew how to build a sawmill and lath factory in the middle of the wilderness, and as the senior partner owned a large stake in the business.[92] Draper inspected the river and measured the speed of the currents, which were about 20 miles per hour, and built a wing dam to regulate the flow and speed of water that powered a waterwheel. It took about a month to lay out a mill site and two months or more to build a wing dam with a gate regulating the water.

Building the dam meant dragging the biggest and heaviest logs to the riverfront with a team of mules, hauling hundreds of heavy rocks to anchor the dam, and forging iron bars from a pile of raw iron ore identified by a surveyor's map. About a dozen men stood in the water week after week while anchoring trees weighing several tons. Their wing dam was eight to twelve feet high.[93] It took about a year to build a mill with some of the gears coming from back east, but a good carpenter could carve them by hand during the winter months from hardwoods.

The typical water-powered mill cut about 3,000 feet a day which means that Draper & Fay's output was around 450,000 board feet per season. The saw had a seven-foot blade that was 3/8 inch thick which, due to primitive metallurgy, left a third of the log on the floor as sawdust.

They were also agonizingly slow. "It was safe to set the saw in motion and go to dinner without any fear it would get through the log before you returned."[94]

In conventional construction, lath was nailed between studs to hold plaster, making it a profitable way to turn scrap into something they could sell. Draper & Fay built a separate "factory" to process about 100,000 feet of lath, and during the winter their workers probably stayed busy splitting shingles from hundreds of two-foot logs using a cleaving axe with a long, wedge-like blade.

During the winter of 1837, Gideon and his loggers cleared a mile and a half pathway heading south from the mill site.[95] What a survey identifies as a "railroad" was actually a plank road through marshy terrain. Logs, probably the trees they chopped down to clear a roadway, were laid across ties for wagons with the sides cut down.[96] These flat beds were pulled by oxen, using some of the wagons his loggers brought with them, because according to a local history, after a couple of years they fell apart due to heavy use.[97]

Trees cleared for a logging plank road and horses pulling wagons loaded with logs to the sawmill. By spring there were several tons of logs piled behind the mill. Pictures courtesy of the History of Logging.

After months of chopping down trees and trimming their branches, they were loaded onto wagons converted to flatbeds. After an agonizingly slow trip back to the sawmill, Draper & Fay turned these logs into lumber, lath, and shingles they could raft down river over 465 miles to a St. Louis lumberyard where they received top dollar.

In a frontier economy that relied on barter, once the lumber arrived in St. Louis, the sawmill, rafters, and loggers would have received a percentage of the sale price. They were paid with a Missouri bank draft, and Gideon received about a half for supplying the logs to the mill with at least two-thirds of that paid to his loggers.[98] This would have been offset by a room and boarding fee that Gideon charged each person, with most of that going in his brother-in-law's pocket for planting and harvesting crops, butchering animals, and running the kitchen. Most of the men who worked in the woods for him would have been anxious to supplement their income by working on one of the rafts, including Gideon and his brother-in-law, Kirkland Torrey.[99]

Creating a Government in the Wilderness, 1839

With so much commercial activity along the Wisconsin River, mill owners pushed for the construction of a roadway that would create a shortcut through the wilderness from Green Bay to the Wisconsin River. This would eliminate a couple of hundred miles and considerable time when hauling equipment and provisions across muddy trails through the thick woods.

Freight from New York City came down the Hudson River to the Erie Canal, and then through the Great Lakes until reaching Green Bay with shipping expenses exceeding the cost of the freight by as much as 200%. A lumberman might have bought gears for his mill for $25 ($6,400 today) back east but spent over a $135 ($34,000 today) to have them shipped to the Wisconsin River.

At Green Bay, the goods were loaded into wagons that followed a complicated 120-mile journey southwest on mostly old Indian trails that were often washed out and deeply rutted, and then 72 miles north until reaching settlers at Point Basse, Grand Rapids, or Draper's Rapids. In 1839, lumbermen along the river petitioned Congress for a road that would run through the woods across the territory.[100] It would cut their travel time and shipping costs in half.

Obtaining territorial funding for a road was complicated due to political rivalries between Democrats along Lake Michigan's shoreline, and the lead mining region in the southwestern corner of the Territory. There was a limited amount of money available, and each region fought hard to get as much as they could for their needs.

The petition they submitted to Congress references twelve mills in operation between Whitney's Rapids and Steven's Point with five more under construction. Furthermore, they state that over 300 people now lived on that 26 mile stretch of the river who were somehow involved in the lumber business.[101]

The settlers along the river also petitioned Congress for mail service, which on January 4, 1840, passed by an overwhelming vote. Thirty-three months later the work began on a post road from Fort Winnebago to Grand Rapids, a few miles downstream from Fay & Draper's mill on the southeast side of the river.[102] A post road was a government thoroughfare over which mail was carried, and they linked hundreds of settlements.

The sale of liquor had become a problem along the river and the French-Canadian trader, John Baptiste DuBay, was making a fortune. "The Indians established an encampment near DuBay's post, partially I suspect because like many traders, he illegally plied them with liquor to win their trade. The highly respected Indian agent, Nicholas Boilvin often complained about such traders, saying of the Indians, 'They drink very much and fight and stab each other.'"[103] Fur traders often used their trading privileges to acquire land from squatters near their trading posts for a pittance.

DuBay was eventually caught red handed on the river with a canoe loaded with several kegs of whiskey. He was acquitted on a technicality when his lawyer claimed that he wasn't selling but transporting the liquor. Trading liquor with the Indians had been a long-standing problem, because according to the records from the American Fur Company, they shipped a total of 8,776 gallons of liquor to their trading posts. When this 180-proof liquor was cut with water it made over 35,000 quarts, enough to fuel thousands of fights, eye-gaugings, and murders on the frontier.[104]

Joshua Draper, partner in the Draper & Fay mill, formed a committee that circulated a pledge that was signed by the local residents. He had twenty employees with plenty of time on their hands during the winters, and didn't need a boarding house full of malcontents and brawlers due to the affects of liquor. Sawmill owners were trying to get settlers to boycott any trading post that sold liquor to spend their money elsewhere, although this had little impact.

"Whereas information has reached us that persons have contemplated bringing spirits into the pinery for the purpose of selling the same to the inhabitants and the Indians residing in and about the area.

"We consider the introduction of liquor for such a purpose as not only highly detrimental to the interests of the people residing here, but as

Richard C. Fritz

to endanger the lives and happiness of all who are in business by the sale of such liquors to the natives who are well known to be reckless of life when under the influence, and that it would retard the growth of this region by preventing others from settling among us.

"We will discourage in every possible way the establishment of any grocery or groceries for the sale of liquor. Should the same be attempted we will not do business with the owners, and will frustrate by every means in our power their wicked purposes. Joshua Draper, Chairman and Daniel Campbell, Secretary."[105] Campbell was a lumberman in the Steven's Point area, upstream from Draper's mill and lath factory.

After becoming a territory, Wisconsin's population jumped from 3,635 (1830) to 30,945 (1840) a decade later. In an attempt to create a government where there had been none, Governor Henry Dodge made the first round of appointments. The Democrats controlled the Wisconsin legislature while the Whigs controlled Congress. Local Democrats in good standing included Harrison Fay, Joshua Draper, Gideon Truesdell, and George Kline, a lumberman from Grand Rapids (Wisconsin Rapids).

At the age of twenty-nine, Gideon was appointed one of four justices of the peace for Portage County, which included much of northern Wisconsin. The position was similar to that of a judge, and the job came with real authority because he was authorized to try civil cases up to $50 ($10,000 today), supervise elections, perform marriages and sign arrest warrants. With nearly everything bartered, there were numerous disputes over the value of what was traded, and "court day" always attracted a curious crowd of onlookers because many of the cases were entertaining, and there wasn't a whole lot of entertainment on the frontier.

County board meetings and territorial courts were held in local taverns, because they had a large room with tables and chairs. Gideon's court was probably held inside his boarding house, and outdoors during warmer weather. The polling place was downstream in Grand Rapids at the house of Edward Bloomer of the Bloomer and Chamberlain mill.

One of the Portage County Constables was Julia Truesdell's brother, twenty-four year old Kirkland Torrey, who served legal papers, investigated deaths, served warrants, arrested people and no doubt worked closely with Gideon to maintain law and order along the river.

The mere fact that Gideon received this appointment suggests that he was a sober young man of sound judgment. Years of physical labor plowing fields, wrestling hogs, and swinging an axe would have made him tough enough to handle himself among the troublemakers living in and around Draper's Rapids because he was a man who didn't tolerate any nonsense.[106]

According to the largest newspaper in the territory that was published a hundred miles south at Madison, the territorial capital, the 1841 Portage County Board of Elections consisted of Gideon Truesdell, Joshua Draper, and Gilbert Conant.[107] The settlement at Draper's Rapids was well represented and had a tight grip over that section of the river.[108]

Election returns from Portage County were disallowed when it was revealed that the polling book was missing after it had been turned over to the Board of Commissioners. Without this book there wasn't a dual control to guard against fraud, which resulted in the entire election being disallowed.[109]

On October 5, 1840, the long-awaited federal survey for the 48 mile stretch of the river that included Draper's Rapids was completed, and Gideon received title to his land after paying $1.25 per acre. By then the sawmills along that stretch of river had already cut and sold six million feet of lumber, but within sixteen months all of them were in financial trouble.[110]

Rafting Lumber from Draper's Rapids to St. Louis, Circa 1839–1841

Wisconsin was so sparsely populated, that the only place to sell the millions of feet of lumber that came from Wisconsin River and St. Croix River sawmills was 184 miles downriver in Galena, Illinois. Eighty percent of the lead (bullets) in the United States came from Galena, and it was the largest city in Illinois. But when it came to lumber, Galena yards didn't pay nearly as much as St. Louis yards.

About 242 miles south of Galena were the St. Louis wholesale and retail yards that paid top dollar, and seldom turned away a raft of lumber. The largest dealers used their riverfront yards to store large inventories they used to supply yards in Memphis, New Orleans, and Baton Rouge. But rafting over 20 tons of lumber from Draper's Rapids to St. Louis required plenty of guts, and it wasn't a trip for sissies. "Some of these rafts cover several acres of surface, and when under motion in a rapid current it requires a great force to stop them."[111]

According to a local history, Joshua Draper piloted Draper & Fay's first raft down the Wisconsin River to the Mississippi and then to St. Louis during the late spring of 1839.[112] This suggests that Draper & Fay were cutting lumber before they received title to their land, not an exceptional infraction in the life of a lumberman along the Wisconsin River. Just as soon as their rafts made it through the rapids below the Draper & Fay mill, they had to steer around thousands of rocks. "It was the worst piece of rapids that I knew anything about; very, very bad."[113]

"From Wisconsin Rapids to the mouth of the Wisconsin River it took us fourteen days to run.... about fourteen hours a day. We used to get started at five o'clock in the morning and tie up at seven in the evening, or start in the morning at six o'clock and tie up about eight, which would give us fourteen hours daylight."[114]

Running the Kilbourn Dam. Each raft had a "sucker line" that ran the length of the raft that a person could grab if he lost his balance. Pictures courtesy of the H.H. Bennett Studio.

The first 60 miles down the Wisconsin was the most dangerous, and where everyone had to pay close attention to the river. There were over twenty rapids along this stretch of the river, dropping from four to six feet with hundreds of twists and turns. About four miles south of Draper's Rapids was a 10 mile stretch where the river dropped an accumulated 60 feet. Once they passed the lower dells their trip calmed down considerably.

According to local historians, Draper & Fay's trip to St. Louis would have been the first from "the pinery." A government survey reveals that in 1839 the water table was unusually low, and old timers recalled that spring was the only time to raft lumber.

"No one that had any amount of lumber to run would undertake any other time than in the spring of the year, when we had the most water while the snow melted. That was the only time in which we would ever try to run a raft. Rafting began as soon as they could get a good stage of water."[115]

This indicates that most of their lumber was rafted downriver in April and May when the water table was at its highest due to melting snow into the river. A few months later, the summer heat and humidity lowered the water table in the rivers, and turned a 30-day trip into a 45-day trip. When a raft got hung up on a sandbar, the men depended on other rafts to stop, and help, not that they had much say in the matter because the stranded raft blocked movement up and down the river.

"I can say that a sand bar in a river will shift inside of twenty-four hours, because while we're sleeping, the Wisconsin River keeps rolling sand, sand, and sand. Where we have run this afternoon into sand tomorrow a raft will come through. I can just make this illustration to show you absolutely how only one-quarter, I might say, of all the day's work was used up by actually running lumber, and three-quarters of the time was used by helping other rafts back into sufficient water where they could run down the river."

St. Louis lumber Wharf where millions of feet of lumber were unloaded, and sold to retail yards along the lower Mississippi River. Picture courtesy of the St. Louis Historical Society.

"From Wisconsin Rapids to the mouth of the Wisconsin River it took us fourteen days to run. You run about fourteen hours a day. We used to get started at five o'clock in the morning and tie up at seven in the evening, or start in the morning at six o'clock and tie up about eight, which would give us fourteen hours run."[116]

A raft was actually six to eight smaller rafts held together by pegs and leather straps, with boards stacked in alternate layers for stability with lath and shingles piled on top. Two mammoth hardwood oars were locked into place at the front and back of the raft; if they got turned around, they could still navigate downriver. When steering 20 tons of lumber through turbulent waters each of the two rear tillers had three men on each oar exerting over 1,200 pounds of muscle.

The men navigating these cumbersome rigs were called pilots and they earned about $100 ($1,100 today) a trip, top dollar in those days.[117] Crew members earned one to three dollars a day, depending on their level of experience. Based on a July 9, 1840 entry in Kirkland Torrey's diary, we know that he and Gideon were in St. Louis, presumably after having worked the tillers, and that "Gid" was sick.[118] Swamp Fever (malaria) was common on the Mississippi River although Kirkland's diary entry doesn't specify Gideon's illness.

The men working on the rafts were called "river hogs." They labored from daybreak to sunset when they tied up for the night after a long, tough day. Some men wore the caulked boots of log drivers but others went barefoot and wore an assortment of ragged shirts, trousers and felt hats. They were in and out of the muddy water throughout the day and it was dirty work.

During their journey downriver the raft's look out scanned the water for boulders, sand bars or other low branches. "I came very near being knocked overboard by the oar getting away from the steersman. No one thrown off at this place has been known to have been saved."[119] The Wisconsin River was 28 feet deep in most parts and ran fast enough to quickly drag a person beneath the water. One morning about a mile downstream from the Draper & Fay mill six men nearly drowned, but were snatched from the river before the currents pulled them under although some of them died a few days later from internal injuries.[120] The river was treacherous as evidenced by the drowning of the Wakelys nine year old son, who fell from a lumber raft and a few years later the drowning of Harrison Fay at the age of forty-two.

There were sections of the river littered with thousand-pound boulders, and during the summer months lumbermen used mules along the riverfront to pull most of them to the shoreline. Boulders too large to move had dams built around them, which allowed rafts to steer around obstacles that could have splintered their rafts. It took about 30 days for them to travel from Draper's Rapids to St. Louis.

After the first few trips downriver, lumbermen constructed slides with timbers secured by massive bins of rocks. This greatly sped up their travel time, and created an amusement ride for teenagers. "When the rafts passed through towns where there was some population, there were always a lot of young fellows waiting at the various eddies for a chance to run the rapids with the crew, but when the water was too dangerous this permission wasn't granted."[121]

When approaching turbulent waters, the eight to ten rafts were disassembled into smaller rafts. After passing Whitney's Rapids, the trip was serene and peaceful until they reached a deadly section of the river frequently referenced by Indians and old fur traders as the "dreaded dells." The river was about a half a mile wide until it narrowed to 54 feet, with fast-moving currents and rock formations on both sides of the river that an out-of-control raft could easily slam into, and splinter into hundreds of pieces.

"In going through the Dells, we disconnected our rafts. Where formerly two men handled a Wisconsin raft (400 to 500 feet long), consisting of three pieces, four men would take one piece through the Dells, run it through below Kilbourn, and gig back. That is, walking back through the Upper Dells. I suppose it is a distance, if I remember right, of about five miles. We will be all day running that lumber through the Dells, and by the time that the last raft comes through, the first raft is possibly almost right opposite Portage, which is about ten miles below."[122]

"We had scarcely got the rafts secured together, when I heard a roaring noise and looking up over the bluffs discovered a large black cloud rolling over us. In less than fifteen minutes we were engulfed in one of the most terrible thunder storms I ever witnessed. The wind blew a gale, the rain fell in torrents, and thunder rolled, and the lightning flashed. The waves rolled upon the raft, and we were in fear of being broken to pieces. It looked still more awful and sublime, because we were floating along under those gigantic bluffs. Night setting in, left us in total darkness, except when the lightning flashed and furnished all the light we had by which to guide the raft. About midnight the storm abated and another set of men took the oars, when I crawled into my bunk, wet as a drowned rat."[123]

After floating through the lower dells with a raft of lumber, David Whitney (1804–1838) went to bed feeling mentally and physically worn out, and woke up feeling tired, weak, and feverish with severe cramps and nausea. The others could see that he was very ill and brought him to Ahira and Jane Sampson, friends who just happened to be staying nearby. It was the onset of the bloody flux; a bacterial or viral form of dysentery that was almost always fatal.

They knew bringing him back to his trading post at Whitney's Rapids was out of the question. Once the parasites attacked his brain, lungs, and liver he would be dead within 24 hours, so a Frenchman paddled upriver to pick up Maria Whitney, then nursing their dangerously sick four year old daughter.

Maria asked their neighbor from across the river, Mary Wakely to watch her five children, before climbing into a birch bark canoe with an Indian and Frenchman paddling downriver a hundred miles. They paddled through the night until arriving the next morning around nine, but by then, David was only a few hours away from death. On August 16, 1838, he died at the age of thirty-four, leaving his widow to raise five children in the wilderness.

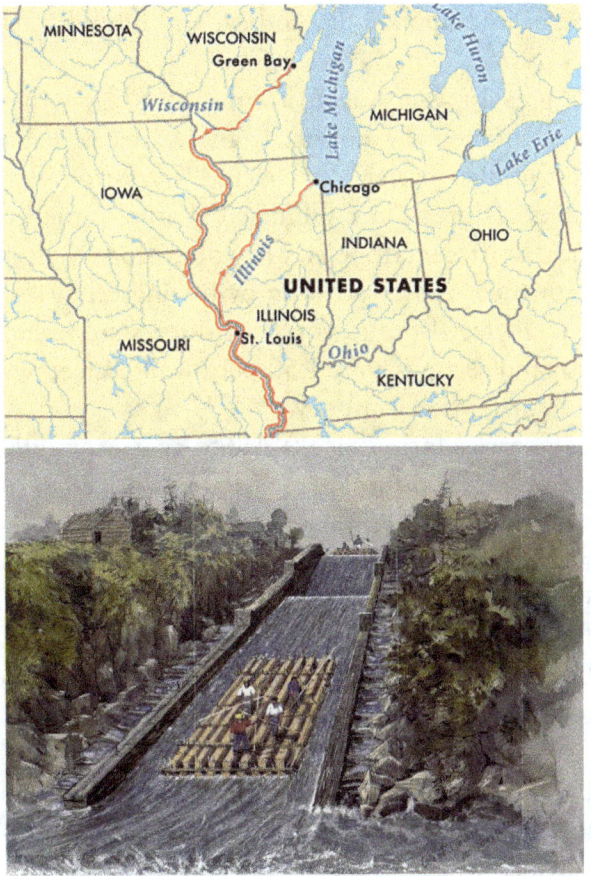

Fox River flows southwesterly from Green Bay to 1.5 miles of the Wisconsin River, which emptied into the Mississippi River. This route was often followed by fur traders, with the Wisconsin River flowing south from Draper's Rapids. Slides built by lumbermen anchored on each side by log-boxes filled with several tons of rocks.

She didn't remain a widow for long, because the following year Justice of the Peace Ahira Sampson presided over the marriage of Maria to Grand Rapids mill owner George Kline. It was the social event of the season and a good excuse for everyone to step away from the hardships of frontier life to relax and let their hair down.

A fully assembled Wisconsin River raft measured about 100 by 30 feet and carried 150,000 feet of lumber or roughly a quarter of a mill's yearly output. After four or five trips to St. Louis, a mill's entire output for that season was sold, and since they had about 90 days before the water levels would begin to evaporate due to heat and humidity, each mill ran a couple of crews to pilot two or three rafts.

St. Louis' greatest asset was its location just below the Missouri and Illinois Rivers, and when the lumber from Draper & Fay arrived at the levee, the largest lumber dealer was Laveille & Morton, who had already made a fortune as architects and builders of some of the foremost public buildings in that frontier metropolis. They didn't loan their money at 10% interest, but kept their money growing by buying yellow pine for $12.00 per thousand board feet from sawmills in three states, retailed "first rate pine" for $5.00, and seconds for $4.50 per hundred feet which generated about a 400% return on their money.[124]

What set George Morton (1790-1865) apart from other Mississippi River wholesale yards was his financial strength. Instead of loaning money at 24% (short term) or 72% (long term) they cleared as much as 400% as lumber dealers. Laveille & Morton became the biggest wholesalers on the Mississippi River. They also owned an interest in several sawmills on the Gasconade River in the Ozarks, a good way to keep their yards on the Mississippi River stocked.[125] Within a few years they would also own a minority interest in several sawmills on the Wisconsin River.

Most yards bought lumber with promissory notes that could be cashed the following spring when the lumber was sold. Laveille & Morton operated a little differently, because they paid cash in the form of a draft that could be cashed at the Bank of the State of Missouri. Unlike other frontier banks, this one survived the "Panic of 1837" unscathed. Rather than letting out-of-state banks take over their economy, the Missouri legislature had the wisdom to charter this bank and owned half of the stock.[126] Its conservative management made their bank notes safe and desirable, because they were traded like cash throughout the Midwest, a sure sign of their soundness.

Dealers like Laveille & Morton continued to buy more lumber than they could sell locally because they were using their St. Louis yards as a temporary holding pen before sending planks, flooring and roof joists to Memphis, Shreveport and New Orleans.

The St. Louis lumber dock was a gathering place for lumbermen, and where information was traded between rivermen. In 1839, Draper piloted his first raft of lumber to Laveille & Morton, where he met George Stevens (1790-1866), who piloted rafts from Pittsburgh down the Alleghany River to the Ohio and then to St. Louis where he sold his lumber for twice what he paid back in Pennsylvania.[127] It was at the lumber wharf that Joshua Draper ran across Robert Wakely, because he had just sold a raft of lumber from Whitneys mill upriver at Point Basse.

Keel boat paintings Harvey W. Johnson. If the wind was strong enough, they sailed upriver; otherwise, they had to propel the raft with oars or poles.

We know how millions of feet of lumber came down the Wisconsin River to St. Louis on rafts, but are far less certain how the men returned to Draper's Rapids. If it was a tough trip coming down the Wisconsin River it was even tougher going upriver against the currents. The weight of evidence suggests that rivermen hooked a ride on one of the sternwheelers on the Mississippi River traveling north to Minneapolis.

Steamships ran up and down the upper Mississippi looking for extra fares, especially for deck passengers, so it wasn't difficult for rivermen to catch a ride to the confluence of the Mississippi and Wisconsin Rivers. Each person paid about $3.20 ($480 today) for deck passage which brought them 382 miles upriver to Prairie du Chien. While a sidewheeler had more power and was easier to steer, anything cruising above St. Louis needed to be a sternwheeler with drafts of as little as two feet, and have enough power to plow through sandbars, shallow water and rocks.

The government had established Fort Crawford at the confluence of the Mississippi and Wisconsin Rivers, where a couple dozen keel boats were beached along the shoreline. We know that David Whitney kept boats there for the trip upriver, indirectly supporting the presumption that most people returning from St. Louis arrived at Prairie du Chien by steamboat. A keel boat had a sail, and if the wind wasn't blowing, they brought out the oars. If they couldn't row, they used the oars to pole the boat through difficult stretches of the river.

Draper, Fay & Company and Gideon Truesdell File for Bankruptcy

Five years after lumbermen arrived, there were thirty-seven mills on the Wisconsin and St. Croix Rivers sending lumber to St. Louis. Supply and demand leveled out, prices dropped to normal levels, and Gideon had to depend on his entrepreneurial skills to earn a living. We know from Kirkland Torrey's diary that he began delivering wagon loads of fruits, vegetables, flour, butter, hams and bacon to "Stevens Landing," where a shanty and barn were used to store provisions for his sawmill and bunkhouse thirty miles north.[128] An Indian trail became a wagon road paralleling the river, and during the winter sleighs brought people and supplies to loggers and mill workers living in Big Bull Falls (Wausau).

Gideon and other lumbermen along the river were dealing with the aftershocks of the "Panic of 1837," which lasted for another five years. His logging company didn't last for long, perhaps three seasons at best, and yet he was probably too stubborn to give up. Manpower was scarce in the pinery as evidenced by a September 29, 1839, letter from George Stevens to his St. Louis partners. "Hands are very scarce, and wages are $25 a month and it's still impossible to get half as many men as we need."[129]

The loggers Gideon brought with him from New York no doubt followed Joshua Draper to Big Bull Falls where wages were higher, and they didn't have to wait seven months to get paid, but finding reliable young men to work in the wilderness or sawmills were still difficult.

Out of desperation, Daniel Whitney hired several men from Quebec as indentured servants.[130] When they walked off the job and refused to return to work despite Whitney having already paid their travel expenses from Canada, he had them arrested as "stubborn servants." Since there wasn't a jail, the Judge ruled that they would be "sold" at auction for two months of labor to the highest bidder with the proceeds going to Whitney.[131]

The quality of workers along the riverfront left a lot to be desired as evidenced by this classified advertisement. "Laborers Wanted! Will hire twelve first rate hands, good choppers and teamsters to work during the coming winter, to good hands fair wages paid, and none but good faithful hands will be employed at Warner's Mill on the south side of the Wisconsin River."[132]

Meanwhile, by 1841 wholesale prices fell to realistic and less profitable levels, and by the end of the third logging season, Gideon began putting his affairs in order. He published the following notice on September 4, 1841, in the *Madison Express*.

"NOTICE, the subscriber would respectfully request all those who are indebted to him for lumber or anything else, to call on him and settle the same without delay, and those who have demands against him will please present them and they will be paid. Gideon Truesdell."[133]

On November 17, 1841, the *Madison Express* printed a foreclosure notice from banker Richard Rising against Paul Kingston, Harrison Fay, and Joshua Draper.[134] Sixty days later, their mill, lath factory, boarding house and land were sold at auction.[135] Ten days later Roswell Morris foreclosed on Harrison Fay's farm on the southeast side of the territory in Racine County.[136]

By the end of 1841, Draper's Rapids had gone from 40 to 50 men living in the two boarding houses to almost none. According to census information there were now 79 people living in the entire county, a significant drop from the 300 counted in a petition submitted to Congress two years earlier.[137]

When the Draper & Fay sawmill became insolvent, Gideon was in trouble because his logging business depended upon his selling logs to their mill, and they were now in foreclosure. On July 8, 1842, Richard Bushnell and Demos Beech sued Gideon for $65 ($7,900 today). Bushnell vs. Truesdell landed before the territorial court, and once a judgment was issued, and after Gideon and Julia settled their affairs, they decided to leave the area.

After five years of back-breaking work in the wilderness, life along the Wisconsin River had lost its appeal. Gideon needed to hire an attorney to protect himself from future litigation, and find somewhere with better prospects to start over. That place was the booming lakefront community of Southport on Lake Michigan's southeastern shoreline.

Why Southport? Gideon and his brother had already visited the area during their 1836 trip between Milwaukee and Chicago. They figured its fertile back country would someday turn it into a prosperous lakeshore community with a large wheat export. During the previous year, Southports population had soared from 875 to 1,820 with 165 building permits issued.[138] Whether Gideon returned to farming or found something else, his prospects were infinitely better in a fast-growing town where a multitude of opportunities were available.

In June or July of 1842, Gideon, Julia, and their adopted son Bradley packed what fit into their wagon, which consisted of essentials like pots, pans, skillets, blankets, and wooden plates and bowls along with a table, two chairs, and a mattress. Julia was six months pregnant as they bounced along deeply rutted trails for at least two weeks, covering 172 miles before reaching the tiny hamlet of Walworth near Big Foot Lake (Lake Geneva). This is where on August 4, 1842, Gideon filed for bankruptcy and papers to legally adopt Bradley as his son.[139]

There were only a few hundred people living at one end of the lake in a settlement made up of a general store, blacksmith shop, church and the Red Lion Hotel. The Pottawattamie Indians were friendly, and shared the land with the white settlers. Why did they pick Walworth instead of Madison, which was 73 miles closer and where there were dozens of lawyers?

We know that Jeremiah Truesdell, who was a year older than his brother, was farming in Walworth although exactly when they arrived is tough to pinpoint. But it would make sense for Gideon and Julia to turn to their family during their time of need. Nobody in their right mind would have had a baby in a place where they didn't know a single person. On October 18, 1842, Julia gave birth to a son, improbably named Geraldine Joshua Truesdell (1842–1922), and he was the only child that survived childbirth.[140]

He was named after a Welsh ancestor, and his name was pronounced Jer-All-Dean, but his parents and just about everyone else called him G.J., although he was often called Dell or Gerald.[141] After G.J. were born that was it for Walworth, Wisconsin.

Gideon and Julia Truesdell Settle in Southport, Wisconsin, 1843

During the spring of 1843, Gideon and Julia left Walworth with their son and infant G.J. for the prosperous community of Southport. It was a brief 33-mile trip along the old Beloit Military Trail which, depending on the condition of the trail was about a two-day trip. According to an early history, new arrivals often lived out of the back of their wagons on Pikes Creek until they figured out their next move.[142] For many, that was filing a preemptive claim on 40 acres for farming.

A newspaper article illustrates just how remunerative fresh soil was to a farmer, and how in 1842 the Carey brothers came to Wisconsin to buy land.[143] They bought 300 acres under the preemption act for $1.25 ($495 today) per acre, and listed their income and expenses as follows:

300 acres: $375.00
Fencing 3 fields of 100 acres each: $300.00
Breaking the soil + plowing: $525.00
Seed, 1.5 bushels per acre: $281.00
Sowing and harrowing: $300.00
Harvesting and stacking: $375.00
Hauling 5,400 bushels to Southport: $810.00
Sale of 5,400 bushels @ 60¢: $3,240.00

1st year profit: $274.00 ($45,000 today.)
2nd year profit: $2,040.00 ($348,000 today.)

After an unbelievable amount of back-breaking work they got their investment back after the first harvest, and cleared a $274 which wouldn't have happened had they stayed in New York. Of course, farmers seldom had more than three good seasons in a row before too much or too little rain, high temperatures burned up their fields, or insects ruined that years harvest. But the law of averages made farming a good way to earn a living, and made farmers an extremely hard working and frugal lot.

The consumption of wheat throughout the Wisconsin Territory accounted for less than 2% of each harvest. The only buyer for that much wheat was one of the many grain elevators in Buffalo at the edge of Lake Erie. Most of the wheat was hauled to four cities on Lake Michigan's shoreline for export; Sheboygan, Milwaukee, Racine, and Southport.

What began as a small export business from farmers within twenty miles of Southport evolved into a very large trade from as far away as seventy miles in the Rock River Valley. Why would a farmer make dozens of trips along a decrepit old trail to Southport? Because it was the closest Lake Michigan port with warehouses that would buy their wheat on consignment, and arrange to have it shipped to Buffalo.

During the 1840s, wheat exports were small enough for local merchants to store bags in their cellars, with merchants combining their shipments so they could afford to rent a schooner that held about 30,000 bushels. As commission agents, they took about a third of the sale price for renting a schooner, finding a buyer, and converting a New York bank note into a something that could be spent back in Wisconsin.[144]

One of the first things a farmer did once he sold his crops was replace his log cabin with a proper house, and wheat exports and lumber imports paralleled each other. With a bank draft or a note from the warehouse that bought his wheat, a farmer made 20 to 30 trips back to his farm with his wagon hauling wheat and returning with lumber. One year a farm house was rebuilt with lumber, then a barn and stable, chicken coop, and hog sheds. In 1843, over 400,000 feet of pine and 500,000 shingles were offloaded in Southport, and sold through four warehouses.[145]

It was the right place for Gideon to start over, although exactly what he did during his first five months is unknown, but probably carpentry or construction. This would have generated enough cash for him to start another business, and by the end of the summer he leased the Wisconsin House on Main Street a few doors north of Charles Durkee & Company He no doubt answered this advertisement in the *Southport American*.[146]

"WISCONSIN HOUSE FOR SALE: The establishment is well situated for a Public House, and will be sold on very reasonable terms. Any person desirous of making a permanent location of this kind will find the present a favorable opportunity. S. & A.W. Doolittle."[147]

We know from a newspaper article that the hotel was poorly furnished, drafty and could be leased on "very reasonable terms."[148] After running a boarding house on the Wisconsin River, this probably seemed like a good fit for Gideon and Julia.

Built in 1837, with squared logs by A.W. Doolittle, it was one of the earliest hotels in the settlement.[149] There was a dining hall and kitchen on the first floor with a dormitory on the second that could sleep 12 guests.[150] There had been a secession of tenants before Gideon came along, and it was described as a "scanty furnishment."[151] Most hotels or taverns from that era had a fireplace at one end of a long room, washstand with a pitcher of water, a brush and comb attached to thick string, a shallow outdoor well, and an outhouse next to the livery stable. They would have served a basic fare of fresh bread, stew, soup, apples or peaches, and strong coffee.

The mortgage was in the hands of Hale & Bullen, who in addition to running a busy mercantile store, reinvested their profits making loans secured by real estate. Two weeks after the "for sale" advertisement ran there was another that notified the public that the hotel had been leased by Gideon Truesdell.[152]

By then, several better inns had been built from milled lumber; the hotel Gideon leased was built from squared logs.[153] To signal a change in management he renamed the business the American Hotel, which catered to travelers looking for a cheap night of lodging. Nearly all of their business would have been travelers aboard a schooner that docked at Southport for the night. When a ship docked, each hotel or tavern sent a wagon to the dock looking for customers, with each person yelling at the weary passengers the attractions of their establishment. This ranged from good food to free moonshine. Gideon's drawing card would have been cheap rates and a wife who was a good cook.

There was a lot of daily chores involved in running a hotel, livery stable, and livestock corral. Whether he needed a partner to share the workload, contribute money or both, Gideon struck a deal with twenty-eight-year-old Charles Bishop, someone he couldn't have known for long, perhaps somebody he worked with, because on September 7, 1843 they ran this advertisement.[154]

American Hotel, Southport, W.T

"THE undersigned would respectfully inform the citizens of Wisconsin, and the traveling public generally, that they have leased this convenient and well-known stand for a term of years, and that they are now prepared to entertain all who may favor them with their patronage, in a style that will merit its continuance.

"THEIR TABLE will be set with every luxury the market affords and their accommodations in rooms and lodging will be pleasant and agreeable and their charges moderate to suit the times. The pleasant location of the American and its neighborhood to the pier will render it the most convenient stopping place for those that travel by the lakes.

"CARRIAGES, will at all times be in readiness to convey passengers and their baggage to and from the boats free of charge. Teams procured to convey freight or passengers to any part of the Territory at reasonable charges; and every facility in the way of information touching the different sections of the Territory, cheerfully afforded to the traveler or immigrant.

Truesdell & Bishop

The hotel was a block away from the harbor in a community where nearly everyone arrived by ship traveling to or from somewhere, because few stayed. Before dusk, most schooners on Lake Michigan stopped for the night at the nearest settlement because sailing vessels weren't outfitted with sleeping quarters. After bouncing around in a cabin all day on uncomfortable benches the passengers needed a break from the rolling seas.

In addition to serving breakfast, Julia Truesdell probably prepared and sold lunches to her guests before they left.[155] She would have filled their jugs with fresh water from a hand pump, ladled stew into a crockery container they brought with them and sold them apples or pears in season. Some innkeepers tried to make a killing, but if the price of lunch was outrageous the traveler walked down the road to the nearest grocery store, and bought crackers with a piece of cheese and filled their jug with cider.

Once Lake Michigan closed for the winter, Truesdell & Bishop would have had to survive for five months on little more than a few permanent borders and a small amount of dining room business from a local clientele.

It's hard to say how Gideon Truesdell met Charles and Harvey Durkee, but it was a life-changing event. He probably walked a block to their store to buy groceries for his kitchen, and they became friends.[156] All he had to do was hand the clerk a list of what he needed, and a few hours later a boy delivered the order using a cart pulled by a donkey. Gideon was struggling to start a new business, and would have needed a certain amount of credit until his summer revenues caught up with his leftover winter expenses.[157] The Durkees obviously trusted him otherwise they wouldn't have extended him credit.

The daily chores would have been divided between the Truesdells and the Bishops, with one couple running the desk, cleaning rooms, and washing the linens and towels while the other ran the kitchen, dining room, and stables. But the partnership didn't last long because four months after their first advertisement the Bishops were no longer partners. In their place, Kirkland Torrey (1817–1895) and his newlywed wife Esther, who came from the Wisconsin River to help Gideon and his sister, Julia, run a business that had become a poorly paid headache.[158]

At the end of the lease, Gideon was so broke he didn't even own a horse, and this would have been his second failure in three years. He turned the hotel over to the mortgage holders and left the business owing money.[159] He was honest, and intended to pay by selling 80 acres of pinelands along the Wisconsin River, but he needed to borrow enough money to buy a horse and provisions so he could travel there.[160] That's how broke he was.

A small amount of cash came from lawyer Volney French who, according to the credit rating agency of R.G. Dun & Company, "skins everyone he touches and makes plenty of money, good but slippery."[161] Many years later Gideon spoke at an Old Settlers picnic, and recalled that Volney French and Harvey Durkee became his endorser, and Julia sold her gold watch. "He procured a team and wagon, laid in a stock of bread and bacon, and started for the Wisconsin River, with a view among other things of selling patent rights. His wife assisted him in cooking meals by the roadside, and he managed to realize money enough to pay what he had borrowed and a little more."[162] The "patent rights" were for land he bought when he came to Wisconsin, and the trees on that land would have had some value.

Gideon returned to Southport in time for the fall harvest, paid his debts, and found work as a field hand at Harvey Durkees farm.[163] He would have spent a couple of months swinging a wheat cradle, shocking wheat on the stone floor of a barn, and shoveling it into 60 pound burlap bags. Where Gideon, Julia, Bradley, and three year old G.J. spent that winter is a mystery but it was probably out at the farm where Harvey Durkee would have had a few cabins for married workers.

Tragically, on March 12, 1846, their fifteen year old son, Bradley, died. It must have been a painful and agonizing good bye for Gideon and Julia because they had raised Bradley since he was a little boy. Without an undertaker in town, the grim task of making his sons coffin no doubt fell to Gideon, with the town's sexton paid to dig a grave in the Durkee plot at the cemetery.[164] Gideon and Julia were religious people, and no doubt asked a Minister to conduct a proper service. At a time when they didn't have much money, they scraped together enough to buy a tombstone marking his grave for the ages. "Bradley S. Truesdell, 15 years old, adopted son of J. & G. Truesdell."[165]

Charles and Catherine Durkee, Circa 1836

Since Gideon's life would become intertwined with Charles and Harvey Durkee on so many levels during the next 30 years, it helps to know a little about them. They grew up poor on a Vermont farm, and like most farm children they worked from dawn to dusk alongside of their parents.[166] Their father was an intelligent and honorable man but was far from affluent, and had eight children to support. When Charles was four years old his mother died, possibly from childbirth, although within a year his father had married again, adopted his wife's two boys, and had two more children with Dolly Durkee.

Charles was a personable young man with enough ambition to get himself elected to the Vermont legislature, which might have been where he met Judge John Winchester Dana, whose brother, Judah, became a U.S. Senator.[167] They inherited significant real estate holdings from their father, and after settling in Cabot the Judge "was largely instrumental in building it."[168] He erected the first sawmill and manufactured bricks.[169] He was wealthy and successful, and when Charles entered his circle of influence it was a life-changing event.

After having opened a general store but moving twice to larger villages because there wasn't enough business, Charles knew he needed money to expand, and turned to Dana as a silent partner. Minority partnerships were profitable when the right young man was running the store, and it was an easy way for the Judge to keep his money growing. He was obviously impressed with his young partner, and had no misgivings when Charles began courting his daughter, which led to their wedding at the Dana residence on May 28, 1833, in Cabot, Vermont.[170]

The Danas were an old Boston Brahmin family that came to America toward the end of the Puritan migration. By the time Charles and Harvey Durkee married into the family they had amassed considerable wealth and influence. Catherines uncle was U.S. Senator Judah Dana (1772–1845), who studied law with Samuel Fessenden. His son was a U.S. Senator and Secretary of the Treasury during the Lincoln Administration.[171] His niece would later marry Charles and Harvey Durkees nephew, John W. Dana II.

A few years after Charles and Catherine Durkee were married, they were on their way to Milwaukee with their life's savings, and possibly with a letter from the Judges bank. They left their friends and family behind for the adventure of a lifetime. Charles was looking for cheap land to buy that could be sub-divided, and then sell to the flood of settlers that were sure to follow. It was a difficult trip that turned into a daily endurance contest.

They bounced around in a stagecoach for 180 miles until reaching the Erie Canal, where they transferred their trunks to a shallow draft boat for a peaceful 10-day voyage to Buffalo at the eastern edge of Lake Erie. This was where thousands of people boarded ships bound for Lake Michigan, and in Chicago they boarded a smaller schooner, the Van Buren, which was sailing north to Milwaukee. This was how shipping lanes worked in those days; passengers traveled to a major destination like Cleveland, Detroit, Green Bay, or Chicago and took a smaller schooner to one of the settlements.

Confined to a claustrophobic, damp, moldy cabin, they suffered the onset of some type of respiratory illness.[172] Charles asked the captain to drop them off at the nearest settlement so she could regain her health. That settlement was Pikes Creek, but this was a complicated stop, because like every other lakeshore settlement there wasn't a dock. The Van Buren had to drop anchor a couple of hundred feet offshore so she wouldn't run aground due to rapidly changing depths and rocks.

Using lanterns to signal the shoreline, the call went for every able-bodied man in the settlement to help launch an unwieldy, heavy yawl that could hold several tons of freight and passengers. If somebody tried to get out of "boat duty," Samuel Hale went to the malingerer's door and kicked it until he answered, and in an unfriendly voice told him to get down to the dock. On the afternoon Charles and Catherine arrived the skies were dark, the seas choppy, and a steady rain and wind had to be contended with. They risked their lives jumping from the higher schooner into the smaller yawl that would have rocked wildly in the heavy seas.

The Durkees original destination had been Milwaukee, where an inland bay could be turned into a harbor away from Lake Michigan's crashing waves, but when Charles learned that speculation had driven land prices to unrealistic levels, he ruled out Milwaukee as a good place to buy land. Buying land was a suckers bet unless it was bought at the right price. The number of ships sailing past Pikes Creek wouldn't have gone unnoticed, so Charles decided to take a chance when he bought a large parcel on the south side of the creek. He believed that this settlement had everything they needed for growth; mostly, a back country with fertile land for farming and an inland basin that could be turned into a harbor.

Charles was described as friendly, ready to help anyone in need but not much of a talker. He was smart enough to amass a fortune with no more than a few years of schooling, which caused some people to regard him as a bit of a dullard. But he wasn't. He was a shrewd judge of character and grasped complicated subjects quickly. Wisconsin's governor, Henry Dodge, wrote a letter to Washington stating that "you will find him [Durkee] a clever man and I would be much pleased to see him succeed."[173]

Once Charles and Catherine decided to stay, they wrote their families and encouraged them to join them on the frontier.[174] As a farmer, Charles knew the quality of the soil would turn the back country into a prosperous farming community with wheat exports creating a strong export trade. By 1843, there were over 20,000 acres in cultivation with over 400,000 bushels of wheat exported from harbors in Racine and Southport.[175] This was about a 500% increase from three years earlier, and in their quest for federal funding for a harbor, they decided to change their name from Pikes Creek, which sounded a bit hickish, to Southport.[176]

That first year, thirty-one year old Charles Durkee was an extremely busy man. He chopped down enough black walnut trees to build a cabin, bought a shipload of lumber from Farnworth's sawmill in Sheboygan, began building a general store on the east side of the basin that emptied into Lake Michigan, and was asked to represent the settlement in the first territorial legislature. When he opened his store money were tight, so a friend from Vermont, Dr. Royal Waldo, bought a minority interest in Charles Durkee & Company.

Among other family members moving to Southport was Charles' twenty-four year old half-brother, Harvey, who came to help him build the store, and start his own farm. Harvey Durkee (1815–1887) was well prepared for frontier life after having been raised on a farm where he worked from dawn to dusk. He was intelligent and had a quick grasp of things but there was definitely an edge to him, and if he brought you into his inner circle, you could have the shirt off his back. At some point, Gideon became one of his closest friends. Within a few years he went from employee to partner, and during the next twenty-five years they made a lot of money together.

Though of slight stature, Harvey was a strong young man after years of plowing fields, wrestling hogs and butchering animals. But it was never a good idea to antagonize him because he tended to settle things with his fists, or worse. Many years later when somebody struck his son with a horsewhip, Harvey grabbed a hatchet, and repeatedly struck him in the face until others pulled him off or he would surely have killed the man. It was never a good idea to pick a fight with Harvey Durkee.

"The dispute grew out of the disposition of a cargo of lumber which was being delivered to Backus & Glover at the foot of Grand Street, near Durkees Coal Yard. Harvey Durkee then attacked Backus with a hatchet, striking him twice on the head and face, destroying one eye and breaking his nose. The injured man was conveyed to his home where he now lies in a critical condition."[177]

Criminal charges were filed but dropped, and a civil trial was held where Backus won a $50 ($1,800 today) judgment. This was far less than the $20,000 he was asking for, and after the trial was over the town wasn't big enough for the two of them. Backus sold his lumberyard, and left town a severely disfigured and disillusioned man.[178]

After his brother's store was completed, Harvey slept in the storage room until he married Martha Dana (1818–1891), his brother's sister-in-law.[179] Charles never got around to farming, at least not in the southwestern corner of the territory, but his brother filed a preemptive claim on 160 acres and planted wheat.[180] The soil was so fertile that his first harvest was a bumper crop that more than paid for the land. In Vermont, 160 acres would have yielded around 6,500 bushels due to the mediocre condition of the soil, and during the first few years, Durkee was able to harvest at least 18,000 bushels.

Hundreds of Easterners broke soil for farming, and since wheat paid top-dollar it created a large export business. In those territorial days the only place to sell shiploads of wheat was at one of the Buffalo, New York, elevators. There wasn't enough demand for farmers to sell their wheat locally, and smaller elevators in Milwaukee or Chicago didn't pay nearly as much as the elevators in Buffalo, which shipped wheat internationally. But only Sheboygan, Milwaukee, Racine, and Southport on the western shoreline of Lake Michigan bought and sold grain, which gave farmers only a few places to sell their crops.

As farms were carved out of the backcountry, small storage buildings were built along Southport's lakeshore where burlap bags of wheat were stored until the next schooner arrived. Merchants like Charles Durkee, Samuel Hale, and C.I. Hutchison sold wheat on commission, which meant that farmers had to make dozens of trips to their warehouses to drop off hundreds of bags of grain. The merchant leased a schooner, shipped their wheat to Buffalo, and took a third of the sale price for storage, transportation, sales commission, and converting a Buffalo bank draft into a currency that could be spent in Southport.

A merchant stored a farmer's wheat, and accumulated enough from other farmers to rent a schooner that could haul about 30,000 bushels in her cargo holds.[181] When the ship was full, the warehouses that leased the schooner made around $2,800 ($340,000 today) after the wheat was sold in Buffalo. Shipping costs averaged half of the cargo's value, and after the warehouses over head was deducted, they cleared around 15% or roughly $850 per schooner. When divided by five warehouses that shared a schooner, each cleared around $175 ($22,500 today). It was a nice piece of seasonal business that generated a respectable profit, and a way for a small town merchant to make a tidy sum for roughly eight weeks of work.

Southport's future lagged for several years while they waited for government funding to improve their decrepit "harbor." Out of desperation the community took matters into their own hands. A year after Reuben Deming arrived, his first wifes cousin, Benjamin Cahoon (1791–1861), built a warehouse in an import/export firm styled as Deming & Cahoon, but their most pressing need was a dock.[182]

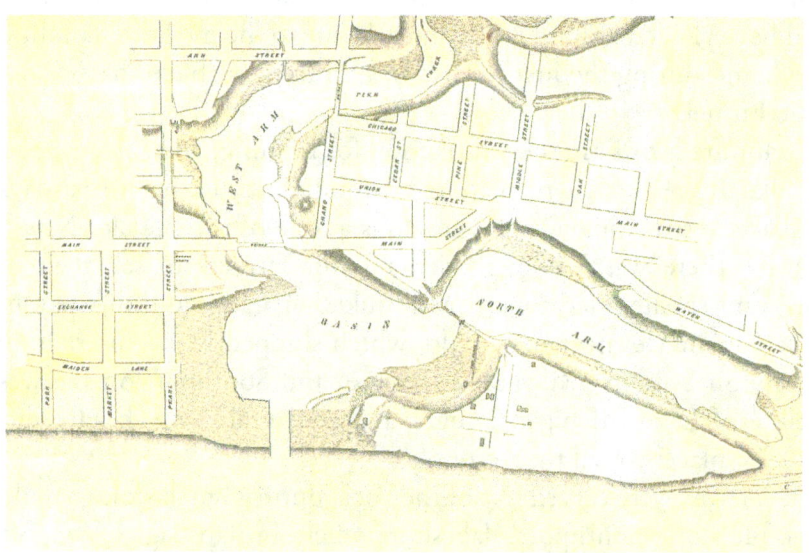

Southport, Wisconsin circa 1840 on the western shoreline of Lake Michigan, with an island on the eastern side of the basin. Charles Durkees first store was located on the west side of the basin. Map courtesy of the U.S. Army Corp of Engineers.

He had considerable experience, because twelve miles south in Waukegan, Illinois, he built a courthouse. The village bartered thirty-eight adjacent lots for his labor which he later sold at a substantial profit when land around the courthouse became quite valuable. When they asked him to finish seven rooms in the basement of the courthouse, they gave him exclusive rights to rent them for six years as payment for his work.[183]

When it came time to build a dock the men in the community helped, and he supervised construction where Pikes Creek emptied into Lake Michigan. The shallow depth (four feet) of the shoreline made this a challenging project until they deepened the land around the dock, and built a breakwater in front of the creek where a sandbar formed. It took two years to complete, and the cost was entirely funded by donations of cash or labor. The largest cash donations came from George Kimball, Charles Durkee, Reuben Deming, and Harvey Durkee.[184] Others contributed smaller sums or their labor, and when finished, the dock didn't look at all seaworthy.

Sailors aboard passing ships predicted that the first big storm would carry the home-made looking pier out to sea. Newspapers called it "Cahoon's Folly," and the captain of the steamer Wisconsin was so sure the dock would collapse that he invited people from other towns for a good laugh. In April of 1842, he tied his twenty-seven ton steamer to the dock. He was positive that once he started his engines the vibrations would wreck the dock, but it didn't budge.[185]

Sketch of Southport, Wisconsin with a pier on the south side of Pikes Creek and the three-story warehouses on either side, circa 1842. Courtesy of the Kenosha History Center Archives.

Probably because Charles Durkee served in the Vermont legislature, he was asked by his neighbors to represent Pikes Creek at the first territorial legislature.[186] They passed laws that got Wisconsin off to a good start, but delegates were far more concerned with obtaining funding for their district with a lot of vote swapping.[187] Many had significant investments in land, and roads or harbor improvements would increase the value of their holdings.

A few days before the first legislature met, construction of a meeting hall and boarding house for the delegates was almost finished. But when they met in November the meeting hall was unfinished, so they had to meet in the basement of the American House. They moved into a partially finished capitol building; the basement was unfinished and James Morrison's hogs had taken it over.[188] While discussing territorial business the delegates could hear his pigs snorting and squealing through the floor boards.

To establish better communications, the government established eighty post offices and thirty-five routes throughout the Wisconsin Territory. Communications with the outside world were almost entirely by mail, and the letter carrier was the best source of information from neighboring communities.

Alexis Clermont (1808–1892) was hired by the U.S. Postal Service to walk a 240-mile route along the Green Bay Military Trail from Green Bay to Chicago, and a round trip took about a month. He traveled with an Oneida Indian with Clermont carrying a 60-pound sack of mail, musket, and bag of parched corn along with a knife, blanket, and snowshoes. His helper carried their provisions, and they shot squirrels and rabbits for food and slept under the stars.

Clermont earned $60 to $65 per trip plus 25¢ per letter, which in those days was paid by the recipient, and he used this extra money to pay for meals along the way when there wasn't wild game or birds to catch and cook along the trail.

There was no such thing as an "envelope" in those days so letters were folded and sealed with wax, and instead of a postage stamp, 25¢ was written next to the address, which was his pay for delivering the mail. Clermont's route began in Chicago where he collected hundreds of letters that had come there from the Detroit Post Office, and once a plank road was completed it only took 30 hours for the mail to arrive by stagecoach from Detroit to Milwaukee.[189]

When rabbits, porcupines, or squirrels became scarce, Clermont and his companion went hungry, and depended on the kindness of others. But owing to the large number of deadbeats traveling along the Green Bay Military Trail, settlers were leery of unexpected and unwanted visitors.

"For the greater part of our diet we relied upon the Indians or what game we could kill; the bags of corn were merely to fall back on in case the Indians had moved away, as they were apt to on hunting and fishing expeditions. At night we camped in the woods wherever darkness overtook us and slept on the blankets which we carried on our backs.

"On the way I came across a house where a woman lived alone. I asked for breakfast, at the same time telling her I was penniless, but being the mail carrier, I would pay her upon my return. 'We don't trust!' On I walked to a house nearby where another woman lived alone.

"This time in asking for breakfast I did not tell of my lack of money until after the meal was eaten, and the women had given me a pair of stockings and mended one of my moccasins. When I admitted my condition, her eyes blazed and she hit me over the head with a broom."[190]

During the early years, letters for people living in Southport were dropped off at Willis' Tavern on the Green Bay Military Trail. This major thoroughfare ran through several towns from Green Bay to Chicago, and Harvey Durkee would ride four miles on horseback to drop off and pick up mail at Willis' Tavern.[191] It was an old trick merchants used to bring customers into their store, and as a storekeeper, Harvey was "always courteous and obliging to his friends and neighbors."[192]

As the population of Southport grew so did Charles Durkee & Company, until they had outgrown the small wood frame storefront they built on the western side of the basin. By 1840 the money was rolling in from land sales and a busy mercantile store, and Charles decided it was time to build a much larger store on the other side of the creek.[193]

His three-story building was at the corner of Main and Market Streets with an office on the ground floor that he rented to his attorney, who also handled his real estate sales.[194] A few weeks after it was built, the brick exterior separated from the front of the building due to soft footings, and thousands of bricks crashed into the street.[195] The exterior had to be re-bricked again.

After the failure of the American Hotel, Gideon found work as a field hand during the 1845 harvest at Harvey Durkees farm.[196] We suspect that Gideon, Julia, and fourteen year old Bradley lived out at the farm where he would have looked after the livestock. That spring, he began working at Charles Durkee & Company's downtown mercantile store.[197]

Charles Durkee & Company, General Merchants.

The town was growing fast. According to an 1841 *Wisconsin Enquirer* article, there were "40 new buildings to be built this spring and summer in Southport.... for this to happen there must be an increased activity in every department of business."[198]

Charles Durkee & Company had become so profitable that Dr. Royal Waldo abandoned his medical practice, and moved to Southport where he opened his own store.[199] At that point, twenty-five year old Harvey Durkee bought his minority interest, and became the managing partner when his brother became busy in politics and the abolitionist movement.[200] His home was a stop in the Underground Railroad, and he was president of the Wisconsin Liberty Association. When he was elected to Congress, his stop in the Underground Railroad was run by his brother-in-law, Reuben Deming, a defrocked minister who ran afoul of the church hierarchy when he questioned the right of another minister to own slaves.

With a new three-story building, Charles Durkee & Company branched into hardware, lumber, and glass from the Essex Glass Company in Bennington, Vermont.[201] He advertised flour that came from Burlington & Richmond Mills in Vermont, and barrels of salt at a time when it was used extensively to preserve meat.[202] No doubt through Harrison Durkee, they had a distributorship with the Albany Nail Factory that allowed them to wholesale kegs of nails to dozens of stores in addition to their own.[203]

Gideon helped run a busy store where a six-month inventory of merchandise was stored on the second and third floors, with over a hundred barrels of flour, salt, and nails stored in the cellar. Merchants could only afford to travel twice a year to New York to buy inventory, but it seems likely that since their business was so extensive, they had to rent more than one schooner. Each ship hauled over ninety tons of merchandise, and once the ship arrived in Southport the cargo was transferred to dozens of wagons. It was hauled several blocks to the second and third floors of the Durkee mercantile, with barrels of flour and salt rolled down a wooden ramp to the cellar. With a street level storefront that ran the length of the building, two floors of storage space and a barn by the harbor for storing wheat, Charles and Harvey lived by the old merchant's adage, "If you don't have it, you can't sell it."

Based on an obscure piece of information, it appears as if Charles Durkee & Company turned over a $10,000 ($4.2 million today) inventory twice a year with about a 300% mark up.²⁰⁴ This is confirmed by notice of a lost check, because each fall Harvey bought their spring inventory and during the spring, he bought his winter inventory. Before a merchant could place an order the previous order had to be paid in full.

"CAUTION. The public are cautioned about receiving or negotiating a note made by myself, and payable to my own order, being properly endorsed, for $5,000 ($800,000 today), which said note was dated Dec. 1, 1848, and payable six months after that date, the said note having been lost or stolen from the mail in Troy, New York, to this place, and payment thereafter having been stopped. HARVEY DURKEE."²⁰⁵

If a merchant ran across a good deal on cast iron stoves, he bought whatever he thought he could sell and yet he still needed to carry a standard inventory. In 1841, Harvey Durkee filed an insurance claim on some damaged plows in a flooded cargo hold aboard a schooner that got stuck on a sandbar on Lake Erie.²⁰⁶

These trips were exhausting because wholesalers in Chicago, Detroit, and Cleveland lacked the selection, quantity and pricing a merchant needed to generate a decent profit. Renting a schooner cost around 50% of the cargo's value although that changed when railroads knocked that down at least two-thirds during the 1850s.

Running out of something sent customers to another store down the street, and buying too much merchandise translated into unsold inventory that tied up cash. An over-stocked store or a depressed economy caused merchandise to sit on the shelves, and created a cash flow squeeze when bills fell due. Mark-ups had to cover deadbeats, slow inventory, merchandise that didn't sell, and a storekeeper's mistakes.

Since barter was how things were bought and sold in those days, Harvey Durkee had to convert hundreds of IOUs and notes from customers into a Chicago or Milwaukee draft from one of the major banks. Throughout the year his customers charged goods and settled their account when they sold their wheat on consignment. Before a government currency, merchants selling wheat in Buffalo cannibalized their commission in exchange fees. We know that Harvey tried to avoid high exchange fees by cashing checks at his brother's Wall Street office.²⁰⁷ His in-laws owned a controlling interest in the Troy Savings Bank, Howard Trust & Banking Company, Troy City Bank, and a minority interest in nineteen other banks along the Hudson River.²⁰⁸

If Charles and Harvey received a $2,000 check from an elevator

Richard C. Fritz   83

drawn on a Buffalo bank, they would have paid a bank back home a 10% exchange fee of $200 ($32,000 today) to convert it to a New York or Chicago note that would have been accepted at face value. Banks had employees who did nothing but board a train with a suitcase filled with bank notes, present them for payment at the bank of origin, and return with a trunk loaded with hundreds of pounds of gold or silver coins. Sometimes they brought their wife and children to camouflage what they were doing. The exchange fee covered his wages, and banks generated a healthy profit clearing paper.

Traveling through the Great Lakes had vastly improved during the past twenty years. According to the *Kenosha Democrat*, in 1838, it took Harvey Durkee fourteen days to sail from Buffalo to Milwaukee aboard the Constitution, but eight years later he made the same trip in a day and a half, lightning speed in those days, aboard an express steamship that only stopped in Cleveland and Detroit instead of six other ports before landing in Milwaukee in a schooner that depended on the wind.[209]

Money was scarce on the frontier and hard to get. Merchants extended credit because few people had enough cash to make daily purchases. They had to "mortgage their future" to a general merchant whom they trusted, and if they were established customers, they received a limited line of credit, and were charged 7% interest. If the customer had a poor reputation, the merchant would have asked him to sign a promissory note secured by his farm, plow, crops, or a co-signer with good credit.

Harvey and Martha Dana Durkee, their mansion overlooking the City Park, and surrounded by a seven-acre orchard. Pictures courtesy of the Kenosha History Center Archives.

A farmer couldn't survive without credit because he charged goods all season long, and settled his bill when his crops were sold. If a farmer lived frugally, he could get ahead of his bills, but a careless person spent a lifetime living from hand to mouth. Although it took a large amount of capital to open a store, merchants were nicely rewarded for waiting for their money.

A merchant's most exhausting job was collecting past due accounts because it was nearly impossible to find a deadbeat. Charge-offs was a part of a merchant's business, and a 15% loss on uncollectable debts meant that he was staying on top of his receivables. But the only way to keep from drowning in unpaid bills was to visit dead-beats each week to collect a small amount on their balance, which sometimes meant taking crops, livestock, tools, or watches in trade. When they refused to pay their debts, the merchant got a court order, and visited their farm with the sheriff. Sometimes he accepted land to settle an account, and that's how many small-town merchants ended up owning a lot of farm land they rented to others.

Charles invested his real estate and mercantile profits building storefronts that generated a monthly income, and his objective would have been creating a pool of tenants who paid him rent every month. He also built a first-class hotel on the southside of the harbor with a restaurant and shops on the first floor, no doubt believing that the rooms and storefronts would add significantly to his monthly rental income.

He actually built two hotels. According to the *American Freeman*, the first hotel was about to open on December 1, 1846 when gale force winds off of Lake Michigan destroyed the building, and caused an estimated $3,200 ($360,000 today) of damage with little insurance.[210] In those days companies limited coverage to 15% to discourage a policy holder from torching an unprofitable business.

"He first put up a three-story building of moderate size, but when nearly completed it crumbled to the ground, a mess of brick and mortar in consequence of insufficient foundations. He re-built in 1848, making it four stories and increasing the number of rooms by the time it opened that fall.[211]

Durkee House at the corner of Main and Pearl by the harbor. The first hotel didn't have storefronts and was only three stories. Amos Truesdell's grocery store occupied the corner storefront. Picture courtesy of the Kenosha History Center Archives.

Charles Durkee was a staunch abolitionist who was elected president of the Wisconsin Liberty Association. This led to his running on the Free Soil ticket for several offices, and after mediocre showings in the past, he defeated Congressman William Pitt Lynde in an upset election nobody expected him to win.

Lynde was a political heavy-weight who graduated from Yale and Harvard Law School, whereas Charles Durkee had a few years at a country school and a few months at the Royalton Academy. Before serving in Congress, Lynde was Wisconsin's Attorney General and a U.S. Attorney. Durkee had served a one year term in the Vermont legislature and two separate one year terms in the Wisconsin territorial legislature before taking his place on the national stage.

Charles Durkee ran on the anti-slavery Free-Soil ticket but received congratulations from an opposition newspaper, the *Oshkosh True Democrat*. "Mr. Durkee has earned the right kind of popularity for he has earned it without seeking it. We have no doubt that hes astonished to learn how well he is regarded. He has never sought office, and never, therefore, endeavored to earn popularity for the sake of it. Durkee stands high because he is known to be just, firm, determined, generous, and a warm friend. His election against the immense vote of Milwaukee is a great triumph."[212]

Upon his upset victory, Charles Durkee hosted a "grand entertainment" for his friends in the recently opened Durkee House dining room, with over a hundred guests attending.[213] But it's doubtful Charles and Caroline had much to celebrate because it had only been a year since their four year old boy, Charles, died.[214] Before leaving for Washington, he turned over the management of his downtown store and land company to his brother, Harvey.

The Origins of Durkee, Truesdell & Company

Luther Whitney (1815–1905) would become closely associated with Gideon Truesdell in many ways for many years to come. He became his longtime accountant, partner in a sawmill, and many years later president of the Truesdell Furniture Company. He came to the frontier with his cousin, David Blish (1814–1847), to work for their uncle who was a frontier heavy weight. At the age of eighteen they began working on one of Daniel Whitney's logging crews, and inside his warehouse inspecting furs.

In 1840, David Blish married Adeline Irwin, whose father was a prominent pioneer with a sawmill and trading post. Three years later, Luther married Rebecca Irwin, Adelines sister. After saving their money both couples struck out on their own, and chose Southport, because it was one of the fastest growing settlements in the territory.

They built a store with a second-floor apartment at the corner of Pearl and Exchange down by the harbor. Soon thereafter, a ship arrived from their uncles warehouse loaded with groceries, mercantile goods and lumber. The earliest mills in the territory were owned by Daniel Whitney, which gave them access to large quantities of lumber.

During their first year, Blish & Whitney sold 200,000 feet of lumber and 30,000 shingles at a huge mark-up.[215] By trading lumber for groceries they used to stock their shelves, they used barter to build a profitable business.

"We will trade lumber for 10,000 bushels of oats, 3,000 bushels of good wheat or 10 tons of pork."[216] Buying anything they could sell at a profit, Blish & Whitney built a profitable business, despite competition from Hale & Bullen, Charles Durkee & Company, Hutchison & Wheeler, and others.

As wheat shipments increased to over 400,000 bushels a year, David Blish knew he needed a private dock due to the decrepit condition of Pikes Creek. If the tide was high schooners could enter the makeshift harbor, but if enough silt and sand created a sandbar, schooners were stuck inside the harbor until the water-level increased. Blish & Whitney solved this problem by buying lakefront property on the less crowded south side of the government dock, but this created its own unique set of problems. They needed to build a warehouse with a basement that could hold 30,000 bushels of wheat, and a freight yard that could stockpile lumber.

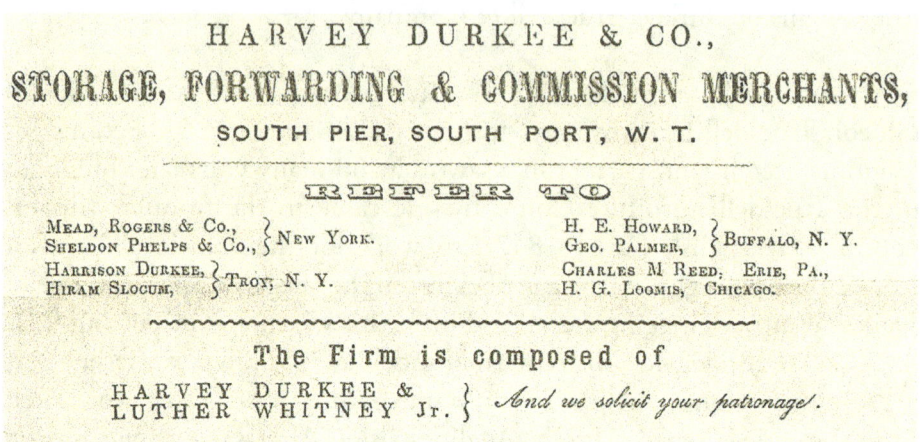

Harvey Durkee & Company letterhead circa 1848. Harrison Durkee was Charles and Harvey's brother. Hiram Slocum was the mayor of Troy, and was a partner in Durkee, Slocum & Company. Letterhead courtesy of the Kenosha History Center Archives.

In those days freight was shipped warehouse-to-warehouse beginning in Troy, New York at the confluence of the Hudson River and Erie Canal. Merchandise moved westward from New York City to Troy, Buffalo, Cleveland, Detroit, Green Bay, Milwaukee, and finally Chicago. Each firm charged a fee for handling the freight passing through their store room. A warehouse would have gone broke had they not been plugged into a circuit with affiliated warehouses in every major town along the way.

Southport merchants had direct access to Lake Michigan, but the water was two to four feet deep along the shoreline. Blish & Whitney's solution was building a 672-foot crib dock that reached water deep enough for ships to dock safely, but it was a long distance to walk when freight was transferred from the warehouse to a schooner.[217] During the fall, crashing waves pummeled the shoreline which took a toll on their dock, and every spring repairs were needed before shipping season began. But this new location allowed them to ship a much larger volume of wheat.

Blish handled lumber, and Luther Whitney bought and sold wheat as a commission agent where he received a percentage of the final price. Blish was "described by those who knew him as genial, intelligent, and devoted to his family and friends."[218] Blish & Whitney were off to a good start when David Blish became a statistic in one of the worst Great Lakes maritime disasters.

On November 11, 1847, a group of immigrants from the Netherlands boarded the steamer Phoenix in Buffalo, bound for Chicago where they would follow maps until reaching Iowa, where they were going to start a farming community.[219] During this late season voyage, the Phoenix was carrying coffee, sugar, molasses, and hardware consigned to merchants in Chicago.

While cruising down the Hudson River the crew played a dangerous game whenever they came upon another steamer. They stoked the boilers with wood for maximum speed, because racing along the river had become a popular but deadly sport. When boilers over heated it caused ships to catch on fire.

As the Phoenix passed through the Straits of Mackinac, she encountered heavy seas before pulling into Manitowoc, Wisconsin, to take on wood for her boilers. By November 21st, the lake had settled down enough for her to continue 25 miles south to Sheboygan.[220]

Early in the morning, a passenger noticed smoke coming from the boiler room, and told a crew member but was rudely told to mind his own business. It was later determined that some of the crew had spent the night in a Manitowoc saloon in the red light district where they became drunk and disorderly.[221]

According to eyewitnesses, when the Phoenix pulled out of Manitowoc, she was fighting hard to get though heavy seas. To give the captain enough speed to fight six to ten foot swells, the men in the boiler room crammed as much wood into the boilers as they could, which gave the wheelsman the necessary power to plow through crashing waves, or at least that's what the surviving sailors said at the coroner's inquest.[222]

Around four o'clock in the morning clouds of smoke came through the deck vents, and a bucket brigade was organized but within minutes the fire was out of control. Forty-five minutes later the ship was engulfed and life boats were launched among mass hysteria.

One panic stricken Norwegian girl jumped into the freezing water, grasping the side of a lifeboat but those aboard, fearing that she would capsize the boat, pried her little fingers loose until she slipped into the water where she drowned.[223]

When onlookers in Sheboygan, less than five miles away, saw 40-foot flames, the entire town was awakened by church bells, the sound of screaming, and pandemonium.

There wasn't enough room in the lifeboats. As the flames became more intense, those left behind were forced to jump into the freezing water. They soon became numb from hyperthermia, which caused them to grow sleepy and, paradoxically, feel warm when their body temperature rapidly dropped. In a minute or two they lost consciousness and quietly slipped beneath the water.

The ship's engineer stayed with the ship until the flames drove him into the water, where he found a floating door to hang onto. Others desperately clung onto floating wreckage until they succumbed to hyperthermia. A young cabin boy was later found dead on a floating ladder, lying on his side, his head resting on his hands as if asleep.[224]

Those stuck aboard realized they might not be alive by the time other boats arrived. Some prayed, others cursed their terrible luck while some sat in their lifeboats stunned in disbelief. The schooner Liberty tried to get underway for rescue but the wind was at a dead calm, so the Captain launched a lifeboat and ordered his men to row as fast as they could towards the burning steamer.[225]

The steamer Delaware fired her boilers, but it took fifteen minutes to build up enough steam before she could get underway.[226] While her boilers were warming up every available craft in the harbor, regardless of size, was racing toward the wreckage.

The Delaware, which took longer than the others to clear the harbor, was the first to arrive due to her speed once she got underway.

By then only three from the Phoenix were alive and the Liberty had to steer around dozens of dead bodies floating in the water. They pulled the frightened survivors aboard, and retrieved several corpses from the icy waters but the burning steamer was sinking fast. It was one of the deadliest disasters on Lake Michigan with 160 dead.[227]

The *Sheboygan Mercury* wrote "Without dwelling too long on the terrible details of the catastrophe, and drawing a veil over acts of selfishness…. acts excused by the direst necessities of the hour…. we cannot forbear singling out the unselfish conduct of one of the passengers, Mr. Blish of Southport. He appears like an angel of mercy…. if one-tenth of what the survivors tell us about the behavior of Mr. Blish in those trying hours is true, that were enough of a shining example of love and sacrifice for others.

"He assisted the injured Captain to the lifeboat, and although by common consent offered a seat in the boat himself, he declined, and said 'there is work left for me here, and I want to take my chances with the rest.' During the trip he made friends with the Hollanders....and especially helped the little ones when they stumbled. He had endeared himself to those children, this merchant, with his large business, his large new warehouse, and his young family at Southport.

Drawing of the Phoenix courtesy of *Harper's Weekly*.

"Mr. Blish concerned himself greatly with these young people, and the report says that he, even on the brink of the other world, tried to console and comfort them. Other reports of Mr. Blish persist. One of them is that when practically the whole boat was aflame, he took up into his arms a bewildered and lost child and protected her, while exposing himself to the devouring element.

"The last we hear of Mr. Blish was that he was extremely active about the little rafts, that he had finally constructed a little raft for himself, and that, holding two children, he clung desperately to it until, and benumbed by the cold he lost hold and perished."[228]

"He was on the steamer and did heroic service in rescuing the helpless. He brought many unconscious and fainting women and children from the hold, which was filling with smoke and flames. He was warned by the captain not to go down again as the steamer weas fast settling, but he insisted in making one more trip, and descended into the hold. He never returned, and was doubtless overcome by the smoke and flames."[229]

The sinking of the Phoenix was one of the worst maritime disasters on the Great Lakes, and Harvey Durkee leased Blish & Whitney's warehouse and dock from David's widow. The partnership was styled Harvey Durkee & Company with Luther Whitney listed as his partner, although according to the credit reporting firm of R.G. Dun & Company, Whitney didn't have much equity.[230] When David's widow married William Strong, they moved to Chicago, and she sold the warehouse and dock to Holbrook, Elkins and Company. This pushed Harvey Durkee out of the lumber and grain business, at least temporarily.

Gideon Truesdell and Joseph Hackley's Trip to California Gold Fields, 1849

After two successive crop failures just about everyone in Southport was struggling, which made optimistic reports from President Polk about a California gold rush impossible to ignore. Throughout his life, Gideon had an infatuation with mining that probably began with the California gold rush. He was one of 41 men who parted with $208 ($38,000 today) of their hard-earned money to travel to the western extreme to see if they could strike gold.[231]

This figure was higher than Gideon could possibly have saved as a clerk at Charles Durkee & Company, so it seems likely that Charles and Harvey paid his expenses in exchange for half of his earnings, a common way for wealthy people to get a piece of the action without getting their hands dirty. If the person they bankrolled struck gold, their return would have been at least 50 times more than what they laid out to cover their expenses.

The prospectors from Southport named themselves the Banner Company, a group where everyone agreed to split the expenses and profits.[232] They were an intelligent group with physicians, attorneys and merchants. About half came from Southport and the others were from northern Illinois. Southport lumberyard owner Elias Lee was "Captain of the Guard," and responsible for the groups safety from Indians or highway robbers.

They were divided into groups of six. One of Gideon's traveling companions was thirty-seven year old Joseph Hackley, a building contractor who would later play a significant role in Gideon's accumulation of wealth.[233] Another was Andrew Dana (1820–1849), a twenty year old Durkee in-law who would never again see Southport after drinking bad water, and dying from typhoid fever in a tent along the American River near Sacramento.[234]

Unlike a lot of ambitious men who rushed into a dangerous 2,000-mile trek across unsettled countryside, the Banner Company was organized, hired an experienced guide, and outfitted themselves with everything they would need to cross the frontier but couldn't buy once they crossed the Missouri River.

Wagons were chosen that could withstand swings in temperatures because the mountain passes through the Sierras were below freezing at the highest points, whereas a few weeks later they were traveling through a desert with 100-degree temperatures.

A *Southport Telegraph* article lists what each man's fee was used for:

8 MULES: $50
6 BOWIE KNIVES: $1.50
900 LBS BACON: $36
600 LBS CRACKERS: $24
160 LBS COFFEE: $16
200 LBS SUGAR: $20
10 LBS TEA: $7.50
1 COFFEE POT: $1
100 LBS SALT: $1
5 LBS OF PEPPER: 62¢
2 CHEESES: $7
10 GAL MEDICINAL BRANDY: $20
1 WAGON & HARNESS: $100
6 SADDLES: $50
SPARE WAGON HARNESS: $150
6 PAIR MACKINAW BLANKETS: $24
6 BUFFALO SKINS: $12
12 PAIRS BOOTS: $18
6 DOZEN WOOL SOCKS: $15
30 YDS OSNABURG: 2 TENTS: $3.75
20 YDS DRILLINGS: $2.00
1 ROPE FOR TENTS: 25¢
2 TENTS SEWING CHARGE: $1.50
6 RIFLES: $120
6 SHARES MILITARY GUIDE FEE: $30

6 REVOLVERS/HOLSTERS: $60
6 INDIA RUBBER CLOAKS: $30
100 LBS LEAD: $3.50
6 AXES: $6
2 KEGS GUN POWDER: $10
1 MEDICINE: $5
6 FARES TO INDEPENDENCE: $60

TOTAL EXPENSES FOR 8 MEN: $1,248.22 ($190,000 today)

The Banner Company traveled roughly 65 miles south from Southport to Chicago, west to Dubuque, and then southwesterly until reaching Independence, Missouri, where a heavily traveled trail began that ran over 1,700 miles to the gold fields. It was a long trip in a three mph world where they averaged 25 miles a day. Independence was a bustling frontier town where everything they needed could be purchased.

On May 10, 1849, the Banner Company pulled out of Independence for the first leg of their journey.[235] By then, the grass was tall enough for the animals to forage, and enough snow would have melted in Sierra Mountains to clear the mountain passes. Had their timing been off they would have suffered a fate similar to the Donner Party.

The trail consisted of two well-traveled ruts though the western territories. As in earlier treks from New York westward with similar gear, these trails took a toll on wagons and animals. Each unit of six men carried spare parts, mostly spindles for broken wheels, water barrels, and heavy ropes. Ordinary chores on the trail consisted of driving wagons and swimming animals across rivers. Each member had specific assignments; guard duty, a physician who tended to the sick or injured, supplies, repairs, preparing meals, and an attorney who kept a fascinating first-hand account of their trip.

We know from a *Southport Telegraph* article that they traveled in groups of six, which meant they bought Conestoga wagons for their cross-country trip, outfitted with three bunk beds lashed together in each wagon. While two men were driving the rig the other four could sleep, play cards, or read a book although it was a bumpy and uncomfortable ride. A Conestoga was 18 feet long, four feet wide, could carry up to 1,200 pounds, and was usually pulled by eight mules. The floor of the wagon curved upward at each end to prevent things from shifting during travel, and the cracks between the boards were caulked to prevent seepage when crossing rivers or streams.

Typical Conestoga wagon from the 1840s with a feed-box attached to the back. These wagons were the finest money could buy and designed for a cross-country trip. Pictures courtesy of the Kansas City Historical Society.

According to the *Southport Telegraph*, "The Banner Company numbered about forty men, several of whom were citizens of this place [Southport]. On May 10, 1849 we left the outposts of civilization on the Missouri River and with the magnetic needle alone, for our guide, launched into the almost trackless wilderness that stretches its thousands of miles toward the Pacific.

"To persons designing to cross the plains I would advise that mule teams are preferable to all others. Wagons should be light and strong. Take just baggage enough to get through, half a dozen shirts, as many pairs of socks, with a change of outside clothing made of strong material. Buffalo robes, blankets, and India-rubber material used for sleeping. The load should not weigh over 1,200 pounds for four men, 6 mules are necessary to a wagon, with a couple extra for the saddle.

"The first part of the journey tried our qualities. It rained a great deal, accompanied with thunder and lightning, and a high wind, which with an occasional snow and hailstorm, and now and then a streak of sunshine, made up our weather. Poor grass and poor water, and frequently none of either. Plains where the dust is impregnated or mixed with a sort of alkali, which of course entered our mouths, noses, and eyes, as also those of our animals.

Once Banner Company reached Fort Kearney, Nebraska, the Platte River guided them into Wyoming.

"On June 3, 1849 we arrived at Fort Laramie. After halting here a short time, we crossed what is called the Black Hills. The country here begins to assume a picturesque, indeed, a magnificent appearance, to a person whose eye has long been familiarized to the monotonous level of Wisconsin scenery. Laramie Peak lifts its head towering to the cloud, while on every side, like silver headed patriarchs, stand the snow-capped mountains.

"On June 9, 1849, we crossed the north branch of the Platte River at the Mormon Ferry. After this, we found the grass scarcer, and the water very much of the character of alkali. Some kinds of game are plenty, particularly a species of Antelope and Buffalo meat is occasionally had, which is quite a treat.

"On June 14, 1849, we had attained an elevation which brought us into a region of snow. We used snow water for coffee, and at night the weather was freezing cold. We used Artemisia or wild sage for firewood.

"On June 15, 1849, we stood upon the summit of the Rocky Mountains. Standing at this elevation, perched upon the backbone of this monster earth, overlooking the whole North American continent, a man is apt to breathe freer and deeper.

"It is something to float on the majestic rivers, and to plough the waves of the inland seas. It is something to stand in this old world among the majestic ruins of time and people that have passed, or among the splendid monuments of the present. All this furnishes food for thought and gives scope to the imagination.

"The mountains are tolerable, but we succeeded in traveling without moving our loads until we came to the Sierra Nevada range, when we were compelled to partially unload, and pack upon mules, drawing our wagons up light. These mountains are from a mile in height, and rocky and rough. Very few teams preceded us; consequently, the road was not very well defined.

"On June 16, 1849, we halted at noon at the forks of the road, and took a vote to see whether we should go by Sublettes Cut-Off, or by Fort Bridger. The company voted to go the cut-off route, which proved the best. There are some very interesting springs.

"On June 26, 1849, we arrived at Fort Hall, where we halted to recruit a little fresh meat, corn bread, and milk. After leaving we found the grass scarcer, and crickets enough to feed a nation of Indians. Some of the rivers were deep and difficult to ford, but we made out to cross them."[236]

Sublettes Cut-Off was a fifteen-day trip through land with little water or grass to feed the animals that shortened their trip by fifty miles and a week of travel.

"On July 4, 1849, we found ourselves camped in Hot Springs Valley. Our thoughts on this day wandered off to friends and home.

"After eating our hard bread, washed down with water, for dinner, and short cake and bacon for supper, a Mr. Morrison gave us a good oration. Seated on the grass, snowcapped mountains around us, we listened to the words of the speaker as he dwelt upon the event which makes this day hallowed in our country's history. At night, a campfire was kindled on the ground, and while the mountain echoed back the music of the violin, and while the dance was going on, in the wilderness of the scene and its excitement, we forgot temporarily, all things else.

"The next point of importance was the Humboldt River, where all accounts led us to expect good grass for feed, but we were disappointed to find it the poorest spot on the route. The river is a peculiarity, losing itself in a small lake from which there is no visible outlet, and from which the water undoubtedly sinks into the earth. Around this lake, or rather end of the river, we cut grass and put it in our wagons, and took some water preparatory to striking across the sandy desert which here commences, and on the morning of July 17, 1849, at half past six, we started across this trackless waste.

"This day was the most difficult of the journey, both for us and the teams. Desert sand beneath our feet, a burning sun over our head, and not a drop of water or a blade of grass, and of these we took on board before we started was soon exhausted. There is no doubt but many of the emigrants will suffer in crossing this desert, particularly those who come at the close of the season.

"After crossing the desert, we found more pleasant traveling and better grass, until we arrived at the Sierra Nevada Mountains, which were near the end of our route. The later part of the journey is the most rugged and difficult, and requires men of energy, perseverance, and go-ahead. In crossing the mountains, we encountered snow several feet deep, through which we were compelled to drag our wagons. Leaving them we approached with much satisfaction the end of our journey.

"On July 28, 1849, we arrived near the diggings. Unparalleled speed, through in 80 days from western frontier. Triumphant! We left the Missouri River on May 10, 1849, and arrived here July 28, 1849, having laid in twelve days, making the entire trip in 68 days without serious accident or loss of animals. We claim that this is the quickest time in which the overland route has been made with wagons; the past can present no parallel to it. It's quicker than any other company will make this season. Over 3,000 teams left the western frontier before us, but in our speed over the plains, deserts, and mountains of the western wilds, have left all but 18 teams behind.

"We have been particularly fortunate for we have not suffered from scarcity of food for ourselves or the animals. The savage and hostile Indians that have harassed others have not molested us. Unexampled good feeling and harmony have existed among the members of our company, and we can make the boast that no member that started with us from frontier left us on the journey.

"Expressing our decided and honest preference for mules over any other kind of teams in traveling this route, mules with reasonable loads, will accomplish the journey much sooner than oxen. We have averaged 25 miles per day for the entire number of days out. Beat this who can!"[237]

The gold rush was a poorly thought out "get rich quick" scheme that attracted 200,000 desperate men into a harsh and unforgiving land, with little knowledge of mining or the risks of cross-country travel. A few of the easterners drawn en masse to the California El Dorado amassed fortunes but not from mining. Merchants made far more money than the miners.

Activity along the American River near Sutter's Mill, circa 1852.
Picture courtesy of the Sacramento Historical Society.

John Studebaker built and sold wheelbarrows to the miners, but returned to South Bend, Indiana, with an $8,000 ($1.2 million today) grubstake to start a carriage business that later became the world's largest. An impeccably dressed Jewish man named Levi Strauss wore tailored suits, but stepped off the boat with a bolt of canvas cloth. He began making the only pants that could stand up to working with rocks all day long. John Armour discovered that feeding people was more profitable than mining, and with his earnings from the gold fields became one of the country's largest meatpackers. While fifteen year old John Folger's brothers were off mining, he started roasting coffee beans and selling fresh coffee to the miners. After failing as a prospector, R.H. Macy cleared $3,000 ($480,000 today) by swapping land deeds, and returned to New York City with enough money to open what eventually became the world's largest department store.

But the California gold rush turned out to be a wild goose chase for thousands of men, women, and children. Many were so poorly prepared that death was inevitable, and for those who made it to Sacramento, the best claims had already been exhausted by the first wave of prospectors.

By the time the Banner Company reached the mining camp, big strikes were few and far between. It was estimated that 99 out of 100 were lucky to make expenses. This created a large population of angry and desperate miners. The tent city along the American River were violent with horse stealing topping the list of crimes. A stolen horse could be sold for around $120 ($6,000 today), but if caught, the thief was immediately hung from the nearest tree as a deterrent to other thieves.

After a month of prospecting the Banner Company cleared about $7,000 or less than $38 ($5,700 today) per man.[238] (Each man paid $156 in traveling expenses.) Nobody was prepared for the laws of supply and demand once they reached the gold fields, because just about everything sold for exorbitant rates. There was also a high mortality rate. About 30% of the miners died of disease, accidents, or violence.

The *Southport Telegraph* wrote, "It must be an immutable law of trade in any mining country, that all things are priced in proportion to the average yields in the mines. Whether it is worthwhile for a man to abandon all the delights of home and friends and civilized life, for a home at hard work in the mines of California, is a question which every man must answer himself."[239]

Notes:

1. Torrey family history, *Hackley & Hume* papers at Michigan State University, Gideon and Julia (Torrey) Truesdell.
2. *Truesdell Family History*, Major General Karl Truesdell, Group C, Gideon Truesdell lost branch, and origins of the family in England.
3. Bannister family history; Gideon R. Truesdell married Polly Bannister who was descended from Mayflower passenger Stephen Hopkins.
4. Ibid.
5. Diane Truesdell Loy research which ties into pension records.
6. *History of Warsaw*, John Truesdell biographical sketch.
7. Diane Leiter research, a descendent of Solomon Truesdell.
8. *Holland Land Office Museum* archives.
9. Ibid.
10. Ibid.
11. *History of the town of Warsaw, New York*, pp. 28. Webster's purchase was entered on 20 June 1803 with the *Holland Land Company*.
12. *Wyoming County Mirror, March 1852*.
13. *Historical Wyoming Quarterly*, 1952, William Webster interview reprinted from an earlier sketch, pp. 97.
14. Ibid, pp. 97
15. Ibid.
16. Ibid, pp. 106.
17. Ibid.
18. Ibid.
19. Over the years there had been considerable debate over when and where he died; one historical sketch titled "The Pathfinder" places his birth in Old Fort #4 in Charleston, his parents being William and Deliverance (Jeason) Truesdell, but this is entirely unsubstantiated. During a 1977 interview with Beebe Truesdell in Cuba, New York, which was forty or fifty miles southeast of South Warsaw, Beebe (a descendant of William and Deliverance) stated that "we always heard we were somehow related to the Truesdells in Warsaw, way back, but never knew how." But there were two different Truesdell branches living in that area—the Gideon Truesdell and Jacob Truesdell families who weren't related.
20. Gideon Truesdell's approximate death is based on the birth of youngest daughter, Thankful Truesdell, who was born in 1800.
21. 1800 federal census, Whitehall, Washington, New York; roll 26, pp.

552, image 275. According to this census "Dorcas Truesdale" was listed as the head of the household, and an 1804 Whitehall tax assessment role references the "Widow Toudesdall" as owning 250 acres of land.

22. *History of Warsaw*. Elizur Webster was John Truesdell's brother-in-law. A few local histories have mistakenly written that he was Betsy's father.

23. Dorcas Truesdell Munger was deaf according to Warsaw Historian John Wilson's file on the Truesdell family.

24. Truesdell Family History, Major General Karl Truesdell, Group C, Gideon Truesdell lost branch.

25. *Historical Wyoming Quarterly*, 1952, William Webster interview, pp. 97.

26. Bannister's Settlement, *Historical Wyoming County Quarterly*, April 1958. Truesdell Road ran behind their farms and into Bannisters. This is present day Silver Springs.

27. Bannister's Settlement is present-day Gainesville.

28. Torrey genealogy, Gideon was married to Julia Ann Torrey.

29. Descendants still living in the area said that this had been long-established family tradition.

30. Family tradition. Dorcas Crandall Truesdell was a deeply religious Baptist who was descended from Elder John Crandall of Rhode Island. Charles Humphrey (1888–1977) was a descendent of John Truesdell. Interview, 1977, Warsaw, N.Y.

31. *History of Warsaw*. Truesdell brothers served in militia.

32. *Historical Wyoming Quarterly*, October 1977. Jeremiah, Solomon, and Gideon Truesdell served from 24 September 1812 to 3 November 1812.

33. Ibid.

34. Diane Truesdell Loy military research.

35. *Holland Land Office Museum* archives, Batavia, New York.

36. Ibid.

37. At this writing five generations of descendants were woodworkers/cabinetmakers by hobby.

38. Julia Torrey was the daughter of Noah and Abigail Torrey. She was born on the family farm in Hamilton, New York until they moved to Mt. Morris.

39. Noah Torrey family history.

40. Truesdell family Bible that was in the possession of Patrick D. Truesdell in 1977, copy of signed marriage certificate by Rev. William Arthur.

41. Rhoda Truesdell reminiscences to son Fayette Truesdell; he was Patrick

D. Truesdell's great, grandfather.
42. Ibid.
43. Of the five Truesdell brothers, Gideon and Amos were the closest in age and lifelong friends.
44. Ibid.
45. Jeremiah Truesdale descendants and census information. He spelled his last name differently than the rest of the family. Family Bible page establishes lineage through several generations. Family legend states that he was a stone mason.
46. Gideon's whereabouts during this period were tough to pinpoint, but information from Rhoda Truesdell's reminiscences helped.
47. Jeremiah Truesdell was a stone mason by trade living on the outskirts of Buffalo with his family.
48. Frank Wyman Sherwood (1866–1927) narrative, pp. 1-4. This fits with Buffalo & Niagara timeline. He was Amos Truesdell's grandson.
49. Ibid.
50. April 21, 1835 infant daughter died, Wyoming Historical Quarterly, May 1952, Portageville Cemetery records.
51. Rhoda Truesdell reminiscences to grandson, Amos Fred Sherwood.
52. *Wisconsin Historical Collections*, Volume XIX, pp. 212-213.
53. Ibid.
54. Ibid.
55. Ibid.
56. WPA history; Narrative of Morgan L. Martin, PP. 406.
57. Amos Fred Sherwood reminiscences, 1940. He was Amos and Rhoda Truesdell's grandson and family historian.
58. History of Deerfield, Illinois-Truesdell Family. Amos sold his Portageville farm to his brother Levi who rented it to others.
59. Amos Fred Sherwood narrative, 1939, pp 1-4.
60. *University of Wisconsin* historical archives, Madison campus. Wisconsin Academy of Sciences, Arts, and Letters, chapter 2, 1837 Treaty with the Chippewa (Pine Tree Treaty).pp, 13–31.
61. *Wisconsin Historical Collections*, Volume XXIV, Daniel Whitney,
62. *The Pinery*, pp. 20
63. Ibid
64. *Pioneers of the Pinery*, Chapter II, The Hathaway survey, pp. 23-39.
65. Ibid.
66. Ibid.

67. *Wisconsin Historical Collections*, Volume XXIV, Daniel Whitney
68. Ibid
69. *Morgan L. Martin*, PP. 399.
70. Daniel Whitney died in 1838 at the age 34, and this would have had a commercial impact on the area.
71. Carolyn Truesdell Siders, 1977 interview. She was descended from Jeremiah Truesdell.
72. Federal census; 1840, Portage County, Wisconsin Territory, roll 580, pp. 131.
73. *Torrey Family Genealogy*, *Hackley & Hume* papers, Michigan State University, Gideon and Julia Truesdell was Julia Hackley's uncle and aunt.
74. *Torrey Family Genealogy*, pp. 836.
75. This is based on when they were in Middlebury, Indiana, and the approximate travel to between there and Chicago.
76. Present-day Wisconsin Rapids.
77. *History of Portage County*.
78. *Old Pulaski: A Lumber Rafting Legacy* by Lynn Morrow. *Old Settlers Gazette Archive*.
79. Bob Fay research, 1999 interview and correspondence. He was descended from Harrison and Isabella Fay and did considerable research.
80. Kirkland Torrey diary. What pages survived are out of order with some missing the year, but still very informative.
81. Sister-in-law remembered Gideon as kindhearted; Rhoda Mills Truesdell papers.
82. Mosquito Creek was an early (1840) designation, and must have been named by Truesdell or Kingston, Fay, or Draper.
83. Malcom Rosholt research; *Portage County Historical Society*.
84. Robert Wakely letters, *Wood County Historical Society*.
85. Ibid.
86. Ibid.
87. *Early Western Days*.
88. Ibid.
89. Bob Fay research, 1999 interview and correspondence. He was descended from Harrison Fay and Paul Kingston.
90. *Madison Express*, 17 November 188841, pp. 4. Richard Rising vs. Harrison Fay et al.
91. *Milwaukee Advertiser*, 15 April 1837, pp. 4.
92. Robert Fay papers, correspondence with Bev Elmshauser, a descendent

of Joshua Draper.
93. Tom Taylor narrative, McMillian Library, Wisconsin Rapids, Wisconsin.
94. *Muskegon Chronicle*, 23 August 1888, pp. 7. Thomas D. Gilbert reminiscences.
95. *The Wisconsin River: An Odyssey Through Time and Space*, pp. 87.
96. Ibid.
97. Ibid.
98. Passim, this was the going rate (1835–1842) for a thousand feet of lumber paid by St. Louis wholesale yards.
99. Kirkland Torrey diary, 1 July 1841.
100. *Territorial Papers of the United States, Volume XXVII, Wisconsin Territory, 1836–1839*, pp. 106.
101. Ibid.
102. *Milwaukee Weekly Sentinel*, 28 Sep 1842, pp. 2.
103. The Wisconsin River: An Odyssey Through Time and Space, pp. 71.
104. Ibid.
105. *Wisconsin Enquirer*, 11 January 1840, pp. 3.
106. Kirkland Torrey dairy.
107. *Madison Enquirer*, 20 February 1841.
108. Ibid
109. *Wisconsin Enquirer*, 13 Feb 1841, pp. 3.
110. The Wisconsin River: An Odyssey Through Time and Space, pp. 20-22.
111. *Lumber rafting on the Wisconsin River*.
112. Malcom Rosholt notes.
113. Tom Taylor narrative, McMillian Library, Wisconsin Rapids, Wisconsin.
114. Tom Taylor narrative, McMillian Library, Wisconsin Rapids, Wisconsin.
115. Ibid.
116. Tom Taylor narrative, McMillian Library, Wisconsin Rapids, Wisconsin.
117. *Old Pulaski: A Lumber Rafting Legacy* by Lynn Morrow. Old Settlers Gazette Archive.
118. Kirkland Torrey diary, July 9, 1840.
119. *Lumber rafting on the Wisconsin River*.
120. The Wisconsin River: An Odyssey Through Time and Space, pp. 24.
121. Tom Taylor narrative, McMillian Library, Wisconsin Rapids,

Wisconsin.
122. Ibid.
123. *Lumber rafting on the Wisconsin River*.
124. *Old Pulaski: A Lumber Rafting Legacy* by Lynn Morrow. Old Settlers Gazette Archive.
125. Ibid.
126. *Branch Banking in Missouri: Past, Present, and Future*, pp. 794.
127. Malcom Rosholt papers, George Stevens correspondence.
128. Kirkland Torrey diary entry, 9 July 1842.
129. Malcolm Rosholt-Robert Wakely letters.
130. *Reminiscences of the Early Northwest*.
131. Ibid.
132. *Grant County Herald*, 27 Sep 1845, pp. 3.
133. *Madison Express*, 4 September 1841, pp. 4
134. *Madison Express*, 17 November 1841, pp. 4.
135. Ibid.
136. *Southport Telegraph*, 27 November 1841, pp. 3.
137. Petition to Washington for the construction of a road into the pinery.
138. *History of Kenosha & Kenosha County, Wisconsin*, pp. 87
139. *Madison Express*, 30 August 1842, pp. 4.
140. Maudine Truesdell. Her husband was G.J. Truesdell's grandson, Len Truesdell Sr.
141. Didn't like his name. Welsh according to his daughter-in-law, Maudine Truesdell 1977 interview.
142. *Kenosha News*, 4 December 1923, "Turn Back the Pages of Kenosha History."
143. *Wisconsin Democrat*, 21 Dec 1843, pp. 3.
144. Ibid.
145. *Kenosha News*, 4 December 1923, "Turn Back the Pages of Kenosha History."
146. This is where the 1st National Bank stood.
147. *Southport American*, Wisconsin House ad for rent, owned by Bullen & Hale.
148. *Daily Milwaukee News*, 1 May 1869, "Old Settlers" article, pp. 4.
149. Hotel built by Doolittle brothers.
150. *Pioneer Life in Kenosha County*, pp. 16–19. Wisconsin House built by Doolittles in 1837; later renamed the American House.
151. *Kenosha Telegraph*, Old Settlers article, 14 May 1869.

152. *Southport American*, 21 August 1843, ad for sale
153. *Kenosha Telegraph*, Old Settlers article, 14 May 1869.
154. *Southport American*, 7 September 1843, pp. 1.
155. This was customary for hotels that catered to the sailing public.
156. This hotel was later called the City Hotel, and located on Main Street and Market.
157. This is based on the fact that Gideon owed them money a few years later when he didn't renew his lease.
158. 1843 Wisconsin census, Runge Collection, Milwaukee Public Library.
159. This is based on his own statements about his early years in Kenosha at an 1869 Old Settlers picnic when asked to speak.
160. *Daily Milwaukee News*, 1 May 1869, Old Settlers article.
161. *R.G. Dun & Company*, Wisconsin ledger, volume 27, pp. 268.
162. Ibid.
163. The Durkee farm was located at the intersection of present-day Sheridan Road and 75th Street all the way to 22nd Avenue.
164. *Green Ridge Cemetery* records, Kenosha, Wisconsin.
165. Ibid.
166. *Kenosha Retrospective, Charles Durkee*, Yankee Idealist chapter, pp. 1.
167. *Wisconsin Free Democrat*, 4 October 1848. Durkee served in Vermont legislature.
168. *History of Cabot, Vermont*. John Winchester Dana biographical sketch.
169. *History of Pomfret, Vermont*.
170. *Society of Durkee*, a comprehensive family genealogy since they came to this country.
171. Dana-Fessenden connection
172. *Kenosha Retrospective, Charles Durkee*, Yankee Idealist chapter, pp. 1. Sailing ships of that era all shared a mold and mildew problem.
173. Territorial Papers of the United States, VOL XXVII Wisconsin Territory, 1836-1841. Pp. 877.
174. Charles and Catherine Durkee letter to Demings about opportunities, *Kenosha Historical Society*, Durkee file.
175. *Milwaukee Weekly Sentinel*, 29 July 1843, pp. 2. Southeastern Wisconsin is present-day Racine and Kenosha harbors.
176. Ibid.
177. *St. Paul Daily Globe*, 8 July 1879. pp. 8.
178. Ibid.
179. Property located at 5125 6th Avenue.

180. Harvey Durkee farm was at the present-day corner of Sheridan Road and 75th street and extended to 22nd Avenue.
181. *Wisconsin Shipwrecks*, the Kate Kelly, pp. 9.
182. Cahoon was Rev. Reuben Deming's deceased first wife's cousin.
183. *History of Lake County*, pp. 192.
184. *Kenosha Telegraph*, 19 February 1911. Mary Ann Deming was close friends with Deming's first wife, who died at a young age.
185. Ibid
186. *Wisconsin Free Democrat*, 4 October 1848. Durkee served in Vermont legislature.
187. WPA Writers Project; Narrative of Morgan L. Martin, pp. 409.
188. *Recollections of the Early History of Wisconsin*, pp. 289.
189. *Milwaukee Weekly Sentinel*, 16 March 1844, pp. 2.
190. WPA History, Clermont's Narrative, pp. 457.
191. *Kenosha Telegraph*, 6 April 1887, Harvey Durkee obituary.
192. Ibid.
193. *Wisconsin Express*, 10 October 1840, pp. 2.
194. Ibid.
195. Ibid.
196. *Daily Milwaukee News*, 1 May 1869, Old Settlers article.
197. Kirkland Torrey dairy entry, 9 March 1846, "Gid started working at Durkee store."
198. *Wisconsin Enquirer*, 20 Mar 1841, pp. 2.
199. *American Argus*, 7 December 1845, pp. 2.
200. This is a presumption based on stray pieces of information; Waldo left around the time Harvey Durkee became the managing partner of his brother's business. After Charles left for Washington, he never really had any involvement in the business.
201. *Southport American*, 3 May 1841.
202. Ibid, 19 March 1841
203. *Milwaukee Weekly Sentinel*, 14 July 1844.
204. *Dutton, Richardson & Company vs. Charles Durkee*. He appears to have been selling $200,000+ of merchandise a year.
205. *Southport Telegraph*, 2 March 1849, pp. 4.
206. *Milwaukee Weekly Sentinel*, 30 Oct 1841, pp. 2.
207. *Durkee vs. City Bank of Kenosha*, 1860 Wisconsin Supreme Court term trnscripts.
208. Troy Historical Society, Hart-Howard family file.

209. *Kenosha Democrat*, 16 September 1853, pp. 2.
210. *American Freeman*, 8 December 1846, pp. 2.
211. *Wisconsin Argus*, 12 November 1848, pp. 2.
212. *Oshkosh True Democrat*, 21 December 1849, pp. 1.
213. *Juneau County Argus*, 9 February 1871, pp. 3.
214. Society of Durkee, Charles Durkee group sheet.
215. *Southport American*, 7 Marche 1843.
216. Ibid, 12 October 1841.
217. 1857 Army Corp of Engineers report, pp. 1,018.
218. *Genealogy of the Blish Family in America: 1637–1905*, pp. 188.
219. *Maritime Disasters*, Phoenix chapter, pp. 113–129.
220. Ibid
221. Ibid
222. Ibid
223. Ibid
224. Ibid
225. Ibid
226. Ibid
227. Ibid
228. Ibid
229. *Genealogy of the Blish Family in America: 1637–1905*, pp. 188.
230. *R.G. Dun & Company*, Harvey Durkee & Company, Wisconsin ledger, volume 27, pp. 192, August 1847 to July 1849 entry.
231. *Southport Telegraph*, 2 November 1849, pp. 1.
232. Ibid.
233. Ibid.
234. Dana genealogy, Andrew Dana died of Typhoid Fever in Sacramento.
235. *Southport Telegraph*, 2 November 1849, pp. 1.
236. Ibid.
237. Ibid.
238. Ibid.
239. Ibid.

2

GIDEON TRUESDELL & COMPANY: 1850–1852

In 1850, Southport petitioned the state to allow the southern half of Racine County to become Kenosha County. They no longer had to spend a day traveling to the Racine courthouse because the seat of government was now nearby. At the same time Southport's name was changed to Kenosha, and a booming Kenosha it was.

Hutchison & Wheeler, Hale & Ayer, Bennett & Selleck, and Harvey Durkee & Company were the largest warehouses, and tough competitors. They under-cut warehouses in neighboring counties by shaving 10% off the price of lumber, and paying 10% more for wheat.[1] No wonder farmers came back year after year until Kenosha cleared the largest tonnage of freight between Milwaukee and Chicago. But it hadn't always been that way because Racine warehouses were only 17 miles north, and a few years earlier they built plank roads that ran deep into Kenosha County so they could siphon wheat exports.

During the 1840s, Charles Durkee & Company had been selling about 150,000 feet of lumber and 250,000 shingles each year from a vacant lot next to their store, but knew the time was right to leverage this into a separate business.[2] He also believed the time had come to spin-off the hardware they sold into a separate business. Most general stores carried common items but nobody offered a full line of hardware.

Charles Durkee had an eye for spotting sharp young men, because during the 1840s he bankrolled two additional mercantile stores.[3] This was a common way for a merchant to keep his money growing while others handled the day-to-day headaches of running a store. He would have provided enough start-up money to rent a storefront, and stock each store.

Each spring and fall on his buying trips to New York City for his own store, he would have tripled his order, and divided the cargo between each store. In addition to interest and principal Durkee would have received a third of the profits.

After working for Charles Durkee for about five years, Gideon had no doubt demonstrated his abilities. He was smart, hard-working, and as honest as the day was long which made him a good candidate for a partnership. Upon Gideon's return from the gold fields and after Harvey lost his lease on the Blish & Whitney warehouse, the Durkees began making plans to expand their hardware sales by spinning this into a separate business. They picked Gideon to become their managing partner, and a few years later, Charles and Harvey Durkee's stake in Gideon Truesdell & Company became incredibly profitable.

Charles knew that pinelands was a solid investment. Two years after he arrived in the Wisconsin Territory, he bought an interest in the Neshoto Lumber Company, one of the earliest Sawmills in Wisconsin. He also invested in a couple of logging syndicates where he and others bought thousands of acres, hired loggers, and shipped the logs to Darling, Fitzgerald & Company where they cleared about a 400% profit. In a May 25, 1851 reply to a friend looking for advice, Durkee explained the strengths and weaknesses of buying and logging large tracts of pinelands. Although there were experienced axmen from the eastern states available, he warned him that most of the logging crews were unskilled or transient workers that were unreliable and sometimes a headache.[4]

While Charles was busy in Washington as a Congressman during a difficult period of history, his brother managed his investments, including the construction of a hardware store on land Charles owned at the corner of Lake and Wisconsin Streets, across from the Blish & Whitney warehouse and dock. The first floor would have been the store with hardware stacked from floor to ceiling, with the second and third floors used for storage of inventory.

Charles Durkee & Company had been distributors of window and plate glass, and had the local market to themselves. They also had wholesale connections for plastering hair, hardware, building supplies, and lumber. Through their brother, Harrison Durkee, they obtained the first distributorship outside of Albany for kegs of nails mass-produced at Erastus Corning's Albany Nail Factory.[5] Based on advertising, these distributorships shifted to the Gideon's hardware store and lumberyard.

On April 5th, 1850, the *Kenosha Telegraph* printed the following notice:

"PARTNERSHIP NOTICE. The undersigned have formed a partnership for the purpose of transacting a lumber business in Southport under the name and style of Gideon Truesdell & Company. Harvey Durkee and Gideon Truesdell."[6]

Most of the business was owned by Gideon although Charles and Harvey Durkee held an interest in the business. They rented him the building he used for a hardware store, and a city block for a retail lumberyard. Between the rental income from the store, lumberyard, and a third of the profits this would have been a good investment for them.

Kenosha was going through a construction boom, and this would have brought builders to Gideon's lumberyard and hardware store when picking up milled lumber across the street. There were other lumberyards nearby that were owned by Theodore Newell & Company, Ryerson & Morris (Elkins Brothers), Leonard & Lay, and smaller yards operated by merchants on a vacant lot next to their stores.[7]

Gideon's niche in a crowded market was having the only hardware store in town, and a yard stocked with different grades of lumber. The other yards were owned or affiliated with mills on the eastern side of Lake Michigan that used them as an outlet to sell their lumber. Most of the trees in the southern half of Minnesota, Wisconsin, and Michigan were hardwoods that weren't suitable for construction, which meant that nearly all of pine used for construction had to be imported by schooners. Gideon stocked construction grade pine from Muskegon, Michigan. A cheaper grade from mills in Kalamazoo and St. Joseph, who milled boards from low-quality trees with lots of knot-holes and sap stains that was suitable for barns, fences, hog sheds, or chicken coops.

Gideon also stocked mass-produced hinges, door knobs, window hardware, and quarter-barrels of white paint powder and a couple hundred tons of animal hair for plaster work. The hardware store was no doubt stocked by Harvey Durkee, and Gideon would have stocked the lumberyard with a wide selection of what contractors needed. Before the opening of navigation in 1850, he placed the following advertisement:

"GIDEON TRUESDELL, dealer in lumber in Southport. I will have constantly on hand, a well-selected assortment of lumber. Also, on

Richard C. Fritz

hand shingles, lath, plastering hair, window sash, glass, etc. Lumber yard opposite the Planing Machine."[8]

According to a November 12, 1851 *Weekly Wisconsin* article, an employee working in their yard was fatally struck in the head by a board "at the lumber yard of Truesdell & Durkee."[9] An 8-foot board was leaning against a pile of lumber, when a gust of wind smashed it into the workers head while crouched over. He never knew what hit him.

After a profitable first year, Harvey and Gideon were able to buy the block-and-half of land they rented from Charles Durkee for $1,900 ($285,000 today), probably with some type of mortgage.[10] This suggests they were immediately successful, but the retail yards of Theodore Newell & Company and Ryerson & Morris (Elkins Brothers) still controlled at least two-thirds of the local market.

Gideon's twenty-two year-old brother-in-law, Allen Torrey, left the family farm in New York to come to Kenosha and manage the yard with a couple of day laborers.[11] Gideon would have spent the day inside the hardware store with a couple of clerks, and strong young men looking for work were hired each morning when a schooner docked. There was no easy way to unload a ship other than board by board, piling them into a wagon, and hauling them across the road to the yard.[12] Since the boards were still green and moist to the touch, they were cross-stacked 20-feet high to dry over the next four to six weeks. Boards that weren't properly seasoned became twisted and warped, and couldn't be sold for anything other than firewood.

During the early 1850s there were three lakefront warehouses; Bennett & Sellick, Hale & Ayer, and Holbrook, Elkins & Company. Henry Elkins lined-up a Boston investor, and bought the Blish warehouse and dock, although a few years later he lost his investor. In 1852, Samuel Hale built a much larger warehouse with two separate docks, and leased half of his building to Elkins. This placed the Blish property back on the market, and Charles and Harvey Durkee were ready to take their investment in Gideon Truesdell & Company to the next level.

Durkee, Truesdell & Company, 1852–1871

The Durkees had long been land rich and cash poor, and Harvey Durkee no doubt regretted not being able to buy the Blish property a few years earlier. When it came back on the market, Charles, Harvey, and Gideon had the funds to leverage a deal.

The new firm was Durkee, Truesdell & Company with Harvey Durkee, Gideon Truesdell, and Charles Durkee each owning 30% of the firm.[13] The remainder was owned by Charles Deming, a nephew by marriage to the Durkees, and he had about five years' experience at the warehouse and freight forwarding firm of owned by his uncle.[14] Several years earlier he learned double-entry accounting, and became Durkee, Truesdell & Company's bookkeeper.

They opened just in time for one of the busiest harvests in recent years. After a three year drought that caused wheat exports to plummet, the local economy was booming again after a bumper-crop. According to U.S. Customs House records for 1852, over $900,000 ($108 million today) of freight was offloaded in Kenosha, and the partners picked a good time to get into the warehouse business.

In 1852, the *Kenosha Telegraph* wrote, "We are informed by merchants that it looks like old times again, and that they have done more business and taken more cash this spring, than they have in any season for the same length of time in three years past. Teams come in with wagons loaded with wheat, oats, etc. and go out loaded with lumber, dry goods and groceries. Farmers drive off whistling with a big smile on their faces."[15]

The August 12, 1852, *Kenosha Times* reported, "The South Pier and Warehouse, late of Ball & Elkins, have been purchased by Durkee, Truesdell & Company, who will continue to run a warehouse, forwarding, and commission firm. The new firm, practical businessmen whose motto is 'always be busy at something' invariably ensures success. We hope this eligible site for business will bring a fair quota of profit to its enterprising proprietors, and we wish success to them."[16]

They inherited a franchise with the Reed Ship Lines, whose ships traveled through the Great Lakes but mostly between Green Bay and Chicago. The partnership had another franchise with the larger Griffith's Western Line, which sailed throughout the Great Lakes, Ohio River and Mississippi River. Durkee, Truesdell & Company were also listed as agents for the Union Transportation Line which ran canal boats from Buffalo to New York City.[17] These franchises were necessary if they were serious about getting into the freight-forwarding business. In those days freight was shipped from warehouse to warehouse, and a freight forwarding company had to be affiliated with warehouses from New York City to Chicago.

It was wheat exports and lumber imports that brought an enormous amount of money into the community, because Kenosha was the closest Lake Michigan harbor for farmers as far away as 70 miles west in the fertile Rock River Valley. During the harvest season hundreds of wagons rolled down the old Beloit Military Trail, loaded with over forty 65-pound bags of wheat for shipment to Buffalo through one of the Kenosha warehouses.[18]

Wheat had to be harvested at the right time or it deteriorated and sold for a lower price. A farmer could tell when it was time to harvest by taste, and when that happened everyone worked around the clock because the market price depended on the quality of the wheat.

Teenagers worked from dawn to dusk on a harvesting crew, and young boys were pressed into action driving wagons loaded with bags of wheat. The last thing a harvest crew did after a grueling sixteen-hour day was load the wagons, because at the crack of dawn, boys hitched up the horses and began a two-day trip to Kenosha. Farmer Elbridge Ayer loaded two wagons at a time, recruiting boys as young as ten years old to drive them to a lakefront warehouse. Rather than return to the farm with an empty wagon, most farmers returned with their wagons loaded with lumber to build fences, barns, hog sheds, and stables.

Before they left, Mrs. Ayer packed each boy a lunch, gave them enough money to stop at a tavern for the night where they were fed and given a bed, and 25¢ ($20 today) so they could pay somebody to unload their wagon at the lakefront warehouse. Once they crossed the Fox River there were a 22 mile stretch of the old Beloit Military Trail where there were taverns, and each had a reputation. A temperance house didn't serve liquor, and others were known for serving excellent meals. At the lower end of the scale were taverns known for gambling and loose women that catered to a sleazier clientele.

A.J. Baethke tavern, Trevor, Wisconsin. The first floor consisted of a dining room and kitchen, with a dormitory on the second floor with 10 to 15 beds. Picture courtesy of the Kenosha History Center Archives.

A large flatbed was used to transport wheat from the warehouse to a schooner for the trip through the Great Lakes to the grain elevators in Buffalo. Picture courtesy of the Buffalo History Museum.

During the fall harvest, 300 to 400 wagons rolled along the old 72-mile Beloit Military Trail that ran from the Rock River to the Kenosha lakeshore. None of the warehouses unloaded wagons, but there were always day laborers standing around looking for this type of work because it paid well. Farmers patronized the warehouse where they had a relationship with the owner, which meant that a newcomer like Durkee, Truesdell & Company would have had to build a clientele.

After breakfast the boys hit the trail, and by noon they reached the

Kenosha city limits, and according to one source, during the harvest season there were wagons backed up a quarter-mile from the warehouses. Once a wagon reached Durkee-Truesdell's warehouse, the driver pulled onto a loading dock where there was a scale beneath a platform that weighed the wagon, driver and wheat. The driver was handed a slip with his gross weight and told to move his wagon to the pier house where it was up to the driver to unload. The wagon was then driven to a second scale where it was weighed again with the difference being the net weight of the wheat. The slip was taken across the street to Durkee-Truesdell's office at the hardware store where they were paid with a bank draft.

The point-spread between what lakefront warehouses paid farmers, and what the Buffalo elevators paid enabled Hale & Ayer, Elkins Brothers, Durkee, Truesdell & Company, and Bennett & Sellick to make money fast. Record-breaking profits wouldn't have been possible without the City Bank of Kenosha, and according to the banks cashier during the 1857 harvest, they turned-over $100,000 ($12 million today) of capital in a single day.[19]

A significant increase in wheat exports coincided with the development of the mechanical reaper. By 1860, Cyrus McCormick was manufacturing 4,000 reapers a year with over 50,000 already in use. In Kenosha, the Elkins brothers had the local franchise for the McCormick Reaper, and Hale & Ayer sold the less expensive Manny Reaper which was manufactured in nearby Rockford, Illinois.

Durkee, Truesdell & Company shipped around 137,000 bushels of wheat, a fraction of what the four older warehouses shipped due to a long list of loyal customers.[20] Based on partial U.S. Customs House records, Gideon sold around 462,000 feet of lumber that year with a gross profit of around $2.85 per thousand feet, which would have generated around $1,316 ($157,000 today).[21] How much their hardware store and freight forwarding business contributed to the top line is anyones guess, but most warehouses cleared over $1,000 ($128,000 today) handling freight, and their hardware store probably cleared about the same since they had most of the local market to themselves.

During their first year, the Durkee-Truesdell partnerships gross profit would have been higher than normal due to a bumper wheat crop, with gross sales falling into the $6,000 range.[22] After subtracting mortgages, wages, inventory, feed, banking fees, insurance, and repairs they probably netted about a 30% net profit, which was typical, or roughly a $1,890 ($226,000 today).

In 1853, we know from a *Milwaukee Sentinel* article that 3,716,817 board feet of lumber, 487,900 feet of lath, 168,290 shingles, and 168,290 fence posts were off-loaded and sold in Kenosha.[23] With Theodore Newell & Company and Ryerson & Morris completely out of the market, Durkee, Truesdell & Company would easily have controlled at least 50% of Kenosha market. The Durkee brothers crapshoot to "go big" when they bankrolled Gideon Truesdell had paid-off handsomely, and would continue to do so for many years to come. In the coming years Gideon would amass a fortune much larger than either of the Durkee brothers.

Schooner Challenge, circa 1854

What a lakefront lumberyard needed most during the 1850s was a schooner to service dozens of undercapitalized sawmills looking for buyers for their lumber. On April 3, 1854, the *Buffalo Daily Republic* wrote "we learn from the *Chicago Democratic Press* that Messrs. Durkee & Truesdell, of Kenosha, have purchased the schooner Challenge from Pratt Brothers for $5,000."[24] ($640,000 today.)

According to the Runge Maritime Collection the Challenge cost $4,500 to build.[25] During the previous year, the ship reported a $2,000 ($240,000 today) profit but her owners knew they could make even more money with a larger ship.[26]

Durkee, Truesdell & Company kept their schooner busy hauling lumber in one direction, and returning to the other side of Lake Michigan with freight. By sending a schooner to an undercapitalized mill, Gideon could lower his wholesale cost by around 12.5% or roughly $1.00 ($125 today) per thousand feet. Based on shipping records the Challenge would have paid for itself in less than two years.

The Challenge could haul about 90,000 feet of lumber and her revolutionary design made her one of the fastest schooners on Lake Michigan with the sharp bow of a clipper ship, and a drop keel for speed. The Challenge was fast with a shallow draft, averaging thirteen miles per hour while carrying 45-tons of lumber with a six-foot draft, which enabled her to easily glide over the sand bars obstructing most Lake Michigan harbors. Because of her design, she averaged three round trips a week between their lumberyard and sawmills in Muskegon at a time when other schooners averaged two.

Life at sea was a mixture of boredom and danger: falling down an open hatch, being crushed by a crashing 300-pound rigging, taking the wrong step 40-feet above while tenting a sail, getting caught between shifting lumber in a cargo hold, or tripping on a rope. An anchor breaking loose from its mooring could rip a hole in the side of the boat and take it to the bottom of Lake Michigan in less than fifteen minutes. The life of a sailor was full of hazards because four out of seven sailors died before reaching retirement.

Sailing on Lake Michigan caused more deaths than all the other Great Lakes combined-she was large enough to encounter heavy seas but small enough to prevent outrunning them. The narrow width of the lake made it treacherous during a storm because swells developed faster, waves crashed at shorter intervals with 16-foot swells that could capsize a 90-ton schooner in the blink of an eye during a deadly storm.

During a storm with gale force winds, an experienced captain didn't attempt to steer a schooner through heavy seas, because it was safer to let the wind blow them off course than try to control the ship through rough seas with 16-to-24-foot swells. After the storm was over, they corrected their course, and slowly made their way back to the shipping lanes. This was the safest place to sail, because if a schooner began to take on water there were other ships nearby to pull crew members out of the water before the ship sank.

Schooner Challenge docked in the Sheboygan, Wisconsin harbor. About 95,000 feet of lumber could be loaded into a cargo bay that was about 8 feet tall with another 30,000 to 50,000 feet chained to the deck. Schooners were floating warehouses that haul as much cargo as several semi-trailers. Pictures courtesy of the Milwaukee Public Library, Herman Runge Collection. Schooner Simpson. Pictures courtesy of the Chicago Maritime Society.

Because fog accounted for most collisions, an experienced captain stationed a crew member on deck who slowly rang the ship's bell. When he heard another bell from a nearby ship, they would yell "ahoy" back and forth until safely passing. The sound of the bell and voice calling-out ahoy told the other ship how close they were, and usually avoided a collision.

The headache of owning a ship is clearly evident by the insurance claims filed by Harvey Durkee and Gideon Truesdell. When the Challenge lost the small boat that hung from its transom, "Mr. Truesdell presented a request to borrow or buy the yawl belonging to the city [Kenosha]. He stated that their vessel was idle from having lost their yawl-none could be bought in Chicago."[27]

The 1854 sailing season was expensive when a mild winter prevented the lake from freezing, and created an unnavigable harbor. In January, "the Challenge was breeched near Manitowoc and had to be towed to Chicago for repairs - $300 ($34,000 today)." On April 30, 1854, the Challenge was docked in Chicago just after gale force winds sent the Maine, Lizzie Throop and Hayden crashing against the breakwater.

The *Chicago Tribune* estimated that over twenty sailors were swept out to sea but, "Captain Ackerman of the Challenge, Captain Drummond of the William Jones, and Peter Johnson brought them all in safely." About an hour later another ship crashed into shoreline and the crew from the Challenge and William Jones again came to their rescue, and after they returned to their ships to get some sleep because they were exhausted, they were called a third time. George Humphrey from the Challenge launched their yawl and pulled the crew out of the water."[28]

The following season, the *Kenosha Telegraph* wrote that, "the schooner Challenge, one of the swiftest little schooners on the lake, with one of the most careful and skillful skippers on the water, came in from her first trip of the season on Saturday afternoon. She went out Wednesday, ran to Manitowoc loaded with wood, made a run to Chicago, discharged her cargo, and was again in the harbor making the run from Chicago to Kenosha in a little over three hours. She is now painted and repaired and rides the waters as gracefully as a swan."[29]

Schooners caught in storm. Pictures courtesy of the Great Lakes Maritime Museum.

Every season had its share of snapped masts, leaks, and collusions which required towing the Challenge to the nearest shipyard for repairs. When damages occurred, it cost the owners a small fortune, but it enabled Harvey Durkee and Gideon Truesdell to take their business to the next level. Toward the end of 1855, however, they reported a serious accident while docked in Kenosha. "One of the hands on the schooner Challenge, by the name of Eastman, while furling the sail at the topmast head, made a misstep and fell, striking upon the head of the winch and bending the shaft. His thigh bone was broken and he was severely injured internally.

Drs. Farr and Johnson attended him and he is now doing well."[30] Dr. Farr was a renowned surgeon, and a close friend of Gideon's.[31]

A few years later, the Challenge got caught in a violent storm near Lake Superior and began taking on water, at which point Captain Ackerman ordered the crew to quickly lighten their load or risk sinking. "The schooner Challenge was at Grand Island, having put in during the gale of Wednesday, after throwing overboard 50 tons of iron-ore...she was reported leaking."[32]

According to an 1854 *Kenosha Telegraph* article, "the schooner Challenge, of this port, loaded lumber at Manitowoc and sailed from there Saturday last. She discharged her freight here and returned to Twin Rivers for a load of lumber, seven miles beyond Manitowoc, in forty-two hours. Sailing distance 247 miles. Time occupied in discharging freight, 6-hours, total sailing time, 36 hours."[33] They kept the Challenge busy on return trips to the eastern side of Lake Michigan as evidenced by a cargo of 50-barrels of lard.[34]

Other ships sailing from Kenosha to Muskegon averaged two-trips a week, whereas the Challenge averaged about three due to her revolutionary design.[35] Without any additional financial outlay she was able to haul a third more than other schooners. Her speed turned her into a real money-maker, and received critical acclaim in an 1856 article published in *Souvenirs de France*.[36]

Based on shipping records, we know that Gideon kept the Challenge zigzagging from Kenosha to sawmills over a hundred miles north, returning with lumber that was off-loaded at their dock. Several tons of provisions, hay, and oats for boarding houses and logging camps were loaded into her cargo bays, and unloaded at Whitehall, Muskegon, or Grand Haven before picking-up another load of lumber.

Although Durkee, Truesdell & Company was profitable, each year they waited anxiously to see what damages they would have to pay for. The two biggest drains on their cash-flow were their unusually long dock, warehouse, and the Challenge.

"The lake was lashed to its utmost fury, and the combined action of the ice and waves came fearfully upon all three piers. That of Durkee & Truesdell, the south pier, suffered the most severely. Some 200-feet of the furthest end are gone, with the pier house, which was filled with pressed hay stored for shipment early in the spring to Lake Superior.

"Although the middle pier, Hale & Ayers, has not been swept away to so great an extent yet it is sadly broken and damaged. Some 80 to 100 feet of the further end of the north pier, Elkins, was washed away. The damage to the piers is probably not short of $3,000."[37] ($384,000 today.)

Damage caused by crashing waves and the after effects of an ice storm. Pictures courtesy of the Kenosha History Center Archives.

A few years later a violent storm weakened the corner of their new warehouse to the point that it fell into the lake during the next storm. The vibrations from the crashing waves during another storm caused their "pier house" to shake. The *Kenosha Tribune & Telegraph* reported, "A CRASH-One of the beams of the second floor of Durkee, Truesdell & Company's warehouse gave way, on Saturday last, letting a large bin of wheat down into the basement and upon the ground. Fortunately, there was no one under at the time. Some 30,000 bushels of wheat came down. Aside from the time and expense of repairing, the loss will not be great."[38]

After three years of operating a schooner, Harvey Durkee and Gideon Truesdell decided to let others have the headaches and expense of owning a schooner. Schooners were profitable, but the Lake Michigan Vessel Owners Association had reduced their rates to reasonable levels, and lumbermen began renting schooners instead of buying them.

In 1857 the partners "sold" the Challenge to their captain, Alfred Ackerman, and his brother Theodore along with George and C.S. Reed for $4,000 ($480,000 today) with Harvey Durkee and Gideon Truesdell holding the note. They also owned the Heligoland, and both ships were almost exclusively used by Durkee, Truesdell & Company.[39]

Based on Lake Michigan shipping records, about 2.2 million feet of lumber was hauled to Durkee, Truesdell & Company's Kenosha retail yards with roughly 4.5 million feet wholesaled to lumberyards between Green Bay and Chicago. By the end of 1854, the wholesale side of their business was larger than their retail sales at their Kenosha yard, and they sometimes ran out of dock space.

Chicago yards that bought lumber were notorious for down-grading the price for an entire shipload, and when that didn't work, they shorted the count. If the schooner left the mill with 90,000 feet of lumber the count at the wholesale dock was often 5,000 to 10,000 feet short. This turned Durkee, Truesdell & Company's Kenosha yards into a destination for smaller mills fed-up with the shenanigans at the Chicago wholesale dock. They always got a better price at one of the three lakefront warehouses, and the Durkee-Truesdell dock was sometimes incredibly busy when several ships were unloaded in a single day.

During the first week of August 1855, four schooners off-loaded 322,000 feet of lumber, and on August 1st the Octavia unloaded 120,000 feet. Three days later the Amelia Smith off-loaded 40,000 feet, on August 8th the Union unloaded 60,000 feet, and the Octavia unloaded 102,000 feet.[40] Sometimes there was so many schooners at the Durkee-Truesdell dock that schooners had to be unloaded at the nearby Elkins dock.[41]

Southport and Beloit Plank Road Company

For warehouses that bought and sold wheat, the condition of a 70-mile trail between the Rock River in Beloit and Kenosha became extremely important. With hundreds of thousands of bushels of wheat hauled along that trail, and lumber moving in the opposite direction this trail was crowded during the fall harvest.

Fall Harvest. Pictures courtesy of the Henry Ford Museum.

If local warehouses wanted to see their volume increase, they needed to improve the trail between both cities with a plank road. Their neighbors 17 miles north in Racine, Wisconsin, was a couple of years ahead of them when it came to building plank roads, which enabled them to siphon a lot of wheat exports from northern Kenosha County township farmers.

There was considerable competition between warehouses in Racine and Kenosha because their harbors were less than 20 miles apart. According to the 1850 census, Racine shipped 250,000 bushels of wheat whereas Kenosha exported a little over 400,000, which caused Racine to covet their neighbors' exports and build plank roads deep into Kenosha County.

Kenosha warehouses knew that a plank road was a game changer, and that it should have been built many years earlier. Samuel Hale led the effort to make the Southport & Beloit Plank Road Company a reality, and three years later he obtained a charter with a $50,000 ($6 million today) capitalization. Their charter granted them permission to raise funds through the sale of stock, charge tolls, collect interest, sign contracts, and pay dividends to investors.

Private control of roads and harbors was allowed, and sometimes welcomed by state and local officials due to their inability to provide adequate funding for improvements. This forced the private sector to take matters into their own hands. The government didn't object because these projects were expensive, but along with a state issued charter came conditions that had to be followed or the charter could be revoked.

Hale & Ayer, Durkee, Truesdell & Company, Elkins & Company, and Bennett & Sellick along with farmers bought stock in the Southport & Beloit Plank Road Company. For lakefront warehouses to see a significant bump in their yearly exports they needed this road, because they were stalled at 400,000 bushels a year. Every farmer left hundreds of bushels of wheat rotting in the fields because he couldn't get it to the warehouses before they closed for the season. Once the lake began to freeze schooners stopped sailing to the Buffalo grain elevators.

Based on costs listed by other plank roads, the Southport & Beloit Plank Road Company would have averaged $1,200 ($144,000 today) per mile depending on land acquisitions, lumber, gravel, and manpower. Their charter allowed them to charge 2¢ a mile for a wagon or carriage pulled by two horses, 1¢ for a sleigh or sled, 1¢ for a horse and rider or a wagon pulled by a single horse, a half cent for a score of sheep or swine or 2¢ for a score of "neat cattle" being driven to market. Trips that had previously taken twenty hours could now be made in ten to twelve.

Plank roads required constant maintenance because after a few years of heavy traffic they fell into disrepair. Boards became loose, missing, warped or rotted with repairs costing 20 to 30% of the original cost. A superintendent had to be hired, toll houses built and staffed with "shunpikes" cutting into their profits. Imaginative crooks created shortcuts that bypassed toll houses so travelers could "shun" paying tolls.

When the plank road was completed, Kenoshas wheat exports increased by about 20%, which meant that with a faster turn-around time farmers could send twenty to thirty more wagons a season. Another 200,000 bushels translated into an additional $30,000 ($3.6 million today) for the four warehouses, and made the construction of this road a worthwhile investment. According to state records, in 1851 they declared a $2,421 ($290,000 today) profit.[42]

Wagons hauling wheat to the Kenosha warehouses sometimes carried a different type of cargo. During the fall harvest, over a hundred wagons a day rolled along the trail to Kenosha, and in addition to bags of wheat some carried runaway slaves on the last leg of their journey to freedom. Once they reached Kenosha, they boarded a schooner sailing to the Buffalo elevators that made a slight detour into Georgian Bay, where there were abolitionists on the Canadian side waiting to help them blend into a racist, but free society.

As a teenager, Theodore Fellows made what he thought was a routine trip to Kellogg's Tavern. His father often made trips to the harbor with his wagon loaded with wheat, but when he couldn't make the trip, he sent his son. Theodore loaded the wagon the previous night, and when he noticed a hollow square in the center of the wagon his father told him the wagon road better that way.

Kellogg's Tavern, a popular stopping point for farmers and a stop on the Underground Railroad. The fee for boarding animals and the driver was 50¢ ($60 today). There was a big brick oven with a fireplace in the basement kitchen, with a dining room that could seat over 40 people on the first floor, and a large dormitory on the second floor. Picture courtesy of the Kenosha History Center Archives.

"The next morning, Fellows set off with instructions to stop at the Fox River bridge to eat his dinner before making his overnight stop. He was told not to arrive at the Kellogg Tavern until after dark. When he drove into the tavern yard, he was greeted by the innkeeper who asked if he was the Fellows boy. Theodore said that he was, and Kellogg told him to drive into the barn and unhitch the ox. 'I was surprised to see Kellogg pull a man from under the bags and hurry him into the house,'"[43]

Durkee, Truesdell & Company, Wholesale Lumber Dealers & Manufacturers, 1854–1858

With so much lumber passing through Kenosha the town needed a planing mill to make doors, windows, and trim. With farmers replacing log cabins with proper farmhouses, a planing mill could sell just about everything they made.

Amos Noyes bought a machine shop across the road from the Durkee-Truesdell yards, and converted it into a planing mill. When he wanted to expand, William Wheeler became the senior partner in the Kenosha Steam Planing Mill. In 1850, they replaced a machine shop with a larger building with steam-powered equipment.[44] At that point they installed saws that milled window sashes, doors, siding, and flooring. When Mr. Wheeler died the partnership was dissolved, and Durkee, Truesdell & Company bought them out.

> "STEAM PLANING ESTABLISHMENT. From our office windows we notice that this establishment at the foot of Park Street, near Durkee & Truesdell's warehouse and lumberyard is undergoing extensive additions and repairs. On inquiry, we learn that it has been purchased by Durkee & Truesdell who are fitting it up to do a large business.
>
> "They will soon have it in running operation, when we expect their facilities for getting large quantities of the best quality lumber, will enable them to furnish planed flooring and work of all kinds which such machines turn out, of a quality and at a price which must command a large share of customers."[45]

It was a logical move, and Gideon enlarged the planing mill so they could add two steam-powered shingle saws, and begin manufacturing "prime cut shingles" that sold for a higher price due to a uniform cut.[46] According to advertisements, this brand of semi-automatic circular saw could cut 20,000 shingles a day, and with two shingle saws this made Durkee, Truesdell & Company one of the largest manufacturers on Lake Michigan with around four million shingles manufactured each year.[47]

At $2 per thousand shingles, they would have grossed at least $800 ($96,000 today) each season just from the sale of shingles, with about half of that dropping to the bottom line. "Pine shingles, of our own manufacture, WARRENTED, besides all qualities manufactured elsewhere, always on hand for sale at the lumber yard of Durkee, Truesdell & Company."[48] Several retail yards between Green Bay and Chicago began advertising Prime Cut Shingles, and Gideon would have used rented schooners to clear stacks of shingles from their dock.

An advertisement for one of the latest shingle machines; all an employee had to do was put a block of wood in the machine and the machine kicked-out twenty to thirty shingles a minute. Picture courtesy of Industrial America.

Working around sharp blades was dangerous, as evidenced by a newspaper article about a nineteen year old. "A worker in Durkee & Truesdell's steam planing and shingle mill by the name of Isaac McKisson, while tending the shingle machine had his fingers caught in the saw, by which one finger was cut off, another so that it merely hung by the skin on one side, and a third badly mangled."[49]

The typical lumber yard stockpiled 300,000 feet of lumber, shingles, fence posts, and lath. Picture courtesy of the Northwest Lumber Museum.

Based on U.S. Customs House records, in 1854 Durkee, Truesdell & Company changed how they bought and sold lumber. They continued to operate one of the largest yards between Milwaukee and Chicago but began buying lumber by the shipload from smaller mills, and selling their output to retail lumberyards using rented schooners to extend their sales territory.[50]

As their business continued to grow, they bought additional lots around their lumberyard until it covered two city blocks. Every square foot of their property had rows of lumber stacked 20 to 30 feet high. After selling his wheat, a farmer could drive his empty wagon between rows of lumber, and a yardman would load his wagon before sending him to the office for payment.

To keep their lumberyards fully stocked, Gideon began buying shiploads of lumber from sawmills that lacked a place to sell their output. Undercapitalized mills couldn't afford to open a retail lumberyard to sell their output and rarely received a fair price at the wholesale dock in Chicago. At this point, Durkee, Truesdell & Company established a relationship with smaller mills who wholesaled their lumber to them. Gideon would have sent a rented schooner to their mill every few weeks to clear their docks.

These undercapitalized mills were still cutting lumber with outdated upright saws, which left their lumber with a wavy, washboard look due to the play in the blade. But there was a large demand for this type of lumber for barns, stables, and hog sheds.

Harvey Durkee and Gideon Truesdell realized if they could match the output from these smaller mills on the eastern side of Lake Michigan with standing orders with smaller retail yards on the western side of the lake, they could substantially increase the amount of lumber they sold using rented schooners.

It was a balancing act: Gideon would have lined-up smaller mills to supply him with 12 million feet of lumber each season at $8.00 per thousand feet, and had retail yards lined-up pay him the market price of $10.00. During a 26-week sailing season, he would have grossed at least $24,000 ($2.8 million today) before deducting his overhead expenses. Using rented schooners, Durkee, Truesdell & Company expanded their sales territory until they were just as big as many of the Milwaukee or Chicago yards.

After years of backbreaking work, false starts and mistakes, Gideon had become one of Kenoshas leading businessmen. But success came slowly because he and his family were still living a spartan life in an apartment over a grocery store on Old Chicago Street. By 1852 they were affluent, but Gideon had to keep plowing his profits back into the business to fund his share of their rapid expansion.

In 1854, he could afford to improve his circumstances, and paid $2,000 ($450,000 today) for one of the nicest homes overlooking the City Park.[51] "This Park, containing some eight acres, if not the veritable 'Garden of Eden' only needs the presence of fruit trees."[52] This is where the wealthiest people in town lived, and without exception all were self-made men who beat the odds through hard-work and smart decisions. On the opposite end of the City Park was the Harvey Durkee residence.

Gideon J. and Julia Truesdell: pictures courtesy of Sidney and Frank Small. Truesdell residence overlooking the City Park, picture courtesy of the Kenosha History Center Archives.

After years where Gideon could barely pay his bills, by 1855 the money was rolling in so fast that he began making loans in $1,000 ($125,000 today) increments.[53] According to court documents, these loans were secured by income-producing assets, which gave him a solid asset he could attach if they defaulted. And we know from court documents that neither Harvey Durkee or Gideon Truesdell were shy about suing people.

At the end of the 1854 season, Durkee, Truesdell & Company probably grossed at least $21,000 for an estimated $6,900 ($831,000 today) gross profit before expenses. After two years of aggressive expansion the partners were making money hand over fist, and the coming of the railroads was about to open new markets.

Richard C. Fritz

During the 1850s, the railroads were about to change everything, and Lake Michigan warehouses understood this. Shipping costs by schooner averaged around 25% of the value of the cargo, but railroads would cut that in half.[54] Schooners would continue to be the backbone of lake traffic, especially with lumber, but railroads were about to open thousands of new interior markets that had previously been inaccessible by water.

In 1855, a lakeshore railroad running from Green Bay, Milwaukee, and Chicago was in its final stages of construction but had a ruinous catch: it wouldn't stop in Kenosha or Racine. Unless a town ponied up a significant amount of money in the way of stock subscriptions, it was all but guaranteed that trains would speed past their communities without stopping. But through political muscle at the state level, each town was able to exert considerable pressure, and get the trains to build stations in their communities.

A bill was presented to the State Senate for the incorporation of the Milwaukee & Chicago Railway Company by Stephen Bennett, a senator who was a political ally with Charles Durkee.[55] Fortuitously amended, the bill included stops in Racine and Kenosha. Bennett argued persuasively that it would be wrong for the people in each town to be asked to raise money for a railroad that didn't stop in their communities.

Senator Bennett also asked that Samuel Hale and Harvey Durkee be added to the list of the railroad's incorporators.[56] Both said the railroad should be built without Racine or Kenosha having to contribute a penny, which the railroad agreed to, but asked them to use their municipal credit to build "feeder" railroads extending west into the states heartland, which would increase the tonnage of freight returning eastbound to the Milwaukee & Chicago yards.[57]

During the previous year, steamships running between Milwaukee and Chicago hauled about $300,000 ($36 million today) of freight. Experts believed that at least twice that amount could be transported by rail.[58]

Harvey Durkee understood that a Milwaukee & Chicago depot in Kenosha would open new markets, and allow them to tap into them by underselling Chicago yards. Due to lower overhead expenses, they could sell lumber 10% cheaper without sacrificing a dime of profit, and the partners bought 2.9 acres for a temporary storage yard on Grand Avenue abutting the Kenosha depot.[59]

Loading a boxcar. Pictures courtesy of the Burton Historical Collection.

Using dozens of freight wagons, they would have hauled lumber from their yards to the Milwaukee & Chicago depot for shipment to northern Illinois yards. Although labor intensive, this arrangement would have opened dozens of new customers. After a couple of rough years, the local economy was booming, and Durkee, Truesdell & Company was booming too.

The *Kenosha Telegraph* reported "Good times for farmers are followed by new barns, sheds, fences, and dwellings in place of log houses. We call attention to the advertisement of Durkee, Truesdell & Company of lumber, found in our newspaper today. We have noticed that they keep piling up shipload after shipload of the choicest lumber brought from the pinery."[60]

"Shall the state of things endure, a few days since Durkee & Truesdell shipped a quantity of lumber 40 miles by a circuitous and expensive route, by rail to Chicago, thence to Woodstock, and thence by wagons twelve miles away. Buying lumber in Kenosha rather than in Chicago the purchaser saved one dollar per thousand feet. ($120 today.)

"Our lumber dealers can sell 10 to 15% cheaper than in Chicago. We are nearer the pine forests of Wisconsin and Michigan from which both places draw their supplies. The expenses of the business are much cheaper here.

"The rent for a lumberyard in Chicago is a small fortune. If we can undersell Chicago with all of the disadvantages of a circuitous, troublesome and expensive route as we have now, what may we expect when we soon have our own railroad?"[61]

Richard C. Fritz   133

"The enormous piles of all kinds of lumber, including lathing and shingles, in the yards of Durkee, Truesdell & Company, we do not know what in the world they are going to do with; but they seem confident of disposing of it by ship load after ship load, which they keep sending for and receiving."[62]

As Durkee, Truesdell & Company continued to double and triple their business each year they needed more operating capital, and based on court records we know that Harvey Durkee and Gideon Truesdell borrowed at least $8,000 ($1.2 million today) a year, undoubtedly more, for cash-flow from the City Bank of Kenosha and private lenders.[63] At the end of the year they paid the interest, rolled over existing notes, and borrowed what they thought they needed for the coming season.[64]

During the early 1850s dozens of towns along Lake Michigan's eastern shoreline, big and small, wanted a railroad that would link their community with the massive Mississippi River trade. Most of these railroads only existed on paper, but there was serious talk underway of a railroad running from the lakefront warehouses in Kenosha and Racine in the southeastern corner of the state. Experts estimated that even though these towns were only 17 miles apart, with their own railroad, each town could haul 6-million bushels of wheat to their warehouses valued at $320 million ($38 billion today).[65]

They also predicted that a railroad could haul 80-million feet of lumber each year to interior markets, which was critical because a railroad had to make a profit in each direction. Hale & Ayer, Elkins Brothers, and Durkee, Truesdell & Company wanted a piece of that action but needed bigger warehouses, better docks with an expensive steam-powered 30-ton crane, larger freight yards, and a railroad spur that ran to the edge of their dock. They decided to merge, but their expansion had more to do with survival than getting rich quick because the Racine, Janesville, & Mississippi and four other railroads was nipping at their heels.

The first step in building a $1.5 million ($180 million today) railroad was lining-up funding. To accommodate the massive increase in imports and exports, Hale & Ayer, Durkee, Truesdell & Company, and the Elkins brothers consolidated their warehouses and docks into a single, well-funded firm.[66] If they failed, their warehouse business was as good as gone because the other railroads under construction would steal most of it, or enough to send these three Kenosha partnerships into receivership.

The Kenosha Pier Company, 1857

The wheat market was changing fast, and by the early 1860s Wisconsin had become the "granary of the north" with over a million acres of wheat in cultivation that produced over 30-million bushels a year. Wisconsin had become the largest wheat producer in the world with Milwaukee replacing Buffalo as the largest international wheat market, with million-bushel grain elevators under construction by wealthy cartels along the Milwaukee River.

With an estimated $320 million ($38 billion today) of wheat harvested each year just in southern Wisconsin, Hale & Ayer, Durkee, Truesdell & Company, Bennett & Sellick and the Elkins Brothers knew they could turn their warehouses and docks into the fourth largest shipping hub on Lake Michigan behind Chicago, Milwaukee, and Michigan City.

They would never get a piece of that $320 million with worn-out plank roads, and farmers still hauling wagons of wheat to the lakefront. They needed to drastically speed-up the travel-time from the farms to their warehouses. But they couldn't just lay tracks wherever they wanted; they had to first obtain permission from the legislature. The Kenosha & Beloit Railroad obtained a charter which gave them the right to pass through the most fertile wheat fields between Beloit and Kenosha.

The City of Racine was way ahead of them after having organized the Racine, Janesville & Mississippi a few years earlier, which forced Kenosha to get serious about building a railroad. If they didn't get moving fast, most of their wheat and lumber business would be swallowed-up by communities serviced by a railroad. With a labyrinth of tracks about to pass through the grain belt there would soon be cut-throat competition. These were warehouses who would do anything to destroy a competitor so they could steal their market share.

The Kenosha & Beloits competitive niche would have been a harbor that didn't require costly tugboat fees, and 30-ton cranes that could load and unload freight directly from the dock into the cargo hold of a ship. This was something that neither Chicago or Milwaukee warehouses could offer, at least not quite yet, and for Kenosha it was a huge competitive edge.

Rather than depleting their bank accounts they decided that merging was less risky, because it was smarter to compete against the Racine, Janesville & Mississippi than each other. On February 20, 1857, Samuel Hale, Ephraim Elkins and Harvey Durkee petitioned the legislature to charter the Kenosha Pier Company with a capitalization of $30,000

($3.6 million today).[67] The three blocks owned by Durkee, Truesdell & Company, Hale & Ayer, and Elkins Brothers were merged.

This merger coincided with a negative Army Corp of Engineers survey that were critical of the three privately-owned docks. Since the length of them was longer than the government dock where Pikes Creek emptied into Lake Michigan, the currents washed sand and silt in front of the entrance to the harbor, creating a semi-permanent sandbar that prevented ships from entering during low tides. Between this sandbar and a 4-foot depth, Kenosha had one of the worst harbors on Lake Michigan, but with enough money invested in a massive dredging operation that would soon change.

The partnership had their three docks removed by Joseph Hackley's contracting firm, and replaced them with a massive single dock with a crane and railroad spur.[68] The crane could unload cargo holds and load flatbeds and boxcars in a single movement, which would have required less manpower and time. The Durkee-Truesdell land east of Lake Street was used as a storage yard for freight, merging the two warehouses gave them storage for over 140,000 bushels of wheat.

According to the *Kenosha Tribune & Telegraph*, "At a meeting of the Kenosha Pier Company, held at the office of Durkee, Truesdell & Company, February 28th 1857, the following men were elected directors for the ensuing year: Harvey Durkee, E.S. Elkins, and J.V. Ayer. At a meeting of the Directors held the same day at the same place the following officers were elected: Harvey Durkee, president; J.V. Ayer, Vice President; J.W. Merrill, Secretary-Treasurer."[69]

The Kenosha Pier Company was a high-powered firm. Samuel Hale was heavily invested in banking and railroads, and about to find himself in the middle of a railroad scandal that would make national headlines. Charles Durkee was a wealthy U.S. Senator with heavy-duty political connections. Henry Towslee was president of the Kenosha Pier Company, principal stockholder in the City Bank of Kenosha, partner in the Chicago law firm of Scales, Bates, & Towslee, and a close friend of Samuel Hales.[70]

And yet it was a peculiar partnership because a few months later, Henry Towslee was sued by Harvey Durkee and Gideon Truesdell, and Towslee counter-sued. A few years earlier, Harvey Durkee sued Samuel Hale, and both men sat on the board of the City Bank of Kenosha.[71] But at the end of the day it was all about the money and together they stood to make a lot of it.

Hale & Ayer was composed of Samuel Hale and John V. Ayer (1812–1877). The latter had arrived in Kenosha penniless after having lost a fortune. Ayer began working for Samuel Hale at his warehouse, but demonstrated a shrewdness that convinced Hale that he better make him a partner before a competitor lured him way. He was a sharp businessman and made Samuel Hale a *lot* of money. He was also Gerald Ford's great, great grandfather.

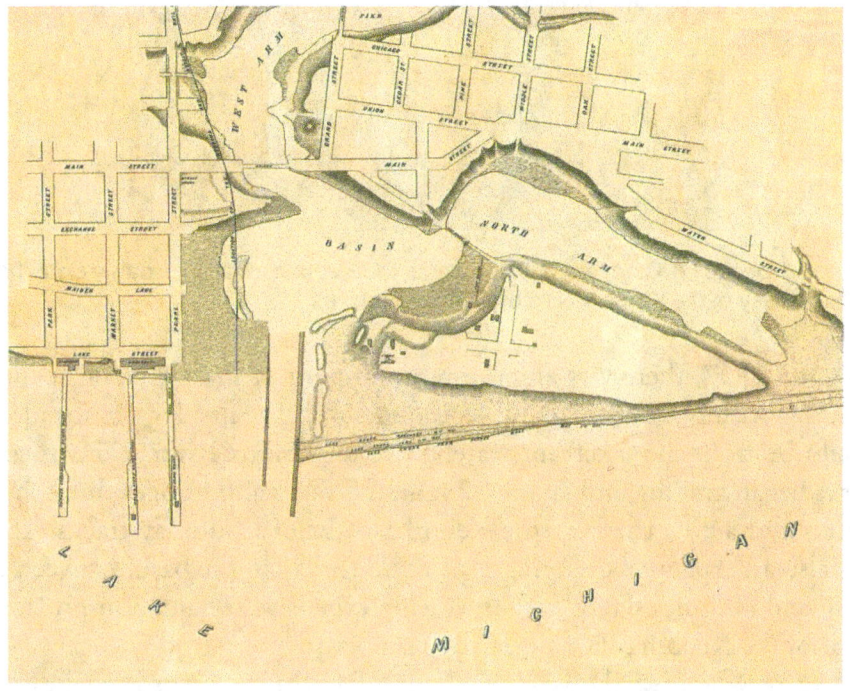

Kenosha, Wisconsin circa 1857. The three privately owned docks belonged to Durkee, Truesdell & Company (L), Hale & Ayer (C), and Elkins Brothers (R) south of the government docks at the mouth of Pike's Creek. Sketch courtesy of the U.S. Army Corps of Engineers.

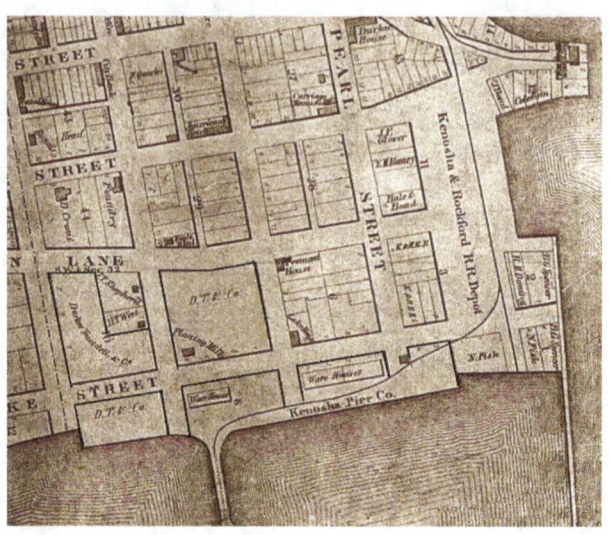

Durkee, Truesdell & Company lumberyard & the Kenosha Pier Company, circa 1857. Map courtesy of the Kenosha History Center Archives.

By 1857, there was an enormous amount of money being spent in Kenosha with two big-ticket projects underway. The first leg of the railroad would be from the lakefront warehouses to the Fox River. Construction crews began grading and laying 22 miles of tracks and bridges through the woods and across rivers so the Kenosha & Beloit could lay tracks. There was also an expensive dredging project underway in the basin between the mainland and the island, and an equally expensive reclamation project in front of the Kenosha Pier Company's property.

Since their warehouses were built a few years earlier so freight could flow to schooners docked along the lakefront, the best place to build railroad tracks was along the lakeshore so they didn't have to reconfigure their warehouses. For that to happen, they needed to reclaim the land in front of their warehouses that had been washed away by erosion. A steam shovel excavated dirt and muck from the basin where they were making the harbor deeper, dumped on barges, pulled by tugboats a quarter of a mile south in front of the warehouses so they could add another 18-feet of shoreline.

Kenosha & Beloit Railroad, 1853

In Kenosha, there was gridlock at meeting after meeting. Railroad promoters ran into strong pushback from property owners about the breathtaking $1.5 million ($180 million today) price-tag. Samuel Hale, the chief promoter, was pushing for the city to borrow against their tax base, but that was overwhelmingly voted-down. Property owners had legitimate concerns about borrowing so much money, and were leery about being dragged into financing a railroad that would make Kenoshas wealthiest men even wealthier. What they failed to grasp was that it would significantly increase Kenoshas tax base, and keep the community from stagnating while other communities prospered.

Community leaders asked Samuel Hale, Harvey Durkee, Alonzo Campbell, E.W. Evans, George Bennett, Josiah Bond and H.B. Hinsdale to come up with alternatives without draining the municipal treasury or ruining land values.[72]

The *Kenosha Democrat* acknowledged the importance of a railroad and warned their readers that time was running out. "Kenosha is better able to build a railroad than Racine. Our location is better for the terminus of a railroad from the west because of our more central position between Milwaukee and Chicago, and because it lies further inland.

"Racine is largely in debt. Why isn't it that Racine, less favorably circumstanced in every way than we are, should go forward and build a railroad to the country back of us, while Kenosha lies upon her backside under the conviction that the enterprise is impracticable? Gentlemen of capital and influence; stir up your rusty muscles. Remember that the future of Kenosha depends upon your enterprise."[73]

Chicago had a crowded and expensive harbor to navigate, but it also had the Michigan & Illinois Canal that linked Lake Michigan with the Mississippi River, and created a direct route to St. Louis, Memphis, Baton Rouge, New Orleans, and the Gulf of Mexico. A large tonnage of lumber was sent downriver on barges, but once the Rock Island Bridge was built across the Mississippi River, lumber could be shipped by train to the western territories with millions of bushels of wheat returning in empty boxcars.

But the Chicago River was already over-crowded, because in 1855, 6,610 ships entered the river loaded with mostly wheat and lumber. Two years later, that number increased to 7,557, and by 1860 that number soared to over 10,000 ships.[74] During daylight hours, a ship entered or left the harbor every two-minutes, and Kenosha was in a position to siphon enough of Chicago's overflow to make their railroad a success.

The Army Corp of Engineers published a report stating that, "the natural facilities for a harbor at Kenosha are superior to those of any place on Lake Michigan."[75] The inland basin between the island and the mainland had great potential but would need extensive dredging, but once completed, 20 to 30 ships could dock inland away from Lake Michigan's crashing waves.

For about $8,000 ($1.2 million today), a modern harbor could be built where Pikes Creek emptied into Lake Michigan, and capable of docking any sized ship in her basin.[76] That would give Kenosha another competitive edge when competing with lakefront cities building railroads to the Mississippi River.

Samuel Hale had been elected to the Wisconsin legislature and promised to do all he could "to secure the privilege of loaning the credit of the county to the railroad. There are enough votes in the back towns of the country, together with all of the votes of the city to secure anything the railroad may want. The proof may be found in the fact that of the election of Levi Grant over Upson, who opposed the loan."[77]

On May 9, 1853, and with only one dissenting vote, Kenoshas City Council voted to loan the Kenosha & Beloit Railroad $150,000 ($18 million today) of their municipal credit to help finance the railroad.[78] The state legislature authorized a railroad "from the City of Kenosha in the County of Kenosha to such a point in the village of Beloit, upon the Rock River as shall be determined by the board of directors and to connect with the Illinois Central in Rockford which runs to the Mississippi River."[79]

It was a gutsy move for a town of only 3,500 people, and yet every major town along Lake Michigan's western shoreline was in a hurry to build a railroad to the Mississippi River, because it would give a significant boost to their economy. But it came at a stunningly high price because most of the capital were raised through reckless financing, and a cost per mile that doubled and tripled until they spiraled out of control. Nobody knew with any degree of certainty how much it would cost to build a railroad. If the land was level and they didn't have to cross dozens of rivers or blast-through rock formations the cost could be controlled, but that rarely occurred.

The Kenosha & Beloit raised capital like most railroads during the 1850s, by selling stock subscriptions to people along the route who used their farms and houses as collateral. But Wall Street bankers weren't interested in thousands of little mortgages as security for the enormous amount of money they were being asked to loan. What they wanted was for a municipality to use their tax base as collateral. Then, if they defaulted, they could attach the city's tax base and force property owners to pay the debt through special tax assessments.

In 1853, the Kenosha & Beloit elected officers and a board of directors that had the talent and energy to launch a $1.5 million ($180 million today) enterprise. It was a lot of money for a 72 mile railroad and yet it had tremendous potential. Kenoshas economy had been struggling for the past decade, and voters viewed this as their last and best chance to turn things around.

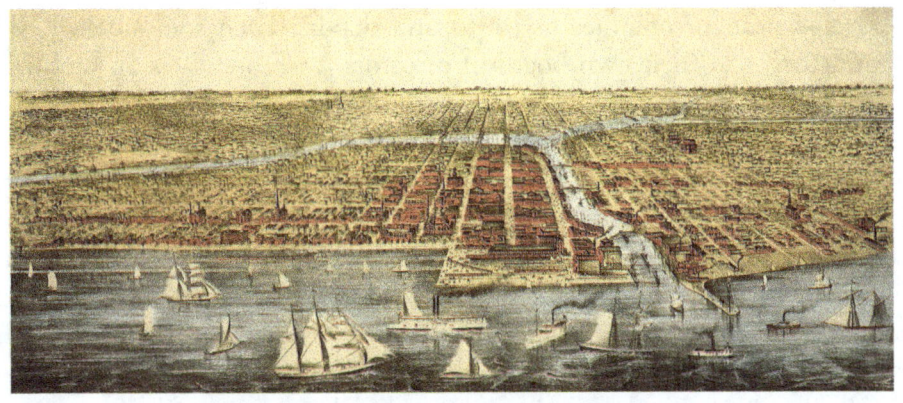

"Rush hour" on the Chicago River, circa 1860.
Map courtesy of the Chicago History Center.

Samuel Hale of Hale & Ayer was listed as President; publisher Charles Sholes as Vice President; attorney Josiah Bond, Secretary; City Bank of Kenosha president Alonzo Campbell, Treasurer; and Gideon Truesdell sat on the board of directors for the next three years.[80] Behind the scenes, Harvey Durkee was involved but held no official position. The *Kenosha Democrat* had mixed feelings about such a mammoth undertaking but gave a balanced endorsement.

"By virtue of the proposed connection between the Southern Wisconsin and the Kenosha & Beloit, and their similarity of gauge, Kenosha necessarily becomes the most accessible point. This ought to give us command of the freighting business between southwestern Wisconsin, and such other freight as there may be within the vicinity of Dubuque for the east by way of the Great Lakes. Besides, the Kenosha & Beloit must carry the freight of a large portion of northern Illinois going in the same direction. The amount will ultimately exceed all present calculations.

"This being so, passenger travel from any point on the Mississippi River north of Dubuque and south of La Crosse is quite likely to find its way over the broad gauge of the Kenosha & Beloit as in any other direction. So much for our views of the Kenosha & Beloit Railroad; if they are half realized the road will pay, and as the country becomes thickly populated it will pay a thousand times over."[81]

In the spring of 1854, there were over 100 men chopping-down trees so they could clear a 22 mile right-of-way from Kenosha to the Fox River through the woods.[82] This was the first leg of the eastern division, and the Kenosha & Beloit had two divisions with each responsible for building a specific number of miles of tracks and depots. Each sold stock, hired contractors, had their own board of directors, with one division building west from the Kenosha harbor, and the other division building tracks east from the City of Beloit.

With four major railroads intersecting with the Kenosha & Beloit, it was no longer a 72 mile "short line" but something much bigger that could reach Lake Superior and the Ohio and Mississippi Rivers through junctions with major lines. The first railroad to the Mississippi River stood to make a fortune, and yet there was plenty of business for everyone. Each community would have more freight business than they could possibly handle, but in the final analysis what it came down to was which group of capitalists would gain control of freight rates.

After the Kenosha & Beloit route was announced, there was enthusiastic support from farmers and businessmen along the right of way, and it was widely believed that this railroad could turn a profit in both directions.

"The railroad will be 30 miles shorter than the Chicago railroad, enough distance to give Kenosha a decided advantage for all heavy freight if facilities there are offered for shipping as cheap as in Chicago. Twenty thousand dollars are already secured for opening a harbor in Kenosha. The work is progressing rapidly under the direction of the City authorities, and it is expected that by fall the best harbor on Lake Michigan will be opened."[83]

Most of the stock was sold to ordinary people, with a salesman telling them their investment would not only benefit them but the communities the railroad passed through. The first day, they sold $61,000 ($7.8 million today) of subscriptions with 10% down and $75 ($9,000 today) a year for the next 20 years.[84] It was a gigantic crapshoot that had great potential but a decade later would boomerang with devastating consequences.

The *New York Journal of Commerce* wrote that "the railroads are moving slowly toward completion in consequence of scarcity of money, but the good ones are sure to be built. Kenosha, in consequence of its roadway to Janesville and its connections to Dubuque and Fond du Lac has a prospect of rising to great importance."[85]

When Janesville dropped out of the Racine, Janesville & Mississippi Railroad, railroad officials approached Beloit, which was only 22 miles south of Janesville, and where they found considerable interest in their railroad. Beloit had nothing but verbal assurances that the Kenosha & Beloit would service their town, but had yet to lay a single track at a time when the "Racine Road" was already running freight and passenger trains to within twenty miles of their city.

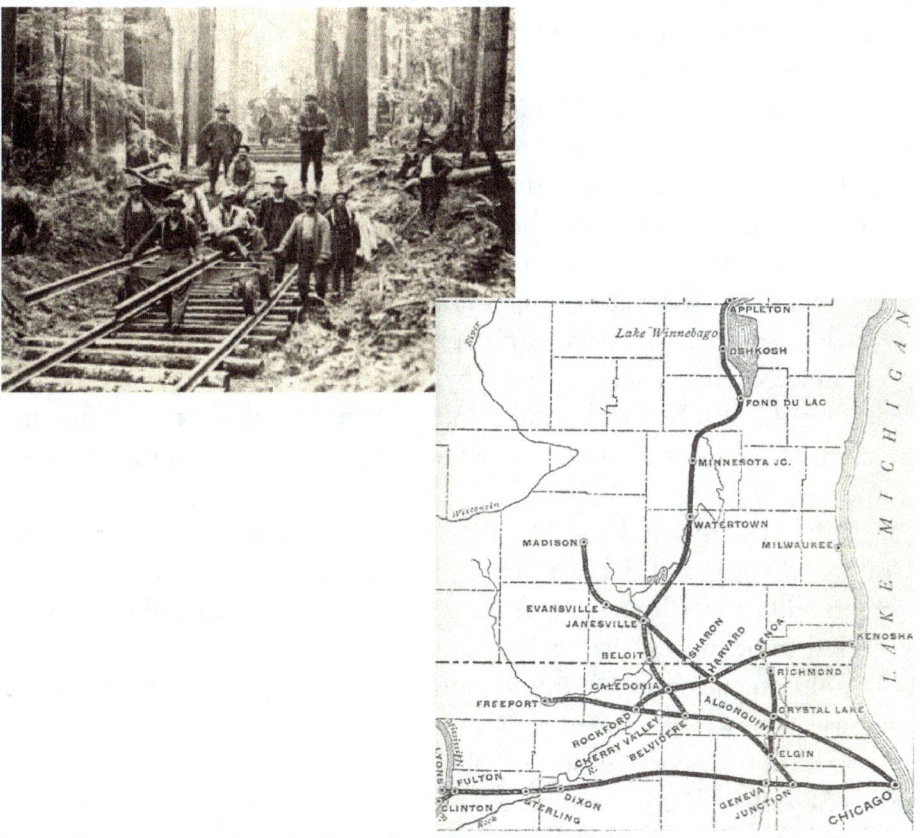

Laying tracks through the wilderness and the Kenosha & Rockford route.

Richard C. Fritz

In 1854, the City of Beloit agreed to buy a block of Racine, Janesville & Mississippi stock to guarantee service to their town. A railroad might pass through a community, but unless they bought a significant block of stock there were no guarantees that it would stop there. Although state-issued railroad charters were for the good of the communities they passed through, there was an unspoken understanding that trains would speed past their town unless they committed to buying at least $50,000 ($6 million today) of capital stock. Once Beloit dropped out, the "Kenosha Road" recruited the City of Rockford as the western end of their railroad.

The following year, and in the midst of construction the Kenosha & Rockford ran out of money. When it was announced that they would have to float another bond issue, Harvey Durkee called a meeting of stockholders. He didn't think more borrowing was necessary, that their budgeting left a lot to be desired, and yet nearly every railroad was living far beyond their means. Shortsighted railroad officials were convinced that once the railroad was completed the end would justify their actions. Once completed the money would start rolling-in, and cover any shortfalls.

By comparison to the Racine, Janesville & Mississippi, which was a highly leveraged railroad, the Kenosha & Beloit was conservatively managed. The "Racine Road" borrowed against every conceivable asset to gain trackage, and to some degree the end justified the means because the more towns they serviced the higher their revenues.

Some property owners didn't think the Kenosha & Beloit would ever be completed, that it was a scheme by insiders to cheat the taxpayers, and that it would ruin Kenoshas land values. When the railroad needed to raise a significant amount of money most voters reluctantly agreed to raise more money.

The *Kenosha Tribune* wrote "There are 150 farmers in Kenosha County who can and ought to raise this sum; and in five years those 150 farmers will be worth one quarter more...if every other railroad in the state is bound to be built while ours is to be abandoned after having expended $100,000...such conduct would be suicidal, cowardly, and penny wise and pound foolish to the last degree."[86]

The second stock subscription fell considerably short when they only raised $84,000 ($10 million today).[87] On August 28th, a special election was held to decide whether Kenoshas municipal credit should be used to indemnify the $66,000 short-fall.[88] They were piling-up a dizzying amount of debt if the railroad failed, but the voters were willing to throw good money after bad.

The second subscription raised enough money to continue when Samuel Hale abruptly resigned as president. Whether this was a forced or planned departure is unknown, but probably forced because Harvey Durkee stepped in as an interim president so decisions could be made. By then, Hale was deeply involved with railroad promoter Byron Kilbourn, a businessman with a shady past who was building a railroad from Milwaukee to the Mississippi River with fraudulent government funds.

Kilbourn understood how land grants worked, and was fairly certain if Congress awarded them to the Wisconsin legislature, he could bribe enough elected officials to get his hands on one of them. After years of political maneuvering the state legislature was about to receive 2,874,000 acres of land to fund a north-south railroad to Lake Superior, and an east-west railroad between Lake Michigan and the Mississippi River. Kilbourn wanted to get his hands on the east-west land grant.

Kilbourn removed rival railroads that existed only on paper with lucrative stock swaps, and camouflaged these bribes as operating expenses. The St. Croix & Lake Superior dropped-out when $1 million of Milwaukee & LaCrosse bonds ended up in Samuel Hales possession, which he deposited for safekeeping in the City Bank of Kenoshas vault. At the appropriate time, these bonds would be used to buy-off St. Croix & Lake Superior's directors. To grease the deal, Governor William Barstow received $87,750 ($10.1 million today), Beriah Brown received $58,500 ($7.2 million today), and Samuel Hale pocketed $31,000 ($3.7 million today).[89]

The *Racine Weekly Advocate* angrily called it what it was: fraud. "They received 40% in LaCrosse bonds on each share of stock pretended to have been held in the St. Croix & Superior Railroad Company. This was all a sham to pluck $1 million dollars ($120 million today) from a public trust fund."[90]

On August 12, 1856, Harvey Durkee stepped-down as president, and was replaced by Josiah Bond.[91] He had been an officer since the railroad's inception, probably needed time to step-away from his law practice, and was highly respected. The new president and the board of directors quickly got things moving in the right direction.

The *Rockford Weekly Register* wrote, "Much of the credit is due to the people of Kenosha and the officers of their railroad for pushing forward their enterprise in the face of numerous obstacles…and we congratulate them that at last they are out of the woods and their railroad project on a safe foundation."[92]

Kenosha residents probably had a different view because the railroad debt caused property taxes to skyrocket. Mayor Michael Frank wrote, "I estimate the taxes to be collected in the following year to double that of this year. The prospect of heavy taxation discouraged business growth…I would without hesitation sell my house and lot for $1,500 if I could get the offer. The past year has been expensive. All kinds of eatables have been higher than ever before since I have lived in this county."[93]

The railroad that was going to breathe new life into Kenoshas faltering economy became a millstone around its neck, and yet according the *American Railroad Journal*, "this road cannot fail to pay."[94]

Long before these small short-line railroads disrupted the balance of power, Chicago and Milwaukee railroads upped the ante significantly. They came up with a flat rate of 8¢ ($9.65 today) a bushel from anywhere as long as the grain ended up at their million-bushel Milwaukee elevator.[95] This was a huge incentive for farmers to bypass smaller elevators, and it was about to have a devastating impact on Racine and Kenosha lakefront warehouses.

With grim determination, the Kenosha & Rockford pushed ahead and took delivery of three new locomotives. They were brought by steamship from Philadelphia to Chicago and driven on the Chicago & Milwaukee tracks until reaching a railroad roundhouse at the Wisconsin state line.[96] They sat there for a few months until driven to a siding near the Kenosha depot where they sat for several more months.

These locomotives remained parked there until December 4, 1856, when they were driven to a Kenosha & Rockford siding. Once the train was placed on the tracks the engineer rang the bell for several minutes while the crowd whistled and cheered.[97]

Specially designed docks at a locomotive factory and tandem cranes that could lower over 100 tons into a ship's cargo hold. Picture courtesy of Library of Congress.

"Look out for the locomotive when the bell rings! We learn from the *Kenosha Telegraph* that iron sufficient to lay ten miles of tracks has been received, that a portion of the track is already laid down, and two locomotives, the Kenosha and Silver Lake placed upon it. All right, it takes President Bond to drive things."[98]

Throughout 1856, over 100 men were at work grading, ballasting, laying ties and spiking iron rails. By September, they finally reached the Fox River but had to stop until the bridge was finished. Before stopping for the winter, they laid twelve more miles of tracks on the western side of the river.[99] They were only 18 miles away from Harvard, Illinois, where they would meet the other end of the railroad running east from Rockford,

Richard C. Fritz   147

Illinois. At the eastern end of the railroad in Kenosha they were busy developing land for a railroad depot, warehouse, and docks. The *Rock River Democrat* reported the following.

"The Company has purchased extensive grounds adjoining the harbor, which they are now docking. Thus, all articles of transportation on the road can be taken right from the cars onto the ship at their own dock at a great savings of time and expense.

"With a harbor capacity equal to its favored neighbors, better improved, and with much easier and safer access, it has a great advantage over all competitors. Kenosha will have a harbor front of nearly four miles with plenty of width and depth of water. The depth of the channel is fifteen feet, and they have an excellent steam dredge digging out the whole principal basin to that depth."[100]

After this basin was dredged there could be as many as twenty ships docked at any time waiting to pick-up or drop-off freight, and with three warehouses equipped with 30-ton steam-powered cranes, they could load or unload ships quickly.

In 1861, there was over forty boxcars and flatbeds hauling freight and passengers from the Kenosha lakefront to Rockford, Illinois, with a 12-hour turn-around time, something none of their competitors could come close to matching.

Shipping freight aboard the Kenosha & Rockford or Racine & Mississippi was about 20% cheaper than railroads controlled by the Chicago monopolies. With over a million pounds of freight shipped each year from Kenosha or Racine, that extra 20% or $200,000 ($25 million today) would soon be deprived of these monopolies, at which point they declared war.

They were going to force these regional railroads out of business so they could dictate freight rates. The previous year, the mammoth Illinois Central shipped $206,230 ($24 million today) from Rockford to Chicago. With Rockford the endpoint for the Kenosha & Rockford, they would soon siphon most of the Illinois Central's outbound freight business from that city, which put them in the cross-hairs of these big city rivals with abundant financial resources.

On December 7, 1856, the eastern branch of the Kenosha & Rockford began service from Kenosha to the Fox River, a distance of 22 miles with ten boxcars and a passenger car.[101] This might not seem like much, but it greatly improved shipping time for farmers hauling wheat to one of the Kenosha warehouses. It also generated some badly needed revenue for the railroad at a time when they really needed it.

Instead of traveling 40 to 60 miles to Kenosha by wagon, farmers from Walworth and Lake Counties only had to travel to the nearest railroad depot, where they could load thousands of bushels aboard the next Kenosha & Rockford train. The trains didn't always stop at depots, because trains would stop at a crossroads along the right-of-way where 20 to 30 wagons were parked waiting for the next train.

The first train left at five p.m. and stopped for the night in Wheatland. It departed at eight a.m. the following morning for the Fox River Bridge on Geneva Road, known as the Beloit Military Trail during territorial times.

A week later, there was a derailment on the eastbound tracks a mile west of the Fox River Bridge, where a locomotive and twelve flatbeds of lumber remained stranded on the tracks when a freight and passenger car derailed.[102] By then they had tracks running through wheat fields in the western end of Kenosha County, but they were still woefully behind the Racine, Janesville, & Mississippi.

Kenosha had made considerable progress after having dredged their harbor. "Main Street particularly has very much been improved by the remodeling and the new finishing of the old business structures and the building of new ones," said the *Rockford Democrat*. "The whole pier interest of the city consolidated itself under the name of the Kenosha Pier Company, and has made a structure which for convenience, strength, and massive neatness is not equaled on the Great Lakes.

"Since the commencement of the railroad and the partial completion of the harbor, much improvement in docking and warehouses has been done. No city in the State has a fairer future before it than Kenosha. With a good harbor and a railroad running through one of the most fertile countries in the world it's certain that good times will return and grow rapidly."[103]

In September of 1857, a nationwide financial crash halted construction of the Kenosha & Rockford and every other railroad. A severe recession followed that would blanket the country through the first few years of the Civil War, and severely complicate finishing a railroad.

Despite two bond issues that raised $234,000 ($30 million today) the eastern division from Kenosha to Harvard, Illinois, was $50,000 ($6 million today) short of what they needed to finish the last 18 miles of tracks.[104] They could no longer borrow from eastern bankers due to the Kenosha & Rockford's heavy debt-load due to a stringency in the capital markets. Yet, the board of directors had to figure a way to get to the finish line, because the western division was already completed and waiting for the eastern section to be finished.

Recession notwithstanding, the City of Rockford and its large manufacturing base was in a stronger position. Kenosha approached them for a loan so they could buy the iron needed to connect both divisions. Not surprisingly, there was opposition because the Kenosha division had a history of problems. But it was imperative that they hurry-up and connect both divisions so they could generate revenues to pay the interest on their debt, but in 1859 the Kenosha & Rockford defaulted on their first payment. Since it was secured by the City of Kenosha the town council authorized a special tax levy, and this became a contentious yearly debate.

The Racine, Janesville & Mississippi and the Kenosha & Rockford competed for half of the same wheat from farmers where rail service overlapped. Each railroad understood this, which led to an ill-advised course of funding for expansion. To gain trackage as quickly as possible, the Racine, Janesville & Mississippi mortgaged their entire railroad from Racine to Beloit so they could borrow $10,000 ($1.2 million today) per mile to fund additional trackage. They knew if they reached Rockford before Kenosha, it would more than pay for itself, but it was a risky move, and they knew gaining distance was the only way they could knock competing railroads out of the ring. And they were right.

Since each railroad was competing for some of the same agricultural customers, there was considerable animosity. The *Racine Advocate* gleefully wrote, "The citizens of Kenosha are desponding on account of all the business prospects this fall. Their grain market does not compare with other places; people predict the ruin of the city on account of taxes to pay for a railroad which does no business."[105]

"The *Kenosha Telegraph* gives the total tax base of Kenosha as $12,153,075, to raise this amount the real estate is bled to the tune of about three cents and two mills on the dollar of the valuation. No wonder city property is cheap there!"[106]

With people mortgaging everything they owned to pay for the railroad, residents of Kenosha, rich and poor alike, found themselves paying inflated prices for groceries, clothing, and rents, essentially becoming slaves to the railroad debt. Nobody in their right mind would buy a house in Kenosha or start a business with the city's tax base mortgaged to the hilt to Wall Street bankers, and the city's tax base began to decline.

At the 1860 stockholders' meeting, Josiah Bond resigned as president after four grueling years. With an empty treasury and no funds to complete the last 18 miles of tracks, they explored the possibility of merging with another railroad, but nobody was interested. There was simply too much competition for a limited amount of business, and the national economy was still in serious trouble.

Teams of mules and oxen pulled this train back on the track. Blacksmiths with portable forges often made repairs in the middle of nowhere. Picture courtesy of Library of Congress.

Josiah Bond was replaced by thirty-two year-old wunderkind Zalmon G. Simmons, who had already loaned the railroad a lot of money.[107] By 1860, he was holding enough secured debt to have an important voice in the railroad's future. He wasn't interested in a merger so he pushed ahead despite staggering odds.[108]

The board gave him complete control, hoping he would find a way to finish the last section of tracks, and get the railroad running from Kenosha to Rockford and the Mississippi River. Once Simmons took over, he discovered that things were far worse than he ever imagined. After a meeting in Harvard, Illinois, he wrote "We had a railroad, but no rolling stock, and no one wanted to buy any. Finally, the stockholders voted to turn the road over to me bodily, and begged me to equip and start it. It was my dark hour, I was bankrupt, though no one knew it. I owed $150,000."[109] ($19.3 million today.)

This suggests that as wealthy as Simmons was, he was holding a fortune in Kenosha & Rockford paper backed by an empty treasury. There were no easy answers; they would soon be competing with the powerful Illinois Central, the Racine, Janesville & Mississippi was running interference, and the Kenosha & Rockford had run out of money. "The subscription of new railroad stock is impossible; the further issuing of bonds is out of the question."[110]

Simmons recruited twenty-seven year-old Samuel Johnson (1833–1919), the son-in-law of a large stockholder, as secretary-treasurer.[111] He had a brilliant mind, and was so convinced the railroad would succeed that he invested half of his salary buying additional Kenosha & Rockford stock.[112] Between Zalmon G. Simmons and Samuel Johnson, the railroad had two of the best and brightest minds in the country working to salvage the railroad.

Simmons asked the Kenosha city council to defer mortgage payments, and came up with a plan to raise money in a depressed economy. He arranged for a group of New Jersey investors to inspect the railroad to verify that they actually had locomotives, tracks, and depots. When railroads ran out of money, some of them got creative with fraudulent loans secured by rolling stock that didn't exist, and by then Wall Street had become very street-smart.

The investors issued a favorable report which cleared the way for issuing 800 five-dollar shares and 3,200 100-dollar 20-year bonds, both of which sold quickly in Eastern markets.[113] This $324,000 ($38.8 million today) of fresh capital was enough to complete the railroad, which was something many people never thought would happen. But it was typical of how Zalmon Simmons pushed through seemly impossible roadblocks with unconventional alternatives.

According to the *Rockford Republican* "We learn that through the efforts of Z. Simmons, the president of the railroad, that iron to complete the road through to Harvard, has been contracted and paid for, including the freight through to Kenosha. We are also assured that the ties are all contracted for, and a good portion of them have already arrived, iron sufficient to finish the road to Genoa is now in this city, and will be laid down as soon as practical. The iron from Genoa to Harvard has been shipped from New York and is now on the way."[114]

After numerous problems that would have defeated lesser men, the Kenosha & Rockford began service on June 7, 1861. By the end of the year, there were fully loaded trains running in both directions pulling 21 boxcars.[115] While one train was hauling over 4,400 tons of lumber, another was moving east hauling thousands of bushels of wheat or manufactured goods from Rockford factories.

In 1861, the *Rockford Republican* reported that most of the freight coming west from Kenosha was lumber. "The amount of freight is very large, the number of cars still being insufficient to accommodate their business. More cars are to be added as soon as they can be obtained."[116]

Most of this lumber was shipped by Martin Ryerson and Gideon Truesdell, who operated a cartel that shipped a large tonnage through the Kenosha Pier Company.[117] By controlling every phase of the lumbering process, they were able to manufacture a thousand feet of lumber for under $5 ($640 today) and wholesale it to lumberyards for twice as much. Once the lumber was unloaded at the Kenosha Pier Company dock, it was sent to Rockford lumberyards with standing orders, who in turn delivered millions of feet each week to retail yards and factories in central Illinois and central Wisconsin.

Although Simmons got the two branches of the railroad finished, he was never able to come-up with a clever scheme to deal with an enormous debt that would strangle the community for the next twenty years. With inbound grain shipments cannibalized by the Milwaukee elevators, and the railroad trying to survive on little more than outbound lumber shipments, the Kenosha & Rockford's future had gone from spectacular to dismal.

By 1863, lumber shipments were so extensive that the Kenosha & Rockford had to lay more tracks at their Kenosha yards. At any given time, they had fifty to sixty flatbeds loaded with lumber sitting in the railroad's lakefront yards waiting for the next train.[118]

According to the *Rock River Democrat*, "the Kenosha Road has laid another track in their yard, which has been very much needed owing to the large amount of lumber that is being shipped over this road to dealers in our city. [Rockford, Illinois.] If business keeps increasing more tracks will have to be laid or the freight yard will be overflowing with wood cars."[119]

After several missed mortgage payments, the Kenosha & Rockford was advertised for sale. Insiders believed that the mammoth Illinois Central would absorb them if for no other reason than to eliminate competition. But it was the Chicago & Northwestern that in 1864 swapped 14,000 shares for the railroad, leaving Kenosha with an enormous debt that had to be paid by the taxpayers over the next 20 years.

The Chicago & Northwestern basically paid for the rolling stock, and received 72 miles of land, tracks, and depots for free. The Kenosha City Council tried to get the balance due reduced, but the U.S. District

Court upheld the $320,000 judgement plus $180,000 ($30 million today) of interest. Although Wall Street often got a black-eye for going after municipalities, they did in fact loan them a huge amount of money, and had the right to get it back.

Every time the Kenosha City Council voted a special tax assessment, lawsuits were filed by property owners, and in one particular lawsuit a group of angry taxpayers attempted to stop the City from collecting an $18,625 ($1.1 million today) levy.[120] One man was so distraught at the thought of everything he made for the rest of his life going to pay the railroad debt that he hung himself.

In an attempt to refinance the railroad debt, Harvey Durkee said if William Goff could raise $1,200 each from a hundred people, he would be one of 40 people to raise the balance of roughly $125,000.[121] "He wanted the debt paid. He (Durkee) had heard enough of the debt and railroad bonds. This debt is a weight on Kenosha business. It keeps capital away and smother's enterprise."[122] (William Goff was a Manitowoc sawmill owner that sold lumber to Durkee, Truesdell & Company.)

Zalmon Simmons might have struck-out as a railroad mogul, but he amassed two spectacular fortunes by spotting undervalued assets. During the 1850s, when Charles Sholes borrowed money from him but couldn't repay the debt, he gave Simmons half of his telegraph company.[123] It wasn't much of a company, just a 79-mile line from Milwaukee to the State capitol. The business wasn't profitable until a few years later when Simmons bought the other half, and turned it into a major enterprise.

Each year, he reinvested a percentage of his profits stringing new lines until they covered 20,000 miles. Twenty years later, Zalmon Simmons sold the Northwestern Telegraph Company to Western Union for $4 million ($6.4 billion today) and took a seat on their board across the table from Harrison Durkee, whose in-laws owned a significant interest in the Albany Telegraph Company.[124]

Simmons struck gold when he accepted a patent for a wire mattress as settlement of a bad debt. After investigating this patent with an eye toward mass-production, he calculated that he could lower the cost of a mattress from $5 to 88¢, which led to his founding the Simmons Mattress Company where he amassed another staggering fortune.

After the Kenosha & Rockford's demise, Simmons loaned the railroad's secretary-treasurer, Samuel Johnson, enough money to go into the hardware business. He developed a paste wax for hardwood floors that he sold door to door, and from these humble beginnings came the family owned multi-billion-dollar Johnson Wax conglomerate.

From the ashes of the Kenosha & Rockford sprang three incredible fortunes.

The City Bank of Kenosha

None of Kenosha's warehouses could have amassed the kind of money they did during the 1850s without a state-chartered local bank Without a bank to cash drafts from a Buffalo grain elevator, warehouses would never have been able to turn-over $100,000 ($12.8 million today) in a single day during the harvest season.

But starting a bank was easier said than done, because the state legislature had outlawed banking during the 1840s. This had more to do with poor management than fraud, and the legislatures desire to protect the public. During a 10-year vacuum 90% of the money supply in Wisconsin was controlled by three capitalists who issued illegal but negotiable promissory notes that were traded like currency.

The *Milwaukee Courier* explained to its readers that anti-banking measures were meant to "protect the weak against the machinations of the powerful."[125] The unsophisticated person would always be at the mercy "of a cunning, overreaching" corrupt minority. There was great distrust of paper money issued by banks, and Democrats recognized the flaws in the system and outlawed banking in the State of Wisconsin to protect the working man.

There was a strong suspicion that if banks had to depend on politicians to get their charters, corruption would inevitably follow. Laws would protect special interests who bribed legislators so they could cheat the working man, and send him to poor house. It wasn't banks that presented the greatest threat but government oversight, or the lack thereof, when legislators accepted bribes from the banking interests.

Without a national currency like the greenback, a currency backed by the government and printed with green ink, there was considerable instability in the money supply. Prior to 1862 when the greenback first appeared, there were over 3,500 banks printing their own currency. In Wisconsin, 106 banks issued different one-, two-, and three-dollar notes that under the law had to be redeemed for gold or silver coins when presented at the bank that issued the note. Had every state or territorial bank operated under the same laws there would have been much greater stability, because these local banks were lax to the point of indifference.

An example was the Bank of Wisconsin, which was organized by a group of politically connected insiders who had no difficulty obtaining a charter from the legislature. In 1835, they listed their capitalization at $200,000 ($40 million today), but in reality, it was less than $15,000 with very little hard-cash, just promissory notes from stockholders.

In 1836, Green Bay attorney and stockholder Morgan Martin instructed their cashier to follow a very conservative policy because the eastern financial markets were unstable. When money became scarce in New York and Boston, he instructed the Bank to stop redeeming notes except for their own. It was sound advice, and it allowed them to weather the panic with the Bank of Wisconsin emerging as one of the strongest banks in the Territory.

The following year the Bank of Wisconsin were in serious trouble despite the legislatures audit committee stating that they were "sound and solvent." They were actually $226,394 ($96 million today) over-drawn, but thanks to their friends in high places they breezed through their most recent audit. Quarter-barrels of nails with layers of coins near the top fooled the auditors, although bribes would have probably accomplished the same outcome. There was an unholy relationship between bankers and territorial auditors that led to the end of banking, at least temporarily, when too many people lost their lifes savings.

What Kenosha warehouses needed most was a bank, because the Buffalo grain elevators paid them large sums of money with a New York draft that had little value in Kenosha. Harvey Durkee used his brother's Wall Street office to clear notes from these elevators, mostly through the Troy Savings Bank, where he was president.[126] A lot of merchants traveled aboard the ship carrying their wheat, and returned home with bags of gold coins because they had universal value anywhere in the country.

Every warehouse had a couple of large safes in their office where they kept trays of gold or silver coins as a means to avoiding cannibalizing their profits with hefty exchange fees. But this required special precautions to prevent robberies, with the office door locked at all times, and a revolver sitting on the bookkeeper's desk cocked and ready.

When Wisconsin became a state in 1848, banking was banned by its constitution, which meant the state wouldn't charter any banks. Four years later, the legislature realized the need for banking because by then two capitalists controlled the states monetary supply. The legislature put the question of legalizing banking on the ballot with 9,126 against and 31,289 in favor.[127] As long as a bank had a charter and met the reserve requirements, they were granted permission by the States Controller of the Currency to print their own currency, make loans and redeem their currency for gold or silver.

The City Bank of Kenosha was organized by Samuel Hale (1799–1877), and without this bank the local warehouses would never have broken the million-bushel mark. This bank was capitalized at $40,000 ($4.8 million today), and the board of directors recruited Alonzo Campbell to serve as president. He quickly turned the City Bank of Kenosha into one of the top banking institutions in the Midwest.[128]

"The officers are gentlemen who command the confidence of the business community," said the *Kenosha Telegraph*. "Of the president, we can only say that he has been long and well known to the community, and we congratulate the stockholders in having secured him for its duties of such acknowledged financial ability and gentlemanly bearing as Alonzo Campbell."[129]

The bank printed one, two, and three-dollar bills with $15,000 ($1.8 million today) in circulation.[130] During the fall harvest, they cleared around $3.4 million ($408 million today) of New York notes from Buffalo grain elevators, and made a fortune in exchange fees.[131]

By 1856, the City Bank of Kenosha was one of the busiest institutions in the state outside of Milwaukee. According to a newspaper advertisement, they bought and sold drafts drawn on New England, Chicago, and Milwaukee exchanges, and wired drafts to England, Ireland, or Scotland.[132] They dabbled in land warrants, which was an easy way to double their money, and something many local mercantile stores did too.

There were over 700,000 land warrants floating around from the Revolutionary War and the War of 1812, and Mexican War soldiers. Since the government didn't have an established army, they relied on state militias where the soldiers were paid a small enlistment bonus, and at the end of the war given a 160-acre land warrant.

This warrant entitled them to obtain land from the federal government. These warrants didn't have any cash value with the government, but during the 1850s they could be bought from former soldiers or their widows for $125. In Muskegon County when Alva Trowbridge was just starting out as a sawmill owner, he bought most of his pinelands with land warrants, which required a certain amount of legwork, and enabled him to buy timber land for less than $1.00 ($120 today) per acre, or about half the going rate.

The City Bank of Kenosha was successful due to its heavy lakefront warehouse business, and Hale & Ayer, Bennett & Sellick, Holbrook, Elkins & Company, and Durkee, Truesdell & Company were major depositors. The Bank was profitable, and a few years later attorney Henry Towslee bought $30,000 ($3.6 million today) of stock, which made him the largest stockholder. The board-of-directors consisted of Alonzo Campbell, H.W. Hubbard, Samuel Hale, Seth Doane, H.B. Towslee, Harvey Durkee, and William Mattocks.[133]

During the eight-week fall harvest, warehouses like Hale & Ayer, Bennett & Sellick, or Durkee, Truesdell & Company converted a total of $75,000 to $100,000 a day of bank drafts from Buffalo elevators. Perhaps the best source of how successful they had become comes from their cashier, Edward Durant, who recalled that during the 1857 fall harvest they turned over $100,000 ($12 million today) in a *single day*.[134]

U.S. Senator Charles Durkee, 1855

At a time when abolitionists were part of the minority, Charles Durkee ran a station in the Underground Railroad, and became a staunch anti-slavery man in Congress at a time when there were only fourteen of them. He worked with Joshua Giddings, who believed slavery had to be abolished before it ruined America.

During the 1840s there was an international awakening to the abolition of slavery, and Durkee was chosen to represent the United States at the Paris Peace Convention. During the summer of 1849 he boarded the steamship Washington, and a few weeks later stepped off the dock in Paris along with Professor Sheppard of Yale; Reverend Phillip Berry, an Episcopal minister from Maryland; Reverend J.W. Parker, a Baptist minister from Cambridge; and Reverend Bidwell of New York.[135]

"Charles Durkee arrived from Wisconsin after traveling 1,500 miles before reaching New York. He is a plain, farmer-looking man of no classical education, and with but little acquaintance with the world. But he is truly an earnest, single-hearted man, and although unable to shine as a speaker his presence will be valuable."[136]

During a floor debate in Congress a reporter wrote that "I saw plain honest noble Charles Durkee. When I look upon that man's face, shake that man's hand; hear that man's voice I am convinced that before me stands a whole souled American, a great son of liberty, an able defender of a free and true democracy. Charles Durkee, that bold and fearless defender of human rights."[137]

In front of world leaders, he had to explain why slavery still existed in the United States, because by then several foreign nations had already outlawed slavery. Many European factories and farms had already switched to indentured servants or sharecroppers, which was little more than slavery by a different name. The United States came under heavy criticism for founding a nation under liberty and justice for all, with slave auction houses within eyesight of their capital building. At the world peace conference, Durkee was asked why slavery continued to flourish in his country.

"The Hon. Charles Durkee, a member of the United States Congress, next addressed the meeting as follows: 'I should not trespass upon the attention of the Congress at this late period, but for the remarks made by a previous speaker, Mr. Brown. I fully agree that slavery is a great curse to our country; but I am happy to say that a great struggle is now going on in America to get rid of this evil."

Charles Durkee had a front-row seat during one of the most painful periods of American history. He voted against the Compromise of 1850 that defused a political confrontation between free and slave states and spoke before Congress where he denounced the Fugitive Slave Act.

"History proves that the most galling oppression that the people have ever suffered has been inflicted by cruel and tyrannical governments...in the long catalogue of public crimes among civilized nations, there is none more cruel or barbarous than the Fugitive Slave Law now in force in this country. The law was called by its friends a healing and peaceful measure; yet time has proven what every candid mind knew it to be...even crueler in its oppression than the guillotine itself.

"This law disregards every principal of justice...who could have imagined that this great Republic would now be engaged in performing the drudgery of slave traders...kidnapping men, women, and children for a slave market! "Who would have believed that this Government could ever be capable of waging a piratical war against innocent, unoffending people, for the sole purpose of enriching the pockets of those who manufacture, and those who use thumb-screws, chains, and fetters.... (who) construct prisons in the maintenance of this horrid traffic? The Fugitive Slave Law is an unrelenting war against the African race; even in Czarist Russia slave families aren't separated."

A reporter from the *New York Tribune* was scribbling-down notes during his speech. "As I write, Mr. Durkee is making the closing speech of the evening. He is a plain man, with no pretentions to oratory having been engaged all his life in mercantile pursuits, but his remarks are being listened to with great reason. He is talking straight-out just as he always does. He dodges nothing."[138]

A reporter from the *Western Citizen* described Durkee standing at the rostrum: "he was a beautiful sight.... his flashing eyes sending streams of light that eclipsed the brilliant chandeliers above him. His soul seemed on fire with earnest thoughts, while his lack of rhetoric, for he is but a plain, limited, educated merchant. The southerners listened to him with the profoundest of respect.... they have come to love him for his child-like simplicity, his undisguised love of liberty. Charles Durkee in a word is one of the few natural men in Congress. He does not know the meaning of the word Aristocracy."[139]

But he was too far out in front in his hatred of slavery, and when he ran for re-election he was in for the fight of his life. He had been targeted by pro-slavery forces as somebody that had to be removed from Congress, and he lost in a three-way race. The *Kenosha Telegraph* wrote, "It is our painful duty to announce the defeat of Charles Durkee. We are not unaware of the extraordinary and unparalleled exertions which were made to defeat him by the friends of slavery."[140]

After his defeat, he returned to Wisconsin and began looking for farms with good soil. He found what he was looking for in Janesville, but at the last minute found better land near the state capitol in Madison, in Windsor Township.

He built a beautiful residence with brand-new barns, outbuildings, and equipped his farm with the latest machinery. It was a rich man's farm, and yet Durkee played an active role in its operations. Each day he could be seen on horseback supervising workers in the barns and out in the fields. His nephew, George Durkee, was "overseer" of over sixty field workers with six mechanical reapers in use.[141]

In 1854 they harvested roughly 4,000 bushels which, at the market price of $1.59 a bushel, would have generated at least $1,600 ($192,000 today).[142] The following year, Georges workers harvested roughly 8,000 bushels, sheared 704 sheep, butchered 63 beef cows, and 112 hogs.[143]

It was the Kansas-Nebraska Act that pulled Durkee back into politics, because it was a brazen attempt to force the spread of slavery from coast to coast. He believed this legislation reversed the Missouri Compromise, and changed the Constitutional landscape. He was still very involved in the Abolitionist movement and the Kansas-Nebraska Act catapulted him back onto the national stage.

After losing his Congressional seat a few years earlier he was lukewarm about running for Governor, and yet he tied for first place on an informal ballot.[144] On two successive ballots he tied with Edward D. Holton (1815–1892), and it was a grudge-match by Free-Soilers to unseat Governor Leonard J. Farwell. The totals were tight; 29 to 29 and then 31 to 31. If Durkee pushed a little harder he might have won but he really wasn't interested in the job.[145]

In 1854 a reporter for the *Daily Argus & Democrat* wrote "We met on the street the Honorable Charles Durkee, ex-Congressman from the 1st District. Mr. Durkee is the owner, occupant, and tiller of a handsome farm a few miles from this place in Windsor. His face is somewhat sunburned, his hands harder and browner, and his form short but muscular. From our conversation we think that he considers Nebraska as an abomination and a wedge to great and dire events."[146]

"If Democrats want a man who is a Democrat in every sense of the word, and.... want one who is a man.... let them take Charles Durkee from the handle of his plough and next winter elect him to the United States Senate."[147]

Many of the states legislators believed Durkees candidacy was doomed from the start because he was such an ultra-abolitionist. He really wasn't known throughout both houses of the legislature, and in those days, they elected their U.S. Senators. The Whigs had double-crossed Durkee during the last election so their support was unlikely.[148] But, earlier in his career he had served in the statehouse as a Democrat, and had a good name within the recently organized Republican Party. Unfortunately, he picked a bad year to run for office.

"The corruption in the election of 1855 was so obvious; we've never seen anything like it since in a gubernatorial race."[149] When incumbent Governor William A. Barstow ran against State Senator Coles Bashford, it looked like Bashford was ahead by 350 out of 72,553 votes, until the Governors hand-picked State Board of Canvassers declared that totals from Bridge Creek and Spring Creek hadn't yet been counted.

"If Barstow received a clear majority nothing was to be done...but if a few hundred votes were needed they were to be manufactured, and if new and unheard-of election precincts were required, they too were to be manufactured as the safest way of multiplying votes."[150]

When the fraudulent totals from Bridge Creek, Spring Creek, and Waupaca were added, Coles Bashford's lead eroded, which put the Governor over the top. The corrupt Board of Canvassers certified Governor Barstow the winner by 157 votes, and he was inaugurated.

Charles Durkee (L) Byron Kilbourn (C) and James Doty (R).
Pictures courtesy of the Wisconsin Historical Society.

Bashford filed a lawsuit contesting the totals. He knew there was widespread fraud, and when independent auditors discovered that the villages of Bridge Creek and Spring Creek *didn't exist* their totals was thrown out. When the totals from Waupaca were re-counted the Governors' 543 vote lead slipped again, and a few days later the Board of Elections ruled unanimously that Bashford had won by 1,009 votes.

On March 25th Coles Bashford arrived at the Capitol to take office. According to the *Wisconsin State Journal* "Bashford, a dignified old gentleman of the old school, leisurely took off his coat, hung it upon the hall tree, and informed MacArthur and his coterie of friends that he had come to take charge of the state government." His term ended abruptly in a railroad bribery scandal that made national headlines, and forced him to flee to the southwest.

Charles Durkee fully comprehended the ramifications of the Kansas-Nebraska Act, and felt he had no alternative but to return to Washington. His candidacy was a longshot, but at just the right time he received a critical boost from C. Lathem and Christopher Sholes, abolitionist friends from Kenosha who were members of the legislature. C. Lathem was somebody people listened to, and perhaps more importantly, he knew when to stop talking.

In 1855, Sholes was elected Speaker of the House, and he and his brother played critical roles in getting their friend elected. During that period, state legislatures elected their Senators to a six year term, because the founding fathers believed that by electing their two Senators, state legislatures would strengthen their ties with the federal government.

"Uncertainty filled the air as the legislature assembled...hotel rooms and boarding houses were jammed with lobbyists."[151] The politically astute *Weekly Wisconsin* wrote 'it is now certain that Mr. Durkee cannot be elected at this session, as the more moderate portion of the Whig section of the Republicans would not support him.'"[152]

C. Lathem Sholes, inventor of the typewriter.
Pictures courtesy of the Kenosha History Center Archives.

At critical times, the Sholes brothers steered Durkees name around petty turf wars. Judge Alexander Randall, just elected to the legislature, pushed Durkees candidacy hard at just the right time. (Randall was Postmaster General in the Johnson Administration.) *Weekly Wisconsin* wrote, "When we predicted the election of Mr. Durkee, we did it in the belief that the silver-gray Whigs elected as Republicans, would vote for him. We were not mistaken."[153] The "silver grays" supported the Compromise of 1850 and were mostly northern conservatives.

Kilbourn and former Governor James Doty were neck-and-neck on the first ballot but on the second day of voting, Doty was ahead of Kilbourn until Charles Durkee pulled ahead, receiving 51-votes and yet he couldn't reach that critical 54-vote threshold.[154]

Kilbourn told the anti-slavery Liberty Party members if they couldn't elect Durkee, they should swing their votes to him because he would give their party $1,000 ($60,000 today). Abolitionist publisher Sherman Booth's astute wife said it was, "better to sacrifice $1,000 than lose the election of Durkee."[155]

The Free Soilers who joined the Republican Party, vindictive after being double-crossed by the Whigs during Durkees re-election campaign, were ready to swing their votes to Kilbourn if the Whigs didn't fall into line. In 1852, the Free Soilers supported Whig candidate Leonard Farwell for Governor, and they expected them to step aside in a tight three-way race that would have given Charles Durkee a third term, but they betrayed his candidacy.

At a critical time when voting was tight, Sherman Booth, Alexander Randall, and Charles Sholes put together a shaky coalition of Whigs, Democrats, and Republicans. After two weeks of voting, the Lt. Governor stepped to the rostrum and announced that Charles Durkee would be their next U.S. Senator. When Durkee made an appearance, the legislature gave him a standing ovation, possibly because after several days of voting they were relieved that it was finally over.[156]

Once again, plain, simple, kindhearted Charles Durkee surprised his critics, and there were many who believed that had it not been for the animosities from the Kansas-Nebraska Act, that an Abolitionist of Durkees stripe wouldn't have been elected. As progressive as Wisconsin was in the abolitionist movement, there were still a lot of people who didn't care. He received a historical footnote as the first Republican elected to the U.S. Senate.[157] The *Washington Era* wrote, "Charles Durkee is an old Liberty man; land reform, free trade, and a progressive. His friends here will give him a warm welcome back to Washington."[158]

Durkee was stepping away from a peaceful life to return to the most contentious periods in American history, and as an ultra-liberal Abolitionist he had a target on his back. After three years of farming, he sold his 1,500-acre property at the top of the market to Isaac DeForest for $25,000 ($3.7 million today), twice what he paid due to the farm's record profits.[159] He built a house in Kenosha with a view of Lake Michigan, and this is where he and his wife lived with their two-year old son, Harvey.[160] While in Washington, he lived at a boarding house with Joshua Giddings, George Julian, and other abolitionists.

Soon after taking office, he became embroiled in the Lecompton crisis that had been brewing in Kansas. He regarded this as a blatant power-grab, and a step to nationalize slavery. In a twisted manifest destiny, they wanted to see the southern half of the country pro-slavery from the Atlantic to the Pacific. This wasn't that far-fetched, because under the terms of the Missouri Compromise and the Kansas-Nebraska Act vote totals could easily be manipulated.

Durkee was disgusted by the sham constitutional convention out in Kansas, and when the constitution came before the Senate for a vote, he said it was weak, vague, and unconstitutional. "I don't believe Congress will pass this bill.... even should it pass, it cannot be enforced. In my opinion, any attempt would light up the flames of a Civil War that would carry with it general devastation and ruin."[161]

The Lecompton bill had enough votes to pass in the Senate but things were less certain in the House of Representatives, until President Buchanan used heavy-duty patronage to grease the deal, sending pro-slavery cabinet members to lobby Congressmen with lucrative government contracts, mail routes, commissions, and even cash. Just about everyone in Washington knew that Buchanan was buying Congressman like hogs.

When the Lecompton bill came up for a vote Durkee said the language was intentionally vague. Although known as a man of few words, on 20 March 1858 he made a speech before the Senate titled the "Lecompton Conspiracy."

"I will say that if you pass the Lecompton Constitution, force it on the people by the army of the United States, and the citizens of Kansas, if the free States tamely submit, I shall be obliged to confess, with shame that the honorable Senator from South Carolina, in his recent speech, was correct when he said that the majority of the people of the free States are already slaves.

"Look at the statute book, and you will see that we have drawn by legislative enactment, a geographical line, and said to all who desire to engage in the slave trade on one side of this line: you may do so with impunity. On the other side of this line, all who dare to engage in this traffic shall suffer death. Has not the Supreme Court just decreed that all the Territories between this and the Pacific shall be open to kidnapping and robbery, provided the victims are of a certain race?

"Now, it should be observed that while we are so reckless of the rights of humanity in the Territories, we are remarkably nice in protecting the rights of property. To illustrate: a colored man emigrates from Massachusetts to Kansas, buys a piece of land, settles on and improves it. Now we have a law saying: 'All persons convicted of horse-stealing shall suffer confinement at hard labor not exceeding seven years.' Here, then, if the white man steals the colored man's horse, he is to be punished as a felon, but if he kidnaps the owner or his family it is right and lawful, being guaranteed by the Constitution. Could anything be more absurdly wicked?

"Mr. President, I cannot believe Congress will pass this bill. And should they it cannot be enforced. In my opinion, any attempt to do so would light up the flames of a civil war that would carry with it devastation and ruin. The path of duty is plain; let the President withdraw troops from Kansas. Let the people make their own Constitution as other States have done in the past. Let the government cease to wage war against an innocent and unoffending people, and return to its duty the protection of the weak against the invasion of the strong."[162]

During his six year (1855–1861) term Durkee witnessed the events leading to secession, and the beginning of a Civil War. In an uncharacteristically gloomy letter to his brother, he knew the end of the republic was near.

"I have been conversant with the Southern mind for twelve years and, though I have been uncompromisingly anti-slavery and outspoken in all my views, yet all this time I have not had an unpleasant discussion with a southern Senator or member of the House; yet, so fully do I understand the designs of southern men, I clearly see a dark cloud is fast gathering over our beloved country; this beautiful land of ours is about to pass through such a terrible, such a scorching and devastating ordeal as history has nowhere furnished a parallel. What a beautiful and happy world this would be if we only all loved one another, and studied each other's happiness and welfare as earnestly as we do our own."[163]

Durkee, Truesdell & Company
Lumber Manufacturers; Muskegon, Michigan, 1856

The railroads were about to change how lumber and wheat was bought and sold, and the Durkee-Truesdell partnership bet heavily on lumber. From the pinelands to their Chicago River lumberyards, Harvey Durkee and Gideon Truesdell would control every phase of the lumbering process.

With their own pinelands, logging camps and the largest sawmill on Lake Michigan, they would be able to manufacture a thousand feet for less than $5 and sell it through their Chicago River wholesale yards at the market price of $10. They would also have the wherewithal to buy shiploads of lumber from smaller mills, sell it to yards and factories in the western territories, and double their money. The only hitch to their masterplan was that it took a lot of money to do business on such a large scale.

There appears to have been a close relationship between mill owner Alva Trowbridge, who was described as a "very nice man," and Gideon Truesdell[164] He began farming in Kenosha, and sold his farm so he could buy a larger farm near Libertyville, Illinois. As a county board member, he engineered a slick property transfer of this farm to the county at a huge mark-up, and was severely condemned.

He invested the money in a portable steam sawmill, built a plank road from Gray's Lake to Waukegan, and began turned logs supplied by farmers into lumber that were sold through Mordechai Brown's retail yard. "I saw Trowbridges mill in '48 cutting lumber in Waukegan…. They moved the whole mill over here (Muskegon) in '49."[165] He was entrepreneurial and resourceful. In 1854, he built a lath mill behind his sawmill, and a year later he built the Trowbridge & Wing mill with his son-in-law, Thomas Wing, with the financing coming from Gideon.[166]

More likely than not, it was through Alva Trowbridge that Gideon heard about a prime lakefront parcel on Muskegon Lake that was for sale. He paid $12,000 ($1.4 million today) for a 6.9-acre lakefront parcel, where they would build one of the largest sawmills on Lake Michigan.[167]

Muskegon was ripe for real estate speculation due to a sharp increase in population with several new mills under construction. On November 10, 1855, Harvey Durkee bought 165 acres on the eastern side of Western Avenue for $7,500 ($900,000 today), which he later sub-divided into Durkees Addition with 1,900 lots for sale.[168]

Lots were sold with nothing down and the balance due in 36 monthly installments with three years of interest pre-paid.[169] When all of them were sold, Harvey Durkee stood to clear around $144,000 ($2.8 million today). Buying land by the acre, sub-dividing, and selling it by the lot had made Charles and Harvey Durkee wealthy after having platted several sub-divisions in Kenosha and Racine counties. During the 1840s and 1850s the Durkees had over 10,000 lots in their inventory that generated a steady return.

When Durkee, Truesdell & Company exited the Kenosha market their lumberyard was still profitable, so they leased this property to Pomeroy, Lewis & Holmes. They also sold them a parcel of land next to their Muskegon mill so they could build a sawmill, and improve their profit-margins by manufacturing what they sold.[170]

This created a significant revenue stream for Harvey Durkee and Gideon Truesdell, who owned a 50% interest in Pomeroy, Lewis & Holmes' Kenosha lumberyard, and a 25% interest in their Muskegon sawmill.[171] In addition to interest and principal, Durkee, Truesdell & Company would have received a percentage of their profits.[172]

The Pomeroy, Lewis, & Holmes mill was pieced together with outdated equipment; an old upright saw, lath saw, and a siding and flooring saw that turned scrap into something they could sell. It had a small daily output of 18,000 board feet and 8,000 feet of lath, and yet they were positioned to make money, with Durkee, Truesdell & Company receiving around $7,200 ($864,000 today) a year from interest, principal and their share of the profits.

Durkee, Truesdell & Company also sold their Kenosha planing mill to E.D. Gillis under similar terms, with the partnership owning a third interest, and holding a $3,450 ($414,000 today) note.[173] They packaged a deal whereby they sold a profitable business, held the mortgage and a minority interest, and created another source of revenue.

According to a May 30, 1856 R.G. Dun & Company report, Durkee-Truesdell's Kenosha partnership was valued at $50,000 ($6 million today), and rated "abundantly good-the firm is wealthy."[174] In just four years the value of their property had increased from $12,000 to $50,000 due to the partial construction of a railroad that would eventually reach the Mississippi River, consolidation of the three largest warehouses along the lakefront, and their third interest in the Kenosha Pier Company.

When Harvey Durkee and Gideon Truesdell expanded, they organized two partnerships. One would finance and build a state-of-the-art mill located in Muskegon with one of the largest outputs on Lake Michigan, and the other would fund a Chicago wholesale yard in the high-rent district along the riverfront where they would buy lumber from other mills by the shipload.

Throughout 1856, Gideon would have been incredibly busy with an architect, machinists and millwrights building a mill with the latest technology that replaced manpower with steam-power. The land, building, and equipment were valued at $56,000 ($6.7 million today) which at the time made it the most expensive mill on Lake Michigan.[175]

There was a third partnership consisting of Charles, Harrison, and Harvey Durkee who bought or more likely optioned 20,000 acres of pinelands along four rivers and tributaries in western Michigan for $2.00 per acre.[176] Given the size of this purchase, it might have come directly from Erastus Corning, whom Harrison and Harvey Durkee knew because during the 1840s they were partners in a land syndicate.[177]

The forests along the Muskegon River consisted of millions of acres of yellow pine and a 300 mile waterway capable of delivering a large tonnage of logs to Muskegon Lake over the next thirty years. The lake was eight miles long and two to four miles wide, depending on where you stood, with 16 sawmills located around the perimeter. By 1855, they manufactured over 92 million feet of lumber, and kept thirty schooners and two steamers moving to and from Chicago River yards.[178] It was the tip of the iceberg, because thirty years later 47 sawmills on Muskegon Lake manufactured 665 million feet each season, enough to build a highway from Boston to Los Angeles. Muskegon became known as the "Lumber Queen of the World" when it became the largest lumber producing city in the world.

Judging from the date on the real estate transfer, Gideon returned to Kenosha just before Lake Michigan closed for the winter, and returned during the spring of 1856 along with a small army of carpenters and millwrights.[179]

While walking down the dirt road in front of his property, Gideon would have had to dodge stumps sticking out of the ground, and noticed wigwams at the edge of the woods. Anyone walking down the Western Avenue after dark did so slowly and cautiously with a whale-oil lantern to avoid stumbling over a tree stump.

One early resident recalled that the Indians were friendly "when the shore and the woods were filed with these kindly, peaceful people.... there was not a bad trait nor a trick in the Indians that was not taught them by the white man.... they were a very religious people.... they pitched their wigwams on Saturday night and made ready for Sunday, during which they would not even pick a berry. All day long they sang and prayed."[180]

Throughout the 1850s the roads were a pool of mud after a good rain. To combat a chronic mud problem the mills began mixing sawdust with mud until it created a solid road surface with the strength of concrete.

The first structure Gideon put his carpenters to work building was a large boarding house overlooking the lake.[181] Once completed, construction workers lived there although furniture, stoves, dishes, and bedding wouldn't arrive for another two months.[182] When completed, it was more like a hotel than a boarding house, with a large first floor lounge with comfortable chairs, and subscriptions to dozens of newspapers and magazines.

After having run a boarding house along the Wisconsin River where loggers had lots of time on their hands, Gideon no doubt knew the importance of giving his workers something to occupy their time other than arguing, drinking, or gambling. Gideon built a cabin where he and his brother slept due to a severe housing shortage, and it became their command post.

North side of Western Avenue from Jefferson toward Terrace Street.
Picture courtesy of the Muskegon Lakeshore Museum.

Most boarding houses had twenty or more men sleeping in a dormitory on the second floor, a dining hall and kitchen below, and an outdoor latrine. Sawmill owners regarded them as necessary but unprofitable, and yet Gideon appears to have cleared large profits from his 32-room boarding house. It was a drawing-card for the best workers in town because they served good food and nobody left the table hungry. At other sawmills, the men ran at full-speed to the boarding house, because the stragglers ended-up with table scraps.

The Durkee-Truesdell boarding house was unusual inasmuch as each person had a private room, and along with their room and board came a laundry service. This amenity was something that no other mill offered. During the Civil war, when he began running his sawmills around the clock, Gideon doubled the size of the boarding house with an addition.

We know from U.S. Customs House records that building materials were shipped from Chicago aboard the Milwaukee & Chicago, transferred to wagons, and hauled to the Durkee-Truesdell dock where they were loaded aboard the next schooner returning to Muskegon. When the ship arrived at the Central Wharf, a steam-powered cargo boom transferred the materials and equipment to wagons that brought them to the building site.

This boarding house was unusual inasmuch as at the end of each 12-hour shift, about fifty men returned home, changed from their dirty clothes into clean, casual attire in a wardrobe room, and dropped their dirty clothes down a chute to the cellar stamped with their locker number. During the night, a large dumbwaiter brought clean clothing from the cellar to their second-floor locker. A small army of women worked through the night washing clothes, towels and bed linens. The day shift washed towels, blankets, and bed linens.

Gideon charged $5.00 ($900 today) a month which covered room, meals and laundry.[183] It was designed to be a home-away-from-home for men with families living elsewhere, and Gideon made it possible for wives and children to occasionally sail across the lake on the Challenge to visit them.[184] They would also forward money across Lake Michigan to their Kenosha office so workers could send money to their families, many of whom lived there.

According to shipping records on July 16, 1856, a 12-ton steam engine, boiler, 5,000 bricks and 5-tons of groceries were shipped to Muskegon aboard the Challenge or Heligoland.[185] On August 14, 1856, the Durkee-Truesdell sawmill was nearing completion, and a *Kenosha Tribune* reporter gave a detailed description of the mill and boarding house.

"The schooner Challenge came into the harbor from Chicago, to take on a lot of brick and stores destined for Muskegon, for Durkee, Truesdell & Company, who are erecting a large steam sawmill at that place. She also takes materials, ready framed and finished, for a large boarding house to accommodate their workmen. Mr. Truesdell, who just came from Muskegon, informs us that they will have their mill in full operation in a few days.

"Nearly all the vessels upon Lake Michigan are engaged from the opening of navigation in the early spring until its close late in the fall in the lumber trade. And this has kept up year after year with a constantly increasing demand, and yet the supply keeps increasing. Where does it all come from? We visited one of the principal lumber manufacturing localities, and we are prepared to answer that query.

"We took passage on the Challenge with Captain Alfred Ackerman for Muskegon, from where is shipped more lumber than any point on Lake Michigan. She has made more trips to Muskegon than any other vessel that sails. We arrived at our destination in due time, after a most pleasant trip, and took a view of the source of Lake Michigan commerce. Muskegon is situated around Muskegon Lake at the mouth of the Muskegon River, which empties into Lake Michigan.

"Muskegon Lake is some five to six miles in diameter. In sight are sixteen sawmills in operation, and others being built in different stages of progress. Most conspicuous among these mills is that of Durkee-Truesdell & Company, which they have just put into operation.

"This establishment is a sample of what energy, skill, and capital will perform when rightly directed. It is now ten months since the site of the mill was decided upon, and the first blow struck in the forests. They now have what is generally conceded to be the most extensive lumbermill on Muskegon Lake, and by the time the twelfth month rolls around, will have cut five or six million feet of lumber.

"The sawmill was built by Mr. Silas Pelton, who has left convincing proof of his skill as a millwright, as well as of his energy and industry. The main building is 40 x 75 feet, with a wing on each side, each 20 x 45 feet, built in the most substantial manner.

"The machinery consists of twelve muley saws and four circular saws for the manufacture of siding and lath, edging lumber, and cutting slabs. All are upon the second floor of the mill, and conveniently arranged for the purpose of the different manufactures.

"This is driven by an engine of 19 inch bore and 24-inch stroke, with a capacity estimated at 100 hsp. with three boilers supplying the steam. About 40,000 - 50,000 feet of lumber are turned out every 24 hours, and 30,000 - 40,000 feet of lath. The slabs are all cut by a circular saw into suitable lengths, for lath and firewood as fast as they accumulate from the different saws.

"The sawdust is carried through chutes, and emptied into handcarts, which as fast as they are filled are wheeled off to the boiler room. This, with a few slabs is all the fuel used to drive the machinery. Everything runs with the regularity of clockwork through a 24-hour period.

"Messrs. Durkee and Truesdell have been fortunate in finding the best employees to run their establishment. It is the result of prompt payment of good wages, and commendable care for the convenience and comfort of their workers. Their boarding house consists of a main section of four stories 24 x 64 feet and a three-story wing 24 x 32 feet. Its furnished with the conveniences of a first-class hotel.

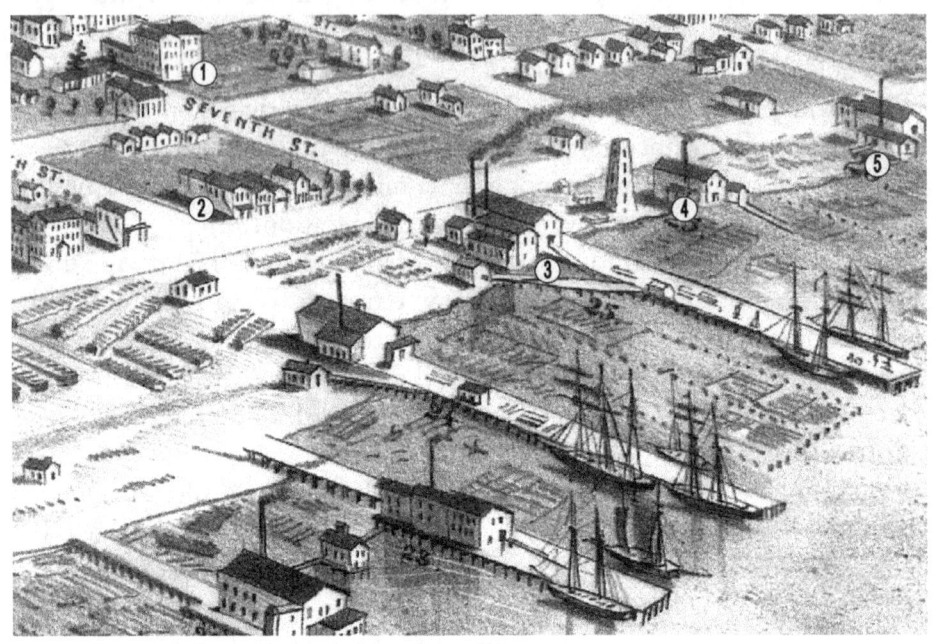

Durkee-Truesdell boarding house (1); mercantile store (2); Durkee-Truesdell mill (3); Durkee-Truesdell shingle mill (4); Pomeroy & Holmes mill (5). This 1868 sketch courtesy of U.S. Department of Interior maps collection.

"On the first floor is a large sitting room for the men, washrooms, and a basement cellar for laundry. On the second floor is the dining room, kitchen, pantry, and wardrobe room. The third and fourth stories are sleeping rooms, which are large and neatly furnished. There are 32 rooms in the main building.

"The building is painted white, set upon the brow of a hill making a fine appearance, and commanding a view of Muskegon Lake. Their workers appreciate all of the comforts of home, and for this Messrs. Durkee and Truesdell are worthy of credit, and offer a good example for all large employers.

"Much of the success of this enterprise is due to the energy and perseverance of Mr. Truesdell, who has given his personal attention to the whole project since its inception. We do not wonder that he feels a commendable pride in the final success of the enterprise. Messrs. Durkee and Truesdell have long been extensive lumber dealers in Kenosha County, and are prepared to add largely to their business.

"Their mill will cut 8,000,000 feet of lumber, which they expect to ship to Kenosha and western markets through this community, and add largely to the business of our city. They ship all their supplies, provisions, produce, and groceries from here and most of their workmen are from here. We view the Sawmill of Durkee, Truesdell & Company as a model establishment in all respects."[186]

Gideon recruited his brother to become the mill's managing partner, and Levi Truesdell (1815–1887) sold his Portageville mercantile store to finance the deal. According to *Michigan's Historic and Eminent Men*, he was "brought up on a farm but left home when he was eighteen, and engaged as a clerk in a hotel where he remained for three years. With seventy-five dollars of savings, he began business in the small village of Portage, New York. He walked, one hundred miles to Rochester to purchase his first stock of merchandise, and from this small beginning his trade increased until he had a profitable business."[187]

Levi bought a 15% stake in the Durkee-Truesdell mill, became Superintendent of their property, and built a general store at his own expense that did about $20,000 ($2.4 million today) of business that first year.[188] His greatest asset would have been a mind that grasped things quickly, a genuine kindness, and his ability to remain calm.[189] He was widely respected, and according to the *Muskegon News & Reporter* he was "one of the foremost of Muskegon's upright businessmen."[190]

Somewhere along the way Levi learned double-entry accounting, where every financial entry has an equal and opposite effect on at least two different accounts, making it infinitely easier to balance the books. A lot of paperwork flowed through his office: production schedules, logging receipts, paperwork from the Muskegon Mill & Log Owners Association, bills of lading for dozens of ships, provisioning orders for the boarding house, hay and oats for the livestock, merchandise for the store, payrolls, and separate sets of books for different partnerships.

Once the mill was ready to begin manufacturing lumber, the most important positions that needed to be filled were the foreman and chief engineer. Throughout his career, Gideon had demonstrated an eye for talent, and several employees went on to become community leaders. William Glue, Mayor; Jacob Hetz, City Treasurer; Augustus Truesdell,

City Treasurer; Joseph Hackley, Village President and County Treasurer; Charles Hackley, Alderman; and James McGordon, Aldermen.

He made an exceptionally good choice when he hired forty-six year-old Joseph Hackley (1810–1874) to run the sawmill, despite having no experience, and yet for many years he ran a large and successful contracting business. As a young man, he worked as a carpenter during the summers and taught school during the winters. When he came to Kenosha, he established himself as a building contractor specializing in harbor work and roads.[191] Hackley knew at a glance how to hire reliable men, manage a crew, stay within budget, and get projects done on time. Those traits alone would have made him the right man for the job at the Durkee-Truesdell mill. In 1851 Kenosha raised $10,000 ($1.2 million today) for "rendering the harbor navigable," and he was given total charge. This major project was under his direction, and he was authorized to sign contracts, disburse funds, and supervise workers.[192]

His contracting firm specialized in "lake work." They built, repaired, and extended docks along with driving pilings into the ground for docks or to protect the shoreline from erosion due to the crashing waves. When the Southport & Beloit Road Company signed contracts, he won a bid to build a 20 mile section of road. Three years later when the three lakefront warehouses consolidated as the Kenosha Pier Company, he removed their three existing docks, and built a massive new dock with a railroad spur running down the middle.[193] This was major contracting work that required an engineering background.

Gideon had known him for several years dating back to when they traveled across the United States in 1849 looking for gold.[194] He was described by the *Muskegon Chronicle* as a man of "great industry and honesty who always retained the respect and confidence of his fellow citizens."[195] He was unpretentious, all business, and had a solid work ethic. A lazy employee wouldn't have lasted long working for him.

According to biographer Louis P. Haight, Joseph Hackley and Gideon Truesdell were "life-long friends" with similar personalities. Both were remembered as men who "carried their business in their hat," which meant they had total recall of facts and figures, and had excellent memories.[196]

Durkee, Truesdell & Company paid Joseph Hackley $1,000 a year, which was top-dollar, but his debts from his failed construction business were such that nearly all of his wages went to pay creditors over the next six years.[197] Biographers have written that he arrived in town broke, and he was definitely broke, but had work lined-up that paid a good wage. Had Hackley filed for bankruptcy he would have been much better off, but turning his back on his financial obligations would never have occurred to him.

The rise and fall of the Kenosha & Rockford ruined Joseph Hackley and hundreds of others. When he landed a large construction contract he needed a partner, and when he emptied the safe in the middle of the night and left town, Joseph Hackley was stuck with at least $5,000 ($600,000 today) of bills.[198] He paid every creditor in full over the next several years, and Joseph was remembered as a quiet, unpretentious man of few words. He also had an analytical mind, and thoroughly studied a problem and the character of the people involved. He knew at a glance what a person was all about, which gave him the wherewithal to run three sawmills and a shingle mill without any major problems. He was very good at hiring solid people.

Gideon hired thirty-one year-old William Glue (1826–1887) as their engineer. He had worked at the Ryerson & Morris mill and had a strong mechanical aptitude. According to one source he was "something of a philosopher," and patented a couple of sawmill devices. When Gideon's son married Sara Louisa Greene, William and Mary Glue were listed as witnesses.[199]

After becoming foreman, Joseph moved his family to Muskegon in installments. The first to arrive was Charley. He came during the spring of 1856, and spent the previous fall with his brother Edwin driving a wagon several miles between Harvey Durkees farm to his lakefront hay press.[200] What little money the family had came from their wages while their father was across Lake Michigan building a dock for the Durkee-Truesdell mill.

"Charley Hackley's father was boss.... and in the spring Charley came down from Kenosha, and his father fetched him up to me on the dock. He said 'this is my boy and I want you to teach him how to work' and he worked well too."[201]

A few months later the Challenge brought Joseph's wife, Salina, seventeen year-old son, Edwin, and seven year-old Porter. They moved into a couple of first-floor apartments at the Durkee-Truesdell boarding house that had been built for the mill's superintendent, foreman, and engineer with a separate entrance.[202]

Joseph Hackley (L), Salina Hackley (CL), and Levi Truesdell (CR), Luther Whitney (R). Pictures courtesy of the Muskegon Lakeshore Museum.

Each apartment had a bedroom and sitting room that was located in a separate wing on the first floor. Arthur Truesdell also recalled an upstairs alcove next to the main dining room, no doubt where the Truesdells, Hackleys, Trowbridges and their guests ate.[203] (All three families lived there.) There were 32 rooms on the third and fourth floors, each with a window with room for a bed, dresser, and a washstand with a porcelain bowl and a pitcher of water. If two men shared a room, and we know they boarded men from the two Trowbridge sawmills, there was enough room for them to live comfortably.

Upon seventeen year-old Edwin Hackley's (1838–1875) arrival he was put to work as a clerk at Gideon Truesdell's general store. A couple of years later when the economy improved, he began working in the Pomeroy & Holmes mill, and eventually supervised the day and night shifts.[204] His mother, Salina Hackley, helped support the family as "mistress" of the boarding house. She was described as 5 feet 3 inches tall, slim, and talkative.[205] She knew the business after having run a small boarding house in Kenosha, and she ran the Durkee-Truesdell boarding house with five full-time women in the kitchen along with two shifts of day laborers who lived elsewhere and washed dishes, pots, and pans.[206]

Muskegon consisted of three settlements carved-out of the woods along the shoreline, and although there was a lakeshore Indian path (Western Avenue), Charles Hackley recalled that it was faster to travel by canoe. There were a certain number of poor, neglected children running around "middle town," and Mrs. Hackley looked after them. After their chores were done, she organized games, and for many children who got lost in the shuffle she was the mother they never had. When she noticed that a child needed a jacket, clothing or shoes, she sent a list to her son Edwin at the Truesdell store.[207]

Every store in town was unfailingly generous to the needy, especially children, although if a man had nothing because he was a drunk or lazy, nobody lifted a finger to help.[208] Some of these down and outers were hired to clean-up the mill's yards, docks, and other menial jobs for which they were often given a bottle or liquor.

But generally speaking, those who could afford to be generous were, and the community looked after each other. Sawmill owner Chauncey Davis was particularly attentive to those in need. "When a case of destitution was discovered there would come a rap at the door and a basket of food would be dropped, and nobody ever knew where it came from. Major Davis was very generous and used to send loads of wood and such things."[209] When a sick employee ran out of money, Mr. Davis supported him until he recovered. "Finally, I came down sick. Major Davis did everything he could for me and said as long as I lived in Muskegon I would be provided for, and he was kind to me until the very last."[210]

Circular saws were becoming standard in modern, well-equipped mills because they squared a log efficiently and quickly. The block of wood was then fed into a gang saw with multiple blades that simultaneously milled it into 10 to 12 boards. A gang saw was so efficient that it cut the boards faster than a circular saw could square the next log. If they wanted to change production runs and cut larger boards or posts, the sawblades could be adjusted to accommodate this.

The men worked an exhausting 11.5-hour day, which was actually more like a 13-hour day because they weren't paid for breaks. It took about 15-minutes for the boilers to warm-up each morning, and once they were at full-power the engineer let out a blast of steam. A full-crew began working from 5:45 a.m. to 8:45 a.m., when the men took an unpaid 15-minute break while the maintenance crew cleaned the pitch from the blades. The men returned to their stations and resumed work from 9:00 a.m. to noon, when the men took another unpaid 30-minute lunch break while the blades were filed. The men walked to the boarding house for lunch, and were back to work from 12:30 to 3:30 p.m. After another unpaid 15-minute while the sawblades were filed, the men returned to work until 6:15 p.m. when their shift ended after a long, hard day of physical demanding labor.

Logs pulled from the sawmill's boom to sawing room by conveyor (L) and logs being squared by a circular saw (R). Picture courtesy of the Burton Historical Collection.

Gang Saw-squared logs were fed into multiple blades that simultaneously milled them into boards. Picture courtesy of the Burton Historical Collection.

In August of 1856 the Durkee-Truesdell mill began manufacturing lumber with thirty-five workers, but increased to fifty at the start of the next season, and one hundred during the war years when Gideon added a night shift.[211] Fifteen years earlier, the old sawmills could cut 450,000 feet a season, but with the latest technology the Durkee-Truesdell mill cut that in nine days. Right from the start their mill was one of the largest in the Midwest, and caught the attention of the *Chicago Tribune*, who on August 14, 1857 published the following article.

"A BIG RUN-Last week the firm of Durkee, Truesdell & Company tallied the amount of lumber sawed in the course of twenty-four hours at their new saw mill. The result exceeded all expectations and will give some idea to the reader of the amount of lumber this firm will turn out in the course of a year.

"Of lumber they sawed the prodigious number of 60,072 feet; of lath 25,200 feet together with a number of pickets not tallied. Now making allowance for the fact that they ran a little faster than they are wont to generally, but an average in round numbers of 50,000 feet daily. In the course of a year, they will have sawed the enormous amount of 15,650,000 feet of lumber. The lath produces a total of 7,887,600 feet.

"This will give the reader a faint idea of the business of this firm, but to truly appreciate it he must first step down into the mill, and make the acquaintance of its courteous and intelligent chief engineer, Mr. Glue, who will escort you around showing and explaining to you everything of interest about its complicated machinery, making it as simple as clockwork."[212]

The process began when a tugboat towed a raft of logs from the booming company's "storage grounds" in the middle of Muskegon Lake, where logs owned by each sawmill were chained together and stored until called for. Each mill had their own holding pen next to their dock, and the outside crew pushed the logs onto a conveyor that brought them to a second-floor sawing room. They were pulled onto a carriage where the log was locked into place, and a sawyer moved the log into a circular sawblade. Once the log was squared it was fed into the gang saw. The Durkee-Truesdell mill was powered by two steam engines weighing 26-tons each, with boilers that transferred power to the saws upstairs through a series of pulleys and belts. One boiler powered two enormous gang saws, and the other powered 24 edgers and trimmers.

A gang saw cut 12 boards simultaneously and once the boards exited the machinery, they were slid to a row of edging saws where the sides were cut to length, and then to a row of trimmers that cut each board to a standard 16 foot length. A large tonnage of lumber was moved downward through the milling process using gravity.

Lumber from the sawing floor slid down a chute to the dock below where it was stacked by four to six dock workers. Prices for different grades fluctuated from $8 to $12 so sorting the boards by grade was important to a mill's bottom line. When Gideon began running the sawmill around the clock, he had two enormous docks that extended over 1,000-feet above the water. This eliminated a bottleneck when the lumber was coming out of the mill faster than schooners were clearing the docks.

Rainy weather or windy days didn't slow the number of boards coming down the chutes from the second-floor sawing floor, because the sawmill rarely closed. There were only so many days in the season before the sawmill closed for the winter, and we know from tax records that Gideon ran each sawmill at maximum capacity.[213] During stormy weather the dock workers wore slickers, and one way or another the lumber got stacked on the dock for that day.

Durkee-Truesdell mill looking north: the smaller addition was where they turned scrap into pickets and lath. Picture courtesy of the Lakeshore Museum Center.

Logs being pulled from the mill's holding pen to the second-floor sawing room by an endless chain powered by one of the steam engines. Picture courtesy of the Burton Historical Collection.

Sawmill boilers and sawdust chutes from the 24 saws and two gang saws upstairs in the sawing floor. Picture courtesy of the Burton Historical Collection.

The layout of a sawmill was designed so they didn't have to move thousands of boards more than once. It all began when logs were pulled to the second-floor sawing room by a conveyor that was designed in Muskegon. Once the logs were turned into lumber the boards slid down a gravity chute to the dock, where workers stacked them onto horse-drawn carts that brought them down a long dock where they were cross-stacked. Unusually long piers extended over Muskegon Lake where as much as 700,000 feet of lumber (1,600 tons) were stacked waiting for the next schooner. According to the *Chicago Commercial Letter*, a commodities newspaper, Gideon kept at least nine schooners sailing between his sawmills and Chicago wholesale yards.

Sometimes a steam whistle from a passing steamer spooked the horses pulling the lumber carts down the dock. When that happened, they had a tendency to charge ahead, pulling the cart over the edge of the dock and into the water.[214] The weight of the lumber cart and the animals pulled both to the bottom on Muskegon Lake. At that point, somebody had to dive into the water, attach ropes to the dead animals, and pull them out of the water using a cargo boom.

Slabs of bark from the circular saw were slid down a chute in the back of the mill where they were stacked along Western Avenue, and by the end of the season they filled several lots. This scrap had value, but not much, and was sold as boiler fuel. The last ships of the season hauled these slabs to factories in Chicago and sold them by the cargo lot as winter fuel.

Docks adjacent to sawmills served as a temporary lumberyard until the next schooner arrived. Pictures courtesy of the Indiana History Center.

Mills with older upright saws where a single blade cut boards from a log had enough play in the blade to leave the board with a washboard cut.[215] Boards like this were sold as construction grade lumber but for a lower dollar. A mill with modern high-speed saws could produce uniform lumber with standard widths and a relatively smooth finish, which permitted a mill to charge a higher price because all a carpenter had to do was cut each board to length.

Each of the 26 saws inside the Durkee-Truesdell sawmill had ductwork that sucked the sawdust into iron bins downstairs behind each of the boilers. The steam engines that ran the saws were fueled by sawdust, and shoveling sawdust into the boilers was a tough job due to the heat and repetitive nature of the work.

Forty years later, the *Muskegon Chronicle* ran articles about the early years, and a couple of Durkee-Truesdell employees contributed. Laurence Flary recalled that the mill ran night and day, each crew working twelve hours. "We received $26 a month and board in the boarding house. The fare was good. On Sundays we rested.

"We had neither a fire department nor water works in those days, and if there happened to be a fire, they put the men in a row from the lake to the fire, and passed pails of water up the line until they had the fire out. With the exception of Pine Street and the road along the shore, the streets ran among the stumps. It was all very well during the daytime, when a man could see to go among the stumps, but at night it had to be moonlight to travel those streets."[216]

Many Durkee-Truesdell employees lived in Kenosha but worked at the mill from March through October. Despite extremely high property taxes, people wanted stay in Kenosha so their children could get a free education. Sometimes an employee sent an envelope with cash aboard the next schooner to Kenosha, where it was brought to Gideon's office.[217] An employees wife would then pick-up the envelope so she had enough money to buy groceries or pay rent. Before Lake Michigan began to freeze, employees caught a ride on the Challenge back home where they lived through the off-season with their families on their accumulated savings.

Some mill employees found winter work chopping-down trees in the woods, but the other employees had their bags packed, and left the boarding house in less than an hour. The clock was ticking, because once the mill closed, they needed to leave by noon the following day or they were charged for another day of room and board. Every sawmill was strict about this because unmarried workers had a tendency to freeload as long as they could get away with it.

Durkee-Truesdell employee Michael Sullivan recalled many years later that, "times were good and wages fair. I got $26 ($2,900 today) a month and board. I had to run to the boarding house...there were men who thought if they did not get to the table first, they would not stand much of a show. Generally, we had beef, pork, or potatoes and beans besides bread, pie, and cake. It was as good as we get now. I think most of it was salt meat...they used to put up a good chuck and plenty of it."[218]

George F. Graves recalled that the lumbermill ran a 12-hour shift that started at 6 a.m. and ended at 6 p.m. with an hour off for lunch—down the road at the boarding house. Employees were paid $1 ($10 today) a day with room and board included.[219]

The men running circular saws earned twice as much as common labors because it was considered skilled work. An incompetent sawyer could wreck a lot of lumber and destroy expensive blades. Due to primitive metallurgy, the blades were brittle and could shatter and snap into several pieces with flying metal slicing-open an arm of taking-out an eye.

It was hard physical work. "We were glad to sleep when we weren't at work…it was awfully bad working in the mills in those days because we had to do everything by hand."[220]

Given the pressure to produce maximum output, it was inevitable that men fed some of their own blood and bone into the saws. Due to the hazards of working around dangerous machinery, drinking or hangovers was grounds for termination, and yet hangovers and drinking were common in every sawmill. But it's doubtful that Joseph Hackley allowed anyone with a hang-over to finish his shift.

Durkee, Truesdell & Company, Chicago Lumber Dealers

Sawmills didn't generate the largest profits but were the vital link between the pinelands and lumberyards. The largest profits came from the ownership of pinelands or at the wholesale end of the business. In 1856, Chicago replaced Albany as the world's largest lumber market, and that year Durkee, Truesdell & Company opened a wholesale lumberyard on the Chicago River to sell the output from their mills.

With twenty-eight railroads passing through Chicago, a retail lumberyard owner from the western territories could come to town, buy a thousand feet for $10, pay $4 for shipping, and sell it for around $60 ($7,200 today) back home. It was a seller's market, and Durkee, Truesdell & Company quickly established themselves as players in the Chicago market.

Durkee, Truesdell & Company also bought lumber by the shipload from other sawmills at the wholesale dock at the confluence of the Chicago River, something they had been doing on a much smaller scale at their Kenosha yards.[221] Once a lumber dealer bought a shipload of lumber it was towed to his yard, unloaded, seasoned for 6-weeks, and then shipped by rail to retail yards in the western territories.

The two largest exporters of lumber were Green Bay sawmills which accounted for 14% of the Chicago market, with 18% coming from Muskegon.[222] About two-thirds of the lumber sold through Chicago came from smaller, undercapitalized sawmills that were always on the look-out for a fast sale so they could pay their bills.

Shoestring operators lived on the ragged-edge with past-due mortgages, taxes, payrolls, and other expenses. For undercapitalized mills, regardless of how many schooners came down the Chicago River loaded with lumber, there was always someone willing to pay cash for their lumber, even for sap-infested lumber or boards full of knot-holes.

Since so much of the lumber from Lake Michigan sawmills ended-up in St. Louis, lumber dealers in that city had a dream of building a canal that by-passed Chicago. This never happened, but they wanted to cut-out the Chicago middlemen who made a fortune handling the lumber before it reached them.[223] A Chicago, Burlington & Quincy's superintendent was 100% correct when he said retail lumberyards in Kansas City, "get their lumber from Chicago because they cannot get it any other way."[224]

The North American lumber market revolved around a 200-foot wharf at the foot of Franklin Street at the confluence of the north and south branches of the Chicago River. This is where schooners carrying lumber from hundreds of mills docked looking for a buyer, and once they struck a deal with a lumber dealer the ship was towed to his yard.

When the lumber dealers out-grew their yards at the confluence of the rivers, the Galena, Burlington & Quincy began developing vacant land for a new lumber district downriver, realizing that in less than five years every parcel of land could be rented at top dollar.

This is where Durkee, Truesdell & Company leased several acres at 17 Lumber Street next to Alvah Trowbridges yard, which Alvah might have sublet from them, because a financial outlay in a high-rent district wouldn't have made sense for him. A sub-lease would have been a clever way for Gideon to defray his rent. Selling a shipload of lumber at the wholesale dock was hit or miss, and depended on how many schooners pulled in ahead of you.

The lumber that wasn't sold to local factories was shipped by rail to customers west of the Mississippi River. Every wholesale yard had a riverfront dock where lumber was unloaded and seasoned since it was shipped green, and six-weeks later loaded aboard a train that would deliver it to buyers in the western territories. Each day the yard's foreman would have ordered the required number of boxcars for the next day's shipments, which were towed to the yard's railroad spur for loading. The railroads wouldn't allow lumberyard employees to load their boxcars, because their people could pack them much tighter, and charged the yard 10¢ ($12 today) per thousand feet for this service.

A Chicago lumber dealer could ship anywhere east of the Missouri River by paying the railroad a flat rate of $4 ($46 today) per 1,000 feet of lumber or roughly 130 boards measuring 16-feet. If the buyer had a good credit rating from R.G. Dun & Company or John Bradstreet & Company, his order was shipped by rail with nothing down but payable in 30-, 60-, and 90- day installments with shipping fees paid in advance.

Schooner Okanagan unloading lumber using the ships winch and pulleys for the sails as a cargo boom.

Lumber district where wholesale yards stockpiled over 300,000 feet of lumber - Schooner Resumption unloading lumber. Pictures courtesy of the Milwaukee Public Library, Runge Collection.

When Durkee, Truesdell & Company opened their yard in 1856, they sent their thirty-three year-old partner, Charles Deming (1828–1912), to run a business where they expected to double their money on every shipload of lumber they bought.[225] We know that Deming brought along his twenty year-old cousin, Benjamin Franklin Deming (1836–1910) to act as his inspector at the wholesale dock.[226] A lot of smaller mills tried to cheat the wholesale yard but lumber dealers knew every trick in the book otherwise they would have gone bankrupt years ago.

When a schooner docked; Frank Deming climbed through the cargo holds to make sure cheap grades weren't buried beneath top grades to improve the over-all price. Once the schooner docked, about eight "dock wallopers," mostly Irish immigrants, unloaded the ship board by board at lightning speed, and they could unload roughly 7,200 boards in about twenty minutes.

Schooner being unloaded by dock workers in Chicago. Picture courtesy of the Chicago History Center.

Boxcar being loaded by yard employees.
Picture courtesy of the Walker J. Cummings Collection.

The Chicago partnership needed a lot of money to buy lumber by the shipload, but after four incredibly profitable years, Durkee, Truesdell & Company could afford to open a wholesale yard. Harvey Durkee, Gideon Truesdell, Charles Durkee, and Charles Deming could each layout at least $2,500 ($300,000 today) each to get things started, because that's about what it took to lease a Chicago River lumber yard, hire workers, and start buying shiploads of lumber for cash.[227]

When it came to borrowing money to fund the purchases of lumber, Durkee, Truesdell & Company seemed to have had no difficulty borrowing from people they knew, and paid them 12% interest. Rather than using their own money, the partners preferred to use somebody elses so they could invest their money elsewhere at a higher rate of return. Banks didn't pay much on balances, so businessmen with funds to invest were likely candidates for loaning them money. We don't know if they paid a flat 12%, the highest rate allowed by law, or if the lender was able to invest in a contract where six or more shiploads had been packaged together with a payout of around 30% interest.

One of the biggest complaints from mills was the low-price Chicago lumber dealers paid at the wholesale dock, which is why the larger mills had their own wholesale yards. If you were a small sawmill using a rented schooner, it was nearly impossible to get a better price when there were over 300-million feet of lumber (1,500 shiploads) sitting in yards along the river. Lumber dealers always kept a buffer to fill thousands of orders just in case weather slowed shipments from the mills, but it also gave them the upper-hand when negotiating prices because they had so much inventory. They could go for a month without buying a single board and still have enough lumber to fill orders from what was sitting in their yards.

A bigger problem for sawmills was over-production. When undercapitalized mills sent as much lumber as they could to generate cashflow, they inadvertently drove prices downward when supply far exceeded demand, and about two-thirds of the mills on Lake Michigan were smaller mills. One might think it was easy to sell lumber in Chicago, but with so many wholesale lumberyards competing for the same customers, cut-throat pricing was always a problem, which kept the price they paid sawmills low. That's why every mill that had the financial wherewithal opened their own Chicago lumberyard.

It took a talented salesman to sell lumber at a higher price than competitors, and nobody did it better than Williams, Ryerson & Company or Charles Mears & Company. "Mr. Williams had the reputation of being the best salesman in the Chicago market, and it was claimed that he could secure better prices for the same grade of product than any other man. His success in building up a Western and Southwestern trade was phenomenal… his trade with St. Louis merchants was the envy of competitors."[228] Williams was so good at moving inventory that Ryerson paid him over $6,000 ($760,000 today) a year in commissions.[229]

Saloons, Whorehouses and Loggers

When Durkee, Truesdell & Company came to Muskegon, it was a quiet town on the verge of becoming one of the largest lumber manufacturing regions in the country. The peaceful years gave way to rougher times, because in 1857 a Protestant minister counted 84 "grog shops or liquor groceries," a tad on the high side for a town of 2,000.[230]

After working a backbreaking twelve-hour shift in the sawmills or booming grounds, the men needed a place to unwind. A night of drinking was how a lot of them kept their sanity; but the spring log drive brought a different type of customer into the saloons. They were young men from the forests along the Muskegon River with a winter's pay in their pockets and a thirst for rock-gut liquor, crooked card games and loose women.

There were two basic types of loggers. Married or those saving their pay so they could get married, and those who were single and poor candidates for matrimony. Married or engaged workers had a greater purpose in life and what logging camps were looking to hire. They were good workers, and a few years later were able to buy land for farming, whereas single men went through their pay like a drunken sailor. They blew their entire pay in about two-weeks.

"I have seen men in camps so mean and penurious that they would pull threads out of an old coffee sack to mend their worn-out socks. Half-sole a sock with a mit, and mit with a sock. Go to their work poorly clad, and suffer the worst pains and penalties the woods could inflict. Borrow, beg and steal tobacco to keep their van bill down, and all to have a big stake in the spring. And when camp breaks up, they go to town.

"First, he rigs himself out in a new suit of clothes and sports a cheap watch and ring, and possibly a pair of patent leather shoes. He then meets a chum, and together they make for the low boarding houses. The hard-earned dollars roll away, till in ten days or two weeks at the most all the boy's money is gone. His watch and ring are gone. The side is out of his new shoe. His coat is torn down the back...watching for some acquaintance to pass from whom he may borrow enough money to get him back to camp."[231]

Men working the log drives were mostly in their late teens or early twenties. The work was very physical and dangerous, and they had to be in peak physical condition to jump from log-to-log as they steered them downriver. For every logger killed by falling limbs in the woods, even more died on the spring log drive.

Saloons were tolerated because loggers came to Muskegon with a winter's pay burning a hole in their pockets. "There was no written law for the place then, and if a man deserved a thrashing, he got it, and that was the end of that."[232] After a few weeks of drinking, fighting and whoring, the town got a significant cash infusion that trickled through the economy.[233]

"My earliest recollection of Muskegon dates back to 1857.... I came from Grand Haven and the stage consisted of a lumber wagon with boards across for seats and without any springs. The road lay through the swamp between here and Grand Haven. We went into a water hole some two or three feet deep, which was too much for iron and wood to stand and we broke our axle. We went down into the water, and from there we walked into Muskegon.

"It was Saturday night.... and after getting up and looking around a little I discovered there was considerable excitement on the street. It turned out that the big drive had just got down. There were perhaps about a hundred drunken men within the space of a single block, in all stages of drunkenness from silly drunk, roaring drunk, fighting drunk, to dead drunk scattered along the street. That continued for three or four days before things quieted down again.

"I expected that the next day the justices' offices would be full of complaints, but not a single complaint was made. The big drive, though somewhat unruly when it got down here for the first few days, was really a necessary institution to Muskegon. We had sawmills down here and the sawmills must have logs, logs must have drivers, and when the drivers got done, they must have drink, and no one complained."[234]

Some of the loggers said they could smell "Muskegon rot-gut" fifty miles away, and the perfume worn by the ugly but friendly "waiter girls" in the saloons.[235] Among the more colorful characters was the proprietor of a Muskegon whorehouse named Big Delia, who at 6'2", tipped the scales at over 250 pounds, chewed Hiawatha tobacco and had a permanent sneer on her ugly face.[236] When a logger refused to remove his muddy boots before entering her run-down dive she slugged him with a powerful roundhouse that broke his jaw.[237]

The Dynamite Saloon in "sawdust flats" was a different type of place, and catered to booming company workers that were underachievers, malcontents or older men that never grew up.[238] They used dozens of tricks to fleece their clientele, from crooked card games to cheap liquor and prostitutes that had to kick-back as much as 80% of their earnings to theowner.[239]

The Canterbury House, which was on the outskirts of the village, was run by Mollie Garde and Jennie Morgan, a couple of tough old whores.[240] They had gambling tables, a dance hall, stage for burlesque shows with an orchestra pit, bar room, and 36 rooms on the second floor they rented to working girls. The only rule was that the "mark" never left with a nickel in his pocket.

Chicago's lumber district also had its share of lively figures, and the meanest by far was "Gentle Anne Stafford, the fattest brothel keeper in Chicago." She was anything but gentle, and cleared out the Prairie Queen when one of her girls defected to a competitor.[241] Her nickname was a joke; Annie had a reputation for beating the hell out of people at the slightest provocation.

The Prairie Queen was several notches above Stafford's place, and according to one source, Annes girl left for better pay and a new dress.

Richard C. Fritz   193

This caused several Madames to retaliate lest their girls get any ideas. They staged a surprise attack on the Prairie Queen, breaking down the front door, busting-up the furniture, chasing away customers, beating-up several girls, and kicking the hell out of Madame Herrick. When the brawl was over "Gentle Anne" straightened her cheap wig, and drove the rest of her girls through the streets back to her brothel like a herd of cattle.[242]

The plight of women in those days was pretty dismal unless they found a husband, and yet for many wives the happiest day was when the undertaker took her husband away. There were so many single women that their wages were low, whether in a saloon or as domestic help in a home. This made it easy for a moderately successful man to staff his residence with servants, and difficult for the servant to ever improve her circumstances unless she found a husband, preferably a rich one.

Having been raised in wealthy home, Harvey Durkees wife, Martha, ran their large home with a domestic staff. A cook worked a 12-hour shift in the kitchen; a scullery maid did nothing but scrub pots, pans, and wash dishes; a maid was responsible for the cleanliness of the house; and a laundress scrubbed clothes and linens by hand with a washboard. The servants lived in small third floor attic rooms away from the family with a separate staircase to the kitchen.

The Truesdell residence on the opposite end of the City Park had its own wing at the back of the house for servants, with a kitchen on the first floor, and servants' quarters upstairs. Every residence had a coach house where horses, carriages, and feed were kept. The chauffer lived upstairs with the horses and carriages below. When the liveryman wasn't driving Gideon or Julia, he washed carriages, groomed the horses, shoveled snow, cut grass, brought firewood into the house, built fires in each of the 8-fireplaces, and late in the afternoon lit the oil chandeliers, table lamps, and wall sconces. It was a comfortable life, and Gideon and Julia had come a long way since their days on the Wisconsin River.

Collapse of Durkee, Truesdell & Company, 1857

When the Kenosha & Rockford ran out of money, Gideon left the board of directors, and probably had no idea when the railroad would be completed.

Things were very strained at their Muskegon mill during their first year of manufacturing. They were over-extended with cash-flow problems, and their foreman, Joseph Hackley, quit, and became Superintendent of the Muskegon Log & Mill Owners Association. His departure would have been a serious blow to the Durkee-Truesdell mill.

Things continued to unravel when the economy crashed in September, and it was a severe and prolonged crash. It was later determined that the recession was caused by several underlying factors, but a railroad debt secured by depreciating land values and weak banking regulations caused most of the damage. The Illinois Central, Erie, Pittsburgh, Fort Wayne & Chicago, and Reading Railroad lines were forced to shut-down due to a significant drop in business. Other railroads were bankrupted or merged with solvent railroads, and the Kenosha & Rockford was in serious trouble.

That fall there were hundreds of runs on banks, with nervous depositors standing in lines for hours to exchange currency printed by the bank for gold or silver coins. The collapse of the national economy caused over 1,400 state banks to fail, and pulled over 5,000 businesses into bankruptcy.

Unemployment soared; railroads went bankrupt, factories closed, businesses had to sell inventory at a loss so they could pay past-due bills, land values crashed, and the working man struggled to put food on the table. Uncertainty swept the country with bankers calling loans, interest rates rising, and speculators finding it impossible to sell their real estate holdings without taking a loss. The economy was bloated with debt from reckless railroad expansion, easy-credit government land sales, and unsound banking practices.

The "Panic of 1857" was deep and prolonged with numerous runs on banks due to a fear that depositors would lose their savings, or get stuck with bank notes of little value. Warehouse owner George Bennett, a director of the City Bank of Kenosha, singlehandedly stopped a run. When depositors began to panic, he walked into the banks crowded lobby carrying a couple of bags with $5,000 ($700,000 today) of gold double-eagle coins, and announced he was depositing all of it.[243] The following day, deposits increased by $16,000 ($1.9 million today) when people realized that the bank wasn't remotely close to going under.[244]

The panic had a devastating impact in Chicago when money stopped circulating. After 53 burglaries in a single week, the *Chicago Tribune* declared that the city "was at the mercy of the criminal class."[245] A gang of grave robbers raided the Old Catholic Burying Ground north of the city, opening graves so they could steal bodies and sell them to medical schools.

Ninety days after the crash, Harvey Durkee and Gideon Truesdell realized they needed to dissolve their partnerships in Kenosha, Muskegon, and Chicago. This would have limited future liability. It also gave Harvey Durkee and Gideon Truesdell time re-organize, and tap into their savings to pay creditors because they were suddenly deeply in debt.

The *Kenosha Tribune & Telegraph* published the following: "DISSOLUTION. The co-partnership heretofore existing between the undersigned, under the name and style of Durkee, Truesdell & Company, is hereby dissolved by mutual consent. All debts and demands owing to said firm must be paid to Harvey Durkee, who is alone authorized to settle the affairs of the firm, and use the name of said firm to liquidation. Harvey Durkee, Gideon Truesdell, Charles Deming, and Charles Durkee. Dated: December 11th 1857."[246]

We know the Muskegon partnership was in trouble before the crash, and Levi Truesdell no doubt realized they had acquired an overwhelming debt-load from expanding too quickly, a common affliction for aggressive businesses.[247] They needed to reorganize with more capital, but Levi decided to assign his shares to his brother, and return to his thriving mercantile business in Portageville when the person who bought his business defaulted.

The solution to Durkee, Truesdell & Company's cash-flow problems was finding a new partner who could invest $10,000 ($600,000 today), or for the existing partners to contribute more capital. Throughout 1857 they were chronically short of money with past-due bills lapsing into default. When Gideon loaned the partnership money, he took the precaution of filing liens, and when the partnership failed it gave him the leverage he needed to negotiate with creditors.[248]

When Levi Truesdell left the partnership, Gideon bought the general store he built across the road from the sawmill. One of the many casualties of the panic was the Pomeroy, Lewis & Holmes mill, who had leased Durkee-Truesdell's Kenosha lumberyard and bought a Muskegon mill from them.

After leveraging assets to buy more assets, the panic nearly bankrupted Harvey Durkee when creditors filed dozens of liens. A wheeler-dealer juggling several balls at the same time, he had more than doubled his net worth during the 1850s. In addition to sub-dividing thousands of acres with his brother, Harvey owned one of the largest farms in Wisconsin and a controlling interest in Forsyth Scales, and was a stockholder and treasurer in the Northwestern Insurance Company.[249] Before the panic, his net worth was comfortably in the $100,000 ($13.6 million today) range, with most of it invested in land that couldn't immediately be turned into cash.[250] When the market crashed the partners placed the following notice in the *Chicago Tribune*:

> "The Co-partnership heretofore existing between the undersigned, under the name and style of Durkee, Truesdell & Company is hereby dissolved by mutual consent. All debts and demands owing to the firm must be paid to Harvey Durkee, who is alone authorized to settle the affairs of said firm, and to use the name of said firm in liquidation. Harvey Durkee, Gideon Truesdell, Charles Deming, Charles Durkee."[251]

The crash caused shipments from Chicago lumberyards to drop by 40% from 444-million feet to 268 the following year. When prices dropped by 60% the panic hit the lumber business particularly hard. The signs were there but nobody wanted to think about a total collapse of the lumber business.

On September 1, 1857 three schooners from a Wisconsin sawmill loaded with flooring, fencing, and siding arrived at the wholesale dock. They sold everything at $14 per thousand feet.[252] The following week, three more ships arrived with flooring and siding but couldn't find a buyer, and sat there for four-days because lumber wasn't selling at any price. Every wholesale and retail yard had a glut of lumber sitting in their yards.

The Kenosha partnership was dangerously over-extended with about $8,000 ($1.2 million today) of notes falling due.[253] Whereas Harvey Durkee had a much larger net worth, Gideon was eminently more solvent due to his conservative investments.[254] Whereas Harvey Durkee was always looking to maximize his investment, Gideon was satisfied making a safe 10% return on loans secured by ample collateral.

When they couldn't pay the mortgage on their freight yard adjacent to the Milwaukee & Chicago depot, they lost a valuable parcel of real estate through foreclosure.[255] Evidently Gideon believed he needed somebody from outside of Kenosha to represent him should things continue to deteriorate. He retained Henry Blodgett, a high-powered Chicago attorney who had an office sixteen miles south of Kenosha in Waukegan, Illinois.[256] It was the beginning of a friendship with somebody who had known Abraham Lincoln from his Illinois circuit court days, and was on a first-name basis with him.[257]

Blodgett & Winston was a premier law firm that represented every major railroad passing through Chicago.[258] Their greatest asset was their political contacts inside the Illinois statehouse, and their ability to walk sweetheart legislation through both houses.

A smaller office, Blodgett & Upton, was located in the sleepy little town of Waukegan where Blodgett lived.[259] During the 1860 presidential race, Abraham Lincoln spent the night at Henry and Althea Blodgett's residence, which was also a stop in the Underground Railroad.[260] Blodgett's law firm had a lot of clients in Kenosha, and their job was to protect Truesdell's assets from creditors, because in those days a partner was responsible for what the other partners couldn't pay.[261]

Gideon was in a much stronger position and had significant cash reserves.[262] We know from court records that when the economy collapsed, he had his money invested in one, two, and three year mortgages in $1,000 ($125,000 today) increments.[263] If the borrower defaulted, he could seize land, crops, or a business that generated an income while he looked for a buyer for the property.

Like other warehouse owners who dealt in large numbers, Harvey Durkee and Gideon would have kept bags of gold coins with as much as $10,000 ($1.2 million today) sitting in a safe at his office or at the City Bank of Kenosha. At a time when money stopped circulating, we know Gideon was paying his employees in gold coins.[264] During the worst of times he had $1,200 ($145,000 today) available to upgrade the saws at the Trowbridge & Wing mill at a time when currency stopped circulating.

Most sawmills and lumberyards didn't survive the crash, but by 1859 the stronger ones resumed operations. Durkee, Truesdell & Company didn't exactly fail but they certainly weren't solvent, and on April 14, 1858 they went into liquidation.[265] The snag was Harvey Durkee. Once he assigned his shares to Gideon, creditors were willing to strike a deal with him because he had dependable cash-flow from investments, and presumably a clean balance sheet. The Muskegon partnership was deeply in debt, and it appears as if Gideon was reluctant to loan them a dime or pay creditors until he had total ownership of the sawmill.

The other problem the partnership faced was that their $56,000 ($6.7 million today) mill was worth about a third less when the economy crashed, and if Gideon took control of the mill, he needed concessions from the creditors that gave him room to maneuver in a bad economy. After two-months of negotiations the creditors came to an agreement, and

Gideon agreed to pay Durkee-Truesdell creditors "dollar for dollar."[266] He eventually paid them in full with interest without declaring bankruptcy. Notably, one of the largest creditors was Gideon.[267]

Perhaps the most critical problem was $8,000 ($1.2 million today) of promissory notes that were called when the economy crashed. Based on court documents from the Towslee vs. Durkee et al suit, we know that as early as 1855, they borrowed heavily to fund cash-flow from City Bank of Kenosha with Harvey Durkee and Gideon Truesdell's signatures securing the loans.[268]

As of October 15, 1857, their outstanding balance with the City Bank of Kenosha were $4,000 ($480,000 today) but nobody seemed concerned.[269] But when the market crashed, Harvey Durkee and Gideon Truesdell owed a significant amount of money because they had 14 demand notes that had been called by the bank.[270]

By paying the interest plus a 1% override fee, Harvey got a 30-day extension on $3,300 ($396,000 today) of their paper, which probably gave him time to pull the rest of the money together.[271] When their account was paid-in-full, he got a nasty surprise when he discovered the bank had charged them 26.7% interest or $841.71 ($100,000 today).[272] By pyramiding fees and exchange rates, the City Bank of Kenosha charged them nearly three times the legal interest rate allowable by state law. Many banks got away with this by manipulating exchange fees on idle balances in correspondent banks in New York, Philadelphia, or Cleveland.

The City Bank of Kenosha kept funds deposited in eastern banks to speed-up clearing checks, and the system was rigged due to a loophole that didn't immediately force banks to redeem their notes unless they were presented in person. This allowed them to sit on large sums of money interest-free, and earn a point or two on what was called "idle balances." This made it easy to exceed the 10% interest rate allowed by law, and it was something nearly every bank did because it was one of the tricks of the trade they used to improve their bottom line.

Harvey Durkee, who sued people at the drop of a hat, filed a lawsuit against the City Bank of Kenosha. The *Wisconsin Free Democrat* wrote that, "Harvey Durkee, of Kenosha, has instituted a lawsuit against the City Bank of Kenosha to determine the question whether the mode some banks have of taking notes payable in New York City, and charging the difference in exchange, realizing 25 to 30% per annum on their accommodations, is usury or not."[273] Oddly enough, Harvey was a stockholder who had previously sat on the board of directors of that bank, and was partners with Samuel Hale and Henry Towslee in the Kenosha Pier Company.

According to Wisconsin law, a bank was permitted to charge no more than 10% interest, but an individual loaning his own money could charge 12%. But banks figured a way to skirt the law and charge what amounted to usury rates. A January 29, 1859 *Daily Milwaukee News* said that Durkee, Truesdell & Company was suing for thousands of dollars of illegal fees.[274]

They lost in the lower courts until their high-profile case reached the Wisconsin Supreme Court: "One filed by former Governor Leonard Farwell against a Madison bank and one filed by Senator Durkee and his partners against a Kenosha bank to recover thousands of dollars of excess fees over the legal rate of interest."[275]

Orson S. Head represented Durkee, Truesdell & Company. He was a brilliant attorney with a quick mind and superb oratory skills with an imposing baritone voice reminiscent of his great grandson, Orson Welles. He contended that the City Bank of Kenosha was purposely vague when stating the terms of the loan and interest rates. Furthermore, there was no way for Harvey Durkee or Gideon Truesdell to have known the actual interest rate or why a New York rate applied.[276] They probably thought they were borrowing short-term funds at 10% interest. There was further confusion over the number of notes that had been paid-off, exchange rates, interest on outstanding loans, and other fees.

When they rolled over existing notes and added new ones, Harvey Durkee and Gideon Truesdell presumed they were signing them under identical terms. Although they agreed to pay an exchange rate if applicable, they figured that since none of their notes were cashed in New York, the East Coast rate wouldn't apply.[277] But with a correspondent bank in New York, the City Bank of Kenosha was able to manipulate charging Durkee, Truesdell & Company a hefty over-ride fee on checks from Harrison Durkees Wall Street office.[278]

The Wisconsin Supreme Court ruled that since the president of the City Bank of Kenosha was a lawyer; he knew what he was doing and each note constituted a "corrupt agreement."[279] They got around the maximum interest by stipulating that Durkee, Truesdell & Company would pay a New York exchange rate when applicable, with the bank deciding when that occurred.[280]

The Court ruled when payment is due a New York bank at the highest allowable rate in Wisconsin, and when its understood by both parties that the notes would *not* be cashed in New York then the bank's intent was to defraud and cheat the borrower.[281] In 1861, Durkee, Truesdell & Company won a $2,806 ($336,000 today) judgment.[282]

The crash hit the partnership hard, and was a mess because Harvey Durkee and Gideon Truesdell leveraged their Kenosha property to borrow some of the money used to build their Muskegon mill. It's difficult to determine what the Muskegon partnership owed but at some point, they turned the heavily indebted property over to Gideon Truesdell.[283]

On April 14, 1858, Harvey signed-over his interest in Durkee, Truesdell & Company's Muskegon partnership to Gideon, which cleared the way for Gideon to pledge his unencumbered assets as security to creditors.[284]

When Alva Trowbridge defaulted on the Trowbridge & Wing mortgage he didn't wait for a lawsuit, and signed over the deed to Gideon along with several lots and a general store that had just been built but not stocked.[285] Trowbridge had built this mill with a $3,550 ($420,000 today) loan from Truesdell dated on January 6, 1855.[286] Most of the loan was secured by a Kenosha farm, 80-acres on Newaygo Road, 14-lots across from the mill site, and a sawmill that had yet to be built.[287]

Once he took ownership of the Trowbridge & Wing mill, Gideon spent $1,200 ($145,000 today) to install a circular saw with a separate boiler.[288] This increased their output from about 18,000 feet per day to 28,000 with another 6,000 feet of lath made from scraps. This confirms that after the financial crash, even with the Durkee-Truesdell mill's financial problems, Gideon wasn't down to his last dollar. Upgrading the saws paid for itself during their first year, because another 10,000 feet per day translated into an extra 432,000 feet per season, and added another $3,888 ($465,000 today) to the mill's top line.

On September 7, 1859 Harvey Durkee transferred 147 lots in Durkees Addition to Gideon for a dollar, which looked like an ordinary transfer where he cancelled debts in exchange for land.[289] But, according to court records, on the same date Gideon sold $5,000 worth of these lots back to him. The following year, Gideon paid $11,000 ($1.3 million today) for all of the lots which suggest he was concealing assets or clearing liens.[290]

Only a few Muskegon sawmills resumed operations in 1859 because the market was still glutted with lumber. Barter ruled the economy, and most mills were so hard-pressed for cash that they paid their men in scrip.

Depending on the reputation of the person issuing the scrip it could be traded around town like cash. Gideon paid his men the difference between their wages and room and board at his boarding house in gold coins that he had sitting in a safe.[291]

The credit-reporting agencies knew little about Gideon Truesdell, which might have been what he preferred. Then as now, businessmen didn't want people poking around their finances.[292] Lumbermen were notorious for pyramiding loans because they dealt in large sums of money, and didn't want anyone calculating their debt. Lawyers frequently checked these credit reports when preparing lawsuits because it gave them an idea of what assets they could go after.

Lumber dealers organized the Chicago Lumberman's Exchange, which circulated weekly lists of delinquent customers, instituted uniform lumber grades and regulated the flow of lumber. Previously, hundreds of sawmills sent boards of different lengths and widths until uniform grades became a necessity.

When tightfisted Charles Mears decided to cut his lumber a little thinner so he could squeeze more boards per log, he thought it would increase his profits. But his Chicago manager warned him that customers was punishing them for selling boards that looked like inferior grades while charging them regular prices.

On June 21, 1858, Truesdell became the sole owner of a heavily indebted sawmill and two smaller mills that were closed, a boarding house with only a few guests, and a mercantile store that was open but not selling anything for cash.[293]

Notes

1. Passim, various newspaper articles during the 1840s–1850s clearly reflect a coordinated pricing arrangement.
2. *Southport Telegraph* 2 January 1844.
3. The other stores were owned by Dr. Royal Waldo (Kenosha), Charles R. Steele (Waukegan), and Cyrus Woodworth (Walworth).
4. The Civil War Era, 1848–1873: *History of Wisconsin*, pp. 99-100.
5. Passim, various newspaper advertisements throughout the 1840s listed them as distributors for various products, including nails.
6. *Kenosha Telegraph*, 5 April 1850, pp. 4.

7. *Southport Telegraph*, 2 January 1844, pp. 3. "Lumber Sold During the Year."
8. *Southport Telegraph*, 3 March 1850, pp. 1, column 1.
9. *Weekly Wisconsin*, 12 November 1851, pp 4, col 1.
10. Kenosha Register of Deeds, 9 November 1851.
11. Herbert Torrey family history narrative that ties into 1850 census.
12. Julia Truesdell 22 May 1850 letter to sister Mary Ann Moore.
13. Kenosha County court records for 1859 when the partners were sued.
14. The partners were Reverend Rueben Deming and his brother-in-law, Benjamin Cahoon.
15. I *Kenosha Times*, 12 August 1852, pp. 3.
16. Ibid.
17. Milwaukee Sentinel, 4 September 1855, Durkee, Truesdale & Co. are listed as their Kenosha agents.
18. Parts of the Beloit Military Trail became Geneva Road, since the roadway went to Lake Geneva, and still later become Highway 50.
19. *History of Racine & Kenosha Counties*, pp. 577. Edward G. Durant biographical sketch, Cashier of City Bank of Kenosha,
20. Based on *U.S. Customs House* records (taxes) and current market prices for wheat and lumber.
21. Based on the current wholesale and retail price of lumber.
22. Based on *U.S. Customs House* records, and the wholesale and Retail price of wheat and lumber.
23. There was a branch of the federal customs house located on Market Street in Kenosha.
24. *Buffalo Daily Republic*, 3 April 1854, pp. 4 column 2.
25. *Milwaukee Public Library, Runge Collection*, schooner Challenge file.
26. *Milwaukee Daily Sentinel* - Monday, April 03, 1854 - Milwaukee, Wisconsin.
27. *Kenosha Telegraph*, 6 January 1854.
28. *Chicago Tribune*, 30 April 1854.
29. *Kenosha Telegraph*, 13 April 1855.
30. *Kenosha Democrat*, 7 September 1855.
31. Gideon had common investments with Dr. Farr.
32. Ibid, 26 October 1859.
33. *Kenosha Telegraph*, 6 June 1854, pp. 2.
34. *Kenosha Telegraph*, 19 May 1854
35. Ibid, 14 August 1856, pp. 3.

36. *Milwaukee Public Library, Runge Collection*, schooner Challenge file.
37. *Weekly Racine Advocate*, 5 Feb 1855, pp. 1
38. *Kenosha Tribune & Telegraph*, 18 September 1856, pp. 4.
39. *Kenosha Telegraph*, 5 March 1857.
40. *Kenosha Tribune & Telegraph*, 9 August 1855
41. Ibid, 7 July 1855.
42. Journal of Proceedings, volume 4, State of Wisconsin- Senate, pp. 387-389.
43. *History of Racine & Kenosha Counties*, pp. 138.
44. *Kenosha Telegraph*, 28 May 1851
45. *Kenosha Tribune & Telegraph*, 12 July 1855, pp. 4.
46. Kenosha Register of Deed's office, volume 2, pp. 34.
47. Milwaukee Sentinel, 12 March 1856.
48. *Kenosha Telegraph*, 12 October 1854, pp. 3.
49. *Wisconsin Free Democrat*, 28 November 1855, pp. 2 col 3.
50. According to weekly maritime lists in the Kenosha Telegraph we know he was using rented schooners.
51. *Kenosha Daily Telegraph* - Wednesday, February 22, 1854.
52. *Rock River Democrat*, 17 Aug 1858, pp. 3.
53. Gideon Truesdell vs. Hiram Bacon, Kenosha County Clerk of Court's records for 1859.
54. During the 1840s freight charges averaged around 50% but with a much larger number of schooners and steamships available, that figure dropped to around 25% in the 1850s.
55. *Wisconsin Racine Advocate*, 2 Feb 1853, pp. 2.
56. Ibid.
57. Ibid.
58. *Cleveland Leader*, 7 May 1855, pp. 2.
59. Kenosha Register of Deed's office, volume 2, pp. 96
60. *Kenosha Telegraph* - Friday, July 28, 1854 - Kenosha, Wisconsin
61. *Kenosha Democrat*, Friday, March 07, 1856 - Kenosha, Wisconsin.
62. *Kenosha Telegraph*, 6 January 1854.
63. Durkee et al vs. *City Bank of Kenosha*, Wisconsin Supreme Court, 1859 session.
64. Ibid.
65. *American Railroad Journal*, Saturday, May 30, 1857, pp. 345-346.
66. Ibid.
67. *Kenosha City Directory*, 1857-58, Kenosha Pier Company biographical sketch.

68. *Kenosha Tribune*, 12 June 1855, pp. 4.
69. *Kenosha Tribune & Telegraph*, 5 May 1857, pp. 4.
70. They were partners in several investments including a Kenosha store.
71. *Kenosha Democrat*, 1 May 1852.
72. *Kenosha Telegraph*, 25 January 1852, pp. 3.
73. *Kenosha Democrat*, 3 December 1852, pp. 4.
74. *Hunt's Merchants Magazine & Commercial Review*, Vol 39, NYC, George Wood.
75. *Report of the Chief of Engineers*, 1856, pp. 1804.
76. Ibid.
77. Ibid, pp. 15 November 1853, pp. 2.
78. *Weekly Racine Advocate*, 18 May 1853, pp. 3.
79. *Steam and Cinders*, pp. 170.
80. *Kenosha Tribune*, 28 December 1854.
81. *Kenosha Democrat*, 6 May 1853, pp. 2.
82. *Steam & Cinders: The Advent of Railroads in Wisconsin*, pp. 175.
83. *Kenosha Tribune*, 23 June 1853.
84. *Steam & Cinders: The Advent of Railroads in Wisconsin*, pp. 175.
85. *Kenosha Tribune*, 17 November 1853, pp. 2. column 3.
86. *Kenosha Tribune*, 3 August 1855, pp. 2, column 4.
87. *Kenosha, From Pioneer Village to Modern City*, pp. 28.
88. Kenosha History Center, Mayor Michael Frank dairy.
89. *Milwaukee Sentinel*, 9 Jun 1858, pp. 2
90. *Racine Weekly Advocate*, 22 Sep 1858, pp. 1
91. *Milwaukee Sentinel*, 6 August 1855, pp. 2, column 2. Harvey Durkee resigns as president of the Kenosha, Beloit, and Rock Island Railroad. On 27 December 1855 Joshua Bond was listed as president.
92. *Rockford Weekly Register Gazette*, 21 May 1857, pp. 2.
93. Kenosha History Center, Mayor Michael Frank diary.
94. *American Railroad Journal*, 1856, pp. 300.
95. *Weekly Racine Advocate*, 7 May 1856.
96. *Weekly Wisconsin Patriot*, 25 April 1857, pp. 3.
97. *Milwaukee Sentinel*, 10 Dec 1856, pp. 2.
98. *Rockford Republican*, 4 December 1856.
99. *Steam & Cinders*, pp. 263.
100. *Rock River Democrat*, 19 August 1856.
101. *Steam and Cinders*, pp. 279.
102. *Weekly Racine Advocate*, 18 December 1856, pp. 3.

103. *Wisconsin Free Democrat*, 30 December 1857.
104. *The History of Wisconsin*, Pp. 38.
105. *Steam and Cinders*, pp. 278.
106. *Weekly Racine Advocate*, 15 Aug 1855, pp. 2.
107. *Rock River Democrat*, 9 February 1860.
108. Fisk was a wealthy land owner with a significant number of shares in the railroad.
109. *Kenosha Retrospective*, Zalmon G. Simmons, Business Innovator chapter, pp. 39.
110. *Steam and Cinders*, pp. 279.
111. He was the son-in-law of Serono Fisk, a wealthy real estate speculator.
112. *Family Pride: 100 Years & Still Shining*, pp. 169.
113. Ibid, pp. 291-292.
114. *Rockford Republican*, 19 July 1860.
115. Ibid.
116. *Rockford Republican*, 12 December 1861.
117. Arthur Truesdell reminiscences, 1902.
118. *Rock River Democrat*, 24 June 1863, pp. 3.
119. Ibid.
120. Campbell vs. City of Kenosha, 1866.
121. *Daily Milwaukee News*, 21 Dec 1869, pp. 4.
122. Ibid.
123. *Kenosha Retrospective*. Zalmon G. Simmons, Business Innovator, pp. 36.
124. Harrison Durkee represented the *Albany Telegraph Company* and Simmons the *Northwest Telegraph Company*.
125. *Milwaukee Courier*, 5 May 1847, pp. 2.
126. Durkee vs. City Bank of Kenosha, 1859.
127. *Triumph of Liberalism in Wisconsin*, pp. 66.
128. *Kenosha Telegraph*, 12 March 1852, pp. 1.
129. Ibid, 3 December 1852, pp. 2
130. Ibid.
131. Estimate based on volume of grain shipped through Kenosha and market price.
132. *Kenosha Telegraph & Gazette*, 28 March 1854.
133. *Kenosha Tribune & Telegraph*, 17 January 1856, pp. 3.
134. *History of Racine & Kenosha Counties*, Edward G. Durant biographical sketch, pp. 577.

135. *Christian Citizen*, 11 Aug 1849, pp. 3.
136. The Advocate of Peace, pp. 150. World Affairs Institute.
137. *Wisconsin Free Democrat*, 11 Apr 1849, pp. 3.
138. *Wisconsin Free Democrat*, 26 June 1850.
139. *Western Citizen*, 21 June 1850, pp. 2.
140. *Kenosha Telegraph*, 5 November 1852.
141. *History of Dane County*, George Durkee biographical sketch, pp. 1133.
142. *Wisconsin Historical Society*, Charles Durkee file.
143. Ibid.
144. *Weekly Racine Advocate*, 15 Jun e 1853, pp. 3.
145. *National Era* (Washington, DC) 16 June 1853, pp. 2.
146. *Daily Argus & Democrat*, 5 May 1854, pp. 2.
147. *Daily Free Democrat*, 20 May 1854.
148. *Weekly Wisconsin* 24 January 1855.
149. Michael Kwas, Wisconsin historian and teacher.
150. Randall, Thomas E., History of the Chippewa Valley, pp. 113.
151. *James Duane Doty*, pp. 337.
152. *Weekly Wisconsin*, 24 January 1855, pp. 2.
153. *Weekly Wisconsin*, 7 February 1855.
154. *James Duane Doty*, pp. 337.
155. *Sherman Booth: Once a Year*. Pp. 9.
156. *Milwaukee Sentinel*, 9 February 1855, pp. 3, col 2.
157. Wisconsin Historical Society, Charles Durkee papers.
158. *National Era*, 8 Feb 1855, pp. 22.
159. Dane County Register of Deeds, volume 1, pp. 72.
160. Society of Durkee. The Ora Caulkin's house had originally bee built by the Durkees.
161. Library of Congress, Congressional Globe, 19 March 1858, Pp. 151-152, Remarks from Mr. Durkee of Wisconsin regarding the Kansas-Lecompton Constitution.
162. *Congressional Globe*, 20 March 1858.
163. Charles Durkee papers, Wisconsin State Historical Society; letter from Charles Durkee to Paoli Durkee.
164. *Muskegon Chronicle*, 14 October 1899, pp. 1. George Easton reminiscences.
165. Ibid, 17 August 1899, pp. 4. "Pioneer Days."
166. Milwaukee County court records, 12 January 1855 where Trowbridge used his Milwaukee lumberyard as security for the loan.

167. *Ottawa County Register of Deeds*, Elias Merrill et al to Gideon Truesdell, volume 2, pp. 234, $12,000.
168. *Ottawa County Register of Deeds*, Elias Merrill et al to Harvey Durkee, volume 2, pp. 234, $7,500.
169. *Muskegon Chronicle*, 29 May 1889 issue reprinted the 16 June 1857 issue.
170. Ibid, Harvey Durkee to John C. Holmes, volume 2, pp. 330, $2,200
171. *Kenosha City Directory* 1857-58 lists land Durkee-Truesdell owned without any legal transfer- either rented or leased lumberyard. According to Kenosha Clerk of Court's documents Harvey Durkee and Gideon Truesdell owned 25% of the mill and 50% of the lumberyard.
172. Kenosha County Clerk of Courts. Gideon Truesdell vs. John C. Holmes et al, 24 May 1858.
173. Ibid, Harvey Durkee and Gideon Truesdell to E.D. Gillis et al, 2 December 1856.
174. *R.G. Dun & Company*, 30 May 1856. Wisconsin ledger, volume 27.
175. 1860 U.S. Census "Products of Industry" value of land was $15,000 and the mill was 40,000. Several other sources also say $56,000.
176. Amos Fred Sherwood family papers, letters, and family narratives. His grandfather was Amos Truesdell.
177. Racine County Register of Deeds, volume 1, pp. 18.
178. Ibid.
179. Ottawa Register of Deeds, Volume 1, pp. 217, on 10 November 1855, John Dana sold this inland parcel to his brother-in-law, Harvey Durkee, for $7,500. This parcel was purchased the previous year for $3,000 by Elias Merrill before he mortgaged it to Dana.
180. *The Life of Charles Henry Hackley*, pp. 99.
181. *Kenosha Times*, 14 August 1856, pp. 3. According to this article there were 32 rooms in the main building, and a much larger wing was under construction or would soon be under construction. During the Civil War years Truesdell added another wing that doubled the size of the first two wings, giving him a total of 144 rooms. Prior to 1874 the entire structure burned to the ground.
182. *U.S. Customs House* records, Kenosha, where nearly everything was brought by train from Chicago.
183. Several historical sketches from the early days agree that room and board was $5.00.
184. Arthur Truesdell reminiscences, 1902.

185. *Kenosha Telegraph & Tribune*, 17 July 1856.
186. *Kenosha Times*, 14 August 1856, pp. 3.
187. *Michigan's Eminent and Historic Men*, Levi Truesdell sketch.
188. *R.G. Dun & Company*, 30 May 1856, Michigan ledger, volume 27.
189. Arthur Truesdell reminiscences, 1902. Levis obituary also described his personality.
190. *Muskegon News & Reporter*, 20 January 1887.
191. *The Life of Charles Henry Hackley*, pp. 41.
192. History of Racine & Kenosha, pp. 525.
193. *The Life of Charles Henry Hackley*, pp. 44.
194. *Southport Telegraph*, 2 November 1849.
195. *Muskegon Chronicle*, 16 January 1874, pp. 1. Joseph Hackley obituary.
196. *The Biography of Charles Henry Hackley*, pp. 48.
197. *Life After Lumbering: Charles Henry Hackley & The Emergence of Muskegon, Michigan*, pp. 23.
198. *Life After Lumbering: Charles Henry Hackley & The Emergence of Muskegon, Michigan*, pp. 17.
199. Gideon obviously respected Glue because he helped finance him when he started his own mill.
200. *The Life of Charles Henry Hackley*, pp. 48.
201. *Muskegon Chronicle*, Louis Ellen's reminiscences, 6 July 1899, pp. 8.
202. Arthur Truesdell reminiscences, 1902.
203. Arthur Truesdell reminiscences, 1902.
204. He worked their full-time until around 1860 when G.J. Truesdell took over because Edwin was needed at one or the other J.H. Hackley mills.
205. *Life After Lumbering: Charles Henry Hackley & The Emergence of Muskegon, Michigan*, pp. 26.
206. 1860 census information.
207. *The Life of Charles Henry Hackley*.
208. The Catholic Church in town did a lot of work for the needy.
209. *Muskegon Chronicle*, 10 June 1899 pp. 2.
210. Ibid, 19 August 1899. "Pioneer Days."
211. *Life After Lumbering: Charles Henry Hackley & The Emergence of Muskegon, Michigan*, pp. 26.
212. *Chicago Tribune*, 14 August 1857, pp. 2.
213. Great Lakes Federal Archives, 1862–1865 tax records. Gideon Truesdell and J.H. Hackley & Company.

214. *Muskegon Chronicle*, 6 June 1863, pp. 3. *Hackley & McGordon* dock.
215. Ibid, 26 June 1857, pp. 3. They gave a description of the mill and its used equipment—an upright saw, lath saw, and flooring saw.
216. *Muskegon Chronicle*, 6 July 1899, pp. 6. Laurence Flary reminiscences.
217. Arthur Truesdell letter to his nephew, 1908.
218. *Muskegon Chronicle*, 23 November 1899, pp. 5. Michael Sullivan reminiscences.
219. *Muskegon Chronicle*, 4 August, 1899, pp. 6. George F. Graves reminiscences.
220. Ibid.
221. The only way they could have justified the expense of a Chicago River yard was if they were buying lumber by the shipload.
222. *Chicago Tribune*, 6 March 1860, pp. 5.
223. Ibid, 19 February 1861, pp. 8.
224. *Natures Metropolis*, pp. 180.
225. 1856 *City of Chicago Directory*.
226. *Chicago Tribune*, 4 April 1910, pp. 18. Benjamin Franklin Deming obituary.
227. Chicago History Center, lumber files.
228. *Industrial Chicago: The Lumber Interests*, pp. 907.
229. Industrial Chicago, pp. 241.
230. *Michigan's Lumber Towns*, pp. 72.
231. Ibid, pp. 71.
232. *Muskegon Chronicle*, 18 December 1900, pp. 1.
233. Ibid, pp. 46. By 1857 there were 16 mills on Muskegon Lake employing 550 men, and based on the output listed in the 1860 "Products of Industry" survey, the annual payroll from upriver loggers and river men would have been in the neighborhood of $60,000, and a conservative estimate.
234. *Muskegon Chronicle*, 25 March 1899, pp.1. Edwin Potter reminiscences.
235. Lumbering Days in Wisconsin, pp. 129.
236. Ibid.
237. Ibid.
238. Ibid.
239. *Michigan's Lumbertowns*, pp. 73. The "black bottle" something the lower-class saloons used to get rid of troublesome customers, usually liquor laced with choral hydrate, which incapacitated the person, but if often killed whomever consumed the drink.

240. Ibid.
241. *Schooner Passage*, pp. 157.
242. Ibid.
243. *History of Racine & Kenosha County*, pp. 578.
244. Ibid.
245. *Murder and Mayhem in Chicago's Vice Districts*, pp. 27.
246. *Kenosha Tribune & Telegraph*, 24 December 1857, pp. 5.
247. *History of Eminent and Self-Made Men of the State of Michigan*, Levi Truesdell biographical sketch, pp. 482.
248. Kenosha County Clerk of Court's records, 1857.
249. Passim, newspaper articles, obituary, credit reports, etc.
250. Passim, real estate deeds, credit reports, and current market prices of over 5,000 acres that included three sub-divisions owned jointly with his brother.
251. *Chicago Tribune*, 2 December 1857, pp. 11.
252. Industrial Chicago, pp. 57.
253. *1860 Wisconsin Supreme Court Cases*, Durkee et al vs. *City Bank of Kenosha*.
254. Passim, various loans secured by farms and the Trowbridge & Wing mill in $1,000 increments.
255. *Kenosha Democrat*, 27 January 1860. William Stanley vs. Durkee, Truesdell & Company et al.
256. Based on Kenosha County court documents Henry Blodgett began handling Gideon's affairs on 12 December 1858.
257. Henry Blodgett autobiography, pp. 29.
258. *History of the Chicago & Northwestern Railroad System*, pp. 65-66.
259. Ibid.
260. *Waukegan Herald*, 8 April 1961, "Lincoln and County Republican Greats."
261. Henry W. Blodgett autobiography, pp. 16.
262. Passim, at a time when money was scarce, he upgraded the Trowbridge & Wing mill.
263. Truesdell vs. Hiram Bacon, Kenosha County.
264. *Life After Lumbering: Charles Henry Hackley & The Emergence of Muskegon*, Michigan. Pp. 29. He must have had a significant amount of gold coins stashed somewhere because he had cash when others didn't.
265. *R.G. Dun & Company*, 21 June 1858, Wisconsin ledger, volume 27, pp. 118.

266. Ibid, 20 January 1859, Michigan ledger, volume 60, pp. 272.
267. Kenosha County Clerk of Court's records, 1856–1857.
268. *1860 Wisconsin Supreme Court Cases*, Towslee vs. Harvey Durkee et al. 27 August 1860
269. Ibid.
270. Ibid.
271. Ibid.
272. Ibid.
273. Wisconsin Free Democrat, 15 December 1858.
274. *Daily Milwaukee News*, 28 January 1859.
275. Ibid.
276. *1860 Wisconsin Supreme Court Cases,* Durkee et al vs. City Bank of Kenosha. 27 August 1860
277. Ibid.
278. Ibid.
279. Ibid.
280. Ibid.
281. Ibid.
282. *Wisconsin Supreme Court Cases*, Durkee et al. vs. City Bank of Kenosha, 27 August 1860.
283. Kenosha Clerk of Court's records, 1856–1859 journal.
284. *R.G. Dun & Company*, 10 November 1858 report, Michigan ledger, volume 60, pp. 272
285. The date on the real estate transfer for the *Trowbridge & Wing* mill was 17 April 1858. According to a 29 July *New York Times* article, in 1859 "I, like so many other lumbermen, got in a tight place." This and other information ties together the reason behind this transfer.
286. University of Wisconsin–Parkside historical archives. 16 January 1855 court records for Kenosha County.
287. Ibid.
288. J.H. Hackley journals; difference between what George Hess and J.H. Hackley & Company paid for the mill.
289. Muskegon Register of Deeds, volume 2, pp. 330, 7 September 1859. Gideon Truesdell to Harvey Durkee, $5,000 for lots.
290. Muskegon Register of Deeds, Volume 2, pp. 330. 7 September 1859 Harvey Durkee pays $11,000 to Gideon Truesdell for lots. Addition, and on that same day Truesdell sold $5,000 of lots back to Harvey Durkee.
291. *Life After Lumbering: Charles Henry Hackley & The Emergence of*

Muskegon, Michigan. Pp. 29.
292. *R.G. Dun & Company*, 10 November 1858 report, Michigan ledger, volume 60, pp. 272. "I have made considerable inquiries and nobody seems to know anything of him."
293. *R.G. Dun & Company*, Wisconsin ledger, volume 27, pp. 146.

3

SURVIVING THE PANIC OF 1857
AND ORGANIZING THE TRUESDELL LUMBER COMPANY

The lumber business had always been far more complicated than just turning logs into boards, and survival after the "Panic of 1857" required heavy-duty cash reserves. In troubled times, poorly capitalized sawmills went into receivership, and this is how Gideon ended up with the Durkee-Truesdell, Pomeroy & Holmes, and Trowbridge & Wing mills. They reverted to him due to financial reversals, and he was more concerned with finding a buyer for the two smaller mills than ownership.

Gideon assumed total ownership of these sawmills during the worst of times, with the aftershocks from the "Panic of 1857" continuing until the second year of the Civil War. He had to push through manpower shortages, higher wages, and a sluggish wholesale market where sales barely covered his overhead expenses. The inevitability of a devastating war caused wages to increase by a third, with demand for lumber dropping to a point where it was difficult for even the strongest mills to show a profit.

"Lumbering was very bad in those days. The lower working classes were quite poor then.... most of them lived in shanties.... the low wages continued through the next two years.... we couldn't get any money only store orders (scrip) so all I received that whole summer was two dollars in money and the rest in store orders. In '58 I asked Mr. Beidler, in whose mill I was working, for two shillings to send a letter to the old country, and he said 'I haven't got two shillings in my office,' money was so scarce."[1]

When Gideon took over Durkee, Truesdell & Company the price of lumber had dropped by 40%, and the firm's Chicago yards had been closed. The wholesale price of lumber had dropped from $10 per thousand feet to $6.00 to $6.50, and a mill owner's biggest dilemma was that what he sold barely covered his costs. "In 1857, '58, and '59 were the hardest times I ever saw in Muskegon. One couldn't get money enough to pay his postage."[2] A year later Gideon got Joseph Hackley and William Glue, to return. What tipped the odds in Gideon's favor were no doubt the bags of gold coins he kept in his safe leftover from the roaring 1850s, and assembling a sharp management staff.

Finding a buyer for an expensive sawmill in the midst of a financial crisis was out of the question, but since Gideon appears to have been Durkee, Truesdell & Company's largest creditor, he had enough leverage to take over the business. In June of 1858, at a meeting in Orson Head's law office above the City Bank of Kenosha, he agreed to pay creditors "dollar for dollar," and assumed ownership of the $56,000 ($6.7 million today) mill which were located 150 nautical miles across from Kenosha, Wisconsin.[3] Out of this wreckage came the Truesdell Lumber Company, and it struggled with a heavy debt load for the next three years.

A few months earlier, when Alva Trowbridge defaulted on a loan, he signed over the deed for the Trowbridge & Wing mill property to Gideon. He also received 80 acres of pinelands along Newaygo Road, 14 lots across from the Trowbridge & Wing mill on Western Avenue, and the deed to a general store that had been built but not yet stocked.[4] Although legal transfer had yet to occur, the Pomeroy & Holmes mill had defaulted on their mortgage, and John C. Holmes was in the process of making an assignment to Gideon Truesdell.

The lumber market was in bad shape, but neither of these mills was making money sitting idle, so Gideon began looking for a buyer for the Trowbridge & Wing property, and packaged a deal with twenty-four-year-old Grand Rapids, Michigan, lumberyard owner George Hess (1834–1907). Although young, he was ready to roll the dice, and significantly increase his net worth although it was a big step for a man of his age. He was a young man of good character and intelligence. At the age of sixteen, he began teaching school back in North Salem, New York.[5] Several years later he was listed as a vestryman in the Catholic Church. He and his younger brother, William, came to Grand Rapids with a small inheritance from their late father, a physician.

Hess knew he could leverage their inheritance into something larger by purchasing pinelands for $1.25 per acre, and within a few years he owned over 5,000 acres of pinelands in Kent and Ottawa County.[6] Each year the Hess brothers cleared more land for farming, had some of the logs turned into lumber at a nearby sawmill at a contract price, and sold it through their Grand Rapids lumberyard.[7]

Gideon continued to hold the mortgage on the Trowbridge & Wing mill, and added $1,200 to the principal so they could upgrade their equipment with a much faster circular saw. An upright saw had a seven-foot blade that was 3/8 inch thick which, due to primitive metallurgy, and left a third of the log on the floor as sawdust. A circular saw was much faster, and would have paid for itself in less than a year. Gideon probably had exclusive sales rights to sell their output through his Chicago yard, and he was the "Company" in George Hess & Company, which meant that he owned a minority interest.[8] In addition to interest and principal Gideon would have also received a percentage of the profits.

Soon thereafter, Gideon received title to the Pomeroy & Holmess delinquent mortgage, which became his when he acquired the assets of Durkee, Truesdell & Company. By then, they owed Harvey Durkee and Gideon Truesdell a lot of money for past-due logging fees.[9] Their sawmill's boiler had been seized for back taxes by the county, and was sitting in a barn downtown.[10] What was left was a sawmill building with used boilers, and equipment that had seen better days.

This was a small sawmill that would have been easy to manage in addition to the Durkee-Truesdell property, and it seems likely that while he was negotiating with creditors, Gideon already had an exit strategy in mind. Even though Joseph Hackley didn't have the money to swing the deal, he was interested in buying the run-down Pomeroy & Holmes mill. This sawmill would have been a tough property to sell in a troubled economy because it needed a lot of work, but Joseph Hackley saw the opportunity of a lifetime, and Gideon was willing to finance the deal. It was an arrangement between two old friends who trusted one another.

Gideon needed a strong person to run a large manufacturing operation while he was away in Chicago selling lumber, and that was Joseph Hackley. By 1860, Gideon had the right team in place, and many years later the *Muskegon News & Reporter* recalled that, "with a wonderful amount of energy and perseverance he paid off the indebtedness, and acquired a handsome property."[11] According to an 1860, R.G. Dun & Company credit report he was "hard up, but I believe he is generally considered as good.... I think is considerably in debt."[12]

Richard C. Fritz

Joseph Hackley, Superintendent of the Durkee, Truesdell & Company Sawmill

Reorganizing the Durkee-Truesdell sawmill wouldn't have been that complicated because it was new, having only ran for ten months before it closed. For unknown reasons, Joseph Hackley left during the spring 1857 to become Superintendent of the Muskegon Log & Mill Owners Association.[13] When Durkee, Truesdell & Company fell on hard times this job might have been arranged by Alvah Trowbridge, who was president of that association, and a close friend of Gideon's.[14] What's peculiar is that he left the mill six months *before* the economy crashed, but in the spring of 1859, he returned to work for Gideon.

Joseph Hackley was probably receptive to returning since the Muskegon Log & Mill Owners Association was in limbo until sawmills obtained new financing. Another young employee with great promise was Joseph Hackley's twenty-year-old son, Charley, who impressed Levi Truesdell as an intelligent person with an aptitude for numbers. He was a bit on the shy side but ambitious enough to apply himself. Charley had been careful with his money, because after two-and-a-half years working a job that paid $25 a month, he saved $156.61 ($19,000 today).[15]

Levi got to know Charley fairly well when he showed up each night after supper to help him with the nightly inventory at his store across the road from the sawmill.[16] He had a profound influence on the young man's life, and became a lifelong friend. Many years later a picture of Levi surfaced in Hackley's private papers with the inscription on the back, "an honorable man" written in his handwriting.

He taught Charley how a beginning inventory plus purchases less sales told them how much merchandise had been sold that day. After totaling the handwritten sales slips from that day, Levi could quickly tell if everything had been accounted for. Hackley's ambition is evident when he asked how he could get ahead. Charley knew his chances for advancement in the sawmill was limited, and Levi urged him to learn double-entry accounting. In those days, the junior partner of a business was usually their bookkeeper, but first Charley would have to learn double-entry accounting.

In the fall of 1857, Levi left the partnership to return to Portageville; evidently, the person who bought his mercantile store in Portageville defaulted. Before Levi left for New York he no doubt spoke to his brother about Charley, and suggested that they find a way to send him to a business school so he could learn accounting.[17] Gideon helped with the tuition, more likely an advance on his wages, and tried to find him a place where he could stay with free room and board.[18] This turned out to be with Charles Deming and his wife in Chicago until Charley changed his plans, and completed a course in Kenosha, where there were many old family friends who would have gladly boarded him.

Durkee-Truesdell sawmill, circa 1872, building closest to Western Avenue was their office. As flooring, siding, and picket saws were added so were addition buildings. Slabs of bark were piled on a vacant lot next to the mill between the roadway and the lakefront. Picture courtesy of the Lakeshore Museum Center.

Although sometimes perceived by writers as one dimensional or poorly educated, Charles Hackley actually received a first-rate education from Professor John G. McMynn, a graduate of Williams College. Kenosha had one of the finest free school systems in the Midwest, and he taught the older students. His use of the language was faultless, and he taught his students how to think rather than merely recite facts. When Hackley graduated at the age of fifteen, he had a solid education that would serve him well.

Charley had probably learned some basic bookkeeping skills from Levi, because he breezed through the bookkeeping course four weeks ahead of the others. But when he returned home, he discovered that Durkee, Truesdell & Company was in receivership while Gideon negotiated with creditors. He put him to work at the store he acquired from his brother where he made lifetime friendships.[19] Once Gideon took control of the sawmill, he put Charley in charge of the payrolls, inventories, purchases, shipping schedules, and several sets of books. It was an incredible opportunity for a young man to learn the inner workings of the lumber business from a "strict businessman."

There was a *lot* of paperwork flowing through the little office in front of the mill on Western Avenue. Gideon systematically paid off creditors, bought out former partners, kept separate books for the boarding house, three mercantile stores, and logging camps. In addition to becoming a first-rate bookkeeper, it gave Charley a chance to see where money was made and lost for a salary of $360 ($43,000 today) a year, plus room and board, a good wage during a bad economy.[20]

It was a life changing event for Charley, because Gideon ran everything by the numbers, and he would have kept dozens of spreadsheets to track income and expenses on what within a few years became a large business. He would have learned analysis, critical thinking, and mathematical cross checks. He sent the journals across Lake Michigan aboard the Challenge to Gideon's Kenosha office, where his head accountant, Luther Whitney, would have reviewed his entries.

There were dozens of internal controls for each mill such as inventories vs. sales; logging tallies vs. booming company reports; tallies from logging camps, bills of lading listing the number of boards that left the mill on a schooner, tallies when the lumber was unloaded at Gideon's Chicago yards; payrolls; docking fees in Chicago, and dozens of other expenses. A lot of sawmill owners were a little fuzzy when it came to recordkeeping, but from various accounts we know that Gideon insisted on a tight set of books.

Gideon inherited a note from the Pomeroy & Holmes mill, which by the spring of 1858 had lapsed into default. It had originated on April 29, 1857, when Gideon split off a narrow strip of land from his Muskegon lakefront property and Harvey Durkee packaged a deal that would have made Pomeroy & Holmes a solid profit.[21]

It would have also made Durkee, Truesdell & Company a healthy profit until the "Panic of 1857" ruined the economy, and by the time Gideon foreclosed the equipment had been seized for back taxes.[22] During a bad economy, Gideon needed to find somebody to buy a broken-down mill that needed a *lot* of work before it could resume cutting lumber, and he turned to Joseph Hackley.

Charles H. Hackley (L) Edwin Hackley (CL) Arthur Truesdell (CR) James McGordon (R). Pictures courtesy of the Lakeshore Museum Center.

Whereas the Trowbridge & Wing note was tied to Gideon personally through a mortgage secured by the sawmill, the Pomeroy note was a bit more complicated. Creditors had filed liens against Durkee-Truesdell assets of which the Pomeroy mortgage was one. On January 21, 1859, Pomeroy & Holmes assigned the mill to Gideon Truesdell who, for some reason, continued as the mortgage holder rather than assuming ownership, but it seems like this was a deliberate financial and legal maneuver.[23]

Many years later Charles Hackley described the mess his father walked into. "The mill was all to pieces at that time, the engine was up town for taxes and the belting one place and another. It was what they called at that time an upright and a siding mill with a lath saw.... Truesdell had a store and we drew on the store and kept the men paid that way."[24]

Joseph Hackley was ready to the roll the dice, and he really had nothing to lose because he had a steady paycheck from the Durkee-Truesdell mill. With Gideon allowing them to use his credit, Joseph knew this was the opportunity he had been looking for since the failure of the Kenosha & Rockford. The Pomeroy & Holmes mill was small, but Joseph would soon have a business that his sons could work their way into, and if they played their cards right the Hackley boys would never have to struggle like their parents.

Gideon sold them this sawmill for $5,500 ($660,000 today), with Joseph contributing $1,311 ($157,000 today) of promissory notes from the Muskegon Log & Mill Owners Association, with Charles' contributing $300 of similar notes and $157 in cash. Gideon knew he would have to bankroll the repairs, and during the first two years owned a 72% equity interest, with Joseph Hackley owning 20%, and Charles Hackley 8%.[25] Due to the poor condition of the wholesale market, the sawmill lost

Richard C. Fritz   221

money during the first two years. Gideon signed a sales agreement with the Hackleys, but he chose not to transfer ownership until the business was on a solid financial footing.

J.H. Hackley & Company burned through the $157 that Charles contributed.[26] During the first ninety days they were strapped for cash, and Gideon loaned the partnership $602.50 ($72,000 today) for additional repairs.[27] He also loaned them the mechanical expertise of the Durkee-Truesdell mill's engineer, William Glue, and after two months of repairs the Pomeroy & Holmes mill was ready to begin cutting lumber with a skeleton crew to save money.[28]

Their first revenue came trickling in on May 17, 1859, when they cut 123,000 feet at $30.75 ($3,600 today) for a pineland owner, which according to their journals required 9.5 days of work.[29] They charged $2.50 ($320 today) per thousand feet, the going rate for sawing lumber owned by others.

Many upriver pineland owners didn't own a mill so they "sawed logs by the halves" with a mill like J.H. Hackley & Company, and half the others on Muskegon Lake. The land owner paid for the logging crew and the expense of rafting the logs to the mill, and the mill paid for turning the logs into lumber and selling them through a Chicago yard. They divided the profits, hence, "sawing logs by the halves." It was the cheapest way for a mill without pinelands to do business in a rough economy, but not necessarily the most profitable.

In a depressed economy where demand was pathetically low, Gideon invested $920 ($118,000 today) to build a separate building on the other side of the Pomeroy & Holmes dock, where he installed a boiler and special saws so they could began turning waste from his three mills into flooring and siding.[30] This was something they had been doing at their Kenosha planing mill, and whenever a sawmill could turn scrap into something they could sell it helped their bottom line.

Mills struggled to break even until 1862, when demand and wholesale prices soared due to pent up demand. Until that happened, Gideon improved the bottom line of each mill by turning scrap into shingles, lath, pickets, flooring, and siding. There was a market for ice in Chicago due to polluted water and open sewers, so he built an icehouse and began cutting ice during the winters. He also contracted with J.H. Hackley & Company to run his logging camps, with Joseph Hackley and his sons spending their winters in the woods.

Chicago Wholesale Lumber Market, circa 1859

Throughout 1858, the four Muskegon mills that Gideon owned remained closed.[31] As the lumber market began to recover, he needed a Chicago River lumberyard to sell millions of feet of lumber, and he leased around 10 acres at Clark and Liberty Street across the river from the old Durkee-Truesdell yard.[32]

Shiploads of lumber arrived at his dock on the riverfront, where Irish dock workers unloaded a ship at the lightning speed of about twenty minutes. Once unloaded, Gideon's men cross-stacked boards so they could dry during the next six weeks. When it was seasoned and ready for shipment, the foreman began pulling inventory from that side of the yard to fill orders. A Chicago yard had to sell a large tonnage every week in order to cover the expense of a Chicago River yard, and Gideon figured a way to double his sales volume.

In addition to selling lumber from his own mills, he became a commission agent for 20 to 30 smaller sawmills that couldn't afford to open a Chicago yard.[33] After buying shiploads of lumber from smaller mills during the past three to four years at their Kenosha dock, Gideon probably knew who to approach, and it was a great opportunity for the sawmill because they now had a Chicago yard acting as their sales agent. They no longer had to put up with rock bottom prices at the wholesale dock.

This would have added at least another twelve million feet of lumber to Gideon's sales volume with a minimal financial outlay, although he probably had to advance payment for renting schooners. In exchange for transportation, sales, and acting as their agent, Gideon would have pocketed about half of the sale price.[34] In addition to selling their lumber he would also have acted as their banker.

Most sawmills were located in small villages where the nearest bank was hundreds of miles away, and long before interstate banking they needed a Chicago office to handle their financial transactions. Lumber that had been sold in Nebraska would have been paid for with an Omaha draft that had little value in Two Rivers, Wisconsin. A check to a creditor from a sawmill in Two Rivers would have had value, but the person accepting it would have discounted it by as much as 50%. A check from a New York City or Chicago bank would have been accepted at face value without a discount fee.

When a check drawn on a Des Moines bank was exchanged, less a 15%

fee, into a Chicago check it would have been accepted just about anywhere. Truesdell had a clerk converting hundreds of drafts drawn on banks west of the Mississippi River into a Chicago specie. If he accumulated $2,500 of bank drafts from the sale of lumber to yards in Iowa or Nebraska, during the next shipment of lumber out west one of his clerks rode along with a suitcase of these drafts, which he cashed at the banks they were drawn on, and returned with a suitcase of gold or silver coins. To avoid robberies, these bank employees sometimes brought along their wife and children as decoys. Upon his return to Chicago, he would have deposited the money in Gideon's First National Bank of Chicago account.

When a schooner docked at Gideon's lumberyard; the captain handed a clerk an envelope from the mill listing the checks they wanted written against the balance in their account. There were blank checks printed for each sawmill that his bookkeeper used to pay bills, and dropped them in the mail.

The wholesale market improved but it was a slow and painful comeback. In October of 1859, Charles Mears wrote that "these are the hardest times for the lumber trade I have ever seen." After the Panic of 1857 the wholesale market was still sluggish, and one of the biggest lumbermen in Chicago, Charles Mears, wrote "I have hardly been able to attend to anything but money matters and have hardly been able to collect enough to pay expenses. Many of the lumber dealers will be obliged to fail if these times last a month longer."[35]

Due to a 39% drop in sales due to the panic, there were still large inventories sitting in every Chicago lumberyard, and by 1860 Chicago dealers knew they had to pursue new markets. Since the opening of the Michigan & Illinois Canal twelve years earlier, St. Louis was where most of the lumber ended up, and a large percentage of their inventories was sold to retail yards in Memphis, New Orleans, Baton Rouge, or the western territories.

According to the *Chicago Daily Herald* "our lumber trade with St. Louis has already assumed colossal proportions, and steadily on the increase. The past year, which everyone knows to have been a very dull one, our St. Louis trade reached the enormous amount of eighty-six and a quarter million feet! Besides this, we sent 71,417,200 shingles and 16,404,175 of lath!

Wholesale yards were small cities with alleys between different grades of lumber. Chicago lumber dealers kept at least 25 million feet in their yards to supply the market during the winter, and to have an ample supply during the spring before the mills began shipping lumber. Pictures courtesy of the Chicago History Center.

"One of our heaviest firms, C. Mears & Company, has been in correspondence with lumber dealers in Nashville, and the result is that two gentlemen from that city have arrived and after careful inspection, bought 200,000 feet of lumber from them. Two boats will be freighted and start for their destination. Nashville dealers were astonished and delighted over the quality of our lumber and the immense supplies."[36]

At the beginning of the Civil War, Gideon had at least nine schooners making two to three "boomerang" trips a week bringing about 2,000 tons of lumber to his Chicago yard.[37] These schooners did nothing but haul lumber from one of his mills, unload at his dock, and return to Muskegon for another load over a twenty-six-week sailing season. We know that at times Gideon had so much inventory on his docks in Muskegon that a few of these schooners were sent to the wholesale dock at the confluence of the Chicago River, where he turned excess inventory into cash.[38]

With his sawmills running smoothly under Joseph Hackley's direction, each spring Gideon and Julia became semi-permanent guests at Chicago's Metropolitan Hotel, which were five blocks from his office. A few years later, they began staying at the Brigg's House, an upscale hotel closer to his office.[39] According to their advertisements they had "always been celebrated for the comfort, neatness, quiet, and the excellence of its table."

Each summer their son joined them for a few weeks, and visited wholesale houses to place orders for their three mercantile stores.[40] We know from court documents that the family dressed expensively. Gideon and his son bought their suits at Brooks Brothers, a high-end Chicago men's store, and Julia and her daughter-in-law shopped at Field, Leiter & Company.[41]

The Brigg's House at the corner of Randolph and Wells and an omnibus. Pictures courtesy of the Chicago History Center.

In 1862, the Chicago market began gaining momentum, and late in the season prices jumped three dollars to four dollars ($348 today) per thousand feet.[42] The pent-up demand from the past five years led to a seller's market where every piece of lumber could be sold for above average prices. Wartime inflation was about to kick-in which caused wholesale prices to skyrocket, and after some extremely tough years it was a good time to be a lumberman.

The larger Chicago lumberyards had two or three clerks who handled a mountain of paperwork. A foreman and assistant foreman hired day laborers to stack lumber, and there were hundreds of men roaming through the lumber district each morning looking for work. In those days lumberyards operated with a skeleton crew with a staff hired at the start of each day.

Inside the office, a clerk did nothing but handle the banking for the smaller mills they represented, wrote checks, and kept journals of deposits vs. withdrawals. At the end of the week, each clerk handed over their journals to a head bookkeeper, who inspected them for accuracy and honesty. On the last day of the season, it was customary for the owner to watch the head bookkeeper make his final entries, because at the stroke of a pen a dishonest person could conceal months of fraud.

One of the daily cross checks would have been incoming checks versus the safes cash balance. Each check written for the dozens of smaller mills could be cashed at the address of Gideon's office, where he had around $175 ($60,000 today) of gold double eagle coins in a safe for that purpose. Many of these checks would have found their way back to his office because they were traded like cash.[43]

This also happened in Muskegon, where at the end of the week merchants traded notes. If Gideon's store was holding $113 of Ryerson & Morris' notes from his store, and Ryerson was holding $149 from Gideon's store, their bookkeepers would have swapped notes and paid the difference in gold coins.

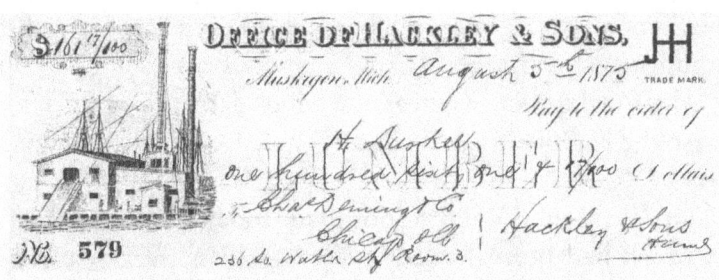

Bank draft from Hackley & Sons payable to Harvey Durkee, and payable through Charles Deming & Company's Chicago office. The Hackley trademark, and sketch of their mill superimposed made it difficult to counterfeit. Reproduction courtesy of Michigan State University, Hackley & Hume papers.

A clerk wrote checks on Gideon's Union National Bank or 1st National Bank of Chicago accounts, which would have been accepted just about anywhere in the country. Today, checks are cleared within hours, but in those days, they had to be taken physically to the bank for payment. The larger banks had a small army of clerks that did nothing but board trains with a suitcase of checks, traveling to their point of origin, and exchanging them at the bank they were drawn on for gold coins or bank notes from one of the larger Chicago banks. The discount rate, a percentage of the check charged for clearing their paper, easily covered the cost of cashing these checks and generated a tidy profit for a bank.

The further the check was from Chicago the higher the discount fee. A check from Milwaukee carried a 5% discount, whereas a bank in Florida would have carried a 60% fee due to distance and/or the soundness of the bank. Every bank and wholesale house printed lists of rejected bank notes, and distributed them to customers as a means of reducing the number of bad checks floating around.

Foreclosing on the Trowbridge & Wing Sawmills and Organizing J.H. Hackley & Company

When Gideon returned to Muskegon during the fall of 1859, the sawmill he sold to George Hess was in financial trouble. It's difficult to say what happened but based on court testimony he "backed out and Mr. Truesdell had to shoulder the responsibility."[44] Regardless of what happened it resulted in an expensive legal battle because Hess wasn't leaving without a fight.

The Pomeroy & Holmes mill had a third of the capacity of the much better equipped Trowbridge & Wing sawmill but sold $25,500 ($2.9 million today) of lumber, whereas the much larger Trowbridge & Wing mill only sold $11,300 ($1.3 million today).[45] Obviously, something was wrong.

Gideon held a $5,500 ($660,000 today) mortgage secured by the mill, which had been deeded to George Hess fractionally from Alva Trowbridge and Thomas Wing. This was how a partnership sold a business in those days, and Gideon was careful to maintain a legal distance from ownership.[46]

Gideon took possession of the property after paying his and Trowbridges $745.26 ($89,000 today) legal bill and an undetermined amount of delinquent taxes.[47] In October 1860, he sold the sawmill for $8,000 ($960,000 today) to J.H. Hackley & Company without any money changing hands.[48] He also sold the vacant Trowbridge & Wing store back to Alva Trowbridge for the amount of the debt he had cancelled a few years earlier when he had a run of bad luck.[49]

The Pomeroy & Holmes and Trowbridge & Wing sawmills were now owned and operated by J.H. Hackley & Company. Money was tight, and in the beginning both mills began cutting lumber with a skeleton crew consisting of Arthur Truesdell, G.J. Truesdell, Edwin Hackley, and Charles Hackley with twelve-year old Porter Hackley stacking the boards on their dock.[50] Their first full-time employee was twenty-three-year-old James McGordon (1836–1880). Jim left home at the age of fourteen, the legal age that a teenager could begin working, and he gravitated to Muskegon Lake looking for work at one of the mills.[51]

He began working at Ryerson & Morris alongside William Glue, and by the time he came to work for Joseph Hackley he had seven years of experience. Tall and lanky but with a muscular build, he was strong enough to pull logs from the mill's holding pens, and at a relatively young age he made top dollar running a circular saw. He had a good work ethic, which earned him the respect of Joseph Hackley, who put him and a helper to work for the winter at the Durkee-Truesdell shingle mill.

They worked a twelve-hour day loading shingle bolts (two-foot block of wood without any knot holes) into two semi-automatic saws. The machines blade automatically gigged back and forth, cutting 40,000 shingles during a twelve-hour day. They manufactured around 1.2 million shingles after the "big mill" closed for the year, because they needed the dock space on all three docks.

The shingle mill was dangerous as illustrated by a newspaper article: "Louis Bowdan, while working in Truesdell's shingle mill on Thursday last, had his left thumb caught in the saw, and was so badly managed as to require its removal close to the hand."[52] Working in the "little mill" was uncomfortable because the building never warmed up beyond 40 degrees with wind and snow blowing off of Muskegon Lake.

Shingles was stacked and over-flowing on all three docks. By springtime, the first schooners of the season hauled them to retail yards with standing orders, and the money was used to fund startup costs for Gideon's three sawmills.

At the end of the season, lumbermen invested their surplus funds upgrading their mills, buying pinelands, or investing in rental properties. At that point in time the stock market wasn't geared for private investors and banks paid low interest rates and were prone to failures.

A tight cash flow meant that every mill had to keep a close eye on their receivables, and winter work like cutting shingles, sawing ice from

Muskegon Lake, or running a mercantile store created cash flow. Gideon would have used the profits from his mercantile stores to fund logging camps along the White, Muskegon, and Grand rivers. The objective was never having to dig too deeply into his own pocket to pay operating expenses.

The cash flow at the two Hackley sawmills continued to be tight as evidenced by several journal entries, and according to an R. G. Dun & Company report Gideon was slow at paying his bills. It wasn't until 1862 that the demand for lumber and pricing increased to a point where profits could be declared.

During the summer of 1861 Jim McGordon loaned J.H. Hackley & Company $119 ($15,000 today) at 10% interest, probably past due wages he allowed the firm to use so they could pay their most pressing bills.[53] The loan was re-paid in 30 days with interest.[54] This tells us that the fast-rising McGordon was careful with his money, and saved nearly every dollar he made until he was able to strike a deal with Gideon for a couple of lots in Durkees Addition, where he built a house for he and his wife within walking distance to the mill.

In 1860, Joseph Hackley started running the Pomeroy & Holmes mill around the clock to boost production, but with a very small pen for holding logs they soon ran out of space.[55] According to the *Kenosha Telegraph*, they had so many logs in their holding pen that he sent McGordon to stand them on end to make room for more.[56]

The Pomeroy & Holmes sawmill had a daily capacity of around 15,000 feet but within a few years Gideon increased that to 28,000 by installing additional saws.[57] That extra 7,000 feet a day translated into a million board feet per season or roughly $10,000 ($1.2 million today) of additional revenues. This translated into an extra 432,000 feet per season.

When a special saw with multiple blades came on the market, it turned thin scraps of waste into pickets, and Gideon installed one at the Durkee-Truesdell mill. A few years later he installed a picket saw at the Pomeroy & Holmes and Trowbridge & Wing mills so he could keep up with the enormous amount of scrap.[58] His Chicago yards had at least 100,000 pickets ready for shipment from a seemingly inexhaustible supply, and in the lumber district he was the largest wholesaler of pickets.

At a time (1859–1861) when the wholesale market was still weak, Gideon made the two Hackley sawmills competitive by improving their bottom line. He did this by adding equipment that would turn scrap into lath, pickets, flooring, and siding, which added about another 20% to their top line. Joseph Hackley continued to improve the volume of lumber each mill manufactured, until the Trowbridge & Wing and Pomeroy & Holmes mills had a combined output nearly equal to the flagship Durkee-Truesdell mill.

Each of the smaller mills continued to show losses during the first three years, but Gideon's financial reserves got them through the lean years until each mill began making record-breaking profits. In the second year of the Civil War, lumber prices stabilized and at the end of 1861 both Hackley mills posted an accumulated (1858-1861) $8,470 ($700,000 today) profit.

Through perseverance Gideon survived the Panic of 1857, and emerged with a supply line that would bring millions of feet of lumber to his wholesale yards. He had no inkling that this would hugely benefit him when lumber prices soared with unprecedented demand during the last three years of the war.

During this period, Joseph Hackley plowed nearly all of their profits back into each mill, replacing old machinery, adding more saws, boilers, and steam engines. By 1864 both Hackley mills were solidly profitable and clearing around $31,000 ($1.8 million today) a year.[59] According to the ledgers at Michigan State University, when the books were closed each year, Gideon took his share in cash, and the Hackleys reinvested theirs to upgrade each mill, which caused the percentages of ownership to change.

After the first distribution of profits in 1861, Gideon's ownership dropped to 43%, giving Joseph Hackley 32%, and his twenty-three-year-old son Charley a 25% interest.[60] The Hackleys now owned a majority interest in each mill. Selling them the Pomeroy & Holmes and Trowbridge & Wing mills on easy terms was the best way for Gideon to cash out two troublesome mortgages during a very unstable economy, but for the Hackleys, it was the opportunity of a lifetime.

Once the economy stabilized toward the end of 1862, J.H. Hackley & Company ended the season with a $2,546 ($254,000 today) profit. By the end of 1863, the book value of the firm had more than doubled due to equipment upgrades, and running a second shift at each mill so they could double their output.[61]

J.H. Hackley & Company declared a profit of $7,000 ($600,000 today), and after two profitable seasons, Gideon formalized the transfer of ownership to each partner at the 1860 book value of $8,000 for the Trowbridge & Wing sawmill.[62] He waited until each mill was on solid ground before transferring the stock, but continued to loan the partnership funds at 10% interest. Twenty-six-year-old Jim McGordon had become invaluable, and Gideon sold him a quarter interest in the Trowbridge & Wing mill for $2,000 ($120,000 today), mostly on credit.

By then McGordon had become indispensable to the Trowbridge & Wing mill, and they couldn't afford to lose him to another sawmill looking for talent. It was never Gideon's intention to own the Durkee-Truesdell, Pomeroy & Holmes, or Trowbridge & Wing mills and pass the ownership to his son. He had an exit strategy in place whereby key employees would buy his interest in each sawmill, and his nephew, Arthur Truesdell, would run a scaled-down version of the Truesdell Lumber Company.

Hackley & McGordon (formerly the Trowbridge & Wing mill) with barrels of water on the ridge board in case the roof caught on fire, and hundreds of logs floating in the mill's holding pen. Picture courtesy of the Lakeshore Historical Museum.

It has been mistakenly reported that McGordon loaned Gideon Truesdell $2,609.92 ($248,000 today), and that he cancelled a debt by transferring ownership in the Trowbridge & Wing mill. There was cancellation of some type of debt, perhaps for work performed at the Durkee-Truesdell mill or scaling logs during the winters. Instead of drawing a salary the partners charged their personal expenses against their share of the business, and when the books were closed each year, they were deducted from their share of the profits. But it's utterly ridiculous to presume that a wealthy businessman would borrow such an enormous sum from an employee, and even if he did, where would Jim McGordon have come up with that kind of money?

Some of the confusion arises from the fact that although the Trowbridge & Wing mill was back in Gideon's hands in 1860, he chose *not* to transfer ownership until each mill was profitable. He would have signed a sales agreement with Joseph Hackley that locked in the price at $8,000, the current book value of the mill at the time of its transfer to J.H. Hackley & Company. But based on what we know about both men a handshake would have sealed the deal.

By 1863, the Trowbridge & Wing mill was solidly profitable, and the mill's book value had doubled to $16,540 ($1.5 million today). Yet, when he transferred ownership on December 21, 1863, he did so at the original $8,000 book value, the difference in book values is where some of the confusion arises, and how it was carried on the books.[63]

Although McGordon was an employee when the mill was "sold" to J.H. Hackley & Company, Gideon sold him a quarter interest at the same price as the other partners, which speaks volumes about what type of person he was. After the books were closed in 1863, and at the stroke of a pen each partner was $2,135 ($195,000 today) richer due to their hard work, and extraordinary perseverance. McGordon's life was truly a rags to riches story that could only have happened in America.

An ambitious fourteen-year-old from a large family left home to find work in a sawmill, learns the business, and when things weren't moving fast enough, he found a job with better prospects at the J.H. Hackley sawmill. He proved himself to be a capable and intelligent employee who demonstrated a solid work ethic, which resulted in his being offered a quarter interest. A decade later, Charles Hackley and Jim McGordon turned the Hackley & McGordon mill into one of the busiest on Muskegon Lake.[64] Thirty years later, Charles Hackley was one of the wealthiest lumbermen in North America.

Life in Lumber Town: Muskegon, Michigan

The Hackleys continued to live at the boarding house where Salina Hackley ran two shifts of kitchen help working a twelve-hour day, cleaning staff, and laundry workers. They were day laborers who lived elsewhere, often sharing a single room in a cheap boarding house until they found a husband, because life as a single woman in those days was one of starvation wages and dismal prospects.

Mrs. Hackley was a kind and loving mother figure to the children living on that end of Western Avenue, feeding hungry youngsters, and putting them to work helping the staff clean rooms, wash dishes, or help in the kitchen. This would have given these children a much-needed sense of purpose, and that nothing in life was free. She also taught them reading, writing, and arithmetic—along with "pleasant evenings and good advice."[65]

Sawmill owners, merchants, and the clergy tried to create wholesome alternatives other than sitting in a saloon. "Social life? The entertainments were very largely in those days boarding house socials, and afterward they developed into church socials. There was very little real social life her in those days."[66]

Once a month during the milling season, the larger mills took a turn hosting a big Saturday night dance at their boarding house, where the dining room stayed open late with the tables pushed aside for dancing. A fiddler was hired, and an elaborate spread of dishes was served with nothing stronger than cider, coffee or tea. With different mills taking their turn, there was always something worthwhile to do on a Saturday night when hundreds of men attended these events.

"Muskegon was a Saturday night town with dinner dances where employees took turns dancing with the wives or daughters of the mill owners, because everyone was on an equal social footing. Nobody dared step out-of-line or used foul language or the others would have dragged him outside and taught him some manners. In those days the man who dared to insult a woman on the street was likely to be knocked down by any passerby.... those were the good old days.... I never saw a drunken man at one of those dances."[67]

When the gregarious and fun-loving Alva Trowbridge took his turn, his parties were remembered as the best in town.[68] On Washington's birthday on February 12, 1863, he hosted a dance at the Durkee-Truesdell boarding house, with admission costing $1.00 and for 25¢ extra he served an oyster dinner, a rare luxury in a mill town. The proceeds went to aid the sick and suffering soldiers.[69]

Each summer, steamboats were rented for a shoreline cruise from Whitehall to Muskegon. Some 250 men and women dressed in their best clothes for this popular social event where a young man sometimes met his future wife. The larger mills contributed cash to defray the expenses, and gave away tickets to their employees. Since the temperatures was hot and humid, a committee of volunteer ladies, many of them the wives or daughters of mill owners, served cake, pie, fresh peaches, ice cold apple cider and desserts.

Fires brought the community together, and when something caught fire a long blast from a mill's steam whistle alerted everyone in town. The faster they responded the less damage to nearby buildings. If a pile of cross-stacked lumber caught on fire it was difficult to extinguish because the flames could burn between layers of boards for days.

Inside every sawmill were buckets of water. In an instant, they could be dumped on the floor when a spark from the machinery set a thin layer of sawdust on fire. Each sawmill had a fireman who periodically ran drills. Each employee had a specific job, some in the cellar where the boilers were located, the second-floor sawing room, and outside on the docks. Sawmills had five to ten large barrels on the roofs ridge board filled with rainfall. If the roof caught fire, employees climbed up a ladder attached to the building so they could kick over barrels of rain water to extinguish the flames.

Due to heavy losses, fire suppression systems came on the market during the war but with a heart-stopping price tag of around $1,800 ($165,000 today). With the turn of a valve, pressure from the steam engine pumped water through a series of perforated pipes running to every level of the building, rooftop, and docks. To prevent boilers on the ground floor from bursting into flames when they became over heated, they were surrounded by a cast iron reservoir of water that kept them from exploding and igniting the floor above.

Once sawmills began running around the clock, they needed indoor and outdoor lighting. Every sawmill with a night shift invested in hundreds of whale oil lanterns. About fifteen were mounted on a wagon wheel chandelier with dozens illuminating the sawing room floor and docks. They were lowered by a rope and pulley system so the mill's maintenance crew could refill the reservoirs, trim the wicks, and light them at dusk for the night shift.

"On entering Muskegon Lake, the stranger beholds on every side the long pipes or chimneys emitting vast clouds of smoke, and unmistakably indicating the active presence of that great mechanical agency, steam."[70] At night, the shoreline was a picturesque sight with red-hot sparks flying out of the smokestacks into the night air, with light streaming through each mill's windows from hundreds of oil lanterns.

The rumbling of twenty-seven steam engines along the lakeshore could be heard day and night, along with the sound of each mill's heavy iron log carriages gigging back and forth as over 500 saws on Muskegon Lake ripped through logs and trimmed thousands of boards, day and night. Anyone walking down Western Avenue could smell the heavy scent of pine, and feel the ground vibrating from the heavy log carriages moving back and forth.

According to 1864 tax returns, the two Hackley sawmills reported a $31,283 ($1.8 million today) income.[71] After six years of living frugally, Joseph Hackley moved his family across the street from the boarding house into a beautiful 3,300 square foot residence that he had built on Clay Avenue.[72] It was built on a double lot that he acquired in 1858 from Harvey Durkee.[73]

Joseph Hackley's 3,300 sq. ft. Italianate residence was completed in 1864 diagonally across Clay Avenue from the Durkee-Truesdell boarding house. Pictures courtesy of the Hackley-Holt House.

After McGordon bought a quarter-interest in the Trowbridge & Wing mill, the new firm was styled Hackley, McGordon & Company. McGordon and Charles Hackley had become friends, and thought nothing of staying out all night. Both were heavy drinkers, although Charley was described as a friendly drunk whereas McGordon was an angry drunk who liked to pick fights. After a decade of sawmill ownership, they marveled at how a couple of poor boys became so rich.

"As they reached a lamp post, Jim reached for it and as he swung around it and fell down, he looked up and said 'Charley, what in the hell is the matter with us anyway?' He replied, 'Jim, I do not know but I guess that we have too much money.'"[74] The moral to this story is that Jim couldn't walk a straight line but Charley could.

On another night of heavy drinking, Charley amused himself by throwing the dishes on his table, and watching them shatter into tiny pieces once they hit the floor. The owner of the saloon came running from the kitchen until somebody stopped him, and explained that when he sobered up Charley would send somebody with a check, and that he never quibbled about the amount. The owner saw this as an opportunity to replace his old chipped plates, and had somebody bring Charley more plates to smash. When Jim and Charley were out on the town nobody could predict how their night would end.

McGordon was likeable enough to get elected to several terms on the Muskegon City Council. But according to family legend, he was an "excessive drinker... involved in unorthodox behavior on many occasions."[75] He had a Jekyll and Hyde personality that got ugly after a night of drinking. One night Jim had been out on the town with Levi Beardsley, and when they reached Frank Scott's saloon, Jim could see that it was closed due to a funeral in the boarding house upstairs. "Jim seized Levi and threw him headfirst into the hearse parked in front of the house, and told the driver to take him to the cemetery, which cost him $10,000 ($250,000 today) when Levi brought suit and collected the damages of an expensive judgement."[76] (Beardsley was a lawyer.)

McGordon dropped dead at the age of forty-four in a Grand Rapids, Michigan, hotel room, and according to the *Isabella County Enterprise*, he "supposedly died of heart disease."[77] This sounds plausible, because his brother also died young of a heart attack, and Jim knew he wasn't well because the previous night before he died, he wrote a new will.

A few months earlier, Jim had been arrested for attempted murder after firing a gun at somebody during a drunken argument. According to court documents, Charles and Porter Hackley posted his $10,000 bond.[78] Two months later, Jim was charged with assault with intent to murder, a serious charge that would have been tough to beat until Jim had the good sense to drop dead.[79] The men running the Truesdell Lumber Company were in their twenties and heavy drinkers, including Gideon's son, who could drink just about anyone under the table.[80]

After a tough day of work a lot of men gravitated to the saloons on Western Avenue, or the rougher joints on Ottawa Street in "sawdust flats" where the men pounded them down just as fast as the bartenders could fill their glasses. One saloon was so busy they had ten bartenders per shift.[81] In a world of low wages and hard physical work this was their pressure valve, and it wasn't a good one.

Death at a young age was common in every mill town, and when a corpse was found floating by the Truesdell dock it turned out to be a booming company employee. "It is supposed that this man was so intoxicated that he did not know land from water, and he tumbled into the lake through his own ignorance."[82] Oddly enough, another body had been fished out of the water by the Truesdell dock two weeks earlier.[83]

G. Truesdell & Son, General Merchants: Croton Township, Michigan

Each year, thousands of loggers blazed through thousands of acres of trees until the early 1860s, when logging operations reached the confluence of the Muskegon and Little Muskegon Rivers forty miles northeast deep in timber country. During the past twenty years loggers had devoured pineland on each side of the river. Since logs were hauled to the riverbank by sleds, logging crews went no further than a mile into the woods. Twenty years later, they would use temporary logging railroads that allowed them to go several miles from the riverfront.

Croton was located at the confluence of the Muskegon and Little Muskegon Rivers, and had a small hotel and a few stores that were the last sign of civilization before entering what became the 5,784-acre Manistee National Forest.[84] To provision his logging camps and dozens of others, Gideon built a large mercantile store that carried everything from groceries to hardware to clothing to patent medicines.[85]

Gideon purchased twelve lots and built a three-story building at 29 River Street with a dock and barn along the riverfront where most of his inventory came from Muskegon Lake.[86] Throughout the summer of 1861, dozens of barges would have been loaded with lumber, bricks, doors, and windows, and towed upriver to the confluence of the Muskegon and Little Muskegon Rivers.

Based on a credit report from R.G. Dun & Company he opened this store in January of 1862, and it was listed as a branch of his Muskegon mercantile business.[87] They had a difficult time nailing down his assets because "his property is so scattered that no person can make a close estimate."[88]

Gideon also opened a store in Whitehall sometime in 1862, although it probably did little more than provision his loggers on the White River.[89] This store was located at 17 Colby Street, and according to R.G. Dun & Company it too was listed as a branch of Gideon Truesdell's Muskegon store. According to Arthur Truesdell, during the war these three stores grossed around $200,000 ($17.1 million today).[90]

We know from an 1856 *Grand River Times* article that there were 3,460 men working in the woods along the Muskegon and Grand Rivers. Schooners brought about 95,000 feet of lumber to Kenosha, and returned with provisions, hay, and oats from the Kenosha Pier Company. Once the supplies reached Muskegon, they were loaded on barges and towed upriver.[91]

Around 1861, Harvey Durkee and Gideon Truesdell started a provisioning business they ran from the Kenosha Pier Company. They assembled large bulk grocery orders, and shipped them aboard empty lumber schooners returning to Green Bay and Muskegon. The following was a typical order:

> 500 tons of hay
> 23,000 bushels of oats
> 170 barrels of pork
> 180 barrels of plate beef
> 8 tons of dry pork
> 14,000 pounds of butter
> 600 pounds of lard
> 80 pounds of coffee
> 450 pounds of bacon
> 110 barrels of sugar
> 10 barrels of salt
> 600 barrels of flour
> 155 barrels corned beef
> 36 barrels of dried apples
> 50 boxes of prunes
> 50 barrels of crackers
> 29 half barrels of syrup
> 82 chests of tea

55 barrels of beans
119 barrels of peas
2,000 pounds of rice
75 boxes of soap
22 barrels of pickles
33 barrels of sauerkraut
17 barrels of vinegar
68 cases of baking powder
16 cases of baking soda
300 pounds of mustard
300 pounds of pepper
11 pounds of all spice
1,800 lbs. chewing tobacco
1,500 lbs. smoking tobacco
250 pairs blankets
66 boxes of axes
71 dozen axe handles

Gideon owned a majority interest in Truesdell, Backert & Company with George Backert (1808–1891).[92] They owned two grist mills where Backert turned wheat into flour and ground oats. He also baled hay for the hundreds of horses used by the logging camps, because horses and mules were the backbone of every logging operation, pulling sleds loaded with several tons of logs to the riverfront.[93]

Each winter, Croton became the headquarters for upriver logging operations with stagecoaches running to Grand Rapids, Big Rapids, and Muskegon. Accounts were set up at G. Truesdell & Son for the men who worked for Gideon, Martin Ryerson, Sextus Wilcox, Alva Trowbridge and others where credit had already been established. A large share of their business was provisioning loggers and their horses throughout the winter.

Logging camps tried to keep their lumberjacks on a short leash, because fighting and drunkenness led to all kinds of problems, including murder, if an angry logger decided to take a swing at somebody with an axe. Each person signed an employment contract that stated they agreed to work for $200 to $250 ($24,000 today) for about one hundred days from dawn to dusk six days a week. Each logger was paid at the end of the season with penalties deducted for a variety of reasons.

Penalties were charged for refusing to get out of bed, drinking, fighting or starting trouble with most of these infractions considered a breach of contract that resulted in termination. If a logger left before the end of his contract or was fired, he was paid for the number of days that he worked less a 20% penalty, and according to the terms of the contract he had to wait until the end of the season to get paid.

After a man was killed in a logging accident, his heartless employer had the audacity to deduct 20% from his accumulated earnings for not completing his contract, but this would have made it extremely difficult for him to hire loggers the following season because word traveled fast in the woods. Then as now, a man's reputation followed him wherever he went.

When a logger was kicked out of the camp his life was in danger, because being stuck in the woods with a large wolf population wasn't a good thing. He might have found work at another camp desperate for loggers, but an experienced foreman knew better than to hire somebody elses headache.

The men usually didn't work on Sundays unless they were behind schedule due to inclement weather, like ice storms. Some of the men spent a few hours on horseback riding into Croton where they charged tobacco or other items at Truesdell's store. Some camps extended credit to their men, and helped them forward money to their families through this store. Gideon and Joseph Hackley went to great lengths to accommodate their loggers because good help was hard to find.

Dishonest employers took advantage of every opportunity to cheat their workers. The two most common were charging a 500% mark up at the company store or selling liquor because the mark-up on that was astronomical. Gideon's store was the only one in Croton, and yet he kept his prices reasonable. According to Michael Sullivan, "we could get things pretty reasonably. We used to pay two shillings for a pair of blue overalls."[94]

If he ran a crooked operation, at the end of the season a logger would have owed for tobacco, clothing, food, and incidentals at an exorbitant mark-up. Tobacco that cost 6¢ in Muskegon cost 92¢ at a company store, and because everything was sold with at least a 500% mark-up a logger left the woods with practically nothing to show for his work. But in those days an angry worker settled the score with a match. The greedy employer might have figured a way to cheat his workers, but it only took one match to set his store on fire during the middle of the night.

Before the winter freeze, tugboats cleared submerged logs from the last log drive. During the winter the icy river was crowded with sleds pulled by dogs bringing supplies to logging camps. According to the *Muskegon Chronicle* "A stage coach ran to Newaygo but a fast walker could beat it, and more than once look back and see it stuck in the mud or tipped over, neither an uncommon occurrence."⁹⁵

The Croton store was run by Gideon's forty-nine-year-old brother, Amos Truesdell (1813–1885), a good businessman with a courteous demeanor who was scrupulously honest. His son, Arthur, was a different story because he had a tougher personality that sometimes rubbed people the wrong way.

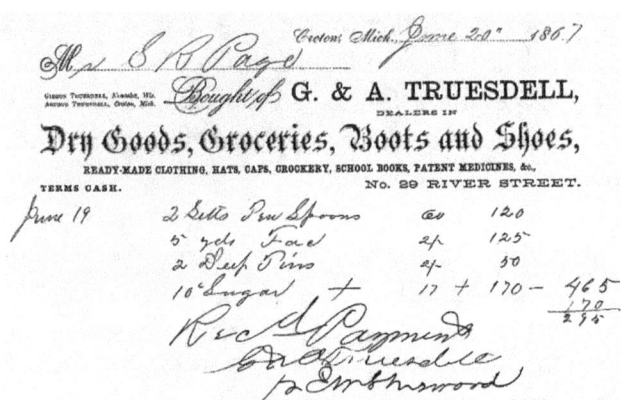

Receipt issued to S.R. Page who was connected with Alva Trowbridges logging operations, and signed by G. & A. Truesdell's manager, Erastus Sherwood. Reproduction courtesy of Michigan State University, Hackley & Hume papers.

Amos Truesdell petitioned the government to locate a post office in their store, and his son, Arthur, was appointed postmaster. This only lasted a few years, because in 1866 "Arthur Truesdell, Esq., Postmaster of Croton, received a suggestive letter from the Post Office Department. He is a true Republican and after writing a response to the letter," said the *Detroit Advertiser*, "he gave Andrew Johnson to understand with what feelings of contempt he is regarded by the loyal portion of the community very quietly sent in his resignation. The trouble is now to find any man so mean as to be willing to take the office."⁹⁶ A few years later Arthur was elected to the Newaygo County Board but resigned before his term ended. He moved to Big Rapids where he supervised logging operations for Gideon and Martin Ryerson.⁹⁷

R.G. Dun & Company gave G. Truesdell & Son an unlimited credit rating of "good for what they want," which meant that whatever they ordered would be paid for. Their report also stated that their real estate consisted of store and lots and grist mills. "Gideon Truesdell alone is worth $100,000 ($8.6 million today). He is doing a heavy lumbering business."[98] In 1865, he sold his nephew, Arthur Truesdell, an interest in his Croton store in a firm styled G. & A. Truesdell.[99]

Logging Camps & Muskegon River Log Drives

In anticipation of the $640,000 ($54 million today) of lumber shipments experts predicted could be sent to the Mississippi River through the Kenosha harbor, Gideon and Martin Ryerson formed an arrangement where they shared logging and milling expenses to create a supply line to wholesale yards in Rockford, Illinois, where a large tonnage of lumber was shipped to interior retail yards along the 299-mile Rock River.[100] It was an arrangement borne of mutual need.

A lumberman could significantly expand his commercial reach with partnerships, and Martin Ryerson was involved in dozens of them.[101] He provided the trees at a time when Gideon didn't have much in the way of pinelands, and as an experienced logger he ran several crews during the winter along the White, Muskegon, and Grand Rivers. After the logs were banked along the river, they were rafted to smaller mills where they were sawed for Martin Ryerson and Gideon Truesdell at a contract price.

Once the logs were turned into lumber, an enormous tonnage was loaded aboard schooners and ferried across Lake Michigan to the Kenosha Pier Company, where they were shipped via the Kenosha & Rockford to Rockford, Illinois wholesale yards.[102]

At some point to facilitate his logging operations along the Grand River, Gideon acquired an interest in Amos Norton & Company in Grand Haven, Michigan.[103] Wealthy lumbermen could acquire an interest in a smaller sawmill with old equipment by writing a check to upgrade their saws, which paid for itself in less than a year, and significantly increased the volume of lumber they could manufacture. It also gave the lumberman a degree of control over a mill's availability to cut logs exclusively for them.

One of the most competent "cruisers" along the Muskegon River was Cornelius Eyke (1834–1900), who landed in Muskegon from the Netherlands at the age of twenty-four.[104] According to the *Muskegon Chronicle* he entered into the employ of "Truesdell & Hackley" on December 3, 1859.[105] He learned how to estimate the quantity of lumber that could be cut from an acre of land, which trees had little value, and became an expert woodsman.

Logging had a standard regimen. Cut the trees during the winter, use the frozen ground to skid them to the riverbank, drop them into the river after the spring thaw, and let the Muskegon Booming Company raft the logs to Muskegon Lake using the millions of gallons of melted snow that created a run-off into the river. Before that happened, a "scaler" measured the length and diameter of each log, and called out the figures to a tallyman who recorded them in a journal.

The foreman knew how many logs the Durkee-Truesdell, Pomeroy & Holmes, and Trowbridge & Wing mills needed to run at full capacity. If the land had more trees than the mill could process, the foreman told his men to stop when they reached a certain point. If they cut too many trees, they had to warehouse them in a lake where the water preserved the wood until next season. If the logs laid in the woods for another year, they would have been worthless due to insect infestation.

To run his three sawmills around the clock, Gideon needed at least 60,000 logs each year. Lumbermen had to replace an enormous number of trees each season, because the 26 mills on Muskegon Lake consumed over a million logs a year.

Much of the upriver logging activities fell to Joseph Hackley, and while the mills were closed for the winter, he and his older sons were busy in the woods. He would have sent a cruiser like Henry Orton, Cornelius Eyke, or Jim McGordon to calculate the amount of lumber they could cut from each parcel.[106] The easiest way to run his calculations was to climb a tree, locate a landmark, and take a compass reading. Once on the ground, he followed his bearings until reaching the landmark, and estimated the yield in board-feet by taking random samplings. He counted the trees, measured the diameter of each trunk, and estimated the yield from a chart that did the math for him.

According to a cruiser's report "North of the line I have marked a line of Pine; the pine stands quite thick and even varying from 25 to 50 trees per acre from 16 inches to 3 feet in diameter and would generally work from 80 to 100 feet. Much of this would be termed cork pine. Good deal of double or thribble pine or buckwheat pine and trees taper rapidly, knots show from the ground, more than one fifth would not pay to cut for logs. Ground is generally pretty level but with some gullies."[107]

In this example, the cruiser calculated that this tract would produce

7,150,000 board feet. That amounted to 12,000 board feet per acre, about twice the states average. He also reported that 20,000 trees were suitable for logging, and 3,500 trees weren't worth the expense of cutting.

Loading 2,000-pound logs on a sled using chains and mules. Pictures courtesy of the Lakeshore Museum Center.

Teams of horses pulled several tons of logs to the riverbank. Pictures courtesy of Michigan State University.

The logging season began sometime in November and ended in late February or early March, when warmer temperatures began melting the snow, which created a run-off that raised the river's water table enough to float 250,000 logs sixty miles downriver to the mills. There was a method to launching that many logs, because the currents had to move thousands of tons through several counties until reaching the sorting pens on Muskegon Lake. Logs first were stacked along the riverfront at the logging camp; wedges against the logs closest to the water were pulled loose by a horse or mule until the weight of the logs caused hundreds of tons to tumble into the water.

The camps furthest upriver put their logs into the water first, and when they floated past the next camp, they dropped theirs into the water until hundreds of logging camps launched an enormous tonnage of logs. The key to keeping the logs floating downriver was a strict timetable of when each camp dropped their logs into the water.

Not a single log could be launched until a Muskegon Booming Company official gave permission, and made a certified count. The number of logs launched needed to match the number of logs tallied at the Muskegon booming grounds. If there was an unaccounted 5,000 feet they were impounded until their driving fees were paid.

The Muskegon River was divided into "beats." The section below Houghton Lake was the Boiling Springs beat, followed by the Jonesville beat, Norway beat, Grindstone beat, Evart beat, Big Rapids beat, Newaygo beat, and Muskegon beat. Each section had its own crew with a foreman responsible for keeping the logs moving. The jam crew rode along the edge of the shoreline looking for the stoppage. Sometimes it was just a matter of chopping a few logs loose. More often than not twenty or more men had to use mules and chains to pull hundreds of logs apart. As a last resort, they used dynamite but it was highly unstable and could blow off a finger or two, and sometimes a hand.

When the Muskegon Booming Company was organized in 1864, a yearly contract for running the log drive went to the lowest bidder, who hired and managed a couple of hundred men to work the drive. Thousands of logs were delivered to the Muskegon Lake sorting grounds where they were sorted by stamp. The booming company charged 3¢ to 16¢ a log depending on its distance from Muskegon.

The firm that won the rafting contract was paid a percentage of the driving fee, which were Odell & Orton (1862–1864), followed by Henry and A.F. Orton (1865–1868) and L.G. Mason (1869–1871).[108]

It's difficult to say how many logs Gideon put into three different rivers because he logged so much land in partnership with others. According to the *Detroit Free Press*, in 1864 he dropped 16.9 million board feet of his own logs into the Muskegon River and J. H. Hackley & Company launched 9,478,040 feet of logs.[109]

Muskegon Booming Company

A year or two after Durkee, Truesdell & Company began logging operations, the number of logs placed in the Muskegon River had become so large that lumbermen formed the Muskegon Log & Mill Owners' Association. "In those days every owner rafted his own logs. There were two booms at the head of the lake, and here every mill owner had to raft his logs after they came down the river. Each mill owner sent his own men to do the work."[110]

During the Civil War, booming companies had to reorganize with new charters that shielded their liability. The Muskegon Booming Company was incorporated in 1864 and, among other things, obtained water rights to Muskegon Lake along with what became known as the sorting grounds at the mouth of the river. This is where logs came floating down the river during the log drive, and were sorted based on the log stamp.

Chauncey Davis was elected president and Joseph Hackley, treasurer. Both had been heavily involved in its predecessor, the Muskegon Log & Mill Owners' Association. They knew more than anyone about booming operations, and simplified a complicated log drive. Within a few years the Muskegon Booming Company floated over 500,000 logs sixty miles to the sorting pens on Muskegon Lake.[111] Of the sixteen stockholders, six were Chicago lumber dealers who owned Muskegon sawmills with "extensive timber holdings in the region."[112]

Chauncey Davis*
Joseph Hackley
Robert H. Foss*
Sextus N. Wilcox*
Charles D. Nelson
Henry Beidler*
Martin Ryerson*

J.H. Swan*
George H. Roberts*
Gideon Truesdell*
R.P. Easton
O.P Pillsbury
Samuel A. Brown
Tunis Ryerson
Lyman G. Mason*
T.J. Rand

*Chicago lumber dealers who owned Muskegon Sawmills and pinelands.

Muskegon Booming Company sporting grounds (L). Picture courtesy of Lakeshore Museum Center. An accumulation of logs after a log drive (R). Picture courtesy of The American Lumberman.

When more funds were needed, they didn't hesitate to raise their capitalization, because two years after their incorporation they employed over 200 men with a payroll of $1.3 million ($78 million today).[113]

The booming company's biggest headache was fraud. It wasn't difficult to drop 20,000 logs into the river and report a lower number to avoid driving fees. Once the logs were in the river, thieves were known to cut off a competitor's log stamp so they could stamp their own. Stealing trees from adjacent tracts was another type of stealing, and called "cutting the big forty," where they accidently cut five acres on each side from surrounding parcels until they had twenty acres of free logs. If caught, the foreman blamed it on foreign born loggers who didn't understand the language, although officials were skeptical and seldom fooled.

The remedy was more inspectors watching what was going on in the woods. A Muskegon Booming Company official needed to see proof of ownership of the land from the camps' foremen, or a logging contract signed by the land owner before he received permission to begin logging operations. Before the log drive, each camp needed to have a certified count, and once the logs reached the sorting grounds the beginning and ending count had to be reasonably close.

The log drive ended at Maple Island near Muskegon Lake, where the logs were sent to an inlet that had been turned into a sorting ground with a couple of hundred pens. It was low tech but effective, with sorters standing on a narrow pier, and using a pole with a hook to pull the log into a pen. When a log mark's pen was full, they were chained together, and a tugboat pulled this floating pen to the "storage yards" in the middle of Muskegon Lake. Since the lake was over 4,000 acres, there was plenty of room in the middle for 500 acres of floating log pens.

Every sawmill had a holding pen next to their mill where logs were muscled onto a conveyor that brought them to the second-floor sawing room. After the logs had been unchained from the floating boom over a thousand pounds of chains were piled on the end of the sawmill's dock, and a couple of tugboats did nothing but retrieve these chains.

Working on a sawmill's boom could be dangerous. "A young man was drowned in White & Swan's boom on Friday afternoon. He was engaged in loading vessels and his haste to get from one dock to another to secure a job from a vessel that had just came in attempted to cross the floating logs. He fell into the water between two logs and they closed over him preventing his rising to the surface. His body was at once recovered but life was extinct."[114]

Upon delivery, the foreman signed a receipt listing the number of logs in each raft, and fees were determined by the distance each log traveled. The Muskegon River was divided into ten sections; the further the logs had to travel the higher the driving fee. About a third of the cost of turning logs into lumber came from rafting, sorting, and delivery fees. We know from booming company reports that Gideon paid as little as 3¢ ($1.80 today) per thousand feet in Muskegon County and 15¢ ($9 today) sixty miles northeast in Mecosta County.[115]

But that wasn't all, because once the logs reached Muskegon Lake the booming company charged the owner of the logs 7¢ to 15¢ per thousand feet for sorting and delivery of the logs to their sawmill. Based on the volume of his mills, Gideon paid around $5,600 ($420,000 today) in rafting fees each year. Each day a booming company official would deliver a bill at the sawmill's office, and find out how many rafts they wanted delivered from the storage yards in the middle of Muskegon Lake. "To maintain operations, the booming company owned a fleet of tugs, a dredge, and pile drivers."[116]

The booming grounds was a sight to behold as evidenced by a *Jackson City Patriot* article: "No person should fail to see how three hundred thousand feet of lumber, belonging to nearly fifty different firms are sorted in the water, made up into rafts, and taken by tugboats to the mill of the rightful owner. After the logs have reached the booming ground, each one of the two hundred men sorts them accurately and expeditiously, and is as familiar with the marks as we are with the alphabet."[117]

In 1868 the booming company's capitalization increased from $40,000 to $100,000 with over 200 men employed, with a $16,000 ($880,000 today) monthly payroll, and ten tugboats in constant operation.[118] It was a big operation.

During the Civil War, whatever logs Truesdell dumped into the White River were processed at a contract price by one of the local mills on White Lake in northern Muskegon County. By 1869, it was possible to tow rafts of logs directly from White Lake to Muskegon Lake. Mason, Pingree, & Lloyd, brought "two large rafts of first-class logs" from the White River, 17 miles north, to Muskegon Lake by towing them on Lake Michigan for Ryerson, Hills & Company. "Another raft is coming this week and in all sufficient to make to make 2,000,000 feet of lumber. Mr. Lloyd says it is just as easy to bring a raft from the White River as it is to tow it on Muskegon Lake."[119]

Schooner being towed through the 2.5 mile channel between Lake Michigan and Muskegon Lake. Picture courtesy of Lakeshore Museum Center.

City of Grand Haven. Picture courtesy of the Michigan Maritime Museum.

By 1870, when several mill owners were dissatisfied over the Muskegon Booming Company fees, they formed the Union Booming Company, hired a Grand Haven firm to build sorting grounds, and put them under contract to sort and deliver logs.[120] Charles Hackley was elected president, although a month later the dispute was resolved, and the new firm disbanded.[121]

Hardwoods weren't typically rafted on the Muskegon River because they were heavier, and tended to sink. But we know from tax records that J.H. Hackley & Company processed hardwoods for Truesdell's Chicago carriage shop on State Street, where Gideon kept a small crew of yard workers busy during the winters building 150 to 200 carriages.[122] According to tax records Gideon declared a $1,000 ($87,000 today) profit.[123]

G.J. and Louisa Truesdell

G.J. Truesdell (1842–1922) was Gideon and Julia's only surviving child, and the heir-apparent to his father's fortune. He was described as a quiet, unassuming young man with a strong work ethic, but lacked his father's shrewd, tough, and pragmatic nature.[124] He was a friendly young man that people liked.[125] The earliest settlers of Kenosha had done something quite extraordinary when they taxed themselves to open the first free school west of the Alleghenies. Any resident could send their children to this school free of charge. This was largely due to the efforts of Reverend Rueben Deming, Charles Durkee, Michael Frank, and Jason Lothrop.

As was the custom of the day, G.J. graduated from high school at the age of fifteen just as his father took over Durkee, Truesdell & Company. He had a bright future but it seems likely that his father realized his easy-going nature was better suited to the mercantile business. It was less demanding, and would allow him to spend time with his family. His cousin, Arthur, was being groomed to take over a scaled down Truesdell Lumber Company when Gideon semi-retired in a few years.[126]

G.J. grew up with his cousins, Adelbert (1838–1878) and Arthur Truesdell (1840–1920), both of whom lived in Kenosha with Gideon and Julia during their teens so they could receive a good education.[127] Their father, Amos, was farming out in Pleasant Prairie about sixteen miles west of downtown Kenosha.[128] Neither of them cared for farming so they began working part-time at the Durkee-Truesdell lumberyard.[129]

Adelbert landed a job on the schooner Challenge and fell in love with the sea.[130] He spent the rest of his life sailing, and saw heavy action during the Civil War along the Atlantic seaboard in the U.S. Navy.[131] He died at age of forty off the coast of Africa during a violent storm when he was pitched overboard.[132] G.J. would name his son, Adelbert J. Truesdell (1882–1973), after him.[133]

At a time when substitutes were hired to take the place of draftees, the Civil War draft didn't touch the men running the Truesdell Lumber Company. Arthur Truesdell, Charles Hackley, Edwin Hackley, James McGordon, William Glue, and G.J. Truesdell worked a twelve-hour day, and with the exception of Glue and Edwin Hackley, spent the night drinking.[134] A few years later Charley signed a temperance pledge which, according to one saloon owner, cost him $1,500 ($38,000 today) a year in business.[135]

During one particular drunken slug-fest, Jim McGordon and Porter Hackley got into a brawl where Porter cut Jim's mouth badly. In a drunken rage he yelled at Jim "now you can drink your whiskey and eat your dinner at the same time."[136] Charles Hackley once recalled that the saloons were just as bad as the boarding house because the same people got on your nerves there, telling the same boring stories and making the same pointless arguments.[137]

According to family legend, G.J. met Sarah Louisa Greene (1846–1921) in Chicago, where she was either staying or living with the Martin Ryerson family at their Michigan Avenue mansion on "millionaires' row."[138] Her father, Samuel, had been his partner in a mill styled Greene & Ryerson until they amicably dissolved their partnership, and went in different directions.[139] She graduated from the Chicago Academy or Nursing at the age of sixteen after completing a one-year course. It was the top wrung of the ladder for a single girl, and she was highly intelligent.[140]

At the age of nineteen, G.J. Truesdell began courting sixteen-year-old Sarah Louisa Greene. She came from a distinguished early American family, and was supposedly descended from Revolutionary War General Nathanial Greene, one of George Washington's most effective field commanders.[141]

In 1843, Greene left to build a water-powered mill on Bear Lake, and opened a retail yard in Kenosha.[142] It was a good business until his mill was damaged by a flood, at which point he opened a "liquor grocery." When he died, Martin Ryerson and Theodore J. Rand were listed as executors for his estate, and although he owned a lot of land, he also owed a lot of money, because when his estate was settled there wasn't much left for his children.

Sam and Louisa Greene were orphans; she was only twelve years old and Sam was fourteen years old when they lost their parents. Upon graduating from high school, Louisa sailed across Lake Michigan where she stayed in Chicago with the Ryersons while attending nursing school.[143] She graduated from the Chicago Academy of Nursing, which was probably the best career path for a single lady. Her whereabouts have been difficult to pinpoint but it seems likely she met her future husband, G.J. Truesdell, at the Ryerson residence.[144]

Charles H. Hackley (CR) and Julia Moore Hackley (R). Picture courtesy of the Lakeshore Museum.

G.J. Truesdell and Louisa Greene Truesdell. Pictures courtesy of the Leonard C. (Maudine) Truesdell family.

After his parent's died, Samuel O. Greene (1844–1891) went to live at George Ruddiman's boarding house, and worked at his sawmill.[145] At the age of fourteen, he was on his own earning a living, and making his own way in the world. According to the 1860 census, at the age of seventeen he was listed as a "chore boy" living at their boarding house.[146] At the start of the war he enlisted in the Michigan 3rd Calvary Regiment (Company I).[147]

After two years of heavy fighting half of his regiment died, and in 1864 Samuel was mustered out of the Union Army as a Sergeant. He re-enlisted in the 3rd Arkansas Cavalry where at a young age he was promoted to First Lieutenant, and became Adjutant to the Commanding General.[148]

While Samuel was fighting, his seventeen-year-old sister married twenty-year-old G.J. Truesdell on June 2, 1863.[149] The wedding brought family and friends to Muskegon including Julia Truesdell's niece, Julia Ann Torrey (1838–1905), who came three months before the wedding, and stayed for four more.[150] After the last of Durkee-Truesdell's bills were paid, Gideon built a beautiful home overlooking Muskegon Lake where Miss Moore stayed for nine months while being courted by Charles Hackley.[151]

In 1862, Gideon Truesdell built a 4,400 sq. ft. Italianate residence nearly identical to the one pictured, overlooking Muskegon Lake with several acres of adjacent acres of orchards. A kitchen and servants quarters were attached to the rear of the house with a stable.

The romance began when Mrs. Truesdell asked Charley to escort her young niece to the wedding.[152] Charley spent a lot of time at their house that summer as a dinner guest, and the Truesdells were pleased with the match.[153] By the time Julia Ann returned to her home in New York for the holidays, she was engaged.[154] The following year they were married in Centerville, New York.[155]

G.J. worked hard under his father's direction, and became a partner in G. Truesdell & Son, a large mercantile store on Western Avenue in Muskegon. This business had grown from the one-room storefront that his uncle opened to one of the larger mercantile stores in town with branches in Whitehall, Croton, and Kenosha. As they expanded into boots, shoes, saddles, clothing, groceries, and livestock feed, Gideon added more buildings until they occupied an entire block across from the mill.[156]

The Typical Life of a Lumberjack in the Woods

The following narrative was published in *Scribner's Magazine*, and gives us a look at life in the woods and the danger they faced from a large wolf population.

"Our camp consisted of two log cabins, each twenty-four feet wide by forty-feet long; just outside the entrance to the sleeping cabin; we dug a well early in the season, into which we put a long wooden pump from which we obtained excellent water.

"The snow fell in great sheets, all day, and at night it was hard work tramping to the cabin after dark. No liquor of any kind was allowed. Anyone found smuggling any in had it forcibly taken from him and emptied on the ground, and was given his pay ticket.

"As Christmas drew near, we all began to feel a little lonelier, and began to think more of home and loved ones for a good many of my men were fine, sturdy fellows of good habits, who had good homes down in the southern part of the state.

"I had some work to do in the woods nearly three-quarters of a mile away. Some of the teams came down late in the afternoon to do a little necessary work, and one of the teamsters urged me to ride home with him on his logging sleigh, telling me he had seen some timber wolves prowling about that afternoon, and we had heard them during the day running deer through the forest, which indicated that they were getting hungry as the snow was so deep as to cut them off from finding any small game.

"I had a rifle; revolver and a small axe with me in the little cabin. I soon finished my work and prepared to take up my lonely walk to the camp. I did not notice the rifle or revolver, the later lying on the desk and the former standing in the corner, but putting my papers in my pocket, I took a light axe, which I carried with me through the woods nearly all the time.

"My lantern was the ordinary one with a glass globe with wires about it and burned whale oil. This lamp was well filled with oil and was burning brightly, I having trimmed the wick well just before dark. I trudged up the road which was simply two trenches in the snow, which was three feet deep and between these trenches. My rubber soles made no sound on the smooth, hard snow and there was scarcely a sound of any kind in the vast forest, the stillness being almost uncanny.

Pictures courtesy of the American Lumberman.

"After walking perhaps one-fourth of a mile, all at once a sound struck my ear like a sort of pit-pat, pit-pat, which attracted my attention to such an extent that I stopped and looked behind me to see if someone was coming. As soon as I stopped, the sound ceased, and listening for a moment and hearing and seeing nothing, I turned about and trudged on. But I soon noticed that as soon as I commenced walking, the pit-pat also commenced. It was weird and at first, I did not think of wolves.

"I noticed the sound was not all behind me but some of it was on either side of the road. At last, the tension became so great that the chills began to run up and down my backbone, and I must confess to feeling a little nervous. I at last stopped to find out what made the noise, and holding up my lantern so that it would shine down a straight stretch of road, I saw the reflection of light in two spots close together in one of the sleigh tracks, and discovered the same in the other track. I raised my lantern a little higher and saw several more pairs of what looked like eyes shining behind the first ones. Quick as a flash, I realized I was being followed by a pack of gray timber wolves.

"I swung the lantern so as to let it shine over the crust of snow, and soon discovered that there were a number of wolves stalking me on either side as well as behind. My first idea was to frighten them back, and swung my lantern, and had the satisfaction of seeing the shining eyeballs disappear in the distance. Turning about, I started on a swift walk up the road toward the camp, shouting as I came nearer, hoping that some of the men might step outside for something.

"Time after time I heard the footsteps of the wolves behind me and alongside, and turned about making a short rush toward them swinging my lantern until they fell back. But every time I did so I found they were nearer than before. At last, I approached the last turn in the road, and across the bend I could see the lights in the camp, and I shouted again for help and thought to myself what a foolish thing I did in leaving my rifle and revolver at the camp.

Richard C. Fritz

"As I turned, I saw about ten feet to the right of the road a small, soft maple tree with the top broken off perhaps a dozen feet or more from the ground. The trunk of the tree was not much larger than an ordinary stovepipe, with some stubs of branches down quite near the ground. I was getting tired, and knew that the wolves would close in if possible before I could reach the camp, which was still an eighth of a mile away.

"I knew if my lantern went out or dropped, they would jump upon me. The rapid whirling of the lantern caused the springs of the lamp to collapse and the lamp fell, of course bottom side up, and went out. With only the stars left shining over me I knew that a hand-to-hand battle with the wolves would follow.

"As my lantern could do me no further good, I dropped it in the road, and seizing my light axe by the handle I had just time as the foremost wolf, a huge brute with tremendous fangs, made a spring for my throat. Swinging the axe and the sharp blade hitting him on the side of his head laid his brain open and he fell on the road with a piercing howl. Quick as a flash it came to me that my only hope was climbing a tree. But the wolves saw me escaping, and those that were on the crest at the side of the road made a dash for me.

"Just as I drew myself up almost out of reach the foremost one made a spring and caught the heel of my right rubber overshoe between his fangs, and made a desperate effort to pull me down; but I had a firm hold on some small branches of the maple, and giving a heavy jerk I pulled my heel out of his mouth. I climbed as near the top of the tree waiting for the onslaught of the entire pack, which I knew would not be long delayed. It came almost instantly, and it seemed to me that the woods were full of big, gray wolves all howling and gnashing their teeth in the hope of picking my bones.

Pictures courtesy of the Western Frontier.

"There I was with no weapon, not even my axe, which I dropped before I started to climb, and still fully an eighth of a mile from camp. The wolves fell to gnawing the tree and fighting, and apparently climbing over one another in their efforts to reach me when I got my second wind. Having a pretty robust voice I let out a loud call for help, and I could plainly see the lights of the camp shining through the windows, and I could even hear the oxen and horses in the barn across the road. I thought if I could hold out until the men were through supper, and the teamsters came out to attend to the horses and oxen I could make them hear me.

"I saw the cabin door open. One of the men stepped outside with a lantern in his hand. I again raised my voice in a robust call for help, and I saw him stop suddenly, listen for a second, and then heard an answering shout as he turned and rushed back into the cabin. In a moment nearly the entire forty men were outside, and I heard him say 'Come on boys, for God's sake, the wolves have got the boss and a dozen lanterns flashed in the night air.

"Several rifle and pistol shots rang out, and it seemed scarcely two minutes before the whole body of men came rushing around the corner of the bend in the road. I called to them to shoot low as I was up a small tree and they began to shoot and I was saved from the wolves that began to run away with disappointed howls. They shot nearly a dozen, killing half that number at least, and wounding as many more that got away in the darkness leaving bloody trails on the snow.

"I looked about for my lantern but found the wolves had practically chewed it all to pieces, crushing the tin lamp, and sucking the whale oil and licking it up from the frozen snow where it had fallen. They managed to break the glass, and had also gnawed the handle off my little axe so that it was almost worthless. With most of the men I tramped on to the cabin, while the rest remained and skinned the dead wolves bringing their pelts to the cabin an hour later."

Chicago's Franklin Street Wholesale Dock

In 1856, Chicago replaced Albany as the world's largest lumber market, with Lake Michigan providing a cheap delivery system from hundreds of sawmills to the wholesale yards along the riverfront. No other city had so many railroads fanning out in all directions or the Michigan & Illinois Canal, which linked their harbor with the Great Lakes and the Gulf of Mexico. The *Wisconsin Lumberman* correctly stated that "no lumber market but this could dispose of an average of three million feet per day."[157]

During the sailing season, 300 to 400 schooners sailed from sawmills on both sides of Lake Michigan, and brought millions of feet of lumber to Chicago lumberyards. A strong wind could bring as many as 200 ships to the Chicago River in a *single day*, passing sixteen bridges that had to be opened or closed by a bridgetender before reaching the lumber district. With so many schooners arriving at the same time, the price at the wholesale dock plummeted, causing one captain to say "the stronger the wind the greater the slaughter."[158]

In 1863, while driving a herd of cattle to the stockyards, a young man found himself on a swinging bridge with his livestock.[159] A bridgetender knew from experience when to open and close a bridge, and a tugboat whistle startled the animals. They stampeded to the other end of the bridge, and their combined weight caused the bridge to creak and snap, with the cattle and pedestrians sliding into the filthy, sewage infested river.[160] People rushed to get boards to those in the water with the sister of the herder drowning, and a $50,000 ($5.4 million today) bridge wrecked.[161]

The North American lumber market revolved around the wholesale dock at the confluence of the north and south branches of the river. Due to excessive property damage when ships collided, an ordinance was passed that schooners had to be towed by a tugboat from the entrance of the river, and each day about 130 ships were towed to the wholesale dock. Most of them came from smaller, independent sawmills that didn't operate their own yard, and needed a place to sell their lumber.

During the 1840s and 1850s independent lumbermen who didn't own a sawmill or a lumberyard were able to buy and sell lumber from the wholesale dock. When Chicago became the world's largest lumber market in 1856, the Chicago Lumberman's Association made it impossible for lumber brokers to buy or sell a single board, because in the past they had disrupted prices. A lumber dealer had to own a lumberyard before he was allowed on the wholesale dock.

A dealer spent a few hours each day down at the wholesale dock buying and selling shiploads of lumber. The bulk of the lumber bought at the wholesale dock was unloaded at the lumber dealers' yard along the river, where it sat for up to six weeks curing in the outdoor air.

Most lumber dealers had an inspector working with them, and before a shipload of lumber had been purchased, it was his job to crawl into the cargo holds to verify the bill of lading, grade of the lumber, and make sure the captain wasn't hiding low-quality lumber beneath a higher grade. He had to know dozens of lumber grades and the specifications for lumber, lath, pickets, fence posts, shingles and other wood products. Reports for every purchase had to be kept on file for one year with the name of the schooner, inspector, tallyman, number boards, and grade of lumber.

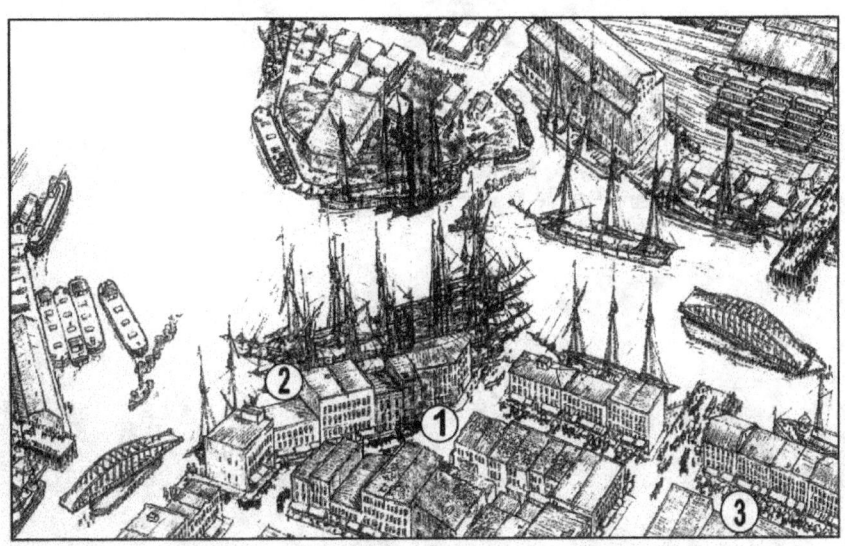

(1) Gideon Truesdell's office at 242 South Water Street at the confluence of the north and south branches of the Chicago River. (2) Wholesale dock where ships were docked 8 to 10 across looking for a buyer.

There were different types of dealers ranging from scrupulously honest to crooked as hell. The most popular scam was "shorting the count" or downgrading an entire shipload of lumber. If a schooner left the mill with 95,000 feet of lumber, a dishonest inspector would short the count by 5%, and by the end of the week he had cheated enough schooners to get what amounted to a free shipload of lumber worth $3,200 ($192,000 today).

The other scheme was downgrading a shipload of lumber, and once the ship was docked in Chicago it was extremely expensive to sail north looking for a buyer in Kenosha, Racine, or Milwaukee. If a mill sent 95,000 feet of #1 common lumber valued at $10 per thousand feet, and the lumber inspectors said it was #2 common he got away with paying a dollar less per thousand feet. During the course of a week, they might have downgraded as many as thirty schooners, with the lumber dealer pocketed around $280 ($24,000 today) for his larceny.

The 248-ton schooner C.H. Hackley was owned by investors from Kenosha with lumber piled below in her cargo bays and chained to her deck. Picture courtesy of the Milwaukee Public Library, Runge Maritime Collection.

Unloading a lumber schooner at the wholesale dock. Pictures courtesy of the Chicago Public Library.

Supply and demand dictated pricing, and lumberyards paid close attention to the *Chicago Tribune* lumber reports. Mills on the upper Mississippi River sent lumber to yards in Iowa, Missouri, and western Illinois, but in 1864 a low water table drastically reduced shipments causing prices to soar in Chicago. This created a bonanza for lumberyards when prices jumped by 36% that year, causing a rapid increase in shipments from Canadian mills.

During the 1860s, a ship entered or left the Chicago harbor every three minutes, and lumberyards needed a faster way to unload ships.

When docked at the mill, the ships crew loaded the schooner. Once the ship arrived in Chicago, a crew of longshoremen leaped into action and unloaded 95,000 feet by hand at the lightning speed of about twenty minutes. A foreman negotiated their pay and kicked-back a percentage to a riverfront boss, who in turn paid off a committeeman who kicked-back a percentage to City Hall. It was a thoroughly corrupt town and yet Chicago truly was the "city that works."

With the retail prices climbing upward, sometime in late 1861, Gideon bought six acres in the warehouse district on State Street where he opened a retail lumberyard.[162] During the war years, after transportation and overhead, he was able to send a thousand feet of yellow pine to this lumberyard for roughly $6.80 per thousand feet. Depending on the time of the year, he would have had no difficulty selling it for $45 to $60 per thousand feet.

In 1862, Gideon moved his wholesale yards from Clark Street to the much costlier Chicago South Branch Canal Company, and rented an office behind the Franklin Street wholesale dock at 242 South Water Street, where he resumed buying shiploads of lumber now that the oppressive Durkee-Truesdell debt were paid. The lumber district gradually evolved during the 1840s and 1850s at the confluence of the river, but with accelerated supply and demand they would have outgrown that area, with the older yards becoming landlocked as the city grew around them.

In 1859, real estate developers paid $600,000 ($72 million today) for 151 acres of pasture on the south branch of the river, a half-mile away from the Michigan & Illinois Canal that linked the Chicago River with the Mississippi River.

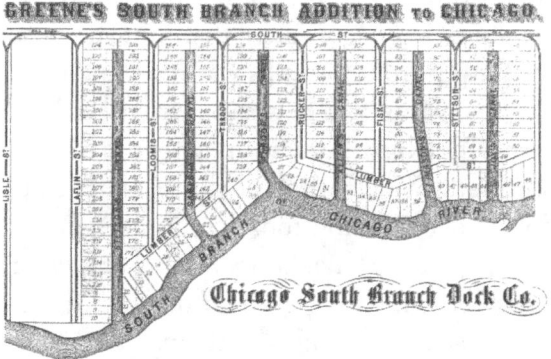

According to insurance maps, Theodore Newell, Martin Ryerson, Gideon Truesdell, and Jacob Beidler each bought yards on Throop Street on Sampson's Canal. Drawing courtesy of Chicago History Center.

Developers hired impoverished Irish day laborers to dig six canals with picks and shovels; each measured 100 feet wide by 244 feet long with a depth of 12 feet. Each canal had about thirty-five yards with a street and railroad spur running behind each of them. Yards were about six acres and rented for $1,000 ($120,000 today) a year, but each yard could also be purchased. From 1862 to 1865, Gideon owned four yards on Throop Street on Sampson's Canal, which gave him about 24 acres of yard space.[163] According to insurance maps, Martin Ryerson, Gideon Truesdell, and Theodore Newell owned adjacent yards on Throop Street.[164]

Each owned schooners, but at the start of the war when independent ship owners dropped their rates to competitive levels, most of them began renting rather than owning ships. According to the *Chicago Commercial Letter*, a commodities newspaper, Gideon kept the Challenge, Heligoland, Telegraph, Illinois, Emma, Kent, Honest John, Lizzie Throop, Mary and others busy during the war years.[165]

According to the *Chicago Commercial Letter*, Gideon often sold what must have been "excess inventory" at the wholesale dock. Throughout the 1862 season, he was paid $10 per 1,000 feet for yellow pine, and $2.75 for shingles, which was the going price.[166] One afternoon, four schooners arrived simultaneously for unloading, a clear indication that he was manufacturing a lot of lumber.[167]

Gideon also began shipping 8-to-10-foot strips of half-inch scrap, which gradually found a market with the manufacturers of shipping crates. Beginning in 1864, he sent at least two ships a week loaded with about 160,000 feet of lath where he received $3,200 ($192,000 today) per shipload. More likely than not, he needed to clear his docks because the output from his mills was more than he could possibly sell through his Chicago yards, and he was able to get a decent price at the wholesale dock.

The North American lumber market revolved around three buildings on South Water Street at the confluence of the river. Over $10 million dollars ($1.2 billion today) of lumber flowed through Chicago yards each year during the Civil War, and this was why nearly every Chicago bank had a lumberman sitting on their board of directors.

Each of the office buildings in the lumber district on South Water Street had a telegraph room. This enabled lumbermen to communicate with factories and lumberyards. Instead of sending a clerk to the local Western Union office to stand in line for an hour or more, messages were brought downstairs and sent by a full-time telegrapher. If a lumberman wanted to buy 20 million feet of Canadian pine from the Winnipeg Exchange, the order was telegraphed, and a couple of weeks later the lumber arrived.

In late 1861, Gideon rented an office at 242 South Water Street across the hall from Martin Ryerson.[168] Both were buying shiploads of lumber and had offices on the first floor, Ryersons in room four and Gideon Truesdell's across the hall in room six. The rent for each office decreased depending on how may flights of stairs they had to climb.

After the collapse of Durkee, Truesdell & Company, Charles Deming left the firm and became a bookkeeper for a Chicago freight forwarding firm. In 1862, Gideon asked him to return, with the understanding that he would sell him a half interest in the business without any money changing hands a few years later when he semi-retired.[169] Gideon would finance his purchase with the profits paying for his percentage of the brokerage, and in the past, Gideon had cleared around $22,000 ($1.7 million today) a year buying and selling shiploads of lumber.[170]

We know Gideon was receiving telegraph orders from yards out west, because he was listed in the *Directory of Kansas & Nebraska Shippers' Guide*.[171] And because he was listed in the *Wisconsin Lumbermens Gazette*, we know that he was buying shiploads from sawmills on the western side of Lake Michigan.[172] U.S. Customs House tax records reveal that he was buying a lot of lumber from smaller sawmills in Sheboygan and Two Rivers, Wisconsin.[173]

Logging Operations Along the White, Muskegon, and Grand Rivers

With the completion of the Kenosha & Rockford in sight, which would occur in June of 1861, Gideon was positioned to begin shipping lumber to interior markets in north-central Illinois and south-central Wisconsin.

After the "Panic of 1857," Gideon didn't have much in the way of pinelands, and he needed a partner with a significant inventory of pinelands. This was Martin Ryerson, and it seems likely that Gideon approached him with an offer that would make them both a lot of money. This joint venture had nothing to do with their Muskegon sawmills, but was an arrangement that would allow them to expand their operations.

Steamship Comet (above) ran from Milwaukee across Lake Michigan to Muskegon and Grand Haven and then across the lake to Kenosha. The steamship Ottawa (below) ran from Muskegon to Grand Haven, and Chicago. Pictures courtesy of the Herman Runge Collection.

The markets in central Illinois and Wisconsin were exploding, and a supply line from the forests to the mills in western Michigan across Lake Michigan was an opportunity to sell an enormous tonnage of lumber using the Kenosha & Rockford. They came to an agreement whereby Ryerson would supply pinelands from his extensive holdings, Gideon would bankroll several logging crews, and together they would raft the logs to small sawmills where they would be turned into lumber at the contract price of $2.50 ($320 today) per thousand feet. Using rented schooners, they shipped millions of feet of lumber to the Kenosha Pier Company, and then using the Kenosha & Rockford flatbeds and boxcars deliver this lumber to wholesale yards in Rockford.

Henry and A.F. Orton ran crews in Osceola County, and Arthur Truesdell ran logging crews in Mecosta County. An arrangement like this was an answer to a prayer for dozens of sawmill owners that didn't own pinelands, and it enabled the partners to process a large tonnage of lumber. It was a shrewd way for Gideon to expand his operations, and declare a net profit of $63,312 ($4 million today) from 1862 to 1865.[174]

Martin Ryerson and Gideon Truesdell were both very aggressive businessmen who knew poverty earlier in their careers. "At one time Ryerson was earning the magnificent salary of eight dollars per month as a Muskegon Township clerk. He used to tell of walking from Grand Rapids to Grand Haven, a distance of about 30 miles, in order to save the stage fare of two dollars ($500 today). With his salary, two dollars meant a weeks work, and a walk of 30 miles was an easy way to earn it."[175]

He came to the Michigan frontier at the age of sixteen, after having walked from his home in New Jersey to the Erie Canal, where he caught a ride on one of the packet boats. After reaching Buffalo he hooked a ride on a schooner sailing to Detroit, and a strong young man could usually work for his passage by helping load or unload the ship.

In Detroit, he began working for Richard Godfrey, an Indian trader, and a year later (1835) he began working for Louis Campau in Grand Rapids. After working for both men in the "Indian trade," Ryerson could see there were large profit margins, so he saved two or three years of wages. At the age of nineteen, he bought a stock of merchandise, paddled up and down rivers across the state in his canoe, trading clothing blankets, and trinkets for furs which he sold to Oliver Newberry's warehouse in Detroit.

In 1839 he began working for Joseph "Truckey" Troutier (1818–1882) at his trading post at the edge of Muskegon Lake. He was a successful but illiterate French-Canadian (his parents emigrated from France to Canada) who kept journals by drawing sketches of what he bought and sold, and ran a large and profitable business. Truckey spent a lot of time paddling up and down rivers visiting Indian settlements from Mackinaw to St. Joseph, and developed a large and diverse business. "It was Truckey who picked up Martin Ryerson when he was sailing into Grand Haven on an old vessel. He kept him in his employment for two years as bookkeeper, then he branched out for himself."[176]

Troutier married and buried three wives, all Chippewas, which brought him deeper into their culture.[177] "Truckey was a man of splendid physique, and weighed 195 pounds."[178] He was always impeccably dressed, and took great pains in selecting his clothes, which were always the finest money could buy. He kept stores at various points along major rivers, and traveled a great deal among the Indians, buying furs and giving merchandise in return."[179] He was held in such high regard by the Indians that he was asked to travel to Washington to help negotiate a treaty whereby they would cede hundreds of thousands of acres north of the Grand River.

Like most frontiersman, Truckey had no use for a thief. "Stealing was unheard of, so Truckey had acquired the habit of keeping large sums of money in the drawer of his desk, which happened to be near the window. There was an epidemic of burglaries, and it was generally believed that some of the men at the nearby lumber camp were responsible. One early morning he heard someone removing the window next to the counter. He lay listening quietly for a moment, and then picking up the hatchet at his side he stole along behind the counter, and as expected, the thief reached in and opened the drawer containing the money, but just as he was about to withdraw his hand with the coveted wealth, Truckey brought down his hatchet neatly chopping off the fingers. With a yell, the man was off, and Truckey went back to bed, glad to have foiled an evildoer so easily."[180]

By 1841, things weren't moving fast enough for Theodore Newell so he leased his general store and steam sawmill to Greene & Ryerson, and moved to Southport where he opened a retail yard for the lumber manufactured from this sawmill. Samuel Greene (1811–1858) was from Ohio who at the age of thirty sold his farm, and landed in Muskegon where he invested his grubstake in real estate. Twenty years later his daughter married Gideon and Julia Truesdell's son.

Even at a young age, Martin Ryerson was widely respected as evidenced by an article published in the *Muskegon Chronicle* many years later. "Martin Ryerson was very poor at first but people had absolute confidence in him and the men would leave a year's wages in his hands, while others would loan him what they had unhesitantly. He was honest to the core and never deceived them."[181]

When Ryerson built a second steam mill on Muskegon Lake, he only had $25 cash leftover and owed $7,000 ($980,000 today), but by the opening of navigation he had a dock full of lumber, and with the proceeds paid off his creditors and had a healthy surplus of money.[182]

Ryerson was totally at ease in the wilderness. As a young man he walked 22 miles from Muskegon Lake to the mouth of the Grand River, and 28 miles northeast to the settlement of Grand Rapids. With little more than a compass he walked until dusk, made a brush tent from twigs and branches, and started a fire where he roasted a raccoon.

Ryerson thought nothing of working 18 hours a day and was a strict taskmaster. When one of his workers was told to move a pile of scrap lumber, it irritated him to see him carrying a few pieces at a time. According to the *Muskegon Chronicle* "Mr. Ryerson, observing this called out to him to throw down his load. The man stood still a minute with a surprised look. Repeating the order with more emphasis, he threw it down. Mr. Ryerson then told the man to go sit in the shade and rest himself until he was able to carry a load as a man ought to carry it."[183]

Martin J. Ryerson (L) Ryerson Physical Laboratory at the University of Chicago, and Martin A. Ryerson Jr. (R). Nobel Prize Winner A.A. Michelson carried out his research at the Ryerson Lab. Pictures courtesy of the University of Chicago.

He might have started with nothing, but Martin Ryerson was intelligent, shrewd, and aggressive enough to amass one of the largest lumber fortunes of his day. He was also a kindhearted man who never forgot his early struggles in life. About a third of the Ryerson fortune came from the lumber business and the remainder from real estate investments and major holdings in the Crane Plumbing Company and the Elgin Watch Company.

His son received an excellent education that included a degree from Harvard Law School. When his father dropped dead of a heart attack, Martin Jr. inherited $5 million ($1.5 billion today). At the age of thirty-one years, this made him the richest man in Chicago.

Martin Jr. sat on the University of Chicago's board of directors with oil tycoon John D. Rockefeller, who was so impressed with his balanced logic and unshakable integrity that he asked him to sit on the board of the Rockefeller Foundation. For several years Martin Jr. sat on the boards of both organizations, with John D. Rockefeller becoming a valued friend.[184]

The Ryerson Charitable Trust was set up by his father to funnel money from at least one Chicago office building to worthy causes, mostly the poor, which had always been important to him. "He made provisions for the distribution of a goodly proportion of his ample wealth among charitable institutions of Chicago."[185] His son's job was to give away his father's fortune, and long after father and son were dead and buried their money would continue to benefit the greater good.

Chicago, Grand Haven & Muskegon Ship Line

By 1863, Gideon had built a small mercantile empire that occupied an entire block on Western Avenue, with stores in Kenosha, Whitehall, and Croton.[186] He might have been following Charles Durkees example, only instead of bankrolling partnerships he owned these stores outright. It was just as easy to stock one store as four, and the Muskegon store was run by his son, On February 17, 1863 the *Muskegon Chronicle* briefly described his store.

"We paid a visit a few days ago to the new store of G. Truesdell & Son and found it to be equal to any store in the county. Dell, (by then Gideon's son was known around town as "Dell") knowing how things are done, has suited up the store in big city style, and keeps on hand a large and beautiful assortment of dress goods, which he is selling very cheap for cash. Give him a call."[187]

Several lumbermen operated stores, and according to the *Muskegon Chronicle*, Martin Ryerson, Theodore Newell, and Chauncey Davis each owned general mercantile stores that sold around $75,000 ($9 million) a year.[188] Gideon, with stores in Kenosha, Muskegon, Whitehall, and Croton sold over $200,000 ($20 million today) during the war years.[189]

Martin Ryerson and Gideon Truesdell came to the conclusion that the freight and passenger service between Muskegon, Grand Haven, and Chicago was underserviced. One of the ships that stopped at each city was the Ottawa, which was owned by Ryerson. Both men realized that a ship traveling in each direction was the best way to service the route, hauling 500 tons of lumber from their sawmills to Chicago, and returning with freight and passengers. Their biggest customer would be themselves, and each ship left Muskegon loaded with lumber, and 30 minutes later docked fourteen miles south in Grand Haven to pick up additional freight and passengers.

In 1856, Grand Haven had become a major transportation artery when the Detroit, Grand Haven & Milwaukee Railroad began running trains across the state from Detroit to Grand Haven. An enormous tonnage of freight going to Chicago, Milwaukee, or Michigan City was routed through several terminals.

The other factor that would have entered into the profit and loss of running two ships were tugboat fees. A skilled captain could sail up and down the Chicago River, but after numerous accidents an ordinance was passed mandating that all schooners had to be towed, because when ships collided it caused over sixty ships to drop their sails and stop moving. It took three separate "pulls" at three dollars ($540 today) a piece to travel downriver to their yards, and three more pulls to clear the Chicago River on their return trip to Muskegon. With six to twelve ships arriving or departing each day from their docks these fees added up, and a couple of large steamships would eliminate them.

In 1863, Martin Ryerson and Gideon Truesdell started the Chicago, Grand Haven & Muskegon Line. Ryerson owned the 578-ton propeller-driven steamer Ottawa, which had seen heavy duty during the past thirteen years hauling cheap Canadian lumber to his yards in Chicago, but had recently been completely refurbished with new above-deck cabins, a major attraction for the passenger trade. Gideon wrote out a check for $50,000 ($5.4 million today) to build a 498-ton steamship he named the G.J. Truesdell. With a steamship coming or going every twelve hours they developed a profitable business with lumber, freight, and passenger service.

According to the *Grand Haven News*, "the propeller Ottawa has been painted anew and refitted while in winter quarters and looks very tasty and inviting to the traveler seeking cleanliness and ease. She will doubtlessly prove a greater favorite than ever before with the traveling public."[190]

Screw propellers had been around for about twenty years but they were expensive to build, and many questioned their seaworthiness. This debate was settled when the screw propeller Rattler and the paddle wheeler Necto, ships of similar size and power, were chained together stern to stern in a bizarre tug-of-war. The 200 horsepower Rattler towed the Necto backward for five miles at 2 ½ knots.

A propeller could plow through heavy swells, make better time and haul a larger tonnage. Most schooners could haul about 95,000 board feet of lumber whereas a steamer could transport five times as much and follow a regular schedule that didn't depend on the wind. The down-side to these steamers was that they rolled awkwardly through rough seas, and caused inexperienced passengers to think that the ship was going to roll over, but the design was seaworthy.

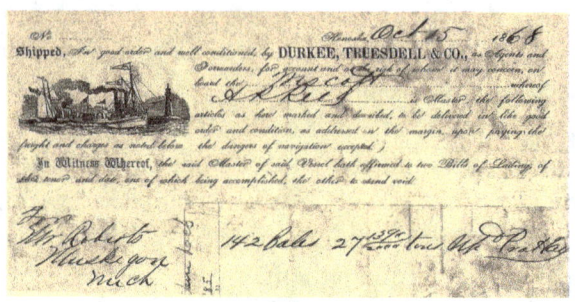

Durkee-Truesdell bill of lading for a load of hay (above). Document courtesy of the Kenosha History Center Archives. Steamship Vernon (below). Picture courtesy of the Herman Runge Collection.

Steamer G.J. Truesdell docked in the Milwaukee harbor. Luggage check from the G.J. Truesdell. Pictures courtesy of the Milwaukee Public Library's Herman Runge Maritime Collection.

According to a Sept. 2, 1863, *Muskegon Chronicle*, "G. Truesdell & Son is having built a large propeller that will run between Chicago and Muskegon on the opening of navigation next spring."

The following spring, the *Chicago Tribune* wrote, "The new steamer G.J. Truesdell, built at Doolittle & Olcott's shipyard on Wells Street near Polk, for Gideon Truesdell Esq. of this city, was launched at four o'clock on Saturday. The G.J. Truesdell is 498 tons and when finished will take her place in the Muskegon, Grand Haven, and Chicago trade."[191]

The G.J. Truesdell was powered by a 270-horsepower engine with 16 passenger cabins. The *Grand Haven News* reported, "A new propeller, the G.J. Truesdell, built and owned by Mr. Truesdell, of Muskegon, has just appeared in this port [Grand Haven]. She is intended for the route from Chicago to Muskegon, touching here each way. She is a model boat with a powerful engine and fixtures, and elegantly fitted for the comfort of passengers."[192]

The G.J. Truesdell advertised itself as a "splendid new UPPER CABIN steamer." Upper cabins had windows, which made them far more desirable than traveling below deck on a schooner. Freight was more important than passengers, and every 24 hours, March thru October, the G.J. Truesdell unloaded about 460,000 feet of lumber at Truesdell's wholesale dock in Chicago. The Ottawa unloaded a slightly larger amount at the Ryerson & Hill's dock, returning to Muskegon with passengers, freight, merchandise for their stores, hay, oats, and groceries for boarding houses and logging camps.

According to the *History of the Great Lakes* the Ottawa and the G.J. Truesdell were the largest steamships on Lake Michigan. In a typical business manuver, Ryerson and Truesdell "sold" their steamships to the Chicago, Grand Haven & Muskegon Line, which was owned exclusively by them.

Charles Hackley's $70,000 Train Ride

Charles Hackley spent most of his time behind a desk making entries in ledgers and analyzing spreadsheets. Each afternoon Charley gravitated toward Judd Moon's saloon a few blocks from his office on Western Avenue, a gathered place for lunch, and a place to unwind after work before people went home for the day.

Charles Hackley's drinking was legendary, and an interesting story from Louis Haight's *The Life of Charles Henry Hackley* reveals just how shrewd he was as a young man.[193] Late one afternoon he stopped by Judd Moons and had a few drinks before going home for dinner. There was a timber cruiser sitting at the bar that had too much to drink, and like most drunks he began talking louder than he realized.

He started bragging about a stand of timber that would make him rich, which got everyones attention. The more he drank the more he talked, and Hackley knew it was just a matter of time before this dullard disclosed the location. Acting as if he was tired, Charley closed his eyes feigning disinterest, and a few hours later the talkative cruiser divulged the location.

Hackley opened his eyes, stretched, and said he was late for dinner. A few hours later he was aboard a train headed for the State capitol and the Auditor General's office. But when he walked into the passenger car, he found his drinking buddies already there.

They had decided to pool their money whereas Hackley had enough cash to swing the deal by himself. They knew they had to neutralize Charley if they were going to buy the land, and figured if they got him drunk, he would be in no condition to bid against them much less find his way to the court house. When they passed around a bottle, which was considered good manners in those days, he tipped the bottle so often that he could barely stand.

By the time the train pulled into a small town for the night, a very drunk Charley Hackley stumbled back to his seat, fell backward, and passed out. The trip to the state capitol required taking a second train in the morning. With Hackley incapacitated the others figured the land was as good as theirs, and one of them laughed, "I guess Charley's going to Detroit."

After the others walked across the road to the hotel, a stone-cold sober Charley opened his eyes, and jumped off the trains rear platform. He ran over to the livery stable, woke up the owner, rented two horses and a wagon, and paid the owner to smuggle him out of town under a load of hay.

Once they reached the edge of town the owner turned the reins over to Hackley, and jumped from the wagon. Charley raced across the countryside during the night, charging the horses so badly they were so crippled that he had to buy them.

When the train pulled into Lansing the following morning, Hackley's traveling companions figured he was still sleeping off a good drunk, and that he was on the east-bound train going to Detroit. But when they reached the Auditor General's office, they were shocked to discover that Charley had already come and gone, and bought the land.

Twenty years later when Louis P. Haight asked him if the story was true, Hackley laughed, and recalled "I did tip their bottles but I did not take one drop." As the train was pulling into the Lansing station the others looked out their window, and saw Hackley waiting for the next train to Junction City.

"One of them yelled 'where in the hell did you come from,' and I said that I walked, which was true because I had to walk those tired old horses the last few miles. That was wonderful pine, and I made just $70,000 ($3.7 million today) by that night's ride."[194]

Gideon Truesdell Semi-Retires from the Lumber Business, 1865

His profits were enormous due to wartime inflation, unusually high demand, and several supply lines in place before demand soared. By 1865, Gideon's net worth was about $1.1 million ($68 million today), and about half came from the rapid escalation of his real estate holdings. During the Civil War, Chicago became one of the hottest real estate markets in the country, and Gideon had the bulk of his profits safely invested there.

Based on research, it appears as if he invested around $95,000 ($8.6 million today) each year from his lumber profits buying storefronts, apartment buildings, and warehouses that not only doubled and tripled in value, but generated a steady yearly income. This was something Martin Ryerson and other Muskegon lumberman were doing with their profits, and it was a solid passive investment.

They managed their real estate holdings through a property manager who collected rents, authorized repairs, and deposited monthly rents into their bank accounts. As property values soared so did Gideon's rents, and by the end of the war these properties were worth over $750,000 ($45 million today).[195] They were the foundation of Gideon Truesdell's wealth.

After working from dawn to dusk since he was a teenager, Gideon could afford to push his life in a different direction, and yet his aggressive, restless nature would stay with him until the day he died. With the bulk of his wealth invested in real estate that returned at least a 10% dividend, and a half interest in the Durkee-Truesdell sawmill and his Chicago lumber brokerage, Gideon Truesdell would have had an unusually high retirement income.

When he scaled down the Truesdell Lumber Company he accumulated $120,000 ($7.2 million today) from the sale of various assets, and made a heavy investment in the emerging dairy industry where profits fell into the 35% range. Although he probably had no desire to become the biggest dairy farmer in the country, during the next few years he spent another $200,000 ($12 million today) to build what became the largest privately owned dairy farm in the United States.[196]

His rapid accumulation of wealth surprised him, because he told a *Milwaukee Sentinel* reporter that "luck favored him beyond his own anticipation."[197] The last two years of the Civil War had made him a rich man, and his wealth gave him the kind of money to become a player in the agriculture, mining, and cattle business.

As a partner in Truesdell & Orton, owners of the former Durkee-Truesdell mill, he wasn't entirely stepping away from the business that made him rich. As more mills were built, Muskegon was about to become one of the largest lumber manufacturing regions in the world.

By 1866, a quarter of the 700 million feet of lumber sold by Chicago lumberyards came from there, and Muskegon sawmills shipped the second largest tonnage on Lake Michigan. During the past ten years, technology improved to the extent that a single shift in a new mill could cut as much lumber as two shifts in an older mill, saving $4,500 ($385,000 today) in wages each year, although this new technology wasn't cheap.

If Gideon intended to spend twenty more years in the lumber business, he would have needed to replace the ten-year-old Durkee-Truesdell sawmill with the latest generation of equipment, which would have required a new, wider building. This would have cost him around $100,000 ($6 million today), but since he was stepping away from the business, he left that decision to his partners. The Durkee-Truesdell sawmill was still profitable but not nearly as efficient as the newer mills. It was described as "a very old mill estimating time as we do here in the west where ten years seems like a half century."[198]

Adjacent to this sawmill was the Durkee-Truesdell shingle mill, and it was "a large, first-class shingle mill capable of cutting 75,000 shingles a day." Between 1868 and 1870, when the price of shingles dropped below production costs due to a huge surplus on the market, Gideon temporarily closed this mill.[199] Even with a ten-year-old mill, Truesdell & Orton cut over ten million feet a year valued at $205,000 ($12.3 million today).[200]

Truesdell was stepping back from the business just when Muskegon sawmills were about to cut an astounding 125 million feet of lumber, 10 million shingles, 20 million feet of beams, 1,000 cords of shingle bolts, 10,000 railroad ties, and 20,000 cedar posts annually.[201]

According to a June 15th 1864 *Grand Haven News* article "the ring of the saw and the sound of the hammer are heard in all directions with some 200 new buildings going up. Muskegon is destined to possess a bridge, a railroad, and a telegraph."[202]

A year before the Hackleys stepped away from the Truesdell Lumber Company, in what appears to have been a carefully planned succession, Gideon's bookkeeper, Luther Whitney, moved from Kenosha to Muskegon to replace Charles Hackley, and take charge of the books. During the past decade Charles had sent their books to him each year for review, and Whitney would have sailed across Lake Michigan to close the books each season.

On February 14, 1866 Gideon sold a half interest in the Durkee-Truesdell mill for $35,000 ($2.1 million today) to Henry Orton (1818–1891) and Alanson F. Orton (1821–1873).[203] They were two of the sharpest lumbermen on the Muskegon River but lacked a sawmill, and they had had a close relationship with Gideon for many years. Truesdell & Orton was immediately rated very high, and described by R.G. Dun & Company as "a tip top firm that can safely be trusted for all they wish,"[204]

According to the *Boston Commercial Bulletin*, "This sale includes one half of the large gang mill, shingle mill, salt well, boarding house, docks, and burning grounds. The Ortons are practical lumbermen and have been engaged in the lumber business at Newaygo for a number of years past. Mr. Truesdell has also sold his interest in the J.H. Hackley mill and his interest in J.H. Hackley's lower mill."[205]

The Pomeroy & Holmes and Trowbridge & Wing mills that were owned by J.H. Hackley & Company had, under the Hackleys' supervision, become quite profitable by the time Gideon sold his interest. According to a *Daily Milwaukee News* article, Hackley & McGordon (Trowbridge & Wing) had invested most of their profits to upgrade their facility, and double their output.[206]

Charles Hackley and James McGordon bought Truesdell's remaining interest in the Trowbridge & Wing mill on credit, paying him 10% interest on the outstanding balance.[207] Joseph Hackley acquired what was left of Gideon's interest in the Pomeroy & Holmes mill with Edwin Hackley acquiring more stock from his father.

In 1870, the *Muskegon Chronicle* described the Trowbridge & Wing mill as "one of the huge institutions of the city—it cuts lumber with amazing rapidity. The firm is counted as one of the wealthiest.... James McGordon is superintendent of the mill and Daniel McGordon is the foreman. The mill is abundantly supplied with all the latest improvements.... the number of men employed are fifty-four."[208]

They built the first fully-automated mill in Muskegon. Lumber was moved from station to station by conveyors with a sawdust carrier that replaced four men shoveling sawdust into the boilers.[209] One of the first semi-automatic tramways in the industry automatically moved the lumber from the Sawmill to the end of the dock where workers cross-stacked thousands of boards. About 60 men were needed to run a single shift and the mill was appraised at $60,000 ($3.6 million today), and scarcely resembled the mill Gideon had acquired from Alva Trowbridge several years earlier.[210]

The Pomeroy & Holmes mill was smaller but profitable, cutting 38,000 feet of lumber and 20,000 shingles during a twelve-hour shift with about 20 employees.[211] This mill was appraised at $30,000. When Gideon sold his remaining interest in J.H. Hackley & Company and Hackley & McGordon, he loaned both partnerships a total of $15,000 ($900,000 today) to buy him out, upgrade each mill's equipment, and to buy pinelands so they could improve their bottom line.[212]

Gideon also helped his longtime engineer, William Glue, start his own sawmill with some of the capital for William Glue & Company coming from him.[213] They bought the old Bushnell & Reed mill, which required a major equipment upgrade before it was ready for operation, and employed about 25 employees. They cut around 30,000 feet a day, 11,000 feet of lath, and the mill was valued at $30,000.[214]

Piecing together Gideon's net worth was made possible by many archival sources, with the best information coming from the J.H. Hackley & Company journals at Michigan State University. Beginning in 1859, they showed entries in Charles Hackley's handwriting for the Trowbridge & Wing and Pomeroy & Holmes mills that included payrolls, production runs, expenses, net profits, and how much each partner received when the books were closed at the end of the year.[215]

When matched with income tax records at the U.S. National Archives (1862–1866), Muskegon Booming Company tallies, court documents, and collateral data it was possible to reconstruct sales. Federal tax return information told us the exact profit declared by each mill although some of the entries were illegible due to sloppy handwriting. The numbers were probably a bit understated to avoid a heavy tax bill—something every businessman did to lower payments of a very unpopular wartime tax.

According to Wisconsin tax returns, we know Truesdell declared a $63,312 ($4 million today) income from 1862 to 1865 for lumber shipped to Rockford, Illinois, through the Kenosha Pier Company aboard the Kenosha & Rockford.[216]

Another tier of research came from the Runge Collection at the Milwaukee Public Library.[217] They have records for just about every ship that ever sailed on Lake Michigan, showing how much cargo capacity each ship had, and when tied into U.S. Customs House tax records, it was possible to estimate how much lumber was shipped when compared to the daily output of each mill and the profits listed on their tax returns.

Additional information came from newspaper articles, and the U.S. Census for 1860 and 1870 "Products of Industry," which list the number of workers and output at each sawmill. The *Chicago Daily Commercial Letter* presented a consistent snapshot of the type and price of lumber Truesdell sold at the wholesale dock, which was much higher than originally estimated from other sources.

From their tally sheet: "schooner Illinois, Muskegon, Truesdell's Sawmill, 80,000 ft good lumber $14.50, 25,000 ft. lath sold for $2.75, May 23rd 1863, 4:30 PM."[218] This tells us that Truesdell received $1,160 for the lumber unloaded and $68.75 for the lath ($73,800 today). It also helps us piece together another layer of information when market prices pinpointed about how much Truesdell made per shipload at the wholesale dock.

It was much harder to figure out exactly what he did with his money, but according to a grandson, Gideon owned considerable property in Chicago. Had there been real estate records there would have been a crosscheck with specific locations, but the Chicago Fire eliminated that source. The best clue we have came from Chauncey Truesdell, who wrote "my parents suffered heavy losses during the Chicago Fire, and the burning of the Michigan prairie."[219] Bankruptcy court records reveal a lot of vacant land that probably had buildings on them before the fire. All we know is there was about a $750,000 hole in Gideon's net worth after the fire, possibly more.

The Truesdell & Orton partnership lasted for three years when the Ortons decided to sell their interest back to Gideon for $30,000 ($1.8 million today).[220] At the time, court records reveal that A.F. Orton was in financial trouble, because in 1870 three judgements totaling $1,801 ($76,000 today) were filed. Furthermore, his health wasn't good, and three years later he was dead at the age of fifty-two. Their departure appears to have been planned as evidenced by an April 10, 1869, *Muskegon Chronicle* article.

"Another New Partner, Arthur Truesdell, of Big Rapids has purchased a quarter interest in the saw and shingle mill of Truesdell & Orton, in this city, paying $20,000 ($1 million today). He will be a valuable acquisition to the already large number of energetic young men who are engaged here in the lumber business."[221]

In 1869, the Ortons sent five million feet of logs from their pinelands to the old Durkee-Truesdell mill where they were cut at a contract price, which suggests a friendly parting. But the wholesale market wasn't in good shape because in July of 1870, thirteen mills on Muskegon Lake had to temporarily close when prices dropped by 20% or two dollars ($79 today) per thousand feet. Sawmills decided the best option, and it wasn't a good one, was to wait until a glut of lumber sitting in Chicago was sold before prices stabilized.

Sawmills in Whitehall, Muskegon, and Grand Haven had long wanted to tap into a railroad that would bypass the Chicago wholesale market, and allow them to ship directly to retail customers throughout the Midwest. According to the May 1, 1868 *Jackson Citizen Patriot* article, "The Muskegon & Ferrysburg Railroad was organized last week. The length of the proposed road is 17 miles, and the capital of $250,000 ($10 million today), in 2,500 shares at $100 each. The officers of the road are as follows: President, Hon. Chauncey Davis; Vice President, Lyman G. Mason; Secretary, Charles H. Hackley; and Treasurer, Henry Beidler."[222]

Mergers were inevitable, and the Muskegon & Ferrysburg Railroad were looking for smaller railroads to merge with until they had tracks running to the mammoth Michigan Central, which tied into dozens of other major railroads. On October 14, 1869, the *Detroit Advertiser & Tribune* wrote, "The movement in Grand Haven, Muskegon and Holland, to connect those three cities with one line of railroad, has at last culminated in a consolidation of three companies then organized into one company called the Michigan Lakeshore Railroad Company."[223]

This 57-mile railroad would run along Muskegon Lakes western lakeshore, with tracks passing between the lakefront and each sawmill, which would require renovations to the Durkee-Truesdell mill. They would have to reclaim the land in front of their sawmill, and relocate their shingle mill to make room for the railroad tracks, although these extensive modifications would have been paid by the railroad. Based on a U.S. Department of Interior map, the tracks passing in front of the Truesdell sawmill were close enough for the lumber to flow out of the lakeside of the mill, and be loaded directly to the boxcars.

Birdseye view (1874) of the Durkee-Truesdell mill (center), recently built J.H. Hackley & Sons (formerly Pomeroy & Holmes) mill to the right and new Roberts & Hull mill to the left. Sketch courtesy of the U.S. Department of Interior.

Richard C. Fritz

An addition to the Durkee-Truesdell mill housed the lath, shingle, flooring, and siding saws, and the building was reconfigured for a smoother flow of lumber. Despite high hopes for this railroad, it never made money, and nearly all of the lumber continued to be shipped by schooners.

In 1870, Arthur Truesdell sold his interest in the old Durkee-Truesdell mill to his cousin, G.J. Truesdell. Levi Truesdell, Luther Whitney, and G.J. Truesdell now owned a third interest in Truesdell Brothers & Company. After selling out, Arthur moved to the upscale suburb of Evanston, Illinois. He commuted to Gideon's downtown Chicago office where he bought and sold lumber contracts for his uncle, and held a position of some type at Charles Deming & Company.[224]

During the 1871–1872 season, there wasn't enough water from melting snow due to a mild winter to increase water levels for a normal log drive. This created a 90-million-foot shortage of logs, which meant every sawmill's output would be lower than anticipated. Mill owners decided to stop manufacturing and take a chance that prices would improve late in the season due to a smaller volume of lumber. The larger mills adjusted their output by starting milling operations a month later and wrapping up their season a month earlier.

According to the *Detroit Advertiser & Tribune*, the only mill that continued to cut and ship large quantities of lumber to Chicago was the one owned by Gideon Truesdell, which reveals just how big his wholesale network was, and his need to service a list of customers with standing orders.[225]

Gideon owned stock in the Union National Bank, First National Bank of Chicago, 1st National Bank of Kenosha, and the Muskegon National Bank.[226] All were profitable but according to court documents filed in 1873, he made more as a private banker with $17,000 ($1 million today) of loans on the books secured by mortgages at 12% interest.[227]

In 1867, the Garden City Manufacturing & Supply Company was organized by a group of mostly Chicago lumbermen. Besides owning the largest planing mill in the world, they also owned pinelands along the Grand River in Michigan. They owned a fleet of ships that brought lumber from their mills across Lake Michigan to their plant at 22nd Street and Morgan. Their factory occupied an entire city block where over 400 men manufactured 60-million feet of windows, doors, flooring and blinds each year.[228]

According to court documents, Gideon owned $8,000 ($450,000 today) of stock in this company.[229] Every penny of its highly leveraged $150,000 of capital was borrowed from the Union National Bank, and secured by loans from its stockholders.[230] This suggests that Gideon's 5% stake might have been acquired with little more than his signature.

In 1865, Andrew Johnson appointed Charles Durkee Territorial Governor of Utah, and while he was out there, he more than doubled his net worth as a partner in John Kerr & Company, Miners National Bank, Kerr & Durkee, and Durkee, Truesdell & Company.

This latest incarnation of the Durkee-Truesdell partnership consisted of Charles and Harvey Durkee, Gideon Truesdell, and Harvey's son-in-law, attorney Franklin Head. They organized a 40,000-acre ranch in Nevada, and invested in a silver mine somewhere north of Salt Lake City.[231] When Gideon cashed out his share was $47,650 ($953,000 today).[232]

Notes

1. *Muskegon Chronicle*, 29 July 1899, pp. 9. E.N. VanBaalen reminiscences.
2. Ibid, 18 November 1899, pp. 3. Michael Hamen reminiscences,
3. *R.G. Dun & Company* report, Harvard University, 18 January 1858, Wisconsin ledger, Volume 27.
4. Muskegon Register of Deeds, 18 November 1860, volume 2, pp.387.
5. Hesss father was Jacob was a physician with $2,500 of property although probably had other assets, died in 1851, in 1850 census George was listed as a teacher at age of 16. 1850 Federal Census, North Salem, Winchester, New York; roll M432_614; page 307A, image 620.
6. Ottawa County Register of Deeds, volume 1, pp. 219.
7. 1860, Grand Rapids, Kent, Michigan; roll M653_550; page 483; image 488. Hesss father was Jacob was a physician with 2500 of property although probably had other assets, died in 1851, in 1850 census George was a teacher at age of 16. 1850 Federal Census, North Salem, Winchester, New York; roll M432_614; page 307A, image 620.
8. Gideon Truesdell owned 100% of *Hess & Company* mortgage plus a third of the partnership plus profits according to *Truesdell vs. Hess*.
9. Kenosha County Clerk of Courts, 12 December 1858, Harvey Durkee et al vs. John C. Holmes et al.
10. Charles Hackley testimony, Littel vs. Hackley interrogatories, Hackley & Hume papers.

11. *Muskegon News & Reporter*, 11 November 1882, Gideon Truesdell obituary.
12. *R.G. Dun & Company*, Michigan ledger, volume 60, pp. 272.
13. *Littell vs. Hackley*, interrogatories about the background of J.H. Hackley & Company.
14. *Romance of Muskegon*, pp. 42.
15. *Life After Lumbering: Charles Henry Hackley & The Emergence of Muskegon, Michigan*, pp. 33.
16. Ibid, pp. 25-26.
17. It was Gideon Truesdell and not his brother Levi that offered to help him with the expenses.
18. According to *Littell vs. Hackley* testimony, he was supposed to attend a business college in Chicago while living with the Deming family, but circumstances changed, and he attended school in Kenosha.
19. The *Life of Charles Henry Hackley*, pp. 26.
20. *Hackley & Hume* papers, Michigan State University.
21. Muskegon County real estate records, Ledger 2, pp. 330. On 29 April 1857 Harvey Durkee sold a portion of the Durkee-Truesdell lakefront property for $2,200 to John C. Holmes of Somers, Wisconsin in Kenosha County.
22. *Life After Lumbering: Charles Henry Hackley & The Emergence of Muskegon, Michigan*, pp. 34.
23. *Hackley & Hume papers*, Michigan State University. J.H. Hackley & Company journal, 1859.
24. Charles Hackley papers, Michigan State University, *Littell vs. Hackley* court transcript.
25. *Life After Lumbering: Charles Henry Hackley & The Emergence of Muskegon, Michigan*, pp. 33.
26. Hackley & Hume papers, Michigan State University. J.H. Hackley & Company journal, 1859.
27. Ibid.
28. Ibid.
29. *Life After Lumbering: Charles Henry Hackley & The Emergence of Muskegon, Michigan*, pp. 35.
30. *Hackley & Hume* papers, Michigan State University. J.H. Hackley & Company journal, 1859.
31. They were the Durkee-Truesdell sawmill, single mill, Pomeroy & Holmes, and Trowbridge & Wing mills.

32. The address where Truesdell opened a yard was owned by the railroad.
33. Julia Moore Hackley biographical sketch, Muskegon Historical Museum, "he uncle (Gideon) went to Chicago to open a yard for smaller mills." This ties into what they were doing at their Kenosha yards.
34. This was a typical commission based on collateral research.
35. *Natures Metropolis*, pp. 169.
36. *Chicago Dailey Herald*, 11 May 1860, pp. 3.
37. Passim, *Chicago Daily Commercial Letter*.
38. Ibid.
39. The Metropolitan and Brigg's House routinely published the names of prominent guests, and Gideon Truesdell was frequently listed.
40. Family correspondence, Julia Truesdell to her brother, Kirkland Torrey, 7 July 1863 letter.
41. Gideon Truesdell bankruptcy papers, Record Group 21, File 26620N3.
42. Industrial Chicago.
43. *Hackley & Hume* papers, copies of Hackley drafts in the J.H. Hackley & Company files.
44. *Hackley & Hume* papers, Michigan State University, Littell vs. Hackley interrogatories.
45. 1860 Products of Industry, U.S. Census, Muskegon, Michigan.
46. 14 October 1860.
47. Joseph H. Hackley & Company journals, 1860, Michigan State University.
48. Ibid.
49. Muskegon County real estate records, Ledger 2, pp. 334.
50. Arthur Truesdell narrative, 1902
51. *Boomer*, Jan, Feb, Mar 1992. Article on James McGordon.
52. *Detroit Advertiser & Tribune*, 13 Feb 1863, pp. 5.
53. Credit reporting agencies listed Gideon as a "slow pay" in 1860 and 1861.
54. *Hackley & Hume* papers, Michigan State University.
55. *Hackley & Hume* papers, Michigan State University.
56. *Kenosha Telegraph*, 25 August 1860.
57. Pomeroy mill increased from 15,000 to 22,000 ft per day.
58. *Hackley & Hume* papers, Michigan State University, J.H. Hackley & Company files, 1859–1865.
59. Federal tax information, 1864 and 1865, Great Lakes Federal Archives.
60. *Hackley & Hume* papers, Michigan State University.

61. *Hackley & Hume* papers, Michigan State University.
62. Muskegon Register of Deeds, 21 December 1863, volume 5, pp. 522-524.
63. Ibid.
64. *Daily Milwaukee News*, 2 June 1871, pp. 2.
65. The *Life of Charles Henry Hackley*, pp. 26.
66. *Muskegon Chronicle*, 16 December 1899, pp. 8. Wesley F. Wood.
67. The *Life of Charles Henry Hackley*, pp.98-99.
68. *Muskegon Chronicle*, 3 December 1892, pp. 4.
69. Romance of Muskegon, pp. 54.
70. *Detroit Advertiser & Tribune*, 6 September 1867, pp. 3.
71. Federal income tax records: 1863, Michigan, line 1,129, Muskegon County. Federal income tax records: 1864, Michigan County, line 1,009.
72. Various sources state that they moved into the house in 1863 or 1864, probably the later.
73. Muskegon Register of Deeds, ledger 2, pp. 330. Hackley paid $50 for each lot.
74. The *Life of Charles Henry Hackley*, pp. 28.
75. *Boomer*, Jan, Feb, Mar 1992
76. The *Life of Charles Henry Hackley*, pp. 19.
77. *Isabella County Enterprise*, 19 December 1880, pp. 2.
78. *Muskegon Chronicle*, 22 November 1880, pp. 3.
79. Ibid.
80. Alcoholism ran in the family, and although Gideon, Amos, and Levi didn't drink, each had a son who was an alcoholic. It was a family curse that skipped through several generations.
81. *Romance of Muskegon*, pp. 125.
82. Ibid, 7 August 1873.
83. Ibid.
84. *Michigan State University, Hackley & Hume* papers, logging camp files. There are several invoices from G. & A. Truesdell; the invoice has been reproduced in this publication.
85. *R.G. Dun & Company*, 18 January 1862, Michigan ledger, volume 54, pp. 10.
86. Newaygo County Register of Deeds, volume 1, pp. 89.
87. *R.G. Dun & Company*, 18 January 1862, Michigan ledger, volume 54, pp. 10.
88. Ibid, 19 July 1864.

89. Whitehall City Directory, 1862-63.

90. Arthur Truesdell wrote his nephew, Amos Fred Sherwood, that their sales were $250,000 but other sources put it at $200,000. Sherwood's father worked for Gideon Truesdell and he was trying to piece together a family history.

91. When wheat exports by-passed Kenosha, Harvey Durkee and Gideon Truesdell began provisioning logging camps and boarding houses in Green Bay and Muskegon. They began doing this as early as 1856.

92. Ibid, 17 October 1867.

93. Ibid.

94. *Muskegon Chronicle*, 23 November 1899, pp. 5. Michael Sullivan reminiscences.

95. *Muskegon Chronicle*, Leonard Eyke reminiscences, 24 Feb 1899, pp. 2.

96. *Detroit Advertiser*, 1 November 1866, pp. 6.

97. Arthur Truesdell letter dated 19 February 1906 to his nephew, Amos Fred Sherwood.

98. *R.G. Dun & Company*, G. & A. Truesdell, 18 February 1865 report. Michigan, volume 54, pp. 10.

99. Ibid, 9 September 1865.

100. Arthur Truesdell narrative, 1902. Right around this time his mother, Rhoda Truesdell (87 years old) began writing down her recollections, her son, Arthur, helped his nephew, Amos Fred Sherwood, research the family history. His father, Erastus Sherwood, helped his father-in-law manage the Croton mercantile. When asked why they opened a big store in the middle of the woods Arthur explained that "Uncle Gid" had some type of arrangement to log, mill, and sell lumber.

101. *Chicago History Center*, Martin Ryerson Sr. papers.

102. This is based on *U.S. Customs House* information throughout the war in *the Kenosha Telegraph*.

103. There existed a close relationship between both men with many of the schooners we know Gideon used docking at *Amos Norton & Company*. When Truesdell organized the *Wisconsin Mining Company* Frederick Ranney sat on the board-of-directors.

104. *Muskegon Chronicle*, 29 March 1900, pp. 1. Cornelius Eyke obituary.

105. Ibid.

106. Passim, all 3 of these men scaled logs for Gideon Truesdell.

107. *Burton Historical Collection, Detroit Public Library*, Lumbering files.

108. *Jackson City Patriot*, 14 November 1888, pp.4.

109. *Detroit Free Press* Truesdell put 7,131,144 feet of logs in the river, J.H. Hackley & Company put 9,478,040. (16,609,184)
110. *Muskegon Chronicle*, 19 August 1899. "Pioneer Days."
111. Chauncey Davis and Joseph Hackley knew one another from Kenosha, where they both started out as builders who found their way to Muskegon. Davis became associated with Theodore Newell and Hackley with Gideon Truesdell.
112. *Michigan Log Marks*, pp. 52.
113. Detroit Advertiser & Tribune, 6 Sep 1867, pp. 3.
114. *Muskegon Chronicle*, 21 Jul 1869, pp. 3.
115. *Michigan State University* historical archives, Hackley & Hume papers.
116. *Life After Lumbering: Charles Henry Hackley & The Emergence of Muskegon, Michigan*, pp. 103.
117. *Jackson City Patriot*, 18 Aug 1869, pp. 2.
118. *Detroit Advertiser & Tribune*, 1 Jul 1869, pp. 2
119. *Muskegon Chronicle*, 21 Jul 1869, pp. 3.
120. *Life After Lumbering: Charles Henry Hackley & The Emergence of Muskegon, Michigan*, pp. 102.
121. Ibid.
122. 1864 federal tax returns, Illinois, Cook County, Gideon Truesdell, line 2,743. Truesdell was listed as a manufacturer of carriages, and carriages made from hardwoods.
123. Ibid, 1863.
124. Erastus Sherwood 9 January 1906 letter to his son, Amos Fred Sherwood. Erastus married Gideon and Julias niece, Ellen, and he worked under G.J. at their Croton mercantile store.
125. Arthur Truesdell narrative, 1902. He and G.J. shared a 2-room apartment at the Durkee-Truesdell boarding house until Arthur got married.
126. Ibid.
127. Ibid.
128. Rhoda Truesdell reminiscences to grandson, Amos Fred Sherwood, and she was Amos Truesdell's widow.
129. Arthur Truesdell narrative, 1902.
130. Ibid.
131. Amos Fred Sherwood family research, 1939. His mother was Gideon Truesdell's niece.
132. Ibid.

133. Truesdell family legend.
134. Truesdell family correspondence; Gideon, Amos, and Levi Truesdell knew they had sons with serious drinking problems.
135. *Grand Rapids Daily Times*, 7 March 1877, pp. 1.
136. The *Life of Charles Henry Hackley*, pp. 61.
137. Ibid, 97. Other articles state that Hackley didn't like wasting his time at the boarding house.
138. Chauncey Truesdell remanences, 1952.
139. Ryerson and T.J. Rand were listed as Executors of Greenes will, and witness several real estate transactions during the 1850s.
140. Chauncey Truesdell correspondence to his nephew, E. Frances Devos, 9 November 1941.
141. 12 September 1940 correspondence between Gideon G. Truesdell (1864–1945) and his nephew, E. Frances DeVos.
142. *Romance of Muskegon*, pp. 121. *Southport American* newspaper advertisements for Greenes lumberyard during late 1840s.
143. Chauncey Truesdell correspondence to nephew Amos Fred Sherwood, 7 June 1939.
144. Letter from Chauncey Truesdell to his nephew, E. Frances DeVos, 19 December 1940.
145. 1860 federal census, Muskegon, Muskegon, Michigan; roll m653__555; page O, image 185.
146. Ibid.
147. *Silver City Enterprise*, 20 Feb 1891, pp. 2, column 4, Samuel O. Greene obituary.
148. Ibid.
149. Marriage certificate on file in Muskegon County Court House.
150. Family correspondence, Julia Torrey Truesdell to her sister, Abigail Torrey Piper.
151. The Life of Charles Henry Hackley, pp. 29.
152. Family correspondence, Julia Torrey Truesdell to her sister, Abigail Torrey Piper.
153. Ibid. Gideon and Julia Truesdell enjoyed extended stays from their nieces, nephews, and friends.
154. *Life After Lumbering: Charles Henry Hackley and the Emergence of Muskegon, Michigan.* Pp. 48.
155. Marriage 3 October 1864, married by Reverend I.K. Torrey. Julia Truesdell's grandfather was a minister.

156. When Levi Truesdell bought the business in 1866 it spanned the entire block on Western Avenue.
157. *Wisconsin Lumberman*, 19 September 1868.
158. Ibid.
159. Karamanski, Theodore J. Schooner Passage, pp. 133.
160. Ibid.
161. Ibid.
162. Chauncey Truesdell reminiscences, 1951.
163. Erastus Sherwood correspondence with Arthur Truesdell, 29 April 1906. Arthur referred to the location as "Sampson's Slip."
164. *Chicago Historical Society*, map room, insurance maps 1869–1871.
165. *Chicago Commercial Daily Letter*, passim.
166. *Chicago Commercial Daily Letter*, commodities newspaper, 19 June, 1862, volume 2384.
167. Ibid.
168. *Wisconsin Directory of Chicago Lumber Dealers*, 1861, Gideon Truesdell, pp. 119.
169. In 1866, Gideon Truesdell's Chicago office became *Charles Deming & Company* with Gideon owning the mortgage, and a 50% interest (Gideon Truesdell bankruptcy papers.)
170. Gideon Truesdell bankruptcy papers, Record Group 21, File 26620N3.
171. *Directory of Kansas & Nebraska Shippers Guide*, Gideon Truesdell, pp. 114.
172. *Directory of Kansas & Nebraska Shippers Guide*, Gideon Truesdell, pp. 371.
173. Passim, U.S. Customs House reports, *Kenosha Telegraph*.
174. This number is the amount listed in the *Milwaukee Sentinel* (1863–1865). They published a list of the largest incomes in the state.
175. *Romance of Muskegon*, pp. 20.
176. Ibid.
177. *Muskegon Chronicle*, 3 June 1897, pp. 4.
178. Ibid.
179. Ibid.
180. Ibid.
181. Ibid, 9 June 1892, pp 8.
182. *Muskegon Chronicle*, 1 September 1893, pp. 1.
183. Ibid, pp. 24.
184. *University of Chicago* archives, board members, and Jennifer L. Condas

thesis, 2014, University of California- Irvine.
185. *Industrial Chicago*, Martin Ryerson biographical sketch, pp. 104.
186. Muskegon City Directory, 1866, L. Truesdell, General Store.
187. *Muskegon Chronicle*, 17 February 1863.
188. *Romance of Muskegon*, pp. 46.
189. *R.G. Dun & Company* reports, passim, Arthur Truesdell recalled that the stores did about $200,000 in a letter to his nephew.
190. *Grand Haven News*, 8 Aug 1863, pp. 4.
191. *Chicago Tribune*, 4 April 1864.
192. *Grand Haven News*, 15 June 1864, pp. 3.
193. Ibid.
194. Ibid.
195. Gideon Truesdell bankruptcy papers, Record Group 21, File 26620N3.
196. *Western Rural Farmer*, 10 March 1870, pp. 1.
197. *Milwaukee Sentinel*, 18 June 1868, pp. 4.
198. *Detroit Advertiser & Tribune*, 29 November 1867.
199. Ibid.
200. Ibid.
201. *Chicago Tribune*, 4 April 1864.
202. Ibid.
203. Muskegon Register of Deeds, volume 8, pp. 566.
204. *R.G. Dun & Company*, Michigan, Volume 60, pp. 272.
205. *Boston Commercial Bulletin*, 23 December 1865, pp. 2.
206. *Daily Milwaukee News*, 2 June 1871, pp. 2.
207. *Hackley & Hume* papers at Michigan State University.
208. *Muskegon Chronicle*, 10 August 1870, pp. 2.
209. Ibid.
210. Ibid.
211. *Daily Milwaukee News*, 2 June 1871, pp. 2.
212. Gideon Truesdell bankruptcy papers, Record Group 21, File 26620N3.
213. Ibid.
214. *Daily Milwaukee News*, 2 June 1871, pp. 2.
215. *Hackley & Hume* papers at Michigan State University.
216. *Milwaukee Sentinel* list of the highest incomes in Wisconsin for 1862 - $6,450; 1863 - $16,395; 1864-$19,378; 1864, $10,355-1865.
217. This extensive maritime collection is housed at the *Milwaukee Public Library*.
218. *Chicago Daily Commercial Letter*, volume 274, pp. 2216.

219. Ibid.
220. Gideon Truesdell bankruptcy papers, Record Group 21, File 26620N3.
221. *Muskegon Chronicle*, 10 April 1869, pp. 3.
222. *Jackson Citizen Patriot*, 1 May 1868, pp. 2.
223. *Detroit Advertiser & Gazette*, October 14, 1869, pp. 3.
224. Gideon Truesdell bankruptcy papers, Record Group 21, File 26620N3.
225. *Detroit Advertiser & Tribune*, 14 Jul 1870, pp. 2.
226. Gideon Truesdell bankruptcy papers, Record Group 21, File 26620N3.
227. *Industrial Chicago: The Building Interests*, pp. 866.
228. Ibid.
229. Gideon Truesdell bankruptcy papers, Record Group 21, File 26620N3.
230. Ibid.
231. Ibid.
232. Gideon Truesdell bankruptcy papers, Record Group 21, File 26620N3.

4

G. TRUESDELL & SON FARMS, CIRCA 1865

Long before the State of Wisconsin became "Americas Dairyland," it had been one of Americas largest growers of wheat. One-sixth of Americas wheat came from there, but after decades of growing nothing but wheat, nitrogen levels dropped and so did crop yields. By 1860, the wheat crop wasn't what it used to be, and farmers knew they had to push their farms in a new direction to survive.

To replace this once profitable cash crop, Wisconsin farmers looked to New York farmers who experienced the same problems a decade earlier. After 30 years of growing the same crops, the soil for many New York farmers had become exhausted, with yields dwindling from 160 bushels per acre to less than 35 in some areas.

It didn't take long for farmers to look for alternatives because they couldn't survive much longer if things stayed the same. Wisconsin and Illinois farmers followed the lead of New York and Ohio farmers when they turned to dairy farming, and began making cheese and butter when pasteurization opened new markets. Cheese now had a shelf life of about a year which made it the most profitable dairy product.

The U.S. Department of Agriculture estimated that dairy sales would soon exceed $400 million ($25 *billion* today) a year. At the time, the national wheat crop amounted to $375 million, hay at $250 million, corn at $450 million, and cotton at $303 million.[1] Clearly, this new industry had a bright future with big profit margins.

The 1860 federal census counted 600 dairies in New York but only 26 in Ohio, 26 in Illinois, 22 in Vermont, and 8 in Wisconsin.[2] When Gideon's dairy plant opened it was larger than anything built in the Midwest, and had a capacity of over a million pounds of cheese a year.

It's likely that Gideon heard about the emerging dairy boom from Harvey Durkee, who in 1839 broke ground for one of the first farms in the town of Pleasant Prairie, five miles west of Kenosha. After serving several terms as president of the Wisconsin Agricultural Society, he was considered one of the best-informed farmers in the state. Those who knew him intimately said he was more of a farmer than a businessman, and yet his business acumen made him wealthy at a young age. The "Panic of 1857" nearly bankrupted him, but through shrewd management of what remained in his portfolio, by 1864, Harvey reported a $5,702 ($364,000 today) income on his federal tax return.[3]

Each summer, Harvey returned to his native Vermont to visit friends and relatives, and then to the World's Fair in New York City. According to an 1853 *Kenosha Democrat* article, "Few, if any of our enterprising businessmen take more interest in adding to their stock of agricultural knowledge than Mr. Durkee. Although he has a fine improved farm of 1,200 acres under a high state of cultivation, having all modern improvements in the way of stock, grain, fruit, and methods of cultivation, still he is in pursuit of more knowledge, not only for himself but for our western farmers."[4]

The dairy boom had an immediate impact, because in 1856, Kenosha County farmers shipped 500,000 pounds of butter valued at $91,236 ($10.9 million now). Ward White, who was the first farmer in Pleasant Prairie to experiment with dairying, recalled a shaky start. "I tried raising grain for two years, and finding that I would lose what little I had if I kept on, I made up my mind that I had to do something else. I milked 70 cows this season, last year 75."[5] He sold 47,000 pounds of milk in a single year and said each cow netted him $100 over expenses. That figure seems unrealistically high but during the early years there were huge profit margins in the dairy business.

Gideon knew how to plant and harvest crops, raise cows and pigs, and how to butcher livestock. When his logging company fell on hard times, he survived by returning to his roots as a farmer, and made a living provisioning logging camps and boarding houses on the Wisconsin River. He raised fruits and vegetables, ground wheat into flour, turned milk into butter, slaughtered pigs and sold barrels of pork up and down the river.[6]

By the end of the Civil War, Gideon was a wealthy man with about a $1.1 million-dollar ($68 million today) net worth.[7] He invested heavily in Chicago real estate, and was about to roll the dice in the emerging dairy industry. With funds from the sale of several lumber-related businesses sitting in his Union National Bank and First National Bank of Chicago accounts, his agricultural investment soared to $345,000 at a time when the entire capital of the 1st National Bank of Kenosha was $304,088.[8] ($17.2 million today.) Clearly, he intended to "go big" in this new industry.

In 1864, he bought a 160-acre farm on the old Green Bay Military Trail and hired his wifes cousin, Derastus Torrey (1820–1896), to turn this property into a dairy farm.[9] After two profitable seasons, Gideon had the proof he needed to make a heavy investment that grabbed the attention of state and national agricultural journalists.

After years of manufacturing an enormous tonnage of lumber, Gideon knew how to fix bottlenecks, pinpoint inefficiencies, replace manpower with machinery, and eliminate logistical problems to maximize output. During the planning stages of his farm, he worked with architects to make sure everything flowed from the corn fields to the dairy barns to the dairy plant, and the wholesale customer.

The average dairy farm consisted of about 160 acres but Gideon was about to build something much, much larger. A nephew recalled "Uncle Gid was going to mass produce dairy products the way he did lumber," and a lot of thought went into the construction of his farm.[10] Within a few years, G. Truesdell & Son Farms had the largest output of dairy products of any privately owned farm in the United States. He streamlined farming to levels never seen before, and in some ways, he was fifty years ahead of the industry. This made his farm the subject of many articles in national publications. The *Western Rural Farmer* wrote that the "farm of Gideon Truesdell....is doubtless the most extensive private farm in the United States."[11]

His first order of business was acquiring land, and piecing together 19 smaller farms until he owned 2,668 contiguous acres in Pleasant Prairie Township. He built two farms; 1,100 acres for himself, 500 acres for his son, and had 1,068 acres of pastures. Gideon hired a small army of workers, and using horse-drawn plows and wagons leveled houses, barns, sheds, and fences to create wide open fields. One of the most striking features of this farm was its self-sufficiency.

The elaborate scale of Gideon's farm was unmatched anywhere in the country. At a time when only the wealthy had indoor running water, the blueprints called for expensive wooden water and sewer lines that ran to his barns, stables, sheep pens, and troughs in the fields.

Water came from wells, and were pumped by a steam engine into three separate 300-barrel towers that in the course of 24-hours pumped a total of 37,800 gallons, which provided constant water throughout the farm. A float valve in each water tower let workers know when each tower was running low. Over a thousand animals drank over 20,000 gallons a day. Building such a large and complex farm was an enormous challenge during the horse and buggy days of farming.

Each barn or stable had floor drains connected to a labyrinth of sewers running under each building, which allowed farmhands to hose down the floors and keep them spotless in a way other farms couldn't. Thousands of feet of expensive commercial sewer lines used in big cities were buried throughout the farm, made from wooden staves eight to ten feet long.

Gideon spent hours relaxing in a greenhouse that was attached to his residence. He enjoyed grafting flowers until he created brilliant colors.[12] It was a hobby, and he had the only private greenhouse in Kenosha County although a few years later his friend, Zalmon Simmons, built one attached to his residence. Gideon bought clusters of trees from a nearby nursery, and had them planted in each pasture to provide shade for grazing because calm, relaxed, and happy cows produced higher yields of milk.[13]

He planting trees around the perimeter of his farm, and kept a couple of men busy building miles and miles of picket fences. An 80-acre apple orchard created a barrier between his residence and a small village of barns, stables, and buildings.[14] According to a niece who lived on the farm, Ellen Truesdell Sherwood (1846–1892), he had a second-floor study with a window that gave him a view of the farms service road, and an observation tower on the rooftop where with a spyglass he could monitor progress in the fields.[15]

One dull, time-consuming, and repetitive job Gideon vastly simplified was grinding feed for over a thousand animals. Processing feed with a hand-cranked mill was exhausting and would have taken a couple of men the better part of a day. Furthermore, once the feed had been ground it had to be loaded into wagons, and forking into feed troughs that required as many as ten farm workers.

Gideon moved an enormous tonnage of lumber from his sawmills down two 1,000-foot docks using strapline tracks and horse-drawn carts. A few years early at the Durkee-Truesdell warehouse in Kenosha, they built a long, wide dock with a railroad track running down the center, making it one of the most efficient warehouses on Lake Michigan.

According to journalists, Gideon significantly reduced his labor cost, and vastly improved the efficiency of his farm by installing a railroad track from his feed barn through his dairy barns, dairy plant, stables and hog pens. A traction engine at each end of the track pulled over sixty feed cars into position, which was something no other farm in the country had, and this railroad track saved thousands of steps every day.

Specially designed feed troughs were attached to axles the width of the rails, brought feed in one direction, and roughly 2,700 gallons of milk in the opposite direction to his dairy plant.[16] His dairy barns had enormous second story storage lofts for hay, corn in the sheaf, and oats, which was brought to the feed barn for processing at the end of the railroad track.

Construction of the two farms began in 1866, when several schooners unloaded lumber at the Kenosha Pier Company dock, and Kenosha & Rockford boxcars delivered over 600 tons of lumber, lath, siding, flooring, shingles and pickets to the Pleasant Prairie train depot. The station was soon flooded with crates of machinery for a state-of-the-art dairy plant that upon its completion became the largest in the Midwest. Boxcars loaded with expensive furniture and carpets also arrived for the two residences under construction.

He knew from selling lumber that wholesale prices would fluctuate based on supply and demand cycles. There would be good years followed by bad years, and he built his farm with that in mind. His farms had fourteen profit centers: cheese, bulk milk, processing milk for other farms, slaughtering livestock, packing meat, selling over 12,000 bushels of apples and pears each season, selling replacement livestock to other farmers, wool, grinding feed for other farmers, manufacturing thousands of barrels of Truesdell's City Mills Flour, barrels of lard, tallow, hay, and selling wagonloads of surplus manure. [17]

We know from a *Milwaukee Sentinel* article that when the price of wool dropped, he butchered two-thirds of his sheep, and expanded his dairy herds.[18] When the price of cheese fell below production costs, he shipped larger quantities of milk to the Chicago Condensed Milk Company, slaughtered and packed a larger tonnage of meat from his hogs, and became a cattle dealer specializing in blooded livestock.

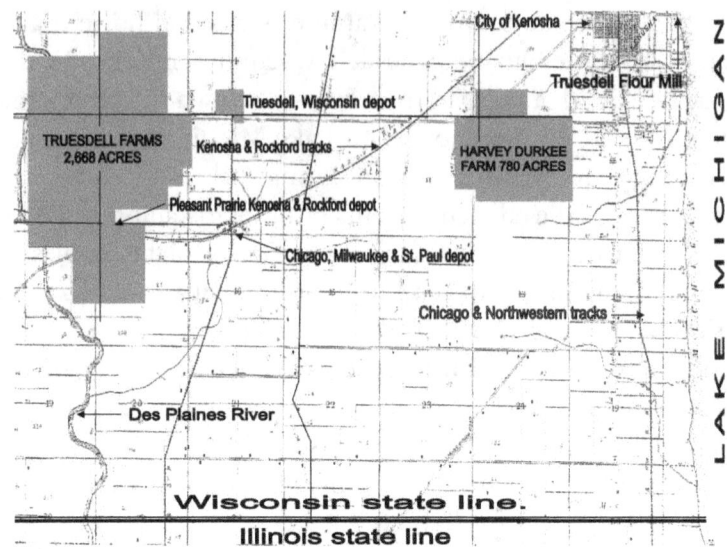
Pleasant Prairie Township, Wisconsin. (Kenosha County)

Every farmer needed to replace older, less productive cows with younger stock, and cattle and horses could be bought much cheaper in Wisconsin. This created a niche for Gideon, who reported making $8,000 ($480,000 today) a year selling blooded horses and cattle.[19] Regardless of what supply and demand did to wholesale prices, Gideon was always able to pivot to where the money was.

Many efficiencies were achieved from the farm's layout, and several journalists were astonished that such a large property was run by eleven full-time employees. According to the *Western Rural Journal*, "Gideon Truesdell, it is said, has his barns and machinery so well arranged that two men can care for 140 head of cattle, doing all the work as to feeding and caring for them."[20]

The farm's superintendent, Derastus Torrey, lived with his wife and sons in a newly constructed two-story house near the dairy plant, with a wing that served as a boarding house where about ten full-time employees lived upstairs with a living room downstairs with comfortable chairs.[21] There was a large dining room in the main house, where Mrs. Torrey served them three meals a day, although during the planting and harvest seasons quite a few more workers needed to be fed. A back porch led to an enclosed walkway to the dairy plant and barns, which made it convenient for feeding and checking on the livestock during a harsh winter or rainy day.[22]

Gideon ran this mammoth farm by the numbers. He ran a highly efficient business because he knew exactly what it cost to feed his cattle, and to make a sixty-pound block of cheese. His farm journals recorded the animals' weight, how much feed they consumed, slaughtering and packing costs, and what each barrel of beef or pork sold for.[23]

During his first year of farming, he appears to have struggled with feed costs until he and other farmers learned how to supplement their feed to lower costs. As a member of the Northwest Dairyman's Association, he participated with other farmers in experimental programs, maintaining feed journals that tracked milk output vs. different types of feed.[24] Gideon discovered that feeding pumpkins to his hogs increased their weight faster, and that he could slaughter them two months earlier than other farmers. He also learned that by mixing corn with hay, oats, and oil cakes he could lower his dairy feed costs.[25]

During another study, they discovered that 32 cows grazing on corn produced four hundred pounds of cheese per cow annually that sold for $1,600, whereas when corn *and* grass were fed to 40 cows, they produced six hundred pounds that sold for $3,000.[26]

All of this information helped Gideon improve the efficiency of his farm, and according to the U.S. Census, four years after breaking ground, his farms grossed an astonishingly high $54,270 ($3.4 million today) gross income.[27]

The centerpiece of his farms was the largest dairy plant in the Midwest with the most expensive equipment money could buy. The average factory was valued at about $2,400 but his was appraised at $15,000 ($980,000 today), and was designed for large commercial output.[28]

According to a *Milwaukee Sentinel* journalist, his factory had the only Fraser's gang press in the Northwest, which could press as many as twenty 60-pound wheels of cheese at a time. Once the cheese looked like a firm gelatin it was placed in a metal hoop where a press applied gentle pressure with jack screws. By the end of the week the cheese was hard enough to be brought to the curing room, where sixty-pound blocks were placed on racks so the air could circulate around wheels of cheese. A few weeks later after frequent turnings they came out perfectly round and firm when they were fully cured. By 1867, Gideon was manufacturing 70,000 pounds or 1,200 sixty-pound blocks of cheese each year, and processing 20,000 gallons of milk from his own herds.[29]

By 1868, there were eight dairy factories in Wisconsin, but two years later that figure soared to sixty-two of which thirty-two were located in Kenosha County, which became one of the largest dairying regions in the country.[30]

Gideon Truesdell Wins 66th Assembly Seat in the Wisconsin Legislature, 1867

Why Gideon subjected himself to the misery of running for public office probably had something to do with the importance of creating a unified dairy market, and getting his hands on funding for what would soon become an international state industry. The legislatures three-man agricultural committee wielded enormous power, and had access to significant state funds and political influence.

Gideon was remembered as a courteous but blunt person, and his wealth rubbed a lot of people the wrong way. Anyone connected with the Kenosha & Rockford railroad debacle immediately had a stigma connected to their name, and Gideon sat on the board of directors for three years. Perhaps more damaging, while taxpayers were struggling to pay for that railroad, he made a *lot* of money shipping lumber to interior markets using this railroad. Right from the start, there were people who believed that taxpayers had built a railroad so a small group of wealthy insiders could become even wealthier. After the railroad crashed, nearly all of the railroad's promoters left the area, including Gideon Truesdell, leaving the taxpayers to clean up their mess.

The Chairman of the Kenosha County Republican convention was Zalmon Simmons, former president of the Kenosha & Rockford, and somebody Gideon knew well because he was the railroad's largest freight customer during the war years.

During the last four years of fighting, Gideon declared an income of $63,312. ($4 million today) on his tax returns from lumber shipped to interior markets using this railroad.[31] This irritated Isaac Webster (1818–1875), a populist attorney who served several terms as mayor and was the publisher of the *Kenosha Union*, a Democratic mouthpiece that would have plenty to say about Gideon's fitness for office.

Zalmon Simmons placed Gideon's name before the convention for an informal vote to see if he had enough support to win. Gideon received 15 of 30 votes, far more than any other candidate, and yet hardly a landslide. But it was strong enough for Simmons to call for a formal vote where

Gideon polled 18, which was enough for the Chairman to ask the delegates for unanimous acclamation.[32]

Isaac Webster resented Gideon's relationship with railroad officials, and it didn't help when the *Milwaukee Journal* published the highest tax returns in the state, revealing that Gideon's was by far the largest in Kenosha County.[33] At a time when the nation's non-farm income averaged $512, his 1865 income was $19,378 ($1.1 million today) for the previous year, and that didn't even include his Muskegon or Chicago income.[34]

The Peoples Party nominated twenty-six-year-old George Hale (1840–1910) to oppose Gideon. He was an eminently qualified candidate, Civil War veteran, and the son of Obed Hale, a farmer from Paris Township who represented a rural district in Kenosha County in the state legislature.[35] While Gideon's son was spending quiet evenings courting Louisa Greene, George was fighting for his life in the Wisconsin Infantry under Captain Lindsey of Kenosha County. Hale was in the battle of Coldwater, which resulted in Lindsey's death, at which point Hale was promoted to Second Lieutenant.

He fought in the Red River campaign that pursued General Price through Arkansas, and he nearly died of typhoid fever which brought him so close to death that he was reported to have died in the Jefferson Barracks Hospital.[36] When his superiors realized that he hadn't died, he was restored to his rank of First Lieutenant, and promoted to Adjutant on the Board of Military Court Martial. In 1865, he was ordered to rejoin his regiment, but the surrender of General Lee ended the war, and he was discharged.[37]

Augustus Coffeen dairy farm, Pleasant Prairie, Wisconsin, and the 1866 Republican Party campaign broadside. Sketches courtesy of the History of Racine & Kenosha Counties.

Richard C. Fritz

Gideon ran as a Radical Republican, a faction of the Republican Party that Charles Durkee belonged too. They believed, among other things, the Confederacy needed to suffer the consequences for starting a war, and were adamant that Negroes were entitled to identical rights as white people. They pushed for the confiscation of southern assets, the imprisoning of Confederate Army leaders including Jefferson Davis, and other retaliatory measures.

The *Kenosha Union* defended Hale as a soldier who "was in the army three years and saw hard fighting. He had a younger brother in the army who died. He is a man against whose character as a soldier, citizen, and friend no man can say a word. We are inclined to think he is no Copperhead."[38] The copperheads were northerners who wanted to negotiate an end to the war before the fighting on both sides destroyed the country.

On October 29, 1866, the populist *Kenosha Union* wrote "we prefer George Hale to the radical candidate [Gideon Truesdell], because he has served his country faithfully in the field, has more than one idea, more sense than money, will not be made the tool of the railroad power, and was nominated by at least 22 delegates instead of 3 men."[39]

They accused Gideon of being a "tool of the railroad power," which had legitimacy since Blodgett & Upton had long represented him in Kenosha County. Henry Blodgett was a railroad attorney who represented the railroads passing through Chicago, and was their "fixer" in the statehouse. Even after he became a judge, Blodgett continued to pull strings for the railroads, and he was a close friend of Gideon's.

Pleasant Prairie Township (five miles west of Kenosha) was on the verge of becoming one of the four largest dairying regions in the country. The *Kenosha Telegraph* wrote "Mr. Truesdell has been an enterprising member of this community for over 20 years, with all his interests blended with the growth and advancement of the county. Though his occupation as an active and hard-working businessman has not given him the ready and glib tongue of the professional stump speaker and politician, he is a man of sound judgment and good sense which are better qualifications for a legislator."[40]

On November 6, 1866, Gideon won 1,510 to 852, the largest margin of anyone elected to the 66th Assembly up until that time.[41] Character assassination notwithstanding, the voters sent the right man to the statehouse.

The *Milwaukee Sentinel* wrote, "Gideon Truesdell (Radical

Republican) is elected to the Assembly over George Hale, conservative Republican run by the Democrats. How much the people care for this type of Republican is shown by the fact that Captain Hale did not run at all ahead of his ticket."[42]

His investment in farming made Gideon's appointment to the powerful Agricultural Committee a logical one. During his one-year term he was listed as "Acting Chairman," and had a strong say in the development of the States newest industry, which was growing rapidly with great economic promise.

Wisconsin Legislature. Gideon Truesdell occupied desk 29.
Picture courtesy of the Wisconsin Historical Society.

Gideon's name was attached to two charters, the Wisconsin Dairyman's Association and the Northwest Dairyman's Association. He also drafted a charter for the Wisconsin Lumberman'ss Association, which was presented by Assemblyman Thomas McDill (1815–1889) and other lumbermen. McDill was somebody Gideon would have known from the Wisconsin River when he was a logger, and his brother was U.S. Congressman Alexander McDill.[43]

The 1867 legislative session was somewhat tedious, but Truesdell seems to have spent his time wisely networking with other legislators, and made an impression on a reporter from the *Milwaukee Sentinel*, because they followed his movements closely.

When Gideon notified the Speaker of House that he would be absent for two weeks to supervise the start of that year's lumber season, the *Kenosha Union* wrote sarcastically that "our Assemblyman has had granted to him a leave of absence for two weeks. He is occupying his time at Muskegon, Michigan, making arrangements for an early run of suckers."[44]

Even after the election was over, Isaac Webster couldn't find anything good to say about Gideon, and obviously wasn't interested in burying the hatchet. At some point in their past the two men clashed, probably over the railroad, because Isaac Webster hated Gideon Truesdell.

Gideon Truesdell & Son Farms, circa 1867

Agricultural journalists described his massive property as a "model farm," one that replaced manpower with the latest equipment, proper crop rotation, and incorporated the latest research. A model farm was pronounced perfect in all its arrangements, a farm that had been thoroughly researched during the planning stages and could scarcely be improved. The *Chicago Tribune* described his farm as the "very best in the United States."[45]

At its peak, Gideon's 2,668 acres supported 300 dairy cows, 250 hogs, 60 horses, 600 sheep, and 10 yokes of oxen.[46] He had 1,600 acres planted in corn with another thousand acres for grazing or the cultivation of hay for winter feed.

He went far beyond the latest technology with his own innovations, which attracted widespread attention from the *Milwaukee Journal, Chicago Tribune, Woodstock Sentinel, Daily Milwaukee News, Western Farmer, Western Rural Journal, National Livestock Journal, American Stock Journal, Cultivator & Country Gentlemen, Plantation (Atlanta), Galveston Tri Weekly*, and other publications.

Running a farm of this magnitude created its own problems, not the least of which was cleaning up after 1,100 animals that produced 33,000 pounds of manure and 2,700 gallons of urine *every 24 hours*. Manure was an essential fertilizer so none of it went to waste, although managing such a large tonnage required a regimented recovery system.

A decade earlier, farmers in New York and Ohio developed a "manure cellar" beneath the feeding floor of a barn. Each stall had a 12-inch opening in the floor where manure was swept into the cellar using gravity. Gideon incorporated this concept into the design of each barn with a few of his own ideas.[47]

Dairy barn with a manure cellar below. The third story attic was used to store hay with lightning rods on the roof. Sketch courtesy of the History of Dairy Farming in America.

He built eight barns on a bluff, creating a roadway behind that abutted the cellars, where manure mixed with peat moss was shoveled into wagons, and dumped along a wide service road behind the barns. There was enough space on the opposite side of the road for hundreds of tons of manure to be dumped throughout the season, where it began to slowly rot in the outdoor air. By springtime, Gideon had enough high-grade manure to fertilize his fields. With over 600 tons of manure piled neatly along one side of the road, it cost him little more than the labor to fertilize his fields.

By springtime, hundreds of loads had been dumped throughout the year with the fresh air decomposing the animal waste. Before winter, a light scattering was spread over 1,600 acres, and then covered with straw. This helped the grass recover faster, and revitalized his corn fields before spring when manure spreaders scattered about 25 tons per acre to bring them back to life. The manner in which he recovered his manure attracted attention from writers. According to an article in the *Cultivator & Country Gentleman*:

"The writer saw a barn constructed like this by Mr. Gideon Truesdell in Kenosha County, Wisconsin to accommodate 306 cows. The barn was 35 feet wide, standing on a wall 7 feet high, forming below a manure cellar, in which the manure is deodorized by muck. A feeding floor ran through the center of the story above, and a row of cows was ranged on each side in stalls.

"In cleaning the ditches from his farm, he had some 300 to 400 loads of muck, which he dumped into the manure cellar. His muck is now in the center between the droppings of his two rows of cows in the manure cellar; and a man goes below every day and spreads a dusting of this dry muck over the droppings."[48]

Inside his barns he used railroad tracks and custom-designed feed troughs that ran from a two-story feed barn that was 112 x 40 feet, and where 200 tons of grain in the sheaf was stored in a loft. Gideon believed that some of the best nutrients were left in the stalk.[49] We also know that he was always looking for ways to lower his feed bill. Using a Richard's Iron Corn Sheller as a sort of 19th century food processor, he ground a natural blend of stalks, rye grass, alfalfa, soybean meal, corn, oats, oats, wild vegetables, and oil cakes.

Using gravity chutes similar to those at his sawmill, stalks came down a chute from a second-floor storage loft to a thresher and sheller that ground corn, stalks, oats, and oil cakes into feed. Commercial corn shellers first came on the market around 1860, and were designed to process corn but Gideon used his to process cattle and hog feed.

On the first floor of the feed barn was a Richard's Iron Corn Sheller powered by a 12-horsepower steam engine, where a single man shoveled stalks and cobs into the machine. A chute brought the ground feed to where it dropped into sixty feed troughs on a railroad track below. The Richard's sheller sold for $475 ($33,000 today), and was designed for high commercial output at warehouses, distilleries, and large farms.[50] It could shell 3,000 to 5,000 bushels per day or roughly 10 bushels per minute. Most farmers did this with a hand-cranked sheller that was slow and exhausting to run.

A separate railroad track ran from his feed barn to his hog pens where, after grinding stalks, corn, pumpkins, eggs, and soy for protein these mobile feed troughs were brough to the pig pens. Special precautions were taken to keep the pigs from rushing to the troughs, and they designed a tailgate that folded down to let the animals run to the troughs when the feed cars had stopped moving.[51]

Most farmers fed their animals "dry" feed, and it would have been much easier had Gideon done this but he followed the example of English farmers. Evidently, he believed the benefits far outweighed the inconvenience. He said on more than one occasion that his cooked feed went much further, and significantly lowered his feed bill.

Instead of using dozens of iron cauldrons to cook his feed, he modified the design of 70 or more rolling feed cars so he could cook the feed in each trough. He accomplished this by running an aerated steam pipe through each trough. Once the troughs were loaded with layers of straw, feed, and oats a pipe was connected to a pipe which was connected to the steam engine in the feed barn. A valve released steam at about 15 psi (121 degrees) that traveled from one end to the last trough, and thoroughly cooked the feed in about twenty minutes.[52]

The *American Stock Journal* said, "Gideon Truesdell told us (and he is a strict businessman) that his savings by cooking his food for such a large stock amounted to $3,000 ($132,000 today) a year."[53] Instead of bringing the feed by wagon to each trough they brought the trough to the animals. In the feed barn, each feed trough moved under a gravity chute, and two men could load over seventy feed cars in about 20 minutes.[54]

These rolling feed troughs did double duty, because with his cows averaging 25 gallons of milk each day, they brought over 7,200 gallons to the dairy plant.[55] The national average for a dairy cow was 9 gallons of milk, but according to the *Milwaukee Sentinel,* Gideon and other Pleasant Prairie farmers were averaging 25 gallons per day by following rigid livestock management.[56]

Milk shipments from neighboring farms arrived in the early morning and late afternoon. Sketch courtesy of the History of Dairy Farming in America.

Smaller farms sold their milk to a nearby dairy for processing, because it didn't make sense for them to invest in their own equipment, and they got a higher price when it was sold to a large Chicago processing plant. Every dairy factory had standards when it came to the quality of milk they accepted, and Gideon insisted that farmers use milk cans he supplied that were made by National Milk Coolers.[57] They were top of the line cans with an ice jacket that kept the milk at cool temperatures even during 90-degree heat, because warm milk could ruin an entire batch of pasteurized milk, butter, or cheese.

Cows were milked twice daily, daytime and evening. By the time the milk arrived at the Truesdell factory it had cooled from 80 degrees to about 60 by immersing pails of milk in cold water.[58] At the next dairyman's convention an expert warned farmers not to mix daytime and evening milk.

By processing milk for others, Gideon was able to keep about a third of the price as a commission, and farmers were happy with this arrangement. Before a single can was unloaded at the Truesdell plant, the milks temperature was measured along with its purity. A sample was poured into a hydrometer, and if the farmer had watered down his milk the entire shipment was refused. There wasn't a market for bad milk at any price.

Ralph's Oneida cheese vat and gang press which made twenty 60 lb. wheels of cheese, and hundreds of 60 lb. wheels of cheese in a curing room. Pictures courtesy of The History of Cheesemaking.

We know that a lot of milk ended up at the Chicago Condensed Milk Company, but they weren't interested in small quantities from a single farmer, and we know Gideon was sending them at least 20,000 gallons a year just from his own herds.[59]

As the industry grew, the New York, Ohio, and Wisconsin Dairyman's Associations ran experimental feeding programs to determine which breeds produced the best quality and quantities of milk.

"Breeding up" was how farmers gradually improved their herds, and the best breeds were Devons, Ayrshires, Herefords, and Alderleys. Gideon's preference for breeding was a purebred Durham bull with ordinary cows that were good milkers.[60]

When Gideon got into the dairy business the Chicago market was wide open, because in 1866, half of the cheese sold there came from New York farmers. This led southeastern Wisconsin farmers to believe they could pirate a large and profitable niche 68 miles away from their farms. But before that occurred, they had to correct a serious image problem.

Most of what Wisconsin farmers had previously sold was homemade cheese or butter made from excess milk, and made by the farmer's wife in her kitchen. Mediocre at best, it was sold or traded for groceries at a rural country store. During the 1850s their milk had a foul odor because farmers let their cows graze on just about anything including turnips and onions. This made their butter gritty, with merchants using inedible shipments to grease their wagon axles.[61] There were other indirect prejudices, because a farmer reported seeing a Milwaukee wholesaler sorting cheese, labeling the best New York and the others Western, which sold for less even if the best came from a Wisconsin dairy.[62]

But the dairy industry held incredible potential for those who manufactured a good product. A huge, untapped niche was southern markets where the land and climate weren't suited for dairy farming. The Northwest Dairyman's Association viewed western states as "significantly underserviced," but within their reach once the trans-continental railroad was completed in a few years due to the invention of the refrigerated freight car. These cars were cooled by ice, which made it possible to ship fruits, meat, butter, and cheese across the country.

Pasteurization was about to open hundreds of international markets in China and the Pacific islands, causing dairymen to believe they would never run out of places to sell their cheese. They were convinced that overproduction or saturated markets would never touch them, but there was a nasty surprise waiting for them just around the corner.

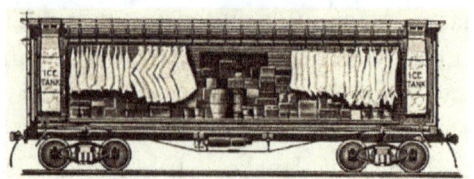
Refrigerated boxcar cooled with ice tanks.

According to a June 18, 1868 *Daily Milwaukee News* article, the previous year the Truesdell factory generated a $6,750 ($400,000 today) profit from the sale of cheddar. An important part in his farm's revenue stream was meatpacking. Hogs multiplied quickly, because sixty pigs could reproduce over 1,800 piglets in twelve months.

According to a reporter at the 1869 Northwest Dairyman's convention, Gideon said he fed his pigs corn, oats, bran and pumpkins, which brought them to slaughtering weight a couple of months early.[63] A smokehouse used hickory or applewood to improve the flavor and kill bacteria, and he packed about 200 to 250 pounds of meat in barrels between layers of salt.[64]

According to a *Western Farmer* article, Gideon sold 18,000 to 24,000 pounds of "plate meat" each year.[65] Smaller meatpackers used a handsaw, but his slaughter barn had a 16-horsepower steam engine that pulled the carcass through a saw that split it in half in a few minutes for butchering.[66] A side of beef had about 200 pounds of sirloin, porterhouse, and T-bone steaks; stew beef, chuck roasts, rib steaks and rib roasts; sirloin tips, cube steaks, rump roasts and ground beef.

Wisconsin livestock dealers had a significant price advantage over eastern dealers, and New York and Ohio farmers could buy blooded stock from them for a third less than at auction barns closer to home. According to the 1870 census, Gideon sold 160 cows for $3,040 and slaughtered and packed $4,000 ($279,000 today) of hogs.[67]

When the Chicago, Milwaukee & St. Paul built a depot near Gideon's farm, they built a livestock pen which made it easier for him to ship animals to New England farmers for 2¢ a pound or $20 ($1,200 today) per animal.[68] New England farmers could buy livestock for about half the price in Wisconsin or Illinois, and even after shipping costs they saved a lot of money. For Gideon, it was easy money.

G. Truesdell & Son Farms packed 18,000 to 24,000 pounds of beef and pork each year, and the G.J. Truesdell farm had over 600 sheep that they sheered for wool, and then butchered for mutton steaks.

According to the *Milwaukee Sentinel*, during the 1867–68 season, Gideon's son sheared 600 sheep, garnering about 15,000 pounds of wool that would have sold for around $4,500 ($270,000 today).[69] When prices dropped significantly, G.J. disposed of the rest of his sheep and increased the number of dairy cows on his farm.[70] At slaughtering time, he would have butchered around 20,000 pounds of mutton.

Harvey Durkee and Gideon Truesdell ran across a potentially lucrative new industry when they discovered peat moss on their farms. They were three-quarters of a mile long and ten feet deep, with enough peat to provide heat for their farms for fifty years.[71]

During the Civil War when the demand for wool was high, Wisconsin farmers raised sheep, and in 1866 Harvey Durkee and Gideon Truesdell considered building a textile mill with the boilers that ran the looms powered by peat moss.[72]

"Peat, again. Mr. Harvey Durkee informed us that he has been in correspondence with Boston parties who have, by the aid of machinery, put their peat beds to practical use, from whom he has received a box of the prepared article, and description of the machinery necessary for its preparation. Mr. Durkee informs us that he intends to have a machine on the ground, and commence cutting and preparing Peat early in the spring. This will be in good time for the New Woolen Factory, if the Peat should turn out to be as valuable for fuel as it is claimed to be."[73]

During the Civil War, a large percentage of wool came from southeastern Wisconsin farmers, and if Harvey Durkee and Gideon Truesdell built a textile mill near their farms in Pleasant Prairie, farmers raising sheep would be able to eliminate shipping costs for their wool. But

Richard C. Fritz

a significant drop in the price of wool made the prospect of a textile mill unworkable. But it shows us that if there was something that had potential for big money, Harvey Durkee and Gideon Truesdell were willing to roll the dice.

On June 18, 1868 the *Milwaukee Sentinel* described Gideon's massive new dairy farm:

GIDEON TRUESDELL'S FARM - KENOSHA COUNTY - BEST IMPROVEMENTS AND LARGEST FARM IN THE STATE OF WISCONSIN

"Gideon Truesdell, the subject of this article and owner of this farm was born in Genesee County, New York, in 1811, and was a resident of that and Allegheny County, until he came west thirty years ago.

"He immediately went into the lumbering business upon the Wisconsin River, and like all other adventurers from the Eastern states has enjoyed prosperity and adversity, but never gave up trying to make his fortune. He has cut cordwood, kept a hotel, went to California to make his fortune and came back thirty dollars poorer.

"About eight years ago he went into the lumbering business at Muskegon, Michigan, and this time luck favored him beyond his own anticipation. Four years ago, he concluded to go into the farming business, and purchased a farm five miles west of Kenosha, and has kept adding to it until he had the largest and most productive farm in the state.

"For the past three years he has been building upon and improving it. If there is another farm that equals the Truesdell farm it has not been found. From his private residence can be seen every foot of land, and he is monarch of all he surveys.

"On the West Side of the road he has built a large two-story residence. There is a cheese curing room 56 x 32 feet, a hog pen 64 x 25 feet, dairy barn with 75 stalls, and an ice house 18 x 18 feet. He has secured one of Fairbanks largest scales for his own use.

"He has built a tool house 20 x 18 feet, where all his farm tools are kept from exposure to storms and sun. There is also a wagon shed 64 x 26 feet, horse barn 76 x 32 feet, hog pen 64 x 28 feet, and a grain barn 112 x 40 feet. In the barn, besides storing grain, he has a thrashing machine, corn sheller, fanning mill, two mills to grind feed for his stock, and a straw cutter.

"Adjoining this barn is an engine house, 18 x 18 feet, where he has a 12-horsepower steam engine which drives all of his farm machinery, steams his feed, saws his wood, and waters his stock. He has built another cow barn, 179 x 34 feet, capable of stalling 110 cows, with stalls on either side of the barn.

"Between these two barns he has a well that furnished water for his entire stock during the past season, which has been the driest in 30 years. Under the 179 x 34 barn, he has a deep cellar, where he gathers all his dirt from ditching and mucking, which he mixes daily with manure from the farm.

"He has 110 cows which he feeds steamed and cut straw, mixing ten bushels of oat meal daily. The daily expense of feeding his cows will not exceed six dollars. He had found that when straw is cut and steamed, his cows leave nothing, and it is the most nutritious food for cattle. He has 276 feet of railroad, with cars to convey the food to his cattle, which he feeds twice daily.

"His cows are taken to pasture twice daily, for drinking and exercising, which is beneficial to their health and comfort. He has a blacksmith shop 18 x 30 feet, packinghouse 18 x 45 feet, and calf and colt sheds 128 x 30 feet. All of his mechanical work is conducted on the farm.

"He has 110 cows and he will milk 120 next season; 27 two-year-old colts, 11 yearling colts, 12 working mares, and he intends to raise 56 calves next season. At the present time he has 160 hogs well fatted. He raises about 120 acres of grain annually, which he heavily manures. During the past year he drew out 2,000 wagonloads, and next spring will draw 3,000 loads of the best kind of manure.

"He is continually improving his stock from the best breeds, and raises horses, cattle and hogs himself, buying none, but continually supplying those who wish to improve their stocks. He thinks he will complete his improvements next season.

"This past season he has harvested 1,200 bushels of apples of the finest grafted variety, and 25 bushels of pears from his orchards. He has slaughtered 67 hogs, with an average weight of 270 pounds, packing 18,097 pounds of meat for shipment.

"He has the largest cheese factory in this part of the country, and has produced 45,000 pounds of cheese this past season. The milk is put into a tin Oneida vat which is heated until it reaches 86 degrees. It is then scalded up to 105 degrees, remaining at that temperature from one to five hours until thoroughly cooked; then it is dipped and wheyed off into a sink settler, and salted with Ashton's Liverpool Salt, which is celebrated for making cheese and curing butter.

"He uses an iron screw press with a Rosa Expansive Hoop, which is used in New York and the northwest. The size of each cheese made is 60 pounds and he usually makes 4 per day. His factory is large, neat, and commodious made exclusively to accommodate the business of his farm, which is the raising of grain and manufacturing cheese. His cheese has been sold at a benefit of $6,500. ($300,000 today.)

"Derastus Torrey, celebrated farmer and cheese maker from Allegheny County, New York is employed as Superintendent and overseer, and their cheese will compare with anything produced in New York or Ohio.

"Last season, Mr. Truesdell built for himself a private 6,300 square foot residence, which is large and commodious and for beauty cannot be surpassed. Beautiful arched doorways of the finest woods, separate parlors and sitting rooms, expensive carpets of the finest variety cover oak floors, and etched leaded glass windows grace this magnificent mansion.

"Off the parlor is a glass conservatory with an abundance of beautiful plants and flowers making this indoor garden a pleasant refuge during the winter. There are six guest bedrooms and the house is built upon an elevation surrounded by native oak and hickory trees.

"The estimated value of Mr. Truesdell's farm buildings are $75,000 ($4.5 million today), exclusive of the stock. He is one of our oldest and respected citizens and an early settler. He represented our citizens at the last session of the State Legislature. His whole soul is now engaged in building and making improvements upon his farm to which he is continually adding buildings and acres.

"He has recently sold his mills in Michigan for $120,000 ($7.2 million today), and in a few years he will retire upon this farm. He intends to spend the remainder of his days in quietude and pleasure and the enjoyment of home, with a competency sufficient to satisfy any reasonable man.

"To G.J. Truesdell, his son, he has given 468 acres, which lie contiguous to his own upon the opposite side of Geneva Road, and he is building for him a beautiful $10,000 ($600,000 today) residence. He has a barn nearly 40 x 30 feet. His sheep barn is 10 x 304, divided into sheep pens, with sufficient water in the center for his stock, which is drawn by a patent pump. His horse barn is 20 x 30 feet.

"The stock on his farm consists of 600 sheep of the choicest breed, 54 cows, 20 calves, 10 colts and 5 horses. He raises grain and wool. His land with improvements is valued at $30,000. He raises a large number of lambs each year, and disposes of his fat withers in the fall. These two farms with their numerous buildings have the appearance of a small village."[74]

Gideon and Julia Truesdell's 6,300 sq. foot residence, Geneva Road, Pleasant Prairie Township, Kenosha County, Wisconsin. Sketch courtesy of the History of Kenosha & Racine County.

Greenhouse attached to the Zalmon G. Simmons' residence and outdoor garden similar to the Truesdell residence. Pictures courtesy of the Kenosha History Center Archive.

Gideon's residence had hand carved oak woodwork, with a beautiful staircase that led to the second floor.[75] Many years after Gideon and Julia died, a newspaper referred to the farmhouse as the "historic old Truesdell residence, one of the show places of the rural districts of Kenosha County,

Richard C. Fritz

and built more than forty years ago for the late Gideon Truesdell who for years he made his home there. The old house was the scene of many historic social gatherings."[76]

Illinois & Wisconsin Dairyman's Association, and Northwest Dairyman's Association

Gideon was a strong believer in trade associations, and thought they were hugely beneficial to a newcomer like himself.[77] He was one of the earliest members of the Fox River Dairy Club, one of the first dairy trade groups in the country. Their first meeting was in 1865 in a vacant courtroom they borrowed for the day in Rockford, Illinois, with about forty farmers attending.[78] The following year they made an effort to recruit new members, and changed their name to the Illinois & Wisconsin Dairyman's Association.

The 1867 convention was once again held in Rockford, which was about a two-hour trip for Pleasant Prairie farmers aboard the Kenosha & Rockford. Gideon attended with his friend, Zalmon G. Simmons.[79] Dairying had become a profitable new industry with affluent physicians, lawyers, and judges investing in dairy farms. Simmons had a knack for spotting opportunities, and sensed that dairy farming was going to become something big. There were many successful men who agreed with Simmons, and viewed dairy farming as a good investment. Judge Sylvester Wilcox, Zalmon G. Simmons, Gideon Truesdell, Judge Henry Blodget and Dr. Joseph Taft had by then bought their own dairy farms.[80]

Most of the discussion at that convention was about butter, because in 1866 Rockford farmers sold over $250,000 ($15 million today), a significant accomplishment. Illinois and Wisconsin dairyman had a competitive advantage because their land and feed costs were cheaper than back east, and cattle could be bought for half what eastern dairymen paid. But there were still a few major image problems that had to be fixed. A Chicago grocer could get $1.20 ($72 today) more per 60-pound wheel of cheese by stamping "New York" instead of "Illinois" or "Wisconsin."[81]

The *Rockford Weekly Register* gave the minutes of the dairymans' convention. "We judge the Convention was composed of practical men, capable of imparting much valuable information upon subjects. We notice among the Vice Presidents the name of the Honorable Gideon Truesdell."[82]

The 1868 convention was held in Belvidere, Illinois, and better organized.⁸³ They spent a lot of time discussing how to recruit new members, because for this organization to gain power they needed at least 200 farmers shipping a large tonnage of dairy products. That would give them enough leverage to get deep discounts from the railroads like other large shippers of commodities.

Each of the ten regional vice presidents visited farmers in their district to explain why they should join, and left them with a pamphlet containing information from the last year's convention. It was an effective recruiting tool with many farmers realizing that the two-dollar ($120 today) membership was money well-spent.

At that year's convention, Gideon was appointed chairman of a steering committee that nominated officers for the next season.⁸⁴ Another special committee was appointed to research feeding programs and compile statistics.

Since so much of their products were shipped by rail, they formed a task force to investigate freight rates. Minneapolis and St. Louis were important distribution points into the territories, but it was cheaper for Illinois and Wisconsin dairymen to send their products to Chicago, and then reship to Minneapolis rather than shipping directly to St. Louis. According to the *Chicago Daily Tribune* it cost 75¢ per 100 pounds to ship cheese from Rockford to St. Louis and 65¢ from Cleveland to St. Louis.⁸⁵

A six-member panel chaired by Gideon Truesdell was asked to vigorously pursue reduced freight rates for dairy farmers.⁸⁶ With a growing tonnage of cheese coming from Illinois and Wisconsin, the railroads were receptive to discounts for large commercial shippers. Gideon's longtime friend and attorney, Henry Blodgett, would have been helpful, because his law firm represented several major railroads passing through Chicago, and he owned a dairy farm in Lake Bluff, Illinois.⁸⁷

At the 1868 Belvidere, Illinois, convention Gideon was asked to speak about his lower feed costs, which he attributed to information from the previous year's convention.⁸⁸ He said that his herds were doing well after mixing hay and corn meal with layers of straw, and that it only took seven bushels a day to feed 100 cows.⁸⁹

During an open forum there were comments from the floor about the quality of milk. After a lengthy discussion, it was agreed that the freshness of the water a cow drank had a major impact on the flavor of the milk. Another farmer said it was a mistake to milk a cow on an empty stomach.

The dairy industry had become lucrative. Compared to other

commodities a pound of cheese could be made for less than a pound of pork, and sold for three times as much. The good news for Wisconsin farmers was that butter shipped from the Rock River Valley near Beloit was now selling for 3¢ more in St. Louis than New York butter, and that butter from northern Illinois was beginning to penetrate the New York market.[90]

This coincided with a major improvement in dairy equipment, and one of the finest pasteurization vats was designed and patented by William Ralph, of Utica, New York. He was at the 1868 Northwest Dairyman's convention, and Gideon tried to convince him to build a manufacturing facility in Kenosha.

"We met Mr. William Ralph at the convention with his celebrated patent, the Oneida Cheese Vat, which is the standard for making good cheese. Factories and dairies are using this vat for over 300,000 cows nationally.

"Mr. Ralph manufactures his vat in Utica, New York. We encouraged him to come to our city to manufacture his vat, it being bulky to ship. Gideon Truesdell, first mentioned the enterprise to Mr. Ralph, and the encouragement Mr. Truesdell gave Mr. Ralph, if he would locate in our city to manufacture is one of the very many noble enterprises that the people of Kenosha should thank Mr. Truesdell for."[91]

During the second day of the convention, Gideon was asked to describe the unusual layout of his farm, and how he operated such a large property with fewer employees than smaller farms. Pleasant Prairie had become one of the largest dairying communities in the country, so they extended an invitation to McHenry County Illinois farmers to visit their farms.

"Perhaps the most important feature of Pleasant Prairie is the extensive cheese dairy of Gideon Truesdell, twenty-five hundred acres of land are maintained for pasturage for a large number of cows, from which butter and cheese are produced in quantity of the finest quality."[92]

One agricultural journalist believed farmers fell into two categories. Young men who became farmers because that's what their father and grandfathers did, and those with a natural feel for farming. Even a twenty-acre farm generated a living, but unsophisticated country folks never achieved the profits of more sophisticated farmers because they didn't stay current on the latest trends. But farmers who took the time to attend conventions, read agricultural journals, and digest the results of studies saw their profits steadily increase each year.

A delegation of McHenry County dairy farmers took the Kenosha & Rockford from Harvard, Illinois, to the Pleasant Prairie depot where they were brought to A.F Coffeen's farm for lunch. A *Woodstock Sentinel* reporter was among the delegation, and on April 23, 1868 wrote an article about their visit.

"A Good Time in The Town of Pleasant Prairie Among the Dairymen."

"After inspecting Mr. Coffeen's farm," it was reported, "with his commodious barn and fine stock of cows we proceeded to the farm of the Honorable Gideon Truesdell one half mile north. This farm consists of 1,600 acres in one body and well does it deserve the name model farm.

"Here we found a village, all buildings belonging to the farm, consisting of two cow barns, one 176 by 56 foot, holding 110 cows, and built in the most modern improved style, with a loft holding nearly 200 tons of hay; another barn, 130 x 32 feet, holding 75 cows.

"One feature that we noticed is that he keeps his manure in the cellar where it is mixed with muck and allowed to rot until spring, when its spread over his fields, the cellar being arranged so that cows pass directly above the center.

"About 100 feet from this and connected by railroad is his grain barn, 112 x 40 feet, two stories high. Grain in the sheaf is kept in the upper story. A railroad track runs the whole length to carry the grain to the threshing machine, which is at one end and run by a 12-horsepower steam engine that occupies an entire engine house some distance off.

"After the grain is threshed it passes through a chute to a hopper in the mill, where it is ground and carried into a steam box, which is mixed with cut straw that has passed through the straw cutter. Steam pipes pass through these boxes and rapidly cook the feed that will be fed to his stock. Mr. Truesdell thinks that cooking adds over one-third to the value of the feed, which more than pays for the added expense.

"Immediately north is a row of hog pens, also connected with his grain barn by railroad with box cars in which the feed is cooked, and so arranged that they can run up and connect with the steam pipes from the boiler, and when cooked pass immediately in front of the hog pens. The ladies admired these pens as they were so arranged that a door passed down and kept the hogs from the trough until they were fed. Everything looked neat and clean and 'a place for everything and everything in its place' appeared to be the rule.

"We next passed to the horse barn and saw some beautiful horses and carriages. Then came his colt and calf shed, which is 100 feet long, each grade having a pen by themselves. His carpenter shop, blacksmith shop, slaughterhouse, sleigh and tool room were all well-arranged and worthy of imitation by any good farmer.

"We then visited his cheese factory which is connected to his cow barns, of which A.E. Torrey is Superintendent, and everything looked neat and clean and the boy looked like he could beat the father, but Derastus Torrey is a hard man to beat. Here we found everything in order with a nice cheese making and curing room of the requisite size for a dairy of 200 cows.

"Having visited over 100 factories during the past month we found here a patent and it must be of great benefit in the manner of pressing their cheese. It is Fraser's Gang Press, where with one screw they can press from one to twenty or more cheeses and all of them alike. This is the only one in the Northwest.

"Mr. Truesdell uses the Oneida vat made by Mr. Ralph of Utica, New York which I think is equal to any cheese vat made. Connected with his cheese house is a dwelling house for his two farm overseers and the fifteen hands that run this farm.

"We next visited the home of his only son, one half mile distant and of 500 acres, who has just completed a beautiful house of modern style, which was thrown open and its hospitalities tendered. We found everything in 'apple pie order' which we might expect from the accomplished lady who adorns it.

"Young Mr. Truesdell keeps about 700 sheep with a barn 430 x 26 feet built in around a square. He has now only 50 cows but is going to enlarge his dairy the coming season and keep less sheep.

"We next visited the mansion of Mr. Gideon Truesdell where we found the latch strings out and the doors wide open. The house was soon filled from cellar to roof, and everyone felt at home and discussed the delicious qualities of his choice apples, and the fine flavor of his cider from an orchard of 2,000 trees occupying an area of 80 acres.

"At 7:00 Gideon Truesdell and Mr. Coffeen proceeded to the Torrey House with a crowd that had increased to nearly fifty couples, and found the tables loaded with a magnificent spread that would have done honor to the

Sherman House in Chicago. The evening was gaily spent discussing cheese and getting acquainted with each another. At a late hour we adjourned to meet the next morning at Mr. Holt's farm and to visit other model farms.

"We had the chance to get acquainted with some whole-souled farmers, and saw our old friend, Harvey Durkee. We are satisfied that such meetings are very useful and that they should happen much more frequently."[93]

The following year, a group of Pleasant Prairie farmers traveled to Richmond, Illinois, to visit their farms. The Kenosha & Rockford left the Pleasant Prairie depot with Sidney and George Derbyshire, G.J. Truesdell, Ward White, R.S. Houston, W.E. Wood, Christopher Holt, and their wives for a 25-mile trip with the delegation staying at the Richmond House.[94]

The Northwest Dairyman's Association knew that by holding their conventions in different communities they would pick up another 20 to 30 new members each year, and the 1869 convention was held in Elgin, Illinois. Over 160 farmers attended, enough for the Chicago Condensed Milk Company to host an elaborate dinner followed by a tour of their facilities.[95] Manufacturers had their farm machinery on display, and a five-man committee that included Gideon was asked to examine this equipment, and report their findings to the convention.[96]

What type of feed farmers fed their cows was the subject of considerable debate, and two neighboring farmers were experts in the ongoing battle between dry versus wet feed. Ward White stressed the importance of dry feed, which he felt was more important than searching for the perfect breed of cow.[97] He advocated feeding meal and dry bran with one to two quarts of oil cake. He thought that buckwheat produced the largest quantity of milk and it was better to feed cows' sweet corn than regular corn. He didn't think an ear of corn was as good as ground corn.

During the 1840s, farmers in England experimented with cooked feed, and found a 25 to 50% increase in winter milk. Most dairy farmers preferred dry feed because of the labor involved, but everything Gideon fed his animals was cooked, which he believed was more nutritious and lowered his feed bill by $3,000 ($132,000 today). Whether they were proponents of dry or wet feed, farmers generally agreed that the more they fed their cows the more milk they produced, and the greater their profits.

Professors from agricultural colleges discussed the latest research, and how costly poor bloodlines were to dairymen.[98] It was often said that a $30 cow was more costly to own than a $100 cow, because the expensive cow produced a much larger volume of milk, whereas the cheaper cow didn't even produce enough to cover its feed bill. A good "milker" produced over 10 gallons a day with a lifespan of about twelve years, although Gideon and other Pleasant Prairie farmers was averaging 25 gallons per day.[99] Experimental feeding programs revealed that when grass was mixed with grain a cow produced 200 pounds more of milk a year.[100]

Keeping their herds healthy was another important subject, and it was discovered that cows living in the city had totally different diseases from those living in the country. A farmer had to be able to recognize the onset of 150 to 200 diseases, and veterinarians spoke at length about the latest studies to keep their animals healthy. Just before a cow gave birth, she was susceptible to fevers, and the remedy was believed to be bleeding six to ten quarts of blood before she went into labor.

Each convention invited marketing experts. The biggest challenge was a fragmented wholesale market that for years had been controlled by brokers. Farmers sold their butter and cheese for cash to a dairy broker, who found buyers, and pocketed a profit. They helped expand the market but they also manipulated prices to the detriment of the dairy farmer. If dairymen were ever going to get a fair price for their products, they needed to drive brokers out of the market, because they would often destroy half of their inventory to create a shortage so they could drive prices upward. These artificial boom-and-bust periods wreaked havoc on wholesale dairy markets.

Northwest Dairyman's Convention, Kenosha, Wisconsin-February 11th and 12th, 1870

In the four years since its founding, the Northwest Dairyman's Association had made great strides, and were drawing large crowds at their conventions. The 1870 convention that was held in Kenosha broke previous attendance records.

The six counties northwest of Chicago (including Pleasant Prairie Township outside of Kenosha) became one of the largest dairying regions in the country. Kenosha farmers produced a large tonnage, which made it a logical place for a convention, and it was held downtown at Simmons Hall above Zalmon Simmons block-long mercantile store.

Free transportation was provided by the Chicago & Northwestern, with several short-line railroads that connected with their trunk line that brought people from rural areas. A reception committee at the Kenosha depot paired visitors with people who put them up for the weekend in their home, making this an affordable convention to attend.

Not surprisingly, three times as many farmers and their wives attended with a large contingent arriving from the Green Bay area. It was the largest dairymans convention in the western states, and Gideon and Julia Truesdell hosted a historic luncheon for over 300 guests at their farm.

Judge Silvanus Wilcox of Kane County, Illinois, presided over daytime and evening sessions. "Mayor Robinson, William Oslege, N. Ratzberger, J.W. Rhodes, Z.G. Simmons, Esquire, and the Honorable Gideon Truesdell were unremitting in their attention, doing everything to make the stay of the delegates pleasant and the convention a success."[101]

On February 11, 1870, a long list of subjects was discussed by experts, including Pleasant Prairie farmer Ward White. He talked about his cows, a native stock crossed with a Durham bull, raised on whey with bran and oats mixed and fed dry.

"In the spring the cows are fed on oil meal and bran…feeding dry is thought important. The cows eat more slowly and get more nutriment from the feed. The cows are not turned to grass until they can get a good bite. By following these rules, a pasture that would keep 50 cows without other feed, will keep 75 in good condition and also add 100 pounds of cheese to each cow's product and $10 to the value of each cow to sell in the market.

A peaceful and serene pastures and barns resulted in higher milk output.

"Mr. White considers it very important to treat cows gently and kindly. His cows are quiet and gentle. The cows are always milked in the stables, fastened with stanchions. As soon as the weather becomes bad in the fall they are kept up at night, but are allowed to run out during the day except in stormy weather. The management of cows is usually followed by his neighbors, who reach the same results."[102]

Gideon was asked to speak, and said he was but four years in the business and was still learning. He said that he profited by attending these conventions and believed they played a significant role in his success.[103]

He stating that he had 258 cows that winter and was feeding them cut straw put into a box with steam pipes running upon the bottom, said his cows were remarkably fond of it, thinks that he can keep 150 cows in that manner cheaper than he could 100, and to give them hay and meal separately.[104]

Gideon said that barley had many beneficial nutrients, and that in his opinion it made the best feed. He also said that corn stalks could be made edible, and even hay could be vastly improved.[105] For late summer he suggested corn ground with green stalks. He said he fed mashed potatoes mixed with bran last year, and found that it soured the milk and spoiled the cheese.[106] He said that it was so bad that even his hogs refused to eat it.

"His speech was listened to with marked attention, and was much applauded for its sound practical common sense. Hes the largest farmer in this region and his experience was interesting."[107]

Professor Welch, editor of the *Prairie Farmer* spoke about a new milk patent by Greenlee & Redfield, which he considered the most important recent invention.[108] It expelled animal odor from milk during the cooling process and was a cheap enough filter for every farmer to buy.

A delegate from the floor suggested placing a cold jar of water inside milk cans to drop the temperature of fresh milk, adding that milk shouldn't be allowed to sit in a pail for more than 45 minutes before being cooled to 58 degrees.[109] Some farmers put their milk cans in a cool spring overnight, and preferred that to expensive milk cans with ice jackets.

The Convention adjourned for lunch and over 300 delegates boarded a specially scheduled Kenosha & Rockford train pulling nine passenger cars for the ride to Gideon's farm. They arrived at the Pleasant Prairie depot at the southern edge of his farm, where he had a dozen horse-drawn omnibuses waiting. Each could accommodate 25 passengers, and ten minutes later they pulled into the circular driveway in front of the Truesdell mansion.

"Mr. Truesdell entertained us with friendly hospitality at his dairy farm, which is the largest in the State. The eager crowd took unlimited range over fields, barns, stables, engine rooms, pigpens, calve stables, and his cheese plant. Here we found perhaps the largest cheese manufacturing establishment in the Midwest."[110] After looking over the premises and stock, they were invited into the house where a sumptuous lunch was spread before them.

Harvesting wheat with a commercial reaper.

"Mr. Truesdell has eight stock barns upon his place, and the cows are brought up and fed twice a day. The manner in which food is conveyed is truly novel. They have a number of rail cars running through the barns, into which chopped straw is placed, then a layer of bran or meal, then straw, then bran, alternately until each car is filled.

"Then a pipe, of which there are many running throughout his barns, is attached, the feed steamed, and the cars are drawn to the barns. Mr. Truesdell has a blacksmith shop, and slaughterhouse in close proximity to the barns, and mechanics constantly employed. In a section of the farm, we found a mill for grinding feed which besides doing their own, they also ground several thousand bushels for neighboring farmers.

"They have a Richard's Corn Sheller, threshing machines which thresh all their grain, and the straw is cut with a mechanical cutter. This machinery is driven by a 15 horse power engine, the house of which is built of brick and stands near the barns. The fuel used in the furnace is mostly cobs from the corn sheller. They manufacture about 480 pounds of cheese per day. The total average per cow for each season is about 500 pounds.

"There is upon this farm 140 head of hogs, and about 300 head of cattle which does not include the calves of which there is 70 head. A windmill draws the water used upon this place from the manufactory of N.D. Nichols.

"In the tower, which is not fully completed, there is a tank, which holds 300 barrels. (12,600 gallons.) The water is forced into the tank, and from there it is conducted in pipes, which run over the whole farm. We saw in the storage room of the factory 230 of the finest cheese ever manufactured.

"The day was beautiful and everybody enjoyed the outdoor entertainment, and was delighted and amazed with the magnificence of this farm. Many visitors felt like the Queen of Sheba, when she went up to see the big temple and the big man that built it, that half the story had not been told. Money and personal enterprise have brought forth this wonderful creation, the pride and glory of Kenosha County. We shall not soon forget Gideon Truesdell, his hospitality, or his farm."[111]

The delegates returned to Simmons Hall where they tendered the appreciation and good will of the Northwest Dairyman's Association to the "Honorable Gideon Truesdell" for the entertainment they enjoyed. The Convention adjourned at 4:30, and most of the delegates took the Chicago train to return to their farms.[112]

The 1870 convention brought national agricultural journalists to Gideon's farm that afternoon, and the *National Livestock Journal* devoted an entire page to describing his farm during their first issue. The *Western Rural Journal* wrote that "during the meeting of the Northwestern Dairyman's Association at Kenosha, a visit was made by most of those in attendance to the farm of Gideon Truesdell, Esq., which is doubtless the most extensive private dairy farm in the United States."[113]

An article about Gideon's feeding program examined the savings from cut stalks, rather than letting cattle forage in the pastures until the fields wore out, and the farmer had to buy hay to feed his animals during the winter.[114] Cutting hay required a lot of work because a farmer had to hitch up a horse drawn mower to cut grass and stalks, load several tons of cuttings into a wagon, and store them in a barn until needed. It required a lot of work, but Gideon was convinced that it paid off.

"On the Gideon Truesdell farm are 316 head of cattle, 35 horses and 250 hogs. Four men cut, thresh, grind, feed and care for these 600 animals.

Mr. Truesdell remarked to a visitor that 'if farming was made an intellectual pursuit, conducted with order, system and taste, farmers' sons would find it an attractive field of labor and seldom leave the old homestead except in search of a new one for themselves.'

"He not only cuts hay for his cattle and horses but cuts clover hay for his hogs, which is steamed with pumpkins, meal, etc. Ten-month-old pigs are dressed at 350 pounds. He cuts his straw as it comes from the threshing machine; and at the same time corn stalks are fed into the machine and cut with the straw."[115]

Cutting Feed for Livestock and Dairy Farming in Kenosha County

"Cutting feed for livestock, Truesdell mixes 16 bushels of meal a day with a proper amount of cut straw and stalks to feed 200 cows, which keeps them in fine condition; in November last they averaged 10 pounds of milk a day.

"This is only two and one-half quarts per cow daily, all the rest is what would be thrown away, burnt, or made of little or no account by many. The meal only costs 4¢ per day for each cow, whereas 25 pounds of hay would cost 10 to 15¢. Their estimate is that they save two-thirds through their cutting and steaming process.

"The question again arises; does it pay? An objector says it requires too much help, but not as much as you think. Mr. Truesdell has 1,100 acres and employs eleven men. (The typical 40-acre farm requires two full-time workers with two more seasonal hands during the planting and harvesting season.) This farm, after adding the cost of buildings and improvements is valued at about $93 per acre.

Here are Mr. Truesdell's figures for 1870:

National Livestock Journal
June, 1871 issue, page 348

INVESTMENT:

        Land- 1,000 acres: $40,000
        Buildings: $62,000
        Livestock: $13,000

Machinery: $10,000

Total: $125,000

INCOME:

Dairy cows (cheese/butter): $11,050
Hogs (slaughtered/packed): $5,000
Young horses (sold): $1,500
Two-year olds (horses): $600
Calves: $1,050

Total: $19,200

EXPENSES:

11 mens wages: $3,025
Making cheese: $789
Other labor: $500
Grain and oil meal: $1,000
Repairs: $500
7% Interest on $125,000: $8,750

Total: $14,564

NET PROFIT: $4,686

"The help is all hired, and we all know this was a hard year to figure up profits. Would this farm have paid had he burned up his straw, and let his stock go out in the winter and pick at dry corn stalks? There, is exactly where the profits came from—from the straw and stalks."[116]

The information in this article is more detailed than the 1870 census information, because Truesdell actually broke out his expenses for the writer. Despite paying cash for his land and improvements, being the rigid businessman that he was he included the interest on his investment.

The *Livestock Journal* analyzed the economics of Gideon's farm. "If a profit can be made upon such an enormous investment in land, buildings and implements in raising live stock in the North, what ought to be done in the South where a large portion of the investment would be unnecessary.

"It will be observed that the wages paid are nearly $300 a year to each laborer. It will also be observed that but eleven regular laborers are employed on this large establishment. Beyond doubt every product of this farm sells at a less rate than it would command at the South. The description of Mr. Truesdell's farm, buildings and operations fills a whole page of the *Livestock Journal*. We give the closing paragraph: DOES IT PAY?

"It is, perhaps, too early to answer this question as he has been constantly building up to this present time; but we will examine his operations for the past year which was an unfavorable season by reason of the severe drought. This $4,686 ($186,000 today) profit is his own salary, so to speak, as the farm manager. How many farms could make a better showing?

"It will be noted that the labor is all hired, and that is a better test as to whether farming will pay than when the labor is performed by the owner's family. The average help upon this farm is eleven men, being more in summer and less in winter. This is one man to 100 acres, and there is more labor performed per acre here than on ordinary farms, as will be seen by the stock kept: 316 head of cattle, 35 horses, 250 hogs and pigs.

Horse drawn mechanical planters.

"This is 29 cows, 3 horses, and 22 hogs to 100 acres. He raised 4,000 bushels of corn, 2,500 bushels of barely, 1,500 bushels of oats, cuts 400 tons of hay which is 727 bushels of grain to 100 acres. His machinery and convenient arrangements greatly cheapen the labor. Four men can thrash, cut, grind, cook, feed, and care for his 600 animals. Where does a man feed so much stock in the usual slip-shod way?"[117]

Not everyone was convinced that farming was as profitable as the

Livestock Journal said. A Vermont farmer took exception "to the example of Gideon Truesdell as showing that farming pays because he had $125,000 ($7.5 million now) to invest in a farm and its appointments. What I want to hear about are the men who have become rich by farming only."

"Well, we shall be gratified.... that a man as sharp as this Vermonter should not have seen that Gideon Truesdell illustrated the most difficult phase of farming.... that of investing a large amount of money, improving a farm with the most expensive machinery, running it with a foreman with hired labor, *and making it pay seven percent* upon the whole investment *with over a $4,000 surplus*, what further proof does he need?"[118]

On August 8, 1872 the *Milwaukee Sentinel* published the following article:

THE DEVELOPMENT OF THE CHEESE-MAKING INDUSTRY IN KENOSHA COUNTY:
The Model Farm of Mr. Gideon Truesdell.

"Last year Wisconsin produced 1,894,688 pounds of cheese, averaging one pound of cheese to every 9.88 pounds of milk, and selling it from 0 to 14¢ a pound; better prices than those gotten for the products of Illinois and Minnesota, and a much larger yield than that of either of them.

"In Kenosha County, this most important branch of husbandry has been developed more than in any other portion of the state. Especially is this true of Pleasant Prairie, some 6 miles from Kenosha and a perfect landscape of beauty. Kenosha County yields 1,000 cheeses per week (60,000 pounds) not to mention large quantities of butter and milk.

"The dairy business began here some dozen years ago, when Mr. White, a Green County farmer of New York, introduced the first cheese press. Since then, it has grown until the Kenosha market is one of the largest in the country.

"The Northwest Dairymens Association has established three markets, one of which is at Pleasant Prairie, where sales are made every other Friday afternoon, quotations from which will be given in this paper. By this means, the dairymen are brought into immediate contact with buyers, getting a better price for their cheese and improving its quality.

"Among a number of large dairy farms perhaps that of Mr. Gideon Truesdell is the most interesting because of the extent of its arrangements. The farm comprises 1,600 acres of land. A village of barns, sheds, workshops, out buildings and dairy houses is located in a convenient part of it.

"Two hundred cows give milk from which twelve cheeses of sixty pounds each are made daily, and two hundred fifty hogs and a number of calves feed on the whey. His cattle are mostly a grade between the Durham and the native cow. They average twenty-five pounds of milk each, from which two and a half pounds of cheese are made. Over $300,000 are invested in this one dairy.

"Mr. Truesdell has successfully fed cooked feed to his cattle but owing to the prejudice of swilled cattle, farmers have refused to boil their feed. This is evidently a mistake. In swill feeding, the evil is not in the boiling but in the character of the article boiled.

"Soft, sloppy food like boiled turnips, and brewer's grain and distillery wash give plenty of serum, but no fat to the milk. But proper food like oats, corn stalks, straw, and meal are doubly nourishing when cooked. This is the experience of Mr. Truesdell, who has two steam engines to boil up and steam his feed. This is also the experience of English dairymen."[119]

Gideon Truesdell Farm:
1870 U.S. Census Products of Industry

Improved land: 1,030 acres
Wooded land: 70 acres
Value of land: $125,000
Value of equipment: $10,000
Value of livestock: $19,075
Wages: $4,800

Horses: 32
Milk cows: 175
Other cattle: 138
Hogs: 200

Corn harvested: 2000 bushels

Oats harvested: 2000 bushels
Barley harvested: 1500 bushels
Potatoes harvested: 300 bushels
Apples harvested: 100 bushels
Hay harvested: 600 tons

Butter manufactured: 500 pounds
Cheese manufactured: 70,000 pounds
Animals slaughtered: $3,500

Farm's gross revenues: $39,520

G.J. Truesdell Farm:
1870 U.S. Census Products of Industry

Improved land: 490 acres
Wooded land: 10 acres
Value of land: $49,000
Value of equipment: $4,000
Value of livestock: $7,160
Wages: $2,000

Horses: 20
Milk cows: 60
Other cattle: 40
Hogs: 46

Corn harvested: 500 bushels
Oats harvested: 2500 bushels
Barley harvested: 600 bushels
Potatoes harvested: 250 bushels
Hay harvested: 300 tons

Milk: 20,000 gallons
Animals slaughtered: $500

Farm's gross revenues: $14,750

According to the *Chicago Tribune* Gideon Truesdell's 1868 net income was $9,054 ($420,000 today), in what was widely regarded as a bad year for farmers.[120] The 1870 census recorded $54,270 ($3.4 million today) of gross revenues for his and his sons' farms, which was incredible for 1,600 acres only four years after he broke ground.[121] But the dairy industry was about to go through a debilitating shake-out for a variety of reasons. Unlike most farms, Gideon's diversified property got him through a tough year where he still managed to show a very large profit.

The November 9, 1870, *Watertown Republican* gave an accurate assessment of the dairy market. "From conversations with dairymen in different parts of the northwest, the past season is represented by all as a very poor one for the dairy business.

"The drought, which was very general during the months when milk is expected, was very severe, greatly lessening the supply of feed and in some sections producing a scarcity of water. As a consequence, the falling off of milk is variously estimated at a fourth to a third of the ordinary amount produced.

"But aside from the small amount of milk produced this season there has been another drawback. The mid-summer months were extremely hot, and a vast amount of cheese has been ruined or its value greatly reduced during the curing process. The late rains have brought up feed in the pastures, but the cows were dried before this change came, and too late to recover."[122]

It was presumed that the dairy industry had an unbeatable future but a dark cloud was approaching. By 1870 everything went haywire. Lopsided supply and demand cycles caused prices to plummet. Too many farmers had converted their farms to dairying, which caused every dairy market in the country to become flooded with milk, butter, and cheese. New York City and Philadelphia were saturated and Chicago was glutted with more cheese than they could possibly sell, but premium grades of butter and cheese sold well.

Gideon Truesdell, (L) Julia Truesdell (LC), Amos Truesdell (CR), and Rhoda Mills Truesdell (R). Gideon and Amos were less than two years apart, and remained close throughout their lives. Julia and her sister-in-law, Rhoda, were also close. Pictures courtesy of the Len (Maudine) Truesdell family.

At the 1873 Northwest Dairyman's convention, it was agreed that the previous season had been profitable, especially for cheese and premium grades of butter. The delegates believed the future looked bright but they needed to improve their standing nationally and internationally. The better the quality of their products the more they sold, and Wisconsin cheese had found a market in New York City, London, and Liverpool.[123]

By 1870, Gideon had come up with an extra sharp cheddar that was comparable to the finest in the world. To get people talking about his special brand he sent a block of his best cheddar in a polished walnut case to influential people, including a 60-pound block to Horace Greeley, the publisher of the *New York Tribune*, which had the largest circulation in the country. He wrote Gideon a thank you letter stating that he thought that his cheese was equal to anything that came out of "old Herkimer County."[124]

Gideon Truesdell Drills for Salt, 1864–1869

The East Saginaw Salt Manufacturing Company drilled its first well on February 7, 1860, and at 706 feet punched into a gigantic cavern. Two years later, there were twenty-three other companies drilling for salt, which at the time was in great demand for seasoning, preserving foods, curing meats, and tanning hides.

Before refrigeration, freshly butchered meat was packed in layers of salt to absorb the moisture and kill bacteria. Once packed in barrels, pork or beef could be shipped much longer distances. This made salt a multimillion-dollar industry for Saginaw, Michigan, when lumbermen discovered massive salt caverns a couple of thousand feet beneath their mills. In Grand Rapids, six wells were drilled at considerable expense, but the quality of the brine was weak, and contained other minerals so they were abandoned.

Thousands of barrels of salt were hauled to docks and railroad depots for shipment. Pictures courtesy of Michigan State University Archives.

During their first year, Saginaw shipping 10,000 barrels of salt, a figure that increased to five million 20-years later. At a time when Gideon was incredibly busy, he delegated the study of the geological similarities beneath his Muskegon Lake property to an engineer.

Based on the results, Gideon believed there were gigantic salt caverns beneath every sawmill on Muskegon Lake. He didn't envision getting rich by cornering the market, but thought he could develop something every sawmill could benefit from, and add another $7,000 to $10,000 ($500,000 today) to their bottom line each year. Lumber mills and salt manufacturing ran on parallel tracks in Saginaw, and made each mill far more profitable.

As early as 1864, possibly earlier, Gideon installed a steam engine next to what a map described as a "salt boring" between the Durkee-Truesdell mill and shingle mill, and hired a firm from Saginaw to sink two shafts at $2.69 per foot. Gideon eventually went down 1,800 feet at a cost of around $10,000 ($600,000 today). By then, the money was rolling in from lumber manufacturing, and he could afford to roll the dice but he lined up partners to defray his startup costs. If they were successful there would be plenty of money for everyone.

On June 4, 1865, the *Grand Haven News* wrote "we are informed that the salt well now being bored by Mr. Truesdell, of Muskegon, has reached a depth of 600 feet and upward, and that the brine obtained contains sixty percent of saline matter. It is the intention of Mr. Truesdell to sink the well to the depth of one thousand feet."[125]

Since Truesdell was funding this experiment with his own money, it seems likely that his ulterior motive was to create enough interest to form a corporation where he could raise $250,000 ($16 million today), which is what Saginaw lumbermen did when they developed five highly profitable salt mines.

Hundreds of sections of pipe were delivered from the other side of the state to the Durkee-Truesdell mill site, where an experienced crew from Saginaw drove them into the ground until they punctured a salt cavern about a quarter-mile below. A 12-horsepower steam engine pumped water from Muskegon Lake into this cavern with a return pipe that forced water and brine to the surface. The salt water was distilled by the sunlight, and a few weeks later all that was left was salt.

According to a January 23, 1866, article "Truesdell's salt well at Muskegon is a success. At about 1,800 feet the brine was found to be of the strongest quality, and in quantity is supposed to be inexhaustible. Mr. Truesdell has gone with a quantity to Syracuse for the purpose of having it tested. (Syracuse was the largest salt producer in the country.) Dr. William H. Allen made from three pints of the brine ten ounces of beautiful salt, and predicts that salt manufacturing at Muskegon will prove a perfect success."[126] Gideon no doubt knew more money was needed as they went deeper, and that a full-time engineer should be hired.

In 1868, about 170 miles southeast, the *Hillsdale Standard* wrote "Truesdell's salt well at Muskegon is a success if all reports are true...the brine was found to be the strongest quality and in quantity inexhaustible. The proprietor has gone to Syracuse for the purpose of having it tested... they made from three pints of brine ten ounces of beautiful salt."[127]

He found salt at 586 feet above tide and at a depth of 1,230 to 1,600 feet in the Monroe beds.[128] The *Muskegon Chronicle* followed his salt well's progress, and reported the following;

"In April 1869, Gideon reported that operations for the raising of brine and for the manufacture of salt were to be resumed as soon as the machinery could be put in working order. He hired an expert from Syracuse, New York, to take charge of the business. It was believed that the brine from this well was far stronger than any found in Saginaw.

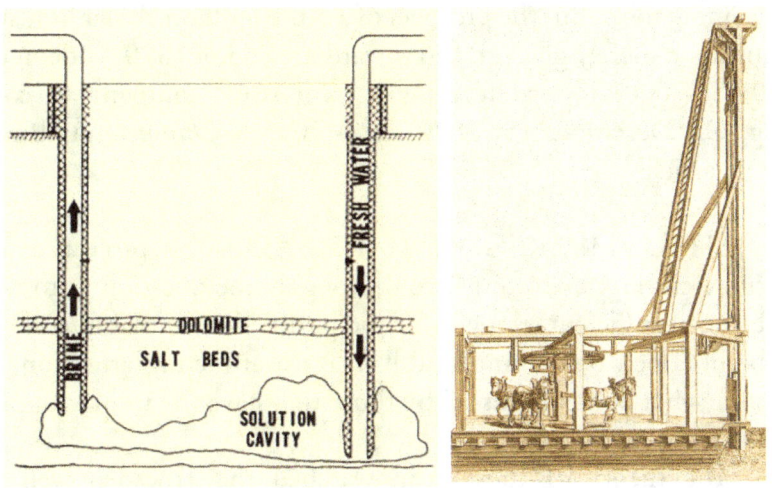

Diagram of a salt boring and a horse-powered pile driver that sank shafts.

"Work at the Truesdell well continued in May of 1869, and by the end of the month a small amount of brine was pumped from the well. When the brine was boiled it produced a salt of great purity."

The brine was of sufficient strength but the quantity was too small to warrant the expense of large-scale manufacture. It was determined that the well should be sunk 1,000 feet further, but when the tools were lost in the shaft, operations temporarily stopped. The tools were recovered, and in August, Gideon's engineer was again experimenting with the brine. This time he said the brine pumped produced two quarts of salt to a gallon.

"However, his attempt to raise enough money to complete the well met with little success. Muskegon was casting envious eyes at Saginaw, whose citizens had exported that year more than 300,000 barrels of salt. Right around that time developers in Alpena, 250 miles northeast on Lake Huron, struck salt at 1,100 feet. There seemed to be no reason why Muskegon should not have 30 wells producing yearly revenue of at least $500,000 ($30 million today), if Truesdell's well should prove a success."[129]

Gideon continued to pour money into salt exploration, and attempted to recruit others with significant resources to invest with him. He was close, because twenty years later the Manistee-Ludington area (60 to 90 miles north) became the largest salt producing region in the state, and Morton Salt Company's largest producer of table salt. In his gut, Gideon believed there was plenty of salt beneath Muskegon.

After six years of trial and error the salt well was abandoned when they lost more tools. But the prospect of a multi-million-dollar industry was too alluring to merely give up, and toward the end of 1870, Gideon offered $1,600 ($67,000) toward forming a joint stock company to continue drilling. On December 15, 1870 the *Muskegon Chronicle* published the following article:

"SHALL MUSKEGON MAKE SALT? The project of raising sufficient money to test here thoroughly the question as to whether brine of sufficient strength for the profitable manufacture of salt can be obtained by sinking a well is again attracting attention, and is somewhat being discussed by those that have the money to put into the equipment.

"The theory of those who watched the Truesdell well closely is that brine strong enough to produce a bushel of salt from the evaporation of forty-five gallons may be obtained at a depth of 900 to 1200 feet. The last time the Truesdell well was pumped out the brine obtained was of sufficient strength to produce a bushel of salt from thirty gallons, and had the owners of the well-received proper encouragement from their neighbors, they would have kept the fresh water out long enough to manufacture at least one bushel.

"But aid was not extended to them, and they abandoned what for them had been a very expensive experiment, and one in which their fellow citizens seemed to have resigned all interest. This much was established by their energy and perseverance of Messrs. Truesdell and Orton in sinking this well—there *is* salt below Muskegon and its manufacture by those who own sawmills can make it a paying speculation.

Salt was pumped from 1,000 to 1,400 below to wooden pipes inside a salt house, where a double block of twenty or more kettles boiled the brine, using sawdust or wood scraps from the sawmill, which evaporated the water until pure salt was distilled. It took one to two days to produce 56 pounds of salt per caldron, and during a 26-week sawing season a mill could manufacture approximately 60,000 pounds of salt. Pictures courtesy of Michigan State University Archives.

"Last summer it was said that L.G. Mason & Company would subscribe a respectable sum towards putting down a well if their neighbors would show like liberality in proportion to their means, the well to be located at any spot that a majority of those subscribing shall select. At the same time, Gideon Truesdell offered to give $1,600 ($67,000 today) for the same purpose. He renews his offer now and adds to it the use of his steam engine. He cares nothing about where the well is located, but is willing to give his money and the use of his machinery to aid in determining whether salt will pay. We urge the moneyed men of this city to unite with him in a spirit as liberal as his. The whole cost of the experiment can be subscribed in a week, and paid in at an early day next spring so that the work may be seasonably commenced.

"It seems to him that every mill on Muskegon Lake should have a salt well attached to it, and a double block of kettles kept in constant operation through the sawing season. It would increase the profits of the mill by $7,000 to $10,000 ($360,000 today) per year. The estimated cost of manufacturing a barrel of salt containing five bushels is $1.00 ($42 today), and from $7 to $12 per ton. Here, fuel would cost nothing for what is now wasted (sawdust) at each mill would keep the brine boiling in two double blocks of kettles. For a market, we would have the whole country west of us as far as the plains and south as far as Mississippi. The supply would not exceed the demand, for there is now imported into this country upwards of 12 million barrels of foreign salt every year."[130]

"The Truesdell well has been as near a success that the fact is demonstrated that we have salt beneath us, and the work will not permanently be abandoned. Our people generally have an interest in this matter and we trust that they will make common cause with Mr. Truesdell in completing the work at which he has labored so long and spent so much money."[131]

After several years of trial and error, the salt well was abandoned when they lost more tools, but Gideon proved there was salt beneath Muskegon, and in 1872 Lyman Mason picked up where he left off by drilling to a depth of 2,627 feet. Martin Ryerson sank a well but met with the same problem; not enough brine to make it a worthwhile enterprise but everyone involved over the years gave it a commendable effort.

Truesdell's City Mills Flour, 1866

Another contributor to the bottom line of Gideon's agricultural empire was a flour mill. There were smaller rural mills that ground feed for farmers and sold much smaller quantities of flour to grocery stores but, like everything Gideon did, his flour mill was designed for large commercial output.

After his farm was completed and during his term in the legislature, Gideon bought the inland peninsula on Pikes Creek owned by Bennett & Sellick, a freight forwarding and grain warehouse that had been built 25 years earlier.[132] Now that Pikes Creek had been dredged to a depth of 9 feet, it was a highly desirable parcel of land with three warehouses that had been built in the 1840s, a Kenosha & Rockford spur, and docking facilities for which Gideon paid $4,000 ($260,000 today).[133]

He spent another $7,690 buying 32 lots south of the warehouses and the four corner lots at Main and Pearl where the old Durkee House stood.[134] In one of the buildings on the Bennett & Sellick property, he installed three 900-pound millstones and a steam engine valued at $11,000 ($672,000 today).[135] Another building was used for storing wheat, oats, and barley waiting to be ground. The third building was used to store barrels of flour and bales and hay or oats awaiting shipment.

A railroad spur linked his property with the Chicago & Milwaukee Railroad and the four railroads that intersected with the Kenosha & Rockford. This cut Gideon's 90-minute trip by horse and buggy from his farm residence to his Kenosha office to 30 minutes, which was lightning fast in a five-mph world.

Each floor stored a specific type of grain; wheat, oats, barley or corn. When the mill stones on the ground floor were adjusted, the men on the upper floors emptied bags of grain down the chutes to the mill stone. Pictures courtesy of the Minnesota Historical Society.

The Kenosha & Rockford gave farmers a direct route to Gideon's lakefront mill from Walworth and Rock County, where wheat was turned into Truesdell's City Mills Flour. On February 28, 1867 the *Kenosha Telegraph* published the following article:

"We understand that the Honorable Gideon Truesdell has purchased the property just below the Main Street Bridge, known as Bennett's Warehouse, for the purpose of turning it into a flouring mill. A large portion of the machinery has already been received, and a strong force of mechanics and millwrights are at work.

"It is the intention of Mr. Truesdell to put up a first-class flouring mill with all the modern improvements, and to have it in operation early in the season. We wish our worthy Assemblyman all success in this enterprise. He has moved his lumberyard to grounds adjacent to the Mill."[136]

Gideon hired George Crane, a young farmer with flour mill experience, and Garrett Van Wagenen. After Gideon bought the flour mill property, he moved his lumberyard to land he purchased surrounding the mill. "Van" was his bookkeeper, ran the lumberyard, and handled Lake Michigan shipping schedules. He supervised a few men working out in the yard, coordinated incoming shipments of grain aboard the Kenosha & Rockford, and outbound shipments of flour, feed, and hay aboard the Pride or Wescott.

Gideon saturated the Kenosha market with barrels of Truesdell's City Mills Flour, which was a good product with a money back guarantee. "Nearly every grocery in the city sells City Mills brands, and we have yet to learn of a single instance where a sack of flour has been returned as poor. It speaks for itself."[137] Smaller mills began to feel the pinch as they lost customers, and a price war began with competitors spreading rumors that Truesdell's City Mills Flour was made from rejected (inferior) wheat.

"MY FLOUR IS MADE FROM NEW WHEAT! To all who purchase of me, should any be dissatisfied, the flour will be taken away and money refunded. The present price of flour will be the basis of my operations. No charge will be made unless warranted by the price of wheat.

"Should wheat advance 10¢ per bushel, we shall be obliged to advance 25¢ per half-barrel. Should wheat decline 10¢ per bushel, my flour will decline by 25¢. Should other dealers charge you any more than $4.50 per half-barrel at the present time, you are paying that difference too much. The difference between their price and the above will be a commission for selling, which you can save by purchasing from me.

"They will be apt to tell you that their flour is better than mine. This is not so, for the flour we offer you is the best grade that comes from wheat—so that pretext is only a game to gull you out of your money.

"Should they offer you flour at these prices it is likely that it will be of an inferior grade, from the fact that good flour cannot be furnished at any lower rates owing to the present price of wheat, unless they should sell without a commission, which they are not likely to do. GIDEON TRUESDELL."[138]

Due to primitive equipment that wasn't much better than a bucket brigade, fires could destroy dozens of buildings before they were extinguished.

When a building caught on fire at the flour mill the church bells rang to alert the community, and early on the morning of December 24th, 1869, the bells began ringing after midnight. The next day, details of a destructive fire were sent out over the wire in a special dispatch to the *Chicago Tribune*, which then was published in the *New York Tribune*, *Cleveland Leader*, *National Republican* in Washington, DC, *Illinois State Journal* in Springfield, Illinois, *Milwaukee Sentinel*, *Lafayette Daily Journal* in Lafayette, Indiana, *Hartford Daily Courant* in Hartford, Connecticut, and the *New Yorker Zeitung*:

"DISASTEROUS FIRE"

"At 12:00 A.M. our citizens were startled by the cry of fire, which proved to be the Truesdell property located by the Main Street Bridge.

By the time any person was able to get there the interior of the mill was completely enveloped by flames.

"Fire companies were early on the grounds, but could do nothing towards saving the mill, but faithful and steady work stayed the progress of the flames, thereby saving a large amount of property, as there were a number of vessels lying in the immediate vicinity, also the lumberyard of Mr. Truesdell's.

"The fire was so hot that it scorched the masts and riggings of the vessels, and charred the outer edges of the piles of lumber stacked high and filling every part of the property. This mill was built about four years ago and cost from $15,000-$16,000 ($960,000 today). There are various conjectures as to the origins of the fire, but the only one that looks probable is the one given by Mr. Truesdell. He thinks someone entered the mill for the purpose of stealing flour and dropped a lighted match.

"There was considerable grain in the warehouse, most of it belonging to Mr. Truesdell, valued at $2,000. There is $10,000 of insurance on the mill. The total loss is about $7,000 ($322,000 today). The fire was first seen in a corner where there had been no fire, and away from the engine. The fire was set by some of the incendiaries who prowl about our city, breaking into our stores and setting our buildings on fire.

"It is hoped that our city authorities will ferret them out and bring them to justice. The fire department did well, considering the poor appliances it has to work with. It is sincerely hoped our city will purchase a steam engine that will protect our property. Mr. Truesdell informed us that it is his intention to rebuild the mill in the spring. This loss is quite heavy on Mr. Truesdell."[139]

Gideon didn't waste any time re-building a bigger and better flour mill, and hired a Chicago architect to design a $27,000 ($1.6 million today) four story grain elevator that would allow him to add four additional stories at a later date.[140] It was the largest grain elevator between Milwaukee and Chicago with farmers shipping wheat by rail from 70 miles east in the Rock River Valley. The old flour mill had a storage capacity of less than 3,000 bushels but the new elevator had a 25,000-bushel capacity.[141]

Since the old warehouses had been built in the 1840s, its location on the property created a bottleneck when shipments of grain had to wait until outbound shipments of flour were loaded aboard schooners. Gideon corrected this problem by moving the railroad spur to the west side of the peninsula, so incoming grain could be unloaded from the train to a mechanical lift that brought wheat, corn, oats, or barley to the second, third, or fourth floor storage bins. When a specific type of grain was refined, an employee dumped 65-pound bags down a chute to the ground floor's stone grist wheels.

"This mill was intended to be the master achievement of Gideon Truesdell. Great pains were taken to embody the best modern improvements and no pains or expense was spared to make it a perfect mill."[142]

On Aug. 11, 1870, the *Kenosha Telegraph* published a description of the mill:

"GIDEON TRUESDELL'S MILL."

"Our citizens felt proud to see this noble building rising from the ashes of the old mill, and even prouder that it's finished, its machinery nearly completed and in running order. The farmers of this county owe a debt of gratitude to Gideon Truesdell for building and furnishing them with the best flouring mill in Wisconsin.

"He is one of our oldest settlers, has been poor but the tides of fortune favored him, and he is now one of the wealthiest men in the county. He does not shut his means up, or loan it for a large interest rate but uses it for the benefit of the people.

"The main building of this mill is 80 x 32, four stories high, and situated at the head of the harbor. The engine building is 60 feet x 16 and contains a 40-horsepower engine built by R.B. Whitaker & Company of this city. There are three runs of stones; two exclusively for flour, and one for buckwheat and feed. The mill will be capable for grinding 300 bushels of wheat and 400 bushels of feed in 10 hours; double that in 24 hours. The mill is furnished by Thomas W. Baxter, of Chicago, furnishes the mill with the best French millstones.

"The Molim Separator manufactured by Wyckoff & Brainerd, also the Dustless machine, blows out all the impurities from the wheat, and discharges the wheat into bins for future use. The machinery of the mill consists of a New York adjustable Smut Machine and

Separator combined which are Trimmer's Patent, Vaughn's Zig-Zag Separator and an oat extractor, and Vandergraft's Centrifugal Feeding Suction Grain Separator & Automatic Grader. They have three Chester bolts; one for merchant work, one for custom, and one for buckwheat. The automatic grader adjusts the mill stone for merchant, custom, and buckwheat.

"The building is furnished in the best style, and anything that is wanted in a first-class mill has been supplied by the proprietor. The storage of the building is 25,000 bushels of wheat. The architect of the building and machinery is F.M. Black, of Chicago, who is one of the oldest and best machinists in the Midwest.

"The millwright who carried out the design of the architect was James McCline, who had twenty-five men under his supervision. The machinist who has put all the machines in running order was Ed Kune, of Chicago, who knows his business and leaves everything in running order.

"The mill runs like clockwork and in the course of 10 days will be completed and ready for customers. This county being a dairy community will be greatly benefited by having a mill with such a large capacity for grinding feed for their cows. The City of Kenosha is proud to have the best mill in the State of Wisconsin within her limits."[143]

Truesdell flour mill and lumberyard. Four story elevator is where grain was stored and one-story building to the right is where stones ground wheat, corn, barley, and oats. View of the Truesdell mill from the harbor. Pictures courtesy of the Kenosha History Center Archives.

The *Kenosha Union* gave a less enthusiastic assessment, and regarded its capacity as a folly. "To keep it running at full capacity would require about 600 bushels of wheat and 1,000 bushels of corn or buckwheat per day. Where is that quantity going to come from? It would seem that Gideon Truesdell has been generous in providing flour for this county, but it would seem that neither this county nor this region could supply the mill."[144]

It's doubtful that the *Kenosha Union* knew that Gideon had warehouse space at the Kenosha & Rockford's Harvard, Illinois depot. During the ten-week fall harvest season, all a farmer had to do was haul his wheat to one of his warehouses, where a clerk wrote them a check, and the next train brought it to his lakefront mill.

According to the *Kansas City Star*, the Truesdell mill was a landmark, and "for many years it was the main grist mill in that section of the state. In the old days farmers came from miles around to have their wheat ground into flour at the mill, and even the Rock River area as far away as Janesville furnished wheat to keep the stones turning."[145]

The mill had an expensive fire system installed similar to the old Durkee-Truesdell mill, with perforated pipes reaching each story, roof, dock, and lumber yard with an outdoor hydrant. An intake pipe sucked water from the harbor and carried it to several hydrants using the mill's steam engine to suck 45 gallons of water per minute which, by the standards of the day was phenomenal.[146] The Bain Wagon Works across the street had a similar system; tragically, both would soon be put to the test.

The Halliday House (formerly Durkee House) Fire, 1871

Oil lamps were widely used for indoor lighting but they were also the source of many, many deadly fires. A hotel like the Sherman House in Chicago would have had hundreds of oil chandeliers in the hallways and rooms, but a desk clerk in a small-town hotel would have had several lamps at the front desk. When a guest checked in the clerk would have lit a lamp, and handed it to the guest so he could find his way to his room. The floors in these older hotels were covered with dozens of coats of varnish, which made them highly flammable. On January 31, 1871, the Haliday House caught on fire, and according to the *New York Times* six people were killed, four of whom were children.[147]

"At about 4:30 this morning, as Capt. Everett and Mr. Bissell were returning from a dance on the north side, they saw smoke coming from the windows of the second story of the Halliday House—a four story brick building on the corner of Main and Pearl streets.

"They immediately ran into the building, and upon reaching the lamp room found flames coming from under the door and up through the floor. They were burning with an intensity that proved they had been burning for some time.

"The floor was saturated with kerosene, owing to the fracture of some of the lamps in the room, which has been used as a storeroom for lamps and kerosene. At the time of the fire there were probably thirty lamps full of the liquid beside a tin container containing five gallons. One of the lamps had been left burning from the previous evening and it was from this that the fire originated.

"Everett proceeded to awaken the proprietor of the hotel, Mr. Smith, and the guests, who numbered about thirty. The alarm was instantly responded to and in a few minutes the whole neighborhood was awakened and rushing to the conflagration. The flames spread rapidly with smoke rushing upstairs filling the hallways with a dense and suffocating heat.

"Two hand engines were promptly brought to the hotel, while men were at work at the two steam jets at the Bain Wagon Works, and the flouring mill of Gideon Truesdell about a block from the fire on the pier. Both were rapidly pouring water upon the flames without any apparent result.

"The night was dark with a strong wind blowing from the north, and a heavy fall of sleet and snow. By the glare of the flames men and women could be seen leaning from the windows and crying for help. Men below were shouting to hold on or descend by the stairs, while others with alacrity brought ladders from nearby barns, rescuing those who had successfully descended to the second story but could go no further.

"An effort was then made to reach the third story but the ladders were all too short. A hundred pair of hands was ready to lash them together but their efforts were fruitless for a long time. Finally, two ladders were firmly lashed together, and two men rushed up but the heat was so intense they were compelled to come back down.

"Mr. Osmond Capron, son of Horace Capron, United States Commissioner of Agriculture was asleep in his room on the third floor when aroused by the flames, the current of air drawing them upwards through the stairwells and fanning them. Those below could see him burst through the fire, clad only in his shirt and drawers, and descend to the second story. He made it to the stairs only to find them burned away with the window his only hope. He leaped into a snow bank, burning garments clinging to him, and half a dozen men came to his assistance and pulled him up.

"He was quite delirious, raving terribly, insisting with the strength of a madman on walking across the street. His frenzy subsided, and he was carried to the house of Henry Andre, on the opposite side of the street, blood dripping from all parts of his body at every step. The lamplight revealed a hideous spectacle; his right cheek was burned clear to the bone with masses of charred flesh dropping from his face. His collarbone protruded, charred and a ghastly white. He is aged 24 years, and employed by his brother, A.B. Capron, flour and feed dealer.

Halliday House (formerly Durkee House) fire that made national headlines. Pictures courtesy of the Kenosha History Center Archives.

"Herbert Chase, a young man recently married, whose wife is now East, was aroused by the smoke, and endeavored to descend by the staircase. His room was in the fourth story, about sixty feet from the ground. He was nearly suffocated in trying to reach the stairs, and returned to his room. He could be seen from the street passing before the window, from which he suddenly leaped. When picked up, it was found that he sustained a compound fracture of the thigh, beside several internal injuries. Surgical aid was on hand. Dr. Wolcott, of Milwaukee, was telegraphed for, and arrived today. He pronounced it the worst fracture he has ever seen, and holds out feeble hopes of his patient's recovery.

"Simeon Fuller, the clerk of the hotel, a man thirty-five years of age, who for the last twenty years has been connected with the establishment, met a tragical end while in the performance of his duty. He was among the first who were alarmed by Capt. Everett. He arose, and, hastily clothing himself, started for the second story in order to save the guests of the hotel. Just as he was passing the fateful lamp room door a terrific explosion was heard, he was thrown upon his face and actually saturated with kerosene, which, igniting, enveloped him literally in a garment of flame. He still preserved sufficient presence of mind to run to the window and throw himself out, when he was taken to an adjoining livery stable, and from thence to the residence of Mr. W. F. Halliday.

"He was burned almost beyond the possibility of recognition, but clung on to life and consciousness in a manner quite phenomenal. He lived in agony until 2 1/2 o'clock this afternoon, when he died peacefully. Simeon Fuller was a faithful servant, and met his end like a hero in the vein attempt to save the lives of others. He was a man of pious character, and enjoyed the confidence not only of his employers, but of every one who knew him. He preserved his full consciousness to the last, and when dying told Mr. Humphrey that he was perfectly satisfied with the course he had taken; that in sacrificing his own life for others he had only done his duty. The only thing he regretted was that he had not succeeded in rescuing Mrs. Merrill and her little ones.

"Col. Fred Lovell of this town was not awakened until the flames had made considerable headway. Opening his door, he was nearly suffocated by the smoke, but crawled on his hands and knees down the back entrance to the building, for which he was no worse for his experience.

"Samuel Ranney occupied a back room on the third floor, and finding his escape cut off by the flames broke his window, lacerating his hand, and jumped to the ground. A mattress broke his fall and he was picked up only slightly hurt. Zack Wilder jumped from the top story to the roof below, and thence to the ground.

"Suddenly the screams of a woman and children were heard above the din of excited voices below, and one more attempt was made to reach the third story by means of the ladders, but again were the brave men driven back by the heat from within. It now became known that the front room on the third story was occupied by Mrs. Merrill and her four little children, the eldest of whom was a child of twelve years of age, and the youngest an infant in arms. Nothing could be seen at the window, but the despairing cries told their own terrible tale.

"Captain Everett was determined to rescue the unfortunate family, even at the risk of his own life, and bravely ran up the stairs until he gained the apartment from which it was stated Mrs. Merrill was endeavoring to escape. He reached it without injury, though nearly suffocated with the smoke. He searched the room, but could discover no one. He cried out, but at first received no reply. Again, he called, and heard a faint and stifled response from some distant portion of the building. Once more the brave man rushed into the suffocating atmosphere of the corridor; but although he heard the cry of anguish from the mother, and the shrieks of terror of the little ones, he could not discover where they were. Feeling himself gradually succumbing to the stifling smoke, he was forced to relinquish the search, and again descended to the ground to meet the eager queries of those below with a terrible negative.

"The fire was put out by eight o'clock this morning. The streams of water continued to play on the ruins in order to cool them, preparatory to the sad task of digging out the remains. By ten o'clock they were sufficiently cooled to commence work. Business was suspended throughout the town, and all who could assist in the search.

"After about an hour's work they came upon the last terrible evidence of the tragic end of Mrs. Merrill and her little ones. Beneath a pile of bricks and beams lay the mother, charred to a cinder, her face so burned as to have lost all semblance of humanity. Clasped tightly to her breast was the little one-year-old girl, also terribly burned. Adjacent were the remains of the three other children, two boys and one girl, forming a group, ghastly yet tender, which drew from the eyes of the strongest men tears which not even their manhood could suppress. Tenderly the little corpses were taken up and placed in coffins, and then the hapless mother was taken up, still clinging to her little one with a grasp that not even an agonizing death could loosen. Mother and child now occupy the same coffin. Mr. Merrill was at South Bend, Indiana. He was immediately telegraphed for, and is expected to-night."[148]

A few days after the fire, Gideon purchased the hotel property with the intention of building two separate brick buildings. On February 15, 1871, Gideon had several wrecking crews at work tearing down the hotel, and hauling the rubble away.[149] Eight months later he built a 20-room hotel and a grocery store. "Upon the ruins of the old Halliday House.... have arisen two fine stores substantially built, and a worthy monument of their enterprising owner, Mr. Gideon Truesdell."[150]

In addition to moving G. Truesdell & Son, Grocers into this new store, he also moved his office there. He rented the old storefront to a general merchant, and opened a reading room on the second floor. He furnishing it with comfortable chairs, and charged a nominal fee to cover the cost of subscriptions, although it's doubtful that he ever came close to breaking even. We know from various sources that Gideon was an inveterate reader of books, magazines, and newspapers. His reading room subscribed to the following publications:

Chicago Daily News
Chicago Daily Journal
New York Tribune
New York Post
New York Herald
New York Times
New York Ledger
Boston Transcript
Boston Traveler
Christian Union
Golden Age
Nation
Scientific American
Die Gastenlaube
Our Young Folks
Harper's Weekly
Harper's Monthly
Galaxy
Popular Science
Atlantic Monthly
Herald of Health
Scribner's Monthly
Chamber's Monthly
Educational Monthly

Finding worthwhile things for young people to do was just as big a challenge then as today, with delinquent teenagers lighting stacks of hay or outhouses on fire. There were gangs who gathered at street corners shooting dice, drinking, and using foul language but Gideon's reading room catered to a different type of young person.

Governor Charles Durkee & the Old Settlers Picnic, May 1st, 1869

From a hectic schedule as a U.S. Senator where there were never enough hours in the day, to a retirement where time seemed to drag. He grew restless and frustrated by his declining health. He was 56 years old when he retired, but rheumatoid arthritis caused him to consider leaving his beautiful lakefront mansion for a dryer climate. He gave serious thought to building a home on the western slope of the Rocky Mountains or in the San Diego area at a time when there were less than a thousand people living there.

When Utah's Governor dropped dead of a heart attack it created an opening. Filling vacancies in the unsettled western territories was complicated, and a lot of positions went to political hacks looking to line their pockets. But Utah was, without question, a place where the lines separating church and state barely existed, with a large Mormon population that had their own economy and system of government that were doing remarkably well. As far as they were concerned, they didn't need any help from the federal government.

When President Andrew Johnson was told of Durkees interest in the position his name moved to the top of the list, but according to *The Bench & Bar of Wisconsin*, he never asked for the position. "President Johnson, without any solicitation on the part of Mr. Durkee, appointed him as Governor Doty's successor."[151] His appointment was probably facilitated by his close friend, Senator James Doolittle, who had a close relationship with the president. Johnson sat a few desks apart from Charles Durkee in the U.S. Senate, and they became friends while serving on the public lands committee.

As Governor, he significantly increased his wealth at least $200,000 ($11.4 million today) with investments in Utah, Nevada, and California. One of his most profitable investments was a Nevada cattle ranch with Gideon Truesdell, Harvey Durkee, and Franklin P. Head in a firm styled

Durkee, Truesdell & Company. The government had millions of acres of land lying dormant that could be leased for 3¢ an acre. The partnership organized a 40,000+ acre ranch and acquired a silver mine near Salt Lake City.[152] (They used the credit rating of the Kenosha partnership by using it as an extension to their cattle and mining activities.)

When soldiers discovered that the Indians had forged bullets from silver, they began looking for the source, which was somewhere in the Oquirrh Mountains. If Harvey hired a mining crew to work their claim, he would have sent their silver ore to Salt Lake City. The closest Union-Pacific depot at that time was in Cheyenne, a 450-mile trip by wagon train before reaching a train going east to Chicago.

A large number of mines in the western territories sent raw gold and silver to Chicago for processing, with many using the Swansea Smelting & Reduction Works. Five years later when Truesdell cashed out his share was $47,650 ($2.1 million today), so it was an excellent investment.[153] We don't know anything about his original investment but it was probably no more than $5,000 ($150,000 today) per partner, which they undoubtedly rolled over when their profits were plowed back into the business so they could keep expanding.[154]

On March 8th, 1869, Governor Durkee requested a leave of absence from officials in Washington so he could return to Kenosha where he was scheduled to host that year's Old Settlers reunion.[155] This was a big social event that was held out at Paddock Lake at the picnic grounds, and where each spring early settlers gathered to reminisce. Durkees health had deteriorated to the point where everyone knew the end was near, including him. "Mr. Durkee spoke with great feeling of this being the last time he should ever be permitted to see another such gathering of old friends and acquaintances."[156]

All of those in attendance had lived through the challenges and deprivations of pioneer life, and the Governor marveled that in their lifetime railroads now ran in all directions, and would soon connect the Atlantic and Pacific. This was unimaginable twenty-five years ago when they arrived at Pikes Creek. The telegraph allowed people to communicate from coast to coast at lightning speed, and so many momentous events had occurred during their lifetimes. Twenty-five years earlier it took a couple of months for a letter to reach Los Angeles, and now it only took a few days for a telegraph message to reach the coast.

About a hundred people attended the picnic, most of them early settlers who arrived during the late 1830s or 1840s, and the Governor asked Volney French, Gideon Truesdell, Isaac George, Jason Lothrop, Judge Jilson, and Reverend John Gridley to speak about their early years.

"Honorable Gideon Truesdell gave his early experiences.... he came here poor, the chief valuables of his household goods consisting of a table and a bed. He first tried hotel keeping on the north side of the creek, managing to get a scanty furnishment for that purpose; but in this business he was quite unsuccessful. He concluded to try his luck in another direction; he borrowed a small sum of money from Judge Volney French, and Harvey Durkee, Esq., consenting to become his endorser.

"His wife sold her gold watch to aid in this new enterprise. He procured a team and wagon, laid in a stock of bread and bacon, and started for the Wisconsin River with the view among other things of selling patent rights. (Land) His wife assisted him in cooking meals along the roadside while on their journey. He managed to realize money enough to pay what he borrowed, and a little more, and after an absence of some months he returned to Kenosha, hired himself to H. Durkee as a laborer, and worked in his employ for four years.

"It is proper here to supply some information Mr. Truesdell omitted. His subsequent course was one of eminent success in business. He is now the owner of the largest, best stocked and most valuable farm. He was modest in closing and not speaking of his great success and his eminently useful labors at present.... very diverse and extensive. It is proper here to supply some history which Mr. Truesdell omitted.... he returns the largest income tax in the county."[157]

The Township of Truesdell, Wisconsin, 1871

During the summer of 1871, Gideon gave the Wisconsin Union roughly three acres of land that had previously been cornfields. It was just down the road from the Bain Station, where a thief had been caught stealing livestock, and neighborhood vigilantes took it upon themselves to tar and feather him.[158] Except for this little bit of vigilante justice, it was a sleepy little farming community, and the Truesdell Station crossed Geneva Road about 1.5 miles east of Gideon's farm.

Sidney Derbyshire was listed as one of the members of a search committee organized to acquire property, and Gideon gave enough land on Geneva Road for the Wisconsin Union to build a passenger, freight depot, and a small business district.[159] Typically, every railroad depot had a post office, and the one just built on Geneva Road was named Truesdell Station with an agent and telegrapher.[160] Truesdell Station was never more than a small farming community with some agricultural related businesses by the depot, and the name was later shortened to Truesdell, Wisconsin.[161]

A *Kenosha News* article stated that, "The name Truesdell—a quirk of fate. Gideon Truesdell was the biggest landowner and probably one of the county's wealthier men when the railroad was built, for he was a human meteor flashing across the countryside briefly, then disappearing. Between father and son, the farms were worth well over $300,000—major wealth in those days."[162] ($13.8 million today.)

The lakeshore railroad that paralleled Lake Michigan between Milwaukee and Chicago had far more freight business than they could handle, and the answer was a second freight line passing through farmland 12 miles west of the lakeshore route. There would be 10 depots along tracks between each city, although more would be added at a later date. The Wisconsin Union was a 37-mile short-line railroad that originated at the Reed Street depot in Milwaukee, and ran to the Illinois-Wisconsin border. At that point the Illinois branch of the railroad were built under a separate charter granted by the Illinois legislature.[163] When the Wisconsin Union was completed, the Wisconsin and Illinois sections was acquired by the Chicago, Milwaukee & St. Paul through a stock swap.

During their first year, they hauled 1.8 million gallons of milk from dairy farmers in northern Illinois and southern Wisconsin to the Chicago market.[164] Between dairy exports, wheat, and livestock shipments to farmers back east, there was more than enough business for this express line to make a profit in both directions.

While still a member of the legislature, and possibly at the request of Judge Henry Blodgett, Gideon filed a petition requesting that they assign the St. Croix canal land grant that had been lying dormant for over 25 years to the Chicago, Milwaukee & St. Paul Railroad.[165] This canal was supposed to link Lake Superior with the Mississippi River, but it never materialized.

The Truesdell Station was built on Geneva Road, and although not quite the transportation artery that it became fifty years later, Geneva Road was part of the old Southport & Beloit Plank Road running seventy miles west to Beloit, Wisconsin.

According to family legend, Gideon asked that the sale of liquor be prohibited in this crossroads community, which is plausible because his son and nephew were heavy drinkers.¹⁶⁶ G.J. and Adelbert Truesdell often enjoyed a night of drinking, but were smart enough to get hammered a discreet distance from where they were known¹⁶⁷ They caught a train at the Pleasant Prairie depot and spent the night drinking in Rockford, Illinois.¹⁶⁸ G.J. was locked up on at least one occasion for being extremely drunk. Evidently, he was a good-natured drunk who cheerfully agreed to sleep it off before catching the next train back to his farm.¹⁶⁹

Harold Nauta, owner of Truesdell Oil Company with the sign from the old Truesdell Station depot. Picture courtesy of the *Kenosha News*.

When railroad service began in late 1872, Pleasant Prairie land values soared, and two years later when the Blodgett Station was built across from Amos Truesdell's 160-acre Deerfield farm, it caused the value of his land to triple.¹⁷⁰ Amos and his son, Arthur, sub-divided this land into residential lots, built houses, and retired comfortably.¹⁷¹

During prohibition, Truesdell became a destination for bootleggers and gamblers, due to its isolated rural location on a railroad that ran far enough away from Chicago to avoid federal law enforcement agents. The Chicago underworld avoided raids by running 10 to 20 high stakes gamblers aboard a special late-night train to Truesdell, where they were safe because they had protection in Kenosha County from a co-operative sheriff.

During prohibition, the Chicago syndicate would send dead bodies riddled with bullets to Truesdell, where they were thrown in front of an oncoming train so the sheriff could record their deaths as "drunk vagrant stumbled in front of a train."¹⁷² The corpses were buried by the county in an unmarked grave in a pauper's field, and the underworld had an easy way to dispose of people they had snuffed-out.

Richard C. Fritz

A tavern down the road from the railroad depot became a major distribution point for illegal liquor.[173] In the basement were concrete vaults with steel doors. The liquor was piped through walls to the second floor from the tanks in the basement.[174] When prohibition agents inspected the property there were no signs of illegal activity but when a panel was removed in one of the dozens of second floor bedrooms liquor bottles could be filled.

There were barns in each of the six townships in Kenosha County where stills ran around the clock and households in the Italian neighborhoods where tin containers of liquor were stored in the attic, which made it nearly impossible for prohibition agents to get ahead of the problem. The rent from bootleggers was how a lot of immigrant widows survived during the depression. A lot of Canadian liquor entered the Port of Kenosha, which during prohibition had become one of the busiest harbors for bootleggers.

CARLOAD OF BOOZE TWICE SHIPPED TO TRUESDEL.

According to a 1920 *Kenosha Evening News* article, "Prohibition may not be prohibiting in Kenosha County, but it is getting to the point where the men who are shipping liquor are beginning to act more cautious. A whole carload of booze, the same sort of wet goods that has been shipped into Kenosha several times during the past year, has twice been on the siding at Truesdell, but both times the owners of the cargo have been wary of unloading it, and have shipped it further along the line in wait for a more propitious time.

Roadhouse in Truesdell, Wisconsin that was a popular rendezvous for bootleggers.
Picture courtesy of the author.

"This was the word brought to Kenosha today. It was added that the homeless booze car is now in a freight yard in Chicago, waiting to be shipped again to this county. The time was when a carload of booze evinced little consternation. The car would be sidetracked at any convenient switch, and unloaded sometimes by night or daytime. Then came the time when the shippers, whoever they are, decided that caution was the better part of valor, and choose Truesdell for their base of operations."[175]

The population peaked during the 1920s when Geneva Road became the main thoroughfare between Kenosha and Lake Geneva. Two passenger trains a day stopped, one in each direction, until 1964 when Truesdell was downgraded to a freight depot only.

Thereafter little more than tank cars of heating oil for Truesdell Oil or fertilizer and feed for Truesdell Feed & Grain arrived by rail.[176] Five years later the station was torn down.

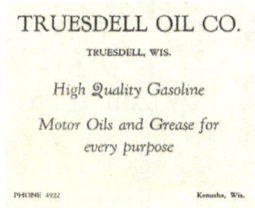

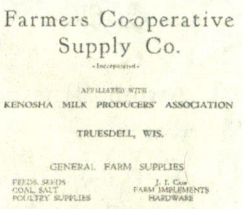

Businesses past and present.

According to Harold "Cap" Nauta, "When I came home from the war in 1946," Truesdell was still the place to go on Saturday night. There was always something going on. There was a popular roadhouse named Bert's Old Time Club east of the railroad tracks, and a second bar, Martin's Tavern, stood just west of the crossing. You went to Bert's on a Saturday night, Martins? That's where the local farmers would go on rainy afternoons and lie about their crops."[177]

Richard C. Fritz

Notes

1. *New England Journal of Agriculture*, 6 August 1870, pp. 2.
2. *Chicago Tribune*, 9 February 1868, pp. 7.
3. *Daily Milwaukee News*, 5 August 1865, pp. 5
4. *Kenosha Democrat*, 16 September 1853, pp. 2.
5. *Milwaukee Sentinel*, 19 July 1867, pp. 6. "A Chapter on Cheese."
6. Kirkland Torrey dairy.
7. His net worth was probably higher but $1.1 million is a safe estimate based on many sources.
8. Passim, several articles estimated the value of his farm at $300,000 but when his lakefront flour mill was added the next asset value of his agricultural property was around $345,000.
9. *History of Kenosha & Racine County*, John Lucas biographical sketch, pp. 706.
10. Arthur Truesdell, 1903 correspondence with nephew Amos Fred Sherwood.
11. *Western Rural Farmer*, 10 March 1870, pp. 1.
12. Gideon was frequently listed as a judge or flowers at the state fair.
13. The beauty of his pastures was described in several articles.
14. *Woodstock Sentinel*, 23 April 1868, pp. 2.
15. Ellen Truesdell Sherwood conversation with her son, Erastus. (The Sherwoods lived on the farm.)
16. 1870 U.S. Census, "Products of Industry," Gideon and G.J. Truesdell farms.
17. Passim, newspaper articles over a 6-year period, census information, Herbert Torrey narrative, etc.
18. Woodstock Sentinel, 23 April 1868, pp. 2.
19. *Western Farmer*, 9 May 1870, pp. 1.
20. *Western Rural Journal*, 22 April 1869, pp. 3
21. 1870 census, Pleasant Prairie Township, Wisconsin.
22. Woodstock Sentinel, 23 April 1868, pp. 2.
23. He was described in a newspaper article as a "strict" businessman, and we know that he kept a tight set of books at the sawmills.
24. *Rockford Weekly Gazette*, 4 April 1869, pp. 2.
25. *Rockford Weekly Gazette*, 13 February 1868, pp. 1.

26. Ibid.
27. 1870 U.S. Census "Products of Industry," Gideon and G.J. Truesdell, Pleasant Prairie, Wisconsin.
28. *Milwaukee Sentinel*, 14 August 1867, pp. 6, "Pleasant Prairie."
29. Ibid.
30. Massachusetts Ploughman and *New England Journal of Agriculture*, 6 August 1870.
31. *Milwaukee Sentinel*, 1863–1866 highest incomes for the 1st Collection District filed by the U.S. Assessor.
32. *Kenosha Telegraph*, 11 October 1866, pp. 3.
33. Milwaukee Sentinel, 12 June 1866 article listing highest incomes for previous year based on tax returns.
34. *Kenosha Telegraph*, 30 May 1867, pp. 3. Highest incomes for the 1st Collection District filed by the U.S. Assessor.
35. History of Kenosha County, George Hale biographical sketch, pp. 284.
36. Ibid.
37. *Kenosha Union*, 18 October 1866, pp. 2 George Hale candidacy.
38. Ibid.
39. Ibid.
40. *Kenosha Telegraph*, 1 November 1866, pp.2.
41. Kenosha Clerk of the Circuit Court, Register of Deeds, 6 November 1866 election results.
42. *Milwaukee Sentinel*, 12 November 1866, pp. 6.
43. *Juneau County Argus*, 13 June 1867, pp.2.
44. *Kenosha Union*, 7 March 1867, pp.2.
45. *Chicago Tribune*, 6 June 1869, pp. 5.
46. Passim, 1870 census, and several newspaper articles although livestock numbers tended to fluctuate based on how many animals were slaughtered or sold.
47. *National Stock Journal*, Volume 1, September 1870, pp. 2.
48. *The Plantation*, Series 1, volume 1, 1872, pp. 233.
49. *Woodstock Sentinel*, 23 April 1868, pp. 2.
50. *Prairie Farmer*, 12 March 1862.
51. *Woodstock Sentinel*, 23 April 1868, pp. 2.
52. *Western Rural Journal*, 3 March 1870, pp. 2
53. *American Stock Journal*, Volume 8, pp. 448.
54. Ibid. 12 April 1871, pp. 3.
55. Different articles written in different years vary as to how many dairy

cows he milked, but by 1870 we know from several sources that it was around 300, although not all of them were dairy cows because he sold blooded stock.

56. *Western Farmer*, 28, May 1869, pp. 1.
57. Herbert Torrey reminiscences, and the standard procedure at other diary plants.
58. Passim, various dairyman's convention minutes about procedures.
59. 1870 U.S. Census, "Products of Industry," Gideon and G.J. Truesdell farms.
60. *Western Farmer*, 12 April 1868, pp. 2.
61. Wisconsin Historical Society, The Rise of Dairy farming papers.
62. Chester Hazen biographical sketch. He organized the Wisconsin Dairyman's Association.
63. *Chicago Daily Tribune*, 12 February 1869, pp. 5.
64. *Western Farmer*, 9 October 1867.
65. *Western Farmer*, 5 June 1871.
66. Herbert Torrey reminiscences
67. 1870 U.S. Census, "Products of Industry," Gideon and G.J. Truesdell farms.
68. *Kenosha News*, 17 September 1983, "Truesdell: Cross-roads community."
69. *Daily Milwaukee News*, 18 June 1868, pp. 4.
70. Woodstock Sentinel, 23 April 1868, pp. 2.
71. *Rockford Weekly Gazette*, 11 November 1865, pp. 2.
72. Ibid.
73. *Kenosha Telegraph*, 14 December 1865, pp. 4.
74. *Milwaukee Sentinel*, 30 December 1868, pp. 4.
75. 1979 interview with Harold Nauta, who remembers stories from family members who were guests at the Werner farm.
76. *Kenosha Telegraph*, 12 October 1920.
77. *Rockford Weekly Gazette*, 13 February 1868, pp. 2. A reported said that Gideon "rejoiced at the information that came from these conventions."
78. *Rockford Weekly Gazette*, 3 April 1865, pp. 2.
79. *Rockford Weekly Register-Gazette*, 6 February 1867, pp. 2.
80. Ibid.
81. *Rockford Weekly Gazette*, 24 March 1867, pp. 2.
82. *Rockford Weekly Register-Gazette*, 6 February 1867, pp. 2.
83. *Rockford Weekly Gazette*, 13 February 1868, pp. 1.
84. Ibid.

85. *Chicago Daily Tribune*, 12 February 1869, pp. 8.
86. *Rockford Weekly Gazette*, 13 February 1868, pp. 2.
87. Blodgett's 370 acre "Crab Tree Farms" was located in Lake Bluff overlooking Lake Michigan.
88. *Rockford Weekly Gazette*, 13 February 1868
89. Ibid.
90. *Chicago Daily Tribune*, 12 February 1869, pp. 8.
91. *Kenosha Telegraph*, 26 March 1868, pp. 3.
92. *Brown's Gazetteer of the Chicago & Northwestern Railway*.
93. Woodstock Sentinel, 23 April 1868, pp. 2.
94. Daily Milwaukee News, 27 Jun 1869, pp. 4.
95. *Chicago Daily Tribune*, 12 February 1869
96. *Western Farmer*, 9 Oct 1869, pp. 1.
97. Ibid.
98. Ibid.
99. *Milwaukee Sentinel*, 14 August 1867, pp. 6, "Pleasant Prairie."
100. *Western Farmer*, 9 Oct 1869, pp. 1.
101. *Kenosha Telegraph*, 7 February, 1870, pp. 2. Northwest Dairyman's Convention.
102. Ibid.
103. *Rockford Weekly Gazette*, 4 April 1869, pp. 2.
104. Ibid.
105. Ibid.
106. Ibid.
107. *Chicago Daily Tribune*, 10 February 1870, pp. 6.
108. Ibid.
109. Ibid.
110. Ibid.
111. Western Rural, 3 March 1870, pp. 1.
112. *Kenosha Telegraph*, 7 February, 1870, pp. 2. Northwest Dairyman's Convention.
113. *Western Rural Journal*, 10 March 1870, pp. 2
114. *Western Farmer*, 9 May 1870, pp. 1.
115. Ibid.
116. *National Livestock Journal*, June 1871, pp. 348.
117. *The Plantation*, June 1872, pp. 233.
118. *Cedar Falls (Iowa) Gazette*, 30 Jun 1871, pp. 2
119. *Milwaukee Sentinel*, 14 August 1872, pp. 6.

120. *Chicago Tribune*, 24 Apr 1869, pp. 3.
121. 1870 census, "Products of Industry," Gideon Truesdell farm.
122. *Watertown Republican*, 9 Nov 1870, pp. 2.
123. *Chicago Daily Tribune*, 24 Jan 1873, pp. 6.
124. *Wisconsin State Journal*, 24 December 1870.
125. *Grand Haven News*,4 June 1865, pp. 1.
126. Ibid, 23 Jan 1865, pp. 4.
127. *Hillsdale Standard*, 23 June 1868, pp.4.
128. *Muskegon Chronicle*, 12 April 1869, Gideon Truesdell drills for salt.
129. Ibid
130. Ibid, 15 December 1870, pp. 3.
131. *Muskegon Chronicle*, 21 Jul 1869, pp. 3
132. *Kenosha Telegraph*, 28 February 1867, pp.3. "New Flouring Mill."
133. Kenosha Register of Deeds records.
134. Ibid."
135. *Rockford Gazette*, 24 April 1867, pp. 2.
136. *Kenosha Telegraph*, 28 February 1867, pp.3. "New Flouring Mill."
137. *Kenosha Telegraph*, 20 October 1870, pp. 9.
138. *Kenosha Telegraph*, 6 February 1868, pp. 4.
139. *Kenosha Union*, 27 December 1869, pp. 1.
140. 1879 Kenosha City Directory, "Manufacturing Interests –Kenosha Flour Mill," pp. 20.
141. Ibid.
142. Ibid.
143. *Kenosha Telegraph*, 1 August 1870, pp. 2. "Gideon Truesdell's Mill."
144. *Kenosha Union*, 9 August 1870, pp. 3.
145. *Kansas City Star*, 17 July 1903. "Kenosha Landmark Destroyed"
146. This estimate is based on advertising for fire systems used in sawmills.
147. *New York Times*, 7 February 1871, pp. 9.
148. *Jackson Citizen*, 7 February 1871, pp. 4.
149. *Kenosha Telegraph*, 16 February 1871, pp. 9.
150. Ibid, 5 October, 1871, pp. 2.
151. *Bench & Bar of Wisconsin*, pp. 207.
152. The partners were Harvey Durkee, Gideon Truesdell, Charles Durkee, and Franklin P. Head.
153. Gideon Truesdell bankruptcy papers.
154. Ibid.
155. *Kenosha Telegraph*, 5 May 1869.

156. *Daily Milwaukee News*, 1 May 1869.
157. *Kenosha Telegraph*, 5 May 1869.
158. Thereafter local residents referred to the spot as "Tar Corners."
159. *Kenosha Republican*, 6 April 1871, pp. 3.
160. *Kenosha News*, Arlene Jensen 16 November 1986.
161. Ibid
162. Ibid.
163. 1871 Wisconsin Union Railroad began survey for tracks
164. *Kenosha News*, 17 September 1983, "Truesdell: Cross-roads community."
165. *Journal of Proceedings of the Annual Session of the Wisconsin Assembly*, pp. 489.
166. Patrick D. Truesdell, 1977 interview.
167. Alcoholism skips through the generations of several different branches of the family.
168. *Janesville Daily Gazette*, 9 July 1868, pp.4.
169. Ibid.
170. Lake County Register of Deeds, "Truesdell's Addition," filed and approved 3 June 1874.
171. Patrick D. Truesdell interview, 1977. His great, grandfather was Fayette Truesdell.
172. Author heard this story from Judge Floyd H. Guttormsen whose father was Chairman of the Kenosha County Board during the depression.
173. Local legend from owners of property
174. Author new the owners they showed basement vaults and copper pipes leading to certain second floor rooms.
175. *Kenosha Evening News*, 4 March 1920. Due to its isolated location, there was considerable bootlegging and gambling.
176. Ibid
177. *Kenosha News*, 17 September 1983, "Truesdell: Cross-roads community."

5

CHICAGO FIRE BANKRUPTS GIDEON TRUESDELL

With roughly two-thirds of his net worth invested in Chicago real estate, Gideon had every reason to believe he could live comfortably for the rest of his life. Fire was a constant threat in those days but with so many properties in his portfolio, his losses would have been limited to one or two buildings unless the entire city burned, and the last time that happened was the Great Fire of London in 1666. With forty-seven storefronts, warehouses, and apartment buildings the odds of Gideon being completely wiped out by a fire were unlikely.

But during the summer of 1871 the Midwest was in its second heat wave. The previous year millions of acres of crops had been ruined by too much heat and not enough rain. During the summer of 1871 there was practically no rainfall combined with prolonged 90-degree temperatures that destroyed another harvest. By October 1871, entire fields were scorched, and the situation had gone from bad to worse. During the past three months, only an inch of rain had fallen, and strong winds blew hot, humid air across Nebraska and Iowa until Chicago felt like a blast furnace.

Kenosha County Farmers Were Trapped in the Second Year of a Devastating Draught.

Temperatures exceeded ninety degrees for fifty-four straight days. Tar roofs bubbled from the midday sun, and telegraph lines snapped due to heat contractions. During extreme heat, trees released moisture, and contributed to dangerous conditions. At the same time, high humidity, in part from Lake Michigan, made the summer of 1871 very uncomfortable for anyone living in Chicago.

After having endured another hot summer, around October, residents started preparing for a typically cold, blustery, snowy Chicago winter by stocking barns and sheds with hay for livestock, firewood for stoves, and kerosene for lamps. The *Chicago Tribune* warned "the absence of rain for three weeks (has) left everything in such a flammable condition that a spark might set a fire which would sweep from end to end of the city."[1]

It wasn't exactly a surprise that, on October 7, 1871, a fire broke out in a boiler room at the Lull & Holmes planing mill at 209 Canal Street. Insurance companies referred to this area as the "red flash district," due to its high combustibility and frequency of claims. Planing mills always had a thin layer of sawdust everywhere, and an arc from a machine could easily ignite the entire floor.

The planing mill fire destroyed four city blocks before it was brought under control, and caused nearly a million dollars of damage. ($68 million today.) It was an expensive fire for the Chicago Fire Department, because several pieces of equipment were warped or wrecked beyond repair. With seventeen engine companies and only 185 firefighters for a city of 300,000, it was just a matter of time before everyones luck ran out.

During the past twenty years, there had been a building frenzy with Chicago growing rapidly with cheaply built wooden houses, buildings, and tenements. Even when brick and limestone cornices were used, window frames, and shingles were still made of wood and highly combustible. Once a fire reached the wooden frame of a building it was soon engulfed by fire within ten minutes, and an entire block could be totally wiped out in twenty minutes, even less if there was a strong wind blowing the flames through the buildings.

Chicago had just installed police and fire alarm boxes throughout the city that communicated with a central station by telegraph. Each station had a box that identified the location of the trouble, but the fire department still relied on an observation tower from which a "fire watcher" with a telescope scanned the skyline looking for smoke.

On October 8th, a watchman saw smoke on the west side of the river but smoldering coal fires made it difficult to pinpoint. Through his telescope, he spotted smoke a couple of miles away near Canalport, and triggered alarm 342 on the fire box. This notified the fire department's telegraph room to send a signal to the engine company closest to that location.[2]

State Street, Police Signal. Pictures courtesy of the Chicago History Center.

As the watchman continued to monitor the fire, he discovered that his bearings were off by a mile, so he struck box 319 which was closer to the fire. The telegrapher refused to change the station number, believing that it would only confuse the firefighters. Since they would pass box 319, they would surely see the fire. It was a mistake of epic proportions.

A disastrously long 45 minutes after the first signal was sent, seven companies were on their way to a barn behind 137 DeKoven Street. The O'Learys claimed that a cow kicked over a lantern but it was later revealed that they kept a still in the barn, and that a very drunk "Peg-leg" O' Sullivan went inside looking for liquor.[3] Unsteady on his wooden leg, he knocked over or dropped his lantern, and ignited bales of hay, or so the story goes. Soon thereafter adjacent houses, stables, pig sheds, and corn cribs were totally engulfed in flames.

Had there not been a northeasterly wind the fire probably would have burned itself out near Conley's Patch, an Irish ghetto on the east side of the river known for open sewers, a violent crime rate and poverty. Instead, the flames raced through a block of shanties. Drunken men staggered through the streets wearing stolen firemens hats, rolling kegs of beer from saloons down the streets and running with as many stolen liquor bottles as they could hold with several crashing to the sidewalk. Firefighters had to stop fighting an out-of-control fire so they could turn their hoses on a disorderly and combative crowd of drunks.

Strong winds sent scraps of burning debris flying through the night air, igniting rooftops or anything else that got in the way. Dozens of planing mills and factories along the riverfront caught fire. Flaming debris crashed into adjacent buildings and the conflagration began to spread. North side hotel guests entertained themselves watching the fire from windows, assured by management that they were in absolutely no danger.

After being awakened and told that the fire was rapidly spreading through the south side, Mayor Roswell Mason arrived at his office around midnight to telegraph nearby towns. "CHICAGO IS IN FLAMES – SEND HELP."[4] When the roof of the million dollar "fireproof" courthouse caught fire, the mayor ordered everyone out of the building including the prisoners in the basement jail cells. As black smoke cascaded through the hallways, frantic screams from the prisoners below echoed through the upstairs hallway. When the bell tower collapsed, the 5,800-pound bell crashed through three floors, clanging erratically until it reached the basement with a loud crash that could be heard throughout the city.

The Great Chicago Fire. Picture courtesy of the Chicago History Center.

As flames spread through city streets frightened horses bucked and kicked; dogs ran in circles barking frantically; and thousands of rats that lived beneath the city wooden sidewalks scurried through the streets. Pigeons circling above the flames were sucked into the vortex and cremated in seconds. Men, women and children ran through the streets ahead of the fire, unable to see a few feet in front of them due to the thick smoke. One survivor recalled that the heat penetrated their backs, as if it was cooking their lungs. When the resins inside the trees exploded, it sent splinters flying in every direction.

The U.S. Weather Office reported wind gusts of a hundred miles an hour as superheated columns of hot air rotated in a tornado-like manner. The wind tunnel blew burning debris far in advance of the flames and instantly ignited hundreds of smaller fires.

Just a few blocks away from Gideon's office at 242 South Water Street it was raining red hot sparks. With a couple of hundred boats docked nearby along the riverfront, tugboats frantically pushed stranded ships out of the way to prevent them from catching fire, waiting their turn to be towed to safety beyond the breakwater. This was far from easy, because they had to dodge parts of bridges that had collapsed and obstructed parts of the river.

The U.S. Weather Signal Office reported winds of 100 miles an hour as superheated columns of hot air rotating in a tornado-like vortex. The wind tunnel blew burning debris far in advance of the flames and ignited hundreds of smaller fires.

The river had become an open sewer for the slaughterhouses. When the fire reached a flammable coating of filth, it spread across the grease and oil-slicked water to the north side of the city. After the fire jumped the river, it raced northward burning everything in its path until it reached Lincoln Park the following morning.

During the next forty-eight hours, somebody died every ten minutes, until over 300 people were dead. Grabbing a stack of papers from his study, attorney Isaac Arnold gathered his family and servants. They walked through crowded streets toward Ogden's Pier where he found a rowboat that could take him to a lighthouse away from the fire.[5] There, he ran into Edward Tinkham, cashier of the Second National Bank, who had a trunk filled with $1.6 million ($64.1 million today) of cash and securities.

Mr. Arnold noticed a tug docked nearby and asked the captain to take them upriver to an unburned part of the city, with women and children placed in the pilothouse with portholes closed tightly. Men crouched on the deck behind the bulwarks to shield themselves from the smoke. With a hose attached to a pump that sucked water from the river, they would have been able to extinguish any part of the ship that caught fire.

The captain steered between two immense clouds of smoke for about a quarter mile, but when he reached the State Street Bridge, he had to slow down to a crawl to steer around another collapsed bridge, but with less horsepower the pumps gave out and the boilers began to seize. Arnold pushed his son to the deck away from clouds of black smoke, and covered his face with a wet handkerchief. The crew began putting out small fires as scraps of burning debris landed on deck. As they steered around the partially submerged Wells Street Bridge, the pilot shouted, "we're through sir," and the air cleared. That morning, Tinkham took a train to Milwaukee and deposited the contents of his trunk in Alexander Mitchell's bank vault.

By Monday, the fire was spreading north to Lincoln Park and south to the elegant mansions along South Michigan Avenue. At a row of townhouses in the path of the fire, servants worked through the night hauling valuables to wagons backed up to the front steps.

The fire left over 100,000 homeless, most of whom found temporary shelter in outlying towns forty to sixty miles away. Among them were Amos and Rhoda Truesdell, who lived on the north side of the Chicago River.[6]

Chicago in flames. Pictures courtesy of the Chicago History Center.

Amos Truesdell and his son, Arthur, were partners in the Truesdell Lumber Company's Chicago River lumberyard. Amos had spent the night of October 8th watching the fire with his youngest sons, nineteen year-old Marcus and thirteen year-old Fayette.[7] At the time, Arthur and his family were living in the upscale suburb of Evanston about twenty miles north of Chicago.

When the fire crossed the river, people lined the sidewalks with furniture thinking they would have time to load their possessions into a wagon, which was a mistake, and created a bonanza for thieves who offered to haul their property to safety. These people never saw their valuables again, and those who were less trusting buried their most valued possessions in their back yards so they could retrieve them after the fire.

Amos and Rhoda packed pictures, documents, and cash.[8] She recalled, "Grandpa feared the fire would spread faster than we could ride. When the fire came across the water, we wasted not a minute...didn't hitch a wagon like some folks...stopped for nothing."[9] For some reason they traveled west of the city instead of twenty miles north to their son's home in Evanston. More likely than not, the fires destruction blocked their path, and the safest place was west of the burning city.

Once they reached the city limits, they kept riding from town-to-town, and finally found a hotel in Aurora, Illinois.[10] With so many families burned out of their homes every room was rented for over 60 miles, and once Amos and Rhoda found a room they telegraphed their son, Arthur, although nearly every telegraph line were overloaded for over a week. During this communications black-out all a family could do was hope for the best, and immediately after the fire the criminal element ran wild.

The *Chicago Evening News* warned "the city is infested with a horde of thieves, burglars, and cut-throats bent on plunder, who will not hesitate to burn, pillage, and murder as opportunity may seem to offer them to do so safely."[11] General Sheridan instituted martial law for the next two weeks while policemen, troops, militia soldiers, and a regiment of volunteers patrolled the streets.

A body count was impossible to make because people were buried beneath buildings or lying at the bottom of the Chicago River. A large number were cremated by a massive wall of flames that swept through the city. A morgue was set up in a livery stable, and over 3,000 desperate people filed past seventy bodies laid on the floor next to a pile of cheap coffins. Once identified, it was up to the family to place the corpse in a coffin, take the body away, and arrange a burial.

The Night America Burned

The night Chicago burned there were other catastrophic fires that destroyed 1.2 million acres of pinelands in western Michigan. Schooners docking for the night in Muskegon told of an unbelievably destructive fire that burned Chicago to the ground, and the thick haze that hung across ninety miles of Lake Michigan. By the time these schooners docked their sails were covered with black soot.

Whether it's possible for scraps of burning debris to travel ninety miles is debatable, but sailors crossing the lake that night recalled tiny holes singed into their sails. After the fires burned themselves out, dark clouds hovered over Lake Michigan for days making navigation difficult for the remaining weeks of the sailing season. Other major fires that night was reported in Iowa, Minnesota, and Indiana, large parts of the Alleghenies, Sierras, Rocky Mountains, Montana, and stretches along the Red River.

For Muskegon sawmill owners the Chicago Fire was a mixed blessing, because the larger manufacturers with wholesale yards and real estate holdings suffered enormous losses. Since the 1871 lumber season was nearly over, and it hadn't been a good one, only a few mills had lumber still on their docks they could send across Lake Michigan for the construction of temporary shacks before it began snowing. Only Hackley & Sons, Hackley & McGordon, and the Mason Lumber Company had unsold lumber on their docks. Gideon set up temporary operations at 15 ½ Franklin Street where he and Charles Deming bought and sold lumber from a shack with a wood-burning stove for heat.[12]

When the Muskegon mills resumed production the following spring, they ran two shifts to keep up with demand. The single largest supply line to Chicago was the 27 sawmills on Muskegon Lake, followed by sawmills along the Wolf River southwest of Green Bay, Wisconsin. By a tragic coincidence, a fire in nearby Peshtigo destroyed the town and surrounding pinelands. The Chicago Fire killed an estimated 300 people but the Peshtigo Fire killed over 1,125, and burned over *two billion* trees.

Thousands of animals were trapped by the flames and died within minutes.

Most of the victims were caught by surprise while walking home from church services when the flames totally engulfed them.[13] Those who survived recalled a rumbling like thunder in the woods just before flames swept through the village.[14] For many, the fire came upon them so quickly they never knew what hit them. Those that managed to get to the Peshtigo River stayed afloat by hanging onto logs, but soon began choking on the smoke and soot until they lost their grip and fell into the water where they drowned.

After the fire destroyed the town, charred bodies were scattered dead in their tracks with their clothing burned off their backs. Some of the bodies were two-thirds of their original size. Some had arms and legs completely burned off. One boy was found in a kneeling position, his head bowed as if in prayer.

There was a boy who survived unharmed while his parents were reduced to cinders just a few feet away.[15] Another body was found nearby fully clothed, seemingly untouched by the fire but dead nonetheless, with the watch in his pocket melting from the intense heat. Survivors recalled objects flying through the air, causing whatever they struck to explode.

At the same time, on the other side of Lake Michigan, a horribly destructive "prairie fire" started in South Haven, Michigan, and was burning northeasterly. It spread rapidly across the state destroying over *five billion* trees, and killing 200 people. The fire burned for 134 miles and wiped out at least 34,000 acres owned by Gideon along the Osceola, White, Muskegon and Grand rivers, worth at least $170,000 ($6.7 million today). This was a total loss since insurance companies didn't insure pinelands.[16] A shift in the wind and the tireless efforts of residents kept the fire away from Muskegon, although Newaygo wasn't as fortunate.

The smoke from the fire spreading north was so thick that by afternoon it looked like dusk. Smoke penetrated houses and businesses to the extent that it was impossible to remain inside for any length of time.

When the fire finally struck, it rolled through the woods and into Newaygo around midnight. Men and women formed bucket brigades, but made no progress. Two hours later, they were saved by a light rain and by daylight the fire was subdued. Farmers in nearby Fremont didn't fare as well even after they tore down fences and dug ditches as a fire break. Several farmhouses and barns were destroyed, and fifty men struggled to save the Darling sawmill.

Not until the first schooners from Chicago docked in Muskegon was anyone aware that most of that city had burned to the ground. As more schooners arrived with the same news, mill owners knew that the wholesale market had been dealt a crippling blow. Not only was Chicago in ruins, but billions of trees in Wisconsin and Michigan were destroyed by fire.

We know from the date on a promissory note that Gideon was in Muskegon when the Chicago fire destroyed over $750,000 ($48 million today) of his property.[17] His immediate concern must have been how much timber property he lost, but when he heard that Chicago had burned, he must have realized that he was in big trouble, because the majority of his income came from buildings that no longer stood.

Total Devastation and Mayhem in Chicago

Chicago had been reduced to eighty blocks of debris when roughly 17,450 buildings were consumed by flames in less than forty-eight hours. The damage was so extensive that fifty-eight insurance companies declared bankruptcy, and Gideon lost at least two-thirds of his net worth that night.

We know from court documents that he insured his properties for about 30% of their value, the maximum coverage in those days, and that Gideon was left with a lot of worthless polices when insurance companies declared bankruptcy in record numbers.[18] Warehouses, apartment buildings, and storefronts were a total loss, causing him to say to say to his brother that "insurance is only profitable for the insurance companies."[19]

The Chicago Fire strained the financial markets with eastern bankers refusing to transfer funds because they believed that would trigger a run on their own banks. Depositors were nervous about their lifes savings, and anxious customers slept in the banks burned-out hallways hoping to withdraw their money. Since fires weren't an uncommon occurrence, bookkeepers locked their journals in a safe each night as a precaution, but the intense heat from the fire made the ink unstable and entries unreadable. During the clean up, firefighters piled safes at the end of each intersection, and it was up to the owner to pick his safe out of the rubble.

After the fire, every bank was closed until October 17th, and even then, none of them had enough cash to meet anticipated runs. Chicago banks simply didn't keep that much money in their vaults, and had most of their funds tied up in mortgages on houses that no longer stood. Only a small percentage of depositors walked away with cash. The Union National Bank was the mightiest of the Midwestern banks but was teetering on the brink of insolvency, and yet Gideon Truesdell walked away with a significant loan secured by his son's farm.[20]

The larger banks resumed business but with very limited reserves, and only allowed their largest depositors to withdraw 25 to 40% of their money. Banks were forced to liquidate securities, dip into their reserves or declare bankruptcy. Older banks with an impeccable record could borrow from European lenders, and in Chicago, attorney J. Young Scammon guaranteed deposits for the Marine Bank from his personal fortune.

Chicago in ruins. Pictures courtesy of the Chicago History Center.

The fire destroyed land deeds so there weren't any records, which meant that landowners had to prove ownership through insurance policies, mortgage records, property tax receipts or affidavits from neighbors. Eighty city blocks of rubble had to be cleared before surveyors could even begin to establish property lines and streets.

The fire also destroyed federal and state courthouse records. In cases pending, new pleadings had to be filed, and only when both sides came forward were judgments restored. Not surprisingly, the vast number of litigants never made it back to the courthouse.

Chicago was a mess with streets obstructed by collapsed buildings, and several pedestrians were killed by falling bricks from burned out shells of buildings. State Street was clogged with bent streetcar rails contorted by the heat, with miles of telegraph wire wrapped around partially burned poles.

Gideon managed to quickly borrow $38,000 ($1.5 million today) from the Union National Bank, with president William Coolbaugh (1821–1877) signing the loan papers.[21] He was probably the only person who could authorize such a large loan that soon after the fire, and Gideon was no doubt a large depositor. Coolbaugh had become one of Chicago's most prominent bankers, with twice as many loans on the books as the First National Bank of Chicago, his closest competitor, making his bank as powerful as any of the big New York City banks.

With millions of acres of pinelands destroyed by prairie fires in the two largest pine belts, Chicago lumbermen called an emergency meeting to determine if their primary source of lumber was gone forever. The loss of an estimated *7 billion trees* caused them to explore importing large quantities of Canadian lumber in the short term, and perhaps forever.

This resulted in the passage of a special bill in Congress that allowed Canadian lumber to come into this country duty free for the next two years while lumbermen determined if their supply line was irreparably damaged.[22] After a thorough investigation, they realized the impact was far less than they originally suspected, and there was another twenty years of standing timber in Wisconsin and Michigan.

Gideon Truesdell Reorganizes Debt, 1872

Although overwhelmed by the fire, Gideon would have still had a significant annual income from the farms, flour mill, sawmill, lumber brokerage, and a mining company. The question was whether Gideon could recover after a rare combination of unpredictable and catastrophic events overwhelmed him.

There was a dark cloud following Gideon, because in 1868 Truesdell & Orton's general store (formerly the Trowbridge & Wing store) burned to the ground. The following year his flour mill was completely destroyed by fire, and the Chicago Fire and the Michigan prairie fires wiped out most of his wealth. The farms, flour mill, sawmill, and lumber brokerage simply couldn't keep up with the enormous losses caused by the fire.

Mother nature crippled Gideon's ability to recoup his losses, because a two-year draught with prolonged 90-degree temperatures burned up the corn fields that supplied corn, oats, and barley for his livestock. His flour mill was similarly affected when high temperatures and only a few inches of rainfall caused farmers to send about 65% fewer bushels of wheat to his flour mill.

His Muskegon mill had a run of bad luck due to a mild winter during the 1871–1872 logging season. A low water table meant there wasn't nearly enough water in the Muskegon River to move logs downriver to the sawmills, and millions of feet of logs had to be warehoused in lakes, rivers, and creeks until the next season. Logs left piled along the riverbanks would have been ruined by worms, insects, and sap by the following year's log drive. Gideon had to warehouse 1.3 million feet of logs in Tamarack Creek in Montcalm County 78 miles northeast of Muskegon.[23]

Gideon's losses continued in Chicago when he had to clear the rubble from forty to fifty vacant lots or risk losing them. Due to a major safety hazard, the City imposed severe penalties on property owners that didn't clean up their land. This created a bonanza for anybody with a wagon and shovel, and farmers flocked to the city and charged exorbitant fees. The going rate per day for a man with a wagon and a strong back was nine dollars ($388 today). Gideon's clean up bill was probably in the neighborhood of $20,000 ($890,000 today). Real estate magnate Potter Palmer received a $5,000 ($38,000 today) bid to clear the six-story Field & Leiter store site, which he thought was outrageous, so he shopped around and found a crew for a thousand dollars.

The question of the day was whether Gideon Truesdell could recover from such a debilitating blow, and his strategy appears to have been getting through the next few years with borrowed funds until his revenues had a chance to catch-up. According to court records he had no difficulty borrowing $163,830 ($6.5 million today) in one-, two-, and three-year notes.[24]

By the end of 1872 he was running out of assets to pledge, so he executed a slick property transfer with the help of Harvey Durkee, a director of the Northwestern Insurance Company. His son's farm had already been used as security for a $38,000 loan from the Union National Bank, and despite living in New Mexico, he "sold" his farm to his father for a dollar. The following day, he sold the farm back to his son with a clean title, which cleared the way to borrow $14,521 ($600,000 today) from the insurance company using the G.J. Truesdell farm as collateral.

Despite catastrophic losses, R.G. Dun & Company gave Gideon an A-1 rating in their Michigan and Wisconsin credit reports, describing his business as a "long standing firm, business devoid of hazard, ample financial means, large wealth outside of business, unlimited credit." This A-1 credit rating bought him a little more time to turn things around, and it's difficult to pinpoint what drained his cash so quickly but what he borrowed the previous year wasn't nearly enough.

Inspecting the damages at LaSalle and Washington Street. Safes piled on Dearborn Street for the owners to retrieve. Pictures courtesy of the Chicago History Center.

In August of 1873 Gideon was desperate enough to list his son's farm for sale with a Chicago broker.[25] "For Sale, one of the best improved farms in Kenosha County, Wisconsin, located 5 miles from Kenosha and 50 miles from Chicago on the Chicago, Milwaukee, & St. Paul Railway containing 490 acres."[26] Since the farm was mortgaged for 127% of its value, his motive might have been to get out from underneath the Union

National Bank and Northwestern Insurance loans before they foreclosed.

Gideon also split off a 225-acre parcel from his farm and sold it to Derastus Torrey for $8,500 when it was actually worth $23,000.[27] More likely than not, Gideon owed him a considerable amount of back pay, and was starting to safeguard family and friends from his financial problems. By then the credit rating firm of R.G. Dun & Company was getting a lot of inquiries on Gideon Truesdell, and on December 12, 1872, they gave subscribers the following information.

"A smart man, about 55 years old, owns 1200 acres of land in Pleasant Prairie with lavish improvements worth at lowest $60,000. More than enough property to pay debts and will keep along unless panic arises among creditors. Owes a great deal of money and hard up for ready means. He is rated very high but too much spread out...farm pays little on investment, $75,000-$100,000 ($3.3 million today) would be considered low, but high enough for safety."[28]

Given the size of his debt, it's highly unusual that throughout 1872 nobody filed a lien against him, but he did pay the interest on a slew of loans secured by solid assets, and got one-, two-, and three-year extensions. By the end of the year, he had very little in the way of assets to pledge for more short term loans, and he was diverting money to southeastern New Mexico where his son was buying assets just in case the family had to start over.[29] Gideon owned a majority interest in the Wisconsin Mining Company in the New Mexico desert just forty miles north of the Mexican border, and with an estimated $900 million ($36 *billion* today) of gold, silver, lead and other precious metals, the southwestern corner of the territory was on the brink of becoming one of the richest mining ranges in the world.

Throughout 1873 Gideon continued to hemorrhage dollars, and he borrowed $96,814 ($3.8 million today) from family and close friends, mostly unsecured, because there was nothing left in the way of collateral.[30] After two years of reorganizing his debt, creditors were growing nervous, and asking questions about his ability to survive.

On July 2, 1873, R.G. Dun & Company updated their report, stating that Gideon "has more than enough property to pay his debts and will keep along unless panic arises among his creditors—he is honest and means to pay—reputed very wealthy—owns immense amount of real estate and personal property of all kinds. Depends on lumber sawed this spring to work out of a tight place—may work this out if not crowded. Cannot give amount of indebtedness as much of it is in notes—his property cannot fall short of $80,000 - $90,000 ($3.6 million today), probably more."[31]

The Panic of 1873

The Panic of 1873 was the end of the road for Gideon Truesdell. Everything he owned was worth a third less when the country was paralyzed by one of the worst recessions in history. Banks called loans, and investors rushed to sell their railroad stocks at a loss just to protect a fraction of their investments. The collapse of Jay Cooke & Company caused a series of bank failures with an abnormally large number of railroad bankruptcies.

Wages dropped 25% across the country, and the financial markets were highly erratic for the rest of the year. Had the economy been a little stronger, Gideon might have worked his way out of his obligations, but by the end of 1873 he was burning through cash at an alarming rate. He was surviving on a day-to-day basis by moving what little money he had to where it was needed the most.

The panic forced the Muskegon National Bank to impose a $50 ($1,500 today) withdrawal limit to prevent a stampede, and the Union National Bank suspended withdrawals altogether until they re-organized. On September 26, 1873, their board of directors stayed up all night assessing the damage. They determined that they had more than enough assets to remain solvent as long as panic didn't cause depositors to push them into a liquidation.

A few days later, six Chicago banks re-opened but the Union National didn't stay open for long, because as the largest bank in the Midwest they were experiencing heavy withdrawals from correspondent banks in other states and territories drawing down their balances. By liquidating their balances from eastern and foreign banks, Chicago bankers were able to move enormous sums of money into their vaults. A bonded express company brought $2 million and a week later another $16 million ($480 million today) to local banks.

But bad news continued when the Garden City Manufacturing & Supply Company became insolvent, leaving Gideon with $3,000 ($1.5 million today) of worthless stock.[32] When the dust settled, they owed creditors an astounding $300,000 ($10 million today).

The panic forced every banker in the country to liquidate assets to remain solvent, including a Grand Rapids banker holding a $5,000 promissory note signed by Gideon. When he bought back the Orton's $30,000 interest in the Durkee-Truesdell mill, he paid them half in cash and the rest in three promissory notes, which they sold to William Ledyard.

When Gideon couldn't pay the final $5,000 ($211,000 today) installment it resulted in a lawsuit that he couldn't possibly win.

During the fall of 1873 the noose tightened when Gideon couldn't pay his tugboat fees in Chicago, Grand Haven, or Muskegon, causing the harbormasters to file liens against his schooners. Until paid, each ship had to pay their towing and docking fees in cash, and he couldn't sell the schooners Pride and Wescott until these liens were cleared.

There were also past due storage fees for over 100,000 feet of logs in Brook's Lake, as well as 1.3 million feet of logs warehoused in Tamarack Creek from the previous winter. Due to a low water table, lumbermen had to store their logs until the following spring log drive. When Gideon's Muskegon Booming Company logging fees became delinquent, he had to forfeit $4,000 ($160,000 today) of his capital stock to cure the default. But it didn't end there because they filed a $2,177 ($92,000 today) lien against his logs, which meant that he couldn't send them to his mill and turn them into lumber until the lien was paid, which affected his ability to send lumber to his Chicago yards to generate badly needed cash. It was a perfect storm with one disaster followed by another.

In August of 1873 farmers began sending thousands of bushels of wheat to his lakefront mill for processing, but before he got too far into the season Zalmon Simmons foreclosed on Gideon's flour mill. He pledged this property as security for a $20,000 ($890,000 today) loan that was now delinquent. The mill had lost a lot of customers in the past year because it needed mechanical upgrades that Gideon couldn't afford. Despite a massive investment, his new mill never lived up to expectations because 100 revolutions per-minute wasn't enough to move three millstones for a uniform milling on larger runs.

"Mr. Z.G. Simmons last week made an extensive purchase of real estate upon the harbor lying from Main Street east and north of Pearl, composed of the Kenosha City Flouring Mill and the ten dock lots connected with it, also the two Truesdell stores and lumber yard property north and east of it. This gives Mr. Simmons control of most of the docking facilities in the city. We have good assurance that the mill will be kept running to its full capacity, giving an additional market to wheat in this city."[33]

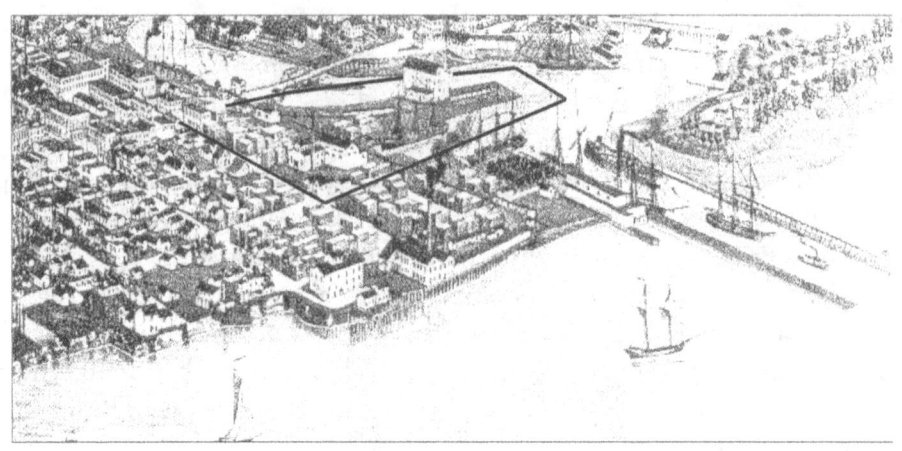

Truesdell's Kenosha flour mill and lumberyard property.
Sketch courtesy of the Kenosha History Center Archives.

Gideon Truesdell's Farm Destroyed by Fire, 1873

A week after Gideon lost his flour mill and downtown properties, mother nature dealt him another crippling blow when the largest barn on his farm was struck by lightning. Powerful gusts of wind accelerated the fire until all of his barns were engulfed in flames, with Gideon rushing outside just after Midnight to the dairy factory where there was a fire hydrant.[34]

While the farm employees were busy driving the animals into pastures, Gideon and Derastus Torrey kept the flames from spreading to nearby buildings, but all they could do was pump water onto the dairy plant's roof.[35] Within the hour all of the dairy barns, stables, and hog sheds were totally consumed by flames.

Given the prominence of Gideon Truesdell's farm, the *Kenosha Telegraph* sent a copy of their story to the *Milwaukee Sentinel*, who telegraphed a special edition to the *Chicago Tribune*. Within a few days this story was dispatched to newspapers around the country:

$75,000 WORTH OF PROPERTY DESTROYED IN KENOSHA COUNTY LAST SUNDAY MORNING.

"On Saturday night at about 11:00, during the heavy storm of that evening, the immense barns of Gideon Truesdell were consumed by fire, by a bolt of lightning, which seemed to have struck the largest barn. There was 250 tons of hay in this barn, and in the grain barn were the products of 93 acres. The wagon house, hog pen, and everything contiguous were consumed. There is about $15,000 ($480,000 today) of insurance upon these buildings, which will cover but a fraction of Mr. Truesdell's losses.

"The news swept through every home in Kenosha, and everybody was anxious to get the particulars of the fire, and the fire has been a subject of great comment and many citizens have visited the ruins. Where last week stood a handsome village of the finest constructed barns, we now find a heap of blackened debris.

"The number of barns destroyed was five, and all of Mr. Truesdell's farm machinery that was operated by steam. The engines, fortunately, were not injured. Besides the destruction of the buildings, a large stock of farm implements was destroyed. Great difficulty was experienced in keeping the fire off the cheese manufacturing plant. Four hogs were found dead in a field nearby, and other animals were found dead.

"The fire originated in the middle of the largest barn, and after a bolt of lightning ignited that barn fires broke out in several places among the barns and sheds. It was impossible to halt the flames until all of the buildings in the vicinity had burned to the ground. The remarkable thing about the fire is these buildings were covered with lightning rods; they're being thirteen upon the longest barn.

A catastrophic fire leveled this farm.

"Mr. Truesdell had spent, we learn, $700 ($29,000 today) for this protection against lightning and it failed him. We fear that we'll have to revise our theories of this subtle agent. Rods directed to the sky presuppose that the fluid comes from the clouds, but does it not come just as often from the ground?

"And even when coming from the clouds or ground, does it go up or down as a rule, does it not go latterly or horizontally just as often? Mr. Truesdell manufactured immense quantities of dairy products at this property, and it is the largest farm in the State. This is a serious loss for Mr. Truesdell."

The failure of these rods caused Gideon to sue the Cleveland Lightning Rod Company for $8,500, and it became one of those lawsuits that acquired a life of its own because it was referenced in a different lawsuit many years later.

"The Cleveland Lightning Rod Company installed lightning rods on buildings owned by Gideon Truesdell & Son in Pleasant Prairie, Wisconsin. Truesdell, on October 9, 1867 paid $700 for the installation and received a written contract insuring the buildings for 10 years against loss or damage by lightning.

"His buildings were destroyed by lightning on August 30, 1873, and Truesdell demanded damages amounting to $8,500. Baker settled the claim in full for $2,000. He was obliged to send an attorney to settle the claim."

Creditors Push Gideon Truesdell into Bankruptcy

Any hope of a financial recovery was lost the night Gideon's "magnificent" farm burned to the ground. The R.G. Dun & Company reports had bought him some time, but with so much of his net worth destroyed by fire, creditors raced to the courthouse to file liens. During the past two years, the best Gideon could do is negotiate extensions and pay the interest on his loans. A month after the farm burned, he defaulted on a $5,812.12 ($185,000 today) note to Henry Moore, an old friend who sold lumber from his mill through Truesdell's Chicago yards.[36]

This note was secured by his interest in the Durkee-Truesdell mill, and although Moore didn't attempt to collect, he did protect himself by filing a lien against the property. The next lien that surfaced was filed by Gideon's nephew, Augustus Truesdell, which must have raised a few eyebrows because he had just served a term as the Muskegon County Treasurer. A few days before Christmas he filed a $7,300 ($233,000 today) lien on behalf of himself and his father, Levi, against the Durkee-Truesdell sawmill, a clear indication that family members were beginning to protect themselves from the inevitable.

Sixty days after the farm burned, the Muskegon National Bank filed a $5,556.57 lien against Gideon's bank stock that had been pledged for a loan that was now delinquent.[37] On December 31, 1873, R.G. Dun & Company issued the following report after the U.S. Bankruptcy Court froze Gideon's assets. "Lots of extensions for 1, 2, and 3 years, owes about $200,000, assets on paper about $260,000 ($10.3 million today) may get out if left alone."[38] This indicates that of the $163,000 that he borrowed a year earlier, all he was able to do was pay $16,330 ($521,000 today) in interest.

The creditor that pushed him over the edge was a Chicago supplier who sold leather belts to sawmills and factories. Part of a salesman's job was to check for liens at the courthouse in his sales territory, and by 1873 Halleck & Wheeler was keeping a close eye on Gideon. They filed a $314.33 ($9,300 today) collection which forced him into bankruptcy court.[39] In district court Halleck & Wheeler filed a "rule to show cause." They said Gideon was indeed insolvent due to unpaid debts to H.D. Moore, Augustus Truesdell and the Muskegon National Bank.[40]

With his old friend Henry Blodgett now sitting on the federal bench, he had to find another top-drawer Chicago attorney to keep him out of bankruptcy. He retained Clarkson & VanShaak, who also represented the Chicago Lumberman's Association.[41] Their first order of business was getting the petition for bankruptcy thrown out, because technically he wasn't broke, just heavily indebted, and not a rare occurrence after the Chicago Fire. Theoretically, he had enough assets to pay his obligations plus interest, but the court ordered an independent audit. They listed $290,000 ($12.3 million today) of assets and $250,000 ($10.6 million today) of debts which left Gideon with a net worth of $40,000 ($1.7 million today), far less than R.G. Dun & Company estimated, but still a respectable amount of money.[42]

When Judge Drummond asked if "right now" he could pay the Henry Moore, Augustus Truesdell, and Muskegon National Bank liens, Gideon admitted that he couldn't. Drummond ruled that Gideon was indeed insolvent, and ordered his assets frozen to protect creditors.[43]

After surrendering his books to an auditor, and at a time when he was prohibited from entering into business transactions, Gideon bent some rules and broke a few laws. More likely than not, most of the money he was scraping together was being sent to Silver City where the Wisconsin Mining Company's operations was in desperate need of cash.

Anticipating a time when he might run out of cash or the Court froze his assets, he wrote himself three promissory notes for $1,000 each ($96,000 today) that were secured by his son's farm.[44] When he walked into the First National Bank, these notes were cashed without question because bank president Zalmon G. Simmons would have had to approve such a large transaction. He had been a close friend of Gideon's for many years, and no doubt presumed that it was him and not his son that was in financial trouble.

Orson S. Head (L) Orson Welles (LC) Judge Henry Blodgett (RC) Zalmon G. Simmons (R). Orson S. Head's great grandson was Orson Welles.

What wasn't immediately known was that every asset G.J. owned had already been tapped by his father. When the first note fell due and wasn't paid, the First National Bank filed a lawsuit although by then father and son were out of reach from the long arm of the law in the New Mexico Territory.[45] The attorneys representing the bank would never have attempted to serve father or son legal papers; it would have required somebody spending two months traveling through the desert to reach them in southwestern New Mexico.

Since everything G.J. owned was mortgaged to the hilt, it made him judgment proof. There were no assets left to sell so the First National Bank withdrew its petition, and waited in line with the other creditors.[46] It was common knowledge that Gideon owned an interest in a New Mexico mining company, but since mining was a boom or bust business, R.G. Dun & Company estimated that his $3,000 ($120,000 today) of capital stock was "probably of little value."[47] And since the mining company was a Wisconsin corporation, Gideon took the precaution of pledging his stock to his longtime accountant for a loan that probably never existed, making it impossible for his creditors to attach.

The next thing Gideon did was illegal, because he was prohibited by the Court from entering into any business transactions, and yet he borrowed $5,000 ($211,000 today) from a Racine County banker who was a longtime friend.[48] Gideon had an impeccable twenty-year record of paying his obligations on time, and he filed one of the largest tax returns in southeastern Wisconsin, which gave him an exceptionally good reputation. Any note signed by Gideon Truesdell was considered as good as gold.

Gideon Truesdell Declared Bankrupt, 1874

According to his brother Amos, too much went wrong at once, and yet he went down swinging.[49] In January 1874, an independent court-appointed auditor came up with a $16,668 ($709,000 today) net worth for Gideon, which was about right because by then three months of interest had been subtracted from the original figure.[50] But he was burning through cash at a furious pace, and was only two to three months away from having a negative net worth.

The Bankruptcy Court for Northern Illinois called a creditors meeting, and nobody wanted the position of "Assignee of Assets" because it was a poorly-paid headache.[51] This person would be responsible for the thankless job of liquidating the estate, and it was a complicated one with assets in three states. With family and friends holding $48,000 ($1.5 million today) of unsecured notes, Arthur Truesdell reluctantly took the job.[52]

Due to the quality of Gideon's assets, the Court stipulated that nothing could be sold for less than 75% of its inventory value.[53] During the next two years, everything was systematically sold, from buildings to livestock to silverware and even the family Bible, with dividends declared by the Court, and paid to creditors until everything was sold. This bankruptcy was unusual inasmuch as the estate generated a significant income during its liquidation. After the 1874 harvest, the farm reported an $8,000 ($339,000 today) profit from the G.J. Truesdell farm, which supports the presumption that with a little more time Gideon could have worked his way out of this mess.[54]

The southern half of the farm owned by G.J. Truesdell was untouched by the fire, and were sold to banker Zalmon Simmons for the bargain price of $30,000, or 37% of its assessed value. All Simmons had to do was put an experienced dairy farmer in charge, which turned out to be Roscoe Torrey, and his investment would generate a solid return. (He was no relation to Derastus Torrey.)

According to the *Green Bay Press Gazette*, "Judge J.H. Howe and Mr. Z.G. Simmons of Kenosha, and Roscoe Torrey, formerly a farmer near Depere and now of Maine, have purchased the celebrated Truesdell Farm six miles west of Kenosha, and will operate it under the management of Mr. Torrey. The farm contains 600 acres in a high state of cultivation, amply supplied with buildings, machinery, water facilities, and is called the model farm of the State."[55]

Jason Howe sat on the board of directors of the First National Bank of Kenosha, and was a former Wisconsin Attorney General, federal judge, nephew of U.S. Senator Timothy Howe, and a close friend of Zalmon Simmons.

The toughest asset to sell was the northern half of the farm where Gideon Truesdell's mansion stood, and where a fire destroyed $75,000 ($240,000 today) of buildings. Two years later, it was sold at a loss to an affluent Evanston, Illinois, livestock dealer. The estate was also having great difficulty finding a buyer for the Durkee-Truesdell sawmill, which never happened, because before a buyer could be found it burned to the ground.

"SAWMILL BURNED – LOSS, $60,000"

"About eight o'clock Thursday evening, the Truesdell mill was discovered to be on fire, and as there was a high wind prevailing at the time, it burned to the ground, without giving our land and marine fire extinguishers an opportunity to save the property.

"The property cost $60,000, and was insured by companies represented by A.G. Smith, for about $20,000. The origin of the fire is unknown, and all sorts of opinions, as to the origin are expressed. The property has been in the bankruptcy court for several weeks, since which time the mill has not been running, and the loss will be sustained by the creditors."[56]

Tragically, there was an expensive fire suppression system with aeriated pipes throughout the sawmill, roof, and docks. With the mill closed, there was nobody there to fire up the steam engines, and yet even if there had been it took twenty minutes for the boilers to reach full steam. By then the entire mill and docks would have been totally engulfed by flames.

About sixty days later, Muskegon suffered a far worse fire when flames "swept through the main section of the city, burning 70 business establishments and leaving about 200 families homeless. Unmindful of the great Chicago Fire of 1871.... overlooking the fact that the city with its lumber piles, heaps of sawdust, and frame houses.... No provisions had been made to assure fire protection. Fires were not uncommon, but people were totally unprepared for the catastrophe that befell them that summer night."[57]

In exchange for an immediate settlement, Arthur Truesdell convinced creditors to withdraw $52,000 ($1.6 million today) of claims and compromise $9,000 of preferred debt.[58] Early in a bankruptcy, creditors are more receptive to deals when it's unclear how much the assets will bring at auction, preferring less money to no money. The Court asked these creditors to forgo any profit if they would agree to reduce their claim to just expenses in the interests of a fast settlement.

Gideon's longtime partners, Charles Deming, Levi Truesdell and Luther Whitney, reduced $49,381 of secured debt by $10,000 ($400,000 today) in exchange for an immediate payment. The estate sold $17,791.66 ($759,000 today) of mortgages held by Gideon to the First National Bank of Kenosha at par value.[59] There was a $47,650 ($2.1 million today) check from Harvey Durkee for Truesdell's quarter-interest in cattle and mining investments, which was used to pay creditors. This was money that could easily have been sequestered by Gideon until he was out of bankruptcy, but he didn't.[60] Auctions in Chicago, Muskegon, Kenosha, and Pleasant Prairie raised $39,758 ($1.6 million today) from the sale of personal property.[61]

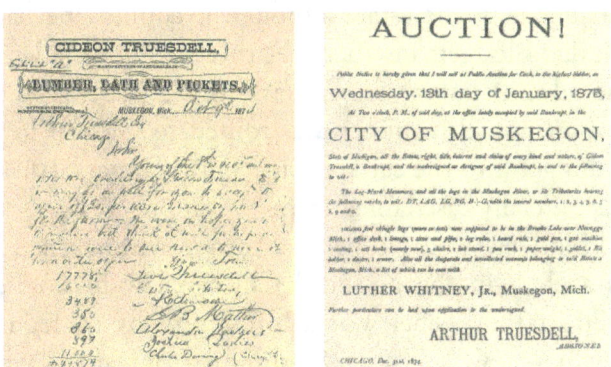

Withdrawal of $49,381 ($2.9 million today) by family and friends, and the Muskegon Auction notice (R). Courtesy of the U.S. National Archives.

There was a $6,800 ($217,000 today) loan to Hackley & McGordon and another for $5,000 to Hackley & Sons ($159,000 today) that were discounted for early payment.[62] By the end of 1874, Gideon's debt had been reduced from $233,302 to $124,873, almost half, during a bad economy.[63] When Gideon learned that there might not be enough assets to pay his debts due to the condition of the economy, he instructed his nephew to sell what was exempted by bankruptcy law, which generated another $1,725 ($52,000 today).[64] As it turned out, Gideon knew almost to the penny how much these assets were worth, and was correct in presuming there were enough assets to pay his creditors. His sister-in-law, Rhoda Truesdell, recalled that it bothered him that people might not get paid, but "he paid everyone, more than he had to under the law."[65]

The one asset that Gideon safeguarded was his 71% interest in the Wisconsin Mining Company. He pledged this asset to longtime bookkeeper and partner, Luther Whitney, for a loan that probably never existed and kept this asset out of reach from creditors.[66] When he left for New Mexico to check on the condition of the mining company, which still had great promise, he was hopeful that it would wipe out his debts, and allow him to buy back from the bankruptcy court the northern section of the farm where his residence was located.[67]

The Chicago Fire bankrupted people in record numbers, and late in the bankruptcy, Gideon's estate was transferred from Judge Drummond's busy court to Judge Blodgetts. Whether this was co-incidental or a slick financial maneuver, it placed the final accounting in the hands of Gideon's longtime friend who had earned a reputation for playing fast and loose. There was a surplus in the estate although it couldn't be paid directly to Gideon, so Judge Blodgett instructed Arthur to submit a letter requesting waiver of the administrator's fee and ask for $2,500 ($106,000 today).[68] More likely than not, this money was routed to Gideon in New Mexico and helped him get into the cattle business. On January 10, 1876, Gideon Truesdell was officially discharged from bankruptcy.[69]

Henry Blodgett was a capable attorney who learned the tricks of the trade as a clerk in the powerful Chicago law firm of Scammon & Judd. Blodgett's father, Israel, was a blacksmith by trade, and a staunch abolitionist who knew J. Young Scammon from anti-slavery meetings. When he was accused of helping slaves escape from law enforcement officers, he was asked in open court what he would do if called upon to be part of a posse to capture fugitive slaves. Scammon replied, "I would certainly obey the summons, but I should probably stub my toe and fall down before I reached him."

There was a longstanding relationship between the Scammon family and Abraham Lincoln, and it was at the Chicago office of Scammon & Judd where Henry Blodgett first met the future president.[70] When this high-powered firm was dissolved, Blodgett & Winston inherited most of their railroad clients. A separate firm, Blodgett & Upton, was located in Waukegan, Illinois, where Henry and Althea Blodgett maintained a residence that was a stop in the Underground Railroad.[71] It was at the Blodgett residence that Abraham Lincoln spent the night in March of 1860 during the Illinois primary.[72] Waukegan was about sixteen miles south of Kenosha, and where Blodgett & Upton had a lot of clients, including Gideon Truesdell.

Blodgett had many admirable qualities, namely, his commitment to the abolitionist cause, and spearheading legislation that gave married women in Illinois control over inherited property. Previously, when a women married, everything she owned or inherited became the property of her husband. As a Judge, Blodgett was seldom reversed, had a "phenomenal memory" that allowed him to listen to days of testimony, and repeat long sections of testimony verbatim.

But it was inevitable that Blodgett's legal shenanigans would run afoul of the Chicago judiciary, and a group of disgruntled attorneys requested a Congressional committee to investigate some very serious charges against him. If they were true, he would have been impeached and quite possibly sent to prison. In *Fifty Years a Journalist*, Melville Stone, founder of the *Chicago Daily News* and manager of the Associated Press, exposed Judge Blodgett's judicial misconduct.

"Henry W. Blodgett was the Judge for the United States District Court in Chicago. He had been a politician (Illinois Senate) for many years standing, and his reputation was not altogether savory. A close scrutiny of his administration as Judge led me to believe him an unjust Judge. A sub-committee of the Judiciary of the House of Representatives.... was appointed to conduct the inquiry.[73]

"Blodgett had for some years been a railroad attorney and a lobbyist on behalf of the railroads.... the atmosphere of the place (Chicago) was murky with influence. The moment the attempt to impeach was disclosed, a large coterie of the leading lawyers in Chicago, who had enjoyed railroad practice, as well as the newspapers competing with the *Chicago Daily*

News…. denounced the three sub-committee members. It thus happened that when the Knott Committee arrived, even before it began work, there was a round of wining and dining for the members, and the whole accusation was stigmatized as an outrage.

"As the hearing went on, however, it was obvious that it was serious. It was clearly shown that there was a backstairs influence which was wholly improper, which undeniably affected Blodgett's judicial actions. It was shown also that he had borrowed money from bankrupt funds in the registry of his Court with which to speculate on Wall Street."[74]

This investigation caused Blodgett to lose an appointment to the U.S. District Court of Appeals, which he wanted, when it became widely known that he used funds from bankrupt estates as his private piggy bank.[75] This caused cases before his court to sit for inordinately long periods until his investments paid off. Attorneys complained about lengthy delays in settling estates in which Blodgett named personal friends as trustees. The Chicago Bar Association wanted him kicked off the bench, but with prior notice he repaid borrowed funds with interest.[76]

"Several years elapsed and then Judge Blodgett faced his deserts. Judge Drummond, the United State Circuit Court Judge…. was about to retire. I went to Washington at once and called upon President Chester Arthur. I asked him to read the record from the Knott Committee. He did so, and when I suggested that Blodgett would be a candidate to succeed Judge Drummond, he very promptly assured me that such an appointment would not be made. Then, as I anticipated, a petition for the appointment of Judge Blodgett for the post was prepared and signed very generally by the railroad lawyers of Chicago and backed by the corrupt forces. It was presented to President Arthur, but was ineffective.[77]

Notes

1. *Chicago Tribune*, 29 September 1871, pp.2.
2. *The Great Chicago Fire*, pp. 36.
3. Ibid, pp. 32-33.
4. Ibid, pp. 37.
5. Ibid, pp. 42.
6. Rhoda Truesdell reminiscences, 1902.
7. Ibid.
8. Ibid.

9. Ibid.
10. Ibid.
11. *Chicago Evening Journal*, 12 October 1871.
12. 1872 *Chicago City Directory*, Charles Deming & Company (Charles Deming & Gideon Truesdell), pp. 381.
13. Ibid.
14. Ibid.
15. Ibid.
16. Gideon Truesdell bankruptcy docket, U.S. Federal Archives, Record Group 21, File 26620N3.
17. The date on a loan signed by Gideon from Joseph Chaddock in Gideon Truesdell's bankruptcy papers.
18. Passim, based on how much insurance he carried on other properties that we know of.
19. Rhoda Truesdell reminiscences, 1902.
20. Gideon Truesdell bankruptcy docket, U.S. Federal Archives, Record Group 21, File 26620N3.
21. Ibid.
22. *Industrial Chicago*, pp. 68.
23. Gideon Truesdell bankruptcy docket, Chicago District Court, Record Group 21, File 26620N3.
24. Gideon Truesdell bankruptcy docket, Chicago District Court, Record Group 21, File 26620N3.
25. *Chicago Daily News*, 20 Aug 1873, pp. 8
26. Ibid.
27. Gideon Truesdell bankruptcy docket, Chicago District Court, Record Group 21, File 26620N3.
28. *R.G. Dun & Company*, 12 December 1872 report. Wisconsin ledger, volume 27, pp. 178.
29. Grant County (New Mexico) Register of Deeds, volume 1 shows property purchased in his son's name.
30. Gideon Truesdell bankruptcy docket, Chicago District Court, Record Group 21, File 26620N3.
31. *R.G. Dun & Company*, 2 July 1873, Wisconsin ledger, volume 27, pp. 210.
32. Gideon Truesdell bankruptcy docket, Chicago District Court, Record Group 21, File 26620N3.
33. *Kenosha Telegraph*, 19 September 1873, pp. 4.

34. Herbert Torrey reminiscences, his father (Derastus Torrey) and Gideon ran out to the fire hydrant and began pouring water on the diary plant's roof.
35. Ibid.
36. Gideon Truesdell bankruptcy docket, Chicago District Court, Record Group 21, File 26620N3.
37. Ibid.
38. *R.G. Dun & Company*, 31 December 1873, Wisconsin ledger, volume 27, pp. 210.
39. Gideon Truesdell bankruptcy docket, Chicago District Court, Record Group 21, File 26620N3.
40. Ibid.
41. Ibid. Joseph Clarkson represented Gideon Truesdell. He also represented the Chicago Lumberman'ss Association.
42. Gideon Truesdell bankruptcy docket, Chicago District Court, Record Group 21, File 26620N3.
43. Ibid.
44. G.J. Truesdell bankruptcy docket "A" number 272, Milwaukee District Court. *First National Bank of Kenosha* vs. G.J. Truesdell.
45. Ibid.
46. Ibid.
47. R.G. Dun & Company, Wisconsin volume 27, pp. 178.
48. Gideon Truesdell bankruptcy docket, Chicago District Court, Record Group 21, File 26620N3.
49. Rhoda Truesdell reminiscences, 1902.
50. Gideon Truesdell bankruptcy docket, Chicago District Court, Record Group 21, File 26620N3.
51. Ibid.
52. Ibid.
53. Ibid.
54. Ibid.
55. *Green Bay Press Gazette*, 21 November 1874.
56. *Muskegon Chronicle*, 2 June 1874, pp. 2.
57. *Romance of Muskegon*, pp. 75.
58. Gideon Truesdell bankruptcy docket, Chicago District Court, Record Group 21, File 26620N3..
59. Ibid.
60. Ibid.

61. Ibid.
62. Ibid.
63. Ibid.
64. Ibid.
65. Rhoda Truesdell reminiscences, 1902.
66. Ibid, the Bankruptcy Court exempted 1 share of stock so Gideon could remain president.
67. Arthur Truesdell narrative, 1902.
68. Gideon Truesdell bankruptcy docket, Chicago District Court, Record Group 21, File 26620N3.
69. Ibid.
70. *Autobiography of Henry W. Blodgett*, pp. 31.
71. Ibid.
72. *Waukegan Sun*, 7, October 1961, pp. 5.
73. Knott Committee.
74. *Fifty Years a journalist*, "The Case of Judge Blodgett, pp. 74-76.
75. Ibid.
76. *Chicago Tribune*, 2 March 1879, pp. 2.
77. *Fifty Years a journalist*, "The Case of Judge Blodgett, pp. 74-76.

6

SILVER CITY, NEW MEXICO, 1871

By the end of 1873, the most valuable asset in Gideon's portfolio was a mining company located forty miles north of the Mexican border. The day after the bankruptcy court appointed his nephew as the "assignee of assets," he boarded a train for the first leg of a 90-day journey that would take him to Silver City.

Three years earlier a couple of ex-Confederate soldiers accidentally discovered silver in the valley of *La Ciénega de San Vicente*, a valley at the foot of the Pinos Altos Mountains. It was later estimated that in that rugged corner of the territory was over $900 million ($36 *billion* today) of gold, silver, copper, lead, and other metals buried beneath the floor of the valley.

After some success in a silver mine northeast of Salt Lake City with the Durkee family, and a few months before the Chicago Fire, Gideon heard about the discovery of silver somewhere in Arizona along the Frisco River or south of an old mining camp in Pinos Altos, New Mexico. He got in on the ground floor of one of the biggest silver strikes in the country, and bought $10,000 ($448,000 today) of claims in the Chloride Flats and Silver Flats mining districts.[1] If just one of his claims hit pay-dirt, he could easily have added another $2 million ($77 million today) to his net worth.[2]

After having lost nearly all of his wealth due to fires, the success or failure of the Wisconsin Mining Company would make or break him. When the Chicago Fire struck, Gideon had already bought a slew of claims, bought a steam quartz mill, and was in the process of shipping it by rail to a remote depot in Kit Carson, Colorado, which were the end of the line for rail service. From there, they would have to load 33,000 pounds of equipment into wagons for the remainder of the trip. The valley known by Spaniards as *La Ciénega de San Vicente* was named Silver City by the first wave of prospectors, and it was just beginning to attract attention.

The *Santa Fe New Mexican* reported, "The discovery of rich and extensive deposits of silver ore in the vicinity of Silver City, has given much needed impetus to the mining men of the territory, and as soon as mills are taken into the district, and several are on the way, there is no doubt but that large shipments of bullion will be made from New Mexico. All things considered, the outlook for our neighbor is encouraging and we hope that mining is to become one of their most reliable and best paying industries."[3]

A tent city of about sixty miners began digging for silver ore which, in some instances was only six feet deep. But it was never a "shack town" because right from the beginning buildings were built of adobe or sun-dried bricks to guard against a fire destroying the entire settlement. The town grew fast; in 1870 there were five buildings and a year later there were eighty.

Pinos Altos Mountains, land surrounding Silver City, New Mexico, and stream in the Pinos Altos Mountains.

A *New York Herald Tribune* reporter wrote, "The quartz is shown to yield on average $300 ($10,000 today) a ton and this with imperfect mechanical equipment, crushing, and washing contrivances. The mines in the vicinity of Silver City, and for hundreds of miles surrounding are the richest and capable of being made the most profitable in the world."[4]

At the age of sixty, Gideon probably had no intention of traveling to New Mexico, which meant that he would have to manage this investment through others, and he selected twenty-seven-year-old Samuel O. Greene (1844–1891). He was his daughter-in-laws brother, and at the start of the Civil War, he enlisted in the Michigan 3rd Calvary Regiment (Company I). After two years of heavy combat half of his regiment died.[5] At the age of twenty, he was mustered out of the Union Army as a Sergeant, and re-enlisted in the 3rd Arkansas Cavalry where he was promoted to First Lieutenant, and Adjutant to the Commanding General.[6] After the war when he was looking for a job, Gideon pegged him as a talented young man, hired him, and sent him to Chicago to run his retail yard. He was somebody the "old man" liked and trusted.

Greene was definitely the right man for the job, because once he left Denver, he would be traveling through a 90-mile desert without any water, and having to protect himself from Apaches who were on a killing spree. This wouldn't be a walk through the park. Silver City wasn't his original destination—more likely it was the Little Colorado River in eastern Arizona.[7] There were rumors of silver having been found, many of which were false and misleading, but the best information indicated that there were enormous deposits of something along the San Francisco River.

In January of 1871, Sam Greene left Chicago with a small group called the Arizona Mining Company.[8] The 28 prospectors agreed to pool their money, share expenses and split any profits although this wouldn't have included Greene.[9] He traveled with them for safety reasons, and would have been discreet about his mission since he would be travelling with Union National Bank drafts, and a letter of introduction from a bank officer. Any bank in Denver would have been able to telegraph the Union National Bank to confirm the legitimacy of this letter.

Banks in Denver became known as the "Wall Street of the Rockies," and most territorial banks used the Union National Bank to clear their paper, which would have made Truesdell's drafts acceptable in Colorado, New Mexico, or Arizona although he would have been charged a hefty discount rate.[10] If he bought $2,500 ($106,000 today) of mining claims he would have paid a 10% fee or $250 ($9,900 today), because the person accepting his note had to travel hundreds of miles to a Denver bank to convert them into greenbacks or more likely deposit them into their own account.

While in Denver buying groceries, the Arizona Mining Company ran across a smaller group traveling in the same direction, and decided to combine resources. One of them was twenty-six-year-old Henry Ailman (1845–1938), and he and Sam Greene became lifelong friends. Before leaving Denver, they bought a wagon loaded with groceries, and hired a guide to get them through the mountains and across the Arkansas River.

The first entry in Ailman's diary mentioning Greene was at the Emery

Ranch about 150 miles south of Kit Carson, Colorado.[11] When the weather turned ugly and their provisions ran low, walking became painful, and even the toughest men were sorely tested. While traveling through the Raton Mountains, black clouds appeared, temperatures dropped and a driving snowstorm with gusty winds slowed them down.[12] By late afternoon, they were totally exhausted after trudging through the snow and slippery ice with winds so powerful that it was difficult to breathe. When the party stopped for the night, they pitched their tents in a blizzard. Snow blew through the tents and the men woke up frozen to their blankets.[13] The following day, they made it as far as the Red River, where they set up camp inside an abandoned shack.[14]

By the time they began riding down through the hills toward the Rio Grande, both groups started bickering. Ailman and Greene decided to go off by themselves with a couple of others, and took the smaller wagon and three yokes of oxen.[15] When they pulled into Albuquerque, a Mexican mercantile center with a large military fort on the Rio Grande, they bought picks, shovels, buckets, groceries, and a winch. As they made their way to an old Indian town called Acoma, they met up with another group, and agreed to travel together for safety reasons.

Albuquerques Business District, Circa 1870.
Picture courtesy of New Mexico State University Archives.

Henry Ailman traded his burro, two pounds of coffee, and a shirt for a mule, but after the Indians stole this animal he was back to walking.[16] They experienced great difficulty finding food, and at Fort Cummings the soldiers offered them $15 ($600 today) for each of their Remington revolvers, which they didn't hesitate to accept, and used the money to buy food.[17] They hadn't found any mining locations, and Ailman noted in his diary that "mining, so far as we could learn, seemed to be dull everywhere."[18] The past 90 days had been incredibly difficult with nothing to eat but hard, crusty bread made without yeast, which made it tasteless, and tough to chew. They supplemented their meals with the occasional rabbit they managed to catch along the trail, but once they got into the desert there were nights when they went to bed and woke up hungry.

Ailman asked about the outcroppings he had heard about near the San Francisco River west of the territorial border in Arizona. He was told there was nothing to the rumors, and that it wasn't worth his time because it was in the middle of Apache country.[19] Therefore, they probably never reached the Little Colorado River but more likely a tributary of the Tularosa River that flowed into that river. Having found nothing on the Arizona side of the border, they decided to ride over to Pinos Altos, New Mexico.

After several days of traveling through the rugged mountains, when they reached Pinos Altos, they found dilapidated cabins leftover from the mining camps heyday.[20] The town sprang up overnight when in 1860, three miners from the California gold rush days stopped to take a drink in Bear Creek, and discovered flakes of gold. Word spread through the mining districts, and soon there were over 700 men digging for gold. By the time Henry Ailman and Sam Greene arrived a decade later, there were still a few men gulch mining but it barely paid enough to keep them alive. They were told to keep riding south until they reached Silver City where several prospectors had struck silver.

They arrived on July 20, 1871, and one of the men in Ailman's posse had little more than the shirt on his back.[21] Some of his men had black spots on their skin, muscle cramps, and bleeding gums from scurvy which was caused by a lack of vegetables in their diet.[22] The mining camp was a little over a year old with mostly tents and a few adobe cabins.[23] The mining boom was in full swing, with prospectors working claims during daylight. What surprised Ailman was that most of the claims were showing good results, and there was an easy-going comradery between the miners.

John Bullard (L) Jim Bullard (CL) Sam Greene (CR) Henry Ailman (R). Pictures courtesy of the Silver City Museum. Sam Greene picture courtesy of the Truesdell family.

Dr. Ashael Farr (L), George Derbyshire (LC), Henry Durkee (RC), Sidney Derbyshire (R). Pictures courtesy of the Kenosha History Center Archives.

The most resourceful settlers were John and James Bullard, who fought in the Civil War as Confederate soldiers, and were now Indian scouts for General George Crook. John had been a Captain, and was described as a "morose, insolent, foul mouth brute."[24] But he also had the trust of the people and was held in high regard by the governor. As Indian scouts they had no equals, and anyone that picked a fight with them was in for the fight of their life.[25] Jim became a close friend of G.J. Truesdell's, and several years later they went prospecting for gold in the Black Hills of South Dakota.[26]

The Bullards were among the first arrivals in Silver City, which for years had been known by the Spaniards as *La Ciénega de San Vicente*, a valley at the foot of the Pinos Altos Mountains. Having filed preemptive claims on land for farming and raising cattle, when they heard about the silver strike in nearby Ralston, they decided to take a look.[27]

Veins of Silver, Gold, and Copper.

The outcroppings looked very familiar to John, who called out to the others "boys, if this is what silver looks like we have plenty of it at home."[28] They chipped a couple chunks of rock from their farm in Silver City, and sent them to Denver, where they assayed at $60 ($1,920 today) per ton.[29] Others assayed at $3,500 ($138,000 today), which was remarkable because they only had to dig a few feet deep before finding underground shafts of silver.[30]

They formed Bullard & Company, with John and James Bullard, John Swisshelm, and Joseph Yankie filing claims on what became the Black Hawk and Legal Tender mines.[31] During the next twenty years, over $3 million ($72 million today) of silver was mined in the Chloride Flats mining district where these claims were located.[32] Each claim were little more than a hole in the ground that the owners would, within a few years, develop with shafts that descended over 160 feet beneath the ground-level.

In September 1871, Sam Greene bought the Two Ikes and six others along with six adjacent lodes for $2,600.[33] He bought another $2,834 of claims from Bennett Brothers & Company, and $5,000 from Florman & Klaus.[34] All totaled, he spent at least $10,458 ($448,000 today) on claims in the Chloride Flats and Silver Flats mining districts in Silver City, although he might also have bought another batch of claims in Georgetown and Clifton, Arizona.

Soon, owing to the absence of steam mills, unrefined silver ore was being shipped from the mining camp 1,276 miles northeast to St. Louis, or 1,570 miles to Chicago where the Swansea had a massive refining plant, or 2,153 miles to Baltimore. Some of the rocks assayed so high that they were shipped across the Atlantic for processing by English syndicates. There were different theories about the origins of the massive silver strike in Silver City.

"A dispatch from Santa Fe, New Mexico, mentions the discovery of certain ancient silver mines in that territory which are supposed to be the 'lost silver mines' of tradition. The silver, it is said, is abundant; the ore according to the best California assay is surpassing in its richness. The remains of an ancient system are plainly visible. Whether these discoveries at Ralston City...are rediscoveries of mines once worked by the Aztecs or the Spaniards time may yet determine."[35]

Like so many other events in Gideon Truesdell's life, the Wisconsin Mining Company was intertwined with the Durkee family. Henry Durkee (1847–1916) got his start as a mining engineer in Utah while his uncle was governor, and studied mining at the Chicago Academy of Science. He learned the business in Stockton, Utah, where he wrote detailed reports for bankers, capitalists and investment syndicates about the potential return of specific mining ranges. Henry was a "confidential man" for H. S. Jacobs & Company in Stockton. Jacobs wrote "hes a mining engineer and assayer... his judgment in mining matters is first class and his reports are reliable." It's quite possible that Gideon had an expert advising him on his mining investments, and at the very least Henry would have been able to tell him what to look for.

Early Prospectors, Apache Depredations, and Primitive Conditions

It was a couple of experienced prospectors from Mexico that put Silver City on the map. When Lorenzo and Juan Carrasco built a smelting furnace at Providencia Ledge, they exported the first silver bullion produced in Silver City, and the high assay value of the silver ore coming out of the Bullard's Legal Tender mine resulted in newspaper articles that were dispatched throughout the county.

The *New York Herald Tribune* wrote, "Within the last six weeks were discovered the richest silver mines in the world, both in quartz and chloride beds or deposits. The quartz taken from the Legal Tender claim has assayed at a little over $3,000 per ton...the rock was taken from a depth of twenty feet. The chloride beds are the richest ever discovered in America, yielding as high as $20,000 ($798,000 today) to the ton, and that from rocks taken only six feet deep."[36]

The *Santa Fe Daily New Mexican* wrote, "They are going to have a big town, whether the mines hold out or not, there has been found some very rich quartz at Lone Mountain lately, the richest I have ever seen, some of the specimens showing native silver. Captain Lowe has had some specimens that he told me would assay at $18,000 to the ton. How is that for high?"[37]

On July 20, 1871, Henry Ailman and Sam Greene arrived in Silver City, where building a settlement was underway with great vigor. Ailman's first impression of the mining camp was that it was friendly, and the owner of an empty shack offered it to him when it looked like rain.[38] It was about the size of a jail cell and was so narrow that two people slept in makeshift bunks with a table that folded against the wall. They stitched together mattresses made from old coffee sacks, stuffing them with whatever was available.[39]

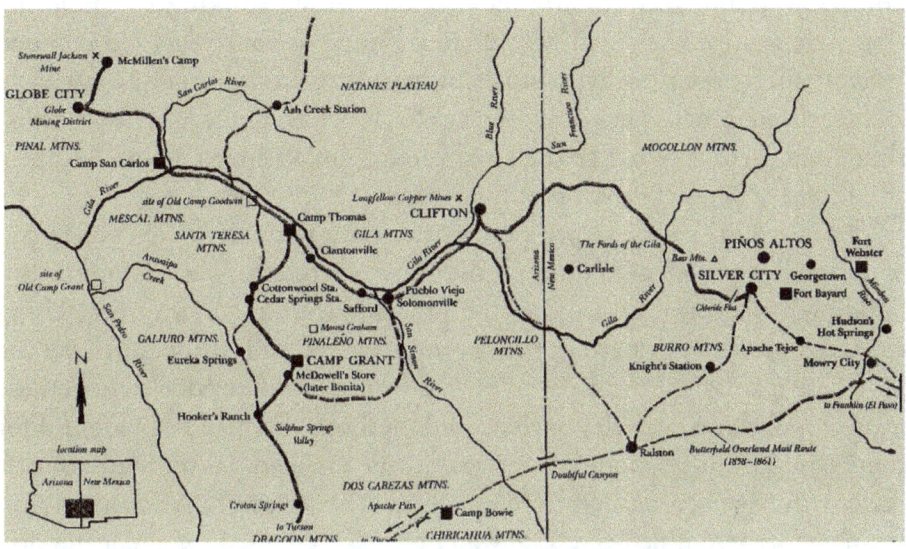

Map courtesy of the Arizona Historical Society.

Getting the rocks out of the ground wasn't complicated; getting the silver out of the rocks was. On June 15, 1871, and without anything in the way of equipment to process their rocks, early prospectors Harvey Whitehill, Silas Tidwell, and Charles Simpson experimented with different methods of refining silver and gold leftover from when the Spaniards were in southwestern New Mexico.[40]

The area had long been known for its copper deposits dating back to when Jose Manuel Carrasco, a Spanish officer stationed in Chihuahua, Mexico, discovered them near Santa Rita about fifteen miles east of Silver City.[41] In 1799, he bought an interest in the mine but five years later sold an interest to a Mexican merchant, who began running mule trains loaded with copper along a trail to Mexico City known as the "copper trail."[42]

Richard C. Fritz   407

The Mexican government built a fort there to guard the people working in the mines from the Apaches. Convicts, political exiles and kidnapped Indians were sent to work in dark, damp and dangerous shafts. They were treated horribly and this was their lot in life until their dying day, which would come soon enough because their captors had absolutely no regard for human life. When copper was re-discovered thirty years later, the miners found skeletons in the shafts which indicated frequent cave-ins and live burials.

When mining resumed many decades later, they found cells with iron rings and chains confirming that the people working in the mines was there against their will. Children as young as four years old chipped away at the copper ore with small picks in tunnels as small as thirty-six inches, passing rocks between their legs for fourteen hours a day to the next child, and were chained to their cell each night so they couldn't escape a childhood of physical and emotional misery.[43]

Silver City's earliest prospectors came up with some inventive ways of processing silver ore. One of the most successful was digging a pit, building a platform, and lining the pit with chunks of silver ore. Using ropes, they hoisted a barrel of rocks into the air, and dropped it into the pit where it smashed the ore into pieces. But they still needed to turn these smaller rocks into particles so they used methods that had been around for centuries in South America. They spread the crushed ore on the floor of a patio with edge boards, and added buckets of water until the consistency of the silver ore resembled clay. Old water barrels were used for amalgamation and crude outdoor arrastras; before steam equipment arrived, everything was done by trial and error and with a strong back and shoulders.

Horses weighing 1,000 pounds trampled over the rocks until it became a pasty compound, and when mercury was added to the sludge, the silver particles clumped to the mercury. When the mercury was washed away, all that was left was nearly pure silver that was heated and poured into 30-pound bars. But this method only netted them $28 per ton ($1,100 today).

Their next experiment used an old whiskey barrel they found along the trail. They mounted it on an axle, and it did a much better job of mixing the silver ore with mercury. Silver ore was crushed in a large pit called an arastra, and then dumped into barrels with water, mercury, salt, and various chemicals. As the barrels were rotated the water washed away the lighter materials while the amalgamated metal sank to the bottom. The mercury was burned off and the remaining silver was poured into bars, which netted them $64 ($2,500 today) from 750 pounds of silver ore.[44] Not fabulous, but promising.

Old water barrels were used for amalgamation and crude outdoor arrastras.

Using these primitive methods, Bullard & Company treated 220 tons which they sold for $25,000 ($1 million today), but they needed steam-powered equipment to take their processing to the next level.[45] Fourteen miles north in Pinos Altos there was a lot of broken-down equipment left over from a short-lived gold rush, and in October of 1872, Bullard & Company purchased an old, worn-out stamp mill. During the first 30 months, Silver City shipped $390,000 ($15.6 million today) of silver that they mined and milled "under the most discouraging circumstances and with the most primitive machinery far from railroads and civilization in general."[46]

One of the most successful prospectors was actually a lumbermen named Martin Bremen (1840–1897). He came to New Mexico with Silas Tidwell (1836–1900), whom he met in Omaha while working for merchant Henry Porter.[47] Five years later Porter opened a general store in Silver City to capitalize on the mining boom.[48]

Upon his arrival in the southwest he had absolutely no interest in mining, and filed a land patent near Pinos Altos where he intended to farm because there was a severe food shortage. He soon realized the land wasn't suitable for farming, and began chopping down trees for support beams that he sold to miners.[49] He brought in a portable steam sawmill and began selling planks at a high mark-up to early settlers.[50]

In the beginning he knew very little about mining, and yet he amassed a fortune buying claims from A.J. Hurlburt (1832–1890) and others, and purchasing an old worn-out mill in Pinos Altos from Reynolds & Griggs. In September of 1871, he moved this equipment to Silver City but could only get five stamps working, and yet he still managed to process 400 tons of silver ore which he sold for $57,000.[51] ($2.2 million today.)

Andrew Hurlburt was another settler who served in the Confederate Army as a Captain, and was remembered for his "coolness and courage."[52] In addition to being one of the most "daring men who ever trod the West," he was also described as a genial, whole souled man who made lasting friendships wherever he went. [53]

In August 1868, he and others organized the Arizona Mining Company, which had nothing to do with the expedition party that Sam Greene traveled with, and they owned the Texas Mine in Pinos Altos.[54] He and Sam became close friends and lived together for a while.[55]

The Texas Mine wasn't remotely successful as evidenced by a judgment for a delinquent $2,000 ($78,000 today) bill for "goods, wares, and merchandise."[56] In 1869, A.J. leased a ranch from W.M. Milby, one of the original founders of Silver City, and two years later filed a claim on 320 acres in the valley with the intention of farming.

But the early prospectors were on a collision course with the Apaches who, for centuries had lived on the land. When Mangas Coloradas tried to find common ground, he walked away dumbfounded when he learned that all the white man wanted was the shiny metal in the ground. The Apaches observed them cutting down trees, digging holes looking for metal, and chasing wild game deeper into the hills. He spoke with the other Apache Chiefs about what he observed, and they agreed to offer the prospectors a gold mine south of the boarder in Mexico if they would leave.

It occurred to the Apaches if they didn't drive the white man away, he would soon take over their land and drive their people away. The Indian culture didn't understand capitalism or the sale of real estate; to them, land was like the oceans or the sky. It could only be shared, never sold. The Apaches targeted A.J. Hurlburt, studied his movements, and lulled him into a false sense of security. On one horrible afternoon while tending his crops he carelessly left his gun inside his cabin.

"Hurlburt...had breakfasted early, and was busy putting in his new crop in full view of his house. Suddenly screams and yells drew his attention in that direction and to his horror, he saw his wife and nine-year-old daughter in the grasp of brutal savages, saw them murdered in a fiendish way, saw his mutilated child tossed from savage to savage, while his wife lay struggling in her last agonies. In his horror he failed to notice these blood-thirsty foes creeping toward him.

"The foremost Apache was within a stones throw when Hurlburt, realizing his danger, turned to the hill behind him and started upon a run up the arroyo...the hills were well timbered and the juniper and oak scrub afforded him some shelter from the bullets of the enemy. It was a long race, ending only when Hurlburt, half naked, torn and bleeding reached the Arizona Mine at the top of the hill near Pinos Altos."[57]

The Apaches were a constant threat, and according to the *Las Cruces Borderer*, "one day last week the Indians made their appearance at Pinos Altos, Bremen's mill, and Silver City. At Pinos Altos they stole some livestock, at Bremen's mill they shot a man and carried away a lot of livestock. At Silver City they made another surprise attack during the daytime, carrying off horses and mules. This can't go on much longer."[58]

According to the *Weekly New Mexican*, "In the spring of 1871 the mining camp of Silver City and the neighboring settlements suffered frequent Apache raids. Following a visit in May of 1871, Governor Pile reported as follows: 'Depredations are almost daily occurrences. Citizens cannot go from one settlement to another, although but a few miles apart....travel and business are almost suspended, mining operations are broken up, and the whole section of the country is in a most deplorable condition.'"[59]

The United States might have acquired this land after the Mexican War but the Indians still regarded it as theirs. And the American prospectors weren't just traveling across their land because they intended to stay, and had no respect for them. As the unwanted interlopers flooded into the area the Apaches studied them from a distance, and at the most opportune time swooped down from the mountain passes at a full gallop, slaughtering them and their horses before they had time to react.

It was an eerie feeling riding through the countryside, day after day not knowing when or where the Apaches might strike, or if they would strike. Every traveler must have died a thousand times in his own mind at the slightest sound, imagining the worst and then realizing that it was nothing. It was an old Apache head-game.

The earliest merchants in the mining camp were Cornelius and Joseph Bennett, who a few years earlier were partners with Jewish immigrants Henry and Charles Lesinsky in a freight and stagecoach business in Las Cruces, about a hundred miles southeast of Silver City, and a major commercial hub. A year after the Treaty of Hidalgo (Mexican War) the United States established a military fort to protect the area. When silver was discovered, the Bennetts and Lesinskys built a store in Silver City at the corner of Hudson and Broadway. They sold mining tools, implements, provisions, patent medicine, clothing, candles, whale oil lanterns, and other mining essentials for prospectors.

The Mercantile Capitol of The New Mexico Territory; Main Street, Las Cruces, New Mexico (L) and Mesilla, New Mexico (R) Were Five Miles Apart. Pictures courtesy of the New Mexico State University.

Bennett Brothers & Company kept their mercantile profits growing by endorsing notes secured by borrowers with good claims, charging them 24% to 72% interest. When the Pope Mill defaulted on a $10,000 mortgage, they acquired the property along with the Bennett Mine about a hundred miles southeast between Silver City and El Paso. As frontier merchants, they made a fortune in the mining business without having to swing a pick-axe or get their hands dirty.

Prospectors accomplished a lot under trying circumstances and ultimately succeeded. According to an August 7, 1872 *Borderer* article, "The news from Silver City is encouraging.... the mines are yielding richly and building is progressing rapidly. Silver City can boast of more fine buildings than any town in the territory. More mills and machinery are on the way there, and parties passed through here on Monday's coach, going east to purchase more machinery. There is no place on the continent where a 40-stamp mill could do as well as at Silver City. Who will bring it along?"[60]

The Two Ikes Mine, Chloride Flats Mining District

Buying mining claims without a geological survey was risky, because there were far more unprofitable than profitable claims, and yet there wouldn't be a government land survey for several years. The best way to unload a bad claim was to sell it to somebody else. The oldest trick in the book was filling a couple of bushels of rich ore from another mine, and scattering it along the shaft of a worthless claim. "Why, this stuff looks as good as the stuff that came out of the Lodestar," which it did, because that's where it came from.

The cornerstone of Gideon's mining company was the Two Ikes, a claim that Sam Greene had purchased from Ike Givens and Ike Stevens. It was described as one of "the best developed of all the mines in this district with galena that assays from $250 to $10,000 per ton." ($10,000 to $400,000 today.) But even a good claim could go bust 20 feet beneath the surface, and there wasn't anything to recommend its purchase other than Sam Greenes gut feeling. But if he had been told by Henry Durkee what to look for, namely other nearby strikes, he would have been in the vicinity of large deposits of silver ore. The Two Ikes were probably happy to sell, because they needed the money to develop other claims.

Greenes gut feeling was dead-on because according to subsequent surveys, there was an estimated $37.5 million ($1.2 *billion* today) of silver in the Two Ikes mine. According to the *Daily New Mexican*, "An assay of the ore from the Two Ikes...was made at the mints in this city yesterday. It gave three,105.15 ounces of silver per ton worth $4,012.02... sixty tons of that in sight and only one hundred feet below the surface of the ground is a pretty good thing to have."[61] It was a fabulous claim and Gideon Truesdell owned it.

The mood in Silver City swung from euphoric to discouraging. One week a successful shipment of silver raised everyones hopes that success was just around the corner, followed by torrential downpours that turned every square foot of the settlement into a pool of mud. News that somebody had been murdered by the Apaches or cattle had been slaughtered left everyone uneasy. One day Silver City was a desert paradise with balmy temperatures followed by stormy weather that confined them to their cabins and tents, and yet the promise of fabulous wealth helped everyone push through some incredibly tough times.

Few of the early prospectors had much experience, and it wasn't unusual for inexperienced miners to walk past rich deposits because they didn't know what to look for. Silver was seldom in plain sight, and prospectors were never sure if they were looking at silver, horn silver, or quartzite streaked with green. Quartzite was considered worthless until the miners discovered that it had considerable value. Fools gold was streaked with alloys resembling gold. Copper had a green or bluish-green tint but rarely did anyone find a chunk sticking out of the ground that looked like copper.

Getting the silver ore out of the ground with a pick and shovel was exhausting, but sending wagon trains to St. Louis, Chicago, or Baltimore was dangerous and expensive. The major players in the emerging mining ranges knew they had to build their own mills near the mines. Instead of sending forty tons of rocks 1,000 to 2,000 miles for processing, they needed to build mills closer to the source of the silver ore, which would enable them to send 20,000 pounds of silver bricks to the U.S. Mint.

Greene filed a 4.7-acre claim across the road from the Bullard's Legal Tender claim on Spring Street between Hudson and Bullard streets.[62] Gideon's attorney used the new corporate form of ownership, and swapped Gideon's $24,000 ($960,000 today) of claims and mill equipment for 181 shares in the Wisconsin Mining Company, which gave him a 71% stake in the company.[63] The corporate form of ownership allowed him to raise large amounts of capital, and at a later date should they strike it rich he would be able to raise another $100,000 ($3.4 million today) of capital to develop such a massive claim.

When they filed a claim on the mill site and dozens of mining claims, they did so before the federal government surveyed the land. Twenty-five years earlier the area had been a Mexican province, and there were thousands of phony land deeds floating around. At the end of the Mexican War, the Treaty of Guadalupe Hidalgo mandated that the United States recognize all legitimate Spanish land decrees in Texas, New Mexico, Arizona, California, Utah, Nevada, and parts of Colorado, which severely complicated the transfer or land.

This created a bonanza in fraudulent land deeds, and in California during a one-year period over 800 claims involving 20 million acres were heard by the Private Land Claims Commission with nearly two-thirds approved. With so much money at stake corruption were inevitable, because even if a 20,000 acre claim was phony, the commissioners and the courts would approve them if a large enough bribe somehow found its way into their pockets.

According to a December 28, 1872, *Las Cruces Borderer* article, "Silver City is the only American town in New Mexico and the most enterprising. A Deputy U.S. Surveyor has arrived to survey the town site and thus relieve the property owners of the uncertain tenure by which real estate has been held. Titles to property can now be regulated, and the rights thus acquired can now be rendered secure."

A few months after Sam Greene bought their claims the laws changed. Now, a prospector had to go down at least ten feet, show evidence of metal, work the claim for one in ten days, post a notice showing the name of the lode, the person who located the claim, and the date when metal was first discovered. This stopped people from unilaterally plastering claims on anything that didn't move, and if nothing was done to improve the claim it reverted back to the government. Investment syndicates couldn't sit on hundreds of claims for fifty years. Claims couldn't exceed 1500 feet in length and 600 feet in width, which made it tougher to steal. These new laws made it tougher to steal as evidenced by the following first-hand recollection:

"We struck outcroppings that crumbled under the pick and showed quartz all streaked with yellow threads. 'Charlie, we have struck it!' But before we sank a shaft, we found something that sent our hearts to our mouths. It was an old shaft, back a little in a claim properly staked out, that covered that very ledge. There was a notification according to the law on one of the posts that Peter Sumner and Joseph Klautzy had taken possession of the 'Big Six' and done the legal assessment work. I sat right down and collapsed, but Charley came back to tell me that it didn't cover half the amount necessary under the law to hold the property for one year. We measured it, and sure enough, it was only down about half the required distance, so we took possession and changed the name to 'The Treasury.'

A horizontal (L) mining shaft and a vertical shaft (R) leading to dozens of underground vertical shafts.

"When provisions began to run short, we didn't both want to leave the claim at once, so it was finally arranged that Charley should go down the creek to a camp about fifty miles and bring a supply. About noon the second day after he left, I was startled by what I thought was a man crossing a little gulch about a half mile away. He was an ugly looking customer, big and brawny, with a flat Scandinavian face, and carried a Winchester on his arm.

Typical Subterranean Mining Claims with Vertical and Horizontal Drifts.

"I had a stick I slipped into the windlass to keep it from turning backward, and leaving the bucket just where it was suspended half way up, I started toward the cabin to get my arms. He covered me with his repeating rifle and ordered me to halt.

"'What are you doing on my claim,' he said. 'I reckon you can see,' I replied putting as good a face on it as I possibly could. 'You mean you've jumped it, you cursed thief?' he said. 'There wasn't enough work on it to hold it, and it was as much mine as anybodys,' I replied. 'You lie!' he said. He looked at me over the sights with his wicked greenish eyes for a full minute, and said, 'Did you ever pray?' Yes, I faltered. 'Then pray now. I'll give you two minutes to do it,' he said.

Winch Above a Mine Shaft That Descended Deep into the Earth.
Picture courtesy of the Palace of the Governor photograph collection.

"By then my mind was clear enough to take in the whole situation, and I had no doubt but he intended to murder me then and there. With me out of the way there would be no one to testify to the insufficient work, and I would simply be regarded as a claim jumper who had been justly dealt with. I felt my knees begin to tremble and tried another trick. 'If you kill me my partner will be back and see that you hang for it,' I said.

"'I'll fix your partner the same way you claim-jumping cuss,' he remarked. 'True enough. Nothing would be easier than assassinating Burk on his return, and we had so jealously guarded the secret of our trip that no one would know where to search for us. We would simply disappear, as hundreds of prospectors do, never to be seen by men again, and speedily to be forgotten.'

"I had no hope of mercy from the cruel man.... I felt with a sickening qualm and a wild drumming in my ears that my time had come. 'Oh, for heaven's sake don't murder me, I will go,' I cried. For a moment my head swam, and then, with a sudden return of my vision that was excruciating in its clearness, I saw him stoop slightly, rest his gun barrel over the windlass (winch) handle, and marked even the slight contraction of the eye lid that always precedes a shot.

"The next instant there was a crash, an explosion, and a cry all mingled into one. I saw the man turning head over heels down the embankment, the Winchester flying through a cloud of smoke up in the air, and all the while heard a whirring noise that was like some gigantic clock running down. I didn't realize at the time what happened: when he rested his gun across the windlass, he dropped the barrel right across the little stick I had thrust in it to prevent it from tumbling and knocked it out.

"I suppose the bucket weighed 150 pounds and the iron handle, swinging clear around, gained such terrific momentum that when it struck him square in the face, which it did, it lifted him off his feet like a cannon ball. The gun was discharged by the shock, but the bullet went nowhere near me. Before I regained my senses, I heard the bucket strike the bottom with a smash. When I picked up the man, he was unconscious, but moaning a little, and blood tricked from his ears."[64]

G.J. Truesdell Brings a Steam Mill Overland to Silver City

By the time Sam Greene returned to Gideon Truesdell's farm during the fall of 1871, he would have arrived just in time for the holidays.[65]

He had a permanent room at G.J. and Louisa Truesdell's 10,000 sq. foot mansion where he was courting his nephews governess, Maggie Walsh.[66] At nineteen, she had lived with the family for several years, and had become an extended member of their family.[67] He would have been shocked to learn the extent of Gideon's losses, and yet he pushed ahead since so much money had already been spent to organize a mining company.

Gideon had already purchased a $12,000 ($512,000 today) steam mill, which was shipped to the railroad depot in Julesburg, Colorado, along with wagons and horses that could be purchased much cheaper in Chicago.[68] The further away from civilization the higher the price of everything, and manpower was nearly impossible to hire so they brought along their own employees.

They recruited strong young men from Kenosha to come with them to New Mexico to work in the mill. Each would receive a share of Wisconsin Mining Company stock to be held in trust as an incentive.[69] If they stayed until the business was profitable a single share had considerable value with yearly dividends that would make them affluent. For an ambitious young man, there was no better opportunity than a share of stock in a mining company.

Gideon sent his twenty-nine-year-old son to bring the mining equipment and employees, and it was a difficult and dangerous trip. Their journey began at the Milwaukee & Chicago depot in Kenosha, and a couple of hours later they reached Chicago, where machinists E.O. Kennedy and Tom Lyons joined the others for a twenty-day trip covering a thousand miles of rail, lightning speed in those days, to Kit Carson, Colorado.[70]

Kennedy had previously worked in a mine in Nevada Gulch near Virginia City. At the age of thirty-two, he developed a strong desire to move to New Mexico where his mechanical skills would be in demand. One of the young men traveling with him was twenty-one-year-old Tom Lyons, a sharp young man who had worked for him at the Swansea Smelting Works, and had previously lived in Kenosha where his immigrant parents ran a grocery store. Tom got to know G.J. during their monotonous trek across the country, and they became lifelong friends.

The first leg of their trip would have been somewhat boring as they traveled by train across Illinois, Iowa, Nebraska, and Colorado. It was a tedious trip as the train crept across poor stretches of tracks at ten to fifteen miles per-hour, covering about sixty to seventy miles a day. Since the Union Pacific and Central Pacific contractors were paid by the mile there were hundreds of miles of unsafe sections caused by sloppy construction. On level ground a train could hit forty miles per-hour, which was incredibly fast during the 1870s, but sometimes wildlife got in the way.

Chauncey Truesdell recalled that it was "a long hard trip... the train was stalled in the western part of Nebraska by thousands of stampeding buffalo that were running away from a prairie fire."[71] There were 30 to 50 million buffalo roaming the central prairies, and although slow and clumsy because each animal weighed a couple thousand pounds, once they began to charge, they could reach speeds of forty miles per hour. A stampede of forty Buffalo could ram a train with 80,000 pounds of force, and knock it completely off the track.

Everything could be bought much cheaper in Chicago, including furniture for the boarding house, tools, plates, dishes, pots, pans, groceries, horses, mules, and wagons. Gideon had already shipped these essential items to the Kit Carson railroad depot. It was a wild frontier town with saloons, gambling dens, and dance halls.

The men would have loaded a reduction mill into freight wagons, saving an estimated $1,700 ($67,000 today), because freight companies were charging five cents a pound by ox or eight cents by mule. The 653-mile trip through Colorado and New Mexico would have been extremely difficult, and pulling heavy freight wagons would have required as many as 20 yoke of oxen to get them through steep mountain passes.[72]

Traveling with heavily loaded wagons at slow speeds would have made them easy targets, and highway robbers made a good living ambushing inexperienced travelers. A couple of heavily armed guards rode with the driver to guard against highway robbers and marauding Apaches. An old Blunderbuss could be packed with nails and broken glass, and when fired, pretty much annihilated the person it was pointed at.

Sometimes an outlaw would wear a fake clerical collar to gain trust by pretending to be a minister. After he lulled his prey into a false sense of security he murdered them, killing a husband, wife, and their children with a cold indifference. After their bodies were stripped of anything they could sell like clothing, shoes and jewelry, their bodies were unceremoniously dumped along the trail. The outlaws would then drive the wagon to the nearest city where they had no trouble selling the horses and wagon for at least $200 ($8,100 today).

When These Freight Wagons Needed to Stop Men Hopped on a Ledge Board Next to Each Brake and Put Their Weight into Pulling It Down. Pictures courtesy of The Old West.

As the convoy reached the Raton Mountain pass just below the Colorado border, all hands were needed to push heavy freighters through the worst stretches of the steep pass. Despite hauling machinery, and at least thirty trunks packed with clothing, dishes, silverware, and other essentials, they made good time.

Once they reached Santa Fe, New Mexico, G.J. hired a different guide who knew the area to get them safely through the mountain passes before dark.[73] Apaches never attacked at night, but travelers had just as much to fear from bands of outlaws who wouldn't think twice about killing a man for his food, clothing, horses or ammunition.

Thirty days after leaving Kenosha, the convoy reached the New Mexico border. According to a February 13, 1872, *Santa Fe Daily New Mexican* article, a "new ten stamp mill for their Silver City mill passed through Albuquerque with a full complement of mechanics to be placed in operation immediately."[74] (It was a Bolthoff pulverizer, the first in the southwest—not a ten-stamp mill.) Once they crossed into New Mexico, they were 358 miles away from Silver City, which meant they covered about twelve miles a day from dawn to dusk. A person could walk about twenty miles a day.

One of the men in their group developed chilblains with open sores on his feet. Since the only doctor along that stretch of the trail was a veterinarian, all he could do was dress the wounds with horse liniment.[75] This caused him to convulse in excruciating pain. The others began to think that the doctor was a quack, but a few days later the sores healed, and they continued through the worst stretch of the desert.

According to Chauncey Truesdell's recollections, after pulling out of

Santa Fe their trip became dangerous due to hostile Apaches looking for white people to slaughter. "The Rio Grande was up and out of its banks, and since it was during the worst of Indian times, we were compelled to travel at night to avoid attacks and get to a place of security by morning."[76] South of Santa Fe, Louisa Truesdell and five-year-old Chauncey became sick after drinking tainted goat's milk.[77] Both became violently ill but the convoy kept moving to make time, with mother and son in the back of the wagon recovering.

The convoy came to what was known as the *Jornada Del Muerto*, Spanish for the Journey of Death, a grueling 90-mile trail through the desert. It was part of a much longer Spanish trail from Santa Fe to Mexico City, and brought the first settlers into New Mexico 22 years before the Pilgrims landed at Plymouth Rock. The Journey of Death ran along a high plateau of the Cabello Mountains where the water wasn't safe for humans or animals. One historian estimated a grave every 500 feet, and it took nerves of steel and plenty of guts to travel across this wide expanse of desert.

Jornada Del Muerto

Travelers and their animals had to survive on the water they had in the barrels strapped to their wagons. If a man were dying of thirst, he took his chances drinking the water from a shallow stream, but four hours later he would have become violently ill with severe diarrhea, and probably died from dehydration. The guide G.J. hired would have known which creeks had clean water, and made sure all wagons' water barrels were topped-off before the start of travel each day.

Lieutenant John Martin had made numerous trips across the Journey of Death, and in 1869 decided to dig a well midway through the harsh desert. He was convinced that if he could punch through volcanic rock, he would find an underground spring. After months of blasting there was no sign of water, and everyone including Martin agreed it was time to admit defeat. "Shall we load up the holes we're putting in and try one more blast?"

They had already gone down 164 feet so Martin told them to go ahead figuring why not, they had nothing to lose. They lit a long fuse, walked over to their wagons for lunch, heard a blast, and thought nothing of it. They were so sure it was another bust they began loading their wagons for the trip back to civilization before checking the hole. One of the men casually walked over to take a look and ran back yelling that it was full of water! Before long, wagon trains stopped at his busy watering hole, and he made a small fortune. Martin charged 25¢ ($10 today) per animal, and with long lines of wagons stopping to water their livestock and passengers his profits multiplied quickly.

The trail running through the Journey of Death was isolated and dangerous.

After G.J. Truesdell's convoy came down through the Raton Mountains at the Colorado-New Mexico border some of the heavy machinery shifted, and a few miles north of Martin's stage stop they snapped an axle. When coming down through the steep mountain pass gravity took its toll: there was too much weight in each wagon. After making a temporary repair, they limped along at slow speeds until reaching the stage stop, where a blacksmith made repairs. Once G.J. reached Martins, he managed to buy additional horses and a smaller wagon so their larger freight wagons could carry less weight.[78]

When they resumed their trip, there were other annoying and dangerous problems, such as microscopic particles of alkali dust and sand blowing through the air. Newspapers frequently attributed poor eyesight to alkali dust that scratched the eyeballs. A horse that had been "alkalied" needed fresh grass and water to cleanse its system before serious digestive problems killed the animal. Too much sun left travelers and their animals dizzy, disoriented, and confused. They had to be careful about unsafe water, and they also had to exercise caution when they left the trail to look for wood or sage brush to start a fire for cooking.

On March 3, 1872, Chauncey Truesdell recalled "we arrived in Silver City… my uncle [Sam Greene] was living with a family named Hurlburt—he was raising vegetables for Fort Bayard and Pinos Altos."[79] By the time they rolled into town, the *Santa Fe Daily New Mexican* reported that "Silver

City is one of the liveliest places in the west. The yield of some of the mines in rich silver ores is truly wonderful."[80]

Their wagons were loaded with a steam engine, Bolthoff pulverizer, Hepburn & Peterson amalgamation pans, settlers, and a Dodge Crusher.[81] The Bolthoff pulverizer was cutting-edge technology because it replaced a 10,000-pound stamp mill, and crushed and amalgamated ores at the same time.

"The pulverizer is cylindrical in form, and the ore is powered by means of iron balls kept in constant motion within the drum. Every quartz miner knows that the chief fault with a stamp mill is its inability to save any but the brightest and purest....as none other will amalgamate."[82]

By the time the equipment arrived, Sam had already built a barn-like building where the equipment was installed. On the edge of their mill site property on what later became known as Bullard Street he supervised the construction of the Wisconsin House, a boarding house for their workers, and a small house close to the mill that was used as an office and living quarters for the managers.

Wisconsin Mining Company

The Wisconsin Mining Company had a sharp group of men to run a large enterprise forty miles north of the border. As was the case in nearly everything Gideon owned, he included his son as a partner, and they owned 71% of the mining company. Much the same as when Gideon drilled for salt in Muskegon, the 29% of the mining companies' stock that were sold to others gave him approximately $7,395 ($295,000 today) of seed money to get started.

George Derbyshire, a close friend of Gideon's who owned a dairy farm down the road from him in Pleasant Prairie, was Vice President. His brother, Sidney, sat on the board of directors of the Kenosha & Rockford railroad with Gideon many years earlier, and was a stockholder with his sons. Sidney owned ten shares, and his sons, twenty-nine-year-old Matthew and twenty-two-year-old Sidney, each owned a share. Behind the Truesdells they were the largest stockholders. Both of Sidney's sons traveled to Silver City to look after their family's investment, but more importantly, to look for commercial opportunities.

Frederick Ranney (1821–1885) was superintendent of the mining company, and he had been a partner in Amos Norton & Company, a Grand

Haven, Michigan, sawmill in which Gideon owned a minority interest. At the end of the Civil War when Gideon semi-retired, so did Ranney, and at age forty-four he moved to Kenosha so his son could receive a first-rate education. He bought a few shares in the mining company, and traveled to New Mexico to help launch a large and complicated enterprise.

The *Kenosha Republican* reported that "G.J. Truesdell and G.S. VanWagenen started for Silver City, New Mexico yesterday. VanWagenen goes there with the intention of making it his permanent home, and takes a position in the office of the Silver City Mining Company. Van is a gentleman of excellent qualities both social and business, and his departure from our midst will be regretted by all of his many friends and acquaintances. Mr. Truesdell goes there to seek a climate for his debilitated physical condition and will return in six months."[83]

Thirty-one-year-old Garrett Van Wagenen (1841–1918), Gideon's bookkeeper who ran his flour mill and lumberyard office, took charge of the mining company's books, and would have sent summaries to Gideon. If he needed to get in touch with him, he would have sent a letter by stagecoach to the telegraph office in Denver, about a two-week trip, where the letter would have been telegraphed to Gideon's office. More likely than not, Gideon would have telegraphed a reply to the Denver office, where it would have been sent to Silver City aboard the next stagecoach. It would have taken about a month to send and receive instructions from Gideon.

As an incentive, the men working for the mining company received a share of stock. If the Two Ikes was as productive as experts predicted, a single share could be worth at least $7,800 ($195,000 today) a year in dividends, and for a young man, it was enough of an incentive to tough it out when the going got rough. The twelve men they brought with them were from Kenosha and would live at the Wisconsin House.[84]

Blake Street, Denver, Colorado, circa 1860s.
Picture courtesy of the Denver Historical Society.

Gideon placed George Coleman in charge of the mill, and he came with considerable experience. Twenty-eight-year-old Sam Greene was placed in charge of the Two Ikes, which was about two miles away from their mill, and where Mexican muleteers kept the mill supplied with dozens of wagons of rocks each day.[85] A mill's location depended on a steady water supply so they could run their amalgamators, which is why the stamp mills in Silver City were located a few miles away from their mines.

In less than thirty days, E.O. Kennedy and Tom Lyons had the steam mill assembled and running smoothly. According to a March 29, 1872 article in *Mining Life*, everyone in the mining camp gathered to watch them fire up the most sophisticated mill in the area. "A bright era is dawning upon our growing town for you can hardly call it a camp. This afternoon Coleman's model mill commenced work. About 200 persons were present when the enterprising and indefatigable owner steamed up, and when the alligator commenced chewing up rock; you should have witnessed the glow of satisfaction which beamed upon the countenance of every one present. The mill is perfect."[86]

Progress was rapid, because by January of 1873 the *Santa Fe Daily New Mexican* reported, "there are two quartz mills at Silver City; that of Mr. Bremen and the Wisconsin Mining Company, both propelled by steam. Mr. Bremen's is a ten-stamp mill of the old pattern that was used in reducing gold in Pinos Altos. Amalgamation is done in barrels according to the Freeberg process.

"Five of the ten stamps run with eight barrels for amalgamation. The capacity of this mill is about twenty tons a week. The ore here is worked from the Seneca Mine and yields on an average of about $100 per ton of two thousand pounds.

"The mill at the Wisconsin Mining Company consists of a rock breaker (Dodge), a ball pulverizer (Bolthoff), and a couple of Hepburn and Peterson pans. This mill works about sixteen tons per week, and has worked ores from the Two Ikes mine."[87]

Bullard & Company, owners of the Legal Tender and Blackhawk mines built a mill across the road from the Wisconsin Mill. William Rynerson (1828–1893) moved his ten-stamp mill from Pinos Altos to Silver City, and placed Ike Stevens in charge.[88] For a brief period, he rented it for $100 ($4,000 today) a day before entering into a more lucrative arrangement with the Bullards.[89]

Gideon waited until the mill was in working order before he incorporated the Wisconsin Silver Mining Company. At $100 ($3,700 today) a share it was a pricey stock, but with the mill already forging 30-pound silver bars its potential for astronomical returns seemed like a sure bet.

On May 23, 1872, the *Kenosha Telegraph* printed the following article:

"The incorporators of the Wisconsin Silver Mining Company met at the office of Gideon Truesdell, Esquire, and perfected an organization under the laws of the State of Wisconsin. A board-of-directors consists of the Honorable Gideon Truesdell, John Yule, George Crane, Sidney Derbyshire, and George Derbyshire."[90]

"Machinery has already been purchased, is now upon the grounds and dislodging metals. Most encouraging reports have been received of the richness and value of the property and those that have invested their money may reasonably hope to realize large returns.

"The officers are Gideon Truesdell, president, George Derbyshire, vice president, Garrett VanWagenen, secretary, and Mayor Ashael Farr, treasurer. The capital stock is represented by 256 shares with a par value of $100."[91] The stockholders are:

S.S. Derbyshire
William Nelson
Abram Slater
G.J. Truesdell
A.P. Read
George W. Head
E.P. Lewis
John Dale
George Derbyshire
George Coleman
F.T. Ranney
Gideon Truesdell
Ashael Farr
George W. Crane
Frank L. Stone
G.S. VanWagenen
Edward L. Richmond

John S. Yule
A.A. Foster
Derastus Torrey
E.L. Hull
Samuel O. Greene

Silver City circa 1872 and the trial to from Silver City to Pinos Altos.
Pictures courtesy of the Silver City Museum.

After a month of heavy use, the Wisconsin Mill's Dodge crusher broke, which closed the mill until this essential piece of equipment was repaired. On April 24, 1872, the *Las Cruces Borderer* reported that "the alligator in Coleman's mill broke his jaw the other day from over feeding, but the repairs have been made, and the old animal will be devouring rock again by Monday."[92]

The quality of the silver coming from the Two Ikes changed as they went deeper, but their biggest headache was a mill that never worked properly. According to an August 7, 1872, *Las Cruces Borderer* article, they needed more equipment because things were backing up during the final stage of the refining process. It was critical enough for George Coleman, Frederick Ranney, and G.J. Truesdell to travel to Denver to buy two additional amalgamators. More likely than not, George returned ahead of the others since he wasn't listed in the following article.

This turned into a three-month trip, as evidenced by a *Las Cruces Borderer*: "Messrs. Ranney, VanWagenen, and Truesdell passed through town on Thursday for Silver City. These gentlemen are connected with the Wisconsin Silver Mining Company and we are glad to welcome them."[93]

On December 7, 1872, the *Las Cruces Borderer* gave the following assessment of the Two Ikes; "this mine has been worked to a sufficient depth to give a faint idea of its magnitude. The peculiar feature of this mine is that silver is found compressed between the layers of slate rock, and take the form of what is known as 'horn silver'" that resembled the color of a cows horns.

"The Holland Company's mill is in running order and certainly one of the finest specimens of mechanical construction on the frontier... Mr. Thomas Lyons has shown great skill in erecting and adjusting the machinery.

"The mill of the Wisconsin Mining Company is still working ore from the Two Ikes mine and getting large profits. Bremen's mill is working ore from Lone Mountain from the celebrated claim recently purchased from William Chamberlain.

"Rynerson's mill is working ore from the New Dexter and turning out enormous yields. The mines are generally jubilant over the future prospects of the country. The Pope Mill will also soon be here—the building is nearly ready to receive it. When spring opens, Silver City will be prepared to assure her claims to superiority as the champion mining town of the frontier.

"Professor (James) Fish arrived last week; he represents the Chicago Mining Company and is so highly pleased with the future outcome of the country he intends making it his home. He intends making preparations for a speedy erection of a smelting works. Furthermore, he says if the country will warrant it, which he says in his opinion it will, he can bring out $5,000,000 ($168 million today) and invest it in mines."[94]

On December 25, 1872, the mining camp gathered to celebrate Christmas, "somewhat boisterously." It had been an incredibly tough year where on many occasions the community pulled together just to survive. Everyone attending relaxed, and forgot about their cares.

"The effects of Mr. Abraham's free eggnog were plainly visible an hour after the incipient draughts was poured. In the afternoon an impromptu horse race was gotten up between the horses of Judge Hudson, Mr. Cohen, and Frank Wilburn. Judge Hudson won. The day was beautiful and the citizens generally in the best of spirits. After dark a dance took place at Mr. Flormans, which was largely attended and passed off very pleasantly."[95]

The Wisconsin Mill

Getting the silver-re out of the Two Ikes wasn't complicated. A stick of dynamite kept four men below ground busy hoisting buckets of rocks to the ground level with a rope tied to a horse, which pulled heavy buckets to the top of the mine shaft.

Mexican teamsters from "Little Mexico" on Chihuahua Hill overlooking the town appeared at the mines each day with a wagon and helpers, and were paid a daily rate to keep the silver ore moving between the Two Ikes and the Wisconsin Mill. During daylight hours, the trail between the mines and the mills on Spring Street were crowded with dozens of wagons loaded with rocks for processing.

"The Two Ikes in Silver City is down 70 feet with a drift [horizontal tunnel along a vein of silver] of 30 feet or more, and the ore keeps increasing in richness. It has since been tested and found to be a superior article. This mine is a Pandoras Box...some rocks contained beautiful virgin silver, and a large piece of slate that was entirely frosted with genuine metal resembling a snow flake."[96]

Four months later, they were working 160 feet below ground level, and the deeper they went the richer the ores. Despite purchasing the latest equipment, the Wisconsin Mill was never able to keep up with the output from their mine. They just couldn't process it fast enough.

Sometimes the blasting deep in the tunnels released underground gases and flooding, and occasionally reptiles found their way into the shafts. The workers were lowered into the tunnels by a winch, and one morning after blasting rock a couple of men were lowered 70 feet to load rocks into buckets until they started screaming, "For god's sake pull us up!"

The men up above reacted quickly, thinking the miners encountered suffocating gases. When the men reached the top, they appeared shaken and were perspiring profusely. When they caught their breath, they told the others there were a bunch of angry rattlesnakes hissing and rattling at the bottom of the shaft.

Someone was lowered to within thirty feet of the snake pit with a stick of dynamite and a long fuse, which he dropped to the bottom of the shaft. After the explosion, 27 dead snakes were found on the floor of the shaft. Evidently the first blast of the day fractured a crevice that led to an underground cavern of snakes. During the next few weeks, the men were extremely careful when blasting.[97]

During the summer of 1873, forty-year-old Henry Lesinsky lowered himself into the Two Ikes to inspect the quality of the silver ore. After working in mines in Australia and California, he was considered a local expert.

"Mr. Lesinsky informs us he was down in the Two Ikes mine to a depth of 150 feet, and at that depth lays an immense body of the richest ore found in this mine. The owners are sacking it up for shipment rather than work it in their mill with the facilities they have for extracting metal."[98]

The only reason Lesinsky would have inspected the Two Ikes was in contemplation of a loan. If he felt the mine had potential, he was prepared to turn over a significant amount of funds in the way of bank drafts indemnified by him. A month after he inspected the mine the news at the Two Ikes was good.

On July 12, 1873, the *Las Vegas Gazette* reported "another very rich deposit of ore has been struck in the Two Ikes mine in Silver City, and it will average a thousand dollars to the ton. 'Go at it while you're young we say.'"[99]

As they went deeper, the quality continued to improve as evidenced by a September 12, 1873, paragraph in the *Santa Fe Daily New Mexican*. "The Two Ikes shows six immense deposits of smelting ore of the richest quality at a depth of one hundred and sixty feet. The deposit is about thirty feet thick."[100]

"At these depths plates of pure silver are found and estimated by measurement, a half a million tons of ore which averages from $60 to $90 ($2,200 today), and with the ease of which the silver is extracted it is easy to see the 'good thing' the owners possess.

"The mine is owned by the 'Wisconsin Mining Company' of which Mr. Frederick Ranney is the gentlemanly manager. Their mill is run extensively on the silver ore from the Two Ikes, and we are informed that they intend putting in new and improved machinery to greatly increase their capacity."[101]

Things ran smoothly until they hit pockets of pure silver so thin, they rolled it like cigarette paper. "The Wisconsin Mill is still working slate from their mine that runs about $40 ($1,600 today) per ton. This is only a third of the silver in the rock according to the assay."[102] The slate was grayish with a layer of "miners talc" that was slippery, decomposed, slate, iron-stained to a reddish yellow that varied in thickness from a few inches to three or four feet.

Only the purest grades of silver ore were processed due to inexperience. During the last stage of the refining process when the silver was extracted from the mercury, there was a large tonnage of waste (tailings) from the amalgamators that unbeknownst to workers still had 20 to 35 ounces of silver per ton. Every mill in town considered them worthless, but discovered when they ran these tailings through their equipment a second time, they were able to extract enough silver to generate a profit.

A constant problem at every mine was theft, because some of the men earned more stealing than working. American workers made about $3.50 ($108 today) a day but Mexicans were only paid $1.50 to $2.00 ($69 today) for the same work, a wonderful incentive to steal. Inspecting lunch pails had a temporary affect. When the men inside the mill spotted a chunk of nearly pure silver sliding down the chute from the crusher, they smuggled it out of the building in a hollow heel of their boot or stuck in their hair. A chunk of pure silver might have been worth as much as $20 ($640 today), and stealing paid better than working for starvation wages.

The mines depended on Mexican muleteers to drive wagons loaded with ore a few miles away to the mills for processing. Somehow the richest pieces accidentally fell from their wagon along the side of the trail, which they discretely retrieved and sold to one of makeshift Mexican smelters that didn't care where it came from.

The Wisconsin Mill was a barn with a large double-door in the back where a pile of silver ore had been dumped from the Two Ikes. The back end of the mill was higher than the front, and gravity moved a large tonnage of heavy rocks through the mill. A man outside shoveled rocks onto a slide that brought them to the Dodge Crusher, with another man shoveling them into the machine so it could turn big rocks into little ones. After they were broken into smaller chunks of rock, they were slid down another chute to the Bolthoff pulverizer, where they were crushed into smaller particles.

The Bolthoff pulverizer replaced heavy stamps, and supposedly had the capacity of an 18-stamp mill.[103] It stood 15 feet tall and five feet wide where "the hardest rock is reduced to a coarse powder which passes into the hopper of a cylinder.... upon which large iron balls grind ore with a tumbling motion."[104]

Other mills used ten-stamp mills that had been around since the California gold rush, where ten 800-pound pestles, five at a time, crushed rocks. The machinery was supported by heavy timbers, and if the stamps weren't properly balanced, the vibrations from 8,000 pounds destroyed the frame in less than twenty minutes. The Wisconsin Mill had a 20-horsepower steam engine that could process two tons of rocks every twenty-four hours.[105]

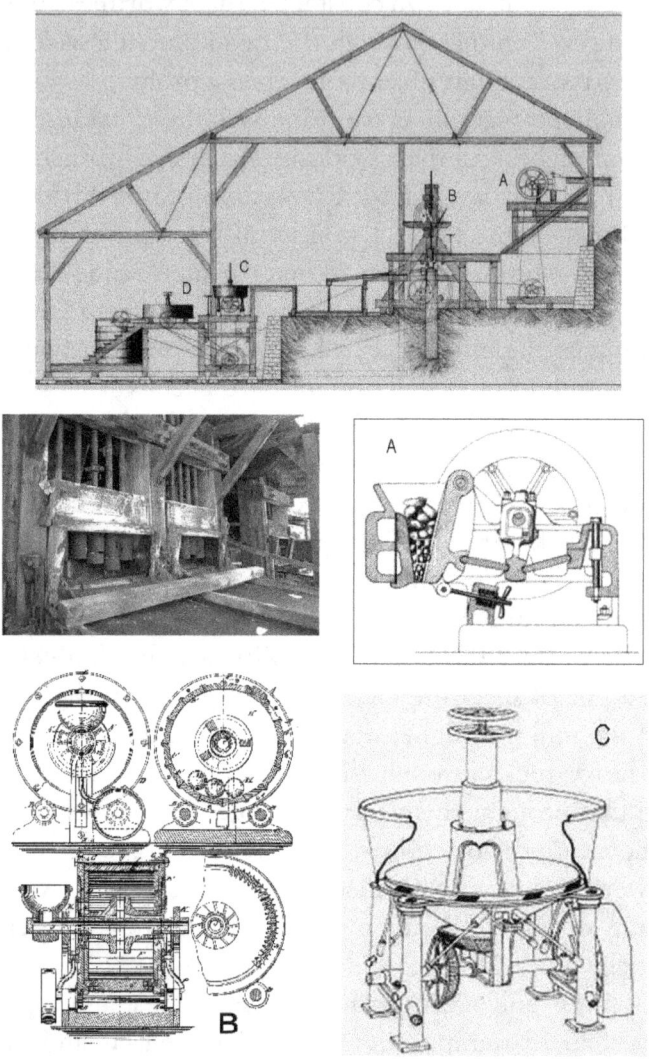

Diagram of the interior of the Wisconsin Mill (L) and an old ten stamp mill (R). Dodge crusher (A), 15-foot Bolthoff pulverizer (B), and Varney pan amalgamator (C).

Pulverized rocks from the Bolthoff Pulverizer were slid down an incline to the Hepburn & Peterson or Varney pans, which were industrial mixers that mixed a half ton of sludge every three hours. Two amalgamators weren't enough to keep up with the output from the Two Ikes. A few months later, they took delivery of another Varney Pan (similar to the Hepburn & Peterson patent) which thoroughly mixed the silver ore pulp with revolving blades that were powered by a belt running to the steam engine.

An employee with a fondness for naps escaped a gruesome death when he crawled into a Varney pan for a snooze; with its high walls nobody could see him napping until he got the surprise of his life when it was fired-up, and the blades began to slowly rotate. When the others heard him yelling, they turned the machine off but by then the blades had ripped off most of his clothing.[106]

Despite the deficiencies of the Wisconsin Mill, Sam Greene continued to pull out a large tonnage of raw silver ore from two main shafts, sending what they couldn't process to other mills with excess capacity.

On July 17, 1873, the *San Diego Union* reported, "the Two Ikes is down 150 feet and at this depth lays an immense body of the richest ore yet found which seems inexhaustible in quality and richness. In fact, the owners are sacking it up for shipment rather than working it in their own mill."[107]

About a week later, *Mining Life* reported that "another rich deposit of ore has been struck at the Two Ikes at Silver City, and it will average a thousand dollars to the ton."[108] ($300,000 today.) By the end of 1873 the future looked promising for the Wisconsin Mining Company but as they tunneled deeper, they transitioned to a more expensive type of mining.

Wisconsin Mining Company Plagued by Problems

The mining business made a lot of men fabulously wealthy but it required a *lot* of operating capital, and the Wisconsin Mining Company's principal stockholder, Gideon Truesdell, was broke. He lacked the funds to make improvements when needed, and the Wisconsin Mill was never able to keep up with the output from the Two Ikes, which had become an enormous moneymaker as evidenced by an 1873 article in the *Las Vegas Gazette*.

"The Two Ikes is now being worked at a depth of 160 feet from the surface, and the ore is constantly growing richer. This lead is curious in many respects, different from the others that I have examined. The silver is in various forms distributed through the slate rock in which it exists. Sometimes it is pure metallic flakes, thin and bright like silver paper; at other parts of the mine in chloride form and in still another peculiar form known as horn silver. This latter seems to be the one that will ultimately prevail in the whole lead below its present depth."[109]

Gideon's financial problems turned a mining company with a bright future into a struggling business that was constantly strapped for cash. Another $20,000 ($620,000 today) would have corrected all of their problems, and before the Chicago Fire, Gideon could easily have sent that and plenty more without straining his bank accounts, but the fire changed everything.

The Wisconsin Mining Company's biggest problem was a mill that couldn't process half of what came out of the Two Ikes. The physical layout, and a major bottleneck at the amalgamators and settlers appears to have been their biggest problem, but what they really needed was a roasting furnace that cooked the rocks before refining. This was something other mills in town didn't know but soon realized was a critical part of the refining process in Southwestern New Mexico.

Roasting had been developed in Nevada, where "cooking" the rocks removed the moisture from the silver ore. A drier rock moved much easier through the pulverizers, and a thoroughly dry chunk of silver ore crumbled apart. The Wisconsin Mill could see the benefits of cooking their silver ore before processing, and in 1873, Sam Greene built a cheaper adobe version of the furnace used by the Tennessee Mill down the street. It was much cheaper but substantial enough to begin cooking their ores.

Mining Life reported that the "WISCONSIN MILL AND FURNACE has this week treated tailings with results not equal to the last report, but still far ahead of working expenses. The furnace, owing to a corner in charcoal, has only treated 1,600 pounds of second-class Two Ikes ore, from which 92 ounces of refined silver was obtained. Mr. Greene is going to employ men to cut wood and burn charcoal, so he will not be at the mercy of those who heretofore monopolized that business."[110]

The *Las Vegas Gazette* reported, "The furnace has been in operation for about forty hours, and treated nearly two tons of ore from the Two Ikes. It is expected to yield considerably more than $800 ($24,000 today) per ton."[111]

Later that year, their luck changed when they ran into a vein of second-class ore valued at $10 to $25 per ton ($690 today), which after processing didn't even cover their expenses. Despite adding more amalgamators, the machinery at their mill was so inadequate they could only treat about 12 tons a week, and in less than a year they went from steady profits to barely breaking even. To generate badly needed operating funds, Sam Greene sent 100 tons of high-grade silver ore across the road to the Cibola and Tennessee mills for processing. They would have kept about half of the market price for processing, and Greene used the remainder to catch up past-due bills. It was an inefficient way to run a mining company, and by the end of 1873, they were on an exhausting treadmill where they never got ahead of their expenses.

A *Silver City Tribune* article tells us why the Wisconsin Mining Company weren't making any money despite owning one of the richest mines in the Southwest.

"The Two Ikes is the best developed of all the mines in this mining district: it has a perpendicular shaft sixty feet deep, passing through a slate formation twenty feet in thickness—width unknown. The slate pays from forty to eleven hundred dollars per ton. Following this slate formation for a short distance they struck galena that assays from $250 to $10,000 per ton. ($8,000 to $34,000 today.) Two hands have taken out of this mine in one night seven tons of rich ore. There could be extracted from this mine alone one hundred tons of ore *per day*. This mine is owned by the Wisconsin Mining Company, but owing to the defectiveness of their machinery at their mill the ore from this mine is rendered almost worthless to the company. It furnishes a poor living and no profits."[112]

About a year later Sam Greene learned a lot, especially from the Tennessee Mill, and Tom Lyons who was a partner. It became apparent that the machinery George Coleman installed was inadequate, and by the time Gideon figured this out he no longer had the money to correct these costly mistakes. At some point Coleman left, and Sam Greene took charge of the steam mill and the Two Ikes. Things slowly improved when he began making long over-due changes.

With salaries much less profits non-existent, the officers of the Wisconsin Mining Company began to leave the firm. At the end of 1873 Frederick Ranney left, and returned home to his family in Kenosha. He probably never intended to stay away for more than a year, but saw this as a chance to make some quick money until he realized it simply wasn't going to happen.

Garrett VanWagenen left but stayed in town, where he opened a store with the backing of the Bennetts, styled Bennett, VanWagenen & Company. The Derbyshire brothers were marginally involved in the mining company, but opened a variety store and news stand, and Sidney Derbyshire already owned an interest in the "Old Store," a large mercantile store in nearby Pinos Altos.[113]

At this point in time the future of the mining company rested on Sam Greenes shoulders, but help was on the way with a badly needed $10,000 ($300,000 today) cash infusion. Gideon and George Derbyshire were about to travel to Silver City to see if things could be turned around, no doubt realizing that there wasn't much time left before the company would fail.

The mill ran until the end of 1873 when Greene shut it down so he could increase capacity. According to *Mining Life* he was waiting for additional equipment to arrive, but 60 days after they closed the mill the Wisconsin Mining Company ran out of money. The Derbyshires sent a message to their father, Sidney, to send money, and he pulled together $1,000 ($40,000 today) but instructed his sons to file liens against some of their undeveloped mining claims.[114]

A crew of mechanics came from Denver to install the new machinery, but poor weather slowed them down. According to *Mining Life*, at the start of 1874 Greene added two more Varney pans and raised them 16 inches to improve the flow through the milling process. The building was enlarged and he moved the steam engine 40 feet to create more floor space. The shaft from the engine that powered a series of belts to six Varney pans were extended, a second settler was installed, and a second water tank was added so they could double their refining capacity.[115]

The mill was closed for ninety days, but the changes boosted production from 12 to 30 tons a week. Within two weeks, Sam Greene was turning out some of the richest silver ever produced by the Wisconsin Mining Company.

On March 21, 1874, *Mining Life* reported that Greene installed another Dodge Crusher, which doubled their pulverizing capacity and sped-up the first step of the refining process. Still, over 100 tons of silver ore were piled behind their mill awaiting processing, which was a magnate for thieves who would load wagons late at night, and sell it to one of the Mexican smelters. The Two Ikes continued sending some of their silver ore to the nearby Tennessee Mill and Martin Bremen's Cibola Smelting & Refining Company.[116]

The Confidence Mill in Graham, New Mexico.
Picture courtesy of the Silver City Museum.

By April 1874, Sam Greene was running two shifts but even then, they were only able to process half of the silver, because by then they had over 200 tons of ore piled at their mill, roughly a months backlog, and a magnate for thieves.

Main Street curled southward into the Cienega, where the chimneys of several smelting furnaces poured an acrid smoke into the sky twenty-four hours a day. The smoke canopied the lower half of the town. One observant mill owner noticed that the Mexican smelters only operated when the American mills ran, which suggested that their silver ore came from men working in their mills.

Once the ore was processed and turned into 30-pound silver bars, each mill had to figure a way to get it to the Denver or San Francisco mint. In 1873 the mills in Grant County shipped about $156,000 of silver, and the following year over $500,000 ($24 million today) as more mills were built.[117] This was an accomplishment, considering the nearest railroad was 750 miles away through deadly Apache country and desolate, lonely trails. This brought nearly every highway robber to the vicinity of Silver City where the pickings were good.

After numerous highway robberies, the mills started casting silver in 300-pound blocks, which barely slowed down the thieves, because they just brought along more pick axes and pack mules. The safest way to ship was surreptitiously. C.P. Crawford wrapped bars in blankets, and loaded them into a freight wagon with a false bottom covered with merchandise. Some mills began using Wells Fargo because they were bonded with heavily armed drivers, but robberies still occurred.

"The Wells, Fargo & Company stage coach lost $7,000 to $8,000 ($200,000 today) of silver after the armed robbery of the Colfax & Grass Valley stage last month. The robbers, four in number, stopped the stage, unhitched the horses, ordered the passengers out and blew open the safe. None of the passengers were molested."[118]

In addition to their own ores, the five mills in Silver City processed a large tonnage from outlying mines 40 to 60 miles away. Eighteen mule team freighters loaded with silver ore came down through the mountains from the Mogollon Mountains. Fifteen miles a day was the most a freighter could cover in good weather before the animals had to be watered, fed, and rested. If one pulled into town after bad weather, there was a good chance they had been on the road for ten straight days in driving rain and wind. A wagon train of goods for Knox & Miller arrived at Fort Bayard after having been on the trail for 105 days with ten oxen dying along the way.[119]

Gideon and Julia Truesdell Arrive in Silver City

By January 1874, the Wisconsin Mining Company was in dire straits, because they had just "lost the lead," which meant they had to relocate this profitable vein. But they couldn't seem to catch a break when their mill was damaged by high winds and torrential rains, leaving a mountain of silver ore water-logged behind the mill.

Gideon realized he needed to travel to New Mexico to see first-hand what their problems were. Once there, he would take control of the last significant asset he managed to pry loose from the bankruptcy court, and he had *everything* riding on its success or failure.

On January 27, 1874, Gideon's nephew, Arthur Truesdell, reluctantly became his Assignee of Assets, and assumed responsibility for a long and complicated bankruptcy. The following week Gideon and his wife and their close friend, George Derbyshire, began a grueling three-month trip from their Pleasant Prairie farms to Silver City.[120] George would never see his farm again. Gideon and Julia were friends of George and Eliza Derbyshire.[121] Their daughter, Charlotte, had recently married Julia's cousin, Herbert Torrey (1851–1931).[122]

They boarded a Union Pacific train in Chicago bound for Kit Carson, Colorado, staying at hotels along the route, before boarding the first of many stagecoaches for the 653-mile journey through Colorado and New Mexico. These stagecoaches were expensive and uncomfortable when traveling up steep grades, across bumpy and dusty trails or through driving rain storms where a certain amount of rain blew through the canvas side curtains.

Traveling by stagecoach was an endurance contest due to the poor condition of the trails, boredom, and passengers who liked to argue. Each stagecoach had a sign warning people not to discuss politics, religion, stagecoach robberies or Indian attacks. If ladies were present, the men were asked to refrain from drinking liquor, smoking cigars, or using profanity.

The trails had long sections that were washed and deeply rutted, and made worse by young and inexperienced drivers who drove too fast. Some people brought along a deck of cards, checker board, chess set or something to read as the coach bounced across hundreds of miles of dusty trails, because they had a *lot* of time to kill before reaching their final destination. After they arrived it seemed like they had been on the road for ten years.

In areas where they were likely to be attacked by Indians or robbers, stagecoaches had three men riding above. The driver sat in the middle steering the rig, with the others riding on either side with shotguns ready to protect the coach from Indians or highway robbers. If the coach hit a rut at the right speed, it sent passengers into the laps of the people seated across from them.

From *This is Silver City, Reprints from the Silver City Enterprise* (page 21):

> If a wagon was ambushed, they only had seconds to escape, and the first thing the Indians did was kill the horses so the passengers had no way of escaping. At Apache Pass, a stagecoach was descending a steep trail when shots rang out from the underbrush, hitting the driver and killing both mules. Passengers created a diversion by opening fire so the driver could cut the dead animals from their harness, and let the coach roll downhill to safety.
>
> Due to a limited number of shallow passes, there were only a few trails running through the mountains. Near the crest at Lancaster Hill there was a narrow pass that two teams could barely fit through, making it a perfect location for an ambush. Compounding the danger was a long descending trail that made a sharp forty-five degree turn through the mountain pass.
>
> Tucked away at the bottom of the hill was the Lancaster stage stop. A young driver in his early twenties, Henry Daly, was attacked just as he neared the summit when the Apaches jumped from a rock formation, and opened fire. The Indians tried to grab the horses bridle, but Daly thought fast and cracked the whip, sending the team charging at a full gallop.

"The air was soon filled with hundreds of arrows flying at him. As we thundered toward the turn, I believed my last moment had come, and I may say that is the only time I have ever had that feeling." When an Apache jumped from a ledge he managed to land on the back of the mules, and while reaching for the bridle of the lead animal was severely injured by quick-thinking young driver.

"I snapped the bullwhip at the Apaches face, sending him to the ground with a deep gash. The next thing I knew the mules were careening around the turn, the wheels left the ground, and the whole coach seemed to swing over space. I could see the harness tighten and strain. Then we hit, on two wheels, careening so that I had to grasp the seat. It required some seconds for me to realize that we were actually on the road, and to this day I don't know how we got there." When the coach pulled into the stage stop, two passengers were wounded, and Daly had two arrows in his back. The coach and mules were so full of arrows that they resembled a pin cushion.

Traveling along worn-out dirt trails all but guaranteed that the horses would kick dust and alkali through the cracks in the floorboards, leaving the inside of the coach stuffy and during high temperatures, suffocating, If it was 90 degrees outside it was hotter inside, and the only saving grace was the cloth side-curtains on the windows that rolled up and permitted a cross-breeze. Men traveled in shirtsleeves and women in a cool, summer dress but it was still uncomfortably hot inside the coach. Since Gideon and Julia were traveling during the spring, the heat probably wasn't that bad.

It wasn't unusual for men to climb on top of the coach for short trips, which added a lot of extra revenue, and a horse could pull 240 pounds but when teamed with another they could pull 720 pounds. Picture courtesy of Stagecoaches & Stage Lines.

When a train ran into the back of another or hit a bad stretch of tracks the damages were extensive. Picture courtesy of the Library of Congress.

Most stagecoaches limited four long-distance passengers to a coach, but there weren't any restrictions for short-distance passengers. In the interests of profits, the stagecoach picked up and dropped off people along the way with young men riding on top of the coach. If you saw youngsters climbing aboard you were in for a rough trip, because they tended to cry and vomit. But lack of sleep was undoubtedly the biggest complaint despite the fact that stage lines advertised a folding seat for sleeping.

It was up to the passengers to pack their meals each day before the coach pulled out of the stage stop, which usually consisted of crackers, beef jerky, and fresh water. Some stage stops sold sandwiches that were outrageously priced, along with an apple or pear, and filled a passenger's jug with cider or coffee. As a general rule, the further away from civilization the worse the stage stop, many of which were dilapidated and filthy because the owner didn't have any competition.

We know that Gideon and Julia and George Derbyshire covered 377 miles in about sixteen days from Denver to Santa Fe. Two years earlier, when G.J. and Louisa made the same trip, it was in a covered wagon and at night for safety reasons. By the time his parents traveled to Silver City the mining boom was in full swing, trails were in better shape, safer, and there were dozens of stagecoach lines running from Kit Carson to Santa Fe and El Paso.

Santa Fe had become a major terminus that saw lots of important people passing through on their way to mining country in Grant County. The *Santa Fe Daily New Mexican* wrote that "Messrs. Truesdell and Derbyshire left on the coach this morning for Silver City. Both of these gentlemen are largely interested in mining operations down in Grant

County, and we should like to see more of the same capitalists coming to our country and making investments."[123]

Santa Fe, New Mexico. Pictures courtesy of New Mexico State University.

A week later their stagecoach arrived in Silver City, where Gideon and Julia would have been warmly greeted by their son and grandchildren, and stayed with them for the next year at the Wisconsin House. This was a primitive ten-room hotel that had been built for the employees. George Derbyshires nephews, Sidney and Matthew, were living at a house next to the mill, and this is probably where George stayed.

A *Santa Fe Daily New Mexican* article described Silver City as a comparatively unknown mining district, "yet, we believe it stands unrivaled in the extent, variety and value of its mines, which contain in great abundance nearly all the valuable metals from gold and silver down to lead and iron. The climate is unsurpassed in any country; it is far enough south to be free of the cold and snows that interfere with operations in winter with our northern mines. Its clear mountain air and low humidity create four gentle seasons. It is high enough in the mountains to be free from the sultry heat of the valleys, and from malaria and diseases that prevail in the low lands of this latitude. A government officer says 'a more delightful, healthful, and cheer-inspiring climate is not to be found under the sun.'"[124]

As a businessman with decades of experience, Gideon no doubt came to the mining camp with a back-up plan. His nephew had a 120-acre dairy farm waiting for him back in Pleasant Prairie, but once Gideon got a chance to look around, he must have realized if the Wisconsin Mining Company failed, there were other ways to recoup his losses. The family had already been moving in that direction, because two years earlier Gideon had sent his son to New Mexico to start a cattle ranch.

"The progress of Grant County has been rapid; mining camps are springing up in every direction and the population is gradually increasing. The town is beautifully situated in a charming little valley, flanked on both sides by rolling hills filled with precious metals and covered with timber and grass. Some of the buildings in Silver City will compare favorably with those of large towns in the East.

"Brick is extensively manufactured, and used almost exclusively for building purposes in the future. The advantage which Grant County possesses over other mining country is its superb climate. No extremes of heat and cold are known throughout the year."[125]

The southwestern corner of New Mexico was starting to attract big money from capitalists with resources. The New Mexico Mining Company had $500,000 ($24 million today) to invest, and sent Professor Fish to scout the area. One of his discoveries was an enormous bed of white marble, and dozens of other rocks and minerals. "Indications of stone coal have been discovered, and the research is to be prosecuted with vigor until this additional treasure shall be brought to light. Nature seems to have provided for every necessity. This country has scarcely been prospected as yet, and no correct idea can be formed of the nature or extent of the mineral deposits here existing."[126]

Within a week of his arrival, Gideon had made up his mind to stay in Silver City, and sent word to his nephew to sell the small farm that had been exempted from his estate. He instructed him to use the proceeds to pay creditors.[127] The town was on the verge of becoming a mercantile metropolis for mining camps within a 200-mile radius, and Gideon probably saw opportunities in every direction.

Its tree-lined streets gave Silver City the appearance of a New England village that had been picked up and dropped into the fertile valley. After traveling across hundreds of miles of desert through mountain ranges, people were utterly shocked when they rolled into town. "We never dreamed of finding large brick residences and storefronts, immense smoke stacks towering over mills, reduction works and foundries, broad and regularly laid out streets in a valley nestled among the high hills which surround the place on all sides."[128]

During the next five years, the population of Grant County soared to over 10,000 with a fully developed mining boom in full swing. Despite its tree-lined streets, when Gideon and Julia arrived, this picturesque town was also known for drunken brawls, shootings and a "violent crime rate." It was actually one of the roughest towns in the old southwest.

During Gideon and Julias first summer in Silver City, there were dozens of shootings in the saloons and gambling halls a block or two west of the Wisconsin House, where three generations of Truesdells lived in primitive circumstances much different than the beautiful mansions they once occupied with servants and liverymen.

Based on correspondence, it seems as if the person who had the toughest time adjusting was G.J.s wife, Louisa, who thought Silver City was an awful place to raise eight-year-old Gideon and six-year-old Chauncey. The Apache problem was a constant threat, and when the call went out to mount a posse her husband often saddled-up. They were a few blocks east of the saloons, dance halls, and poker tables, which meant when their windows were open at night, they could hear silly, drunken simpletons shooting up the streets in a reckless way.

Apache raids were an ongoing threat, as evidenced by this letter from a local resident to Alice Hoffman. "Our Indian troubles are again commencing...last summer somebody was killed nearly every day, but no one has been murdered so far this season although a man came very near it yesterday."

"Their favorite method is to watch the road from some high bluff, and when a man comes along alone, they steal down into a bush close to the road ahead and shoot him as he comes along. They generally succeed in taking a man unawares, and never attack unless there are three of four of them to one white."[129]

In addition to problems with the Apaches, it didn't take long for the criminals, gamblers, and mining riffraff to find their way to Silver City. Three shifts of bartenders worked around the clock with gambling becoming a major pastime. Silver City was a "wide open" frontier town, and at Joe Dyers Orlean's Club the pots hit $1,000 ($40,000 today) during the early morning hours.

The days when frontiersman like Ike Givens and Ike Stevens could discover mining claims gave way to sophisticated investor syndicates. During this period of incredible growth, the low-paid workers in the mills and mines often turned to drinking and gambling. "Everywhere on the frontier, nearly all men drank nearly all the time, which made nearly all men more or less drunk most of the time."[130] For that matter, Gideon's son could drink just about anyone under the table, and get up the next morning refreshed and ready for another long day.[131]

When Gideon and Julia arrived, there were about 1,500 people living in the valley, two-thirds of whom were Mexicans who worked in the mines, drove wagons to and from the mills, and worked as extremely low-paid help. The area had been a part of Old Mexico and still had a strong Spanish influence. Not surprisingly, a "little Mexico" of adobe huts and cantinas sprang up on Chihuahua Hill. Many of the Mexican settlers came north from Chihuahua, a sovereign state on the southern side of the United States border. They played their own music, cooked Mexican dishes and consumed vast sums of homemade tequila. On Saturday nights the men gathered at the end of the road to bet on cock fights with the mauled losers tossed into a roaring fire pit.

Adding to the mix were Chinese opium dens, a large Mexican population, and the Negro soldiers stationed at Fort Bayard. After the Civil War, there were several Negro units, and some were re-assigned to the southwest. The Americans were the newcomers.

Fifteen saloons, dance halls and gambling rooms were packed around the clock with drunk and disorderly patrons. McGary & Dyer on Main Street added a ten-pin alley to their saloon with pot games and side bets adding to the fun. Their dance hall was crowded seven nights a week, and the bar receipts averaged around $100 ($3,200 today) a night.[132] It was a busy frontier town full of trouble with scruffy miners who lacked any type of moral compass. Historian and author Michael Wallis "noticed that the homicide rate in the New Mexico Territory was 47 times higher than the national average, with gunshot wounds the leading cause of death. Grant County was responsible for 15% of all murders in the nation."[133] The Truesdells were starting over in a very rough town.

During a mid-day scuffle behind McGary's Saloon a drunk refused to give the sheriff his gun, which accidently discharged and struck a bystander.[134] Down the street Billy Wilson pulled a knife and slashed saloon owner Joe Dyers face.[135] Innkeeper Peter Ott dodged a bullet during a robbery attempt at the Keystone Hotel and shot his attacker dead.[136] Merchant David Abraham shot and killed a burglar in his home; when a drunk walked into his store with a gun drawn he emptied both barrels into his gut.[137] The driver of several wagons loaded with provisions for John Morrells store was attacked just outside of town, his lifeless body unceremoniously dumped along the trail.[138] His horses were killed, and the contents of the wagons were scattered along the trail in an ugly display of the Apaches hatred for the white man.[139]

The saloons attracted a lively mix, and Alice Ivers or "Poker Alice" was at the top of the list. She emigrated from England, buried a husband who was killed in a mining accident, and was legendary on the poker circuit. She sipped on a shot glass of whiskey, smoked cigars, was "proficiently foul-mouthed" to hold her own with the boys, and carried a revolver which was always cocked and ready.[140]

Poker Alice Ivers and the boys playing poker game in the old west.

During a late-night game one of the players got up from the table, and walked behind the man she was playing when Alice noticed he was about to stick a knife in his back. With one eye on her cards and the other on his movements, at just the right time she reached for her gun and fired a bullet into his forehead causing his knife to drop to the floor. He collapsed into a pool of blood; a couple of bartenders carried him away, and with a slight smile, Alice went back to her cards.

Quarrels were settled outside or the troublemakers were told to find somewhere else to do their drinking. "Two soiled doves had a misunderstanding on Broadway yesterday and went at each other...the claret flowed freely, hair and false teeth promiscuously scattered around when a Good Samaritan parted the belligerent damsels, who skipped out to avoid arrest."[141]

Another lady of the night pulled a gun and accidentally shot a stranger in the foot. Bessie Harper rolled a rock in a towel and went looking for Ruby Fowler whom she "knocked senseless, beating her in a shameful manner, cutting her scalp and face, clear through to the bone in several places."[142] Most of this behavior occurred a few blocks away from the Wisconsin House where there were numerous bars and dance halls doing a land office business.

The people of New Mexico were a mixture of Spaniards, Mexicans, and Indians, but Mayor James Corbin observed they were "an unhappy compound of both races, and partaking of all the bad qualities of both and only a few of the good. Of course, there are among them the Mexicans whose blood is nearly pure Castilian (Spanish) but they are few. There are some nice people among the better classes of Mexicans, courteous and hospitable, and as far as genuine politeness is concerned, I think the whole Mexican race, except for the peons, is naturally and habitually the politest race on earth."[143]

Gideon Truesdell Reorganizes The Wisconsin Mining Company, 1874

By the time Gideon arrived, the change in management had a profound affect, and the mining company was finally moving in the right direction. Sam Greene was considered one of the most competent mining engineers in the area, although much of what he did at the Wisconsin Mill was common-sense.[144] One of his closest friends was Tom Lyons, who no doubt helped him make changes to the mechanical equipment. After he changed the layout, Greene added more equipment which doubled their output and enabled them to recover more silver per ton.

At the start of 1874, it was clear that a significant infusion of money was necessary. Before leaving his farm, Gideon asked for a 50% special assessment from Wisconsin Mining Company stockholders.[145] Since father and son owned 71% of the stock, they would have had to pull together $10,000 ($383,000 today), which wouldn't have been easy because Gideon was under close scrutiny from the bankruptcy court.[146] The "old man" would have known the dangers of coming into something this big undercapitalized, and given their scale of operations he knew he would have to throw a lot of money at their problems to correct them.

The larger merchants in Silver City were also private bankers, and after a couple of highly profitable years, they had plenty of money to lend but only if the borrower had first-rate collateral. Since they were so far away from civilization, the standard interest rate on the frontier was 24% for long-term, and 72% for short term loans with solid security.

If anyone could squeeze blood out of a turnip it was Gideon, because he had decades of experience at pyramiding loans with other peoples money.[147] He borrowed $2,800 ($69,000 today) at 18% from Bennett Brothers & Company, which was actually a good interest rate, and secured by mining claims. But this low interest rate came with a catch; he had to sign five separate "suicide notes" falling due every 90 days.[148] If he missed a single payment the entire loan fell due.

He also signed a $4,000 ($96,000 today) note at 24% with merchant Henry Porter, pledging the Wisconsin Mill's machinery as collateral.[149] He even borrowed another $1,000 ($30,000 today) secured by six tanks of mercury nitrate enroute from Denver, fifty cords of firewood, and fifty tons of raw silver ore piled behind the mill site.[150]

Pledging assets enabled him to pull together another $7,800 ($250,000 today). Between a special stockholder assessment and borrowed money, Gideon raised over $20,000 ($633,000 today) in a very unstable economy. Meanwhile, Sam Greene reported that the main shaft at the Two Ikes had "pinched out" at 160 feet, and going 100 feet deeper was the only way to solve this problem.[151] The million-dollar question was whether it would be enough to turn things around before the first "suicide note" fell due.

Upon his arrival in town, Gideon would have looked to Sam Greene and Tom Lyons for answers, and both urged him to build a brick roasting oven because it would pay for itself. Roasting raw ores in Colorado had been a great success, and the Tennessee Mill had already built a furnace with gratifying results.

Soon after Gideon's arrival he placed an order for firebricks so they could begin building a furnace, which would net them roughly 20% more silver per ton, and speed up the volume of silver ore they could run through their equipment each day.

According to a July 7th, 1874 article in the *Borderer*, "Messrs. Youman and Bouden drew the fire from their kiln on Monday morning and hauling commenced on Wednesday morning, when Peter Hall put a force of masons to work laying brick, and from present appearances not many days will elapse before the furnace will be ready to commence roasting ore.

"This company has an immense amount of ore in sight at the mine that cannot be treated by raw amalgamation. This will pay in the hundreds of dollars per ton after roasting, and the yield will be controlled only by the capacity of the machinery for reduction and amalgamation."[152]

On July 25, 1874, the new furnace cooked its first batch of rocks. The *Denver Mirror* wrote that "the Wisconsin Mill's roasting furnaces were fired last week with great success. The ore from their Two Ikes mine yields a much greater amount of silver after roasting, and does not require so long for amalgamation, consequently, the capacity of the mill has been greatly increased."[153]

More good news came when the *Santa Fe New Mexican* reported, "the Wisconsin Mining Company has opened another large chamber of first-class silver ore in their Two Ikes mine. This makes about twenty of these large masses of ore in sight but not worked out."[154] Good things were happening until they "lost the lead" several weeks before the first suicide note would fall due.

Gideon knew extensions wouldn't be granted so he hired experts to sink a deeper shaft. According to the September 24, 1874, *Santa Fe Daily New Mexican*, "Truesdell has contracted to sink shaft #1 at the Two Ikes until minerals are reached. This shaft is 120 feet deep now, and it is believed that minerals will be reached within another 100 feet."

As extensions pierced through underground springs the water level in a few of the shafts began rising, which were compounded by escaping gases with a foul odor. The men working in the mine would have spent a few days hoisting hundreds of buckets of water to ground level, until the shaft was somewhat dry. Once they went deeper, they found thick shafts of silver ore. *Mining Life* reported that "the Two Ikes, at a depth of over 170 feet has developed metal. There is every indication of a large bed."[155] (A 170-foot mine shaft is the equivalent of a 12-story building. They were working deep beneath ground level.)

The silver assayed at $300 a ton, which meant that each week until the silver ran out, they could expect to ship over $10,000 ($375,000 today) of silver. During the next 52-weeks they stood to process over $500,000 ($24 million today.) But on November 19, 1874, the first suicide note fell due, and Gideon didn't have the cash. It was all over and he knew it.

Gideon began putting the mining company's affairs in order, satisfied liens, and salvaged assets to pay creditors. The company was buried beneath a complicated mess of mortgages and notes that had to be untangled.

Martin Bremen and C.P. Crawford had been waiting for this day, realizing that it was better to wait until the Wisconsin Mining Company ran out of money than to foreclose. If they had taken over the company a year earlier it would have forced them to use their own money to fix problems. By waiting, they reaped the benefits of $20,000 ($798,000 today) of repairs and upgrades. Bremen was holding the oldest note, and had already filed a mechanic's lien for the lumber they bought on credit to build their mill and boarding house two years earlier.

Bremen paid Henry Porter $4,000 ($150,000 today) for the delinquent note he was holding that was secured by the mill's machinery. C.P. Crawford knew the Two Ikes was a highly desirable property, and bought it with Martin Bremen by cancelling debts, and organized Bremen & Tidwell to run the Wisconsin Mill. They reaped the rewards of the recent discovery of several large shafts of silver ore, and began sending rocks with a very high assay value to their mill.

During the summer of 1875 the *Las Vegas Gazette* reported that "the Wisconsin Mill is running on ore from Chloride Flat (Two Ikes) and is paying BIG."[156] Three months later the same newspaper wrote "the Wisconsin Mill...is full of silver bearing ore."[157] Had Gideon been able to hang on for another 90 days he would have struck it rich, and he almost made it.

Tragically, on October 3rd, 1874, George Derbyshire died of Typhoid Fever, leaving behind a wife and children in Pleasant Prairie, Wisconsin. It's easy to see why he was such a good friend to anyone who knew him. "All who knew him can testify to his quiet and unobtrusive manners, his kind heart, his willingness to help others that needed assistance, and his steadfast integrity. He was a man that loved his home, his friends, and all enterprises that improved society and the general good. Few leave more friends and a better record. He never had an enemy, and was patient and industrious through life."[158]

It was a sad year for Gideon and Julia because just a few weeks before they left their farm for Silver City, their dear friend, Joseph Hackley, died of pneumonia. His death was a shock to the entire community, and according to a newspaper account there were over 350 mourners walking behind the hearse with three brass bands playing a funeral dirge.

"Never before was there so large an attendance at a funeral in this city, though the day was cold and unpleasant."[159] Services were held at the

Universalist Church, and although it was one of the largest in town it was "not half large enough to contain the multitude in attendance. Through energy, industry and honesty he obtained what may be considered a large fortune. He forced his way up from poverty without at any time trying to put another man down—his unpretending, cordial manner bringing him friends year by year."[160]

Gideon Truesdell Starts Over at the Age of Sixty-four

Gideon was starting over with a ten-room hotel, Truesdell's Star Hotel, which had a busy dining room, a farm twenty miles east along the Mimbres River, and some undeveloped land in Clifton, Arizona. As part of the dissolution of assets, he swapped notes secured by real estate for twelve lots along Bullard Street and the deed to the Wisconsin House.

This was a boarding house with a small first floor sitting room, dining room, kitchen, and a two-room apartment tacked onto the back where G.J. and Louisa slept with their two boys. The second floor had ten small rooms that generated a steady income because there was a shortage of rooms in town. If each border paid the standard rate advertised in Santa Fe newspapers, they would have paid around $11 a month, which would have generated $1,500 a year ($45,000 today). This would have been an easy property to run with a live-in Mexican couple working for a pittance, and yet back in impoverished Chihuahua, this would have been big money.

A greater source of income was Truesdell's Star Hotel, which G.J. acquired in November or December of 1873. It was built the previous year by Samuel Eckles, who had recently begun bankrolling prospectors, and was making a much larger income as a private banker. In October of 1873, he placed the following advertisement in the *Las Cruces Borderer*;

"Private Sale: The undersigned will offer at a private sale his property in Silver City, on the corner of Spring and Hudson streets and known as the Star Hotel, consisting of ten rooms including a large kitchen and bar room. Large corral and excellent water on the premises. The property fronts 100 feet on Hudson and 76 feet on Spring. S.H. Eckles."[161]

Throughout 1874, G.J. seems to have leased the hotel to somebody, and changed the name to Truesdell's Star Hotel. After the mining company failed, he took charge of the business, updated the interior, and turned it into an upscale property that catered to people with money. There were lots of affluent people passing through town to check on their mining investments. G.J. ordered nicer furniture, washstands, pictures, stationary, linens, glassware, china, and silverware.

Most guests arrived at the hotel by stagecoach, and across Spring Street was a livery stable where they could rent a horse, buggy, or wagons. The hotel had a dining room that served good food, and the Truesdells even had their ten-year-old boy delivering meals to merchants working late. After remodeling the property, they re-named it the Exchange Hotel.

"The Exchange Hotel has passed into the hands of G.J. Truesdell and a great change is the pleasing result. The comfort of his guests is the proprietor's greatest care. The hotel appears like a well-furnished home and this is the feeling that pervades its guests. Citizens and strangers will appreciate the attention so lavishly bestowed by G.J. and his estimable lady."[162]

They doubled the size of their livery stable across the street (see add below), bought more wagons from a Denver wholesaler, purchased additional horses, and sold hay and oats to people living in town. More likely than not, G.J. hired a Mexican couple to run the stable and clean the rooms. Many impoverished Mexicans came up from Chihuahua looking for work, and even a miserly wage was better than what they could earn back home.

Exchange Stables. Opposite Exchange Hotel, Silver City, New Mexico.

"Our stables having been remodeled and we now offer the best accommodations for stock in the Territory. Horses boarded by the day, week, or month. OUR LIVERY DEPARTMENT is now complete with double and single buggies, spring wagons and hacks for hire at reasonable rates. Careful drivers furnished when required."[163]

According to a March 13, 1875, *Grant County Herald*, "the Exchange Hotel, kept by the man in the steeple-crowned hat is full and running over. Our town is filled with newcomers and we have no buildings sufficient to accommodate them although many new ones have been put up within the last two months." The situation was so desperate that people were sleeping in the lobby at the Keystone Hotel down the street.

It's hard to say just how much the hotel made, but at full occupancy and based on advertised rates in Santa Fe, the Exchange Hotel would have grossed around $7,665 a year from rooms, $1,720 from the livery stable, and perhaps another $5,470 from the dining room. It was a real moneymaker but a lot of work for G.J. and Louisa. Based on collateral research of other frontier hotels, the Exchange Hotel probably grossed $14,000 ($300,000 today), with about half dropping to the bottom line after expenses.

The Exchange Hotel after Louis Timmer purchased the property, and the exterior adobe walls bricked. Picture courtesy of the Silver City Museum.

Another source of income came from sixty-one-year-old Julia Truesdell, who opened a millenary shop in a vacant building next to their hotel. When she arrived in town, she observed that women were wearing the same clothing they brought with them a year or two earlier. As Silver City became a major mercantile hub, the wives and daughters of business owners had money to spend, but the larger mercantile companies only carried bolts of fabric. Mrs. Truesdell ordered merchandise from a Denver or Chicago wholesaler, hired a Mexican seamstress, and was successful.

A reporter for the *Las Cruces Borderer* wrote, "we visited the millinery shop of Mrs. G. Truesdell on Hudson Street. We being the male of course cannot give the right name and uses of all the various articles of ornament on display. The stock is large and presided over by a lady of experience and rare taste."[164]

Although lumber had made Gideon wealthy, he decided that livestock and groceries held the greatest potential for a fast recovery. Throughout 1874 and 1875, the entire family were busy accumulating enough cash to get into both businesses. Gideon understood the pedigreed stock business, because according to the *Western Farmer*, he made over $8,000 ($480,000 today) a year selling blooded livestock from his Pleasant Prairie farm.

The cattle business was bound to explode as miners flooded into the southwestern corner of New Mexico, and there were already big ranchers like Dick Hudson, R.V. Newsham, Harvey Whitehill, and others that owned herds in excess of a thousand animals. With over 10,000 horses or mules at work in the mines in Grant County, there was a constant need to expand herds to meet demand. Although a horse had about a 25-to-30-year lifespan, horses were lost due to accidents or theft. Mostly theft.

The only drawback to entering the replacement stock business was that it required buying blooded stock from a Kentucky dealer, and Gideon didn't have that kind of money, at least not just then. But he was stockpiling profits from the hotel and boardinghouse, and would soon have a nest egg of at least $25,000 ($980,000 today) to launch a livestock, grocery, and provisioning business.

Truesdell Ranch, Circa 1875

This seems like a logical move since father and son understood the livestock business, and after Gideon's success out in Nevada with the Durkee brothers, he sent his son to Silver City to start a large ranch. In 1872, G.J. bought around a thousand acres overlooking Silver City, but by then his father was struggling to pay the interest on borrowed money. All he could do was breed mediocre scrub cows that had been roaming the frontier for generations. If his father wanted to get into the replacement livestock business he would need blooded stock, because ranchers weren't in the market for sickly cattle.

Men on horseback charging across the open range.

The first blooded stock in the valley arrived several months earlier from Denver, when Harvey Whitehill brought 15 Durham short-horns and a bull to Silver City. The Durham was an excellent beef cow with superior bloodlines. During the spring of 1875, Gideon sent his son with $3,000 ($84,000 today) to buy a couple hundred cows and three bulls from a Lexington, Kentucky, cattle dealer. It was his intention to breed blooded stock with native cows that produced a bigger, healthy cow with about 30% more marketable beef. G.J. and their ranch foreman, George Wood, traveled to Lexington, and drove their cattle 1,400 miles back to Silver City.

Most of the land in southeastern New Mexico wasn't suited for farming but could be used for grazing. The land was covered with blue grama grass interspersed with creeks and streams that made that part of New Mexico a gigantic feedlot. Gideon must have realized he could make a good living raising blooded stock, and he was trying to create a comfortable living that his grandsons could step into.

Most of the cows roaming the southwest were sickly, underweight cows bred from scrawny bulls. A successful rancher, much the same as a successful dairy farmer, had to know how to breed animals with pedigreed stock. After years of raising cattle, horses, and hogs, Gideon and his son knew how to expand herds while improving their bloodlines.

Given the course of events during the next five years, theres absolutely no doubt that had Gideon been a younger man, he would have organized a ranch with 40,000 or more cows much the same as he and the Durkees had done out in Nevada. By the time they arrived in Silver City, they simply didn't have the kind of money they would have needed to become cattle barons. They did, however, have enough money to go into the replacement stock business, selling breeding stock to ranchers that needed to expand their herds. They already owned 1,000 acres with water and mineral rights, and could lease another couple of thousand acres from the government at 3¢ ($1 today) an acre. A cow needed about five acres of forage land, and a rancher could lease 10,000 acres for as little as $300 ($9,000 today) a year, which made New Mexico ideal for cattle ranching, and why European capitalists invested in "the wild west."

G. Truesdell & Son, Grocery & Provisioning.

The other component to Gideon's plan was a grocery store that serviced the local trade, and shipped wagon-loads of provisions to the mining camps over 50 miles away. Most of these wildcat camps sent freighters loaded with silver ore to Silver City for processing, and returned empty. This would have made it relatively easy for Gideon to have sent grocery orders, hay, oats, and barley to mining camps.

In 1872, G.J. bought 160 acres of land for farming twenty miles east along the Mimbres River near the Santa Rita copper mines.[165] About 70 years earlier, a Chihuahua banker founded Santa Rita del Cobre, and the raw copper ore was shipped to Mexico City by pack mules. The area was peaceful until a stupid American trader named John Johnson ambushed a band of Apaches, and murdered them so he could collect the bounty paid by the Mexican government for their scalps. This infuriated the Apaches, and the Santa Rita copper mines became the primary target of Mangas Colorado, a fierce and deadly adversary. They retaliated by murdering twenty-two fur trappers, and severing the supply lines to the mines. The 40 miners who fled the area were brutally murdered before they could get away. Copper mining resumed in 1873 when Cochise signed a peace treaty, although the area was still subject to attacks from Geronimo, Victorio, and other Apaches who weren't about to forgive and forget.

From *This is Silver City, Reprints from the Silver City Enterprise* (page 19):

> Soldiers from nearby Fort Bayard killed several Apaches along the trail, and when a seven-year old Apache boy was found hiding in the bushes, he showed no emotion after seeing so many of his people murdered, because violent deaths was a part of his culture. The boy was the son of Chief Mangas, and his capture was a tactical win for the settlers. They brought him back to Silver City to live with the Eckles family, and once they went to bed, he would rake the coals from the fireplace, and sleep on the warm bricks.
>
> At some point the Eckles' turned him over to a Mrs. Webb, who made the mistake of asking him to watch her baby. When she looked out the window, she was horrified to see him holding a hammer above her child's head, ready to cave her skull like he had seen his people do so many times before to Americans. Smashing the skull of a baby was

a way of life for him. The boy had been around the Apaches for too long to change his ways, so the military returned him to his people. As an adult, he became one of the most cunning, cruel, and forward-thinking Chiefs, and his brief stay with the Americans in Silver City gave him a unique perspective into the white man's world.

The fertile soil along the Mimbres River was ideal for farming, and with the signing of the peace treaty, G. J. Truesdell bought 160 acres of fertile land. His land had an abundant supply of water, and its proximity to the copper mines guaranteed a source of income from boarding houses in nearby Georgetown, Fort Bayard, Santa Rita, and Silver City. It appears as if G.J. delegated the operation of this farm to impoverished farmers from Chihuahua who were grateful to work for very little pay. It seems likely that a convoy of wagons brought provisions sixty miles west to Silver City, although a couple of years later the Truesdells sold the farm to Matthew Derbyshire. He and his brother were looking for investments that would generate a steady return, and a farm that close to the Santa Rita copper mines would have been a solid investment.

In conjunction with his cattle ranch overlooking Silver City, Gideon was about to open a first-class grocery store. With a population of 1,500, this store would make money right from the start, because local residents had been buying their food from Mexican peddlers who drove wagons up from Chihuahua. Businessman A.H. Morehead recognized the need for a full-service grocery store that sold eggs, butter, cheese, vegetables, fruits, and meat.

Morehead was doing a booming business, and two years later Gideon decided there was room for another grocery store in town, which he built in 1875 on a lot his son bought from A.J. Hurlburt a few years earlier. Porter & Crawford had just built a larger two-story building next to their old store, and while waiting for his store to be built, Gideon rented their vacant storefront at the corner of Main and Spring behind the Exchange Hotel.

The December 15, 1875, *Grant County Herald* reported, "Gideon Truesdell has opened a green grocery establishment, corner of Spring and Main streets, where everything in the way of fruit and vegetables can be had at the cheapest rates. He also has on hand a large supply of flour."

Like most grocery stores of the day, there was a coffee grinder and scale on a long counter running along one wall. Nearly everything was bought in bulk, but sold in much smaller quantities. Coffee was an essential commodity because people didn't trust the water without boiling it first. Bins underneath the counter stored bulk coffee beans, tea, flour, sugar, crackers and the like. According to newspaper advertisements, Gideon sold salted pork, beef, sausage, and slabs of bacon that no doubt came from his farm. He also sold cigars and tobacco, crockery, pots and pans, cooking utensils and dishes. When he had beehives shipped from a farmer in Missouri, Gideon was able to sell about 120 pounds of honey each year, something that simply wasn't available anywhere else in the southwest but at his store.

The grocery store was at the intersection of Main and Broadway, where there were a few other stores, and built a single-story building on an unusually deep lot. Behind the store was a large storage room for assembling bulk orders for mining camps, and behind that a small apartment that opened onto an alley. This is where Gideon and Julia would live, and it would have been a big improvement over their room at the Wisconsin House.

Probably the biggest reason why the Truesdells sold their Mimbres River farm was that they could buy fruits, vegetables, flour, poultry, butter, cheese, cigars, and Mexican silver dollars from Mexican farmers who drove up from Chihuahua and Sonora with goods loaded on pack mules. A wagonload of American goods could be traded with an exchange rate that guaranteed Silver City merchants a nice profit.

When Gideon opened his store flour was selling for the grossly inflated price of $12 ($156 today) a barrel due to scarcity, but according to an advertisement he didn't take advantage of this shortage.[166] Gideon had always been a "low price—high volume" merchant, and a wise grocer never capitalized on shortages.

If Gideon's grocery business serviced two hundred families, he would have grossed about $26,000 ($1.2 million today) a year, and like the Mimbres River farm, replacement stock ranch, and provisioning business, his downtown grocery store would have been run by a manager with clerks and a delivery boy. It was a business he thoroughly understood after 30 years of running multiple locations, and a business he learned from Charles and Harvey Durkee.

Between raising replacement stock, provisioning, and a grocery store, Gideon had carefully built a revenue stream that would enable his family to live comfortably, and with enough surplus revenues to buy real estate. (He somehow ended up owning Clifton, Arizona, between the Morenci and Longfellow mining ranges, where he collected rents from everyone living in that town.) As Grant County's population doubled his sales would have steadily increased.

The mills were a block south clustered along Spring Street near the creek, where a small business district developed on Main Street. For about a block between Spring and Broadway there were several stores built from fireproof adobe or brick. There were five general stores, a drug store, two adobe hotels, four livery stables, and saloons with dance halls. The people running Silver City began to use manure, of which there was plenty, to patch deep pot-holes on Main Street, and cover the patch with dirt.[167] And yet, it was a fast-growing frontier town with a lot to offer, and looked like a New England town that somebody dropped in the middle of the desert.

Eastside of Main Street, Silver City circa 1878. One-story building on the far left is the Truesdell grocery store next to a vacant lot that he owned, Phillips Building, Derbyshires new store and old store, Porter's new store and their old store.

A Typical Grocery Store from That Era.

"Some of the buildings in Silver City will compare favorably with large towns in the East. Brick is extensively manufactured, and used almost exclusively for building purposes in the future. The great advantage which Grant County possesses over every other mining region is its climate. No extremes of heat and cold are known here during the year."[168]

The mining boom turned a tent city into the second largest mercantile hub in New Mexico, with Silver City merchants shipping hundreds of wagons loaded with merchandise, hardware, and provisions to the eastern half of Arizona along dangerous trails. When the Apaches were on the warpath, dead bodies and burned wagons were scattered along the trail as a reminder to the white man that they didn't belong there.

The Apaches weren't pleased to see the Americans take over that corner of the territory, but Mexican tradesmen and farmers were able to develop a lucrative trade where there had once been none. They sent $300,000 ($10 million today) of merchandise each year to Silver City merchants, and it was a volume no other town in New Mexico could match. It wasn't unusual to see wagon trains coming north from Chihuahua that had come to depend on the "American trade."

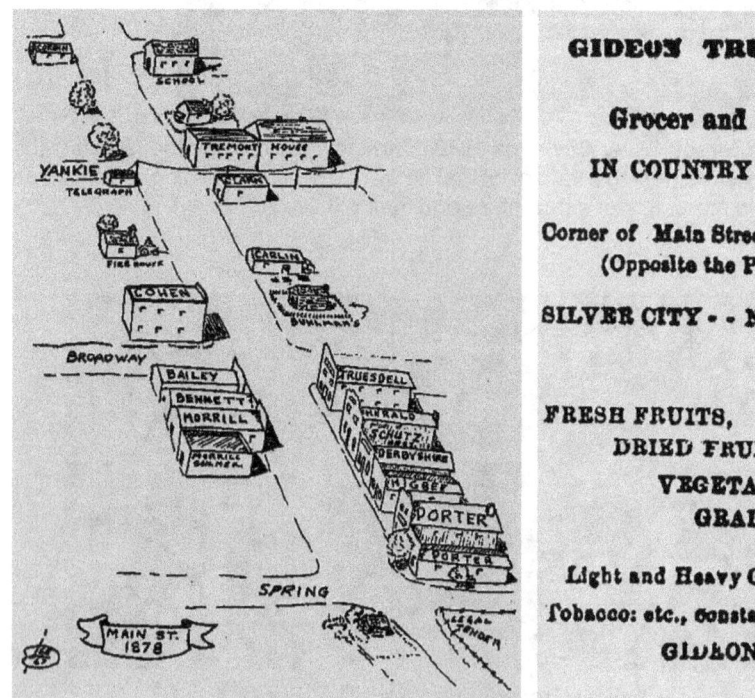

Sketch circa 1878 of Main Street courtesy of Lee Lundwall, and an advertisement courtesy of Mining Life.

There was a lot of money floating around Silver City, and merchants kept their money growing by investing in partnerships that needed funds to expand. Businessmen like the Bennetts and Lesinskys had the wherewithal to invest $10,000 in a business or mining company as minority partners. Gideon didn't have that kind of money but he understood real estate, and began buying downtown lots for back taxes. He paid as little as $40 to $60 ($1,500 today) but, when necessary, paid full price for adjacent parcels until he owned blocks or half blocks. Within a few years he owned half of a block between Bennett and Corbin Streets, a half block on the opposite side of the street and a block between Main and Pope Streets for which he paid $1,600, but later sold for $8,000 ($185,000 today).

Clifton, Arizona and The Longfellow Copper Mine

There was a commercial link between Silver City merchants and Clifton, Arizona, about a hundred miles west, with many of the same businessmen listed in both towns, including Gideon Truesdell. Prior to the Civil War, copper was discovered along the San Francisco River at Clifton, but nobody attempted to file claims because the mines were in Cochises backyard.

Parts of New Mexico fell under Confederate rule, and when Robert Metcalf was discharged from the Confederate Army, he returned home only to find his farm burned out and his wife and children gone.[169] He never did find them. After searching but never finding a trace of them and desperate for work, he turned to ranching and prospecting with his brother, Jim. They followed the cattle boom to Texas before ending up in New Mexico and Arizona.

The Apaches frequently stole horses and livestock from the settlers which caused them to retaliate. On one occasion, Joe Yankie, Jim and Bob Metcalf and others followed their tracks along the Gila River to the San Francisco River in eastern Arizona.[170] They saw clouds of smoke from the top of a mountain, and wondered if the Apaches had pinpointed their location and were signaling others their whereabouts.[171] They followed tracks for over a hundred miles until they reached the San Francisco River, where they pitched tents for the night in a grove of trees by the river.

While drinking from the creek they saw flakes of gold at the bottom of the bed, and began looking for its source in the hills above. Some of the men in the posse believed the area was loaded with minerals and Ike Stevens, an experienced prospector, went looking for promising claims to acquire at the land office. When they accidently ran across a small band of Apaches, they quickly backed away, and quietly left the area.

In the fall of 1872, Cochise signed a peace treaty and the agreement was honored. While tracking Indians that had stolen about 20 horses, the Metcalfs and others in their posse camped out at the confluence of the San Francisco River and Chase Creek. They didn't find the horses that had been stolen, but they did find two deposits of bluish-green rocks in the mountainside.[172]

He returned to Silver City with samples they chipped from the mountain, and took them to Eugene Goulding, who managed the Silver City branch of H. Lesinsky & Company. He sent them to their Las Cruces store where Henry Lesinsky gave them a thorough inspection. He hadn't seen this type of rock before but he knew they were a mineral of some kind, and whatever it was it were nearly pure. He wanted to see where it came from, so he traveled to Silver City where he picked up Goulding and a few others who were willing to risk their lives riding into Apache country.

They followed Indian trails that took them northwesterly toward the San Francisco River. Two men rode ahead of the others scanning the hillsides with a spy glass looking for ambushes, with three men riding in the middle with pack mules loaded with food and utensils, and Metcalf and Lesinsky bringing up the rear.

Pack mules in Silver City and pack mules on a trail. Pictures courtesy of the Silver City Museum and the New Mexico State University.

Metcalf refused to travel across ridges where they could be spotted by the Apaches. On the fourth day, he noticed fresh moccasin tracks, which made him even more nervous. He packed just enough food for the day and when they built a fire for cooking, he insisted they make the least amount of smoke possible.

Once their evening meal was over, they packed up, and moved deeper into the woods to a secluded spot so they could sleep in peace because the Apaches never attacked at night. Had they stayed where they built a campfire, the Indians would have pinpointed their location, and the next morning they would have been scalped at sunrise with their corpses left to rot in the mid-day sun.

On one particular morning Lesinsky wanted to keep moving but Metcalf insisted that they stay there for the entire day and travel at night. Six days later they arrived where Lesinsky found the source of the greenish blue rocks, which turned out to be copper, and it was *massive*. It was so immense they would be pulling copper out of several ranges for the next 150 years, and it was one of the largest deposits in the world.

When Lesinsky saw the deposits, he knew it was copper and there were millions of dollars of it lodged in the mountainside. What he didn't know was whether they would live long enough to get their hands on it because they were intruding on land that Cochise had always regarded as his own.

On June 21, 1873, the *Las Cruces Borderer* wrote, "About two weeks ago Henry Lesinsky and William Grant started a trip to the Francisco Mountains to examine the copper mines. They have returned and give us some information in regard to their trip. They started from Silver City with a light wagon, loaded with the necessities of the trip and drove that as far as the country would allow.

"Then after packing some burros, they road to Goulding's camp. Lesinsky, Grant, Metcalf, and Abraham then left for the mine about eight miles distant. In the foot of the mountain where the lead is situated, they found the ruins of an old furnace and house. In this they camped at night and seeing no traces of Indians left their burros, blankets, and provisions the next morning and climbed about two miles to the inspect the copper deposits.

Copper Ore, Shaft of Copper Ore, and a Vein of Turquoise which was sometimes mistaken for copper.

"After a pretty thorough examination of an immense deposit of copper nearly pure, they descended to camp with the sharpest kind of appetite for supper, but a sickening sight met their gaze. The canned meat and fruits had been cut open and their contents emptied upon the ground. Their plates had been doubled up, the blankets, knifes, and flour that had been nicely packed upon the burros had been driven off by five Apaches in the direction of Cochises camp.

"Tired, hungry, and despondent they laid under a tree and sheltered themselves from the cold mountain air...while Grant started off to Goulding's camp for rations with which he arrived next morning. The Indians had too long a start to make a successful pursuit and the party concluded to adopt Grant's peace policy and returned home minus about two hundred dollars' worth of effects.

"Goulding employs at his camp about ten Mexicans and has about ten tons of copper out. The rough nature of the area makes it necessary to pack this on burros about fifteen miles before it can be loaded into wagons. The deposits of copper are simply immense, and no description can convey an adequate idea of the extent of these mines.

"But in the present dangerous condition of the country it is almost impossible to get men to remain there. With the danger gone, thousands of men could find profitable employment at good wages, and wagon trains from this country would be loaded on their trips to the railroad with cargoes of copper."[173]

Lesinsky told Metcalf that in his opinion, the Apaches wouldn't allow anyone to get that close to the property, but was willing to roll the dice if the price were right. When Metcalf raised the subject again, Lesinsky remained skeptical until he agreed to buy a controlling interest in what became the Longfellow Mine for $10,000 ($275,000 today), but only if Metcalf matched his investment in provisions and tools. It was the beginning of an acrimonious relationship that didn't end well for Metcalf.

Lesinsky returned to his mercantile store, and offered family members an interest in the Longfellow, but warned they could just as easily make or lose a fortune.[174] Their biggest challenge would be hauling copper 700 miles to the nearest railroad depot across washed out trails through dangerous countryside prone to Apache attacks.

After several conversations it was agreed that all three would own equal shares, although it was Freudenthal that kept the mining operation alive with substantial loans. Henry Lesinsky was listed as president of the Longfellow Copper Mining Company, Charles Lesinsky, Vice President, and Julius Freudenthal, Treasurer with David Abraham, Eugene Goulding, and Cornelius and Joseph Bennett listed as stockholders.[175] The Lesinskys had a long association with the Bennetts in Bennett Brothers & Company, and Cornelius Bennett was listed as superintendent of the mine.

The copper ore was sent by mule trains 80 miles to Las Cruces, New Mexico, where the Lesinsky family owned a large mercantile business. Freight wagons hauled these unrefined rocks 600 miles from Las Cruces to Denver where it was transferred to an eastbound train to a mill in Baltimore, Maryland.

Once mines were organized, the area along Chase Creek turned into a small village because it was one of the few areas where houses could be built in this rugged canyon. There was a good water supply, and the settlement was named Clifton. It was prime real estate located between the Longfellow and Morenci mining ranges.

"As our flourishing little town of Clifton is composed principally of citizens from your town (Silver City), I am persuaded that a few lines from this section will be read with interest by your many readers. A permanent camp was established at the mouth of Chase Creek, on the Francisco River, in January last.

"Since which time, mining and smelting copper ore has been carried on successfully by the Gila Copper Mining Company. They have recently made a large shipment of copper made from ores from the Longfellow Mine...and they have the richest mines ever discovered in this country.

Clifton, Arizona. Pictures courtesy of the Arizona Historical Society.

"The Detroit Company also has a rich and extensive copper mine in this vicinity. Gold and silver are also in abundance in this district. The gold placers are paying well six miles from here, on the Francisco River, and extensive preparations are being made for taking out a ditch, which will accommodate several hundred miners."[176]

Stagecoaches and freighters began running 90 miles from Silver City to Clifton, detouring through Mule Creek where there was a shallow mountain pass a freighter could navigate. The trip through the mountains was anything but safe, and when the Apaches were on the warpath, one of their favorite ways of demonstrating their disgust toward the Americans was to savagely tie each passenger to a wagon wheel, and set the wagon on fire.

By 1874, there were six mines in operation with two Mexican furnaces turning out 1,200 to 1,500 pounds of copper *per day* that was 60% pure, although most of it was 20% pure.[177] The Longfellow spent $40,000 to open their mine and build roads to the reduction works about six miles away on the river.[178] Until their mill was completed, they used small adobe furnaces and were able to ship $35,000 ($980,000 today) of copper.[179]

Somehow, the Truesdells ended up owning land where Clifton was built along the river, and for a year or two, houses and shops built paid rent to them.[180] Theres no telling how much money Gideon's claims were worth, but limited finances caused this to be his second near-miss in the southwest. It wasn't a total loss, because he owned 18 acres of prime land adjacent to Chase Creek.[181]

In the Yavapai County courthouse there were dozens of entries as father and son sued each other. There were Truesdell vs. Truesdell lawsuits for defaulted mortgages, evictions, foreclosures, and attachments.[182] In an unsettled area without case law they were establishing precedents, and the fact that they had to do this clearly indicates that they were collecting rents and selling land.

The Longfellows existence was threatened during the first year due to a boundary dispute with the White Mountain Indian Reservation. During the summer of 1874 the matter was resolved, when the Clifton and Morenci mining ranges were restored to the public domain, but six months later, property owners were still waiting for a survey so they could file land patents.[183]

Henry Lesinsky's headaches continued when the Apaches attacked his mines and smelters, causing them to shut down until the nearest military fort sent troops. The Detroit Copper Company decided to close permanently after their food were stolen, smelters shot full of holes, and several of their men were murdered. The price tag was simply too high.

Silver City was the closest shipping hub for mines within a 200-mile radius, with freighters hauling several tons of ores for processing. At times the winding and dangerous 80-mile trail from Clifton to Silver City was closed due to marauding Apaches looking for Americans to murder. There were times when wagons leaving Clifton were never seen again, with badly decomposed bodies and a burned wagon frame found at the bottom of a canyon.[184]

The situation was so dangerous that the Longfellow had to temporarily close when thirty of their mules were stolen. Three detachments from the U.S. Army posts were sent to follow the Apaches, who were trailed to Knight's Ranch about twenty miles south of Silver City where 40 of them were killed.[185]

After 20 years of difficulties, the Lesinskys and Freudenthals sold the Longfellow to a European syndicate. Lesinsky moved to New York City a wealthy man, but admitted that he had "a native restlessness which was the true cause of my success. I felt stranded in a foreign land. The language was strange to me. I found no sympathy among my new associates. It was rush and toil, care and competition, and fraud and cheating such as I had never dreamed of. I felt like one dropped from the moon."[186]

Henry Antrim a.k.a Billy the Kid and Truesdell's Star Hotel

A few blocks north of the Exchange Hotel was a cabin on Main Street owned by Catherine Antrim (1829–1874) and her husband, William.[187] A few years earlier they had been living in Wichita, but not together.[188] Already a mother with two boys to raise, this upbeat and cheerful lady who hadn't had an easy life made a living doing laundry for hotels, brothels and affluent families. She made enough money to buy a quarter section of land in Wichita for $200 ($24,000 today), a rare occurrence for a single lady on the frontier.[189]

Catherine and William Antrim were married in Santa Fe before coming to Silver City, and he was reportedly an indifferent and distant husband with no involvement with his step-sons. It was probably New Mexico's cohabitation law that forced them to get married. Catherine came to New Mexico seeking relief from tuberculosis, but she also worried about her boys' safety in Wichita.[190]

Catherine's husband wasn't much help after they moved to Silver City, and stayed away for long periods. Chauncey Truesdell recalled that, "he worked around at different jobs...gambling mostly."[191] By contrast, Louis Abraham said, "Mr. Antrim was a man of good character and was highly respected." He recalled that Antrim wasn't much of a drinker, and didn't care for rude jokes or crude behavior.

Much the same as she had done in Wichita, after she arrived in Silver City Catherine found work doing laundry for guests at the Southern Hotel.[192] Since G.J. and Louisa Truesdell ran a hotel and boarding house it seems likely that she offered the same services for their guests, and that's how they met. Mary Hudson recalled that Catherine was a "sweet, gentle little lady, as fond of her boys as any mother could be."[193] Perhaps one of the best descriptions of Mrs. Antrim came from Ash Upson, who knew her well.

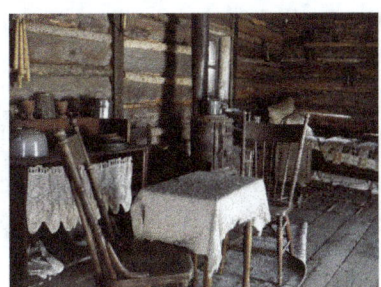

Restored Interior of the William and Catherine Antrim Cabin in Silver City.

"She was about medium height, straight and graceful in form, with regular features, light blue eyes, and luxuriant golden hair. She was not a beauty, but what the world calls a fine-looking woman. She kept boarders in Silver City, and her charity and goodness of heart was proverbial. Many a hungry tenderfoot has had cause to bless the fortune which led him to her door. In her deportment she exhibited the unmistakable characteristics of a lady; by instinct and education.

"There were very few American boys living in Silver City...therefore the few boys that were here ran together all of the time. The Antrim house was the place where the boys gathered most of the time. Mrs. Antrim always welcomed the boys with a smile and a joke. The cookie jar was never empty...each afternoon we made straight for the Antrim home to play."

Chauncey Truesdell recalled that Henry "was quiet as I remember, and never swore or tried to act bad like some of the other kids."[194] And they did act badly. After school, a group of kids played baseball, bummed around town looking for things to do, and often getting into trouble.

Silver City earned a well-deserved reputation as a rough boomtown with saloons, brothels, and gambling halls that contributed to an escalating crime rate. There were two groups that were especially antagonistic toward the other, because the Americans and Mexicans didn't get along.

During one late night foray, the Angelo boys broke into a saloon and stole cash along with a couple of buckets of whiskey, which they either drank or sold. A newspaper editor dubbed them the "Village Arabs."[195] The reporter thought they "ought to be put to work sweeping the streets by day and locked up in the new jail by night."[196]

According to Sheriff Whitehill's journal, the troublemakers were Louis and Hyman Abraham, John and Vincent Mays, Gideon and Chauncey Truesdell, Henry and Joe Antrim, Dan Rose, Charley and Albert Stevens and the sheriff's own son, Harry.[197]

Wayne Whitehill recalled that on Main Street, behind the Keystone Hotel, "there was an adobe building where a Chinaman had a laundry. People gave us orders to chase all the Chinamen out of town, they didn't want Chinaman there. And they said 'rock him' every time we (would) see a Chinaman, rock him and make him leave.

"Manuel Taylor was half Mexican and half Anglo and owned a mining claim in the Chloride Flats district. One day he got a rock and peeked around and after a while he threw it. And when we looked around to see what he'd done with that rock the Chinaman was floppin' around like a chicken with his head cut off. We knew damn well the Chinaman was killed all right. Well, there was never a thing said about it at all."[198]

Tensions with a Mexican teenager nearly cost nine-year-old Chauncey Truesdell a leg.[199] "The leg of the boy became accidently caught in the loop of the rope or lariat, which he had tied to the neck of the burro, which was young and sprightly and upon being purposely frightened by a mischievous Mexican, the burro ran up Bullard Street dragging the boy, at its utmost speed until caught by Mr. J.O. Syme of this office. We are happy to say that the boy, though still confined to bed, is rapidly convalescing."[200]

After the transcontinental railroad was completed, there were 2.5 million Chinese laborers looking for work, and they were excellent workers with many of them migrating to the southwest to work in the mines. The town's first "Chinaman" came in 1874, when twenty-four-year-old Charlie Sun moved from Albuquerque where he ran a hand laundry. When he opened his own laundry, he ran into tough competition. Nellie Johnson ran a laundry, and wasn't pleased to see him taking so much of her business. "Boys, that Chinaman can't do as well for you as I can. Bring your washing to Texas Street."[201]

According to Frederick Nolan "the residents of Silver City looked on their presence and the opium dens in 'Hop Town' with great displeasure, believing that they created problems for the town. The Chinese who patronized these opium dens would get incredibly high, and pass out or fall asleep."[202] It didn't take long for the Village Arabs to realize nobody cared about the Chinese, so rocking a Chinaman became a popular pastime.

Adding to the racial tensions was the Negro Calvary that had been stationed at nearby Fort Bayard during the Civil War. They fought valiantly, and were a rugged lot who were sent to protect the frontier.

Charlie Sun did not endear himself to the townspeople when his Mexican wife became pregnant, and gave birth to a child. He was celebrating at the saloon "and when the baby was born it was a nigger...he had an old sow out in the backyard and he took that baby and threw it in there and the sow killed it. No, there wasn't anything done about it," recalled Sheriff Whitehill's son, Wayne.[204]

Before tuberculosis confined Catherine to a bed, she and her son Henry frequently showed up at Wards for the big Saturday night dance.[205] The Antrims were good dancers and Catherine, who enjoyed being around people, could do the Highland fling. Catherine left Ireland at the age of seventeen, and came to America where she had to push her way into a prejudiced society where being Irish put her at the bottom of the social ladder. Historians are reasonably sure she settled in the slums of New York, and that it was where both of her sons were born, although probably not by the same father. Given the high mortality rate for young Irishmen he probably died at a young age, and left Catherine with a son to raise.

Most Irish girls found work as low-paid scullery maids, the lowest ranked kitchen help who wasn't even allowed to eat at the same able as the kitchen staff. They spent their days scrubbing floors, cleaning the cast iron stove and washing pots and pans.

Catherine would have arrived at the Truesdell's hotel and boarding house at the crack of dawn with bread, rolls, cakes and pies for that day's dining room trade. Tying up a wood burning cook stove in a short-order kitchen for a couple of hours of baking would have been unheard of.[206] When she walked in the back door of the kitchen, Catherine must have been a welcome sight. Both ladies were trapped in bad marriages with sons they were trying to raise in a dangerous frontier town full of temptations.

During the summer of 1874, Catherine's tuberculosis grew worse, and she began coughing up blood. Louisa Truesdell graduated from the Chicago Academy of Nursing before marrying her husband, and understood what Catherine was going through.[207] She knew the end was near, and that it would be a painful and frightening way to die so she sat by her bed every night until dawn. Chauncey recalled seeing Henry by his mother's side trying to comfort her.[208]

On September 16, 1874, Catherine died at the age of forty-five. "She said she was leaving two boys in a wild country," recalled Chauncey Truesdell, "and she made my mother promise to look out for them if anything should happen to her...Henry came to live with us and waited on tables at the Star Hotel."[209]

"Clara (Louisa) washed the body, combed her hair, and dressed the dead women in the best dress she owned. Besides Catherines sons, members of the town's leading families, the Truesdells, Stevens and Whitehills attended a simple service."[210]

Instead of staying by his dying wifes side, William Antrim left for parts unknown and couldn't be reached in time for the funeral. When he returned, he moved his things out of the cabin, and headed for Clifton, Arizona, where there was a mining boom. His last piece of business was sending eleven-year-old Joe and fifteen-year-old Henry to live with either the Hudsons or Knights.[211] Both were good families, but the arrangement didn't last long because Antrim decided to split up the boys.

Joe went to live with saloonkeeper Joe Dyer, where he cleaned the bar, burned trash, stocked liquor and served drinks for his room and board.[212] At a young age Joe was observed drinking, gambling, and smoking in one of the Chinese opium dens.[213] It was hardly the life Catherine Antrim wanted for her son.

Henry did better when he went to live with the Truesdells at the Wisconsin House. He slept in the same room as Gideon and Chauncey, and worked in their father's hotel helping in the dining room and kitchen.[214] The Truesdells treated Henry no differently than their own sons, and G.J. said Henry was the only boy who never stole anything.[215] He accurately pegged the boy as a free spirit. "He said he wasn't a bad boy but one whose nature was wild."[216]

According to Dick Clark, Henry was an easy-going teenager who was pleasant to be around and had a quick mind. "His eyes were full of fun... he was generous and kind to everyone until someone did him dirty, then he would seek revenge."[217]

Author and historian Jerry Weddle believed that the descriptions of Henry made him seem unrealistically wholesome. He "liked to dress well, and everyone noticed his neat appearance and clean habits. He was unfailingly courteous, especially to the ladies. Like his mother, he was a spirited singer and dancer. He had an alert mind and could come up with a snappy answer for every occasion. He read well and wrote better than most adults."[218]

"His rambunctious sense of humor always got a laugh, whether it was on himself of someone else. Because of his small stature he took a lot of ribbing from those bigger and stronger, but what he lacked in size he made up with tremendous energy and quick reflexes. Anxious to please, eager to impress, willing to take extraordinary risks, [Henry] would dare anything to prove his worth. The school kids soon realized that he had genuine courage."[219]

As much as Henry liked Mr. and Mrs. Truesdell, their home was a battleground due to a bad marriage with nightly arguments and yelling that lasted until the early morning hours. With G.J. unwinding in a saloon each night and probably coming home after the bars closed, there would have been plenty for them to argue about. Some of the hostilities no doubt came from Louisas unhappiness with living in Silver City, but she had a knack for stirring things up because a son recalled that she could be a difficult person.[220] After only five months of living with the Truesdells, Henry left at the ripe old age of sixteen.[221]

Antrim paid a price for his freedom because after he left the Truesdells he began stealing to survive. He knew that he was always welcome in their home, and on more than one occasion that's where he went when he was in trouble.[222] There were other families that would have gladly put a roof over his head, and he had a network of safe places to go when he needed help because he was a likeable kid. People around town were sympathetic to his being orphaned, and willing to help.

He was a bright young man who could have succeeded at a traditional occupation, although Sheriff Harvey Whitehill was convinced that he had a criminal mind, and he might have been right. Henry's first dishonest act was stealing butter from a wagon parked in front of a store on Main Street, and selling it to a local grocery store.[223]

His next larceny occurred while walking past Matt Derbyshires storefront where he saw some cheap costume jewelry on display.[224] He hatched a plan to steal it and sell it in Mexico, which was only 40 miles away. He talked sixteen-year-old Charles Stevens (1859–1930) into helping, but he had second thoughts and told his father, Ike Stevens, who marched him over to Derbyshires store to confess, and notify the sheriff.[225] Charlie told his father "He had me hypnotized."²²⁶ Sheriff Whitehill observed a few tell-tale character flaws. "He was a schemer, always trying to figure out some way of putting something over to get money."²²⁷ Like any good conman, Henry studied people and was good at spotting flaws. The sheriff also recalled "dancing eyes" that were constantly eyeballing people and taking in his surroundings.²²⁸

Broadway Street, circa 1876. Picture courtesy of the New Mexico State.

Wagons parked along Broadway Street. Picture courtesy of the Silver City Museum.

At various gambling halls Henry learned how to play Monte and poker, and noticed older men figured him for an easy mark due to his age and boyish appearance. He used this to his advantage, and often walked away with a pocket full of their money.

Henry started hanging around a loser named George Schaefer or "Sombrero Jack," because of the distinctive sombrero that he wore. Schaefer was in his twenties, a heavy drinker and a pathological liar who worshipped the ground Henry walked on. He thought Henry was the smartest man that ever lived.

Late one night George broke into a laundry, stole a pair of revolvers, blankets and clothing, rode 15 miles east to Georgetown where he hid the clothing in an old stamp pit near Crawford's Mill. He offered Henry a share of the loot if he would smuggle it back into Silver City.[229] Henry made the mistake of hiding the stolen laundry in his room at the boarding house. While cleaning his room the stolen loot was found, and Sheriff Whitehill was immediately notified.

"Henry McCarthy [McCarthy was his birth name], who was arrested on Thursday and committed to jail to await the action of a grand jury, upon the charge of stealing clothes from Charley Sun and Sam Chung, celestials, sans cues, sans Joss sticks, escaped from prison yesterday afternoon through the chimney. It is believed that Henry was simply the tool of sombrero Jack,' who done the stealing whilst Henry done the hiding. Jack has skinned out."[230]

Sheriff Whitehill was a powerfully built man with a deep voice, highly intelligent, and a lawman with a kind heart. But this teenage gang, the Village Arabs, was getting out of hand, and he knew they were spiraling out of control.

"Whitehill knew his own sons were just as bad if not worse than Antrim, but Henry was getting so wild after his mother's death that Whitehill thought that by locking him up for the night, he might get Henry to thinking and possibly do him some good."[231]

When Louisa Truesdell heard that Henry was sitting in jail, she tried to get him released into her custody. There were other townspeople, including the sheriff's wife, who insisted that jail was too harsh a punishment for the young teenager. Harriet Whitehall told her husband to bring Henry home for breakfast, and he would have because he agreed with his wife.[232] It was never his intention to lock him up and throw away the key.

The thought of serving time in jail with the dregs of society unnerved

Henry, because in those days the insane, vagrants, alcoholics, and deviants served their time there. After several hours of confinement, Henry came to the realization that this wasn't going to blow over, and if things didn't go well at the trial he might be sent to the territorial prison. He knew his case would be heard by Ike Givens, Justice of the Peace and a strict law and order man who had no use for a thief.

"One day the 'Kid' complained to me," said Sheriff Whitehill, "that the jailer was treating him roughly and kept him in solitary confinement in his cell without any exercise. So, I ordered that he be allowed to remain in the corridor for a limited time each morning. You must remember that he was only a boy, scarcely over 15 years of age. Yet he made the mistake of leaving him alone for a short half hour. When we returned and unlocked the heavy oaken doors of the jail the 'Kid' was nowhere to be seen.

"I ran outside and a Mexican standing on a ridge asked whom I was hunting. I replied in Spanish 'a prisoner.' He came out of the chimney,' answered the Mexican. I ran back into the jail, looked up the big old-fashioned chimney and sure enough could see where in an effort to obtain a hold his hands had clawed into the thick layer of soot which lined the side of the flue. The chimney hole itself did not appear as large as my arm and yet the lad squeezed his frail slender body through it and gained his liberty," recalled Whitehill.[233]

Award winning author and historian Michael Wallis thought that "Of all the people Henry might have turned to, the most plausible candidate was Clara [Louisa] Truesdell. Chances are good that after he made his escape, he went straight to the Truesdell home."[234] This was a small two-room apartment behind the Wisconsin House, and he knew he could count on her to get him out of this jam.

Seventy-five years later Chauncey recalled, "It was the kind scrape any boy might have got mixed into. Father had gone up to the Black Hills gold rush...it was not long before he rapped on our window one night. Mother washed Henry's clothes and dried them by the stove. My brother Gideon, Henry, and I slept on the floor that night. The next morning Mother stopped the stage as it passed our door and asked the driver to take Henry to Globe City, Arizona. Mother gave Henry all the money she had and a little lunch to eat."[235]

Louisa Truesdell believed things would have been different had her husband been in town, because he was friends with Sheriff Whitehill and

Ike Givens.²³⁶ The sheriff didn't exactly know what to do with Henry, and probably would have welcomed placing him in G.J.s custody. Whitehill later said "I did all I could for the orphaned boy, after all, he was somebody's son and a boy who didn't need to go wrong."²³⁷

The sheriff followed him to Ed Moulton's mill in the mountains but by then Henry was lost in the wind. Nobody knew where he was but several accounts place him in Clifton, Arizona, where his stepfather worked. At a young age he was on his own in an unfriendly land, found work at a ranch, and earned extra cash playing poker in the saloons.

Henry spent the next year or two working on ranches and at the age of eighteen he got a job driving a wagon at Fort Grant. He continued to make extra money playing cards and got along with most people except a fat, loud-mouthed slob named Windy Cahill. He liked to talk a lot so people began calling him "Windy."

He didn't like the brash teenager, possibly because Henry had an annoying way of needling people he didn't like, making fun of them until others started to laugh at him. Windy began calling him derogatory names, pinned him to the floor, and started slapping his face. "You are hurting me.... Let me up." Cahill yelled back "I want to hurt you.... That's why I got you down." Henry reached around his fat belly, grabbed his revolver, and shot him dead.

Henry continued to earn a living working on ranches at a time when range wars weren't uncommon, but the Lincoln County War was unusually deadly and propelled him into legendary fame. It began in late 1876, when a wealthy Englishman named John Tunstall came to Lincoln County, New Mexico, to start a cattle ranch with John Chisum. Together, they controlled the land along the Pecos River with over 100,000 head of cattle.

Lawrence Murphy and James Dolan controlled Lincoln County, and having the governor and attorney general in their pocket caused them to run that area as their private fiefdom. An outsider like Tunstall didn't stand much of a chance.

A violent cattle war was triggered over the disposition of an insurance policy when Tunstall's assets were attached by Sheriff Brady, who was on L.G. Murphy & Company's payroll. Dolan hired some of the most violent outlaw gangs to steal cattle from Tunstall's ranches and kill anyone who got in their way.

On February 18, 1878, a sheriff's posse caught up with Tunstall while he and ranch hands Dick Brewer, Henry Antrim, John Middleton, Henry Newton Brown, Robert Wiedemann, and Fred Waite were herding horses. Tunstall was shot and killed in front of Dick Brewer and Henry Antrim. Based on their testimony, arrest warrants were issued from Lincoln County Justice of the Peace John B. Wilson.

Antrim and two others went looking for Sheriff Brady, and when they attempted to serve him an arrest warrant, he became angry and arrested them. A U.S. Marshall who was a friend of Henry's came to their rescue with a detachment of soldiers, arrested the guards who jailed them, and freed Henry and Dick Brewer.

Aware that law and order didn't exist in Lincoln County, Tunstall's men organized a posse called the Regulators, which eventually numbered 50 or 60, and who eventually caught two of his killers, both of whom were shot and killed while trying to escape.

A few days later there had been a shootout, and on July 19, the Regulators gathered in a house in Lincoln County when a deputy set fire to the building, forcing the men trapped inside to shoot their way out. Henry and the others escaped but two Regulators were shot and killed, with Henry returning fire and killing Robert Beckworth.

Henry and three others escaped to the Mescalero Indian Agency where their bookkeeper was murdered. Henry and the others were indicted for murder despite evidence that the bookkeeper was actually shot by Constable Atanacio Martinez, but they were in a county where law and order no longer existed.

On April 1, the Regulators ambushed Sheriff Brady and his deputies. This was the beginning of the end for Henry, because they killed Brady and his deputy, George Hindman. Arrest warrants were issued for Henry and several others even though nobody could say for certain who fired the shot that killed them.

These indictments were later dropped except for Henrys, due to his role in the murder of a crooked sheriff with heavy-duty political connections. When outlaw Jesse Evans ran into attorney Huston Chapman, who were a nuisance and threat to the L.G. Murphy faction, they forced Henry to watch them murder him and set his corpse on fire.

To end the bloody and controversial Lincoln County War, Governor Lew Wallace issued a proclamation of amnesty that didn't include Henry, who wrote the Governor that he was willing to trade his testimony in the

Chapman murder for amnesty. Antrim met with the Governor, and was promised clemency and protection if he would testify in front of a grand jury.

He allowed himself to be arrested by Sheriff George Kimball, but after he testified, the district attorney had second thoughts, and Henry figured the Governor would follow his lead. As unbelievable as it sounds, on June 17, 1879, Henry walked out of the temporary jail where he was being held prisoner.

Around that time Henry discretely returned to Silver City and stopped by the Truesdell Ranch looking for his brother, only to learn their ranch house was under quarantine because fifteen-year-old Gideon had contracted smallpox.[238] Henry was told that his fourteen-year-old brother, Joe, was staying out at the Nicolai Ranch near Georgetown with twelve-year-old Chauncey Truesdell.

"I never heard any more about Henry until one morning down on Charlie Nicolais (1836–1882) ranch on the Mimbres River, where Joe and I were trying to get some milk for breakfast. We had roped a cow and tied her head to the post, tied her hind legs so she could not kick, and I had her tail while Joe milked her. We were in the act of taking about a half a tomato can of milk when three men came riding into the corral. They were right on top of us before we saw them.

"They had red bands tied around their hats. That is the way Indians had of showing they were peaceful. I can well remember how carefully Joe sat the milk can down on the floor, and came up with an old Henry rifle and was about to take a shot at the leader, who called to Joe 'hold on Joe, don't you know your own brother?' It was Henry, and he stayed and visited Joe that night, and after sending his regards to Mother, they went away by way of Bear Canyon. That was the last I saw of Henry Antrim. My mother promised Mrs. Antrim she would try to help her boys and she certainly did," recalled Chauncey Truesdell.[239]

Henry stayed out of trouble until January 10, 1880, when he shot and killed Joe Grant, possibly in self-defense, because Grant vowed to murder him. With nerves of steel, Henry walked over to the man that vowed to kill him, admired his revolver, and asked if he could see it. Before handing it back he noticed it only had three shells, and deftly positioned the hammer so it would land on an empty chamber.

When Grant pointed the gun at Henry's face and pulled the trigger it landed on an empty chamber, which gave him the advantage and he fired a bullet in Grant's face. The *Las Vegas Optic* quoted Henry as saying "it was a game of two and I got there first."[240]

On December 13, 1880, Sheriff Pat Garrett and a posse captured Henry. He was shackled with another prisoner and brought to Las Vegas, New Mexico, where a crowd of onlookers eyeballed them. When Deputy Romero demanded that Henry be turned over to him, Garrett refused and after a tense stand-off, he agreed to let the sheriff and two others take them to the jail in Santa Fe.

In an interview, Henry said he was unafraid and that "if I only had my Winchester, I'd lick the whole crowd." During a jailhouse interview the *Las Vegas Gazette* described Henry as looking relaxed and asked him if his capture bothered him. "What's the use of looking on the gloomy side of everything?"[241]

He went on trial in Mesilla where he was convicted of murdering Sheriff Brady during the Lincoln County War, the only conviction against any of the Regulators who did nothing more than even the score after their boss was murdered by the opposition.

Henry had been before Judge Warren Bristol's circuit court before in Silver City, and he found nothing to like about the charismatic young man. The feeling was mutual, and on April 13, 1881, he sentenced Henry to hang until he was "dead, dead, dead." Henry yelled back "and you can go to hell, hell, hell."[242] Henry managed to escape to Fort Sumner where he had friends.

In 1881, he was staying at the Maxwell residence, where the mostly Hispanic villagers held him in high regard. Sheriff Pat Garrett had heard a rumor that Henry's girlfriend, Paulita Maxwell, was expecting his child, which caused him to believe Henry might be somewhere in Fort Sumner.

Henry was popular with the young Mexican women, and he did father children but not with Paulita.[243] As was the custom of wealthy Hispanic single women in those days, she was chaperoned everywhere. But it was at the Maxwell residence where Pat Garrett shot him dead in his tracks, and yet according to unsubstantiated information it was a young Mexican who resembled Antrim that was shot, which is plausible, but not likely.

About six months earlier, a *Las Vegas Gazette* reporter gave a more accurate description of the unlikely desperado. "There was nothing mannish about him…he is five foot eight or nine inches tall, slightly built and lithe, weighing about 140 pounds; frank open countenance looking like a school boy with the traditional silky fuzz on his upper lip; clear blue eyes with a roguish snap about them, light hair and complexion. He is, in all, quite a handsome looking fellow, the only imperfection being his two front teeth, slightly protruding like squirrel's teeth, and he had agreeable and winning ways."[244]

Witness Jesus Silva was certain that it was Billy the Kid that had been shot that night. He "picked up the lifeless body of Billy and walked into a large hallway in the Maxwell home, laid his body on a long table. I examined him again and ascertained without doubt he was dead. The body was then removed to a carpenter shop where it was laid out. Of course, an inquest had to be held. There was no justice of the peace…so we dispatched a messenger for Alejandro Seguro, justice of the peace at a little town ten miles up the river. Seguro came and the inquest was held."

Soon after the shooting a number of people gathered at the carpenter's shop with several women crying. Billy was laid on a workbench where the women placed candles around him, and arranged for a proper burial.[245]

Said Paco Anaya, "Don Pedro took the $25 and…went to the latter's store and bought a beige suit, a shirt, an undershirt, shorts, and a pair of stockings. I, the writer, and my brother and several others of those that were there, dressed Billy with these clothes then we laid him on a high bed, one of those narrow ones, and we took him to the saloon where they held dances. There we watched, and on the next day we buried him."[246]

Several WPA oral histories from people who had first-hand knowledge doubt that Pat Garrett killed him, and theres enough conflicting information to raise doubts. Some of the conflict came from the book he wrote, but historian and author Jerry Weddle did a good job reconciling "a hostile press…. with the perceptions of those who actually knew him."[247]

Friends from Silver City remembered an easygoing teenager with a friendly smile and a "wonderful sense of humor." One of his saving graces was his ability to keep a cool head during tense moments, think clearly while analyzing the situation, and stay several steps ahead of his adversaries.

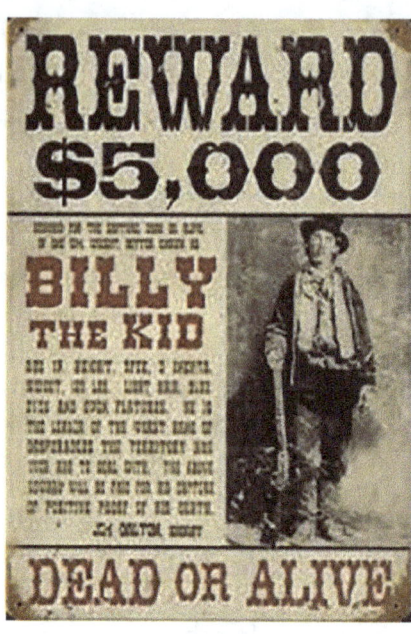

"I never liked the picture, I never thought it does Billy justice," recalled Paulita Maxwell. This souvenir poster with the inverted photo never existed—the reward was actually $500.

Those who knew him as a teenager were angered by the false and misleading articles and sensational dime novels written about him. Henry was no angel but so much of what was written had been fabricated by writers trying to sell a story. "Mr. Moulton would never read an article about Billy because he would become angry and said 'they write so many lies about that boy, and I know the ones are false about his killings in Grant County.'"

The Truesdells felt the same way, and refused to talk to reporters or journalists, although in 1902 a writer located G.J. looking for a juicy story. The only quote he got was that Henry was a good kid, and he didn't steal the silverware from the hotel like most employees. The Truesdells never had a bad thing to say about him.

Many decades later, Chauncey's son, who in 1951 was Vice President of Zenith, sent him a television. One of the programs asked viewers from the old west to send in their recollections, and after he did, much to Chauncey's annoyance he was deluged with curiosity seekers.

"It was only accidental that I was first induced to write about the Kid. That was when an old gentleman, Chauncey O. Truesdell, then living in Phoenix, wrote me that he had known Billy as a boy in Silver City, New Mexico.

"That was early in December of 1951. I visited Truesdell in his home, and obtained such an interesting and apparently authentic account of his playmate days with the Kid I wrote a story for the *Arizona Republic*. Shortly after the appearance of my article I received letters from writers scattered all over the country, who were collecting data on the Kid. Unfortunately, Mr. Truesdell died shortly after I interviewed him."[248]

Chauncey reluctantly agreed to sit down with historian Robert Mullins, who knew if the stories were authentic, he had just unearthed an important piece of Billy the Kid history.

"It would seem that Chauncey Truesdell has brought to light for the first-time little-known phases of the Kid's early life. His statements disagree with most writers, but since he actually lived with the Kid at one time, and even though he was a child of eight to twelve during their acquaintanceship, his account must be reckoned with.

"The writer found Truesdell somewhat reluctant to talk of his family's relationship with Billy the Kid. A check reveals that Truesdell is a man of substance and integrity, with children and many friends who vouch for his honesty and reliability. The writer is convinced that Mr. Truesdell speaks from the truth of his recollections. He also freely admits that the passage of many years dims ones memory regarding details. What he does recall, however, he is positive about. Mullins would come back to his earlier statements, ask questions a different way, and was convinced that his memory was accurate and that he was of sound mind. 'I was impressed with his obvious sincerity and straight forwardness in answering questions.'"[249]

Mercantile Hub of the Southwest, Circa 1875

By the time Gideon and Julia arrived in Silver City, there was an established mercantile hub consisting of about a dozen merchants who became successful through their own perseverance. The settlement was only two years old when Joseph and Cornelius Bennett came to the mining camp to capitalize on the mining boom. They had served as officers during the Civil War; Cornelius enlisted in Iowa and Joseph in California. At the age of 32, Joseph became Assistant Adjutant General of the California column and were assigned to the New Mexico headquarters in Santa Fe. After the war, he returned to Dubuque and started a small manufacturing business. Joseph stayed in New Mexico where he opened a store in Mesilla, and a few years later Cornelius joined him.

Cornelius had been a partner in Henry Lesinsky's profitable but dangerous Santa Fe-Silver City-El Paso-Tucson freight and passenger line. Using stagecoaches but mostly wagons, they moved freight and people between each city. Lesinsky and Eugene Cosgrove, future Silver City businessman started the New Mexico & Arizona Stage Company, running coaches from La Mesilla to Tucson where it crossed trails with stagecoaches traveling west to California.

The Bennett brothers and Henry Lesinsky knew the recent discovery of silver in Silver City was going to turn that area into a major mercantile hub. They moved quickly, and paid Ike Stevens $400 ($12,000 today) for block 16 at the corner of Broadway and Hudson. In April 1872, they began construction of a large brick store which they opened for business seven months later. They sold mining equipment, tools, provisions, loaned money, and had a small logging camp and sawmill in the mountains. The Bennetts eventually acquired a large inventory of claims, usually when somebody defaulted on a loan, and owned the famous Bennett Mine near Las Cruces in Dona Ana County.[250]

Jewish immigrant Henry Lesinsky (1834–1924) arrived in the

southwest as a young man who was looking for a fresh start after years of failures. He told a son that his childhood in Poland was one of "bitterness, poverty, and tears." When he was fourteen, the Lesinsky boys were told to make their own way in the world because their family could no longer feed them. Henry joined his brother in England where he learned how to become a stonemason.

When he heard about the 1851 Australian gold rush, he convinced the Church of England Society to pay his passage to Australia. They were sponsoring "good Christians to counteract the influx of convicts and criminals in the mining regions. He made and lost a small fortune before returning home frustrated and broke.

In 1858, he worked his way to San Francisco as a steward aboard a ship. He had missed the Gold Rush by a decade but tried his luck working some panned-out placer mines near Sutter's Mill, but came up empty-handed. His uncle, Julius Freudenthal (1830–1910), older by only four years, urged him to come to New Mexico where there were unlimited opportunities, and few prejudices against his Jewish ancestry.

Freudenthal had fled Kaiser Wilhelm's oppressive rule of Germany for New York City. At the age 31, he invested his lifes savings to build a general store in Socorro on a major crossroad that ran through southeastern New Mexico. He landed a contract to sell grain and deliver mail which he turned over to Henry, who started a stagecoach line passing through dangerous Apache country. Moving freight in one direction and grain in the other while dodging bullets and arrows, he made a good living.[251]

During the Civil War, parts of New Mexico fell under Confederate rule, which made it a difficult time for merchants due to illegal seizures, terrible wartime economy, rampant inflation, and stealing. Soldiers took whatever they wanted, and paid for it with Confederate dollars that had no value.

After the war Henry went to New York City "wife shopping," not an uncommon practice since there were so few eligible Jewish women on the frontier. Henry returned to Las Cruces with a kindhearted and intelligent Jewish bride, and the two lived a Spartan lifestyle in the back room of his store while saving money to invest in other ventures.

He wasn't home much because he was running stagecoaches through 600 miles of Apache country with his partner, Cornelius Bennett, hauling freight to several military forts, grinding corn and selling it to Mexican merchants, hauling freight and passengers, and carrying the mail between dozens of towns they serviced. They owned a couple of stagecoaches, but ran mostly wagons from Trinidad, Colorado, to Julius Freudenthal's general stores in Paraje, Socorro, and Silver City, New Mexico; Ysleta, Texas; and Juarez, Mexico.

Bennett Brothers & Company at Hudson Street and Broadway, and Bullard Street south of market. Pictures courtesy of the Silver City Museum.

Broadway Street (above) courtesy of the Palace of Governors for New Mexico Collection. Bullard Street (below) looking northwest from Broadway. Picture courtesy of the Silver City Museum John Harlan collection.

Two years after the Bennett Brothers & Company built their store in Silver City, Lesinsky figured there was enough business to open his own store as a branch of his family's Las Cruces store. This gave Henry the opportunity to loan money secured by mining claims, and sometimes he took a percentage of ownership with the right to buy them out if they defaulted. (Lesinsky was the brains behind the family's success in the southwest.) Isaac Cohen, another Jewish immigrant from Jerusalem, landed a job as a clerk at Lesinsky's Las Cruces store before opening his own store in Silver City with Henry's financial backing.

Another Jewish immigrant was David Abraham who, at the age of 47, left his native Poland and spent some time in London before arriving in New York City. He eventually ended up in Silver City with his lifes savings, which he shrewdly invested buying mining claims and opening a general store. He kept his money growing by buying the Centennial Saloon and Southern Hotel and leasing them to others while he ran his store.

C.P. Crawford, who was a clerk at Henry Porter's Elizabethtown, New Mexico, store came to Silver City in 1873 to run a store that was a branch of his frontier mercantile empire. He was an enterprising young man, and he built a thriving wholesale and retail business for his employer. He handled Porter's mining interests in southern New Mexico and eastern Arizona, and opened a bank as a branch of their business."[252]

None of the early merchants came from wealth or privilege, and the men who put Silver City on the map were tough pioneers that had been tested time and again by adversity. As a group, the Jewish residents made the right decisions, and as a group they worshiped together, socialized, and at times pooled their capital.

Law and Order in Southwest New Mexico

Silver City was nestled in the valley of the Pinos Altos Mountains, and a long way from law and order. The criminal element knew there was lots of money floating around town, and stage coaches hauling silver bars to Denver or San Francisco, which made Silver City a magnate for thieves. The mining riff-raff that inevitably finds its way to every boom town took its toll on the town, and it wasn't long before the southwestern corner of the territory was unsafe in every direction.

One of Silver City's founders was Isaac "Ike" Stevens, who discovered the Two Ikes (Ike Stevens and Ike Givens) and other mining claims including the Stevens Group of copper mines in eastern Arizona. But his greatest contribution might have been the men who married his daughters; Dick Hudson (1839–1912) and Harvey Whitehill (1838–1906). Both played extraordinarily critical roles in the early history of Grant County.

Hudson was Silver City's first sheriff, and he arrived in America as an orphan at the age of thirteen. At a young age he somehow found his way from England to the United States, and traveled from Brooklyn to California looking for opportunities. When the Civil War broke out, he joined Californias First Calvary, who was responsible for maintaining law and order in the lower Rio Grande Valley. Governor Lew Wallace made him a major in the New Mexico National Guard until he was promoted to the brevet rank of Colonel.

Pinos Altos, which were 14 miles north of Silver City, was a run-down mining camp that had seen better days. There were still men working claims but with poor results, and during the late 1860s just about everyone regarded Silver City as a farming community due to its fertile soil. To supplement mediocre earnings from mining, Hudson started a stagecoach and freighting business, and was elected sheriff of Grant County, which at the time covered 9,000 square miles in the southwestern corner of the territory. Dick's toughness and tenacity became obvious during a gunfight with the Navajos, because after taking a bullet in each arm he continued to fight.[253]

After the silver strike, he moved to Silver City where he started a livery and freighting business. While exploring the landscape, he discovered a natural hot spring about 20 miles south, which he bought and turned into a successful resort. He was also a sharp businessman because after acquiring over 5,000 acres, he ranged over a thousand head of cattle.

In 1874, his brother-in-law, Harvey Whitehill (1838–1906), succeeded him as sheriff, and Grant County was lucky that he did. He was "exactly what he appeared, a whole souled, honest and straightforward man.... he never missed an opportunity to aid a friend or extend a favor and many were the recipients of his unostentatious charitable acts. He possessed a remarkable power of making friends of everyone he came in contact.... he fought a good fight and fought it well."[254]

He brought law and order to a mining town that was just as rough and lawless as any of the famous towns in the southwest. Whitehill was successful at dealing with the criminal element, and used paid informants to stay one step ahead of them, which didn't always please the people who elected him. His methods might have been questionable but he always got results. "According to Governor Miguel Otero, Whitehill arrested more culprits than any man in the territory."[255]

A double hanging of a black man who fatally stabbed a Fort Bayard soldier, and Barney O'Toole who gunned down a man in Georgetown just because he felt like it. There was considerable controversy over a black man being hanged next to a white man with about 400 spectators. Picture courtesy of the Silver City Museum.

There came a time during the late 1870s when Silver City was at the mercy of the outlaws, and Sheriff Whitehill knew he needed some tough deputies to bring law and order to a town that was getting a well-deserved reputation for gun fights. One of his most controversial appointments was Dan Tucker, who had already killed a man in Colorado and perhaps another in nearby Dona Ana County. When he arrived, the criminal element was shooting up the streets. The pillars of the community were fed up, and wanted this lawlessness to end by any means necessary.

After a few months on the job, Tucker killed one man who resisted arrest and put a bullet in the back of another who had just knifed a man. A few weeks later, he shot an armed drunk, gunned down two horse thieves, and wounded another. By the end of the year the criminals steered clear of Silver City, and people loved or hated the new deputy. At least eight men were shot dead by Dan Tucker, and Silver City's leading citizens didn't object to his methods.

To stop drunken shooting sprees an ordinance was passed prohibiting gunfire within the city limits. When an angry Mexican ignored the law and began shooting up the streets Tucker ordered him to stop; when he didn't, he shot him dead in his tracks.

When he found a Mexican trying to murder his son, Tucker charged inside with his gun drawn. After the man knocked the revolver out of his hand with a blunt object, Dan used his other hand and shot him dead. By the end of the year, Henry Whitehill had brought order back to what had become a dangerous mining town, and the criminal element knew Dan Tucker was nobody to fool with. He'd shoot you in a heartbeat and probably enjoy doing it.

G.J. and Louisa Truesdell

When G.J. arrived in Silver City during the spring of 1872 he had little involvement in the Wisconsin Mining Company. He was there to keep an eye on his father's money, and start a cattle ranch that would supply beef to the anticipated influx of miners.

Based on family information, G.J. was most comfortable as a farmer, but learned the hotel business, and turned out to be a successful innkeeper. People called him "Dell," and at the end of the day he spent a fair amount of time in the saloons. He could drink just about anyone under the table, and still maintain a friendly disposition.[256] People gravitated to G.J. because he was capable of intelligent conversation, good natured, and had an easy-going personality.[257]

While traveling to New Mexico with wagons loaded with mining equipment, he became a lifelong friend of Tom Lyons, who later became one of the biggest cattle barons in the southwest, and one of the wealthiest men in Grant County. In 1873, at a meeting in Henry Porter's store, the town's leading men organized a chapter of the Masonic Lodge. In attendance were prominent members of the community that included Cornelius Bennett, I.N. Cohen, Eugene Goulding, Sam Eckles, Alexander H. Moorhead, George W. Bailey, Robert Florman, G.S. VanWagenen, Sam Greene, John B. Morrill, Harvey Whitehill, and George W. Holt.[258]

It was an ancient fraternal order with membership by invitation only, and G.J. was listed as an officer. He had been a member of the Masonic

Lodge in Kenosha along with G.S. Van Wagenen, Ashael Farr, Erastus Sherwood, Sam Greene, and the Derbyshires.[259] Had G.J.s drinking been out of control he would never have been invited to join this select organization, much less become an officer.

After the hotels were sold G.J. became editor of the town's newspaper, *Mining Life* and was often selected for jury duty when the circuit court was in session. On more than one occasion he also saddled-up with other young men when Sheriff Whitehill organized a posse to pursue Apaches or outlaws. A few years later he was appointed Deputy Clerk of Courts, and was a solid member of the community. Award winning historian and *Billy the Kid* author, Michael Wallis, described the Truesdells as "pillars of the community."[260]

But G.J. and Louisa were trapped in a bad marriage almost from the beginning. She never warmed to Silver City, thought it was the worst place on the planet to raise two young boys, and judging from newspaper articles she wasn't too far off the mark. Their lives had changed considerably from a life of privilege in a 10,000 square foot mansion to sharing two rooms in a cheap boarding house, and yet G.J. and Louisa were integral to the family's financial recovery. The hotel and boarding house generated the cash Gideon needed to get into the livestock, grocery, and provisioning business.

They renovated Truesdell's Star Hotel, doubled the size of the livery stable, and turned it into a moneymaker. But this came at a cost because G.J. and Louisa worked around the clock. A Mexican couple probably ran the Wisconsin House, a staff of Mexicans would have run the livery stable and livestock pens.[261] In a town where two-thirds of the population were from Mexico, none of the mines, mills, or businesses could have functioned without them. And they were happy for the work because the standard of living on the other side of the border was dismal. The toughest job was running the kitchen and dining room, which fell to Louisa, and the hotel had a reputation for serving good food.

Once his father had accumulated enough capital to get into the cattle, provisioning, and grocery business, they sold the hotel to Louie Timmer.[262] At that point, G.J. bought the American House, and continued to run the Wisconsin House for another year before selling them so he could join his father in the cattle business.[263] With the hotels and boarding house gone, G.J. and Louisa decided to put an end to their misery and divorced.

In 1876, G.J. and Jim Bullard left Silver City with others for South Dakota to the rough and tumble mining town of Deadwood.[264] On Christmas Day, 1877, Louisa married Georgetown merchant George Holt (1845–1920), a member from their social circle and a judge for the eastern half of Grant County. If her marriage to G.J. was strained and difficult, this marriage lasted for decades, and appears to have been happy.

Holt owned several mining claims in Georgetown where he was a partner in Holt, Moulton & Company, which owned part of the McGregor Mine. He also owned the Pinion Claim which he leased to others with a 50/50 split of the profits, and was a partner with Tom Lyons and Eugene Cosgrove in a Silver City saddle and leather shop.

G.J. was a regular church-goer, and the most remarkable thing happened when soon after his divorce, he met Callie Schallenberger (1851–1886). She was a teacher who came to New Mexico with her uncle, Reverend George Murray, to open a missionary school in Silver City.

They fell in love, and after a seven-month courtship they were married in nearby Fort Bayard.[265] This marriage appears to have been a perfect match. His son Gideon recalled many years later that Callie, "was all a mother could be to me and I loved her as much as any son could... God Bless her."[266] It's almost a certainty that G.J stayed out of the saloons and stopped drinking. They had three children: Julia Eleanor Truesdell (1878–1959); Zoe Truesdell (1880–1964); and Adelbert J. Truesdell (1882–1972).

Callies eighteen-year-old brother, John Schallenberger (1860–1881), came to live with them at the Truesdell Ranch, and clerked at Gideon's store when his health permitted because he was dying of tuberculosis.[267] Like so many others with this deadly affliction, he came to New Mexico hoping that a dry climate would help, and became an extended member of their family until he died at the age of twenty-one.

G.J. and Callie were expecting their first child when his mother, Julia Truesdell, passed away. This was not unexpected because she had been very ill throughout 1876, and really not well since she arrived in Silver City four years earlier.[268] A sister-in-law wrote "poor Gid just doesn't know what to do without Julia."[269] The *Grant County Herald* published the following obituary;

"Truesdell, Mrs. Julia, wife of Gideon Truesdell, died at the Truesdell ranch, just beyond the city limits on Saturday, the 12th instant. She was buried Sunday the 13th. Reverend N.H. Gale conducted the funeral services, and a large concourse of friends followed the remains to their last resting place.

"Mrs. Truesdell was born in Hamilton County, New York, on the 10th of September, 1813. She was married in 1833, and, with her husband, immigrated to Wisconsin in 1837. The family removed to New Mexico four years ago and located in Silver City. Mrs. Truesdell left a large circle of friends and relatives to mourn her loss."[270]

Soon thereafter, G.J. leased a stage stop from Richard Knight at Knight's Ranch, twenty miles south of town along a major trail that at times was menaced by Apaches.[271] It was a good business on a major thoroughfare, and he was tough enough to protect the hotel while making a good living, but his new wife was adamant about leaving the area.[272] She was no more impressed with Silver City than G.J.s first wife, and never felt safe at the ranch because it was so isolated.[273] A letter dated December 15, 1880, from another early settler gives a revealing look at life during an Apache uprising.[274]

G.J. and Callie Truesdell circa 1878. Pictures courtesy of Helen Oglesby.

"I took the stagecoach at Albuquerque for the south. Stories of Indian outrages were numerous, and many of them no means unfounded. The recent massacre had pretty effectually checked travel and I entered the coach alone. Along the road are frequent Mexican villages but they only serve to make the scenery drearier.

"At Paraje, the road leaves the river and enters the Jornada del Muerto (Journey of Death). This valley is ninety miles long and runs parallel with the river, but separated from it by a chain of mountains. Until recently not a drop of water could be obtained throughout the entire ninety miles. Now there is a well and stage station in the middle of it...this station is the only house in the valley.

"Sometime during the forenoon, we passed a lot of dead cattle lying in a heap by the roadside. Upon inquiry, we were told that the cattle had been killed by the Indians a short time before, and the stones and the cross marked the death scene and resting place of eleven Mexicans who had fallen in the affray.

"By sundown we arrived at Fort Cummings. Here, there were more passengers to get on the coach, and we were crowded during the night. We had not gone far, when a groan from an old man at my side indicated, afterward learned, that we were passing the place where but a few days before the Indians had killed his son.

"Not far from this place our nostrils were greeted by the fetid odor of decaying flesh, and were informed that it arose from the bodies of unburied Indians who had been killed shortly after the tragedy mentioned. Not long after my arrival in Silver City the coach was again attacked, some distance beyond Fort Cummings, and the driver and two passengers left dead by the roadside."[275]

In a letter Callie revealed that she and "Dell" would like to leave the area but did not want to leave Gideon alone.[276] Her father had just built a beautiful farm house outside of Carthage, Missouri, and had served a term in the Missouri legislature.

G.J. was prepared to invest some of his hotel money in Carthage, where he would open a general store, and live with his family at the Schallenberger farm. According to a diary entry, G.J. and Callie repeatedly asked Gideon to join them, but he wanted to be buried next to his wife of 45 years.[277] More likely, declining heath notwithstanding Silver City was his home. He had become a member of the business community, made hundreds of friends, and just finished building a new store, ranch house, and didn't want to spend his last days in a rocking chair.

Apache Depredations

In 1879, Victorio, a warrior and chief of the Warm Springs band of Apaches and his sister, who many believed had clairvoyant powers that allowed her to pinpoint the location of the enemy, began a series of violent attacks within 150-mile radius of Silver City that led to the death of over three hundred people. This would have put the Truesdell Ranch in the middle of harm's way since it was isolated along a trail that led to Pinos Altos.

Sergeant James C. Cooney had been sent by the U.S. Calvary to take back part of the Wheeler Survey, which had been attacked by a band of Apaches.[278] In 1876, he located claims, and three years later he was shipping silver ore for processing to Silver City.

In April 1880, Victorio attacked the Cooney mine as the men were quitting work for the day. Three were killed, another, Mr. Taylor was shot in the leg. Taylor hid out in a cave...the rest of the men scattered into the hills.

According to Frances E. Totty's account, "We children slept in the wagon as the only house we had were a lean to. When I went out to the wagon to go to bed, I heard a strange noise up in the hills. I ran into the house and said 'there is something up in the hills.'

"The entire family came to listen, and when they didn't hear anything, they tried to make me believe that it was the frogs in the swamp. After the family went to bed I could not sleep because I kept thinking about the noise in the hills. I heard some loud talking, and soon decided that it was over at the Robert's house.

Apaches blended into the underbrush wearing buckskins while waiting to ambush travelers on horseback or stage coach.

"I was ready to wake up mother when I heard a horse coming. The horse came up the far side of the lean to, and I called 'we are on this side of the house' A man rode around the house and asked 'where is your father?' I replied in the house, asleep. 'Go wake him, and tell him that the Apaches are out, that he had better get all of his stock in the corral at once and get ready for an attack. I haven't the time to awaken him as I must go warn others.'

"I ran to the house to wake father...the family was soon busy. Father put the stock in the corral and went after my brother and uncle that slept in the store across the creek. When the men came back my uncle and oldest brother stayed at the corral to guard the stock. Mother and I started molding bullets for our old 44 Winchester. Mr. Cooney and another man called Chick came down from the hills, and told us that they had been hiding in the hills after the attack at the mine.

"When night came the Indians began to howl so the dogs would bark and they could get their bearing, thereby explaining the noise that I had heard. Mr. Cooney had been an Indian scout for five years, and said that we need not worry that the Indians would raid their cabins and not bother the settlers. We did not worry as we thought that Mr. Cooney knew what the Indians were likely to do.

"We laughed and molded bullets the rest of the night...next morning Chick wanted to go back to the mine. Mr. Cooney said that the Indians will just raid the cabin, and that it is not safe to go up there now as the Indians are still in the country. Chick insisted that he was going, and finally rather than let him go alone Mr. Cooney consented to go if they could borrow some horses to ride.

"The Apaches raided James Keller's and Jim Roberts' ranch houses, and killed William Wilcox and seriously wounded James Murray. Mr. Ashenfelter of the *Grant County Herald* was pinned inside with the others, and wrote that there were 150 to 250 Indians. Eventually 85 men from Silver City and 20 from other parts mounted up and rode to their rescue. After several hours the horses returned rider less with blood on them...the men were ambushed by the Indians.

"The Indians feared Capt. Cooney and when they saw that they killed him they rejoiced. The warriors left the squaws to mutilate the bodies of Cooney and Chick. When the horses returned rider less the Roberts family decided to send out an alarm. A man rode over to our house and told us to hurry to the Roberts' house. Mother insisted that we go on over to the

Roberts' Ranch...my brother said that he would stay with the stock at the corral. We finally got the two white mules to the wagon and started for the ranch.

"We saw some cattle standing still on a hill...the cattle were watching something. Mother said 'Paw drive faster, the Indians are coming, the cattle are watching them.' He said 'Oh mother, there is plenty of time, those cattle are watching us. The Indians aren't near yet.' Paw would not hurry, and mother would urge him to drive faster. We were leisurely driving along when we came to the top of a hill, and the cattle started to run and bullets starting flying past us as the Indians were coming toward us.

"I grabbed the old Springfield but Paw called 'it isn't loaded...the shells are in my belt.' Paw was driving very fast...I was pointing the gun at the Indians in hopes that they would stay back if they saw a gun. If I had been able to load the gun, I could never hit the Indians as the gun was bouncing around so, as father was really making a race for the Roberts' ranch now. I yelled to the family to lie down in the wagon so the Indians couldn't hit them...bullets were whizzing all around us...the Indians were getting nearer all the time.

"My brother was standing at the corral watching the attack but he could not help us as his gun was not a long-range gun. The men at the Roberts' Ranch saw the trouble that we were in and six of the men rode out to help us risking their lives. We had to pass by the house, and pulled up behind an old log shed. Just as we halted one of the white mules fell dead, the first shot of the Apaches to take effect for they were sure shooting wild.

"To get to the house we were going to have to leap a ditch, the men told us soon as there was a slack in the firing to make for the house. The firing ceased and we knew the Indians were surrounding the place. We made a dash for the house...there were thirty-one men in the house. Luck was surely with us for bullets hit all around us, and not a one was injured.

"The Indians were able to keep up a constant fire as fifteen would drive up and fire, then drop back to reload their guns, and another fifteen would take their place thereby keeping up a constant fire as they were always moving in a circle...there were two hundred thirteen warriors.

"The Indians surrounded the house, some shooting down the hill and many shots lodged on the dirt roof. Others knocked holes in the wall making it unsafe to move about as the Indians could see any movement inside the house through the cracks. I asked 'brother do you want me to take your place for a while?' He said 'no, it is too dangerous as the Indians have nearly hit me several times through the cracks in the wall.'

"Mr. Wilcox was standing on the other side of the cupboard spoke up and said, 'Agnes, when you start back across the room you go as fast as possible. Those Indians are shooting at everything they see move.' Before I started back Mr. Wilcox saw his partner out in the yard trying to get to the house. Mr. Wilcox stepped to the door to aid his partner in getting to the house by exposing himself. Mr. Wilcox cried 'my God, boys I'm shot.' He stood his gun down by the door, and walked over to the fireplace and lay down...before anyone could reach him, he was dead.

"Mr. Murray had gone into the hills early that morning to round up some cattle, and when he heard the firing, he knew the Indians had attacked and hid out in the hills. Late in the afternoon he decided that it was time to try to make it to the house, but he tried to come in too early. The boys sure did have to do some real shooting to make the Indians stay back in order for Mr. Murray to get to the house.

"Mr. Foster understood the Apache language and signs, and he told the boys that Victorio was trying to get his warriors to rush down to the house. The warriors made several rushes for the house but the boys made it too hot for them to get too close. The Apaches are superstitious about fighting at night, and when dark came the Indians made camp at the present site of Alamo. That's when the yelling and whooping started...they really danced and made merry for they had the white settlers penned.

"Our men soon became tired of their merry-making, and sent a few shots over in their direction. The Indians moved a little farther away, and no more was heard of them. We figured we were in for a siege, and had better fill everything with water. If the Indians were to cut the ditch we would probably have to give up the fight from thirst.

"Two men volunteered to try to get through to Silver City for help and ammunition but to go there they must go by the Indian camp. The men came around and told us good bye...they never expected to come back and I don't think anyone in the room expected to see them again. The men arrived in Silver City early the next day and gave the alarm, and rushed over to Fort Bayard.

"Captain Madden had been out on an Indian scouting trip and was just returning to the post with thirty-five of his troops, and ordered his men to turn and march to the Frisco Valley. The men marched by Silver

City where seventy-five citizens joined the troops. The men were tired but they never let this hinder their rush to the settlers. The morning after the...Apaches sent a runner over to the San Carlo's reservations for more warriors.

"The men decided to try to bury Mr. Wilcox...they built a wooden coffin and decided to bury him on the hill behind the house. If the Indians were seen a shot was to be fired from a pistol. The men were carrying the coffin up the hill when a shot was heard and the men hastily placed the body under a tree and made a run for the house. When the men had gathered at the house it was discovered that one of the men had accidentally dropped his gun, and made it go off. Many days later we laughed about it but it sure wasn't funny then.

"When Captain Madden came in sight he could see the ranch with his field glasses... 'we are early enough for I see white men.' The cry of rejoicing went up from that group could be heard for many miles. The Indians had moved into the hills for they apparently heard that soldiers were coming. They went where the Mexican sheepherders were and killed thirty-five men. The Indians were angry because the sheep men had told them that the new settlers could be easily taken.

"Sheriff Whitehill was in the valley at the time of the attack and came on to the ranch, and father sent us back to Silver City with him. Sometime after the fight an Apache scout came into the mining camp with Chick's coat on...the one he had on the day he was killed.

"The boys took the scout as prisoner and took possession of his horse. One morning the boys told the Indian that he was to follow them. The Indians asked, 'Where are you taking me?' One of the boys answered, 'Going to show you the trail.' The Indian said, 'Yes, I know the trail that you will show me, and it will be a long one.' The boys took the scout out and hung him.

"Over at Copper Creek miners and ranchers had to 'fort-up,' with Sheriff Whitehill and his son Harry who just happened to be in the area on business. They remained trapped for ten days while the Apaches raided and set everything on fire."[279]

Forty-year-old Jim Cooney was one of the casualties, and G.J. Truesdell, Tom Lyons and others saddled up and went looking for his corpse so they could give him a decent burial.[280] When they found poor old Mike, the stench from his body was so bad the men had to cover their noses with a handkerchief, dig the grave, and push him into a grave with poles. When the men returned to town, they buried their clothes and took baths but the stench still lingered. Tom was told to cut the hairs in his nose and only then did the stench of death go away.

Cooney wasn't the only casualty that year. Richard Knight and John Connors had a contract with Fort Bayard to deliver hay for their horses. While driving along a deserted trail just after sundown, they discovered the king bolt from a wheel had come loose and was missing. They unhitched their teams, and knowing that it was unsafe to spend the night along the trail, rode back to Silver City where they spent the night.

At daybreak they returned to look for the bolt, bringing Connors' son and a Mexican to help. John Connors and the Mexican helper were not far from Knight's Ranch, when a nut came off the axle and pretty soon the wheel came off.[281] Once they reached their wagon John Connors was shot and killed in an Apache ambush.[282] When the Indians saw the abandoned wagon, they knew it belonged to white people, and after waiting in the brush for hours they shot and killed the entire party. Chauncey Truesdell recalled hearing about this ambush from his father: "Mr. Conner went back down the road to look for the nut, and when he did not come back for quite a spell, the Mexican went back to look for him. He found Mr. Conner dead of Indian poisoning. The Indians had not torn his guts out with cactus the way the Mexicans did to Mike Cooney at Cooney's pass. But they had to rope Conners' dog before they could lift the corpse into the wagon."[283]

By 1880, the attacks had become so frequent that stagecoaches approaching Silver City were met by an armed escort several miles from the city limits, shotguns ready since the Indians were looking for people to slaughter. Every woman in town carried a pistol in case she was attacked because women were greatly mistreated by the Apaches.

When a group of prospectors were camping in the Black Range, they received word that a party of hostile Apaches was coming their way. One of the men with an off-beat sense of humor decided to leave an ammunition belt on the side of the trail, knowing that an Indian wouldn't pass up free bullets. He loaded some empty shell casings with gun powder but added a small amount of dynamite that the prospectors used in the hills for mining.

He dropped the gun belt along the trail heading into Silver City and a few days later a couple of Indians were captured. The prospector who planted the gun belt asked one of them if he found a gun belt along the trail, and he said that he had. They divided the ammunition and soon thereafter one of them spotted a deer. When asked what happened the Apache said, "Ugh, heap bad cartridge. Kill gun. Kill pony. Damn near kill Injun."

Indian attacks were totally out of control, and in 1881, Silver City residents agreed to pay a $100 bounty ($2,000 today) for every Indian captured, with ties to the tribe that murdered American settlers.[284] Thirty-seven people pledged money for this bounty, including Gideon and G.J. Truesdell.[285]

Truesdell, Lyons, & Campbell Cattle Company, Tombstone, Arizona circa 1879

It's hard to say when Gideon made his first trip to Tombstone, Arizona, but it was sometime in late 1879 after news of a silver strike spread throughout the southwest. At the age of 67, he traveled over 160 miles where he found exactly what he expected. A once in a lifetime opportunity to start a provisioning company in a boom town where the population was about to explode.

Two years earlier, prospector Ed Shefflin walked into the mountains looking for silver, but was told by a local "the only rock you'll find is your tombstone." What he found was $25 million ($694 million today) of silver ore deposits.

By 1881, there were over 4,000 people in the hills prospecting for silver, and a year later the population jumped to over 10,000. In the blink of an eye, Tombstone became the largest town between St. Louis and San Francisco with all of the problems of an overnight boom town.

The *Chicago Tribune* wrote that the silver strike "caused a rush like that of early Nevada and Colorado. Tombstone will grow. It is nearer to Sonora [Mexico] than Tucson by 75 miles, and it is bound to receive a portion of the Sonora trade which is worth $2 million annually."[286] In 1881, the Arizona Telephone Company began installing poles and stringing lines to Tombstone as one of the first telephone companies in the Southwest.

Trail outside of Tombstone, Arizona.

It wasn't long before investment syndicates bought up a stack of mining claims and hired cheap immigrant labor to work a twelve-hour shift for $4 ($60 today). This type of mining was easy because the silver ore was near the surface, and at its peak about 6,000 people were hard at work in the mines and mining $168,000 ($4.2 million today) of silver ore every seven days.

During its heyday Tombstone had 110 saloons, 14 gambling halls and dozens of dance halls and brothels. It was a wild and crazy frontier town with gunfights and Indian depredations, where three superintendents at the nearby mines were murdered by the Indians.

There was a fortune to be made provisioning the thousands of miners, but bankers rarely loaned money to ranchers because their herds could be wiped-out by anthrax, contagious diseases, drop in the price of cattle at the stock yards, and livestock theft. But there were also huge profit margins, and a bank's largest depositors were often cattlemen. Gideon didn't have the wherewithal to become a rancher, but with borrowed capital he could build a slaughterhouse and meatpacking operation in Tombstone, and buy cattle and hogs from farmers along the Santa Rita River.

In late 1879, Gideon organized the Truesdell, Lyons, & Campbell Cattle Company with a capital stock of at about $12,000 ($300,000 today).[287] The Truesdells put up half of the capital with Lyons & Campbell contributing the rest.[288] By then, twenty-eight-year-old Tom Lyons, a close family friend and his partner, Angus Campbell, had already made a fortune in the mining business.[289] The partners were Gideon and G.J. Truesdell,

Tom Lyons and Angus Campbell, and Sam Greene.[290] A few miles away from Tombstone they built a stockyard, slaughterhouse and office in the village of Richmond, Arizona, near the rugged Richmond Basin.[291]

With thousands of people flooding into the area the demand for food was incredible, and they bought horses, cattle, and hogs from ranchers along the Santa Rita River. Since the area was mostly inhabited by Mexicans that had lived along the river for generations, Gideon probably hired them to butcher and pack beef, hams, slabs of bacon, and ribs in barrels of salt much the same as he had back at his dairy farm more than a decade earlier.

They also dealt in hay and oats for livestock, and bought fruits, vegetables, flour, and lard from farmers on the other side of the border. Within a few months they had a provisioning business with a supply line from the Santa Rita valley, and were positioned to make money fast.

Ranchers would have driven their herds to the Truesdell, Lyons & Campbell corrals where they were inspected, and paid. With over 10,000 people in the mining camps needing to eat, the partners would have turned their capital over several times. After looking for something that would recoup his losses from the Chicago Fire, Gideon had finally found it in Tombstone.

A side of beef had about 200 pounds of sirloin, porterhouse, and T-bone steaks; stew beef, chuck roasts, rib steaks and rib roasts; sirloin tips, cube steaks, rump roasts and ground beef. At 21¢ a pound, they would have grossed around $168 per cow with about half dropping to the bottom line which made it highly profitable. Collateral research suggests that after two busy years each of the four majority partners walked away with at least $21,000 ($500,000 today).[292]

Tombstone turned into a rough cattle town with saloons, brothels, and gambling halls but there was an enormous amount of money floating around. It's also where the Earp brothers and Doc Holiday gunned down the Clanton gang, although the "gunfight" only lasted thirty seconds before the three Clantons were lying dead in an alley. Their funeral attracted three hundred mourners and an estimated 2,000 people lined the funeral route to the cemetery, causing the Earp gang to leave town as quickly as they could without arousing attention.

The Earps snuck out of Tombstone to avoid arrest or more likely to save their skin, traveling by horseback to Silver City before catching a train to Colorado. Wyatt Earp knew the Arizona authorities would put him in jail, so he and his companions followed an illogical route to Silver

City, giving false names when they tried to sell their horses. Had Sheriff Whitehall's deputy, Dan Tucker ran across them, theres a good chance they would have disappeared because when it came to outlaws, he was legendary for shooting first and asking questions later.

According to the *Grant County Herald*, "last Saturday evening at ten o'clock, the Earp Boys' party and Doc Holliday were in Silver City. They went at once to the Exchange Hotel to find a stage agent to make arrangements to leave the next morning on the Deming coach. They slept in a private house up town and took breakfast the next morning in the Broadway restaurant, as they had not registered at any hotel it was not known they were in town until after their departure."

They stabled their horses at the Elephant Corral and based on eyewitness accounts they were heavily armed. When one of the men at the stable asked for a name one of them answered John Smith, and the other said Bill Snooks.

The owner was leery, and when they offered to sell six of their horses for $300, he was suspicious because they were worth far more, and turned them down. They finally sold them to a man named Miller who was starting a livery stable. That done, they talked to the Elephant Corral's proprietor about hiring horses to take them to Fort Cummings, but he advised them to travel by stagecoach, which they did.

At the end of 1881 the partners went their separate ways but remained close friends. The Truesdells partnered with George Andrews, and organized the Andrews & Truesdell Cattle Company.[293] When combined with other income-producing properties, the Truesdells were once again affluent, something they had been working toward since arriving in the southwest.

Lyons & Campbell had been dabbling in the cattle business, but were about to make an enormous investment when they sold their Cosette Mine for $50,000 ($1.2 million today), and used the proceeds to "go big" in the cattle business. They organized the famous LC Ranch, which a few years later consisted of over 1.5 million acres of pastures with 60,000 cows roaming 2,400 square miles.[294] Their ranch was twice the size of Rhode Island, and they immediately became major players in the cattle business with an office in New York City.

Only a few cattlemen in New Mexico had the brains and guts to build million-acre ranches, and despite the romance of the cattle business those who survived were shrewd, pragmatic, and tough as nails. It wasn't a business for sissies and cattle barons ran their private fiefdoms with an iron fist. John Chisum controlled the Pecos River with 100,000 head; John Grayson controlled Socorro County with 40,000 head; and Lyons & Campbell controlled isolated pockets of Socorro, Sierra, and nearly all of Grant County with 60,000 head.

Gideon Truesdell, Dead at the Age of 71

Poor health notwithstanding Gideon remained busy right up until the end of his life. His grocery store was successful with a large and steady clientele, and as a farmer he knew how to cultivate the tastiest fruits and vegetables in town. He smoked slabs of bacon and hams with applewood and cured his beef with hickory wood.[295] Gideon was about to move this store into a building on Bullard Street, and lease the store at the corner of Broadway and Main now that his son was living in Carthage, Missouri. He also turned some fertile land out at his ranch into a small garden to supply his grocery store with fresh fruits and vegetables.

"On the southern edge of the wide bottom, just north of town, which should have been selected as the town site of Silver City, Gideon Truesdell has chosen a spot for his garden. He has built an adobe wall four and a half feet high, resting upon a heavy stone foundation, and enclosing at least an acre and a half of ground. He has also built a good house of two rooms, in the southwest corner of the enclosure.

"His well is 35 feet deep, and furnishes an abundance of water for irrigating purposes. A heavy brick wall was built along the outside of the foundation on the north side and extending south some 20 feet along the east side, for the purpose of protecting the property from floods. A line of cottonwood trees, planted at proper distances, and eight feet distant from the walls, surrounds the property.

"The garden is planted in all the spring and early summer vegetables, and Mr. Truesdell has just received an assortment of bush roots, such as carrots, raspberries, gooseberries, blackberries, etc. which he will set out at once. He will also put in large beds of pie plant, celery, etc. The garden has been so planted that, with the aid of hot beds, the proprietor feels confident that he will be able to supply this market with fresh vegetables throughout the entire year.

"His windmill and an oscillating corn grinder connected therewith, have been shipped from the end of the railroad, and will probably arrive within a month. Mr. Truesdell has spent hundreds of dollars upon this garden, and we believe that the returns will fully equal his expectations."[296]

After cashing-out of the Truesdell, Lyons & Campbell Cattle Company, Gideon decided to push his provisioning business in a new direction. Ranching was gradually replacing mining as New Mexico's leading industry, and every rancher needed a store that acted as a financial clearing house. Gideon were about to build a two-story building on a vacant lot he owned next to his grocery store, and in addition to provisioning mining camps, he would also provision ranchers.

He organized Truesdell & Lyons, Dealers in Provisions, and when Tom bought cattle from ranchers, he would have paid them in scrip, which could be cashed at C.P. Crawford's bank, or exchanged for provisions, hardware, tools, barbed wire, saddles, or gold or silver coins at Truesdell & Lyons.

Architect Robert Black designed and built a brick storefront nearly identical to the Phillips Building next door. Gideon used his equity in lots 14 and 16 as collateral for a $2,000 loan from banker C.P. Crawford with Tom Lyons co-signing the note.[297] After the building was completed in November 1881, Gideon had carpenters build offices on the second floor that generated a monthly rental income from physicians and lawyers. When finished, this property was known as the Truesdell Building.

Tom got a fully stocked store, and Gideon turned a vacant lot into an income-producing asset for his son. Upon his death, Gideon's estate agreed to sell his 50% interest in Truesdell & Lyons, and about a thousand acres to Tom Lyons for $20,000 ($918,000 today), payable to his son in Lyons & Campbell notes that would have generated a yearly income for the next ten years.[298]

By 1881, Silver City had become a major distribution center for the southwest, and in just seven years Gideon had figured a way to insert himself into the business community. Each week hundreds of wagons hauling merchandise from a railroad depot in Colorado through the desert, mostly by mule trains, arrived in town. The merchandise flowing through Silver City amounted to $300,000 to $600,000 ($20 million today) a year, and one store took delivery of ten tons of merchandise in a single week. Everything could be bought in Silver City, and as an example of how big the town's trade had become, one afternoon 69 freight wagons unloaded at H. Lesinsky & Company.

In 1881, Gideon ran for mayor but lost to James Corbin in an election that went down in history as one of the most uninspired races in the southwest. More likely than not Gideon allowed his name to be used so Corbin didn't have to run unopposed; Corbin ran as a Democrat and Gideon Truesdell as a Republican.[299]

The *Tombstone Epitaph* wrote an article about an election with only a 19% voter turnout. "Silver City, New Mexico, has just passed through the trying ordeal of a heated municipal election, that is, the people have elected a mayor. We have always had considerable respect for our sister city, but since the returns of the late election were made public through the columns of the Chronicle of that place, our respect has given rise to admiration. The vote was most astounding.

"It appears there were three candidates, who polled respectively the following votes: James Corbin (69), Gideon Truesdell (19), and Mr. Scattering (1). Totals—89 votes! Just think for a moment what this enormous vote represents. First, of course, it represents an incorporated city with all the paraphrenia of councilmen, marshal, police, judge, assessor, tax collector, treasurer, and city attorney. Second, it should represent 446 souls, big and little, great and small, estimating upon the usual basis of five to the voter. The fact is, Silver City, New Mexico, almost rivals our Salt River city of Phoenix."[300]

While the new store was under construction, Gideon replaced his ranch residence with a "quite substantial two-story brick house, which Truesdell, a prosperous grocer, had built."[301] He remained busy until August of 1882 when he suffered a massive heart attack, and was more or less confined to this residence.

G.J. and Callie took a series of stagecoaches from Carthage to Silver City with their two, and four-year-old daughters and stayed at the ranch. "Young Gid" who was eighteen-years-old and living with his grandfather, worked in his garden and grain mill.[302] What he really wanted was to follow in his father's footsteps, and get into the newspaper business. For a couple of years G.J. Truesdell was editor of the *Daily Southwest*, and "Young Gid" became Editor of the *Lakewood Press*.

On November 4, 1882, Gideon Truesdell passed away at his ranch house. Matt and Sidney Derbyshire, old family friends from Pleasant Prairie, Wisconsin, had just entered the furniture and undertaking business, and brought a coffin out to the ranch where they laid out their old friend for what promised to be a well-attended funeral.

Tom Lyons, "Cattle Baron of the Southwest," (L), sketch of the Lyons-Campbell townhouse that was built at the Truesdell ranch—the highlighted wing was the house Gideon built in 1881. Pictures courtesy of the Silver City Museum.

An Episcopalian service was performed by Reverend N.H. Gale, a close friend of Callie Truesdell, followed by graveside services at the Masonic Cemetery. Gideon's pallbearers loaded him into the back of a new hearse that had just arrived from the states for Derbyshire Brothers. The procession brought him from the ranch down to Main Street past Truesdell & Lyons, and out to the cemetery beyond the city limits where he was laid to rest next to Julia, his wife of 45 years.

On November 11, 1882, the *Muskegon News & Reporter* wrote that, "We are pained to announce the death of Gideon Truesdell, one of the early settlers of this city and well known in Muskegon, died at Silver City, New Mexico, on the second instant. The immediate relatives and friends were not unprepared for this intelligence, as he had been ailing for some four months.

"Mr. Truesdell was born in Genesee County, New York, in 1811, where he remained until 1837, employed in farming. He then removed to Steven's Point, Wisconsin, and engaged in the lumber business, going thence to Kenosha, Wisconsin.

"In 1855, he entered into partnership with Charles and Harvey Durkee, Levi Truesdell, now of this city, and Charles Deming, under the firm name of Durkee, Truesdell & Company, and commenced building the sawmill in this city, since burned down, known as the Truesdell mill, which was one of the best mills on Muskegon Lake at that time.

"The firm continued until 1858, when Mr. Truesdell purchased the interest of his partners, and with a wonderful amount of energy and perseverance paid off the indebtedness and finally acquiring a handsome property.

"In 1859, Mr. Truesdell entered into partnership with Joseph H. and Charles H. Hackley, under the firm name of J.H. Hackley & Company. This firm was continued until 1866, when the deceased sold his interest to his other partners, still retaining the Truesdell mill. He removed to Kenosha, Wisconsin where he purchased two large farms.

"During the time of his connection with the lumber business in this city, he displayed a great amount not only of energy but of business enterprise, as shown by the fact of his being the first to put in a gang of saws in this part of the State, and also the building of what was then a very fine propeller, the G.J. Truesdell, which is still running on Lake Michigan. He sunk the first salt well in Muskegon. He was never a politician, although he was elected to the Legislature of Wisconsin when he resided in Kenosha.

"Instead of sinking under discouragement at the loss of his property, he started out again in 1874 with all the energy of a young man, although he was nearly sixty years old, and went to Silver City, New Mexico, and again commenced business without capital.

"We are pleased to learn that he succeeded and at the time of his death had acquired considerable property. Those who knew Mr. Truesdell will agree that he was regarded as an honest, upright man, true to his friends, and there are several in this city who are ready to admit that through him, they received their first start in business."

On November 4, 1882, the *Daily Southwest* published the following obituary:

"The funeral of the late Gideon Truesdell took place yesterday from his residence just beyond town, and the sincerity of the respect in which he was held was evidenced by the large concourse of his fellow citizens who followed his remains to his last resting place in the Masonic graveyard.

"Although Mr. Truesdell died at a ripe old age, having reached just beyond the Biblical standard of the duration of life, three score and ten, his decease, outside of the personal grief it caused, was regretted because by it Silver City lost an energetic man of business who, had his life been saved, would not only have amassed considerable wealth but by his enterprise would have benefited the town.

"Although struggling to conduct business with small capital he made every dollar count. The bold Chicago operator, the man who in former years had handled money by the hundreds of thousands, could easily be seen in the merchant of limited resources who dwelt with us. Even in the ashes burn the fire.

"When past sixty he came to Silver City as a member of the Wisconsin Mining Company. The unsuccessful workings of this enterprise swallowed up the pittance he had saved. Despite his growing years and approaching infirmities nothing daunted the old gentleman, who opened a produce store. By shrewd management he amassed a competency before death summoned him to that world beyond, where trade, traffic, and the laying of earthly treasures are unknown."[303]

"His familiar figure will be missed but his career belongs to the early history of our town. Mr. Truesdell leaves a son, G.J. Truesdell. As a tribute to his memory, all places of business in town closed at half past one and did not re-open until after the funeral."

A couple of weeks later, his son returned to Silver City to settle the estate, and the *Daily Southwest* wrote that "Dell Truesdell, an old timer of Silver City but late of Carthage, Missouri, has been busy shaking hands with his many friends in this city for the past few days."[304]

His father left an estate of around $67,000 ($1.9 million today) with nearly all of it already in his son's name. Just about everything Gideon had amassed during the past few years had been converted into income-producing assets for his son. The income from the Andrews & Truesdell Cattle Company produced profits for another two years until the price of silver collapsed, and Tombstone turned into a town that had fallen on hard times.

Block nine in Silver City between Pope and Main Street consisted of 16 lots, and was sold to Sam and Maggie Greene for $1,100 ($23,000 today) at 12% interest without any money changing hands.[305] He sold Tom Lyons 16 lots in block 260 and 267 on Bennett Street for $1,000 payable in Lyons & Campbell Cattle Company notes.[306]

Gideon and Julia Truesdell's grandsons; Gideon Gerald Truesdell (1864–1945) (L), Chauncey Octavius Truesdell (1866–1952) (C), Adelbert J. Truesdell (1882–1972) (R). Pictures courtesy of the Mrs. Len (Maudine) Truesdell Sr. and Hattie Truesdell Hector families.

Yearly interest and principal from these notes plus the sale of other assets would have given G.J. about an $8,000 ($169,000 today) annual income, and yet ten years later he was broke after having made a string of ill-advised investments. In 1886, his wife Callie died from pneumonia, and G.J. went on a seventeen-year bender where he became known as Carthage's town drunk. It was a sad and tragic time for G.J.s children with the girls placed in an orphanage outside of Silver City.[307] Their older half-brothers, Gideon and Chauncey, stayed in touch and did what they could although by then they had their own families.[308] It was a situation for which they never really forgave their father.

During periods of brief sobriety, G.J. would visit his daughters, but they recalled their years in an orphanage as "sad and lonely."[309] For some reason Adelbert was raised by his grandmother on the Schallenberger farm where, at the age of nine he lost an arm in a farming accident. This gave G.J. another reason to drown his sorrows in liquor until his twenty-one-year-old son, Adelbert, and his newly-wed wife asked him to come live with them.[310] A few years earlier, G.J. did something few people have the mental or physical ability to do, and that was quit drinking although by then his son said "father drank his inheritance."[311]

Living with his son's family turned his life around, and "Grandpa Truesdell" helped raise their children. He was remembered as a "kind and loving grandpa," and a granddaughter believed he had finally found the peace that had eluded him since his wife died.[312]

Notes

1. Grant County Deed Book, volume 1.
2. There was an estimated $30 million ($460 million today) of silver in the Two Ikes mine.
3. *Santa Fe New Mexican*, 17 Jan 1871, pp. 1.
4. *New York Herald-Tribune*, 21 December 1870
5. *Silver City Enterprise*, 20 Feb 1891, pp. 2, column 4, Samuel O. Greene obituary.
6. Ibid.
7. *Pioneering In Territorial Silver City*, pp. 28.
8. Ibid, pp. 12.

9. Ibid.
10. Ibid
11. Ibid, pp. 16-17.
12. Ibid.
13. Ibid
14. Ibid.
15. Ibid, pp. 21.
16. Ibid, pp. 34.
17. Ibid, pp. 30.
18. Ibid, pp. 34.
19. Ibid, pp. 27.
20. Ibid, 28-29.
21. Ibid, pp. 36.
22. Ibid, pp. 35.
23. Ibid, pp. 36.
24. *Early History of the Great Southwest*, pp. 83.
25. *Santa Fe Daily New Mexican*, 8 Mar 1871, pp. 1.
26. Chauncey Truesdell reminiscences, 1951.
27. *The Story of Mining in New Mexico*, pp. 51.
28. Ibid.
29. *Las Vegas Gazette*, 7 Jun 1873, pp. 2.
30. *El Paso Post-Herald*, 28 May 1936, pp. 4.
31. *The Story of Mining in New Mexico*, pp. 51.
32. Ibid.
33. Grant County Deed Book, Volume 1.
34. Ibid.
35. *Pittsfield Herald*, 25 August 1870.
36. *New York Herald Tribune*, 27 November 1870.
37. *Santa Fe Daily New Mexican*, 4 April 1871, pp. 1.
38. *Pioneering in Territorial Silver City*, pp. 36.
39. Ibid, *pp. 37.*
40. *Las Vegas Gazette*, 7 June 1873, pp. 2.
41. Jose Manuel Carrasco
42. Ibid.
43. Children dug ore and passed them between legs.
44. Ibid
45. Ibid.
46. *Santa Fe Daily New Mexican*, 16 September 1872, pp. 1.

47. *Arizona Silver Belt*, Martin Bremen obituary, 4 November 1897, pp. 3. *Arizona Silver Belt*, 8 February 1900 Silas Tidwell Obituary.
48. Ibid.
49. *The Story of Mining in New Mexico*, pp. 51.
50. Ibid.
51. Ibid.
52. *Silver City Enterprise*, 25 July 1890, Andrew Hurlburt obituary.
53. *Silver City Enterprise*, 25 July 1890, Andrew Hurlburt obituary.
54. The *Arizona Mining Company* was composed of Andrew Hurlburt, William Smith, James McGhee, John Wagoner, Charles Mankey, and Isaac Langston.
55. Chauncey Truesdell reminiscences, 1951.
56. Jenerett & Milby, general merchants, Pinos Altos.
57. Jacob Bennett D.A.R. chapter, Silver City, 1904, paper read on town's early history as read by Mrs. Ashenfelter.
58. *Borderer*, 31 Aug 1872, pp. 2.
59. *The Weekly New Mexican*, May 23, 1871.
60. *Borderer*, 7 August 1872.
61. *Daily New Mexican*, 6 May 1873.
62. Grant County Deed Book, Volume 1, bordered by Spring Street, Hudson Street, and Bullard Street. Cibola Mill was across the street (Bullard) and next to where the Tennessee Mill would be built a short time later.
63. Gideon Truesdell bankruptcy docket, U.S. Federal Archives, Record Group 21, File 26620N3.
64. *This is Silver City, New Mexico*. Articles published in the *Silver City Enterprise*, 1885–1887, pp. 49.
65. Family correspondence, Greene spent the holidays with his sister's family, and had been courting Maggie Walsh.
66. Julia Truesdell to her sister, Abigail Piper, 2 December 1872.
67. Chauncey Truesdell reminiscences, 1951.
68. Ibid.
69. This is a presumption based on collateral research. Many of the young men listed as stockholders in a *Kenosha Telegraph* article couldn't possibly have afforded to buy a share. More likely than not, their single share was an incentive to assume the risks of traveling to New Mexico and working in a mill in the heart of Apache country.
70. Alice Foster Hill and Ida Foster Campbell notes from Tom Lyons' diary.

71. Chauncey Truesdell reminiscences, 1951.
72. *Dairy of a Freighting Trip from Kit Carson to Trinidad in 1870.*
73. Ibid.
74. *Santa Fe Daily New Mexican*, 13 February 1872.
75. Ibid.
76. Chauncey Truesdell reminiscences, 1951.
77. Ibid.
78. Ibid.
79. Ibid.
80. *Santa Fe Daily New Mexican*, 16 Sep 1872, pp. 1.
81. Chauncey Truesdell reminiscences, 1951.
82. Congressional Serial Set, pp. 339.
83. *Kenosha Republican*, 7 January 1872.
84. Alice Foster Hill and Ida Foster Campbell notes, pp. 5-6. Tom Lyons and E. O. Kennedy briefly lived there.
85. Passim, various newspaper articles, two tons was what others mills also processed.
86. *Mining Life*, 29 March 1872
87. *Santa Fe New Mexican*, 18 January 1873.
88. *Six Guns and Single Jacks*, pp. 98.
89. Ibid.
90. *Kenosha Telegraph*, 23 May 1873.
91. Ibid
92. *Las Cruces Boarder*, 24 April 1872
93. *Borderer*, 26 Oct 1872, pp. 2.
94. Ibid, 4 January 1873, pp. 1.
95. Ibid.
96. *Las Cruces Borderer*, 1 February 1873.
97. *Lost Treasures & Old Mines: A New Mexico Federal Writers Project*, pp. 231.
98. *Las Cruces Borderer*, 21 June 1873.
99. *Las Vegas Gazette*, 12 July 1873
100. *Santa Fe Daily New Mexican*, 12 September 1873
101. *Las Cruces Borderer*, 7 December 1872
102. *Silver City Tribune*, August 1873.
103. Congressional Serial Set, pp. 339.
104. *Black Hills Weekly Pioneer*, 21 Oct 1876, pp. 4.
105. *Borderer,* 7 December 1873.

106. *Mining Life*, 11 July 1874.
107. *San Diego Union*, 17 July 1873, pp. 1.
108. *Las Vegas Gazette*, 12 July 1873, pp. 2.
109. *Las Vegas Gazette*, 21 June 1873, pp. 1
110. Ibid.
111. *Las Vegas Gazette*, 13 Sep 1873, pp. 2.
112. Ibid.
113. *The Pinos Altos Story*, pp. 53.
114. Mining deed liened by Sidney Derbyshire in the Grand County Register of Deeds office.
115. *Mining Life*, 31 January 1874.
116. The Cibola mill was across the road from the Wisconsin Mill, and the Tennessee Mill was on the other side of the Cibola property.
117. *Las Vegas Gazette*, 7 Nov 1874, pp. 2.
118. *Las Vegas Gazette*, 13 September 1873.
119. *Mining Life*, 28 February 1874.
120. George Derbyshires daughter, Charlotte, married Herbert Torrey, Julia Truesdell's cousin's son.
121. Georges parents were from Bennington, Vermont, and in 1838 traveled to southeastern Wisconsin with Harvey Durkee and Reverend Reuben Deming.
122. *History of Kenosha and Racine County*, pp. 707.
123. *Santa Fe Daily New Mexican*, 27 April 1874.
124. Ibid, 16 May 1873, pp. 2.
125. *Executive Documents of the U.S. House of Representatives, 1st session of the 47th Congress, 1881–82, Grant County, New Mexico*. pp. 329-331.
126. Ibid, 1 Feb 1873, pp. 1.
127. Arthur Truesdell replies to 24 March 1911 letter from Amos Fred Sherwood.
128. *New Mexico in 1876–1877: A Newspaperman's View*. Pp. 116
129. *Pioneering in Territorial Silver City*, Burlingame letter to Alice Hoffman, June 6, 1873.
130. *The Darkest Period: The Kanza Indians and their Last Homeland*, pp. 103.
131. Passim, family legend, from all accounts he wasn't a sloppy drunk and could hold his liquor.
132. *Six-Guns and Single-Jacks*, pp. 64.
133. *The Short Life of illy the Kid*, pp. 118.

134. *Sheriff Harvey Whitehill: Silver City Stalwart*, pp. 22
135. *Antrim was my Stepfather's Name: The Boyhood of Billy the Kid*, pp. 11.
136. *Sheriff Harvey Whitehill: Silver City Stalwart*, pp. 22
137. Ibid.
138. *Las Vegas Gazette*, 19 August 1873
139. Ibid.
140. *Old West Legends*, Poker Alice Ivers.
141. *True Tales Volume 1, 1882–1883*. Articles published in the *Silver City Enterprise*, pp. 37.
142. *This is Silver City, New Mexico*. Articles published in the *Silver City Enterprise*, 1885–1887, pp. 72.
143. Silver City Museum, James Corbin file.
144. *Pioneering in Territorial Silver City*, pp. 137.
145. *Kenosha Republican*, 30 December 1873, pp. 2.
146. When the shares Gideon held in trust for employees was added he probably controlled 80% of the capital stock.
147. Gideon Truesdell bankruptcy docket, U.S. Federal Archives, Record Group 21, File 26620N3.
148. Grant County Register of Deeds, foreclosure on assets owned by the *Wisconsin Mining Company*.
149. Ibid.
150. *Borderer*, 6 June 1874, pp. 2.
151. *Santa Fe Daily New Mexican*, 18 July 1874, pp. 1.
152. *Borderer*, 7 July 1874, pp. 2.
153. *Denver Mirror*, 23 August 1874.
154. *Santa Fe Daily New Mexican*, 31 Aug 1874, pp. 1.
155. *Las Vegas Gazette*, 5 September 1874, pp. 2.
156. Ibid, 17 April 1875.
157. *Las Vegas Gazette*, 24 July 1875
158. *Kenosha Telegraph*, 22 October 1874, pp. 9.
159. *Muskegon Chronicle*, 15 January 1874. JHH funeral.
160. Ibid.
161. *Las Cruces Borderer*, 23 October 1873, pp. 1.
162. *Mining Life*, 23 January 1875.
163. Ibid, 7 June 1874, pp. 2.
164. *Borderer,* 31 October 1874
165. Grant County deed book, pp.6.
166. This property was later sold to Matthew Derbyshire.

167. *Articles Compiled from the Land*, pp. 157.

168. *Mine and Mining in the States and Territories West of the Rocky Mountains, Chapter IX, New Mexico*. Rossiter W. Raymond, United States Commissioner of Mining Statistics, Washington, 1873, pp.

169. Passim, stray pieces of information in the files of the Silver City Library, historical museum, and histories of the early years in the Clifton-Morenci mining district.

170. Ibid.

171. *Borderer*, 21 Jun 1873, pp. 2.

172. *The History of Morenci*, 1956 Masters Thesis, Roberta Watt, pp. 27-28.

173. Ibid.

174. Ibid.

175. *The History of Morenci*, 1956 Masters Thesis, Roberta Watt, pp. 27-28.

176. *Silver City Tribune* 20 September 1873, published the following article from *Ed's Tribune* in Clifton

177. *Las Vegas Gazette*, 1 Aug 1874, pp. 3.

178. *Arizona Citizen*, 21 Nov 1874, pp. 2.

179. Ibid.

180. Historian, Jerry Weddle interview 19 August 1990.

181. Yavapai County Register of Deeds, Volume 1, pp. 18.

182. Historian, Jerry Weddle interview 19 August 1990.

183. *Arizona Citizen and Weekly Tribune*, 22 November 1873

184. The History of the Clifton-Morenci Mining District, James Colquhon, London, 1924, pp 6-7

185. Ibid.

186. *Jewish Pioneers of New Mexico*, pp. 9.

187. *Six-Guns and Single Jacks*, pp. 77.

188. *Billy the Kid*, by Michael Wallis, pp. 16.

189. Ibid, pp. 21-23.

190. Ibid, pp. 30.

191. Robert N. Mullin collection, 9 January 1952, Chauncey Truesdell interview,

192. *Billy the Kid*, by Michael Wallis, pp. 64.

193. *Billy the Kid*, by Michael Wallis, pp.76.

194. Chauncey Truesdell reminiscences, 1951.

195. *Antrim was my Stepfather's Name: The Boyhood of Billy the Kid*, pp.

12-14.
196. Ibid.
197. Ibid.
198. Pioneers Foundation Oral History Collection, Wayne Whitehill interview.
199. Family legend- amputation was discussed with doctor but Louisa refused.
200. *Grant County Herald*, 14 November 1875.
201. *Billy the Kid*, pp. 31. (Michael Wallis-author)
202. Ibid, pp. 85.
203. Wayne Whitehill narrative.
204. Pioneers Foundation Oral History Collection, Wayne Whitehill interview.
205. *Billy the Kid*, pp. 75. (Michael Wallis-author)
206. A presumption based on the fact that Louisa Truesdell and Catherine Antrim became very close friends, and the common denominator was the kitchen at the *Exchange Hotel* and the *Wisconsin House*.
207. Passim, Chauncey Truesdell reminiscences and Billy the Kid author Michael Wallis (pp. 78).
208. *Billy the Kid*, by Michael Wallis, pp.77-78.
209. Chauncey Truesdell reminiscences, 1951.
210. *Billy the Kid*, pp. 78. (Michael Wallis-author)
211. Ibid, pp. 82.
212. Ibid.
213. *Antrim was my Stepfather's Name: The Boyhood of Billy the Kid*, pp.19.
214. Chauncey Truesdell reminiscences, 1951.
215. Interview with an unknown journalist around 1902. Article was published in a newspaper or magazine.
216. Ibid.
217. *Antrim was my Stepfather's Name: The Boyhood of Billy the Kid*, pp. 23-24.
218. Ibid, pp. 21.
219. Ibid, pp. 8.
220. Gideon G. Truesdell (1864–1945).
221. *Billy the Kid*, pp. 87. (Michael Wallis-author)
222. Chauncey Truesdell reminiscences, 1951.
223. *Billy the Kid*, pp. 87. (Michael Wallis-author)
224. Ibid, 77.

225. Ibid.
226. *Antrim was my Stepfather's Name: The Boyhood of Billy the Kid*, pp. 17.
227. Ibid.
228. Ibid, pp. 30.
229. *Billy the Kid*, pp. 88. (Michael Wallis-author)
230. *Silver City Herald*, 26 September 1875.
231. *Antrim was my Stepfather's Name: The Boyhood of Billy the Kid*, pp. 27.
232. Ibid.
233. Ibid, pp. 27-28.
234. *Billy the Kid*, pp. 92. (Michael Wallis-author)
235. Chauncey Truesdell reminiscences, 1951.
236. Passim, based on family information there was a degree of love and respect between G.J. Truesdell and Henry. Both G.J. and Louisa deeply regretted what happened to Antrim after he left Silver City, and generally refused to talk to journalists who tracked them down.
237. *Billy the Kid*, pp. 88. (Michael Wallis-author)
238. Chauncey Truesdell reminiscences, 1951.
239. Ibid.
240. *Las Vegas Optic*, 14 February 1881.
241. *Billy the Kid*, pp. 240. (Michael Wallis-author)
242. *Judge Henry Warren Bristol: A Man of his Time and Place?*
243. Jerry Weddle interview, 1991.
244. *Las Vegas Gazette*, 28 December 1880.
245. Deputy John Poe recollections.
246. Paco Anaya recollections.
247. *Antrim was my Stepfather's Name: The Boyhood of Billy the Kid*. Introduction by author Jerry Weddle. pp. xvi.
248. *Arizona Republic*, 18 November 1956, pp. 116. "More About the Kid."
249. Ibid.
250. *History and Biographical Record of North and West Texas*, volume 1, pp. 443-445.
251. *New York Times*, 25 April 1924, Henry Lesinsky obituary.
252. *Pioneering in Territorial Silver City*, pp. 158.
253. *Six Guns and Single Jacks*, pp. 36
254. *Sheriff Harvey Whitehill, Silver City Stalwart*, pp. 283-284.
255. *Deadly Dozen; Twelve forgotten gunfighters of the Old West.*
256. Hattie Truesdell Hector interview, 1983, Gilmer, Texas. She was G.J.s granddaughter.

257. Arthur Truesdell replies to 24 March 1911 letter from Amos Fred Sherwood.
258. *Six Guns and Single Jacks*, pp. 76.
259. Proceedings of the Grand Lodge of Wisconsin, Kenosha Lodge #47, pp. 244-245.
260. *Billy the Kid*, pp. 84. (Michael Wallis-author)
261. A presumption based on the fact that most Angelo settlers came to work in the mills. The mining camp depended heavily on the Mexican population.
262. Chauncey Truesdell reminiscences, 1951.
263. The *American House* was bought by G.J. from *McGary & Slocum*.
264. Chauncey Truesdell reminiscences, 1951.
265. Callie Truesdell diaries.
266. Gideon G. Truesdell 29 July 1940 letter to nephew, E. Frances DeVos.
267. Callie Truesdell diaries.
268. Passim, letters, newspaper clippings, and family tradition.
269. Mrs. Amos (Rhoda) letter to her sister-in-law, Mrs. Levi (Mary Ann) Truesdell, 12 March 1879.
270. *Grant County Herald*, 19 October 1878.
271. Ibid, 16 November 1878.
272. Callie Truesdell diary entries.
273. Ibid.
274. *Port Royal Times*, February 3 and 10 1881.
275. Ibid.
276. Ibid.
277. E Francis DeVos- Callies grandson.
278. *The Story of Mining in New Mexico*, pp. 54.
279. Frances E. Totty narrative, 1936, WPA writers project.
280. Chauncey Truesdell reminiscences, 1951.
281. Ibid.
282. *Lost Treasures & Old Mines: A New Mexico Federal Writers Project*, pp. 235.
283. Chauncey Truesdell reminiscences, 1951.
284. *Los Angeles Daily Herald*, 4 Feb 1881, pp. 5.
285. Ibid.
286. *Chicago Tribune*, 17 May 1880, pp. 6
287. This is an estimate based on collateral research of other cattle operations during that period.
288. Gideon G. Truesdell 29 July 1940 letter to nephew, E. Frances DeVos

about how the family got into the cattle business in Tombstone.
289. In addition to owning hundreds of mining claims, they also owned the Cosette Mine and a quartz mill in Globe City, Arizona.
290. Ibid.
291. Gideon G. Truesdell 29 July 1940 letter to nephew, E. Frances DeVos about how the family got into the cattle business in Tombstone.
292. This is based on other cattle operations, and the fact that Gideon and G.J.s standard of living greatly improved around 1881.
293. *Phoenix Evening Gazette*, 10 July 1945, Gideon G. Truesdell obituary.
294. Passim, this is widely repeated in several articles about the size of the LC ranch.
295. *Milwaukee Sentinel*, 6 August 1869, pp. 7.
296. *Grant County Herald*, 24 May 1879.
297. Alice Foster Hill and Ida Foster Campbell notes, pp.5.
298. Ibid, pp. 6.
299. *History of New Mexico: Its Resources and People*, pp. 738.
300. *Tombstone Epitaph*, 19 December 1881, pp. 6.
301. *Built to Last, An Architectural History of Silver City, New Mexico*, pp. 30.
302. 1880 federal census.
303. *Daily Southwest*, 4 November 1882.
304. *Daily Southwest*, 23 November 1882.
305. Grant County land records, 20 December 1882, G.J. Truesdell & wife to Samuel Greene & wife. $1,100 promissory note due on 20 December 1885.
306. Grant County land records, 2 December 1882, G.J. Truesdell & wife sell lots to Lyons & Campbell for $1,000.
307. Beatrice DeVos Davidson letter, 19 July 1993. She was Zoe Truesdell DeVos' daughter.
308. Hattie Truesdell Hector (1920–1990) 20 October 1983 interview, Gilmer, Texas, 1983. She was G.J. Truesdell's granddaughter.
309. Ibid.
310. Hattie Truesdell Hector (1920–1990) 20 October 1983 interview, Gilmer, Texas, 1983.
311. Sidney and Frank Small interview.
312. Hattie Truesdell Hector (1920–1990) 20 October 1983 interview, Gilmer, Texas, 1983.

TRUESDELL GENEALOGY CHART

Gideon Truesdell (1756–1799/1800) – Dorcas Crandall (1758–1824)

Children:
Jeremiah (1782–1837), John (1784–1838), Solomon (1787–1850), Gideon R. (1789–1847), Timothy L. (1790–1818), Dorcas (1791–1868), Assenath (1793–1840), Thankful (1800–1827)

Gideon R. Truesdell (1789–1847) – Polly Banister (1787–1856)

Children:
Polly Diadama (1809–1902), Jeremiah (1810–1860), Gideon J. (1811–1882), Amos (1813–1885), Levi (1815–1887), Ezra (1817–1895), Clarissa (1819–1893)

Gideon J. Truesdell (1811–1882) – Julia Ann Torrey (1813–1878)

Children:
Maude (1835–1835), Bradley – adopted (1831–1846), Geraldine J. "G.J." (1842–1922)

Geraldine J. (G.J.) Truesdell (1842–1922) – Clara Louisa Greene (1846–1920)
Divorced: 1877

Children:
Gideon G. (1864–1945), Chauncey O. (1866–1952)

Geraldine J. (G.J.) Truesdell (1842–1922) – Callie Schallenberger (1851–1886)

Children:
Julia E. (1878–1959), Zoe (1880–1964), Adelbert J. (1882–1972)

Amos Truesdell (1813–1885) – Rhoda Mills (1815–1905)

Children:
Adelbert (1838–1878), Arthur (1841–1920), Ellen (1846–1891), Emma (1849–1938),
Marcus (1852–1934), Fayette (1858–1938)

Levi Truesdell (1815–1887) – Mary Ann Chaddock (1818–1892)

Children:
Augustus C. (1840–1915), Frances E. (1843–1889), Frederick G. (1852–1887)

BIBLIOGRAPHY AND SOURCES

Archival Sources:

Dossin Collection; Great Lakes Museum.
Detroit, Michigan. Information on the steamers *Truesdell* and *Ottawa, and schooners Challenge, Wescott, Pride,* and *Henry Moore.*

R.G. Dun & Company Collection.
Baker Library, Harvard University Graduate School of Business Administration, Cambridge, Massachusetts. Confidential credit reports (1840–1880) on firms and individuals.

Charles Durkee papers.
Wisconsin State Historical Society, Madison, Wisconsin. File of family letters and documents.

Charles Mears (1814–1895) papers, Chicago Historical Society.

Durkee family papers.
Kenosha History Center, Kenosha, Wisconsin. File of family papers from Charles and Harvey Durkee with pictures of the Durkee, Deming, and Dana families.

Hackley & Hume papers.
Michigan State University, Lansing, Michigan. Business papers of Charles H. Hackley and Thomas Hume (55 boxes) that included financial journals and ledgers dating back to 1859 when Gideon Truesdell purchased the Trowbridge & Wing and Pomeroy & Holmes mills.

John Harlan collection.
Silver City Museum, Silver City, New Mexico. This photo collection contains over 12,000 pictures of the town's history.

Richard P. Hart papers.
Rensselaer Historical Society, Troy New York. The Hart mansion is headquarters for the Societies archives, which include the private papers from Richard and Betsey Howard Hart's estates. Amelia Hart married Harrison Durkee.

Moses Strong papers.
Wisconsin Historical Society, Madison, Wisconsin. Extensive collection detailing the early history of the Territory as well as Strong's business and political career.

Durkee Family.
Society of Genealogy of Durkee, Long Beach, California. Extensive genealogy of the Durkee family.

Herman J. Runge Collection.
Milwaukee Public Library, Milwaukee, Wisconsin. Very detailed information and pictures of over 7,000 ships that sailed the Great Lakes. Collection includes data on the schooner *Challenge* and steamers *Truesdell* and *Ottawa*.

Wisconsin Magazine of History collections; 1922–1949, volumes 6–32. Bound reprints of *Wisconsin History Magazine*.

Territorial and State Records:

Arizona Land Records:
Pima County, Tucson, Arizona. 1871–1885.

Michigan Land Records:
Muskegon County, Muskegon, Michigan. 1861–1875.
Ottawa County, Grand Haven, Michigan. 1839–1861.

New Mexico Land Records:
Grant County, Silver City, New Mexico. 1871–1885.
Territorial records, Santa Fe, New Mexico. 1870–1885.

Department of the Interior: Bureau of Land Management preemptive claim records:
Portage County, Steven's Point, Wisconsin. 1841–1845.
Wood County, Wisconsin Rapids, Wisconsin. 1841–1845.
Kenosha County, Kenosha, Wisconsin. 1850–1875.
Racine County, Racine, Wisconsin. 1839–1850.

Territorial Papers of the United States, Volume XXVII, Wisconsin Territory, 1836–1839. National Archives, publisher, 1975. Very detailed information from the Wisconsin Territory's earliest records.

Territorial Papers of the United States, Volume XXVIII, Wisconsin Territory, 1839–1848. National Archives, publisher, 1975. Very detailed information from the Wisconsin Territory's earliest records.

Federal Records:

Department of the Interior, Washington, DC.
Ariel observation balloon maps circa 1868–1874; Muskegon, Michigan.
Ariel observation balloon maps circa 1856–1871; Chicago, Illinois.

U.S. Census information from "Products of Industry" surveys for 1860 (mill) and 1870 (farm).

Library of Congress, Washington, DC.
U.S. Federal Census; 1790–1880,

U.S. Federal Archives, Great Lakes Region, Chicago, Illinois.
Federal income taxes; Michigan, Illinois, and Wisconsin 1864–1868.
First National Bank of Kenosha vs. Geraldine J. Truesdell, Involuntary Bankruptcy, Milwaukee, Wisconsin, 19 February 1874.
Gideon Truesdell bankruptcy docket, U.S. Federal Archives, Great Lakes Region, Chicago, Illinois. Record Group 21, File 26620N3.

Published Sources:

Acuna, Rudolfo. *Corridors of Migration: The Odyssey of the Mexican Laborers, 1600–1933*. University of Arizona Press, 2007.

Adams, Charles. *When in the Course of Human Events, Arguing the Case for Southern Secession*. Bowman & Littlefield, New York, New York. 2000.

Alexander, Bob. *Dangerous Dan Tucker*. High Lonesome Books, 2001, Silver City, New Mexico.

Alexander, Bob. *Sheriff Harvey Whitehill, Silver City Stalwart*. High Lonesome Books, 2005, Silver City, New Mexico.

Alexander, Bob. *Six-Guns and Single-Jacks*. Gila Books, 2005, Silver City, New Mexico.

Andreas, A.T. *Excerpts From the History of Northern Wisconsin, Portage County*. Western Historical Company, Chicago, Illinois. 1881.

Andreas, A.T. *Excerpts From the History of Northern Wisconsin, Wood County*. Western Historical Company, Chicago, Illinois. 1881.

Andreas, A.T. *The History of Chicago, 1839–1900*. Western Historical Company, 1884, Chicago, Illinois.

Asbury, Herbert. *The Gangs of Chicago*. Knopf, Inc. New York, New York. 1940.

Bailey, Harry H. *When New Mexico Was Young*. Las Cruces Citizen, Las Cruces, New Mexico. 1946.

Roy P. Basler, editor, *Collected Works of Abraham Lincoln*, Letter from Abraham Lincoln to James R. Doolittle, January 22, 1863, January 22, 1863, Volume VI, p. 70.

Berquist, Goodwin and Bowers, Paul C. *Bryon Kilbourn and the Development of Milwaukee*. Milwaukee County Historical Society, Milwaukee, Wisconsin. 2001.

Berry, Susan and Russell, Sharman Apt. *Built to Last, Architectural History of Silver City, New Mexico*. Silver City Museum Society, Silver City, New Mexico. 1986.

Bishop, Lewis H. *The South Warsaw Story*. Historical Wyoming Quarterly, October 1965.

Bordewich, Fergus M. *Bound for Canaan*. Harper, New York, New York. 2005.

Boyd, Eva. *That Old Overland Stage Coaching*. Republic of Texas Press, Plano, Texas. 1993.

Bruce, William George. *History of Milwaukee City and County*, Volume 1. Clark Publishing, Milwaukee, WI. 1922.

Burckel, Nicholas, John Neuenschwander, Don Jensen. *Kenosha Retrospective*. University of Wisconsin Archives, Kenosha, Wisconsin. 1981.

Ida Campbell and Alice Hill. *Triumph and Tragedy*. High Lonesome Books, 2001. Silver City, New Mexico.

Casey, Robert. *The Story of the Chicago & North Western System*. McGraw-Hill, New York, New York. 1948.

Coffin, Levi. *Reminiscences of Levi Coffin*, Ayer Company, Salem, Massachusetts, reprinted in 1968.

Colquhon, James. *The History of the Clifton-Morenci Mining District*, John Murrey, William Clowes & Son, London, England. 1924.

Cooper, William J. *Jefferson Davis, American*. Vintage Civil War Library, New York, New York. 2000.

Cronon, William. *Natures Metropolis*. Norton & Company, New York, New York. 1991.

Cropley, Carrie. *Kenosha, From Pioneer Village to Modern City*. Kenosha County Historical Society, Kenosha, Wisconsin. 1958.

Curry, J. Seymour. *Chicago: Its History and Its Builders, Vol. IV*. Franklin H. Head.

Deshon, George. *Guide for Catholic Women Especially for those who Earn Their Own Living*, Columbus Publishing Company, New York, 1863.

Deyle, Steven. *Carry Me Back: The Domestic Slave Trade in American Life*, Oxford Press, New York, New York, 2005.

Duckett, Kenneth W. *Frontiersman of Fortune: Moses M. Strong of Mineral Point*. State Historical Society of Wisconsin, Madison, Wisconsin, 1957.

Einhorn, Robin L. *Property Rules, Political Economy in Chicago 1833–1872*. University of Chicago Press, Chicago, Illinois. 2004.

Ewing, Wallace K. *Chronological Directory of Industries, Businesses, and Other Organizations in Northwest Ottawa County*. Tri-Cities Historical Museum, Grand Haven, Michigan. 1999.

Farrow, Anne; Lang, Joel; Jennifer Frank. *Complicity: How the North Promoted, Prolonged, and Profited from Slavery*. Ballantine Books, New York, New York. 2005.

Fehrenbacker, Don E., *Chicago Giant*, the biography of John Wentworth, American History Research Center, Madison, Wisconsin, 1957.

Forrest, Alexander F. *The Kimballs of Kenosha*. Holke Press, Barrington, Illinois. 1994.

Fries, Robert. *Empire in Pine, The Story of Lumbering in Wisconsin, 1830–1900*. William Claxton, Ltd. Ellison Bay, Wisconsin. 1951.

Genovese, Eugene. *The Political Economy of Slavery*, Wesleyan University Press, 1989.

Greene, Lorenzo Johnston. *The Negro In Colonial New England 1620–1776*, Columbia University Press, New York City, 1942.

Hagadorn, Ann. *Beyond the River: The Untold Story of the Heroes of the Underground Railroad*. Simon & Schuster, New York City, 2002.

Hager, Albert D. *History of Early Chicago, Modern Chicago, and Its Settlement, Early Chicago and the Northwest.* Western Publishing, Chicago, Illinois. 1892.

Haight, Louis P. *The Life of Charles Henry Hackley*. Dana Publishing, Muskegon, Michigan. 1948.

Harms, Richard. *Life After Lumbering: Charles Henry Hackley & The Emergence of Muskegon, Michigan*. University Press, Lansing, Michigan, 1984.

Harpster, Jack. *The Biography of William B. Ogden*, Southern Illinois University Press, Carbondale, Illinois, 2009.

Henderson, Frederic W. Free Trade, *The Confederacy, and the Political Economy of the South*. The American Almanac, 1991.

Hill, Libby. *The Chicago River*. Lake Claremont Press, Chicago, Illinois. 2000.

Hotchkiss, George W. *Industrial Chicago*. Goodspeed Publishing Company, Chicago, Illinois, 1894.

Hubbard, Gurden S. *The Autobiography of Gurden Saltonstall Hubbard*. Citadel Press, New York, New York. 1969.

Hummel, Jeffrey Roders and Barry R. Weingast, *The Fugitive Slave Act of 1850: Symbolic Gesture or Rational of Guarantee?* Doctoral Thesis, Sanford University, 2006.

Hunt, Gaillard. *Israel, Elihu, and Cadwallander Washburn, A Chapter in American Biography*. MacMillin & Company, New York, New York. 1925.

Hunt, Robert. *Early Milwaukee*. Wisconsin State Historical Society, Madison, Wisconsin. 1977.

Industrial Chicago: The Building Interests, Goodspeed Publishing, Chicago, Ill, 1891.

Ilminen, Gary. *The Great Chiefs: Black Hawk: Tactical Genius of the Sauk & Fox. Native Peoples*, Vol 19, No. 5, September/October 2006, pp. 74-76.

James, Cyril F. *The Growth of Chicago Banks*. Harper, New York, New York. 1938.

Jensen, Don. *Kenosha Kaleidoscope: Images of the Past*. Kenosha Community History Committee, Kenosha, Wisconsin. 1985.

Julian, George Washington. *Life of Joshua R. Giddings*, A.C. McClurg, Chicago, 1892.

Karamanski, Theodore J. *Schooner Passage: Sailing Ships and the Lake Michigan Frontier*. Wayne State University Press, Detroit, Michigan. 2000.

Keyes, Alice Prescott. *Romance of Muskegon*. Muskegon Heritage Association, Muskegon, Michigan. 1937.

Kilar, Jeremy W. *Michigans Lumbertowns: Lumbermen in Saginaw, Bay City, and Muskegon*. Wayne State University Press, Detroit, Michigan. 1990.

Kinzie, Juliette. *Wau-Bun*. The National Society of Colonial Dames in Wisconsin, 1968, Menasha, Wisconsin. Edited by Louisa Phelps Kellogg.

Lacy, Anne and Anne Valley-Fox, editors. *Lost Treasures & Old Mines, A New Mexico Federal Writers Project Book*. Sunstone Press, Santa Fe. 2011.

Lorenzesonn, Axel S. *Steam and Cinders: The Advent of Railroads in Wisconsin, 1831–1861*. Wisconsin Historical Society Press, Madison, Wi. 2009. Perhaps the best historical record of railroads in that state.

Lundwall, Helen. *Pioneering in Territorial Silver City.*

Lyman, Frank. *The City of Kenosha and Kenosha County, Wisconsin: A Record of Settlement.* S.J. Clarke Publishing, Chicago, Illinois. 1916.

Mansfield, J.B. *The Maritime History of the Great Lakes*, J.H. Beers & Company, Chicago, 1899.

McGraw, Arthur. *Reminiscences of Levi Coffin: The Reputed President of the Underground Railroad.* Western Tract Society. Cincinnati, Ohio. 1876.

Mitchell, Mary Irwin. *Reminiscences of the Early Northwest* as published in a series of articles in the Menomonee (Michigan) Herald, October 16, 18, and 20, 1899. She was the daughter of Robert Irwin, and sister of Mrs. David Blish and Mr. Luther Whitney.

Morgan, Edmund S. *The Genuine Article; A Historian Looks at Early America.* Norton & Company, New York, New York. 2004.

Munson, John M. *Michigan's White Pine Era: 1840–1900.* Michigan Historical Commission, Lansing, Michigan. 1964.

Musgrove, Jon. *Slaves, Salt, Sex & Mr. Crenshaw.* Illinois History.com, Marion, Illinois. 2004–2005.

Northrup, Solomon, *Twelve Years a Slave*, Derby & Miller, Buffalo, New York, 1853. Northrup was kidnapped in Washington, DC in 1841, and rescued in 1853 from a cotton plantation near the Red River in Louisiana.

Norris, James D. *R.G. Dun & Company 1841–1900.* Greenwood Press, Westport, Connecticut. 1978.

Poole, Ernest. *Giants Gone, Men Who Made Chicago.* McGraw-Hill, New York, New York. 1943.

Pugach, Dr. Noel. *Jewish Pioneers of New Mexico: The Freudenthal, Lesinsky and Solomon Families*, 2003. New Mexico Jewish Historical Society.

Ornish, Natalie. *Pioneer Jewish Texans*. Texas A & M University Press, College Station, Texas. 1989.

Quaife, Milo Milton. *Chicago and the Old Northwest 1673–1835*. University of Illinois Press, Chicago, Illinois. 1913.

Raynor, Ted. *Old Timers Talk in Southwestern New Mexico*. Texas Western Press. El Paso, Texas. 1960.

Read, Frederic. *A Long Look at Muskegon*. Patterson College, Benton Harbor, Michigan. 1976.

Rosholt, John G. *A Standard History of Portage County Wisconsin*, Lewis Publishing, Chicago, 1919.

Rosholt, Malcom. *Pioneers of the Pinery*, Rosholt House, Steven's Point, WI. 1979.

Selitzer, Ralph. *The Dairy Industry in America*. Dairyfield, New York, New York. 1976.

Shindlar, Hal. *The Territorial Governors: Charles Durkee (1865–1869)*. The Salt Lake Tribune, 7 January 1996.

Simmons, Marc. *Massacre on the Lordsburg Road*. Texas A & M University Press, College Station, Texas. 1997.

Simmons, Marc. *Ranchers, Ramblers & Renegades, True Tales of Territorial New Mexico*. Ancient City Press, Santa Fe, New Mexico. 1984.

Smith, Alice Elizabeth. *James Duane Doty, Frontier Promoter*. State Historical Society of Wisconsin, Madison, Wisconsin. 1954.

Spooner, Harry L. *Lumbering in Newaygo County. Cooper Press*, Grand Rapids, Michigan. 1946.

Stampp, Kenneth M. *American in 1857*. Oxford University Press, 1990, New York, New York.

Stewart, John J. *The Iron Trail to the Golden Spike*, Deseret Book Company, Salt Lake City, Utah, 1969.

Strong, Moses. *History of the Wisconsin Territory From 1836–1848*. Democrat Printing Company, Madison, Wisconsin. 1885.

Young, Andrew W. *History of the Town of Warsaw, New York*. Sage & Sons, Buffalo, New York. 1869.

Walker, August. *Early Days on the Lakes, With an Account of the Cholera Visitation of 1832*. Cornell University Library Digital Collections, 1994.

Wallis, Michael. *Billy the Kid*. Norton & Company, New York, New York. 2007.

Weddel, Jerry. *Antrim Was My Stepfather's Name: The Boyhood of Billy the Kid*. Arizona Historical Society, 1993, historical monograph #9.

Wells, Robert W. *This is Milwaukee*. Doubleday, Garden City, New York. 1970.

Wendt, Lloyd. *swift Walker' Biography of Gurden Saltonstall Hubbard*. Regency Books, Chicago, Illinois, 1986.

Weissend, Patrick R. *The Life and Times of Joseph Ellicott*, Holland Purchase Historical Society, Batavia, New York, 2002.

Western Publishing. *History of Eminent and Self-Made Men of the State of Michigan*. Western Publishing, Cincinnati, Ohio, 1878.

Western Historical Publishing Company. *The History of Racine and Kenosha Counties, Chicago, Illinois*. 1879.

Wink, Jay. *April 1865, The Month that Saved America*. Harper-Collins, New York, New York. 2000.

Wisconsin Magazine of History, *The Burning of the Steamer Phoenix*, 1924.

Works Project Administration. *Michigan Log Marks*. Michigan State College, Lansing, Michigan. 1942.

Wyman, Mark. *The Wisconsin Frontier*. Indiana University Press, Bloomington, Indiana. 1998.

Privately Published Sources:

Blodgett, Henry W. *Autobiography of Henry W. Blodgett*. Waukegan, Illinois. 1906.

Durkee Newsletter, Society of Durkee, Long Beach, California.

Dewey, James S. Works Progress Administration project; *Michigan Log Marks*. Michigan State College Agriculture Experimental Station (Michigan State), Memoir Bulletin #4, 1941.

Early Western Days, Madison, WI. 1897. Information about the Kingston family. (Draper, Fay & Company.)

Historical Wyoming Quarterly, Warsaw, New York, 1952.

Mears, Carrie Ellen. *Charles Mears, Pioneer of the White Lake Area*. 1952.

Kellogg & Thayer. *Crandall Family Record*. 1949.

Kirschbaum, Joseph. *Lumbering Days in Wisconsin*. WPA project, 1936.

Mygatt, Wallace. *Early History of Kenosha*. 1874.

Purvis, J.B. *Biron, Old and New*, Consolidated News, 1927.

Reeve, Paul. *Mormons, Miners, and Southern Paiutes*. Chapter 2, Power, Place, and Prejudice. Utah Historical Society.

Rosholt, Malcolm Leviatt, *Those Who Came First: Our County our Story of Portage County*, Portage County Board of Supervisors, 1959, Worzalla

Publishing, Steven's Point, Wisconsin.

Simmons, H.M. *Pioneer Life in Kenosha County*, 1876.

Stanley, F. *The Georgetown, New Mexico Story*. Pep, Texas, 1963.

Truesdell, Karl. *Truesdell Genealogy*. 1955. Comprehensive family history listing every Truesdell, Trousdell, Truesdale, and Truesdell branch in America. Copy available at *New York Genealogical & Biographical Society*, New York, New York.

Manuscripts

Martin Bremen. Ellen Cline, 1978. Manuscripts file, The Library, Silver City, New Mexico.

Yakes, Daniel J. and Hornstein, Hugh A. *The Many Lives of Muskegon*, 1979, Muskegon Community College.

Newspapers

Allegan Daily Times, 1905
Allegan Journal and Tribune, 1887
Allegan Gazette, 1904
Boston Commercial Bulletin, 1865
Buffalo Daily Republic, 1854
Chicago American, 1835–1837
Chicago Daily American, 1839–1842
Chicago Democrat, 1833–1834
Chicago Democrat, 1842–1845
Chicago Inter-Ocean, 1874–1875
Chicago Journal, 1844–1875
Chicago Times, 185–1875
Chicago Tribune, 1847–1875
Daily Milwaukee News, 1871
Detroit Advertiser & Tribune, 1865–1872

Detroit Free Press, 1864–1868
Ed's Tribune, 1873. (Clifton, AZ.)
Grand Haven News, 1864–1869
Grant County Herald, 1881–1885
Jackson City Patriot, 1869
Kenosha Democrat, 1850–1861
Kenosha Republican, 1872–1873
Kenosha Telegraph, 1851–1854.
Kenosha Telegraph Courier, 1858–1871
Kenosha Times, 1857–1863
Kenosha Tribune, 1852–1858
Kenosha Union, 1866–1875
Kenosha Telegraph, 1871–1875
Las Cruces Boarder, 1871–1873.
Madison Express, 1840–43
Madison Enquirer, 1842
Milwaukee Sentinel, 1840–1875
Milwaukee Courier, 1847
Mining Life, 1873–1877
Muskegon Daily Chronicle, 1882
Muskegon Enterprise, 1870–1873
Muskegon Journal, 1857
Muskegon Morning News, 1882
Muskegon News & Reporter, 1870–1882
Muskegon Reporter, 1859–1864
Racine Advocate (Racine, Wi.) 1851–1859
Real Estate Record & Builders Guide, 1866–1869
Rock River Democrat (Rockford, Il.) 1850–1856
Rockford Weekly Register Gazette, 1856–1859
Rockford Republican, 1856–1859
Silver City Enterprise, 1877–1881
Silver City Tribune, 1877–1877.
Southport American, 1841–1849
Southport Telegraph, 1840–1850
Weekly Racine Advocate, 1854–1859
Wisconsin Argus, 1848–1854
Wisconsin Free Democrat, 1854–1857

Interviews:

Jean Crump interview, June 2005, Minneapolis, Minnesota. She is descended from Diadema Truesdell King (1809–1905), who was Gideon Truesdell's older sister. Ms. Crump conducted extensive research on Diadema King and Ezra Truesdell, both of whom settled in Minnesota with scraps of information about their brother, Gideon Truesdell.

Beatrice DeVos Davidson interview, July 1991, Webster Groves, Missouri. She was the great granddaughter of Gideon and Julia Truesdell. Her brother, Frank Devos, collected information over a fifty-year period with correspondence to and from various family members.

Robert Fay (1954–2011) interview, September 2000, Kenosha, Wisconsin. He is descended from Harrison Fay, and conducted extensive research on the Fay & Draper mill with the assistance of Draper descendents.

Richard H. Harms interview, February 1991, Grand Rapids, Michigan. He spent a great deal of time sifting through fifty-five boxes of the Charles Hackley papers (1859–1905) at *Michigan State University*, and had researched the Durkee-Truesdell and Truesdell-Hackley partnerships.

Hattie Truesdell Hector (1922–1990) interview, October 1983, Gilmer, Texas. She was the granddaughter of G.J. and Callie Truesdell. Her grandfather (G.J. Truesdell) lived with her family during the last twenty years of his life. She had heard stories from her father, Adelbert J. Truesdell (1882–1973), mostly about the family's years in Silver City.

Alice Hill and Ida Campbell interview, August 1995, Silver City, New Mexico. They are the granddaughters of Angus Campbell and Tom Lyons. When Angus Campbell died their grandmother married Lyons. They had extensive family papers on the origins of the Lyons & Campbell cattle empire, and were able to located real estate deeds detailing property sold by Gideon and G.J. Truesdell to Tom Lyons and Angus Campbell.

Charles Humphrey interview, January 1977, Warsaw, New York. He was a great, great grandson of John Truesdell. Although advanced in age he was able to shed some light on Wyoming County family members, and repeat stories he had heard that were passed through the generations.

Dianne Leiter (1922–1998) interview, March 1991, Phelan, California. She is descended from Solomon Truesdell, and spent her retirement years researching the Truesdell branch of her family.

Diane Truesdell Loy interview, February 1991. She complied some of the best information on the Truesdell family circa 1630–1930. Her files were detailed and she followed the highest standards of research.

Helen Oglesby interview, 17 February 2017, Willits, CA. Her great, grandparents were G.J. and Callie (Schallenberger) Truesdell. She supplied the circa 1878 pictures of G.J. and Callie.

Sidney and Frank Small interview, May 2006, Silver City, New Mexico. They are the grandsons of Gideon Truesdell (1864–1945). Because he was older Sid knew his grandfather better, and was able to repeat what he heard, mostly from his mother, about the Truesdell side of his family.

Arthur Truesdell (1920–1990) interview, October 1976. Fremont, Nebraska. He was Arthur Truesdell's (1840–1920) grandson.

Patrick D. Truesdell (1940–2000) interviews, 1976–1977. Sacramento, California. He had correspondence from Rhoda Truesdell (1815–1905) who was married to Amos Truesdell, that included family research that began while she was still living and living with her son, Fayette Truesdell (1858–1939), who was Patrick Truesdell's great, grandfather. His letters included ones from Rhoda Truesdell, Amos Fred Sherwood (grandson of Rhoda), and Arthur Truesdell, Rhodas son who was closely associated with his uncle, Gideon Truesdell.

John Truesdell interview, January 1977, Ithaca, New York. He is descended from Hiel Truesdell, and compiled some preliminary research that led him to believe that the "Warsaw branch" was somehow related. "Down through the years we always knew that we were somehow related to the family living in Warsaw," he remarked.

Carolyn Truesdell Siders (1926–1994) interview, December 1976. Newaygo, Michigan. She was descended from Jeremiah Truesdell, had a picture of the Truesdell Hotel painted on a serving tray, and knew about the South Warsaw family as well as Gideon Truesdell (1811–1882).

A. Bruce Truesdell interview, February 1977. Omaha, Nebraska. He is a great, great grandson of Gideon and Julia Truesdell. His grandfather was Chauncey Truesdell.

Maudine Truesdell interview, February 1977. Kansas City, Missouri. She was married to Leonard Truesdell and was able to share information that came from her late husband's knowledge of his family. (Chauncey Truesdell was her father-in-law.) She supplied copies of the Truesdell family circa 1870 and sent them for inclusion in this biography.

Jerry Weddle interview, November 1991. Catalina, Arizona. He researched and wrote a biography on Billy the Kid, and was able to share his impressions of early Silver City and the most probable relationship Henry Antrim would have had with the Truesdell family.

Family Papers:

Frederick Amos Sherwood (1864–1940) family sketch, 1939. This is a seven-page history written by a grandson of Amos and Rhoda Truesdell. His father was employed by Gideon Truesdell in various positions in Muskegon, Croton and Kenosha. His reminiscences came from stories he heard from his grandmother, mother, and father. Ellen Truesdell Sherwood (his mother) was close to Gideon and Julia, and she and her family were extended members of their family. His father worked for G. & A. Truesdell & Company at their Croton store (1865–1869), moved to Pleasant Prairie and lived on a Geneva Road farm near Gideon and Julia Truesdell (1869–1875), and eventually moved to Rodgers Park, Illinois where he owned a grocery store. There were nineteen letters written by Rhoda Truesdell late in life to family members, and some of them referenced the family's early years on the Portageville farm. These letters are considered part of the "Frank Sherwood family sketch."

Kirkland Torrey diary, 1837–1841. Incomplete with many missing pages but still very helpful. He was Julia Truesdell's younger brother, and traveled with them to the Wisconsin River. He appears to have managed Gideon's livestock, and his 16-acre garden. He spent at least one summer working aboard a lumber raft.

Herbert Torrey reminiscences, 1903. This is a small collection of scraps of notes, pages from farm journals, and an undated diary that is presumed to have been kept by his mother, Mrs. Derastus (Jane) Torrey in the early 1870s. He also left behind a crude map of the Truesdell farm in Pleasant Prairie. Herbert Torrey married George Derbyshires daughter, Charlotte, but he left behind nothing about the Wisconsin Mining Company.

Arthur Truesdell (1900–1991) interview, 1976. His grandfather was closely associated with Gideon Truesdell, and he had a lot of general information that he had heard. His nephew, John Reeves, supplied pictures of Amos and Rhoda Truesdell as well as a copy of their 1835 marriage certificate that was signed by President Arthur's father.

Callie Schallenberger Truesdell diary, 1880–1881. This diary was kept by G.J. Truesdell's second wife and references various family members.

Chauncey Truesdell narrative, 1952. This is a three-page summary that for years has been widely used by Billy the Kid researchers. Almost everything in this narrative checks out, historically, and is considered by old west historians to be an important source document. Minor errors were no doubt due to the normal confusion that occurs after the passage of time, and despite the fact that Chauncey was in his eighties, historian Robert Mullin found his memory and recollection of dates and events from that period (1872–1882) to be correct.

A copy of this narrative as well as an interview conducted by historian Robert N. Mullin, and part of the "Mullin Papers" at the Haley History Center in Midland, Texas. The topic of Billy the Kid wasn't discussed much by Truesdell family members who knew him, and from various bits and pieces of information floating around the family, Louisa Truesdell carried a degree of guilt and regret with her over his fate until the day she died. She once said that had her husband been in town and not in Deadwood, South

Dakota when Antrim got into trouble, she was certain that he would have straightened things out.

Chauncey's brother, Gideon, probably knew Antrim's older brother Joe better than Henry, and it seems as if the family knew Henry from his brief stay with the family and the two or three years he was in school with Gideon and Chauncey Truesdell.

Gideon G. Truesdell correspondence, 1940. This is a one-page letter written to his nephew, Frank DeVos, in response to a request for family information. Much of the information is incorrect (Truesdell was 76 years old and in poor health) but theres enough solid data for this letter to hold significance. He recalls that his mother said they were descended from General Nathaniel Greene, and had her lineage traced when she became a member of the Daughters of the American Revolution.

Family Interviews:

Maudine Truesdell, Kansas City, MO September 8th, 1977.
Bruce Truesdell, Omaha, NE, October 12th, 1977.
Sidney Small, Silver City, NM.
Frank G. Small, Silver City, NM.
Diane Truesdell Loy, Brookfield, WI.
Dianne Leiter, Riverside, CA.
Patrick D. Truesdell, Sacramento, CA.
Beebe Truesdell, Cuba, NY.
Charles Humphries, Warsaw, NY.
Hattie Truesdell Hector, Gilmer, TX.
Beatrice DeVos Davidson, Webster Groves, MO.
Shaun Fisher, Las Vegas, NV.
Kellie Truesdell Robbins
Helen Oglesby
Arthur Truesdell, Fremont, NE, 6 October 1976.
Jean Crump, Dennison, MN.
Phyllis Metzger, Solomon.

City Directories:

Chicago, Illinois (1856–1874) Polk & Company. Chicago Historical Society.
Kenosha, Wisconsin (1859–1873) Polk & Company. Kenosha History Center.
Muskegon, Michigan (1873) A. Bailey & Company. Hackley Public Library.

www.ingramcontent.com/pod-product-compliance
Lightning Source LLC
Chambersburg PA
CBHW061339300426
44116CB00011B/1925